Contents

REPAIRS AND OVERHAUL

Engine and associated systems

SOHC petrol engine in-car repair procedures	Page	**2A•1**
DOHC petrol engine in-car repair procedures	Page	**2B•1**
Diesel engine in-car repair procedures	Page	**2C•1**
Engine removal and overhaul procedures	Page	**2D•1**
Cooling, heating and air conditioning systems	Page	**3•1**
Petrol engine fuel systems	Page	**4A•1**
Diesel engine fuel system	Page	**4B•1**
Emission control and exhaust systems – petrol models	Page	**4C•1**
Emission control and exhaust systems – diesel models	Page	**4D•1**
Starting and charging systems	Page	**5A•1**
Ignition system – petrol engines	Page	**5B•1**
Pre-heating system – diesel engines	Page	**5C•1**

Transmission

Clutch	Page	**6•1**
Manual transmission	Page	**7A•1**
Automatic transmission	Page	**7B•1**
Driveshafts	Page	**8•1**

Brakes and Suspension

Braking system	Page	**9•1**
Suspension and steering systems	Page	**10•1**

Body equipment

Bodywork and fittings	Page	**11•1**
Body electrical systems	Page	**12•1**
Wiring diagrams	Page	**12•20**

REFERENCE

Dimensions and weights	Page	**REF•1**
Conversion factors	Page	**REF•2**
Buying spare parts	Page	**REF•3**
Vehicle identification numbers	Page	**REF•3**
General repair procedures	Page	**REF•4**
Jacking and vehicle support	Page	**REF•5**
Disconnecting the battery	Page	**REF•5**
Tools and working facilities	Page	**REF•6**
MOT test checks	Page	**REF•8**
Fault finding	Page	**REF•12**
Glossary of technical terms	Page	**REF•19**

Index

Index	Page	**REF•24**

Many people see the words 'advanced driving' and believe that it won't interest them or that it is a style of driving beyond their own abilities. Nothing could be further from the truth. Advanced driving is straightforward safe, sensible driving - the sort of driving we should all do every time we get behind the wheel.

An average of 10 people are killed every day on UK roads and 870 more are injured, some seriously. Lives are ruined daily, usually because somebody did something stupid. Something like 95% of all accidents are due to human error, mostly driver failure. Sometimes we make genuine mistakes - everyone does. Sometimes we have lapses of concentration. Sometimes we deliberately take risks.

For many people, the process of 'learning to drive' doesn't go much further than learning how to pass the driving test because of a common belief that good drivers are made by 'experience'.

Learning to drive by 'experience' teaches three driving skills:

- ☐ Quick reactions. (Whoops, that was close!)
- ☐ Good handling skills. (Horn, swerve, brake, horn).
- ☐ Reliance on vehicle technology. (Great stuff this ABS, stop in no distance even in the wet...)

Drivers whose skills are 'experience based' generally have a lot of near misses and the odd accident. The results can be seen every day in our courts and our hospital casualty departments.

Advanced drivers have learnt to control the risks by controlling the position and speed of their vehicle. They avoid accidents and near misses, even if the drivers around them make mistakes.

The key skills of advanced driving are **concentration,** effective all-round **observation, anticipation** and **planning.** When **good vehicle handling** is added to these skills, all driving situations can be approached and negotiated in a safe, methodical way, leaving nothing to chance.

Concentration means applying your mind to safe driving, completely excluding anything that's not relevant. Driving is usually the most dangerous activity that most of us undertake in our daily routines. It deserves our full attention.

Observation means not just looking, but seeing and seeking out the information found in the driving environment.

Anticipation means asking yourself what is happening, what you can reasonably expect to happen and what could happen unexpectedly. (One of the commonest words used in compiling accident reports is 'suddenly'.)

Planning is the link between seeing something and taking the appropriate action. For many drivers, planning is the missing link.

If you want to become a safer and more skilful driver and you want to enjoy your driving more, contact the Institute of Advanced Motorists at www.iam.org.uk, phone 0208 996 9600, or write to IAM House, 510 Chiswick High Road, London W4 5RG for an information pack.

Working on your car can be dangerous. This page shows just some of the potential risks and hazards, with the aim of creating a safety-conscious attitude.

General hazards

Scalding

• Don't remove the radiator or expansion tank cap while the engine is hot.
• Engine oil, automatic transmission fluid or power steering fluid may also be dangerously hot if the engine has recently been running.

Burning

• Beware of burns from the exhaust system and from any part of the engine. Brake discs and drums can also be extremely hot immediately after use.

Crushing

• When working under or near a raised vehicle, always supplement the jack with axle stands, or use drive-on ramps. *Never venture under a car which is only supported by a jack.*

• Take care if loosening or tightening high-torque nuts when the vehicle is on stands. Initial loosening and final tightening should be done with the wheels on the ground.

Fire

• Fuel is highly flammable; fuel vapour is explosive.
• Don't let fuel spill onto a hot engine.
• Do not smoke or allow naked lights (including pilot lights) anywhere near a vehicle being worked on. Also beware of creating sparks (electrically or by use of tools).
• Fuel vapour is heavier than air, so don't work on the fuel system with the vehicle over an inspection pit.
• Another cause of fire is an electrical overload or short-circuit. Take care when repairing or modifying the vehicle wiring.
• Keep a fire extinguisher handy, of a type suitable for use on fuel and electrical fires.

Electric shock

• Ignition HT voltage can be dangerous, especially to people with heart problems or a pacemaker. Don't work on or near the ignition system with the engine running or the ignition switched on.

• Mains voltage is also dangerous. Make sure that any mains-operated equipment is correctly earthed. Mains power points should be protected by a residual current device (RCD) circuit breaker.

Fume or gas intoxication

• Exhaust fumes are poisonous; they often contain carbon monoxide, which is rapidly fatal if inhaled. Never run the engine in a confined space such as a garage with the doors shut.
• Fuel vapour is also poisonous, as are the vapours from some cleaning solvents and paint thinners.

Poisonous or irritant substances

• Avoid skin contact with battery acid and with any fuel, fluid or lubricant, especially antifreeze, brake hydraulic fluid and Diesel fuel. Don't syphon them by mouth. If such a substance is swallowed or gets into the eyes, seek medical advice.
• Prolonged contact with used engine oil can cause skin cancer. Wear gloves or use a barrier cream if necessary. Change out of oil-soaked clothes and do not keep oily rags in your pocket.
• Air conditioning refrigerant forms a poisonous gas if exposed to a naked flame (including a cigarette). It can also cause skin burns on contact.

Asbestos

• Asbestos dust can cause cancer if inhaled or swallowed. Asbestos may be found in gaskets and in brake and clutch linings. When dealing with such components it is safest to assume that they contain asbestos.

Special hazards

Hydrofluoric acid

• This extremely corrosive acid is formed when certain types of synthetic rubber, found in some O-rings, oil seals, fuel hoses etc, are exposed to temperatures above 400°C. The rubber changes into a charred or sticky substance containing the acid. *Once formed, the acid remains dangerous for years. If it gets onto the skin, it may be necessary to amputate the limb concerned.*
• When dealing with a vehicle which has suffered a fire, or with components salvaged from such a vehicle, wear protective gloves and discard them after use.

The battery

• Batteries contain sulphuric acid, which attacks clothing, eyes and skin. Take care when topping-up or carrying the battery.
• The hydrogen gas given off by the battery is highly explosive. Never cause a spark or allow a naked light nearby. Be careful when connecting and disconnecting battery chargers or jump leads.

Air bags

• Air bags can cause injury if they go off accidentally. Take care when removing the steering wheel and/or facia. Special storage instructions may apply.

Diesel injection equipment

• Diesel injection pumps supply fuel at very high pressure. Take care when working on the fuel injectors and fuel pipes.

⚠ *Warning: Never expose the hands, face or any other part of the body to injector spray; the fuel can penetrate the skin with potentially fatal results.*

Remember...

DO

• Do use eye protection when using power tools, and when working under the vehicle.
• Do wear gloves or use barrier cream to protect your hands when necessary.
• Do get someone to check periodically that all is well when working alone on the vehicle.
• Do keep loose clothing and long hair well out of the way of moving mechanical parts.
• Do remove rings, wristwatch etc, before working on the vehicle – especially the electrical system.
• Do ensure that any lifting or jacking equipment has a safe working load rating adequate for the job.

DON'T

• Don't attempt to lift a heavy component which may be beyond your capability – get assistance.
• Don't rush to finish a job, or take unverified short cuts.
• Don't use ill-fitting tools which may slip and cause injury.
• Don't leave tools or parts lying around where someone can trip over them. Mop up oil and fuel spills at once.
• Don't allow children or pets to play in or near a vehicle being worked on.

VW Bora TDi Saloon

The Golf and Bora models covered by this manual date from late 2001 to the end of 2003.

Models have been produced with a wide range of engines, from the economical 1390 cc petrol engine, to the performance-orientated 1781 cc 20-valve turbo petrol engine, as well as normally-aspirated and turbocharged diesel engines. All petrol engines use fuel injection, and are fitted with a wide range of emission control systems. All the engines are of a well-proven design and, provided regular maintenance is carried out, are unlikely to give trouble.

Golf models are available in 3- and 5-door Hatchback, and 5-door Estate bodystyles, whilst Bora models are available in 4-door Saloon form. In some countries, the Bora is available as a 5-door Estate.

Fully-independent front suspension is fitted, with the components attached to a subframe assembly; the rear suspension is semi-independent, with a torsion beam and trailing arms.

A five-speed manual gearbox is fitted as standard to all models, with a four-speed automatic gearbox available as an option for some petrol and diesel models.

A wide range of standard and optional equipment is available within the model range to suit most tastes, including an anti-lock braking system and air conditioning.

For the home mechanic, Golf and Bora models are straightforward vehicles to maintain, and most of the items requiring frequent attention are easily accessible.

Your Golf and Bora Manual

The aim of this manual is to help you get the best value from your vehicle. It can do so in several ways. It can help you decide what work must be done (even should you choose to get it done by a garage). It will also provide information on routine maintenance and servicing, and give a logical course of action and diagnosis when random faults occur. However, it is hoped that you will use the manual by tackling the work yourself. On simpler jobs it may even be quicker than booking the car into a garage and going there twice, to leave and collect it. Perhaps most important, a lot of money can be saved by avoiding the costs a garage must charge to cover its labour and overheads.

The manual has drawings and descriptions to show the function of the various components so that their layout can be understood. Tasks are described and photographed in a clear step-by-step sequence.

References to the 'left' and 'right' of the vehicle are in the sense of a person in the driver's seat facing forward.

Acknowledgements

Thanks are due to Draper Tools Limited, who provided some of the workshop tools, and to all those people at Sparkford who helped in the production of this manual.

This manual is not a direct reproduction of the vehicle manufacturer's data, and its publication should not be taken as implying any technical approval by the vehicle manufacturers or importers.

We take great pride in the accuracy of information given in this manual, but vehicle manufacturers make alterations and design changes during the production run of a particular vehicle of which they do not inform us. No liability can be accepted by the authors or publishers for loss, damage or injury caused by any errors in, or omissions from, the information given.

VW Golf 5-door Estate

VWW Golf 5-door Hatchback

The following pages are intended to help in dealing with common roadside emergencies and breakdowns. You will find more detailed fault finding information at the back of the manual, and repair information in the main chapters.

If your car won't start and the starter motor doesn't turn

☐ Open the bonnet and make sure that the battery terminals are clean and tight.
☐ Switch on the headlights and try to start the engine. If the headlights go very dim when you're trying to start, the battery is probably flat. Get out of trouble by jump starting (see next page) using a friend's car.

If your car won't start even though the starter motor turns as normal

☐ Is there fuel in the tank?
☐ Is there any moisture on electrical components under the bonnet? Switch off the ignition, then wipe off any obvious dampness with a dry cloth. Spray a water-repellent aerosol product (WD-40 or equivalent) on ignition and fuel system electrical connectors.

A Check the condition and security of the battery connections.

B Check the fuses and fusible links in the fusebox located on top of the battery.

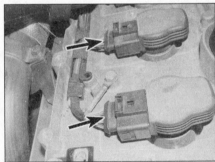

C Check the wiring to the ignition coils beneath the engine top cover (petrol models only)

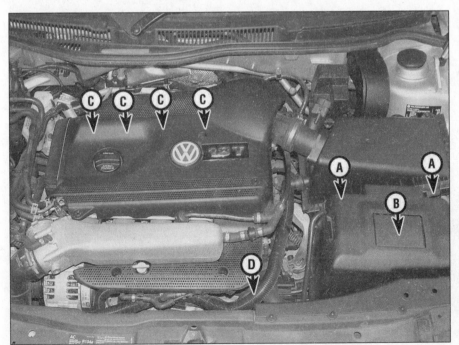

Check that electrical connections are secure (with the ignition switched off) and spray them with a water-dispersant spray like WD-40 if you suspect a problem due to damp

D Check that the starter motor wiring is secure

Jump starting

When jump-starting a car using a booster battery, observe the following precautions:

✔ Before connecting the booster battery, make sure that the ignition is switched off.

✔ Ensure that all electrical equipment (lights, heater, wipers, etc) is switched off.

✔ Take note of any special precautions printed on the battery case.

✔ Make sure that the booster battery is the same voltage as the discharged one in the vehicle.

✔ If the battery is being jump-started from the battery in another vehicle, the two vehicles MUST NOT TOUCH each other.

✔ Make sure that the transmission is in neutral.

 HAYNES HINT *Jump starting will get you out of trouble, but you must correct whatever made the battery go flat in the first place. There are three possibilities:*

1 The battery has been drained by repeated attempts to start, or by leaving the lights on.

2 The charging system is not working properly (alternator drivebelt slack or broken, alternator wiring fault or alternator itself faulty).

3 The battery itself is at fault (electrolyte low, or battery worn out).

1 Connect one end of the red jump lead to the positive (+) terminal of the flat battery

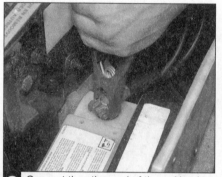

2 Connect the other end of the red lead to the positive (+) terminal of the booster battery.

3 Connect one end of the black jump lead to the negative (-) terminal of the booster battery

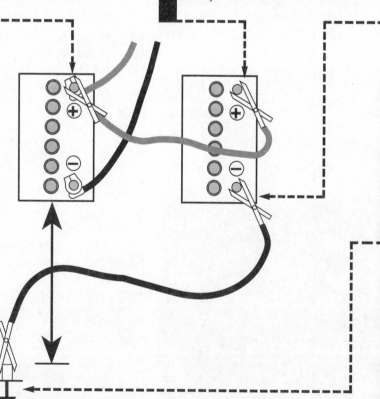

4 Connect the other end of the black jump lead to a suitable metal part of the engine on the vehicle to be started.

5 Make sure that the jump leads will not come into contact with the fan, drivebelts or other moving parts of the engine.

6 Start the engine using the booster battery and run it at idle speed. Switch on the lights, rear window demister and heater blower motor, then disconnect the jump leads in the reverse order of connection. Turn off the lights etc.

Wheel changing

Some of the details shown here will vary according to model

 Warning: Do not change a wheel in a situation where you risk being hit by another vehicle. On busy roads, try to stop in a lay-by or a gateway. Be wary of passing traffic while changing the wheel - it is easy to become distracted by the job in hand.

Preparation

☐ When a puncture occurs, stop as soon as it is safe to do so.

☐ Park on firm level ground, if possible, and well out of the way of other traffic.

☐ If you have one, use a warning triangle to alert other drivers of your presence.

☐ Apply the handbrake and engage first or reverse gear, or P on automatic transmission models.

☐ Use hazard warning lights if necessary.

☐ If the ground is soft, use a flat piece of wood to spread the load under the jack.

Changing the wheel

1 The spare wheel and tools are stored in the luggage compartment. Release the retaining strap, and lift out the jack and wheel changing tools from the centre of the wheel.

2 Unscrew the retainer and lift out the wheel.

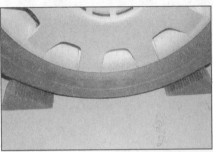

3 For safety, chock the diagonally opposite wheel – a couple of large stones will do for this.

4 Use the wire hook and wheel brace to remove the wheel trim. Where applicable, the hook can be used to remove the small central trim or wheel bolt caps.

5 Slacken each wheel bolt by half a turn.

6 Locate the jack below the reinforced point on the sill (don't jack the vehicle at any other point of the sill) and on firm ground, then turn the jack handle clockwise until the wheel is raised clear of the ground.

7 Unscrew the wheel bolts (using the box spanner provided) and remove the wheel. Fit the spare wheel, and screw in the bolts. Lightly tighten the bolts with the wheelbrace then lower the vehicle to the ground.

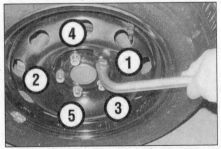

8 Securely tighten the wheel bolts in the sequence shown then refit the wheel trim/hub cap. Stow the punctured wheel back in the spare wheel well. Note that the wheel bolts should be tightened to the specified torque at the earliest possible opportunity.

Finally...

☐ Remove the wheel chocks.

☐ Stow the jack and tools in the spare wheel.

☐ Check the tyre pressure on the wheel just fitted. If it is low, or if you don't have a pressure gauge with you, drive slowly to the next garage and inflate the tyre to the correct pressure.

☐ Have the damaged tyre or wheel repaired as soon as possible.

Identifying leaks

Puddles on the garage floor or drive, or obvious wetness under the bonnet or underneath the car, suggest a leak that needs investigating. It can sometimes be difficult to decide where the leak is coming from, especially if the engine bay is very dirty already. Leaking oil or fluid can also be blown rearwards by the passage of air under the car, giving a false impression of where the problem lies.

 Warning: Most automotive oils and fluids are poisonous. Wash them off skin, and change out of contaminated clothing, without delay.

 The smell of a fluid leaking from the car may provide a clue to what's leaking. Some fluids are distinctively coloured. It may help to clean the car carefully and to park it over some clean paper overnight as an aid to locating the source of the leak. Remember that some leaks may only occur while the engine is running.

Sump oil

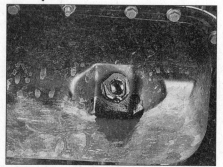

Engine oil may leak from the drain plug...

Oil from filter

...or from the base of the oil filter.

Gearbox oil

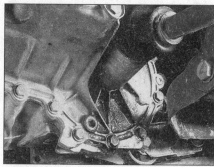

Gearbox oil can leak from the seals at the inboard ends of the driveshafts.

Antifreeze

Leaking antifreeze often leaves a crystalline deposit like this.

Brake fluid

A leak occurring at a wheel is almost certainly brake fluid.

Power steering fluid

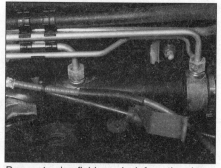

Power steering fluid may leak from the pipe connectors on the steering rack.

Towing

When all else fails, you may find yourself having to get a tow home – or of course you may be helping somebody else. Long-distance recovery should only be done by a garage or breakdown service. For shorter distances, DIY towing using another car is easy enough, but observe the following points:

☐ Use a proper tow-rope – they are not expensive. The vehicle being towed must display an ON TOW sign in its rear window.

☐ Always turn the ignition key to the 'on' position when the vehicle is being towed, so that the steering lock is released, and that the direction indicator and brake lights will work.

☐ On models with automatic transmission, do

not exceed 30 mph (50 kph) and do not tow for more than 30 miles (50 km). If in doubt, do not tow, or transmission damage may result.

☐ Before being towed, release the handbrake and select neutral on the transmission.

☐ Only attach the tow-rope to the towing eyes provided.

☐ Note that greater-than-usual pedal pressure will be required to operate the brakes, since the vacuum servo unit is only operational with the engine running.

☐ Because the power steering will not be operational, greater-than-usual steering effort will be required.

☐ The driver of the car being towed must

keep the tow-rope taut to avoid snatching.

☐ Make sure that both drivers know the route before setting off.

☐ Only drive at moderate speeds and keep the distance towed to a minimum. Drive smoothly and allow plenty of time for slowing down at junctions.

☐ The front towing eye is supplied as part of the toolkit stored in the luggage compartment. To fit the eye, remove the vent/cover from the front bumper. Screw the eye into position anti-clockwise (it has a **left-handed** thread), and tighten using the wheelbrace handle.

☐ The rear towing eye is located beneath the right-hand side of the rear bumper.

Introduction

There are some very simple checks which need only take a few minutes to carry out, but which could save you a lot of inconvenience and expense.

These *Weekly checks* require no great skill or special tools, and the small amount of time they take to perform could prove to be very well spent, for example:

☐ Keeping an eye on tyre condition and pressures, will not only help to stop them wearing out prematurely, but could also save your life.

☐ Many breakdowns are caused by electrical problems. Battery-related faults are particularly common, and a quick check on a regular basis will often prevent the majority of these.

☐ If your car develops a brake fluid leak, the first time you might know about it is when your brakes don't work properly. Checking the level regularly will give advance warning of this kind of problem.

☐ If the oil or coolant levels run low, the cost of repairing any engine damage will be far greater than fixing the leak, for example.

Underbonnet check points

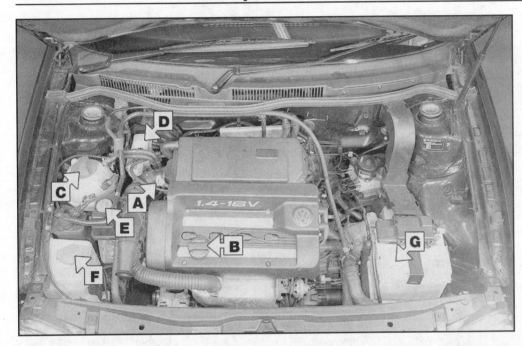

◀ 1.4 litre 16-valve petrol

A *Engine oil level dipstick*

B *Engine oil filler cap*

C *Coolant expansion tank*

D *Brake (and clutch*) fluid reservoir*

E *Power steering fluid reservoir*

F *Screen washer fluid reservoir*

G *Battery*

* *Manual transmission only*

◀ 1.8 litre 20-valve petrol

A *Engine oil level dipstick*

B *Engine oil filler cap*

C *Coolant expansion tank*

D *Brake (and clutch*) fluid reservoir*

E *Power steering fluid reservoir*

F *Screen washer fluid reservoir*

G *Battery*

* *Manual transmission only*

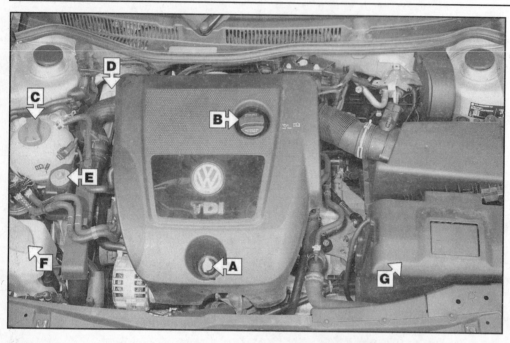

A *Engine oil level dipstick*

B *Engine oil filler cap*

C *Coolant expansion tank*

D *Brake (and clutch*) fluid reservoir*

E *Power steering fluid reservoir*

F *Screen washer fluid reservoir*

G *Battery*

* *Manual transmission only*

Engine oil level

Before you start

✔ Make sure that your car is on level ground.
✔ Check the oil level before the car is driven, or at least 5 minutes after the engine has been switched off.

 If the oil is checked immediately after driving the car, some of the oil will remain in the upper engine components, resulting in an inaccurate reading on the dipstick.

The correct oil

Modern engines place great demands on their oil. It is very important that the correct oil for your car is used (See *Lubricants and fluids*).

Car Care

● If you have to add oil frequently, you should check whether you have any oil leaks. Place some clean paper under the car overnight, and check for stains in the morning. If there are no leaks, the engine may be burning oil.

● Always maintain the level between the upper and lower dipstick marks. If the level is too low severe engine damage may occur. Oil seal failure may result if the engine is overfilled by adding too much oil.

1 The dipstick is often brightly coloured for easy identification (see *Underbonnet check points* for exact location). Withdraw the dipstick, then use a clean rag or paper towel to wipe the oil from it. Insert the clean dipstick into the tube as far as it will go, then withdraw it again.

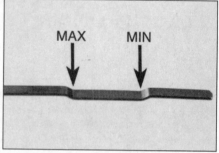

2 Note the level on the end of the dipstick, which should be between the upper (MAX) and lower (MIN) mark.

3 Oil is added through the filler cap aperture. Unscrew the cap.

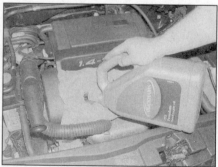

4 Place some cloth rags around the filler cap aperture, then top-up the level. A funnel may help to reduce spillage. Add the oil slowly, checking the level on the dipstick frequently. Avoid overfilling (see *Car care*).

Coolant level

Warning: DO NOT attempt to remove the expansion tank pressure cap when the engine is hot, as there is a very great risk of scalding. Do not leave open containers of coolant about, as it is poisonous.

Car Care

● With a sealed-type cooling system, adding coolant should not be necessary on a regular basis. If frequent topping-up is required, it is likely there is a leak. Check the radiator, all hoses and joint faces for signs of staining or wetness, and rectify as necessary.

● It is important that antifreeze is used in the cooling system all year round, not just during the winter months. Don't top-up with water alone, as the antifreeze will become too diluted.

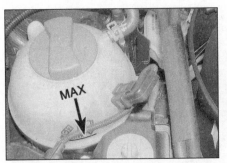

1 The coolant level varies with the temperature of the engine. When the engine is cold, the coolant level should be between the MIN and MAX marks.

2 If topping-up is necessary, wait until the engine is cold. Slowly unscrew the cap to release any pressure present in the cooling system, and remove the cap.

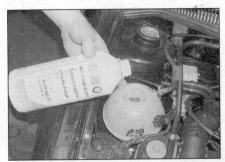

3 Add a mixture of water and the specified antifreeze (see Lubricants and fluids) to the expansion tank until the coolant level is halfway between the level marks. Refit the cap and tighten it securely.

Brake (and clutch*) fluid level

*On manual transmission models, the fluid reservoir also supplies the clutch master cylinder with fluid.

Warning:
● Brake fluid can harm your eyes and damage painted surfaces, so use extreme caution when handling and pouring it.
● Do not use fluid that has been standing open for some time, as it absorbs moisture from the air, which can cause a dangerous loss of braking effectiveness.

Before you start

✔ Make sure that your car is on level ground.

✔ Cleanliness is of great importance when dealing with the braking system, so take care to clean around the reservoir cap before topping-up. Use only clean brake fluid.

Safety First!

● If the reservoir requires repeated topping-up this is an indication of a fluid leak somewhere in the system, which should be investigated immediately.

● If a leak is suspected, the car should not be driven until the braking system has been checked. Never take any risks where brakes are concerned.

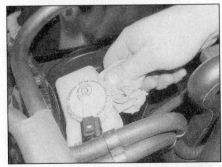

1 The MIN and MAX marks are indicated on the reservoir. The fluid level must be kept between the marks at all times. Note that the level will drop naturally as the brake pad linings wear, but must never be allowed to fall below the MIN mark. If topping-up is necessary, first wipe clean the area around the filler cap to prevent dirt entering the hydraulic system.

2 Unscrew and remove the reservoir cap.

3 Carefully add fluid, taking care not to spill it onto the surrounding components. Use only the specified fluid (see Lubricants and fluids); mixing different types can cause damage to the system. On completion, securely refit the cap and wipe away any spilt fluid.

Tyre condition and pressure

It is very important that tyres are in good condition, and at the correct pressure - having a tyre failure at any speed is highly dangerous. Tyre wear is influenced by driving style - harsh braking and acceleration, or fast cornering, will all produce more rapid tyre wear. As a general rule, the front tyres wear out faster than the rears. Interchanging the tyres from front to rear ("rotating" the tyres) may result in more even wear. However, if this is completely effective, you may have the expense of replacing all four tyres at once! Remove any nails or stones embedded in the tread before they penetrate the tyre to cause deflation. If removal of a nail does reveal that the tyre has been punctured, refit the nail so that its point of penetration is marked. Then immediately change the wheel, and have the tyre repaired by a tyre dealer.

Regularly check the tyres for damage in the form of cuts or bulges, especially in the sidewalls. Periodically remove the wheels, and clean any dirt or mud from the inside and outside surfaces. Examine the wheel rims for signs of rusting, corrosion or other damage. Light alloy wheels are easily damaged by "kerbing" whilst parking; steel wheels may also become dented or buckled. A new wheel is very often the only way to overcome severe damage.

New tyres should be balanced when they are fitted, but it may become necessary to re-balance them as they wear, or if the balance weights fitted to the wheel rim should fall off. Unbalanced tyres will wear more quickly, as will the steering and suspension components. Wheel imbalance is normally signified by vibration, particularly at a certain speed (typically around 50 mph). If this vibration is felt only through the steering, then it is likely that just the front wheels need balancing. If, however, the vibration is felt through the whole car, the rear wheels could be out of balance. Wheel balancing should be carried out by a tyre dealer or garage.

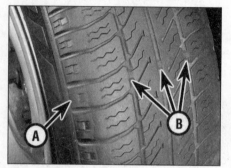

1 Tread Depth - visual check
The original tyres have tread wear safety bands (B), which will appear when the tread depth reaches approximately 1.6 mm. The band positions are indicated by a triangular mark on the tyre sidewall (A).

2 Tread Depth - manual check
Alternatively, tread wear can be monitored with a simple, inexpensive device known as a tread depth indicator gauge.

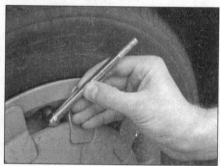

3 Tyre Pressure Check
Check the tyre pressures regularly with the tyres cold. Do not adjust the tyre pressures immediately after the vehicle has been used, or an inaccurate setting will result.

Tyre tread wear patterns

Shoulder Wear

Underinflation (wear on both sides)
Under-inflation will cause overheating of the tyre, because the tyre will flex too much, and the tread will not sit correctly on the road surface. This will cause a loss of grip and excessive wear, not to mention the danger of sudden tyre failure due to heat build-up.
Check and adjust pressures
Incorrect wheel camber (wear on one side)
Repair or renew suspension parts
Hard cornering
Reduce speed!

Centre Wear

Overinflation
Over-inflation will cause rapid wear of the centre part of the tyre tread, coupled with reduced grip, harsher ride, and the danger of shock damage occurring in the tyre casing.
Check and adjust pressures

If you sometimes have to inflate your car's tyres to the higher pressures specified for maximum load or sustained high speed, don't forget to reduce the pressures to normal afterwards.

Uneven Wear

Front tyres may wear unevenly as a result of wheel misalignment. Most tyre dealers and garages can check and adjust the wheel alignment (or "tracking") for a modest charge.
Incorrect camber or castor
Repair or renew suspension parts
Malfunctioning suspension
Repair or renew suspension parts
Unbalanced wheel
Balance tyres
Incorrect toe setting
Adjust front wheel alignment
Note: *The feathered edge of the tread which typifies toe wear is best checked by feel.*

Washer fluid level

● Screenwash additives not only keep the windscreen clean during bad weather, they also prevent the washer system freezing in cold weather – which is when you are likely to need it most. Don't top up using plain water, as the screenwash will become diluted and will freeze in cold weather.

 Warning: On no account use coolant antifreeze in the washer system - this could discolour or damage paintwork.

1 The screenwash fluid reservoir is located on the right-hand side of the engine compartment, behind the headlight. Pull up the filler cap to release it from the reservoir.

2 When topping-up the reservoir, a screenwash additive should be added in the quantities recommended on the bottle.

Battery

Caution: Before carrying out any work on the vehicle battery, read the precautions given in Safety first! at the start of this manual.

✔ Make sure that the battery tray is in good condition, and that the clamp is tight. Corrosion on the tray, retaining clamp and the battery itself can be removed with a solution of water and baking soda. Thoroughly rinse all cleaned areas with water. Any metal parts damaged by corrosion should be covered with a zinc-based primer, then painted.

✔ Periodically (approximately every three months), check the charge condition of the battery as described in Chapter 5A. A 'magic eye' charge indicator is fitted to the standard battery – if the indicator is green in colour, the battery is fully charged, however, if it is colourless, it should be recharged. If it is yellow in colour, the battery should be renewed.

✔ If the battery is flat, and you need to jump start your vehicle, see *Jump starting*.

1 The battery is located in the front left-hand corner of the engine compartment. Remove the cover from the heat protective jacket by pressing the side buttons to gain access to the battery terminals. The exterior of the battery should be inspected periodically for damage such as a cracked case or cover.

2 Check the security and condition of all the battery and fuse connections. The exterior of the battery should be inspected periodically for damage such as a cracked case or cover.

3 If corrosion (white, fluffy deposits) is evident, remove the cables from the battery terminals (refer to *Disconnecting the battery* in the Reference chapter at the end of this manual), clean them with a small wire brush, then refit them. Automotive stores sell a tool for cleaning the battery post . . .

4 . . . as well as the battery cable clamps. **Note: VW specifically prohibit the use of grease on the battery terminals.**

Electrical systems

✔ Check all external lights and the horn. Refer to the appropriate Sections of Chapter 12 for details if any of the circuits are found to be inoperative, and renew the fuse if necessary.

✔ Visually check all accessible wiring connectors, harnesses and retaining clips for security, and for signs of chafing or damage.

 If you need to check your brake lights and indicators unaided, back up to a wall or garage door and operate the lights. The reflected light should show if they are working properly.

1 If a single indicator light, brake light or headlight has failed, it is likely that a bulb has blown and will need to be renewed. Refer to Chapter 12 for details. If both brake lights have failed, it is possible that the brake light switch operated by the brake pedal has failed. Refer to Chapter 9 for details.

2 If more than one indicator light or headlight has failed, it is likely that either a fuse has blown or that there is a fault in the circuit (see *Electrical fault finding* in Chapter 12). The main fuses are in the fusebox beneath a cover on the right-hand end of the facia panel. Use a small screwdriver to prise off the cover. The circuits protected by the fuses are shown on the inside of the cover. Additional heavy duty fuses and fusible links are in the fusebox located on top of the battery.

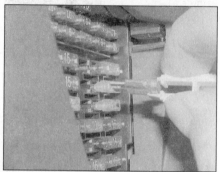

3 To renew a blown fuse, pull it from its location in the fusebox, using the plastic pliers provided. Fit a new fuse of the same rating, available from car accessory shops. It is important that you find the reason that the fuse blew (see *Electrical fault finding* in Chapter 12).

Wiper blades

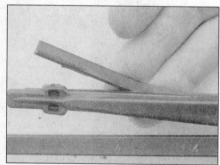

1 Check the condition of the wiper blades; if they are cracked or show any signs of deterioration, or if the glass swept area is smeared, renew them. For maximum clarity of vision, wiper blades should be renewed annually, as a matter of course.

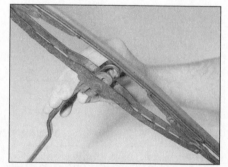

2 To remove a windscreen wiper blade, pull the arm fully away from the screen until it locks. Swivel the blade through 90°, press the locking tab with your fingers, and slide the blade out of the hooked end of the arm.

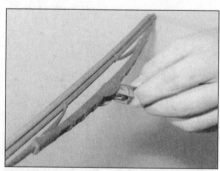

3 Where applicable, don't forget to check the tailgate wiper blade as well. To remove the blade, depress the retaining tab and slide the blade out of the hooked end of the arm.

Lubricants and fluids

Engine (petrol)
Standard (distance/time) service interval . . . .   Multigrade engine oil, viscosity SAE 5W/40 to 20W/50, to API SG/CD

LongLife (variable) service interval . . . .   VW LongLife engine oil part number VW 503 00*

Engine (diesel)
Standard (distance/time) service interval . . . .   Multigrade engine oil, viscosity SAE 5W/40 to 20W/50, to API SG/CD

LongLife (variable) service interval . . . .   VW LongLife engine oil part number VW 506 00**

Cooling system . . . .   VW additive G12 only (antifreeze and corrosion protection)
Manual transmission . . . .   VWG50 gear oil, viscosity SAE 75W/90 (synthetic)
Automatic transmission:
Main transmission (01M) . . . .   VW ATF
Final drive (01M) . . . .   VWG50 gear oil, viscosity SAE 75W/90 (synthetic)
Main transmission and final drive (09A) . . . .   VW ATF
Braking system . . . .   Hydraulic fluid to SAE J1703F or DOT 4
Power steering reservoir . . . .   VW hydraulic oil G 002 000

* A maximum of 0.5 litres of standard VW 502 00 oil may be used for topping-up when LongLife oil is unobtainable
** A maximum of 0.5 litres of standard VW 505 00 oil may be used for topping-up when LongLife oil is unobtainable

Choosing your engine oil

Engines need oil, not only to lubricate moving parts and minimise wear, but also to maximise power output and to improve fuel economy.

HOW ENGINE OIL WORKS

• Beating friction

Without oil, the moving surfaces inside your engine will rub together, heat up and melt, quickly causing the engine to seize. Engine oil creates a film which separates these moving parts, preventing wear and heat build-up.

• Cooling hot-spots

Temperatures inside the engine can exceed 1000° C. The engine oil circulates and acts as a coolant, transferring heat from the hot-spots to the sump.

• Cleaning the engine internally

Good quality engine oils clean the inside of your engine, collecting and dispersing combustion deposits and controlling them until they are trapped by the oil filter or flushed out at oil change.

OIL CARE - FOLLOW THE CODE

To handle and dispose of used engine oil safely, always:

• **Avoid skin contact with used engine oil. Repeated or prolonged contact can be harmful.**
• **Dispose of used oil and empty packs in a responsible manner in an authorised disposal site. Call 0800 663366 to find the one nearest to you. Never tip oil down drains or onto the ground.**

Tyre pressures

Note: *The recommended tyre pressures for each vehicle are given on a sticker attached to the rear of the fuel filler flap. The pressures given are for the original equipment tyres – the recommended pressures may vary if any other make or type of tyre is fitted; check with the tyre manufacturer or supplier for latest recommendations. The following pressures are typical.*

	Front	Rear
Golf models		
Normal load	1.9 bars (28 psi)	1.9 bars (28 psi)
Full load:		
175/80R14 tyres	2.2 bars (32 psi)	3.0 bars (44 psi)
All other tyres	2.1 bars (30 psi)	2.6 bars (38 psi)
Bora models		
Normal load	1.9 bars (28 psi)	1.9 bars (28 psi)
Full load	2.1 bars (30 psi)	2.8 bars (41 psi)

Notes

Chapter 1 Part A:
Routine maintenance and servicing – petrol models

Contents

Air filter element renewal 24
Airbag unit check 19
Antifreeze check 9
Automatic transmission final drive oil level check 29
Automatic transmission fluid level check 28
Auxiliary drivebelt check 8
Auxiliary drivebelt check and renewal 26
Battery check 17
Brake (and clutch) fluid renewal 31
Brake hydraulic circuit check 10
Brake pad check 4
Coolant renewal 32
Driveshaft gaiter check 15
Engine management self-diagnosis memory fault check 21
Engine oil and filter renewal 3
Exhaust system check 6

Headlight beam adjustment 11
Hinge and lock lubrication 18
Hose and fluid leak check 7
Introduction 1
Manual transmission oil level check 13
Pollen filter element renewal 12
Power steering hydraulic fluid level check 27
Regular maintenance 2
Resetting the service interval display 5
Road test and exhaust emissions check 23
Spark plug renewal 25
Steering and suspension check 16
Sunroof check and lubrication 22
Timing belt renewal 30
Underbody protection check 14
Windscreen/tailgate/headlight washer system check 20

Degrees of difficulty

Easy, suitable for novice with little experience

Fairly easy, suitable for beginner with some experience

Fairly difficult, suitable for competent DIY mechanic

Difficult, suitable for experienced DIY mechanic

Very difficult, suitable for expert DIY or professional

Lubricants and fluids

Refer to end of *Weekly checks* on page 0•17

Capacities

Engine oil – including filter (approximate)

1.4 litre engine	3.2 litres
1.6 litre engine	
SOHC engine	4.5 litres
DOHC engine	3.2 litres
1.8 litre engine	4.5 litres
2.0 litre engine	4.0 litres

Cooling system (approximate)

1.4 litre engine	6.0 litres
1.6 litre engine	
SOHC engine	5.0 litres
DOHC engine	6.0 litres
1.8 and 2.0 litre engines	5.0 litres

Transmission

Manual transmission:	
Type 02K	1.9 litres
Type 02J	2.0 litres
Automatic transmission (Type 01M):	
Main transmission	5.3 litres
Final drive	0.75 litres
Automatic transmission (Type 09A):	
Main transmission unit incl final drive	7.0 litres

Power-assisted steering

All models	0.7 to 0.9 litres

Fuel tank (approximate)

All models	55 litres

Washer reservoirs

Models with headlight washers	5.5 litres
Models without headlight washers	3.0 litres

Cooling system

Antifreeze mixture:	
40% antifreeze	Protection down to -25°C
50% antifreeze	Protection down to -35°C

Note: *Refer to antifreeze manufacturer for latest recommendations.*

Ignition system

Spark plugs:	Type	Electrode gap
1.4 litre engine	Bosch F 7 HPP 222	1.0 mm
	NGK BKUR6ET-10	1.0 mm
	VW 101000033AA	1.0 mm
1.6 litre engine:		
8-valve:		
Codes AEH and AKL	Bosch FR 7 LD+	0.9 mm
	NGK BKUR6ET-10	1.0 mm
	VW 101000033AA	1.0 mm
Code AVU	Bosch F 7 HPP 222	1.0 mm
	NGK BKUR6ET-10	1.0 mm
	VW 101000033AA	1.0 mm
Code BFQ	NGK BKUR6ET-10	1.0 mm
	VW 101000033AA	1.0 mm
16-valve, codes AZD and BCB	Bosch F 7 HPP 222	1.0 mm
	NGK PZFR5D-11	1.1 mm
	VW 101000062AB	1.1 mm
1.8 litre engine	Bosch F 7 HPP 222 T	0.8 mm
	NGK PFR6Q	0.8 mm
	VW 101000063AA	0.8 mm
2.0 litre engine	Bosch F 7 HPP 222	1.0 mm
	NGK BKUR6ET-10	1.0 mm
	VW 101000033AA	1.0 mm

Brakes

Brake pad minimum thickness:
Front . . . . 7.0 mm (including backing plate)
Rear . . . . 7.5 mm (including backing plate)

Torque wrench settings

	Nm	lbf ft
Automatic transmission level plug	15	11
Manual gearbox filler/level plug	25	18
Roadwheel bolts	120	89
Spark plugs	30	22
Sump drain plug:		
1.4, 1.6 and 2.0 litre engines	30	22
1.8 litre engine	40	30

Maintenance schedule

The maintenance intervals in this manual are provided with the assumption that you, not the dealer, will be carrying out the work. These are the minimum intervals recommended by us for vehicles driven daily. If you wish to keep your vehicle in peak condition at all times, you may wish to perform some of these procedures more often. We encourage frequent maintenance, since it enhances the efficiency, performance and resale value of your vehicle.

When the vehicle is new, it should be serviced by a dealer service department, in order to preserve the factory warranty.

All VW Golf/Bora models are equipped with a service interval display indicator in the instrument panel. Every time the engine is started the panel will illuminate for approx-imately 20 seconds with service information. With the standard non-variable display, the service intervals are in accordance with specific distances and time periods. With the LongLife display, the service interval is variable according to the number of starts, length of journeys, vehicle speeds, brake pad wear, bonnet opening frequency, fuel consumption, oil level and oil temperature, however the vehicle **must** be serviced at least every two years. At a distance of 2000 miles (3000 km) before the next service is due, 'Service in 2000 miles' (or '3000 km') will appear at the bottom of the speedometer, and this figure will reduce in steps of 100 units as the vehicle is used. Once the service interval has been reached, the display will flash 'Service' or 'Service Now'. Note that if the variable (LongLife) service interval is being used, the engine must **only** be filled with the recommended **long-life** engine oil (see *Recommended lubricants and fluids*).

After completing a service, VW technicians use a special instrument to reset the service display to the next service interval, and a print-out is put in the vehicle service record. The display can be reset by the owner as described in Section 5, but note that for models using the 'LongLife' interval, the procedure will automatically reset the display to the 10 000 miles/15 000 km 'distance' interval. To have the display reset to the 'variable' (LongLife) interval, it is necessary to take the vehicle to a VW dealer who will use a special instrument to encode the on-board computer.

Models using distance and time intervals

Note: *The following service intervals are only applicable to models with a PR number of QG0 or QG2 (shown in the vehicle Service Schedule booklet or on the Next Service sticker located on the driver's door pillar).*

Every 250 miles (400 km) or weekly

☐ Refer to *Weekly checks*

Every 5000 miles (7500 km) or 6 months

☐ Renew the engine oil and filter (Section 3)

Note: *Frequent oil and filter changes are good for the engine. We recommend changing the oil at the mileage specified here, or at least twice a year if the mileage covered is a less.*

Every 10 000 miles (15 000 km) or 12 months, whichever comes first – 'Oil' on display

In addition to the items listed above, carry out the following:

☐ Check the front and rear brake pad thickness (Section 4)
☐ Reset the service interval display (Section 5)

Every 20 000 miles (30 000 km) or 2 years, whichever comes first – '01' on display

In addition to the items listed above, carry out the following:

☐ Check the condition of the exhaust system and its mountings (Section 6)
☐ Check all underbonnet components and hoses for fluid and oil leaks (Section 7)
☐ Check the condition of the auxiliary drivebelt (Section 8)
☐ Check the coolant antifreeze concentration (Section 9)
☐ Check the brake hydraulic circuit for leaks and damage (Section 10)
☐ Check the headlight beam adjustment (Section 11)
☐ Renew the pollen filter element (Section 12)
☐ Check the manual transmission oil level (Section 13)
☐ Check the underbody protection for damage (Section 14)
☐ Check the condition of the driveshaft gaiters (Section 15)
☐ Check the steering and suspension components for condition and security (Section 16)
☐ Check the battery condition, security and electrolyte level (Section 17)

Every 20 000 miles (30 000 km) or 2 years, whichever comes first – '01' on display (continued)

☐ Lubricate all hinges and locks (Section 18)
☐ Check the condition of the airbag unit(s) (Section 19)
☐ Check the operation of the windscreen/tailgate/headlight washer system(s) (as applicable) (Section 20)
☐ Check the engine management self-diagnosis memory for faults (Section 21)
☐ Check the operation of the sunroof and lubricate the guide rails (Section 22)
☐ Carry out a road test and check exhaust emissions (Section 23)

Every 40 000 miles (60 000 km) or 4 years, whichever comes first

☐ Renew the air filter element (Section 24)
☐ Renew the spark plugs (Section 25)
☐ Check the condition of the auxiliary drivebelt (Section 26)
☐ Check the power steering hydraulic fluid level (Section 27)
☐ Check the automatic transmission fluid level (Section 28)
☐ Check the automatic transmission final drive oil level (Section 29)

Every 60 000 miles (90 000 km)

☐ Renew the timing belt (Section 30)

Note: *VW specify timing belt inspection after the first 60 000 miles (90 000 km) and then every 20 000 mile (30 000 km) until the renewal interval of 120 000 miles (180 000 km), however, if the vehicle is used mainly for short journeys, we recommend that this shorter renewal interval is adhered to. The belt renewal interval is very much up to the individual owner but, bearing in mind that severe engine damage will result if the belt breaks in use, we recommend the shorter interval.*

Every 2 years

☐ Renew the brake (and clutch) fluid (Section 31)
☐ Renew the coolant (Section 32)*

***Note:** This work is not included in the VW schedule and should not be required if the recommended VW G12 LongLife coolant antifreeze/inhibitor is used.*

Models using 'LongLife' variable intervals

The LongLife variable service intervals are only applicable to models with a PR number of QG1 (shown in the vehicle Service Schedule booklet or on the Next Service sticker located on the driver's door pillar). The occurrence of the service on the display unit will depend on how the vehicle is being used (number of starts, length of journeys, vehicle speeds, brake pad wear, bonnet opening frequency, fuel consumption, oil level and oil temperature). For example, if a vehicle is being used under extreme driving conditions, the 'oil' service may occur at 10 000 miles, whereas, if the vehicle is being used under moderate driving conditions, it may occur at 20 000 miles. It is important to realise that this system is completely variable according to how the vehicle is being used, and therefore the service should be carried out when indicated on the display. When an OIL CHANGE SERVICE ('Oil') or INSPECTION SERVICE ('01') is due, follow the relevant procedure described for the normal 'distance and time' intervals.

Every 250 miles (400 km) or weekly

☐ Refer to *Weekly checks*

Every 5000 miles (7500 km) or 6 months

☐ Renew the engine oil and filter (Section 3)

Note: *Frequent oil and filter changes are good for the engine. We recommend changing the oil at the mileage specified here, or at least twice a year if the mileage covered is a less.*

'Oil' on display

In addition to the items listed above, carry out the following:

☐ Check the front and rear brake pad thickness (Section 4)
☐ Reset the service interval display (Section 5)

'01' on display or every 2 years, whichever comes first

In addition to the items listed above, carry out the following:

☐ Check the condition of the exhaust system and its mountings (Section 6)
☐ Check all underbonnet components and hoses for fluid and oil leaks (Section 7)
☐ Check the condition of the auxiliary drivebelt (Section 8)
☐ Check the coolant antifreeze concentration (Section 9)
☐ Check the brake hydraulic circuit for leaks and damage (Section 10)
☐ Check the headlight beam adjustment (Section 11)
☐ Renew the pollen filter element (Section 12)
☐ Check the manual transmission oil level (Section 13)
☐ Check the underbody protection for damage (Section 14)
☐ Check the condition of the driveshaft gaiters (Section 15)
☐ Check the steering and suspension components for condition and security (Section 16)
☐ Check the battery condition, security and electrolyte level (Section 17)
☐ Lubricate all hinges and locks (Section 18)
☐ Check the condition of the airbag unit(s) (Section 19)

'01' on display or every 2 years, whichever comes first (continued)

☐ Check the operation of the windscreen/tailgate/headlight washer system(s) (as applicable) (Section 20)
☐ Check the engine management self-diagnosis memory for faults (Section 21)
☐ Check the operation of the sunroof and lubricate the guide rails (Section 22)
☐ Carry out a road test and check exhaust emissions (Section 23)

Every 40 000 miles (60 000 km) or 4 years, whichever comes first

☐ Renew the air filter element (Section 24)
☐ Renew the spark plugs (Section 25)
☐ Check the condition of the auxiliary drivebelt (Section 26)
☐ Check the power steering hydraulic fluid level (Section 27)
☐ Check the automatic transmission fluid level (Section 28)
☐ Check the automatic transmission final drive oil level (Section 29)

Every 60 000 miles (90 000 km)

☐ Renew the timing belt (Section 30)

Note: *VW specify timing belt inspection after the first 60 000 miles (90 000 km) and then every 20 000 mile (30 000 km) until the renewal interval of 120 000 miles (180 000 km), however, if the vehicle is used mainly for short journeys, we recommend that this shorter renewal interval is adhered to. The belt renewal interval is very much up to the individual owner but, bearing in mind that severe engine damage will result if the belt breaks in use, we recommend the shorter interval.*

Every 2 years

☐ Renew the brake (and clutch) fluid (Section 31)
☐ Renew the coolant (Section 32)*

* Note: *This work is not included in the VW schedule and should not be required if the recommended VW G12 LongLife coolant antifreeze/inhibitor is used.*

Underbonnet view of a 1.8 turbo model

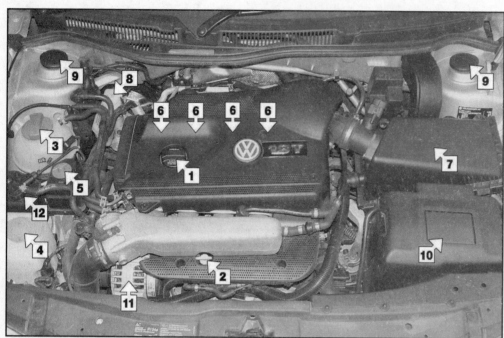

1 Engine oil filler cap
2 Engine oil dipstick
3 Coolant expansion tank
4 Windscreen/headlight washer fluid reservoir
5 Power steering fluid reservoir
6 Ignition coils and spark plugs (beneath top cover)
7 Air cleaner
8 Brake master cylinder fluid reservoir
9 Front suspension strut upper mountings
10 Battery
11 Alternator
12 Evaporative emission charcoal canister

Front underbody view of a 1.4 model

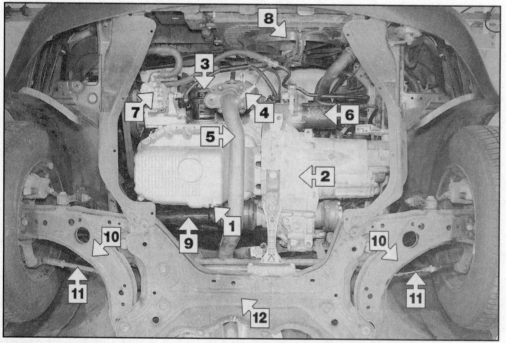

1 Sump drain plug
2 Manual transmission
3 Oil filter
4 Oxygen sensor
5 Exhaust front pipe
6 Starter motor
7 Power steering pump
8 Radiator and electric cooling fan
9 Driveshafts
10 Front suspension lower arms
11 Steering track rods
12 Crossmember

Rear underbody view of a 1.4 model

1 Fuel tank
2 Fuel filter
3 Rear axle assembly
4 Rear axle front mountings
5 Rear suspension coil springs
6 Handbrake cables
7 Rear suspension shock absorbers
8 Exhaust rear silencer and tailpipe

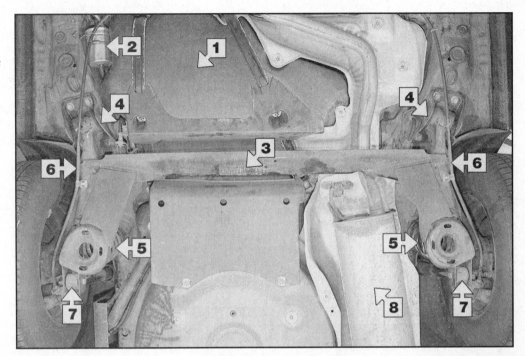

1 Introduction

This Chapter is designed to help the home mechanic maintain his/her vehicle for safety, economy, long life and peak performance.

The Chapter contains a master maintenance schedule, followed by Sections dealing specifically with each task in the schedule. Visual checks, adjustments, component renewal and other helpful items are included. Refer to the accompanying illustrations of the engine compartment and the underside of the vehicle for the locations of the various components.

Servicing your vehicle will provide a planned maintenance programme, which should result in a long and reliable service life. This is a comprehensive plan, so maintaining some items but not others will not produce the same results.

As you service your vehicle, you will discover that many of the procedures can – and should – be grouped together, because of the particular procedure being performed, or because of the proximity of two otherwise unrelated components to one another. For example, if the vehicle is raised for any reason, the exhaust can be inspected at the same time as the suspension and steering components.

The first step in this maintenance pro-gramme is to prepare yourself before the actual work begins. Read through all the Sections relevant to the work to be carried out, then make a list and gather all the parts and tools required. If a problem is encountered, seek advice from a parts specialist, or a dealer service department.

2 Regular maintenance

1 If, from the time the vehicle is new, the routine maintenance schedule is followed closely, and frequent checks are made of fluid levels and high-wear items, as suggested throughout this manual, the engine will be kept in relatively good running condition, and the need for additional work will be minimised.
2 It is possible that there will be times when the engine is running poorly due to the lack of regular maintenance. This is even more likely if a used vehicle, which has not received regular and frequent maintenance checks, is purchased. In such cases, additional work may need to be carried out, outside of the regular maintenance intervals.
3 If engine wear is suspected, a compression test (refer to the relevant Part of Chapter 2) will provide valuable information regarding the overall performance of the main internal components. Such a test can be used as a basis to decide on the extent of the work to be carried out. If, for example, a compression test indicates serious internal engine wear, conventional maintenance as described in this Chapter will not greatly improve the performance of the engine, and may prove a waste of time and money, unless extensive overhaul work is carried out first.
4 The following series of operations are those most often required to improve the perform-ance of a generally poor-running engine:

Primary operations

a) Clean, inspect and test the battery (See 'Weekly checks').
b) Check all the engine-related fluids (See 'Weekly checks').
c) Check the condition and tension of the auxiliary drivebelt (Section 8).
d) Renew the spark plugs (Section 25).
e) Check the condition of the air filter, and renew if necessary (Section 24).
f) Check the condition of all hoses, and check for fluid leaks (Section 7).
5 If the above operations do not prove fully effective, carry out the following secondary operations:

Secondary operations

All items listed under Primary operations, plus the following:
a) Check the charging system (see Chapter 5A).
b) Check the ignition system (see Chapter 5B).
c) Check the fuel system (see Chapter 4A).
d) Renew the ignition HT leads (where applicable).

3.3 The engine oil drain plug location on the sump

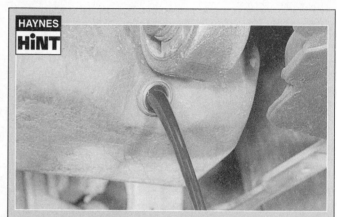

Keep the drain plug pressed into the sump while unscrewing it by hand the last couple of turns. As the plug releases, move it away sharply so the stream of oil issuing from the sump runs into the container, not up your sleeve.

Every 5000 miles or 6 months

3 Engine oil and filter renewal

1 Frequent oil and filter changes are the most important maintenance procedures which can be undertaken by the DIY owner. As engine oil ages, it becomes diluted and contaminated, which leads to premature engine wear.

2 Before starting this procedure, gather all the necessary tools and materials. Also make sure that you have plenty of clean rags and newspapers handy, to mop-up any spills. Ideally, the engine oil should be warm, as it will drain better, and more built-up sludge will be removed with it. Take care, however, not to touch the exhaust or any other hot parts of the engine when working under the vehicle. To avoid any possibility of scalding, and to protect yourself from possible skin irritants and other harmful contaminants in used engine oils, it is advisable to wear gloves when carrying out this work. Access to the underside of the vehicle will be greatly improved if it can be raised on a lift, driven onto ramps, or jacked up and supported on axle stands (see *Jacking and vehicle support*). Whichever method is chosen, make sure that the vehicle remains level, or if it is at an angle, that the drain plug is at the lowest point. Undo the retaining screws and remove the engine undershield(s), then also remove the engine top cover where applicable.

3 Using a socket and wrench or a ring spanner, slacken the drain plug about half a turn **(see illustration)**. Position the draining container under the drain plug, then remove the plug completely **(see Haynes Hint)**. Recover the sealing ring from the drain plug.

4 Allow some time for the old oil to drain, noting that it may be necessary to reposition the container as the oil flow slows to a trickle.

5 After all the oil has drained, wipe off the drain plug with a clean rag, and fit a new sealing washer. Clean the area around the drain plug opening, and refit the plug. Tighten the plug to the specified torque.

6 If the filter is also to be renewed, move the container into position under the oil filter, which is located on the left-hand side of the cylinder block.

7 Using an oil filter removal tool if necessary, slacken the filter initially, then unscrew it by hand the rest of the way. Empty the oil in the filter into the container.

8 Use a clean rag to remove all oil, dirt and sludge from the filter sealing area on the engine. Check the old filter to make sure that the rubber sealing ring has not stuck to the engine. If it has, carefully remove it.

9 Apply a light coating of clean engine oil to the sealing ring on the new filter, then screw it into position on the engine. Tighten the filter firmly by hand only – **do not** use any tools.

10 Remove the old oil and all tools from under the car. Refit the engine undershield(s), tighten the retaining screws securely, then lower the car to the ground. Also refit the engine top cover where applicable.

11 Remove the dipstick, then unscrew the oil filler cap from the cylinder head cover. Fill the engine, using the correct grade and type of oil (see *Lubricants and fluids*). An oil can spout or funnel may help to reduce spillage. Pour in half the specified quantity of oil first, then wait a few minutes for the oil to run to the sump. Continue adding oil a small quantity at a time until the level is up to the maximum mark on the dipstick. Refit the filler cap.

12 Start the engine and run it for a few minutes; check for leaks around the oil filter seal and the sump drain plug. Note that there may be a few seconds delay before the oil pressure warning light goes out when the engine is started, as the oil circulates through the engine oil galleries and the new oil filter (where fitted) before the pressure builds-up.

⚠ *Warning: On turbocharged engines, do not increase the engine speed above idling while the oil pressure light is illuminated, as considerable damage can be caused to the turbocharger.*

13 Switch off the engine, and wait a few minutes for the oil to settle in the sump once more. With the new oil circulated and the filter completely full, recheck the level on the dipstick, and add more oil as necessary.

14 Dispose of the used engine oil safely, with reference to *General repair procedures* in the *Reference* section of this manual.

4.1 The outer brake pads can be observed through the holes in the wheels

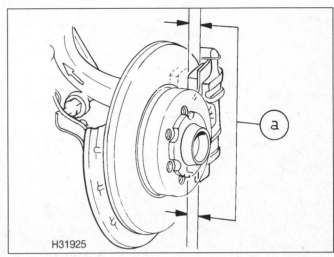

4.3 The thickness (a) of the brake pads must not be less than the specified amount

Every 10 000 miles or 'Oil' on display

4 Brake pad check

1 The outer brake pads can be checked without removing the wheels, by observing the brake pads through the holes in the wheels **(see illustration)**. If necessary, remove the wheel trim. The thickness of the pad lining and backing plate must not be less than the dimension given in the Specifications.

2 If the outer pads are worn near their limits, it is worthwhile checking the inner pads as well. Apply the handbrake then jack up vehicle and support it on axle stands (see *Jacking and vehicle support*). Remove the roadwheels.

3 Use a steel rule to check the thickness of the brake pads (including the backing plate), and compare with the minimum thickness given in the Specifications **(see illustration)**.

4 For a comprehensive check, the brake pads should be removed and cleaned. The operation of the caliper can then also be checked, and the condition of the brake disc

itself can be fully examined on both sides. Refer to Chapter 9.

5 If any pad's friction material is worn to the specified minimum thickness or less, *all four pads at the front or rear, as applicable, must be renewed as a set.*

6 On completion of the check, refit the road-wheels and lower the vehicle to the ground.

5 Resetting the service interval display

1 After all necessary maintenance work has been completed, the service interval display must be reset. VW technicians use a special dedicated instrument to do this, and a print-out is then put in the vehicle service record. It is possible for the owner to reset the display as described in the following paragraphs, but note that the procedure will automatically reset the display to a 10 000 mile (15 000 km) interval. To continue with the 'variable' intervals which take into consideration the number of starts, length of journeys, vehicle

speeds, brake pad wear, bonnet opening frequency, fuel consumption, oil level and oil temperature, the display must be reset by a VW dealership using the special dedicated instrument.

2 To reset the standard display manually, switch off the ignition, then press and hold down the trip reset button beneath the speedometer. Turn the digital clock reset knob clockwise, and the trip display will now show 'service - - -'. Depress the clock reset knob as required to alternate between individual services, however, do not zero the display otherwise incorrect readings will be shown.

3 To reset the LongLife display manually, switch off the ignition, then press and hold down the trip reset button beneath the speedometer. Switch on the ignition and release the reset button, and note that the relevant service will appear in the display. Turn the digital clock reset knob clockwise, and the display will now return to normal. Switch off the ignition to complete the resetting procedure. Do not zero the display otherwise incorrect readings will be shown.

Every 20 000 miles, 2 years or '01' on display

6 Exhaust system check

1 With the engine cold (at least an hour after the vehicle has been driven), check the complete exhaust system from the engine to the end of the tailpipe. The exhaust system is most easily checked with the vehicle raised on a hoist, or supported on axle stands, so that the exhaust components are readily visible and accessible (see *Jacking and vehicle support*).

2 Check the exhaust pipes and connections for evidence of leaks, severe corrosion and damage. Make sure that all brackets and mountings are in good condition, and that all relevant nuts and bolts are tight. Leakage at any of the joints or in other parts of the system will usually show up as a black sooty stain in the vicinity of the leak.

3 Rattles and other noises can often be traced to the exhaust system, especially the brackets and mountings. Try to move the pipes and silencers. If the components are able to come into contact with the body or

suspension parts, secure the system with new mountings. Otherwise separate the joints (if possible) and twist the pipes as necessary to provide additional clearance.

7 Hose and fluid leak check

1 Visually inspect the engine joint faces, gaskets and seals for any signs of water or oil leaks. Pay particular attention to the areas

A leak in the cooling system will usually show up as white- or rust-coloured deposits on the area adjoining the leak.

around the camshaft cover, cylinder head, oil filter and sump joint faces. Bear in mind that, over a period of time, some very slight seepage from these areas is to be expected – what you are really looking for is any indication of a serious leak. Should a leak be found, renew the offending gasket or oil seal by referring to the appropriate Chapters in this manual.

2 Also check the security and condition of all the engine-related pipes and hoses. Ensure that all cable-ties or securing clips are in place and in good condition. Clips which are broken or missing can lead to chafing of the hoses, pipes or wiring, which could cause more serious problems in the future.

3 Carefully check the radiator hoses and heater hoses along their entire length. Renew any hose which is cracked, swollen or deteriorated. Cracks will show up better if the hose is squeezed. Pay close attention to the hose clips that secure the hoses to the cooling system components. Hose clips can pinch and puncture hoses, resulting in cooling system leaks.

4 Inspect all the cooling system components (hoses, joint faces, etc) for leaks **(see Haynes Hint)**. Where any problems of this nature are found on system components, renew the component or gasket with reference to Chapter 3.

5 Where applicable, inspect the automatic transmission fluid cooler hoses for leaks or deterioration.

8.2 Checking the underside of the auxiliary drivebelt with a mirror

6 With the vehicle raised, inspect the petrol tank and filler neck for punctures, cracks and other damage. The connection between the filler neck and tank is especially critical. Sometimes a rubber filler neck or connecting hose will leak due to loose retaining clamps or deteriorated rubber.

7 Carefully check all rubber hoses and metal fuel lines leading away from the petrol tank. Check for loose connections, deteriorated hoses, crimped lines, and other damage. Pay particular attention to the vent pipes and hoses, which often loop up around the filler neck and can become blocked or crimped. Follow the lines to the front of the vehicle, carefully inspecting them all the way. Renew damaged sections as necessary.

8 From within the engine compartment, check the security of all fuel hose attachments and pipe unions, and inspect the fuel hoses and vacuum hoses for kinks, chafing and deterioration.

9 Where applicable, check the condition of the power steering fluid hoses and pipes.

8 Auxiliary drivebelt check

1 Apply the handbrake, then jack up the front of the vehicle and support it on axle stands (see *Jacking and vehicle support*).

2 Using a socket on the crankshaft pulley bolt, turn the engine slowly clockwise so that the full length of the auxiliary drivebelt can be examined. Look for cracks, splitting and fraying on the surface of the belt; check also for signs of glazing (shiny patches) and separation of the belt plies. Use a mirror to check the underside of the drivebelt **(see illustration)**. If damage or wear is visible, or if there are traces of oil or grease on it, the belt should be renewed (see Section 26).

9 Antifreeze check

1 The cooling system should be filled with the recommended G12 antifreeze and corrosion protection fluid – **do not** mix this antifreeze with any other type. Over a period of time, the concentration of fluid may be reduced due to topping-up (this can be avoided by topping-up with the correct antifreeze mixture – see Specifications) or fluid loss. If loss of coolant has been evident, it is important to make the necessary repair before adding fresh fluid.

2 With the engine **cold**, carefully remove the cap from the expansion tank. If the engine is not completely cold, place a cloth rag over the cap before removing it, and remove it slowly to allow any pressure to escape.

3 Antifreeze checkers are available from car accessory shops. Draw some coolant from

the expansion tank and observe how many plastic balls are floating in the checker. Usually, 2 or 3 balls must be floating for the correct concentration of antifreeze, but follow the manufacturer's instructions.

4 If the concentration is incorrect, it will be necessary to either withdraw some coolant and add antifreeze, or alternatively drain the old coolant and add fresh coolant of the correct concentration (see Section 33).

10 Brake hydraulic circuit check

1 Check the entire brake hydraulic circuit for leaks and damage. Start by checking the master cylinder in the engine compartment. At the same time, check the vacuum servo unit and ABS units for signs of fluid leakage.

2 Raise the front and rear of the vehicle and support it on axle stands (see *Jacking and vehicle support*). Check the rigid hydraulic brake lines for corrosion and damage. Also check the brake pressure regulator in the same manner.

3 At the front of the vehicle, check that the flexible hydraulic hoses to the calipers are not twisted or chafing on any of the surrounding suspension components. Turn the steering on full lock to make this check. Also check that the hoses are not brittle or cracked.

4 Lower the vehicle to the ground after making the checks.

11 Headlight beam adjustment

1 Accurate adjustment of the headlight beam is only possible using optical beam-setting equipment, and this work should therefore be carried out by a VW dealer or service station with the necessary facilities.

2 Basic adjustments can be carried out in an emergency, and further details are given in Chapter 12.

12 Pollen filter element renewal

1 The pollen filter is located on the bulkhead, in front of the windscreen – on RHD models it is on the left-hand side, and on LHD models it is on the right-hand side.

2 Ease off the rubber seal and undo the four screws, then pull up and withdraw the cover **(see illustrations)**. The cover may be quite tight and the use of a wooden wedge or suitable lever may be required to release it from the bulkhead panel.

3 Release the clips and withdraw the filter frame, then remove the element from the frame **(see illustration)**.

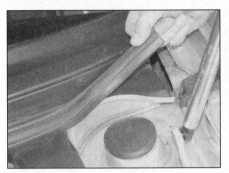

12.2a Ease off the rubber seal . . .

12.2b . . . remove the cover . . .

12.3 . . . and remove the pollen filter

4 Locate the frame into the end laminations of the new element, then fit to the housing, making sure that the lugs engage with the recesses.
5 Refit the cover and secure with the screws, then press down the rubber seal.

13 Manual transmission oil level check

1 Park the car on a level surface. For improved access to the filler/level plug, apply the hand-brake, then jack up the front of the vehicle and support it on axle stands (see *Jacking and vehicle support*), but note that the rear of the vehicle should also be raised to ensure an accurate level check. The oil level must be checked before the car is driven, or at least 5 minutes after the engine has been switched off. If the oil is checked immediately after driving the car, some of the oil will remain distributed around the transmission components, resulting in an inaccurate level reading.
2 Undo the retaining screws and remove the engine undershield(s). Wipe clean the area around the transmission filler/level plug which is situated in the following location:
  a) *1.4 and 1.6 litre engines (02K transmission) – the filler/level plug is situated on the left-hand end of the transmission casing* **(see illustration).**
  b) *1.8 and 2.0 litre engines (02J transmission) – the filler/level plug is situated on the front of the transmission casing* **(see illustration).**

3 The oil level should reach the lower edge of the filler/level hole. A certain amount of oil will have gathered behind the filler/level plug, and will trickle out when it is removed; this does **not** necessarily indicate that the level is correct. To ensure that a true level is established, wait until the initial trickle has stopped, then add oil as necessary until a trickle of new oil can be seen emerging. The level will be correct when the flow ceases; use only good-quality oil of the specified type.
4 If the transmission has been overfilled so that oil flows out when the filler/level plug is removed, check that the car is completely level (front-to-rear and side-to-side), and allow the surplus to drain off into a suitable container.
5 When the oil level is correct, refit the filler/level plug and tighten it to the specified torque. Wipe off any spilt oil then refit the engine undershield(s), tighten the retaining screws securely, and lower the car to the ground.

14 Underbody protection check

Raise and support the vehicle on axle stands (see *Jacking and vehicle support*). Using an electric torch or lead light, inspect the entire underside of the vehicle, paying particular attention to the wheel arches. Look for any damage to the flexible underbody coating, which may crack or flake off with age, leading to corrosion. Also check that the wheel arch liners are securely attached with any clips provided – if they come loose, dirt may get in behind the liners and defeat their purpose. If there is any damage to the under-seal, or any corrosion, it should be repaired before the damage gets too serious.

15 Driveshaft gaiter check

1 With the vehicle raised and securely supported on stands, slowly rotate the roadwheel. Inspect the condition of the outer constant velocity (CV) joint rubber gaiters, squeezing the gaiters to open out the folds. Check for signs of cracking, splits or deterioration of the rubber, which may allow the grease to escape, and lead to water and grit entry into the joint. Also check the security and condition of the retaining clips. Repeat these checks on the inner joints **(see illustration).** If any damage or deterioration is found, the gaiters should be renewed (see Chapter 8).
2 At the same time, check the general condition of the CV joints themselves by first holding the driveshaft and attempting to rotate the wheel. Repeat this check by holding the inner joint and attempting to rotate the driveshaft. Any appreciable movement indicates wear in the joints, wear in the driveshaft splines, or a loose driveshaft retaining nut.

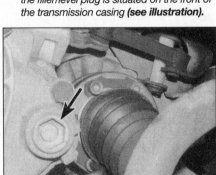

13.2a Filler/level plug location on the 02K manual transmission

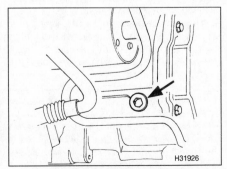

13.2b Filler/level plug location on the 02J manual transmission

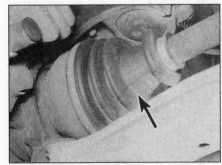

15.1 Check the condition of the driveshaft gaiters (arrowed)

16.4 Check for wear in the hub bearings by grasping the wheel and trying to rock it

16 Steering and suspension check

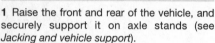

1 Raise the front and rear of the vehicle, and securely support it on axle stands (see *Jacking and vehicle support*).
2 Visually inspect the track rod end balljoint dust cover, the lower front suspension balljoint dust cover, and the steering rack-and-pinion gaiters for splits, chafing or deterioration. Any wear of these components will cause loss of lubricant, together with dirt and water entry, resulting in rapid deterioration of the balljoints or steering gear.
3 Check the power steering fluid hoses for chafing or deterioration, and the pipe and hose unions for fluid leaks. Also check for signs of fluid leakage under pressure from the steering gear rubber gaiters, which would indicate failed fluid seals within the steering gear.
4 Grasp the roadwheel at the 12 o'clock and 6 o'clock positions, and try to rock it **(see illustration)**. Very slight free play may be felt, but if the movement is appreciable, further investigation is necessary to determine the source. Continue rocking the wheel while an assistant depresses the footbrake. If the movement is now eliminated or significantly reduced, it is likely that the hub bearings are at fault. If the free play is still evident with the footbrake depressed, then there is wear in the suspension joints or mountings.
5 Now grasp the wheel at the 9 o'clock and

17.1 Removing the battery cover

3 o'clock positions, and try to rock it as before. Any movement felt now may again be caused by wear in the hub bearings or the steering track rod balljoints. If the inner or outer balljoint is worn, the visual movement will be obvious.
6 Using a large screwdriver or flat bar, check for wear in the suspension mounting bushes by levering between the relevant suspension component and its attachment point. Some movement is to be expected as the mountings are made of rubber, but excessive wear should be obvious. Also check the condition of any visible rubber bushes, looking for splits, cracks or contamination of the rubber.
7 With the car standing on its wheels, have an assistant turn the steering wheel back-and-forth about an eighth of a turn each way. There should be very little, if any, lost movement between the steering wheel and roadwheels. If this is not the case, closely observe the joints and mountings previously described, but in addition, check the steering column universal joints for wear, and the rack-and-pinion steering gear itself.
8 Check for any signs of fluid leakage around the front suspension struts and rear shock absorber. Should any fluid be noticed, the suspension strut or shock absorber is defective internally, and should be renewed. **Note:** *Suspension struts/shock absorbers should always be renewed in pairs on the same axle to ensure correct vehicle handling.*
9 The efficiency of the suspension strut/shock absorber may be checked by bouncing the vehicle at each corner. Generally speaking, the body will return to its normal position and stop after being depressed. If it rises and returns on a rebound, the suspension strut/shock absorber is probably suspect. Examine also the suspension strut/shock absorber upper and lower mountings for any signs of wear.

17 Battery check

1 The battery is located in the front, left-hand corner of the engine compartment. Where a heat protective jacket is fitted, unclip the cover and remove the jacket to gain access to the battery **(see illustration)**.
2 Where necessary, open the fuse holder plastic cover (squeeze together the locking lugs to release the cover) to gain access to the battery positive (+) terminal and fuse holder connections.
3 Check that both battery terminals and all the fuse holder connections are securely attached and are free from corrosion. **Note:** *Before disconnecting the terminals from the battery, refer to 'Disconnecting the battery' in the Reference Chapter at the end of this manual.*
4 Check the battery casing for signs of damage or cracking and check the battery retaining clamp bolt is securely tightened. If

the battery casing is damaged in any way the battery must be renewed (see Chapter 5A).
5 If the vehicle is not fitted with a sealed-for-life maintenance-free battery, check the electrolyte level is between the MAX and MIN level markings on the battery casing. If topping-up is necessary, remove the battery (see Chapter 5A) from the vehicle then remove the cell caps/cover (as applicable). Using distilled water, top the electrolyte level of each cell up to the MAX level mark then securely refit the cell caps/cover. Ensure the battery has not been overfilled then refit the battery to the vehicle (see Chapter 5A).
6 On completion of the check, clip the cover securely back onto the fuse holder and close up the insulator cover (where fitted).

18 Hinge and lock lubrication

1 Lubricate the hinges of the bonnet, doors and tailgate with a light general-purpose oil. Similarly, lubricate all latches, locks and lock strikers. At the same time, check the security and operation of all the locks, adjusting them if necessary (see Chapter 11).
2 Lightly lubricate the bonnet release mechanism and cable with a suitable grease.

19 Airbag unit check

Inspect the exterior condition of the airbag(s) for signs of damage or deterioration. If an airbag shows signs of damage, it must be renewed (see Chapter 12). Note that it is not permissible to attach any stickers to the surface of the airbag, as this may affect the deployment of the unit.

20 Windscreen/tailgate/ headlight washer system check

1 Check that each of the washer jet nozzles are clear and that each nozzle provides a strong jet of washer fluid.
2 The tailgate jet should be aimed to spray at the centre of the screen, using a pin.
3 The windscreen washer nozzles should be aimed slightly above the centre of the screen using a small screwdriver to turn the jet eccentric.
4 On Golf models, the headlight inner jet should be aimed slightly above the horizontal centreline of the headlight, and the outer jet should be aimed slightly below the centreline. On Bora models, the headlight jet should be aimed slightly below the horizontal centreline of the headlight. VW technicians use a special tool to adjust the headlight jet after pulling the jet out onto its stop.

5 Especially during the winter months, make sure that the washer fluid frost concentration is sufficient.

21 Engine management self-diagnosis memory fault check

This work should be carried out by a VW dealer or diagnostic specialist using special equipment. The diagnostic socket is located behind a cover beneath the central part of the facia. The cover is clipped in position.

22 Sunroof check and lubrication

1 Check the operation of the sunroof, and leave it in the fully open position.
2 Wipe clean the guide rails on each side of the sunroof opening, then apply lubricant to them. VW recommend lubricant spray G 052 778.

23 Road test and exhaust emissions check

Instruments and electrical equipment

1 Check the operation of all instruments and electrical equipment including the air conditioning system.
2 Make sure that all instruments read correctly, and switch on all electrical equipment in turn, to check that it functions properly.

Steering and suspension

3 Check for any abnormalities in the steering, suspension, handling or road 'feel'.
4 Drive the vehicle, and check that there are no unusual vibrations or noises which may indicate wear in the driveshafts, wheel bearings, etc.
5 Check that the steering feels positive, with no excessive 'sloppiness', or roughness, and check for any suspension noises when cornering and driving over bumps.

Drivetrain

6 Check the performance of the engine, clutch (where applicable), gearbox/transmission and driveshafts.
7 Listen for any unusual noises from the engine, clutch and gearbox/transmission.
8 Make sure the engine runs smoothly at idle, and there is no hesitation on accelerating.
9 Check that, where applicable, the clutch action is smooth and progressive, that the drive is taken up smoothly, and that the pedal travel is not excessive. Also listen for any noises when the clutch pedal is depressed.
10 On manual gearbox models, check that all gears can be engaged smoothly without noise, and that the gear lever action is smooth and not abnormally vague or 'notchy'.
11 On automatic transmission models, make sure that all gearchanges occur smoothly, without snatching, and without an increase in engine speed between changes. Check that all the gear positions can be selected with the vehicle at rest. If any problems are found, they should be referred to a VW dealer.
12 Listen for a metallic clicking sound from the front of the vehicle, as the vehicle is driven slowly in a circle with the steering on full-lock. Carry out this check in both directions. If a clicking noise is heard, this indicates wear in a driveshaft joint, in which case renew the joint if necessary.

Braking system

13 Make sure that the vehicle does not pull to one side when braking, and that the wheels do not lock when braking hard.
14 Check that there is no vibration through the steering when braking.
15 Check that the handbrake operates correctly without excessive movement of the lever, and that it holds the vehicle stationary on a slope.
16 Test the operation of the brake servo unit as follows. With the engine off, depress the footbrake four or five times to exhaust the vacuum. Hold the brake pedal depressed, then start the engine. As the engine starts, there should be a noticeable 'give' in the brake pedal as vacuum builds-up. Allow the engine to run for at least two minutes, and then switch it off. If the brake pedal is depressed now, it should be possible to detect a hiss from the servo as the pedal is depressed. After about four or five applications, no further hissing should be heard, and the pedal should feel considerably harder.
17 Under controlled emergency braking, the pulsing of the ABS unit must be felt at the footbrake pedal.

Exhaust emissions check

18 Although not part of the manufacturer's maintenance schedule, this check will normally be carried out on a regular basis according to the country the vehicle is operated in. Currently in the UK, exhaust emissions testing is included as part of the annual MOT test after the vehicle is 3 years old. In Germany the test is made when the vehicle is 3 years old, then repeated every 2 years.

Every 40 000 miles or 4 years

24 Air filter element renewal

Engine codes other than AZD, BCA and BCB

1 Unscrew the bolts and remove the cover from the air filter housing. If preferred, the cover may be removed from the inlet duct.
2 Note how the element is fitted, then remove it.
3 Remove any debris and wipe clean the interior of the housing.
4 Fit the new air filter element in position, ensuring that the edges are securely seated **(see illustration)**.
5 Refit the cover and secure with the bolts.

Engine codes AZD, BCA and BCB

6 The air filter is incorporated in the engine top cover. First, disconnect the warm-air hose, then lift the cover to release the rubber mounting grommets.

7 With the cover upside down on the bench, undo the screws and remove the air filter housing, noting the location of the seal.
8 Note how the element is fitted, then remove it.
9 Remove any debris and wipe clean the interior of the housing.
10 Fit the new air filter element in position, ensuring that the edges are securely seated.
11 Refit the seal followed by the air filter housing, and tighten the screws securely.
12 Refit the engine top cover and reconnect the warm-air hose.

25 Spark plug renewal

1 The correct functioning of the spark plugs is vital for the correct running and efficiency of the engine. It is essential that the plugs fitted are appropriate for the engine (a suitable type is specified at the beginning of this Chapter). If this type is used and the engine is in good condition, the spark plugs should not need attention between scheduled renewal intervals. Spark plug cleaning is rarely necessary, and should not be attempted unless specialised equipment is available, as damage can easily be caused to the firing ends.

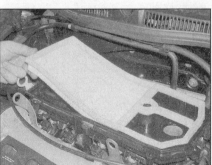

24.4 Removing the air filter element (1.6 litre AEH engine)

25.6 Engine top cover retaining screws (1.8 litre AUM engine)

25.7a Undo the nut and move the vacuum reservoir to one side, then unbolt the bracket . . .

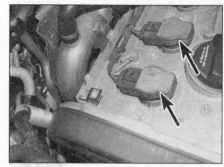

25.7b . . . and remove the ignition coils from the spark plugs

1.4 & 1.6 litre DOHC engines

2 Undo the bolts and remove the cover from the top of the engine, then unscrew the oil filler cap.

3 Disconnect the HT lead connectors and lift the leads from the channels in the cover, then slightly pull the cover upwards. Alternatively, the cover can be removed together with the leads by pulling on each connector in turn using a hook made from welding rod.

1.6 & 2.0 litre SOHC engines

Note: *The spark plugs are located beneath the inlet manifold upper section, and are very difficult to access. VW technicians use a special tool to disconnect the HT leads, together with a universally-jointed spark plug socket to unscrew the spark plugs. If these tools are not available, the alternative method is to remove the inlet manifold upper section (see Chapter 4A).*

4 Carefully lever off the caps with a screwdriver, then unscrew the nuts and remove the engine top cover. Similarly remove the second engine cover where fitted. Where necessary on 2.0 litre engines, also disconnect the wiring from the 1st and 4th fuel injectors.

5 Disconnect the HT lead connectors from the spark plugs. To do this, VW technicians use special tool T10029 to disconnect Nos 1 and 4 leads, and ordinary spark plug lead pliers to disconnect Nos 2 and 3. The special tool is approximately 30 cm in length with a bayonet-type claw at the bottom, which

engages the HT lead connectors. If this tool is not available, or if an alternative tool cannot be fabricated, the upper inlet manifold section must be removed to improve access.

1.8 litre turbo DOHC engine

6 Undo the screws (or release the clips) and lift the cover from the top of the engine **(see illustration)**.

7 Where applicable, undo the nut and move the vacuum reservoir to one side, then unbolt and remove the reservoir bracket. Remove the ignition coils and conncetors from the spark plug - according to the engine type, the coils may be clipped in position or it may be necessary to unscrew the retaining bolts **(see illustrations)**.

All engine codes

8 It is advisable to remove the dirt from the spark plug recesses using a clean brush, vacuum cleaner or compressed air before removing the plugs, to prevent dirt dropping into the cylinders.

9 Unscrew the plugs using a spark plug spanner, suitable box spanner or a deep socket and extension bar. Keep the socket aligned with the spark plug - if it is forcibly moved to one side, the ceramic insulator may be broken off. The use of a universal joint socket will be helpful. As each plug is removed, examine it as follows.

10 Examination of the spark plugs will give a good indication of the condition of the engine. If the insulator nose of the spark plug is clean and white, with no deposits, this is indicative

of a weak mixture or too hot a plug (a hot plug transfers heat away from the electrode slowly, a cold plug transfers heat away quickly).

11 If the tip and insulator nose are covered with hard black-looking deposits, then this is indicative that the mixture is too rich. Should the plug be black and oily, then it is likely that the engine is fairly worn, as well as the mixture being too rich.

12 If the insulator nose is covered with light tan to greyish-brown deposits, then the mixture is correct and it is likely that the engine is in good condition.

13 The spark plug electrode gap is of considerable importance as, if it is too large or too small, the size of the spark and its efficiency will be seriously impaired. On engines fitted with multi-electrode spark plugs, it is recommended that the plugs are renewed rather than attempting to adjust the gaps. On other spark plugs, the gap should be set to the value given by the manufacturer.

14 To set the gap on single electrode plugs, measure it with a feeler blade and then bend open, or closed, the outer plug electrode until the correct gap is achieved. The centre electrode should never be bent, as this may crack the insulator and cause plug failure, if nothing worse. If using feeler blades, the gap is correct when the appropriate-size blade is a firm sliding fit **(see illustrations)**.

15 Special spark plug electrode gap adjusting tools are available from most motor accessory shops, or from some spark plug manufacturers **(see illustration)**.

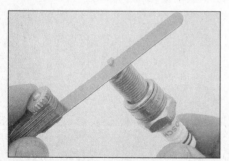

25.14a If single electrode plugs are being fitted, check the electrode gap using a feeler gauge . . .

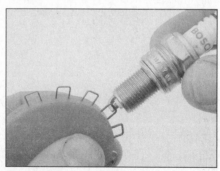

25.14b . . . or a wire gauge . . .

25.15 . . . and if necessary adjust the gap by bending the electrode

It is very often difficult to insert spark plugs into their holes without cross-threading them. To avoid this possibility, fit a short length of rubber hose over the end of the spark plug. The flexible hose acts as a universal joint to help align the plug with the plug thread, the hose will slip on the spark plug, preventing thread damage to the aluminium cylinder head.

16 Before fitting the spark plugs, check that the threaded connector sleeves are tight, and that the plug exterior surfaces and threads are clean. It's often difficult to screw in new spark plugs without cross-threading them - this can be avoided using a piece of rubber hose **(see Haynes Hint)**.

17 Remove the rubber hose (if used), and tighten the plug to the specified torque using the

26.4 Release the tensioner and insert a drill

spark plug socket and a torque wrench. Refit the remaining spark plugs in the same manner.

18 Reconnect the HT leads/ignition coils using a reversal of the removal procedure.

26 Auxiliary drivebelt check and renewal

Checking

1 See Section 8.

Renewal

2 For improved access, apply the handbrake, then jack up the front of the vehicle and support it on axle stands (see *Jacking and vehicle support*).

26.5 Removing the auxiliary drivebelt

3 Remove the right-hand front roadwheel, then remove the access panel from the inner wheel arch.

4 On 1.6 litre SOHC, 1.8 and 2.0 litre engines, use a spanner on the lug provided and turn the tensioner clockwise. Lock the tensioner in its released position by inserting a drill through the lug into the tensioner body **(see illustration)**.

5 On 1.4 litre and 1.6 litre DOHC engines, use a spanner to turn the tensioner central bolt clockwise to release the tension on the drivebelt **(see illustration)**.

6 Note how the drivebelt is routed, then remove it from the crankshaft pulley, alternator pulley, power steering pump pulley, and air conditioning compressor pulley (where applicable) **(see illustrations)**.

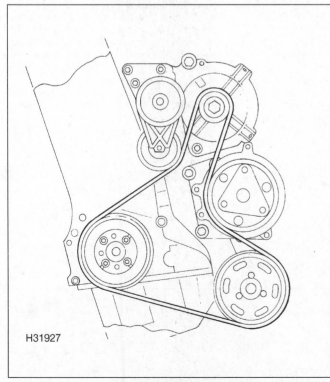

H31927

26.6a Auxiliary drivebelt configuration – 1.6 litre SOHC, 1.8 and 2.0 litre engines with air conditioning

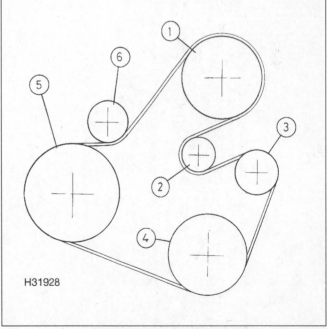

H31928

26.6b Auxiliary drivebelt configuration – 1.4 and 1.6 litre DOHC engines with air conditioning

1 *Power steering pump pulley*	4 *Air conditioning compressor*
2 *Idler roller*	5 *Crankshaft pulley*
3 *Alternator pulley*	6 *Tensioner*

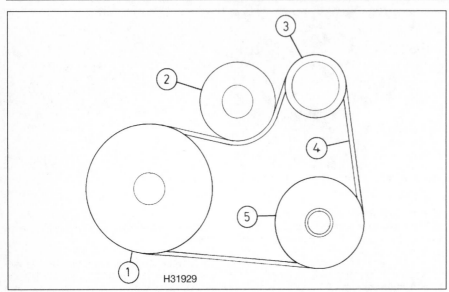

26.6c Auxiliary drivebelt configuration – 1.4 and 1.6 litre DOHC engines without air conditioning

1 Crankshaft pulley	3 Alternator pulley	5 Power steering pump
2 Tensioner	4 Drivebelt	pulley

7 Locate the new drivebelt on the pulleys, then release the tensioner. Check that the belt is located correctly in the multi-grooves in the pulleys.

8 Refit the access panel and roadwheel, and lower the vehicle to the ground.

27.2 Unscrew the cap from the hydraulic fluid reservoir, and wipe clean the integral dipstick with a clean cloth

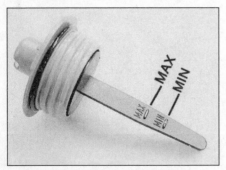

27.3 Screw on the cap hand tight then unscrew it again and check the fluid level on the dipstick

27 Power steering hydraulic fluid level check

1 Turn the front roadwheels to the straight-ahead position without starting the engine. If the vehicle has been left standing for an hour or more, the power steering fluid will be cold (below 50°C), and the 'cold' level markings must be used. If, however, the engine is at normal temperature (above 50°C), the fluid will be hot, so use the 'hot' level markings.

2 The reservoir is located on the right-hand side of the engine compartment, next to the coolant expansion tank. The fluid level is checked with a dipstick attached to the reservoir filler cap. Using a screwdriver, unscrew the cap from the hydraulic fluid reservoir, and wipe clean the integral dipstick with a clean cloth **(see illustration)**.

3 Screw on the cap hand tight then unscrew it again and check the fluid level on the dipstick. If the fluid is cold (below 50°C), it must be in the 'hashed' cold area indicated on the dipstick. If the fluid is hot (above 50°C), it must be between the hot MAX and MIN marks indicated on the dipstick **(see illustration)**.

4 If the level is above the maximum level mark, syphon off the excess amount. If it is below the minimum level mark, add the specified fluid as necessary *(see Lubricants and fluids)*, but in this case also check the system for leaks. On completion, screw on the cap and tighten with the screwdriver.

28 Automatic transmission fluid level check

Note: *An accurate fluid level check can only be made with the transmission fluid at a temperature of between 35°C and 45°C, and if it is not possible to ascertain this temperature, it is strongly recommended that the check be made by a VW dealer who will have the instrumentation to check the temperature and to check the transmission electronics for fault codes. Overfilling or underfilling adversely affects the function of the transmission.*

1 Take the vehicle on a short journey to warm the transmission slightly (see Note at the start of this Section), then park the vehicle on level ground and engage P with the selector lever. Raise the front and rear of the vehicle and support it on axle stands (see *Jacking and vehicle support*), ensuring the vehicle is kept level. Undo the retaining screws and remove the engine undershield(s) to gain access to the base of the transmission unit.

2 Start the engine and run it at idle speed until the transmission fluid temperature reaches 35°C.

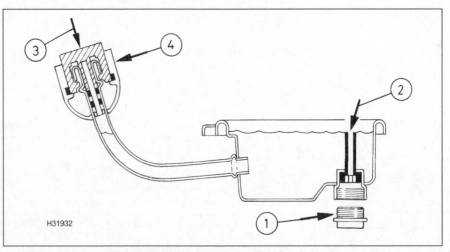

28.3 Automatic transmission fluid level check

1 Level plug	2 Level tube	3 Filler cap	4 Retaining clip

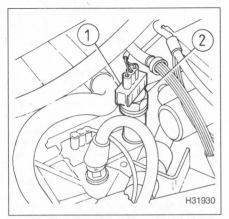

29.2 Disconnect the wiring (1) from the speedometer drive (2)

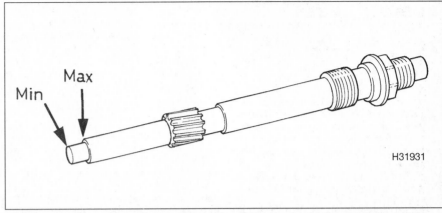

29.4 The automatic transmission final drive oil level is checked on the bottom of the speedometer drive

3 Unscrew the fluid level plug from the bottom of the transmission sump **(see illustration)**.

4 If fluid **continually** drips from the level tube as the fluid temperature increases, the fluid level is correct and does not need to be topped-up. Note that there will be some fluid already present in the level tube, and it will be necessary to observe when this amount has drained before making the level check. Make sure that the check is made before the fluid temperature reaches 45°C. Check the condition of the seal on the level plug and renew it if necessary by cutting off the old seal and fitting a new one. Refit the plug and tighten to the specified torque.

5 If no fluid drips from the level tube, even when the fluid temperature has reached 45°C, it will be necessary to add fluid as follows while the engine is still running.

6 Using a screwdriver, lever off the cap from the filler tube on the side of the transmission sump. **Note:** *On some models the locking device will be permanently damaged and a*

new cap must be obtained. On other models, the cap securing clip must be renewed.

7 With the cap removed, pull out the filler tube plug then add the specified fluid until it drips out of the level tube. Check the condition of the seal on the level plug and renew it if necessary by cutting off the old seal and fitting a new one. Refit the plug and tighten to the specified torque.

8 Refit the filler tube plug and the new cap or cap securing clip.

9 Switch off the ignition then refit the engine undershield(s), tighten the retaining screws securely, and lower the vehicle to the ground.

10 Frequent need for topping-up indicates that there is a leak, which should be found and corrected before it becomes serious.

29 Automatic transmission final drive oil level check

Note: *This work only applies to the 01M transmission.*

1 Apply the handbrake, then jack up the front of the vehicle and support it on axle stands (see *Jacking and vehicle support*), but note that the rear of the vehicle should also be raised to ensure an accurate level check.

2 The final drive level check is made by removing the speedometer drive. First, disconnect the wiring from the sender on the top of the speedometer drive **(see illustration)**.

3 Unscrew the speedometer drive and withdraw it from the transmission. There is no need to remove the sender unit from the top of the drive.

4 Wipe clean the lower end of the drive, then re-insert it and screw it fully into the transmission. Remove it again and check that the oil level is between the shoulder and the end of the drive **(see illustration)**.

5 If necessary, add the specified oil through the drive aperture until the level is correct.

6 Refit the drive and tighten securely, then reconnect the sender wiring.

7 Lower the vehicle to the ground.

Every 60 000 miles

30 Timing belt renewal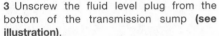

Note: *VW specify that the timing belt tensioner roller is also renewed on 1.8 litre models.*

Inspection

1 Release the clips and remove the upper

timing belt cover (refer to Chapter 2A or 2B).

2 Using a spanner or socket on the crankshaft pulley bolt, turn the engine slowly in a clockwise direction. **Do not** turn the engine on the camshaft bolt.

3 Check the complete length of the timing belt for signs of cracking, tooth separation, fraying, side glazing, and oil or grease contamination. Use a torch and mirror to check the underside of the belt.

4 If there is any evidence of wear or damage

as described in the last paragraph, the timing belt **must** be renewed. A broken belt will cause major damage to the engine.

5 After making the check, refit the upper timing belt cover and remove the spanner/socket from the crankshaft pulley bolt.

Renewal

6 Refer to Chapter 2A or 2B for details.

Every 2 years

31 Brake (and clutch) fluid renewal

⚠️ **Warning: Brake hydraulic fluid can harm your eyes and damage painted surfaces, so use extreme caution when handling and pouring it. Do not use fluid that has been standing open for some time, as it absorbs moisture from the air. Excess moisture can cause a dangerous loss of braking effectiveness.**

1 The procedure is similar to that for the bleeding of the hydraulic system as described in Chapter 9, except that the brake fluid reservoir should be emptied by syphoning, using a clean poultry baster or similar before starting, and allowance should be made for the old fluid to be expelled when bleeding a section of the circuit. Since the clutch hydraulic system also uses fluid from the brake system reservoir, it should also be bled at the same time by referring to Chapter 6, Section 2.

2 Working as described in Chapter 9, open the first bleed screw in the sequence, and pump the brake pedal gently until nearly all the old fluid has been emptied from the master cylinder reservoir.

HAYNES HINT Old hydraulic fluid is often much darker in colour than the new, making it easy to distinguish the two.

3 Top-up to the MAX level with new fluid, and continue pumping until only the new fluid remains in the reservoir, and new fluid can be seen emerging from the bleed screw. Tighten the screw, and top the reservoir level up to the MAX level line.

4 Work through all the remaining bleed screws in the sequence until new fluid can be seen at all of them. Be careful to keep the master cylinder reservoir topped-up to above the MIN level at all times, or air may enter the system and greatly increase the length of the task.

5 When the operation is complete, check that all bleed screws are securely tightened, and that their dust caps are refitted. Wash off all traces of spilt fluid, and recheck the master cylinder reservoir fluid level.

6 On models with a manual transmission unit, once the brake fluid has been changed the clutch fluid should also be renewed. Referring to Chapter 6, bleed the clutch until new fluid is seen to be emerging from the slave cylinder bleed screw, keeping the master cylinder fluid level above the MIN level line at all times to prevent air entering the system. Once the new fluid emerges, securely tighten the bleed screw then disconnect and remove the bleeding equipment. Securely refit the dust cap then wash off all traces of spilt fluid.

7 On all models, ensure the master cylinder fluid level is correct (see *Weekly checks*) and thoroughly check the operation of the brakes and (where necessary) clutch before taking the car on the road.

32 Coolant renewal

Note: *This work is not included in the VW schedule and should not be required if the recommended VW G12 LongLife coolant antifreeze/inhibitor is used. However, if standard antifreeze/inhibitor is used, the work should be carried out at the recommended interval.*

⚠️ **Warning: Wait until the engine is cold before starting this procedure. Do not allow antifreeze to come in contact with your skin, or with the painted surfaces of the vehicle. Rinse off spills immediately with plenty of water. Never leave antifreeze lying around in an open container, or in a puddle in the driveway or on the garage floor. Children and pets are attracted by its sweet smell, but antifreeze can be fatal if ingested.**

Cooling system draining

1 With the engine completely cold, unscrew the expansion tank cap.

2 Firmly apply the handbrake then jack up the front of the vehicle and support it on axle stands (see *Jacking and vehicle support*). Undo the retaining screws and remove the engine undershield(s) to gain access to the base of the radiator.

3 Position a suitable container beneath the coolant drain outlet which is fitted to the coolant bottom hose end fitting. Loosen the drain plug (there is no need to remove it completely) and allow the coolant to drain into the container. If desired, a length of tubing can be fitted to the drain outlet to direct the flow of coolant during draining. Where no drain outlet is fitted to the hose end fitting, remove the retaining clip and disconnect the bottom hose from the radiator to drain the coolant (see Chapter 3, Section 2).

4 On engines with an oil cooler, to fully drain the system also disconnect one of the coolant hoses from the oil cooler which is located at the front of the cylinder block.

5 If the coolant has been drained for a reason other than renewal, then provided it is clean, it can be re-used, though this is not recommended.

6 Once all the coolant has drained, securely tighten the radiator drain plug or reconnect the bottom hose to the radiator (as applicable). Where necessary, also reconnect the coolant hose to the oil cooler and secure it in position with the retaining clip. Refit the

undershield(s), tighten the retaining screws securely.

Cooling system flushing

7 If the recommended VW coolant has not been used and coolant renewal has been neglected, or if the antifreeze mixture has become diluted, the cooling system may gradually lose efficiency, as the coolant passages become restricted due to rust, scale deposits, and other sediment. The cooling system efficiency can be restored by flushing the system clean.

8 The radiator should be flushed separately from the engine, to avoid excess contamination.

Radiator flushing

9 To flush the radiator, first tighten the radiator drain plug.

10 Disconnect the top and bottom hoses and any other relevant hoses from the radiator (see Chapter 3).

11 Insert a garden hose into the radiator top inlet. Direct a flow of clean water through the radiator, and continue flushing until clean water emerges from the radiator bottom outlet.

12 If after a reasonable period, the water still does not run clear, the radiator can be flushed with a good proprietary cleaning agent. It is important that their manufacturer's instructions are followed carefully. If the contamination is particularly bad, insert the hose in the radiator bottom outlet, and reverse-flush the radiator.

Engine flushing

13 To flush the engine, remove the thermostat (see Chapter 3).

14 With the bottom hose disconnected from the radiator, insert a garden hose into the coolant housing. Direct a clean flow of water through the engine, and continue flushing until clean water emerges from the radiator bottom hose.

15 When flushing is complete, refit the thermostat and reconnect the hoses (see Chapter 3).

Cooling system filling

16 Before attempting to fill the cooling system, ensure the drain plug is securely closed and make sure that all hoses are securely connected and their retaining clips are in good condition. If the recommended VW coolant is not being used, ensure that a suitable antifreeze mixture is used all year round, to prevent corrosion of the engine components (see following sub-Section).

17 Remove the expansion tank filler cap and slowly fill the system with the coolant. Continue to fill the cooling system until bubbles stop appearing in the expansion tank. Help to bleed the air from the system by repeatedly squeezing the radiator bottom hose.

18 When no more bubbles appear, top the coolant level up to the MAX level mark then securely refit the cap to the expansion tank.

19 Run the engine at a fast idle speed until the cooling fan cuts in. Wait for the fan to stop then switch the engine off and allow the engine to cool.

20 When the engine has cooled, check the coolant level with reference to *Weekly checks*. Top-up the level if necessary, and refit the expansion tank cap.

Antifreeze mixture

21 If the recommended VW coolant is not being used, the antifreeze should always be renewed at the specified intervals. This is necessary not only to maintain the antifreeze properties, but also to prevent corrosion which would otherwise occur as the corrosion inhibitors become progressively less effective.

22 Always use an ethylene-glycol based antifreeze which is suitable for use in mixed-metal cooling systems. The quantity of antifreeze and levels of protection are indicated in the Specifications.

23 Before adding antifreeze, the cooling system should be completely drained, preferably flushed, and all hoses checked for condition and security.

24 After filling with antifreeze, a label should be attached to the expansion tank, stating the type and concentration of antifreeze used, and the date installed. Any subsequent topping-up should be made with the same type and concentration of antifreeze.

25 Do not use engine antifreeze in the windscreen/tailgate washer system, as it will damage the vehicle paintwork. A screenwash additive should be added to the washer system in the quantities stated on the bottle.

Chapter 1 Part B:
Routine maintenance and servicing – diesel models

Contents

Air filter element renewal 27
Airbag unit check 22
Antifreeze check 12
Automatic transmission final drive oil level check 32
Automatic transmission fluid level check 31
Auxiliary drivebelt check and renewal 29
Auxiliary drivebelt check 11
Battery check 20
Brake (and clutch) fluid renewal 35
Brake hydraulic circuit check 13
Brake pad check 5
Coolant renewal 36
Driveshaft gaiter check 18
Engine management self-diagnosis memory fault check 24
Engine oil and filter renewal 3
Exhaust system check 7
Fuel filter renewal (vehicles using high sulphur diesel fuel) 10
Fuel filter renewal (vehicles using standard diesel fuel) 28
Fuel filter water draining (vehicles using standard fuel) 9

Fuel filter water draining (vehicles using high sulphur fuel) 4
Headlight beam adjustment 14
Hinge and lock lubrication 21
Hose and fluid leak check 8
Introduction 1
Manual transmission oil level check 16
Pollen filter element renewal 15
Power steering hydraulic fluid level check 30
Regular maintenance 2
Resetting the service interval display 6
Road test and exhaust emissions check 26
Steering and suspension check 19
Sunroof check and lubrication 25
Timing belt and tensioning roller renewal (engines with injection pump) 34
Timing belt and tensioning roller renewal (engines with 'unit' injectors) 33
Underbody protection check 17
Windscreen/tailgate/headlight washer system check 23

Degrees of difficulty

Easy, suitable for novice with little experience	Fairly easy, suitable for beginner with some experience	Fairly difficult, suitable for competent DIY mechanic	Difficult, suitable for experienced DIY mechanic	Very difficult, suitable for expert DIY or professional

Lubricants and fluids

Refer to the end of *Weekly checks* on page 0•17

Capacities

Engine oil (including filter)

1.9 diesel engine . . . .   4.5 litres

Cooling system

1.9 diesel engine . . . .   6.0 litres

Transmission

Manual transmission:

    Type 02K . . . .   1.9 litres

    Type 02J . . . .   2.0 litres

    Type 02M . . . .   2.3 litres

Automatic transmission:

    Type 01M:

        Main transmission unit . . . .   5.30 litres

        Final drive . . . .   0.75 litres

    Type 09A:

        Main transmission unit including final drive . . . .   7.0 litres

Power-assisted steering

All models . . . .   0.7 to 0.9 litres

Fuel tank (approximate)

All models . . . .   55 litres

Washer reservoirs

Models with headlight washers . . . .   5.5 litres

Models without headlight washers . . . .   3.0 litres

Engine

Timing belt wear limit . . . .   22.0 mm wide

Cooling system

Antifreeze mixture:

    40% antifreeze . . . .   Protection down to -25°C

    50% antifreeze . . . .   Protection down to -35°C

Note: *Refer to antifreeze manufacturer for latest recommendations.*

Brakes

Brake pad minimum thickness:

    Front . . . .   7.0 mm (including backing plate)

    Rear . . . .   7.5 mm (including backing plate)

Torque wrench settings

	Nm	lbf ft
Automatic transmission level plug	15	11
Manual gearbox filler/level plug	25	18
Oil filter cap	25	18
Roadwheel bolts	120	89
Sump drain plug	30	22

Underbonnet view

1 Engine oil filler cap
2 Engine oil dipstick
3 Oil filter
4 Coolant expansion tank
5 Fuel filter
6 Windscreen/headlight
   washer fluid reservoir
7 Master cylinder brake fluid
   reservoir
8 Front suspension strut
   upper mounting
9 Air cleaner housing
10 Battery
11 Alternator
12 Brake vacuum pump
13 Power steering fluid
   reservoir
14 Power steering pump
15 Vacuum reservoir for inlet
   manifold flap valve

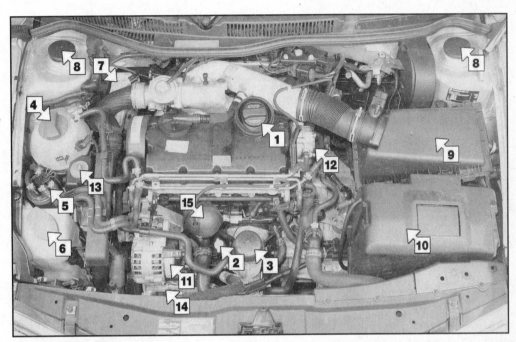

Front underbody view

1 Sump drain plug
2 Oil cooler/filter base cap
3 Manual transmission drain
   plug
4 Air conditioning
   compressor
5 Driveshaft
6 Radiator
7 Intercooler
8 Front suspension lower
   arm
9 Crossmember
10 Steering track rod
11 Front brake caliper
12 Exhaust pipe

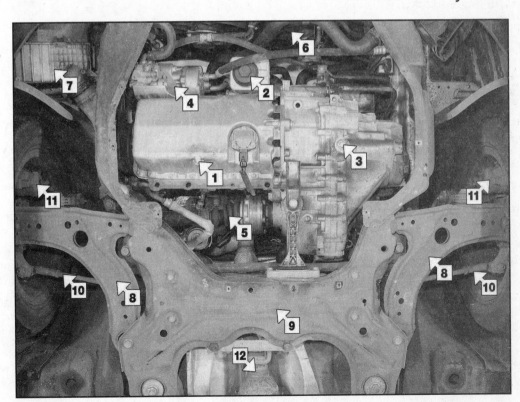

Rear underbody view

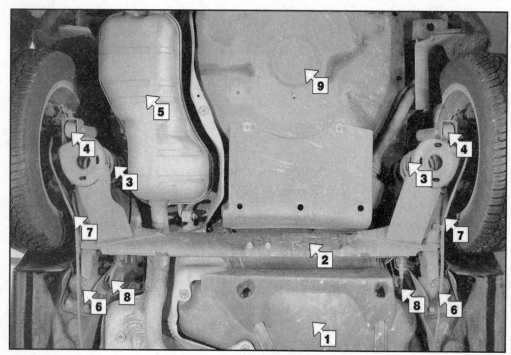

1 Fuel tank
2 Rear axle assembly
3 Rear suspension coil spring
4 Rear shock absorber
5 Exhaust rear silencer
6 Rear axle assembly front mountings
7 Handbrake cables
8 Hydraulic brake line
9 Spare wheel well

Maintenance schedule

The maintenance intervals in this manual are provided with the assumption that you, not the dealer, will be carrying out the work. These are the minimum intervals recommended by us for vehicles driven daily. If you wish to keep your vehicle in peak condition at all times, you may wish to perform some of these procedures more often. We encourage frequent maintenance, since it enhances the efficiency, performance and resale value of your vehicle.

When the vehicle is new, it should be serviced by a dealer service department, in order to preserve the factory warranty.

All VW Golf/Bora models are equipped with a service interval display indicator in the instrument panel. Every time the engine is started the panel will illuminate for approx-

imately 20 seconds with service information. With the standard non-variable display, the service intervals are in accordance with specific distances and time periods. With the LongLife display, the service interval is variable according to the number of starts, length of journeys, vehicle speeds, brake pad wear, bonnet opening frequency, fuel consumption, oil level and oil temperature, however the vehicle **must** be serviced at least every two years. At a distance of 2000 miles (3000 km) before the next service is due, 'Service in 2000 miles' (or '3000 km') will appear at the bottom of the speedometer, and this figure will reduce in steps of 100 units as the vehicle is used. Once the service interval has been reached, the display will flash 'Service' or 'Service Now'. Note that if the

variable (LongLife) service interval is being used, the engine must **only** be filled with the recommended **long-life** engine oil (see Recommended lubricants and fluids).

After completing a service, VW technicians use a special instrument to reset the service display to the next service interval, and a print-out is put in the vehicle service record. The display can be reset by the owner as described in Section 6, but note that for models using the 'LongLife' interval, the procedure will automatically reset the display to the 10 000 miles/15 000 km 'distance' interval. To have the display reset to the 'variable' (LongLife) interval, it is necessary to take the vehicle to a VW dealer who will use a special instrument to encode the on-board computer.

Models using distance and time intervals

Note: *The following service intervals are only applicable to models with a PR number of QG0 or QG2 (shown in the vehicle Service Schedule booklet or on the Next Service sticker located on the driver's door pillar).*

Every 250 miles (400 km) or weekly

☐ Refer to *Weekly checks*

Every 5000 miles (7500 km) or 6 months

☐ Renew the engine oil and filter (Section 3)

Note: *Frequent oil and filter changes are good for the engine. We recommend changing the oil at the mileage specified here, or at least twice a year if the mileage covered is a less.*

Every 10 000 miles (15 000 km) or 12 months, whichever comes first – 'Oil' on display

In addition to the items listed above, carry out the following:

☐ Fuel filter water draining* (Section 4)
☐ Check the front and rear brake pad thickness (Section 5)
☐ Reset the service interval display (Section 6)

* *Only when using high sulphur diesel fuel not conforming to DIN EN 590 or when using RME fuel (diester)*

Every 20 000 miles (30 000 km) or 2 years, whichever comes first – '01' on display

In addition to the items listed above, carry out the following:

☐ Check the condition of the exhaust system and its mountings (Section 7)
☐ Check all underbonnet components and hoses for fluid and oil leaks (Section 8)
☐ Fuel filter water draining* (Section 9)
☐ Renew the fuel filter** (Section 10)
☐ Check the condition of the auxiliary drivebelt (Section 11)
☐ Check the coolant antifreeze concentration (Section 12)
☐ Check the brake hydraulic circuit for leaks and damage (Section 13)
☐ Check the headlight beam adjustment (Section 14)
☐ Renew the pollen filter element (Section 15)
☐ Check the manual transmission oil level (Section 16)
☐ Check the underbody protection for damage (Section 17)
☐ Check the condition of the driveshaft gaiters (Section 18)
☐ Check the steering and suspension components for condition and security (Section 19)

Every 20 000 miles (30 000 km) or 2 years, whichever comes first – '01' on display

☐ Check the battery condition, security and electrolyte level (Section 20)
☐ Lubricate all hinges and locks (Section 21)
☐ Check the condition of the airbag unit(s) (Section 22)
☐ Check the operation of the windscreen/tailgate/headlight washer system(s) (as applicable) (Section 23)
☐ Check the engine management self-diagnosis memory for faults (Section 24)
☐ Check the operation of the sunroof and lubricate the guide rails (Section 25)
☐ Carry out a road test and check exhaust emissions (Section 26)

* *Only when using diesel fuel conforming to DIN EN 590*
** *Only when using diesel fuel not conforming to DIN EN 590 or when using RME fuel (diester)*

Every 40 000 miles (60 000 km) or 4 years, whichever comes first

☐ Renew the air filter element (Section 27)
☐ Renew the fuel filter* (Section 28)
☐ Check the condition of the auxiliary drivebelt on vehicles fitted with an automatic tensioner (Section 29)
☐ Check the power steering hydraulic fluid level (Section 30)
☐ Check the automatic transmission fluid level (Section 31)
☐ Check the automatic transmission final drive oil level (Section 32)

* *Only when using diesel fuel conforming to DIN EN 590*

Every 60 000 miles (90 000 km)

☐ Renew the timing belt and tensioner roller on engines with 'unit' injectors, ie, without an injection pump (Section 33)

Every 80 000 miles (120 000 km)

☐ Renew the timing belt and tensioner roller on engines with an injection pump, ie, without 'unit' injectors (Section 34)

Every 2 years

☐ Renew the brake (and clutch) fluid (Section 35)
☐ Renew the coolant* (Section 36)

* **Note:** *This work is not included in the VW schedule and should not be required if the recommended VW G12 LongLife coolant antifreeze/inhibitor is used.*

Models using 'LongLife' variable intervals

The LongLife variable service intervals are only applicable to models with a PR number of QG1 (shown in the vehicle Service Schedule booklet or on the Next Service sticker located on the driver's door pillar). The occurrence of the service on the display unit will depend on how the vehicle is being used (number of starts, length of journeys, vehicle speeds, brake pad wear, bonnet opening frequency, fuel consumption, oil level and oil temperature). For example, if a vehicle is being used under extreme driving conditions, the 'oil' service may occur at 10 000 miles, whereas, if the vehicle is being used under moderate driving conditions, it may occur at 20 000 miles. It is important to realise that this system is completely variable according to how the vehicle is being used, and therefore the service should be carried out when indicated on the display. When an OIL CHANGE SERVICE ('Oil') or INSPECTION SERVICE ('01') is due, follow the relevant procedure described for the normal 'distance and time' intervals

Every 250 miles (400 km) or weekly
☐ Refer to *Weekly checks*

Every 5000 miles (7500 km) or 6 months
☐ Renew the engine oil and filter (Section 3)

Note: *Frequent oil and filter changes are good for the engine. We recommend changing the oil at the mileage specified here, or at least twice a year if the mileage covered is a less.*

'Oil' on display
In addition to the items listed above, carry out the following:
☐ Fuel filter water draining* (Section 4)
☐ Check the front and rear brake pad thickness (Section 5)
☐ Reset the service interval display (Section 6)

* Only when using high sulphur diesel fuel not conforming to DIN EN 590 or when using RME fuel (diester)

'01' on display or every 2 years, whichever comes first
In addition to the items listed above, carry out the following:
☐ Check the condition of the exhaust system and its mountings (Section 7)
☐ Check all underbonnet components and hoses for fluid and oil leaks (Section 8)
☐ Fuel filter water draining* (Section 9)
☐ Renew the fuel filter** (Section 10)
☐ Check the condition of the auxiliary drivebelt on vehicles not fitted with an automatic tensioner (Section 11)
☐ Check the coolant antifreeze concentration (Section 12)
☐ Check the brake hydraulic circuit for leaks and damage (Section 13)
☐ Check the headlight beam adjustment (Section 14)
☐ Renew the pollen filter element (Section 15)
☐ Check the manual transmission oil level (Section 16)
☐ Check the underbody protection for damage (Section 17)
☐ Check the condition of the driveshaft gaiters (Section 18)
☐ Check the steering and suspension components for condition and security (Section 19)
☐ Check the battery condition, security and electrolyte level (Section 20)

'01' on display or every 2 years, whichever comes first (continued)
☐ Lubricate all hinges and locks (Section 21)
☐ Check the condition of the airbag unit(s) (Section 22)
☐ Check the operation of the windscreen/tailgate/headlight washer system(s) (as applicable) (Section 23)
☐ Check the engine management self-diagnosis memory for faults (Section 24)
☐ Check the operation of the sunroof and lubricate the guide rails (Section 25)
☐ Carry out a road test and check exhaust emissions (Section 26)

* Only when using diesel fuel conforming to DIN EN 590
** Only when using diesel fuel not conforming to DIN EN 590 or when using RME fuel (diester)

Every 40 000 miles (60 000 km) or 4 years, whichever comes first
☐ Renew the air filter element (Section 27)
☐ Renew the fuel filter* (Section 28)
☐ Check the condition of the auxiliary drivebelt on vehicles fitted with an automatic tensioner (Section 29)
☐ Check the power steering hydraulic fluid level (Section 30)
☐ Check the automatic transmission fluid level (Section 31)
☐ Check the automatic transmission final drive oil level (Section 32)

* Only when using diesel fuel conforming to DIN EN 590

Every 60 000 miles (90 000 km)
☐ Renew the timing belt and tensioner roller on engines with 'unit' injectors, ie, without an injection pump (Section 33)

Every 80 000 miles (120 000 km)
☐ Renew the timing belt and tensioner roller on engines with an injection pump, ie, without 'unit' injectors (Section 34)

Every 2 years
☐ Renew the brake (and clutch) fluid (Section 35)
☐ Renew the coolant* (Section 36)

* Note: This work is not included in the VW schedule and should not be required if the recommended VW G12 LongLife coolant antifreeze/inhibitor is used.

1 Introduction

This Chapter is designed to help the home mechanic maintain his/her vehicle for safety, economy, long life and peak performance.

The Chapter contains a master maintenance schedule, followed by Sections dealing specifically with each task in the schedule. Visual checks, adjustments, component renewal and other helpful items are included. Refer to the accompanying illustrations of the engine compartment and the underside of the vehicle for the locations of the various components.

Servicing your vehicle will provide a planned maintenance programme, which should result in a long and reliable service life. This is a comprehensive plan, so maintaining some items but not others will not produce the same results.

As you service your vehicle, you will discover that many of the procedures can – and should – be grouped together, because of the particular procedure being performed, or because of the proximity of two otherwise unrelated components to one another. For example, if the vehicle is raised for any reason, the exhaust can be inspected at the same time as the suspension and steering components.

The first step in this maintenance programme is to prepare yourself before the actual work begins. Read through all the Sections relevant to the work to be carried out, then make a list and gather all the parts and tools required. If a problem is encountered, seek advice from a parts specialist, or a dealer service department.

2 Regular maintenance

1 If, from the time the vehicle is new, the routine maintenance schedule is followed closely, and frequent checks are made of fluid levels and high-wear items, as suggested throughout this manual, the engine will be kept in relatively good running condition, and the need for additional work will be minimised.
2 It is possible that there will be times when the engine is running poorly due to the lack of regular maintenance. This is even more likely if a used vehicle, which has not received regular and frequent maintenance checks, is purchased. In such cases, additional work may need to be carried out, outside of the regular maintenance intervals.
3 If engine wear is suspected, a compression test (refer to Chapter 2C) will provide valuable information regarding the overall performance of the main internal components. Such a test can be used as a basis to decide on the extent of the work to be carried out. If, for example, a compression test indicates serious internal engine wear, conventional maintenance as described in this Chapter will not greatly improve the performance of the engine, and may prove a waste of time and money, unless extensive overhaul work is carried out first.
4 The following series of operations are those most often required to improve the performance of a generally poor-running engine:

Primary operations

a) Clean, inspect and test the battery (See 'Weekly checks').
b) Check all the engine-related fluids (See 'Weekly checks').
c) Drain the water from the fuel filter (Section 4).
d) Check the condition and tension of the auxiliary drivebelt (Section 11).
e) Check the condition of the air filter, and renew if necessary (Section 27).
f) Check the condition of all hoses, and check for fluid leaks (Section 8).

5 If the above operations do not prove fully effective, carry out the following secondary operations:

Secondary operations

All items listed under *Primary operations*, plus the following:

a) Check the charging system (see Chapter 5A).
b) Check the preheating system (see Chapter 5C).
c) Renew the fuel filter (Section 10) and check the fuel system (see Chapter 4B).

Every 5000 miles or 6 months

3 Engine oil and filter renewal

1 Frequent oil and filter changes are the most important preventative maintenance procedures which can be undertaken by the DIY owner. As engine oil ages, it becomes diluted and contaminated, which leads to premature engine wear.
2 Before starting this procedure, gather all the necessary tools and materials. Also make sure that you have plenty of clean rags and newspapers handy, to mop-up any spills. Ideally, the engine oil should be warm, as it will drain better, and more built-up sludge will be removed with it. Take care, however, not to touch the exhaust or any other hot parts of the engine when working under the vehicle. To avoid any possibility of scalding, and to protect yourself from possible skin irritants and other harmful contaminants in used engine oils, it is advisable to wear gloves when carrying out this work. Access to the underside of the vehicle will be greatly improved if it can be raised on a lift, driven onto ramps, or jacked up and supported on axle stands (see *Jacking and vehicle support*). Whichever method is chosen, make sure that the vehicle remains level, or if it is at an angle, that the drain plug is at the lowest point. Undo the retaining screws and remove the engine undershield(s), then also remove the engine top cover where applicable.
3 Slacken the sump drain plug about half a turn. Position the draining container under the drain plug, then remove the plug completely **(see illustration and Haynes Hint)**. Recover the sealing ring from the drain plug.
4 Allow some time for the old oil to drain, noting that it may be necessary to reposition the container as the oil flow slows to a trickle.
5 After all the oil has drained, wipe off the drain plug with a clean rag, and fit a new sealing washer. Clean the area around the drain plug opening, and refit the plug. Tighten the plug securely.

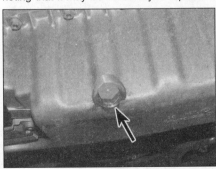

3.3 Sump drain plug

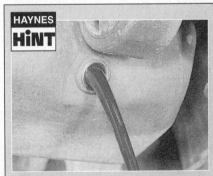

Keep the drain plug pressed into the sump while unscrewing it by hand the last couple of turns. As the plug releases, move it away sharply so the stream of oil issuing from the sump runs into the container, not up your sleeve.

3.7a Unscrew the cap . . .

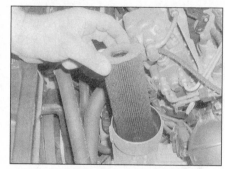

3.7b . . . and remove the filter element

3.7c Remove the sealing ring from the cap

3.11 Pour in half the specified quantity of oil first, wait, then add the rest

6 Remove the engine top cover(s) (see Chapter 2C) to gain access to the oil filter housing. Place absorbent cloths around the filter housing to catch any spilt oil.
7 Unscrew and remove the cap from the top of the oil filter housing using an oil filter strap or suitable spanner. Recover the large sealing ring from the cap, and the small sealing ring

from the centre rod. Lift out the filter element **(see illustrations)**. Dispose of the element.
8 Using a clean rag, wipe all oil and sludge from the inside of the filter housing and cap(s).
9 Insert the new element. Fit new sealing rings to the cap, then refit it and tighten to the specified torque. Also, as applicable, refit the lower cap and drain plug and tighten to the

specified torque. Wipe up any spilt oil before refitting the engine top cover(s).
10 Remove the old oil and all tools from under the car then refit the undershield(s) and lower the car to the ground. Also refit the engine top cover.
11 Remove the dipstick, then unscrew the oil filler cap from the cylinder head cover. Fill the engine, using the correct grade and type of oil (see *Lubricants and fluids*). An oil can spout or funnel may help to reduce spillage. Pour in half the specified quantity of oil first **(see illustration)**, then wait a few minutes for the oil to run to the sump (see *Weekly checks*). Continue adding oil a small quantity at a time until the level is up to the maximum mark on the dipstick. Refit the filler cap.
12 Start the engine and run it for a few minutes; check for leaks around the oil filter cap and the sump drain plug. Note that there may be a few seconds delay before the oil pressure warning light goes out when the engine is started, as the oil circulates through the engine oil galleries and the new oil filter (where fitted) before the pressure builds-up.

⚠️ **Warning: Do not increase the engine speed above idling while the oil pressure light is illuminated, as considerable damage can be caused to the turbocharger.**

13 Switch off the engine, and wait a few minutes for the oil to settle in the sump once more. With the new oil circulated and the filter completely full, recheck the level on the dipstick, and add more oil as necessary.
14 Dispose of the used engine oil safely, with reference to *General repair procedures* in the *Reference* section of this manual.

Every 10 000 miles or 'Oil' on display

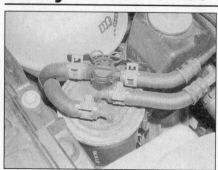

4.2 The fuel filter is mounted on the inner wing, above the right-hand wheel arch

4 Fuel filter water draining (vehicles using high sulphur fuel)

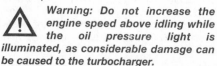

Note: *Carry out this procedure at this interval only when using high sulphur diesel fuel not conforming to DIN EN 590 or when using RME fuel (diester). This fuel is not available in the UK.*

1 Periodically, the water collected from the fuel by the filter unit must be drained out.
2 The fuel filter is mounted on the inner wing, above the right-hand wheel arch **(see illustration)**. At the top of the filter unit,

release the clip and lift out the control valve, leaving the fuel hoses attached.
3 Slacken the screw and raise the filter in its retaining bracket
4 Position a container below the filter unit and pad the surrounding area with rags to absorb any fuel that may be spilt.
5 Unscrew the drain valve at the base of the filter unit, until fuel starts to run out into the container. Keep the valve open until about 100 cc of fuel has been collected.
6 Refit the control valve to the top of the filter and insert the retaining clip. Close the drain valve and wipe off any surplus fuel from the nozzle.

7 Remove the collecting container and rags, then push the filter unit back into the retaining bracket and tighten the bracket securing screw.

8 Run the engine at idle and check around the fuel filter for fuel leaks.

9 Raise the engine speed to about 2000 rpm several times, then allow the engine to idle again. Observe the fuel flow through the transparent hose leading to the fuel injection pump and check that it is free of air bubbles.

5 Brake pad check

1 The outer brake pads can be checked without removing the wheels, by observing the brake pads through the holes in the wheels (see illustration). If necessary, remove the wheel trim. The thickness of the pad lining and backing plate must not be less than the dimension given in the Specifications.

2 If the outer pads are worn near their limits, it is worthwhile checking the inner pads as well. Apply the handbrake then jack up vehicle and support it on axle stands (see *Jacking and vehicle support*). Remove the roadwheels.

3 Use a steel rule to check the thickness of the brake pads (including the backing plate), and compare with the minimum thickness given in the Specifications (see illustration).

4 For a comprehensive check, the brake pads should be removed and cleaned. The operation of the caliper can then also be checked, and the condition of the brake disc itself can be fully examined on both sides. Refer to Chapter 9.

5 If any pad's friction material is worn to the

5.1 The outer brake pads can be observed through the holes in the wheels

specified minimum thickness or less, *all four pads at the front or rear, as applicable, must be renewed as a set.*

6 On completion of the check, refit the roadwheels and lower the vehicle to the ground.

6 Resetting the service interval display

1 After all necessary maintenance work has been completed, the service interval display must be reset. VW technicians use a special dedicated instrument to do this, and a print-out is then put in the vehicle service record. It is possible for the owner to reset the display as described in the following paragraphs, but note that the procedure will automatically reset the display to a 10 000 mile (15 000 km) interval. To continue with the 'variable' intervals which take into consideration the number of starts, length of journeys, vehicle speeds, brake pad wear, bonnet opening

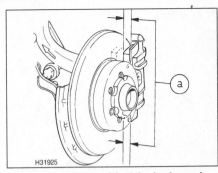

H31925

5.3 The thickness (a) of the brake pads must not be less than the specified amount

frequency, fuel consumption, oil level and oil temperature, the display must be reset by a VW dealership using the special dedicated instrument.

2 To reset the standard display manually, switch off the ignition, then press and hold down the trip reset button beneath the speedometer. Turn the digital clock reset knob clockwise, and the trip display will now show 'service - - -'. Depress the clock reset knob as required to alternate between individual services, however, do not zero the display otherwise incorrect readings will be shown.

3 To reset the LongLife display manually, switch off the ignition, then press and hold down the trip reset button beneath the speedometer. Switch on the ignition and release the reset button, and note that the relevant service will appear in the display. Turn the digital clock reset knob clockwise, and the display will now return to normal. Switch off the ignition to complete the resetting procedure. Do not zero the display otherwise incorrect readings will be shown.

Every 20 000 miles, 2 years or '01' on display

7 Exhaust system check

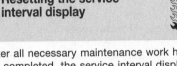

1 With the engine cold (at least an hour after the vehicle has been driven), check the complete exhaust system from the engine to the end of the tailpipe. The exhaust system is most easily checked with the vehicle raised on a hoist, or suitably supported on axle stands, so that the exhaust components are readily visible and accessible (see *Jacking and vehicle support*).

2 Check the exhaust pipes and connections for evidence of leaks, severe corrosion and damage. Make sure that all brackets and mountings are in good condition, and that all relevant nuts and bolts are tight. Leakage at any of the joints or in other parts of the system will usually show up as a black sooty stain in the vicinity of the leak.

3 Rattles and other noises can often be traced to the exhaust system, especially the brackets and mountings. Try to move the pipes and silencers. If the components are able to come into contact with the body or suspension parts, secure the system with new mountings. Otherwise separate the joints (if possible) and twist the pipes as necessary to provide additional clearance.

8 Hose and fluid leak check

1 Visually inspect the engine joint faces, gaskets and seals for any signs of water or oil leaks. Pay particular attention to the areas around the camshaft cover, cylinder head, oil filter and sump joint faces. Bear in mind that, over a period of time, some very slight seepage from these areas is to be expected –

what you are really looking for is any indication of a serious leak. Should a leak be found, renew the offending gasket or oil seal by referring to the appropriate Chapters in this manual.

2 Also check the security and condition of all the engine-related pipes and hoses. Ensure that all cable-ties or securing clips are in place and in good condition. Clips which are broken or missing can lead to chafing of the hoses, pipes or wiring, which could cause more serious problems in the future.

3 Carefully check the radiator hoses and heater hoses along their entire length. Renew any hose which is cracked, swollen or deteriorated. Cracks will show up better if the hose is squeezed. Pay close attention to the hose clips that secure the hoses to the cooling system components. Hose clips can pinch and puncture hoses, resulting in cooling system leaks.

4 Inspect all the cooling system components

A leak in the cooling system will usually show up as white- or rust-coloured deposits on the area adjoining the leak.

(hoses, joint faces, etc) for leaks **(see Haynes Hint)**. Where any problems of this nature are found on system components, renew the component or gasket with reference to Chapter 3.

5 Where applicable, inspect the automatic transmission fluid cooler hoses for leaks or deterioration.

6 With the vehicle raised, inspect the petrol tank and filler neck for punctures, cracks and other damage. The connection between the filler neck and tank is especially critical. Sometimes a rubber filler neck or connecting hose will leak due to loose retaining clamps or deteriorated rubber.

7 Carefully check all rubber hoses and metal fuel lines leading away from the petrol tank. Check for loose connections, deteriorated

hoses, crimped lines, and other damage. Pay particular attention to the vent pipes and hoses, which often loop up around the filler neck and can become blocked or crimped. Follow the lines to the front of the vehicle, carefully inspecting them all the way. Renew damaged sections as necessary.

8 From within the engine compartment, check the security of all fuel hose attachments and pipe unions, and inspect the fuel hoses and vacuum hoses for kinks, chafing and deterioration.

9 Where applicable, check the condition of the power steering fluid hoses and pipes.

9 Fuel filter water draining (vehicles using standard fuel)

Note: Carry out this procedure at this interval only when using diesel fuel conforming to DIN EN 590 (standard fuel in the UK).

Refer to Section 4.

10 Fuel filter renewal (vehicles using high sulphur diesel fuel)

Note: Carry out this procedure at this interval only when using diesel fuel not conforming to DIN EN 590 or when using RME fuel (diester). This fuel is not available in the UK.

1 The fuel filter is mounted on the inner wing, above the right-hand wheel arch **(see illustration)**. Position a container underneath

the filter unit and pad the surrounding area with rags to absorb any fuel that may be spilt.

2 At the top of the filter unit, release the clip and lift out the control valve, leaving the fuel hoses attached to it **(see illustrations)**.

3 Slacken the hose clips and pull the fuel supply and delivery hoses from the ports on the of the filter unit. If crimp-type clips are fitted, cut them off using snips, and use equivalent size worm-drive clips on refitting. Note the fitted position of each hose, to aid correct refitting later.

Caution: Be prepared for an amount of fuel loss.

4 Slacken the securing screw and raise the filter out of its retaining bracket **(see illustrations)**.

5 Fit a new fuel filter into the retaining bracket and tighten the securing screw.

6 Refit the control valve to the top of the filter and insert the retaining clip.

7 Reconnect the fuel supply and delivery hoses, using the notes made during removal – note the fuel flow arrow markings next to each port. Where crimp-type hoses were originally fitted, use equivalent size worm-drive clips on refitting **(see illustration)**. Remove the collecting container and rags.

8 Start and run the engine at idle, then check around the fuel filter for fuel leaks. **Note:** *It may take a few seconds of cranking before the engine starts.*

9 Raise the engine speed to about 2000 rpm several times, then allow the engine to idle again. Observe the fuel flow through the transparent hose leading to the fuel injection pump and check that it is free of air bubbles.

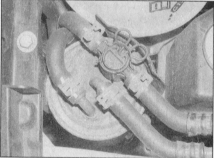

10.1 The fuel filter is mounted on the inner wing, above the right-hand wheel arch

10.2a Release the clip . . .

10.2b . . . and lift out the control valve, leaving the fuel hoses attached to it

10.4a Loosen the securing screw . . .

10.4b . . . and raise the filter out of its retaining bracket

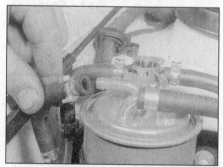

10.7 Reconnect the fuel supply and delivery hoses

11 Auxiliary drivebelt check

Note: *This procedure at this interval only applies to vehicles not fitted with an automatic tensioner.*

Checking

1 Apply the handbrake, then jack up the front of the vehicle and support it on axle stands (see *Jacking and vehicle support*).
2 Using a socket on the crankshaft pulley bolt, turn the engine slowly clockwise so that the full length of the auxiliary drivebelt can be examined. Look for cracks, splitting and fraying on the surface of the belt; check also for signs of glazing (shiny patches) and separation of the belt plies. If damage or wear is visible, or if there are traces of oil or grease on it, the belt should be renewed (see Section 29).

12 Antifreeze check

1 The cooling system should be filled with the recommended G12 antifreeze and corrosion protection fluid – **do not** mix this antifreeze with any other type. Over a period of time, the concentration of fluid may be reduced due to topping-up (this can be avoided by topping-up with the correct antifreeze mixture – see Specifications) or fluid loss. If loss of coolant has been evident, it is important to make the necessary repair before adding fresh fluid.
2 With the engine **cold**, carefully remove the cap from the expansion tank. If the engine is not completely cold, place a cloth rag over the cap before removing it, and remove it slowly to allow any pressure to escape.
3 Antifreeze checkers are available from car accessory shops. Draw some coolant from the expansion tank and observe how many plastic balls are floating in the checker. Usually, 2 or 3 balls must be floating for the correct concentration of antifreeze, but follow the manufacturer's instructions.
4 If the concentration is incorrect, it will be necessary to either withdraw some coolant and add antifreeze, or alternatively drain the old coolant and add fresh coolant of the correct concentration (see Section 36).

13 Brake hydraulic circuit check

1 Check the entire brake hydraulic circuit for leaks and damage. Start by checking the master cylinder in the engine compartment. At the same time, check the vacuum servo unit and ABS units for signs of fluid leakage.
2 Raise the front and rear of the vehicle and support it on axle stands (see *Jacking and vehicle support*). Check the rigid hydraulic brake lines for corrosion and damage. Also check the brake pressure regulator in the same manner.
3 At the front of the vehicle, check that the flexible hydraulic hoses to the calipers are not twisted or chafing on any of the surrounding suspension components. Turn the steering on full lock to make this check. Also check that the hoses are not brittle or cracked.
4 Lower the vehicle to the ground after making the checks.

14 Headlight beam adjustment

1 Accurate adjustment of the headlight beam is only possible using optical beam-setting equipment, and this work should therefore be carried out by a VW dealer or service station with the necessary facilities.
2 Basic adjustments can be carried out in an emergency, and further details are given in Chapter 12.

15 Pollen filter element renewal

1 The pollen filter is located on the bulkhead, in front of the windscreen – on RHD models it is on the left-hand side, and on LHD models it is on the right-hand side.
2 Ease off the rubber seal and undo the four screws, then pull up and withdraw the cover **(see illustrations)**. The cover may be quite tight and the use of a wooden wedge or suitable lever may be required to release it from the bulkhead panel.
3 Release the clips and withdraw the filter frame, then remove the element from the frame **(see illustration)**.
4 Locate the frame into the end laminations of the new element, then fit to the housing, making sure that the lugs engage with the recesses.
5 Refit the cover and secure with the screws, then press down the rubber seal.

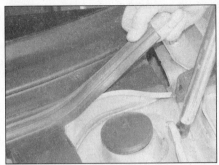

15.2a Ease off the rubber seal . . .

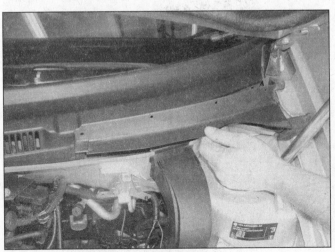

15.2b . . . remove the cover . . .

15.3 . . . and remove the pollen filter

16.2a Filler/level plug location on the 02K manual transmission

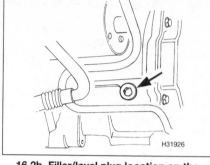

16.2b Filler/level plug location on the 02J manual transmission

17 Underbody protection check

Raise and support the vehicle on axle stands (see *Jacking and vehicle support*). Using an electric torch or lead light, inspect the entire underside of the vehicle, paying particular attention to the wheel arches. Look for any damage to the flexible underbody coating, which may crack or flake off with age, leading to corrosion. Also check that the wheel arch liners are securely attached with any clips provided – if they come loose, dirt may get in behind the liners and defeat their purpose. If there is any damage to the underseal, or any corrosion, it should be repaired before the damage gets too serious.

16.2c Filler/level plug location on the 02M manual transmission

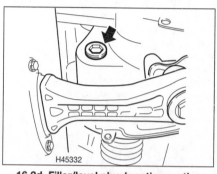

16.2d Filler/level plug location on the 02T manual transmission

18 Driveshaft gaiter check

1 With the vehicle raised and securely supported on stands, slowly rotate the roadwheel. Inspect the condition of the outer constant velocity (CV) joint rubber gaiters, squeezing the gaiters to open out the folds. Check for signs of cracking, splits or deterioration of the rubber, which may allow the grease to escape, and lead to water and grit entry into the joint. Also check the security and condition of the retaining clips. Repeat these checks on the inner joints **(see illustration)**. If any damage or deterioration is found, the gaiters should be renewed (see Chapter 8).
2 At the same time, check the general condition of the CV joints themselves by first holding the driveshaft and attempting to rotate the wheel. Repeat this check by holding the inner joint and attempting to rotate the driveshaft. Any appreciable movement indicates wear in the joints, wear in the driveshaft splines, or a loose driveshaft retaining nut.

16 Manual transmission oil level check

1 Park the car on a level surface. For improved access to the filler/level plug, apply the handbrake, then jack up the front of the vehicle and support it on axle stands (see *Jacking and vehicle support*), but note that the rear of the vehicle should also be raised to ensure an accurate level check. The oil level must be checked before the car is driven, or at least 5 minutes after the engine has been switched off. If the oil is checked immediately after driving the car, some of the oil will remain distributed around the transmission components, resulting in an inaccurate level reading.
2 Undo the retaining screws and remove the engine undershield(s). Wipe clean the area around the transmission filler/level plug which is situated in the following location:
  a) *02K transmission – the filler/level plug is situated on the left-hand end of the transmission casing* **(see illustration)**.
  b) *02J transmission – the filler/level plug is situated on the front of the transmission casing* **(see illustration)**.
  c) *02M transmission – the filler/level plug is situated on the front of the transmission casing* **(see illustration)**.
  d) *02T transmission – the filler/level plug is situated on the right-hand rear of the transmission casing* **(see illustration)**.
3 The oil level should reach the lower edge of

the filler/level hole. A certain amount of oil will have gathered behind the filler/level plug, and will trickle out when it is removed; this does **not** necessarily indicate that the level is correct. To ensure that a true level is established, wait until the initial trickle has stopped, then add oil as necessary until a trickle of new oil can be seen emerging. The level will be correct when the flow ceases; use only good-quality oil of the specified type.
4 If the transmission has been overfilled so that oil flows out when the filler/level plug is removed, check that the car is completely level (front-to-rear and side-to-side), and allow the surplus to drain off into a suitable container.
5 When the oil level is correct, refit the filler/level plug and tighten it to the specified torque. Wipe off any spilt oil then refit the engine undershield(s), tighten the retaining screws securely, and lower the car to the ground.

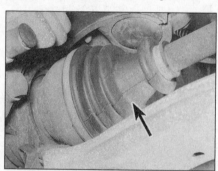

18.1 Check the condition of the driveshaft gaiters (arrowed)

19 Steering and suspension check

1 Raise the front and rear of the vehicle, and securely support it on axle stands (see *Jacking and vehicle support*).
2 Visually inspect the track rod end balljoint dust cover, the lower front suspension balljoint dust cover, and the steering rack-and-pinion gaiters for splits, chafing or deterioration. Any wear of these components will cause loss of lubricant, together with dirt and water entry, resulting in rapid deterioration of the balljoints or steering gear.
3 Check the power steering fluid hoses for chafing or deterioration, and the pipe and hose unions for fluid leaks. Also check for signs of fluid leakage under pressure from the steering gear rubber gaiters, which would

indicate failed fluid seals within the steering gear.

4 Grasp the roadwheel at the 12 o'clock and 6 o'clock positions, and try to rock it **(see illustration)**. Very slight free play may be felt, but if the movement is appreciable, further investigation is necessary to determine the source. Continue rocking the wheel while an assistant depresses the footbrake. If the movement is now eliminated or significantly reduced, it is likely that the hub bearings are at fault. If the free play is still evident with the footbrake depressed, then there is wear in the suspension joints or mountings.

5 Now grasp the wheel at the 9 o'clock and 3 o'clock positions, and try to rock it as before. Any movement felt now may again be caused by wear in the hub bearings or the steering track rod balljoints. If the inner or outer balljoint is worn, the visual movement will be obvious.

6 Using a large screwdriver or flat bar, check for wear in the suspension mounting bushes by levering between the relevant suspension component and its attachment point. Some movement is to be expected as the mountings are made of rubber, but excessive wear should be obvious. Also check the condition of any visible rubber bushes, looking for splits, cracks or contamination of the rubber.

7 With the car standing on its wheels, have an assistant turn the steering wheel back-and-forth about an eighth of a turn each way. There should be very little, if any, lost movement between the steering wheel and roadwheels. If this is not the case, closely observe the joints and mountings previously described, but in addition, check the steering column universal joints for wear, and the rack-and-pinion steering gear itself.

8 Check for any signs of fluid leakage around the front suspension struts and rear shock absorber. Should any fluid be noticed, the suspension strut or shock absorber is defective internally, and should be renewed. **Note:** *Suspension struts/shock absorbers should always be renewed in pairs on the same axle to ensure correct vehicle handling.*

9 The efficiency of the suspension strut/ shock absorber may be checked by bouncing the vehicle at each corner. Generally speaking, the body will return to its normal position and stop after being depressed. If it rises and returns on a rebound, the suspension strut/shock absorber is probably suspect. Examine also the suspension strut/shock absorber upper and lower mountings for any signs of wear.

20 Battery check

1 The battery is located in the front, left-hand corner of the engine compartment. Where a heat protective jacket is fitted, unclip the cover and remove the jacket to gain access to the battery **(see illustration)**.

2 Open the fuse holder plastic cover (squeeze together the locking lugs to release the cover) to gain access to the battery positive (+) terminal and fuse holder connections.

3 Check that both battery terminals and all the fuse holder connections are securely attached and are free from corrosion. **Note:** *Before disconnecting the terminals from the battery, refer to 'Disconnecting the battery' in the Reference Chapter at the end of this manual.*

4 Check the battery casing for signs of damage or cracking and check the battery retaining clamp bolt is securely tightened. If the battery casing is damaged in any way the battery must be renewed (see Chapter 5A).

5 If the vehicle is not fitted with a sealed-for-life maintenance-free battery, check the electrolyte level is between the MAX and MIN level markings on the battery casing. If topping-up is necessary, remove the battery (see Chapter 5A) from the vehicle then remove the cell caps/cover (as applicable). Using distilled water, top the electrolyte level of each cell up to the MAX level mark then securely refit the cell caps/cover. Ensure the battery has not been overfilled then refit the battery to the vehicle (see Chapter 5A).

6 On completion of the check, clip the cover securely back onto the fuse holder and close up the insulator cover (where fitted).

21 Hinge and lock lubrication

1 Lubricate the hinges of the bonnet, doors and tailgate with a light general-purpose oil. Similarly, lubricate all latches, locks and lock strikers. At the same time, check the security and operation of all the locks, adjusting them if necessary (see Chapter 11).

2 Lightly lubricate the bonnet release mechanism and cable with a suitable grease.

22 Airbag unit check

Inspect the exterior condition of the airbag(s) for signs of damage or deterioration. If an airbag shows signs of damage, it must be renewed (see Chapter 12). Note that it is not permissible to attach any stickers to the surface of the airbag, as this may affect the deployment of the unit.

23 Windscreen/tailgate/ headlight washer system check

1 Check that each of the washer jet nozzles are clear and that each nozzle provides a strong jet of washer fluid.

2 The tailgate jet should be aimed to spray at the centre of the screen, using a pin.

19.4 Check for wear in the hub bearings by grasping the wheel and trying to rock it

3 The windscreen washer nozzles should be aimed slightly above the centre of the screen using a small screwdriver to turn the jet eccentric.

4 On Golf models, the headlight inner jet should be aimed slightly above the horizontal centreline of the headlight, and the outer jet should be aimed slightly below the centreline. On Bora models, the headlight jet should be aimed slightly below the horizontal centreline of the headlight. VW technicians use a special tool to adjust the headlight jet after pulling the jet out onto its stop.

5 Especially during the winter months, make sure that the washer fluid frost concentration is sufficient.

24 Engine management self-diagnosis memory fault check

This work should be carried out by a VW dealer or diagnostic specialist using special equipment. The diagnostic socket is located behind a cover beneath the central part of the facia. The cover is clipped in position.

25 Sunroof check and lubrication

1 Check the operation of the sunroof, and leave it in the fully open position.

2 Wipe clean the guide rails on each side of the sunroof opening, then apply lubricant to them. VW recommend lubricant spray G 052 778.

20.1 Removing the battery cover

26 Road test and exhaust emissions check

Instruments and electrical equipment

1 Check the operation of all instruments and electrical equipment including the air conditioning system.
2 Make sure that all instruments read correctly, and switch on all electrical equipment in turn, to check that it functions properly.

Steering and suspension

3 Check for any abnormalities in the steering, suspension, handling or road 'feel'.
4 Drive the vehicle, and check that there are no unusual vibrations or noises which may indicate wear in the driveshafts, wheel bearings, etc.
5 Check that the steering feels positive, with no excessive 'sloppiness', or roughness, and check for any suspension noises when cornering and driving over bumps.

Drivetrain

6 Check the performance of the engine, clutch (where applicable), gearbox/transmission and driveshafts.
7 Listen for any unusual noises from the engine, clutch and gearbox/transmission.

8 Make sure the engine runs smoothly at idle, and there is no hesitation on accelerating.
9 Check that, where applicable, the clutch action is smooth and progressive, that the drive is taken up smoothly, and that the pedal travel is not excessive. Also listen for any noises when the clutch pedal is depressed.
10 On manual gearbox models, check that all gears can be engaged smoothly without noise, and that the gear lever action is smooth and not abnormally vague or 'notchy'.
11 On automatic transmission models, make sure that all gearchanges occur smoothly, without snatching, and without an increase in engine speed between changes. Check that all the gear positions can be selected with the vehicle at rest. If any problems are found, they should be referred to a VW dealer.
12 Listen for a metallic clicking sound from the front of the vehicle, as the vehicle is driven slowly in a circle with the steering on full-lock. Carry out this check in both directions. If a clicking noise is heard, this indicates wear in a driveshaft joint, in which case renew the joint if necessary.

Braking system

13 Make sure that the vehicle does not pull to one side when braking, and that the wheels do not lock when braking hard.
14 Check that there is no vibration through the steering when braking.
15 Check that the handbrake operates

correctly without excessive movement of the lever, and that it holds the vehicle stationary on a slope.
16 Test the operation of the brake servo unit as follows. With the engine off, depress the footbrake four or five times to exhaust the vacuum. Hold the brake pedal depressed, then start the engine. As the engine starts, there should be a noticeable 'give' in the brake pedal as vacuum builds-up. Allow the engine to run for at least two minutes, and then switch it off. If the brake pedal is depressed now, it should be possible to detect a hiss from the servo as the pedal is depressed. After about four or five applications, no further hissing should be heard, and the pedal should feel considerably harder.
17 Under controlled emergency braking, the pulsing of the ABS unit must be felt at the footbrake pedal.

Exhaust emissions check

18 Although not part of the manufacturer's maintenance schedule, this check will normally be carried out on a regular basis according to the country the vehicle is operated in. Currently in the UK, exhaust emissions testing is included as part of the annual MOT test after the vehicle is 3 years old. In Germany the test is made when the vehicle is 3 years old, then repeated every 2 years.

Every 40 000 miles or 4 years

27.3 Removing the air filter element

27 Air filter element renewal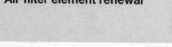

1 The air filter is housed in the air cleaner, which is situated on the left-hand side of the inner wing, behind the battery.
2 Undo the screws and lift the cover from the top of the air cleaner body.
3 Lift out the air filter element **(see illustration)**.
4 Remove any debris that may have collected inside the air cleaner.

5 Fit a new air filter element in position, ensuring that the edges are securely seated.
6 Refit the air cleaner top cover and secure with the screws.

28 Fuel filter renewal (vehicles using standard diesel fuel)

Note: Carry out this procedure at this interval only when using diesel fuel conforming to DIN EN 590 (standard fuel in the UK).
Refer to Section 10.

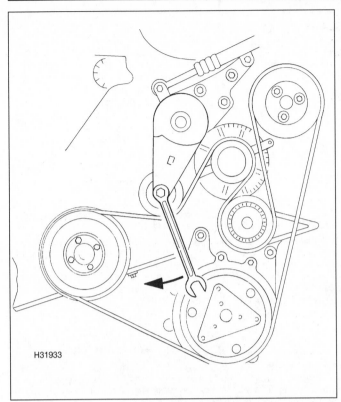

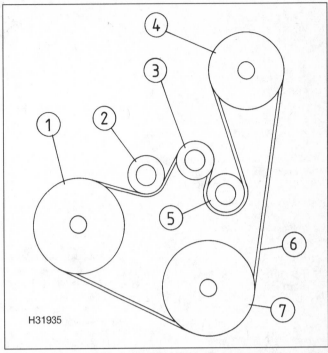

29.4 Turn the tensioner central bolt clockwise to release the tension on the drivebelt

29.5a Auxiliary drivebelt configuration on injection pump models

1 Crankshaft pulley
2 Tensioner
3 Alternator pulley
4 Power steering pump pulley
5 Idler
6 Auxiliary drivebelt
7 Air conditioning compressor pulley

29 Auxiliary drivebelt check and renewal

Check

1 See Section 11.

Renewal

2 For improved access, apply the handbrake, then jack up the front of the vehicle and support it on axle stands (see *Jacking and vehicle support*).
3 Remove the right-hand front roadwheel,

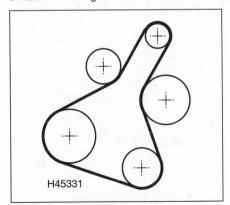

29.5b Auxiliary drivebelt configuration on unit injector models

then remove the access panel from the inner wheel arch.
4 Use a spanner to turn the tensioner central bolt clockwise to release the tension on the drivebelt (see illustration).
5 Note how the drivebelt is routed, then remove it from the crankshaft pulley, alternator pulley, power steering pump pulley, and air conditioning compressor pulley (where applicable) (see illustrations).
6 Locate the new drivebelt on the pulleys, then release the tensioner. Check that the belt is located correctly in the multi-grooves in the pulleys.
7 Refit the access panel and roadwheel, and lower the vehicle to the ground.

30 Power steering hydraulic fluid level check

1 Turn the front roadwheels to the straight-ahead position without starting the engine. If the vehicle has been left standing for an hour or more, the power steering fluid will be cold (below 50ºC), and the 'cold' level markings must be used. If, however, the engine is at normal temperature (above 50ºC), the fluid will be hot, and the 'hot' level markings must be used.
2 The reservoir is located on the right-hand side of the engine compartment, next to the

coolant expansion tank. The fluid level is checked with a dipstick attached to the reservoir filler cap. Using a screwdriver, unscrew the cap from the hydraulic fluid reservoir, and wipe clean the integral dipstick with a clean cloth (see illustration).
3 Screw on the cap hand tight then unscrew it again and check the fluid level on the dipstick. If the fluid is cold (below 50ºC), it must be in the 'hashed' cold area indicated on the dipstick. If the fluid is hot (above 50ºC), it must be between the hot MAX and MIN marks indicated on the dipstick (see illustration).
4 If the level is above the maximum level mark, syphon off the excess amount. If it is below the minimum level mark, add the

30.2 Unscrew the cap from the hydraulic fluid reservoir, and wipe clean the integral dipstick with a clean cloth

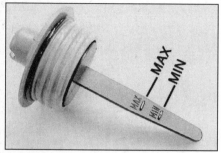

30.3 Screw on the cap hand tight then unscrew it again and check the fluid level on the dipstick

specified fluid as necessary (see *Lubricants and fluids*), but in this case also check the system for leaks. On completion, screw on the cap and tighten with the screwdriver.

31 Automatic transmission fluid level check

Note: *An accurate fluid level check can only be made with the transmission fluid at a temperature of between 35°C and 45°C, and if it is not possible to ascertain this temperature, it is strongly recommended that the check be made by a VW dealer who will have the instrumentation to check the temperature and to check the transmission electronics for fault codes. Overfilling or underfilling adversely affects the function of the transmission.*

1 Take the vehicle on a short journey to warm the transmission slightly (see Note at the start of this Section), then park the vehicle on level ground and engage P with the selector lever. Raise the front and rear of the vehicle and support it on axle stands (see *Jacking and vehicle support*), ensuring the vehicle is kept level. Undo the retaining screws and remove the engine undershield(s) to gain access to the base of the transmission unit.
2 Start the engine and run it at idle speed until the transmission fluid temperature reaches 35°C.
3 Unscrew the fluid level plug from the bottom of the transmission sump **(see illustration)**.

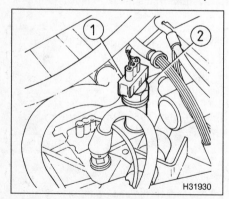

32.2 Disconnect the wiring (1) from the speedometer drive (2)

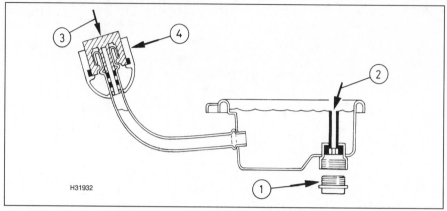

31.3 Automatic transmission fluid level check

1 Level plug   2 Level tube   3 Filler cap   4 Retaining clip

4 If fluid **continually** drips from the level tube as the fluid temperature increases, the fluid level is correct and does not need to be topped-up. Note that there will be some fluid already present in the level tube, and it will be necessary to observe when this amount has drained before making the level check. Make sure that the check is made before the fluid temperature reaches 45°C. Check the condition of the seal on the level plug and renew it if necessary by cutting off the old seal and fitting a new one. Refit the plug and tighten to the specified torque.
5 If no fluid drips from the level tube, even when the fluid temperature has reached 45°C, it will be necessary to add fluid as follows while the engine is still running.
6 Using a screwdriver, lever off the cap from the filler tube on the side of the transmission sump. **Note:** *On some models the locking device will be permanently damaged and a new cap must be obtained. On other models, the cap securing clip must be renewed.*
7 With the cap removed, pull out the filler tube plug then add the specified fluid until it drips out of the level tube. Check the condition of the seal on the level plug and renew it if necessary by cutting off the old seal and fitting a new one. Refit the plug and tighten to the specified torque.
8 Refit the filler tube plug and the new cap or cap securing clip.
9 Switch off the ignition then refit the engine undershield(s), tighten the retaining screws securely, and lower the vehicle to the ground.

10 Frequent need for topping-up indicates that there is a leak, which should be found and corrected before it becomes serious.

32 Automatic transmission final drive oil level check

Note: *This work only applies to the 01M transmission.*

1 Apply the handbrake, then jack up the front of the vehicle and support it on axle stands (see *Jacking and vehicle support*), but note that the rear of the vehicle should also be raised to ensure an accurate level check.
2 The final drive level check is made by removing the speedometer drive. First, disconnect the wiring from the sender on the top of the speedometer drive **(see illustration)**.
3 Unscrew the speedometer drive and withdraw it from the transmission. There is no need to remove the sender unit from the top of the drive.
4 Wipe clean the lower end of the drive, then re-insert it and screw it fully into the transmission. Remove it again and check that the oil level is between the shoulder and the end of the drive **(see illustration)**.
5 If necessary, add the specified oil through the drive aperture until the level is correct.
6 Refit the drive and tighten securely, then reconnect the sender wiring.
7 Lower the vehicle to the ground.

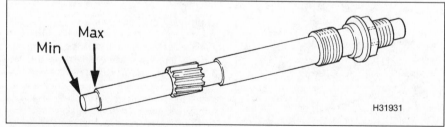

32.4 The automatic transmission final drive oil level is checked on the bottom of the speedometer drive

Every 60 000 miles or 6 years

33 Timing belt and tensioning roller renewal (engines with 'unit' injectors)

Note: *This work at this interval applies only to engines with 'unit' injectors (see Chapter 4B).*
1 Refer to Chapter 2C for details of renewing the timing belt and tensioning roller.

Every 80 000 miles or 8 years

34 Timing belt and tensioning roller renewal (engines with injection pump)

Note: *This work at this interval only applies to engines with an injection pump (see Chapter 4B).*
1 Refer to Chapter 2C for details of renewing the timing belt and tensioning roller.

Every 2 years

35 Brake (and clutch) fluid renewal

Warning: Brake hydraulic fluid can harm your eyes and damage painted surfaces, so use extreme caution when handling and pouring it. Do not use fluid that has been standing open for some time, as it absorbs moisture from the air. Excess moisture can cause a dangerous loss of braking effectiveness.

1 The procedure is similar to that for the bleeding of the hydraulic system as described in Chapter 9, except that the brake fluid reservoir should be emptied by syphoning, using a clean poultry baster or similar before starting, and allowance should be made for the old fluid to be expelled when bleeding a section of the circuit. Since the clutch hydraulic system also uses fluid from the brake system reservoir, it should also be bled at the same time by referring to Chapter 6, Section 2.
2 Working as described in Chapter 9, open the first bleed screw in the sequence, and pump the brake pedal gently until nearly all the old fluid has been emptied from the master cylinder reservoir.

HAYNES HiNT *Old hydraulic fluid is often much darker in colour than the new, making it easy to distinguish the two.*

3 Top-up to the MAX level with new fluid, and continue pumping until only the new fluid remains in the reservoir, and new fluid can be seen emerging from the bleed screw. Tighten the screw, and top the reservoir level up to the MAX level line.
4 Work through all the remaining bleed screws in the sequence until new fluid can be seen at all of them. Be careful to keep the master cylinder reservoir topped-up to above the MIN level at all times, or air may enter the system and greatly increase the length of the task.
5 When the operation is complete, check that all bleed screws are securely tightened, and that their dust caps are refitted. Wash off all traces of spilt fluid, and recheck the master cylinder reservoir fluid level.
6 On models with a manual transmission unit, once the brake fluid has been changed the clutch fluid should also be renewed. Referring to Chapter 6, bleed the clutch until new fluid is seen to be emerging from the slave cylinder bleed screw, keeping the master cylinder fluid level above the MIN level line at all times to prevent air entering the system. Once the new fluid emerges, securely tighten the bleed screw then disconnect and remove the bleeding equipment. Securely refit the dust cap then wash off all traces of spilt fluid.
7 On all models, ensure the master cylinder fluid level is correct (see *Weekly checks*) and thoroughly check the operation of the brakes and (where necessary) clutch before taking the car on the road.

36 Coolant renewal

Note: *This work is not included in the VW schedule and should not be required if the recommended VW G12 LongLife coolant antifreeze/inhibitor is used. However, if standard antifreeze/inhibitor is used, the work should be carried out at the recommended interval.*

Warning: Wait until the engine is cold before starting this procedure. Do not allow antifreeze to come in contact with your skin, or with the painted surfaces of the vehicle. Rinse off spills immediately with plenty of water. Never leave antifreeze lying around in an open container, or in a puddle in the driveway or on the garage floor. Children and pets are attracted by its sweet smell, but antifreeze can be fatal if ingested.

Cooling system draining

1 With the engine completely cold, unscrew the expansion tank cap.
2 Firmly apply the handbrake then jack up the front of the vehicle and support it on axle stands (see *Jacking and vehicle support*). Undo the retaining screws and remove the engine undershield(s) to gain access to the base of the radiator.
3 Position a suitable container beneath the coolant drain outlet which is fitted to the coolant bottom hose end fitting. Loosen the drain plug (there is no need to remove it completely) and allow the coolant to drain into the container. If desired, a length of tubing can be fitted to the drain outlet to direct the flow of coolant during draining. Where no drain outlet is fitted to the hose end fitting, remove the retaining clip and disconnect the bottom hose from the radiator to drain the coolant (see Chapter 3, Section 2).
4 To fully drain the system also disconnect one of the coolant hoses from the oil cooler which is located at the front of the cylinder block (see Chapter 2C).
5 If the coolant has been drained for a reason other than renewal, then provided it is clean, it can be re-used, though this is not recommended.
6 Once all the coolant has drained, securely tighten the radiator drain plug or reconnect the bottom hose to the radiator (as applicable). Also reconnect the coolant hose to the oil cooler and secure it in position with the retaining clip. Refit the undershield(s), tighten the retaining screws securely.

Cooling system flushing

7 If the recommended VW coolant has not been used and coolant renewal has been neglected, or if the antifreeze mixture has become diluted, the cooling system may gradually lose efficiency, as the coolant passages become restricted due to rust, scale deposits, and other sediment. The cooling system efficiency can be restored by flushing the system clean.

8 The radiator should be flushed separately from the engine, to avoid excess contamination.

Radiator flushing

9 To flush the radiator, first tighten the radiator drain plug.

10 Disconnect the top and bottom hoses and any other relevant hoses from the radiator (see Chapter 3).

11 Insert a garden hose into the radiator top inlet. Direct a flow of clean water through the radiator, and continue flushing until clean water emerges from the radiator bottom outlet.

12 If after a reasonable period, the water still does not run clear, the radiator can be flushed with a good proprietary cleaning agent. It is important that their manufacturer's instructions are followed carefully. If the contamination is particularly bad, insert the hose in the radiator bottom outlet, and reverse-flush the radiator.

Engine flushing

13 To flush the engine, remove the thermostat (see Chapter 3).

14 With the bottom hose disconnected from the radiator, insert a garden hose into the coolant housing. Direct a clean flow of water through the engine, and continue flushing until clean water emerges from the radiator bottom hose.

15 When flushing is complete, refit the thermostat and reconnect the hoses (see Chapter 3).

Cooling system filling

16 Before attempting to fill the cooling system, ensure the drain plug is securely closed and make sure that all hoses are connected and are securely retained by their clips. If the recommended VW coolant is not being used, ensure that a suitable antifreeze mixture is used all year round, to prevent corrosion of the engine components (see following sub-Section).

17 Remove the expansion tank filler cap and slowly fill the system with the coolant. Continue to fill the cooling system until bubbles stop appearing in the expansion tank. Help to bleed the air from the system by repeatedly squeezing the radiator bottom hose.

18 When no more bubbles appear, top the coolant level up to the MAX level mark then securely refit the cap to the expansion tank.

19 Run the engine at a fast idle speed until the cooling fan cuts in. Wait for the fan to stop then switch the engine off and allow the engine to cool.

20 When the engine has cooled, check the coolant level with reference to *Weekly checks*. Top-up the level if necessary, and refit the expansion tank cap.

Antifreeze mixture

21 If the recommended VW coolant is not being used, the antifreeze should always be renewed at the specified intervals. This is necessary not only to maintain the antifreeze properties, but also to prevent corrosion which would otherwise occur as the corrosion inhibitors become progressively less effective.

22 Always use an ethylene-glycol based antifreeze which is suitable for use in mixed-metal cooling systems. The quantity of antifreeze and levels of protection are indicated in the Specifications.

23 Before adding antifreeze, the cooling system should be completely drained, preferably flushed, and all hoses checked for condition and security.

24 After filling with antifreeze, a label should be attached to the expansion tank, stating the type and concentration of antifreeze used, and the date installed. Any subsequent topping-up should be made with the same type and concentration of antifreeze.

25 Do not use engine antifreeze in the windscreen/tailgate washer system, as it will damage the vehicle paintwork. A screenwash additive should be added to the washer system in the quantities stated on the bottle.

Chapter 2 Part A:
SOHC petrol engine in-car repair procedures

Contents

Balancer shaft assembly (2.0 litre AZJ engines) – removal and refitting 22
Camshaft – removal, inspection and refitting 9
Camshaft cover – removal and refitting 4
Camshaft oil seal – renewal 11
Compression test – description and interpretation 2
Crankshaft oil seals – renewal 16
Crankshaft pulley – removal and refitting 5
Cylinder head – removal, inspection and refitting 12
Engine assembly and valve timing marks – general information and usage 3
Engine oil cooler – removal and refitting 18
Engine/transmission mountings – inspection and renewal 17
Flywheel/driveplate – removal, inspection and refitting 15
General information 1
Hydraulic tappets/roller rocker fingers – removal, inspection and refitting 10
Oil level/temperature sender – removal and refitting 21
Oil pressure relief valve – removal, inspection and refitting .. 19
Oil pressure warning light switch – removal and refitting 20
Oil pump, drive chain and sprockets – removal, inspection and refitting 14
Sump – removal and refitting 13
Timing belt – removal and refitting 7
Timing belt covers – removal and refitting 6
Timing belt tensioner and sprockets – removal and refitting ... 8

Degrees of difficulty

Easy, suitable for novice with little experience	**Fairly easy,** suitable for beginner with some experience	**Fairly difficult,** suitable for competent DIY mechanic	**Difficult,** suitable for experienced DIY mechanic	**Very difficult,** suitable for expert DIY or professional 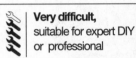

Specifications

General

Manufacturer's engine codes*:	
1595 cc	AEH and AKL
1595 cc (with roller rocker fingers)	AVU and BFQ
1984 cc	APK, AQY AZH and AZJ
Maximum power output:	
1.6 litre engines:	
AEH and AKL	74 kW at 5600 rpm
AVU and BFQ	75 kW at 5600 rpm
2.0 litre engines:	
APK and AQY	85 kW at 5200 rpm
AZH and AZJ	85 kW at 5400 rpm
Maximum torque output:	
1.6 litre engines:	
AEH and AKL	145 Nm at 3800 rpm
AVU and BFQ	148 Nm at 3800 rpm
2.0 litre engines:	
APK and AQY and AZH	170 Nm at 2400 rpm
AZJ	172 Nm at 3200 rpm
Bore:	
1.6 litre engines	81.0 mm
2.0 litre engines	82.5 mm
Stroke:	
1.6 litre engines	77.4 mm
2.0 litre engines	92.8 mm
Compression ratio:	
1.6 litre engines (except BFQ)	10.2 : 1
1.6 litre BFQ engines	10.5 : 1
2.0 litre engines	10.5 : 1
Compression pressures:	
Minimum compression pressure	Approximately 7.5 bar
Maximum difference between cylinders	Approximately 3.0 bar
Firing order	1 – 3 – 4 – 2
No 1 cylinder location	Timing belt end

* Note: *See 'Vehicle identification' at the end of this manual for the location of engine code markings.*

Lubrication system

Oil pump type	Gear type (rotor type on AZJ engine), chain-driven from crankshaft
Oil pressure (oil temperature 80°C):	
At 2000 rpm	2.7 to 4.5 bar

Camshaft

Camshaft endfloat (maximum)	0.15 mm
Camshaft bearing running clearance (maximum)	0.1 mm
Camshaft run-out:	
1.6 litre engines (maximum)	0.01 mm
2.0 litre engines (maximum)	0.05 mm

Torque wrench settings

	Nm	lbf ft
Ancillary (alternator, etc) bracket mounting bolts	45	33
Auxiliary drivebelt pulley bolts	25	18
Auxiliary drivebelt tensioner securing bolt	25	18
Balancer shaft chain tensioner mounting bolts	15	11
Balancer unit-to-cylinder block:		
2.0 litre AZJ engines:		
Stage 1	15	11
Stage 2	Angle-tighten a further 90°	
Big-end bearing caps nuts/bolts (on engines with bolts, renew bolts):		
Stage 1	30	22
Stage 2	Angle-tighten a further 90°	
Camshaft bearing cap/ladder nuts	20	15
Camshaft cover nuts/bolts	10	7
Camshaft sprocket bolt	100	74
Clutch pressure plate/driveplate mounting bolts*:		
1.6 litre engines:		
Stage 1	60	44
Stage 2	Angle-tighten a further 90°	
Coolant housing-to-cylinder head bolts	10	7
Coolant pump bolts	15	11
Crankshaft oil seal housing bolts	15	11
Crankshaft position sensor wheel-to-crankshaft bolts*:		
Stage 1	10	7
Stage 2	Angle-tighten a further 90°	
Crankshaft pulley bolts	25	18
Crankshaft sprocket bolt*:		
Stage 1	90	66
Stage 2	Angle-tighten a further 90°	
Cylinder block oil gallery plug	100	74
Cylinder head bolts*:		
Stage 1	40	30
Stage 2	Angle-tighten a further 90°	
Stage 3	Angle-tighten a further 90°	
Cylinder head oil gallery plug	15	11
Driveplate mounting bolts*:		
Stage 1	60	44
Stage 2	Angle-tighten a further 90°	
Engine mountings:		
Left-hand mounting-to-body bolts:		
Large bolts*:		
Stage 1	40	30
Stage 2	Angle-tighten a further 90°	
Small bolts	25	18
Left-hand mounting-to-transmission bolts	100	74
Right-hand mounting-to-body bolts*:		
Stage 1	40	30
Stage 2	Angle-tighten a further 90°	
Right-hand mounting bracket-to-body bolts (small bolts)	25	18
Right-hand mounting-to-engine bracket bolts	100	74
Right-hand mounting bracket-to-engine bolts	45	33
Rear engine/transmission mounting:		
Bracket-to-subframe bolts*:		
Stage 1	20	15
Stage 2	Angle-tighten a further 90°	

Torque wrench settings (continued)

	Nm	lbf ft
Engine mountings (continued):		
Rear engine/transmission mounting (continued):		
Bracket-to-transmission bolts*:		
Stage 1	40	30
Stage 2	Angle-tighten a further 90°	
Exhaust manifold nuts	25	18
Exhaust pipe-to-manifold nuts	40	30
Flywheel*:		
Stage 1	60	44
Stage 2	Angle-tighten a further 90°	
Inlet manifold (lower part) nuts	10	7
Main bearing cap bolts*:		
1.6 litre engines:		
Stage 1	40	30
Stage 2	Angle-tighten a further 90°	
Main bearing cap bolts*:		
2.0 litre engines:		
Stage 1	65	48
Stage 2	Angle-tighten a further 90°	
Oil baffle plate securing bolts	15	11
Oil cooler securing nut	25	18
Oil drain plug	30	22
Oil filter housing-to-cylinder block bolts*:		
Stage 1	15	11
Stage 2	Angle-tighten a further 90°	
Oil level/temperature sender bolts	10	7
Oil pick-up pipe-to-oil pump bolts	15	11
Oil pressure relief valve plug	40	30
Oil pressure warning light switch	25	18
Oil spray jet/pressure relief valve bolts	27	20
Oil pump chain tensioner bolt	15	11
Oil pump cover securing bolts:		
2.0 litre AZJ engines	8	5
Oil pump securing bolts:		
All except 2.0 litre AZJ engines	15	11
Oil pump sprocket bolt	20	15
Roadwheel bolts	120	89
Sump:		
Sump-to-cylinder block bolts	15	11
Sump-to-transmission bolts		
1.6 litre engines	25	18
2.0 litre engines	45	33
Thermostat cover bolts:		
All except engine code AZJ	10	7
Engine code AZJ	15	11
Timing belt outer cover bolts	10	7
Timing belt rear cover bolts:		
Small bolts	15	11
Large bolt	20	15
Timing belt tensioner nut	20	15
Vent pipe-to-cylinder head bolt:		
Engine codes AVU and BFQ	10	7

*Note: Use new bolts

---

1 General information

Using this Chapter

Chapter 2 is divided into four Parts; A, B, C and D. Repair operations that can be carried out with the engine in the vehicle are described in Part A (SOHC petrol engines), Part B (DOHC petrol engines), and Part C (diesel engines). Part D covers the removal of the engine/transmission as a unit, and describes the engine dismantling and overhaul procedures.

In Parts A, B and C, the assumption is made that the engine is installed in the vehicle, with all ancillaries connected. If the engine has been removed for overhaul, the preliminary dismantling information which precedes each operation may be ignored.

Engine description

Throughout this Chapter, engines are identified and referred to by their capacity and, where necessary, by the manufacturer's code letters. A listing of all engines covered, together with their code letters, is given in the Specifications.

The engines covered in this Part of the Chapter are water-cooled, single-overhead camshaft (SOHC), in-line four-cylinder units.

The 1595 cc engine has an aluminium alloy cylinder block fitted with cast-iron cylinder liners and the 1984 cc engine has a cast-iron cylinder block with integral cylinder bores. Both engines have an aluminium alloy cylinder head and are transversely mounted at the front of the vehicle, with the transmission unit on their left-hand end.

The crankshaft is of five-bearing type, and thrustwashers are fitted to the centre main bearing to control crankshaft endfloat.

The camshaft is mounted at the top of the cylinder head and is driven by a toothed timing belt from the crankshaft sprocket. On most engines it is secured in place by bearing caps, except the 1.6 litre AVU and BFQ engines, which have a retaining ladder frame to hold the camshaft in place.

The valves are closed by coil springs, and the valves run in guides pressed into the cylinder head. The camshafts actuate the valves directly via hydraulic tappets on most engines, except the 1.6 litre AVU and BFQ engines, which have roller rocker fingers to operate the valves.

The oil pump is driven via a chain from a sprocket on the crankshaft. Oil is drawn from the sump through a strainer, and then forced through an externally-mounted, renewable filter. From there, it is distributed to the cylinder head, where it lubricates the camshaft journals and hydraulic tappets, and also to the crankcase, where it lubricates the main bearings, connecting rod big-ends, gudgeon pins and cylinder bores. A coolant-fed oil cooler is fitted to all engines.

On the 2.0 litre AZJ engine, there are balancer shafts fitted between the cylinder block and the main sump casting. The unit consists of two counter-rotating balance shafts driven by the crankshaft

On all engines, engine coolant is circulated by a pump, driven by the timing belt. For details of the cooling system, refer to Chapter 3.

Operations with engine in car

The following operations can be performed without removing the engine:

a) Compression pressure – testing.
b) Camshaft cover – removal and refitting.
c) Crankshaft pulley – removal and refitting.
d) Timing belt covers – removal and refitting.
e) Timing belt – removal, refitting and adjustment.
f) Timing belt tensioner and sprockets – removal and refitting.
g) Camshaft oil seal – renewal.
h) Camshaft and hydraulic tappets – removal, inspection and refitting.
i) Cylinder head – removal and refitting.
j) Cylinder head and pistons – decarbonising.
k) Sump – removal and refitting.
l) Oil pump – removal, overhaul and refitting.
m) Crankshaft oil seals – renewal.
n) Engine/transmission mountings – inspection and renewal.

o) Flywheel – removal, inspection and refitting.
p) Balancer shaft assembly (2.0 litre AZJ engines) – removal and refitting.

Note: *It is possible to remove the pistons and connecting rods (after removing the cylinder head and sump) without removing the engine. However, this is not recommended. Work of this nature is more easily and thoroughly completed with the engine on the bench, as described in Chapter 2D.*

2 Compression test – description and interpretation

Note: *A suitable compression tester will be required for this test.*

1 When engine performance is down, or if misfiring occurs which cannot be attributed to the ignition or fuel systems, a compression test can provide diagnostic clues as to the engine's condition. If the test is performed regularly it can give warning of trouble before any other symptoms become apparent.

2 The engine must be fully warmed-up to normal operating temperature, the battery must be fully-charged and the spark plugs must be removed. The aid of an assistant will be required.

3 Disable the ignition system by disconnecting the wiring plug from the DIS unit or removing fuse, see Chapter 12.

4 Referring to Chapter 4A, depressurise the fuel system – this is necessary, in order to prevent unburnt fuel from passing into the catalytic converter during cranking.

5 Fit a compression tester to the No 1 cylinder spark plug hole. The type of tester which screws into the plug thread is preferred.

6 Have the assistant hold the throttle wide open and crank the engine for several seconds on the starter motor. **Note:** *On models fitted with an throttle position sensor instead of a cable, the throttle will not operate until the ignition is switched on.* After one or two revolutions, the compression pressure should build-up to a maximum figure and then stabilise. Record the highest reading obtained.

7 Repeat the test on the remaining cylinders, recording the pressure in each.

8 All cylinders should produce very similar pressures. Any difference greater than that specified indicates the existence of a fault. Note that the compression should build-up quickly in a healthy engine. Low compression on the first stroke, followed by gradually increasing pressure on successive strokes, indicates worn piston rings. A low compression reading on the first stroke, which does not build-up during successive strokes, indicates leaking valves or a blown head gasket (a cracked head could also be the cause). Deposits on the undersides of the valve heads can also cause low compression.

9 If the pressure in any cylinder is reduced to the specified minimum or less, carry out the

following test to isolate the cause. Introduce a teaspoonful of clean oil into that cylinder through its spark plug hole and repeat the test.

10 If the addition of oil temporarily improves the compression pressure, this indicates that bore or piston wear is responsible for the pressure loss. No improvement suggests that leaking or burnt valves, or a blown head gasket, may be to blame.

11 A low reading from two adjacent cylinders is almost certainly due to the head gasket having blown between them and the presence of coolant in the engine oil will confirm this.

12 If one cylinder is about 20 percent lower than the others and the engine has a slightly rough idle, a worn camshaft lobe could be the cause.

13 If the compression reading is unusually high, the combustion chambers are probably coated with carbon deposits. If this is the case, the cylinder head should be removed and decarbonised.

14 On completion of the test, refit the spark plugs, and reconnect the DIS unit.

3 Engine assembly and valve timing marks – general information and usage

General information

1 TDC is the highest point in the cylinder that each piston reaches as it travels up and down when the crankshaft turns. Each piston reaches TDC at the end of the compression stroke and again at the end of the exhaust stroke, but TDC generally refers to piston position on the compression stroke. No 1 piston is at the timing belt end of the engine.

2 Positioning No 1 piston at TDC is an essential part of many procedures, such as timing belt removal and camshaft removal.

3 The design of the engines covered in this Chapter is such that piston-to-valve contact may occur if the camshaft or crankshaft is turned with the timing belt removed. For this reason, it is important to ensure that the camshaft and crankshaft do not move in relation to each other once the timing belt has been removed from the engine.

4 On some models, the crankshaft pulley has a marking which, when aligned with a corresponding reference marking on the timing belt cover, indicates that No 1 piston (and hence also No 4 piston) is at TDC **(see illustration).**

5 The camshaft sprocket is also equipped with a timing mark. When this mark is aligned with the OT mark on the rear timing belt cover, No 1 piston is at TDC on the compression stroke **(see illustrations).**

6 Additionally, the flywheel/driveplate has a TDC marking, which can be observed by removing a protective cover from the transmission bellhousing. The mark take the form of a notch in the edge of the flywheel on

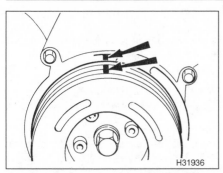

3.4 Crankshaft pulley TDC mark aligned with mark on timing belt lower cover

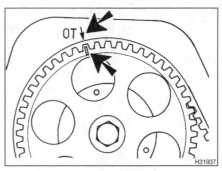

3.5a Camshaft sprocket TDC mark aligned with timing mark on timing belt rear cover . . .

3.5b . . . 1.6 litre engine set to TDC (as seen in-car)

manual transmission models, or an O marking on automatic transmission models **(see illustrations)**.

Setting No 1 cylinder to TDC

7 Before starting work, make sure that the ignition is switched off (ideally, the battery negative lead should be disconnected).

8 Where applicable, remove the engine top cover.

9 If desired, the make the engine easier to turn, remove all of the spark plugs as described in Chapter 1A.

10 Remove the upper timing belt cover as described in Section 6.

11 Turn the engine clockwise, using a spanner on the crankshaft sprocket bolt, until the TDC mark on the crankshaft pulley or flywheel/driveplate is aligned with the corresponding mark on the timing belt cover or transmission casing (as applicable), and the mark on the camshaft sprocket is aligned with the corresponding mark on the rear timing belt cover.

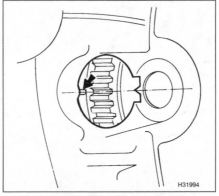

3.6a Flywheel TDC marking aligned with pointer on transmission casing – manual transmission model

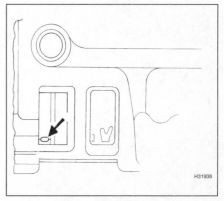

3.6b Driveplate TDC marking aligned with window in transmission casing – automatic transmission model

---

4 Camshaft cover – removal and refitting

Note: *On all engines except 1.6 litre AVU and BFQ engines, VW sealant (D 454 300 A2 or equivalent) will be required to seal the joints between the camshaft front bearing cap and the cylinder head on refitting.*

Removal

1 Where applicable, remove the upper part of the inlet manifold, as described in Chapter 4A.

2 Release the spring clip securing the breather hose at the rear, then twist the camshaft cover breather housing clockwise, and withdraw it from the camshaft cover **(see illustration)**. **Note:** *On 2.0 litre AZJ engines the breather housing is part of the camshaft cover and cannot be removed.*

3 To improve access, remove the upper timing belt cover with reference to Section 6.

4 Unscrew the nuts/bolts securing the camshaft cover to the cylinder head, starting from the outside and working inwards. Note the location of any support brackets secured by the camshaft cover nuts, then (where fitted)

remove the two reinforcement strips along the edge of the cover.

5 Lift the camshaft cover from the cylinder head, and recover the gasket.

6 Lift the oil deflector from the camshaft cover or the top of the cylinder head, as applicable.

Refitting

7 Inspect the camshaft cover gasket, and renew if worn or damaged.

8 Thoroughly clean the mating surfaces of the camshaft cover and the cylinder head, then lay the oil deflector in position over the camshaft bearing caps.

9 On all engines except 1.6 litre AVU and BFQ engines, working at the front (timing belt end) of the cylinder head, apply VW sealant

4.2 Removing the breather housing

(D 454 300 A2 or equivalent) to the two points where the front camshaft bearing cap contacts the cylinder head.

10 Carefully lay the camshaft cover gasket on the cylinder head, then refit the camshaft cover. Where applicable, lay the reinforcement strips in position, then locate any support brackets that where removed.

11 Tighten the nuts/bolts progressively to the specified torque, starting from the inside and working outwards.

12 Refit the upper timing cover, with reference to Section 6.

13 Check the condition of the camshaft cover breather housing seal, and renew if necessary. On all engines except 2.0 litre AZJ refit the breather housing, and twist it clockwise to lock it in position.

14 Where applicable, refit the upper part of the inlet manifold, as described in Chapter 4A.

---

5 Crankshaft pulley – removal and refitting

Removal

1 Disconnect the battery negative lead. **Note:** *Before disconnecting the battery, refer to 'Disconnecting the battery' at the rear of this manual.*

2 For improved access, raise the front right-

5.3 Removing the wheel arch liner access panel

hand side of the vehicle, and support securely on axle stands (see *Jacking and vehicle support*). Remove the roadwheel.

3 Remove the securing screws and withdraw the engine undershield(s) and wheel arch liner access panel **(see illustration)**.

4 If necessary (for any later work to be carried out), turn the crankshaft using a socket or spanner on the crankshaft sprocket bolt until the relevant timing marks align (see Section 3).

5 Slacken the bolts securing the crankshaft pulley to the sprocket **(see illustration)**. If necessary, the pulley can be prevented from turning by counterholding with a spanner or socket on the crankshaft sprocket bolt.

6 Remove the auxiliary drivebelt, as described in Chapter 1A.

7 Make a note of the fitted position of the pulley, then unscrew the bolts securing the pulley to the sprocket, and remove the pulley.

Refitting

8 Refit the pulley to the sprocket, locating the small offset hole over the sprocket peg as noted on removal, then refit the pulley securing bolts.

9 Refit and tension the auxiliary drivebelt as described in Chapter 1A.

10 Prevent the crankshaft from turning then tighten the pulley securing bolts to the specified torque.

11 Refit the engine undershield and wheel arch liner as applicable.

12 Refit the roadwheel and lower the vehicle to the ground, tighten the wheel to its correct torque setting.

13 Reconnect the battery negative lead.

6.1a Release the clip at the front and rear of the cover . . .

5.5 View of the crankshaft pulley, showing the four securing bolts

---

6 Timing belt covers – removal and refitting

Upper outer cover
Removal

1 Release the securing clip at the front and rear of the cover, and lift the cover out of the section below it, noting how it fits **(see illustrations)**.

Refitting

2 Refitting is a reversal of removal. Engage the base of the cover correctly (this is a fiddly operation) before trying to secure the upper clips, or they will not engage.

Centre outer cover
Removal

3 Remove the upper outer cover as described previously in this Section.

4 Remove the two bolts and nut securing the right-angled bracket fitted above the auxiliary drivebelt tensioner, and remove the bracket to improve access.

5 Unscrew the securing bolts, and withdraw the cover from the engine.

Refitting

6 Refitting is a reversal of removal.

Lower outer cover
Removal

7 Remove the upper and centre covers as described previously in this Section.

6.1b . . . and lift off the upper cover

---

8 Remove the crankshaft pulley as described in Section 5.

9 Unscrew the securing bolts, and withdraw the cover from the front of the engine.

Refitting

10 Refitting is a reversal of removal.

Upper inner cover
Removal

11 Remove the upper outer cover as described previously in this Section. Note on some models it may be necessary to remove the camshaft sprocket to remove the inner cover (see Section 8 for removal of camshaft sprocket).

12 Unscrew the nuts/bolts securing the inner cover to the camshaft cover, and remove the inner cover from the engine.

Refitting

13 Refitting is a reversal of removal.

Lower inner cover
Removal

14 Remove the timing belt as described in Section 7.

15 Unscrew the securing bolts and remove the timing belt lower inner cover.

Refitting

16 Refitting is a reversal of removal, but refit and tension the timing belt as described in Section 7.

---

7 Timing belt – removal and refitting

Removal

1 Remove the engine top cover(s). Depending on model, these may be clipped in position or removal by prising up the circular covers and removing the nuts/screws underneath. On some models, the engine front cover may be secured by a further nut on the right-hand side.

2 Remove the auxiliary drivebelt as described in Chapter 1A.

3 Unscrew the securing nut and bolts, and remove the right-angled bracket over the auxiliary drivebelt tensioner; the tensioner is now held by one further bolt at the top – remove the bolt and withdraw the tensioner from the engine.

4 Unbolt the coolant expansion tank, and move it clear of the working area, leaving the hoses connected.

5 Unbolt the power steering fluid reservoir, and move it clear of the working area, leaving the hoses connected.

6 Remove the timing belt upper outer cover, with reference to Section 6.

7 Turn the crankshaft to position No 1 piston at TDC, as described in Section 3.

8 Attach a hoist and lifting tackle to the

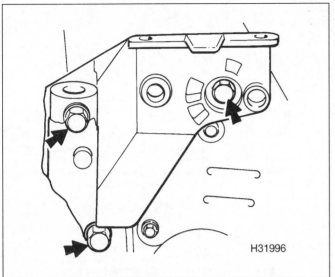

7.11 Right-hand engine mounting bracket-to-engine bolts (arrowed)

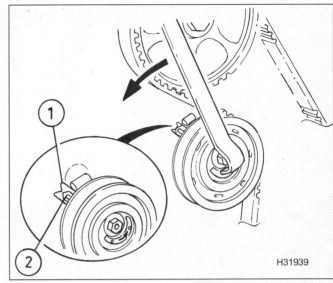

7.20 Tension the timing belt so that the tension indicator pointer (2) is aligned with the centre of the indicator notch (1)

engine lifting brackets on the cylinder head, and raise the hoist to just take the weight of the engine.

9 Unscrew the securing bolts and remove the right-hand engine mounting assembly, with reference to Section 17.

10 Remove the crankshaft pulley, with reference to Section 5. Before finally removing the pulley, check that No 1 piston is still positioned at TDC (see Section 3).

11 Unbolt the right-hand engine mounting bracket from the engine. Note that it may be necessary to raise the engine slightly, using the hoist, to allow access to unscrew the engine mounting securing bolts (once the bolts have been unscrewed, it will probably be necessary to leave the bolts in position in the bracket until the bracket has been removed) **(see illustration)**.

12 Remove the timing belt centre and lower outer covers, with reference to Section 6.

13 If the timing belt is to be refitted, mark its running direction.

14 Slacken the timing belt tensioner securing nut to release the tensioner, then withdraw the timing belt from the sprockets.

15 Turn the crankshaft a quarter-turn (90°) anti-clockwise to position Nos 1 and 4 pistons slightly down their bores from the TDC position. This will eliminate any risk of piston-to-valve contact if the crankshaft or camshaft is turned whilst the timing belt is removed.

Refitting

16 Check that the camshaft sprocket timing mark is aligned with the corresponding mark on the rear timing belt cover (see Section 3), then turn the crankshaft a quarter-turn (90°) clockwise to reposition Nos 1 and 4 pistons at TDC. Ensure that the appropriate crankshaft timing marks are aligned. If it is not possible to view the flywheel/driveplate timing marks, temporarily refit the crankshaft pulley and

timing belt cover, and turn the crankshaft to align the mark on the pulley with the corresponding mark on the belt cover.

17 Fit the timing belt around the crankshaft sprocket, coolant pump sprocket, tensioner, and camshaft sprocket. Where applicable, observe the running direction markings.

18 The timing belt must now be tensioned as follows.

19 Engage a pair of angled circlip pliers, or a similar tool, with the two holes in the centre of the tensioner pulley, then turn the pulley back-and-forth from the clockwise stop to the anti-clockwise stop, five times.

20 Turn the tensioner pulley anti-clockwise to its stop, then slowly release the tension on the pulley until the tension indicator pointer is aligned with the centre of the indicator notch **(see illustration)**. It may be necessary to use a mirror to view the tension indicator alignment.

21 Hold the tensioner pulley in position, with the pointer and notch aligned, and tighten the tensioner nut to the specified torque.

22 Turn the crankshaft through two complete revolutions clockwise until the No 1 piston is positioned at TDC again, with the timing marks aligned (see Section 3). It is important to ensure that the last one-eighth of a turn of rotation is completed without stopping.

23 Check that the tension indicator pointer is still aligned with the centre of the indicator notch. If the pointer is not aligned with the centre of the notch, repeat the tensioning procedure given in paragraphs 19 to 23. If the pointer and notch are correctly aligned, proceed as follows.

24 Refit the timing belt lower and centre covers, with reference to Section 6.

25 Refit the crankshaft pulley, with reference to Section 5, and tighten the securing bolts to the specified torque.

26 Refit the right-hand engine mounting bracket, and tighten the securing bolts to the specified torque (slide the securing bolts into position in the bracket before offering the bracket up to the engine).

27 Refit the right-hand engine mounting assembly, and check the mounting alignment as described in Section 17. Once the mounting alignment is correct, tighten the securing bolts to the specified torque.

28 Disconnect the hoist and lifting tackle from the engine.

29 Refit the timing belt upper outer cover.

30 Refit the power steering fluid reservoir and the coolant expansion tank.

31 Refit the auxiliary drivebelt tensioner, and tighten the securing bolts to the specified torque, then refit the auxiliary drivebelt as described in Chapter 1A.

32 Refit the engine top cover.

8 Timing belt tensioner and sprockets – removal and refitting

Camshaft sprocket

Removal

1 Remove the timing belt as described in Section 7.

2 Where necessary, unscrew the securing nut and remove the timing belt upper inner cover.

3 The camshaft must be held stationary as the sprocket bolt is slackened, and this can be achieved by making up a tool, and using it to hold the sprocket stationary by means of the holes in the sprocket face **(see illustration)**.

4 Unscrew the sprocket bolt and withdraw it, then withdraw the sprocket from the end of the camshaft. Recover the Woodruff key if it is loose.

8.3 Using a home-made tool to hold the camshaft sprocket (tool shown being used when tightening bolt)

8.11a Unscrew the securing bolt . . .

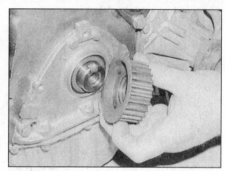

8.11b . . . and withdraw the sprocket from the crankshaft

Refitting

5 Prior to refitting, check the camshaft oil seal for signs of leakage, and if necessary renew the seal as described in Section 11.

6 Where applicable, refit the Woodruff key to the end of the camshaft, then refit the sprocket.

7 Tighten the sprocket bolt to the specified torque, preventing the sprocket from turning using the method used on removal.

8 Where applicable, refit the upper rear timing belt cover, then refit the timing belt as described in Section 7.

Crankshaft sprocket

Note: *A new sprocket securing bolt will be required on refitting.*

Removal

9 Remove the timing belt as described in Section 7.

10 The crankshaft must be held stationary as the sprocket bolt is slackened. On manual transmission models, engage top gear and apply the footbrake pedal firmly. On automatic transmission models, unbolt the starter motor and use a wide-bladed screwdriver engaged with the driveplate ring gear to hold the crankshaft stationary.

11 Unscrew the sprocket bolt (note that the bolt is very tight), and withdraw the sprocket from the crankshaft **(see illustrations)**.

Refitting

12 Locate the sprocket on the crankshaft, with the flange against the oil seal housing, then tighten the securing bolt to the specified torque, whilst holding the crankshaft stationary using the method employed during removal.

 Warning: Do not turn the crank- shaft, as the pistons may hit the valves.

13 Refit the timing belt as described in Section 7.

Coolant pump sprocket

14 The coolant pump sprocket is integral with the coolant pump, and cannot be removed separately. Refer to Chapter 3 for details of coolant pump removal.

Tensioner assembly

Removal

15 Remove the timing belt as described in Section 7.

16 Unscrew the securing nut and recover the washer, then withdraw the tensioner assembly from the stud on the engine.

Refitting

17 Offer the tensioner assembly into position over the mounting stud, ensuring that the lug on the tensioner backplate engages with the corresponding cut-out in the cylinder head.

18 Refit the securing nut, ensuring that the washer is in place, but do not fully tighten the nut at this stage.

19 Refit and tension the timing belt as described in Section 7.

---

9 Camshaft – removal, inspection and refitting

Note: *New camshaft seal(s) should be used on refitting.*

Removal

1 Remove the camshaft cover as described in Section 4.

2 Remove the timing belt as described in Section 7.

3 Remove the camshaft sprocket as described in Section 8.

All engines except 1.6 litre AVU and BFQ

Note: *VW sealant (AMV 174 004 01 or equivalent) will be required to coat the cylinder head mating face of No 1 camshaft bearing cap on refitting.*

4 Check the camshaft bearing caps for identification markings. The bearing caps are normally stamped with their respective cylinder numbers, and have an elongated lug on one side. The numbers should be readable from the exhaust side of the cylinder head, and the lugs should face the inlet side of the cylinder head. If no marks are present, make suitable marks using a scriber or punch. The caps should be numbered from 1 to 5, with No 1 at the timing belt end of the engine. Note on which side of the bearing caps the marks

are made to ensure that they are refitted the correct way round.

5 Unscrew the securing nuts for Nos 1, 3 and 5 bearing caps and remove the caps.

6 Working progressively, in a diagonal sequence, slacken the nuts securing Nos 2 and 4 bearing caps. Note that as the nuts are slackened, the valve springs will push the camshaft up.

7 Once the nuts securing Nos 2 and 4 bearing caps have been fully slackened, lift off the bearing caps.

8 Lift the camshaft from the cylinder head, then remove the oil seal from the end of the camshaft and discard it. A new seal will be required for refitting.

9 To remove the hydraulic tappets, see Section 10.

1.6 litre AVU and BFQ engines

Note: *VW sealant (D 188 800 A1 or equivalent) will be required to seal the joints between the camshaft retaining frame and the cylinder head on refitting.*

10 Unscrew the securing nuts, and remove the retaining ladder frame from top of the camshaft **(see illustration opposite)**. Note, number 1 bearing cap is at the timing belt end of the engine.

11 Progressively slacken the nuts securing numbers 5, 1 and 3 bearing caps, then 2 and 4, using an alternating diagonal sequence. Note that as the nuts are slackened, the valve springs will push the camshaft up.

12 Once the nuts securing Nos 2 and 4 bearing caps have been fully slackened, lift off the retaining ladder frame.

13 Lift the camshaft from the cylinder head, then remove the oil seal and the sealing cap from the ends of the camshaft and discard them. New seals will be required for refitting.

14 To remove the hydraulic tappets and roller rocker fingers, see Section 10.

Inspection

15 With the camshaft removed, examine the bearing caps/retaining frame and the bearing locations in the cylinder head for signs of obvious wear or pitting. If evident, a new cylinder head will probably be required. Also check that the oil supply holes in the cylinder head are free from obstructions.

16 Visually inspect the camshaft for evidence of wear on the surfaces of the lobes and journals. Normally their surfaces should be smooth and have a dull shine; look for scoring, erosion or pitting and areas that appear highly polished, indicating excessive wear. Accelerated wear will occur once the hardened exterior of the camshaft has been damaged, so always renew worn items. **Note:** *If these symptoms are visible on the tips of the camshaft lobes, check the corresponding tappet/rocker finger, as it may probably be worn as well.*

17 If the machined surfaces of the camshaft appear discoloured or blued, it is likely that it has been overheated at some point, probably due to inadequate lubrication.

18 To measure the camshaft endfloat, temporarily refit the camshaft to the cylinder head, then fit Nos 1 and 5 bearing caps or the ladder and tighten the retaining nuts to the specified torque setting. Anchor a DTI gauge to the timing belt end of the cylinder head. Push the camshaft to one end of the cylinder head as far as it will travel, then rest the DTI gauge probe on the end face of the camshaft, and zero the gauge. Push the camshaft as far as it will go to the other end of the cylinder head, and record the gauge reading. Verify the reading by pushing the camshaft back to its original position and checking that the gauge indicates zero again **(see illustration)**. **Note:** *The hydraulic tappets must **not** be fitted whilst this measurement is being taken.*

Refitting

19 Ensure that the crankshaft has been turned to position Number 1 and 4 pistons slightly down their bores from the TDC position (see Section 7). This will eliminate any risk of piston-to-valve contact.

20 Refit the hydraulic tappets/roller rocker fingers as described in Section 10.

21 Lubricate the camshaft and cylinder head bearing journals with clean engine oil **(see illustration)**.

22 Carefully lower the camshaft into position in the cylinder head making sure that the cam lobes for No 1 cylinder are pointing upwards.

All engines except 1.6 litre AVU and BFQ

23 Fit a new oil seal to the camshaft. Make sure that the closed end of the seal faces the camshaft sprocket end of the camshaft, and take care not to damage the seal lip. Locate the seal against the seat in the cylinder head.

24 Oil the upper surfaces of the camshaft bearing journals, then fit Nos 2 and 4 bearing caps. Ensure that they are fitted the right way round and in the correct locations (see paragraph 4), then progressively tighten the retaining nuts in a diagonal sequence to the specified torque. Note that as the nuts are tightened, the camshaft will be forced down against the pressure of the valve springs.

25 Ensure that the mating faces of bearing cap No 1 and the cylinder head are clean and free from traces of old sealant, then smear the

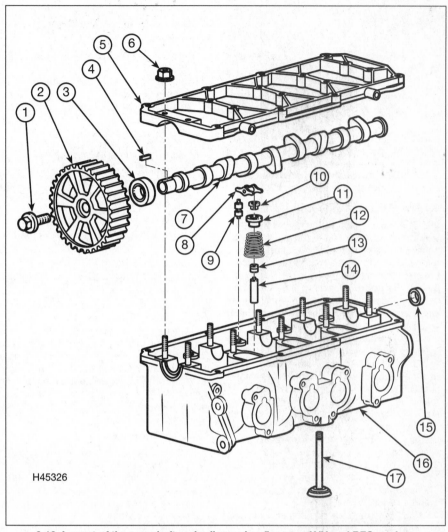

H45326

9.10 Layout of the camshaft and roller rocker fingers – AVU and BFQ engines

1 Bolt	7 Camshaft	12 Valve spring
2 Camshaft sprocket	8 Roller rocker finger	13 Valve stem seal
3 Oil seal	9 Support	14 Valve guide
4 Parallel key	10 Collets	15 Camshaft end sealing cap
5 Retaining ladder frame	11 Upper valve spring	16 Cylinder head
6 Retaining nut	washer	17 Valve

cylinder head mating surfaces of bearing cap No 1 with sealant (VW sealant – AMV 174 004 01 or equivalent) **(see illustration)**. Fit bearing caps 1, 3 and 5 over the camshaft and progressively tighten the nuts to the specified torque.

9.18 Checking the camshaft endfloat using a DTI gauge

9.21 Lubricate the camshaft bearings with clean engine oil

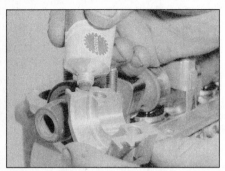

9.25 Smear the mating surfaces of bearing cap No 1 with sealant

1.6 litre AVU and BFQ engines

26 Fit a new oil seal to the camshaft. Make sure that the closed end of the seal faces the camshaft sprocket end of the camshaft, and take care not to damage the seal lip. Locate the seal against the seat in the cylinder head.

27 Oil the upper surfaces of the camshaft bearing journals in the retaining ladder frame, without getting oil onto the sealing surface, where it meets the cylinder head.

28 Ensure that the mating faces of the cylinder head and retaining frame are clean and free from traces of old sealant, then apply an even bead of sealant (VW sealant – D 188 800 A1 or equivalent) to the groove in the lower surface of the retaining frame. **Note:** *The frame must be ready to tighten down without delay, as soon as it comes into contact with the cylinder head surface the sealant begins to harden immediately.*

29 Before the frame is tightened down, fit a new sealing cap to the transmission end of the camshaft, fitting it flush to the end of the cylinder head.

30 With the frame in position, tighten the retaining nuts for bearing caps 2 and 4, using an alternating diagonal sequence. Then fit and tighten the nuts for 1, 3 and 5 progressively in a diagonal sequence. Note that as the nuts are tightened, the camshaft will be forced down against the pressure of the valve springs.

31 Tighten the retaining nuts to the specified torque in sequence **(see illustration)**.

All engines

32 Refit the camshaft sprocket as described in Section 8.

33 Refit and tension the timing belt as described in Section 7.

34 Refit the camshaft cover as described in Section 4.

---

10 Hydraulic tappets/roller rocker fingers – removal, inspection and refitting

Removal

1 Remove the camshaft, as described in Section 9.

Hydraulic tappets

2 Lift the hydraulic tappets from their bores in the cylinder head, and store them with the valve contact surfaces facing downwards, to prevent the oil from draining out.

3 It is recommended that the tappets are kept immersed in oil for the period they are removed from the cylinder head. Make a note of the position of each tappet, as they must be refitted in their original locations on reassembly – accelerated wear leading to early failure will result if the tappets are interchanged.

Roller rocker fingers

4 As the components are removed, keep them in strict order, so that they can be refitted in their original locations **(see illustration 9.10)**. Accelerated wear leading to early failure will result if the tappets and rocker fingers are interchanged.

5 Note the fitted position, then unclip the rocker fingers from the hydraulic tappets and lift them from the cylinder head.

6 Carefully lift the tappets from their bores in the cylinder head. It is advisable to store the tappets (in the correct order) upright in an oil bath whilst they are removed from the engine.

Make a note of the position of each tappet, as they must be refitted in their original locations on reassembly – accelerated wear leading to early failure will result if the tappets are interchanged.

Inspection

7 Check the cylinder head bore contact surfaces of the tappets for signs of scoring or damage. Similarly, check the tappet bores in the cylinder head for signs of scoring or damage. If significant scoring or damage is found, it may be necessary to renew the cylinder head and the complete set of tappets.

8 Inspect the hydraulic tappets for obvious signs of wear or damage, and renew if necessary. Check that the oil holes in the tappets are free from obstructions.

9 On 1.6 litre AVU and BFQ engines, check the valve, tappet and camshaft contact faces of the rockers for wear or damage, and also check the rockers for any signs of cracking. Renew any worn or damaged rockers.

10 Inspect the camshaft, as described in Section 9.

Refitting

11 Smear some clean engine oil onto the sides of the hydraulic tappets, and offer them into position in their original bores in the cylinder head. Push them down until they are seated correctly and lubricate the upper surface of the tappet.

12 On 1.6 litre AVU and BFQ engines, oil the rocker contact faces of the tappets, and the tops of the valve stems, then refit the rockers to their original locations, ensuring that the rockers are securely clipped onto the tappets.

13 Lubricate the camshaft lobe contact surfaces and refit the camshaft as described in Section 9.

---

11 Camshaft oil seal – renewal

Note: *The oil seals are a PTFE (Teflon) type and are fitted dry, without using any grease or oil. These have a wider sealing lip and have been introduced instead of the coil spring type oil seal.*

1 Remove the timing belt as described in Section 7.

2 Remove the camshaft sprocket as described in Section 8.

3 Drill two small holes into the existing oil seal, diagonally opposite each other. Take great care to avoid drilling through into the seal housing or camshaft sealing surface. Thread two self-tapping screws into the holes and, using a pair of pliers, pull on the heads of the screws to extract the oil seal.

4 Clean out the seal housing and the sealing surface of the camshaft by wiping it with a lint-free cloth. Remove any swarf or burrs that may cause the seal to leak.

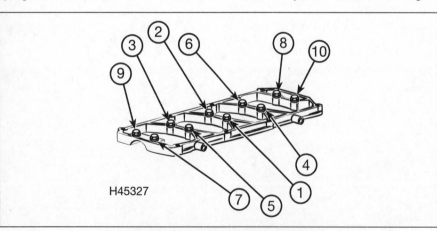

H45327

9.31 Tightening sequence for camshaft ladder – AVU and BFQ engines

5 Carefully push the seal over the camshaft until it is positioned above its housing. To prevent damage to the sealing lips, wrap some adhesive tape around the end of the camshaft.

6 Using a hammer and a socket of suitable diameter, drive the seal squarely into its housing. **Note:** *Select a socket that bears only on the hard outer surface of the seal, not the inner lip which can easily be damaged.* Remove the adhesive tape from the end of the camshaft after the seal has been located correctly.

7 Refit the camshaft sprocket with reference to Section 8.

8 Refit and tension the timing belt as described in Section 7.

12 Cylinder head – removal, inspection and refitting

Note: *The cylinder head must be removed with the engine cold. New cylinder head bolts and a new cylinder head gasket will be required on refitting.*

Removal

1 Disconnect the battery negative lead. **Note:** *Before disconnecting the battery, refer to 'Disconnecting the battery' at the rear of this manual.*

2 Remove the engine top cover(s). Depending on model, these may be clipped in position or by prising up the circular covers and removing the nuts/screws underneath. On some models, the engine front cover may be secured by a further nut on the right-hand side.

3 Drain the cooling system as described in Chapter 1A.

 Warning: The fuel lines are under pressure. Before disconnecting the fuel lines, depressurise the fuel system as described in Chapter 4A.

4 Squeeze the quick-release end fittings, and disconnect the fuel supply and return hoses. Note the positions of the fuel lines (on some models the fuel supply pipe has white markings and the return pipe has blue markings). Clamp or plug the fuel hoses and the open ends of the fuel rail to prevent fuel loss and dirt entry.

5 Remove the upper part of the inlet manifold as described in Chapter 4A.

6 Where applicable, remove the exhaust gas recirculation pipe as described in Chapter 4C.

7 Disconnect all relevant coolant hoses from around the cylinder head, then unbolt the coolant distribution housing or connecting piece, as applicable, from the transmission end of the cylinder head.

8 Move any wiring harnesses away from the cylinder head, noting their fitted position.

9 On models with secondary air injection, disconnect and remove the secondary air injection system pipes, and remove the pressure pipe bracket. Remove the secondary air injection pump and mounting bracket, with reference to Chapter 4C.

10 Disconnect the hose from the charcoal canister solenoid valve at the right-hand side of the engine compartment.

11 On all models, except 1.6 litre AEH and AKL engines, remove the following components:
a) *Spark plug HT leads.*
b) *Camshaft position sensor wiring connector.*
c) *Unscrew the securing nut and bolts, and remove the right-angled bracket and auxiliary drivebelt tensioner from the engine.*

12 Remove the exhaust front section, complete with the catalytic converter and the manifold support bracket, as described in Chapter 4C.

13 Remove the auxiliary drivebelt as described in Chapter 1A.

14 Remove the timing belt as described in Section 7.

15 As the engine is currently supported using a hoist and lifting tackle attached to the right-hand engine lifting bracket on the cylinder head, it is now necessary to attach a suitable bracket to the cylinder block, so that the engine can still be supported as the cylinder head is removed. Alternatively, the engine can be supported using a trolley jack and a block of wood positioned under the engine sump.

16 If the engine is to be supported using a hoist, bolt a suitable bracket to the cylinder block. Attach a second set of lifting tackle to the hoist, and adjust the lifting tackle to support the engine using the bracket attached to the cylinder block. Once the engine is supported using the bracket attached to the cylinder block, disconnect the lifting tackle from the lifting bracket on the cylinder head.

17 Remove the camshaft cover as described in Section 4.

18 Make a final check to ensure that all relevant wiring, pipes and hoses have been disconnected to facilitate cylinder head removal.

19 Progressively slacken the cylinder head bolts, by one turn at a time, in order **(see illustration)**. Remove the cylinder head bolts.

20 With all the bolts removed, lift the cylinder head from the block, together with the exhaust manifold, and the lower section of the inlet manifold. If the cylinder head is stuck, tap it with a soft-faced mallet to break the joint. **Do not** insert a lever into the gasket joint.

21 Lift the cylinder head gasket from the block.

22 If desired, the exhaust manifold and the lower section of the inlet manifold can be removed from the cylinder head with reference to Chapters 4C and 4A respectively.

Inspection

23 Dismantling and inspection of the cylinder head is covered in Part D of this Chapter.

Refitting

24 The mating faces of the cylinder head and block must be perfectly clean before refitting the head.

25 Use a scraper to remove all traces of gasket and carbon, also clean the tops of the pistons. Take particular care with the aluminium surfaces, as the soft metal is easily damaged.

26 Make sure that debris is not allowed to enter the oil and water passages – this is particularly important for the oil circuit, as carbon could block the oil supply to the camshaft and crankshaft bearings. Using adhesive tape and paper, seal the water, oil and bolt holes in the cylinder block. To prevent carbon entering the gap between the pistons and bores, smear a little grease in the gap. After cleaning a piston, rotate the crankshaft to that the piston moves down the bore, then wipe out the grease and carbon with a cloth rag. Clean the other piston crowns in the same way.

27 Check the head and block for nicks, deep scratches and other damage. If slight, they may be removed carefully with a file. More serious damage may be repaired by machining, but this is a specialist job.

28 If warpage of the cylinder head is suspected, use a straight-edge to check it for distortion, as described in Part D of this Chapter.

29 Ensure that the cylinder head bolt holes in the crankcase are clean and free of oil. Syringe or soak up any oil left in the bolt holes. This is most important in order that the correct bolt tightening torque can be applied, and to prevent the possibility of the block being cracked by hydraulic pressure when the bolts are tightened.

30 Ensure that the crankshaft has been turned to position Nos 1 and 4 pistons slightly down their bores from the TDC position (refer to timing belt refitting in Section 7). This will eliminate any risk of piston-to-valve contact as the cylinder head is refitted.

31 Where applicable, refit the exhaust manifold and the lower section of the inlet manifold to the cylinder head with reference to Chapters 4A and 4C.

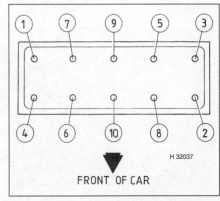

12.19 Cylinder head bolt slackening sequence – SOHC engines

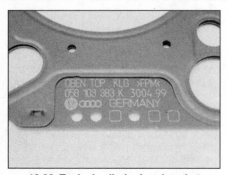

12.32 Typical cylinder head gasket markings

32 Ensure that the cylinder head locating dowels are in place in the cylinder block, then fit a new cylinder head gasket over the dowels, ensuring that the part number is uppermost. Where applicable, the OBEN/TOP marking should also be uppermost **(see illustration)**. Note that VW recommend that the gasket is only removed from its packaging immediately prior to fitting.

33 Lower the cylinder head into position on the gasket, ensuring that it engages correctly over the dowels.

34 Fit the new cylinder head bolts, and screw them in as far as possible by hand.

35 Working progressively, in sequence, tighten all the cylinder head bolts to the specified Stage 1 torque **(see illustration)**.

36 Again working progressively, in sequence, tighten all the cylinder head bolts through the specified Stage 2 angle.

37 Finally, tighten all the cylinder head bolts, in sequence, through the specified Stage 3 angle.

38 Reconnect the lifting tackle to the engine right-hand lifting bracket on the cylinder head, then adjust the lifting tackle to support the engine. Once the engine is adequately supported using the cylinder head mounting bracket, disconnect the lifting tackle from the bracket bolted to the cylinder block, and unbolt the improvised engine lifting bracket from the cylinder block. Alternatively, remove the trolley jack and block of wood from under the sump.

39 Refit the camshaft cover as described in Section 4.

13.4 Disconnect the wiring connector (arrowed) from the oil level/temperature sender

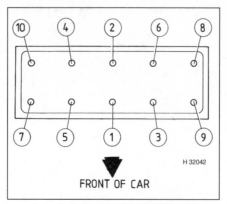

12.35 Cylinder head bolt tightening sequence – SOHC engines

40 Refit and tension the timing belt as described in Section 7.

41 Refit the exhaust front section as described in Chapter 4C.

42 Where applicable, refit the secondary air injection pump and pipes, with reference to Chapter 4C.

43 Refit the coolant distribution housing or connection piece, and reconnect the coolant hoses.

44 Reconnect the charcoal canister solenoid valve hose.

45 Reconnect the fuel supply and return hoses.

46 Refit the exhaust gas recirculation pipe, as described in Chapter 4C.

47 Refit the auxiliary drivebelt as described in Chapter 1A.

48 On all models, except 1.6 litre AEH and AKL engines, refit the following components:
a) *Spark plug HT leads.*
b) *Camshaft position sensor wiring connector.*
c) *Refit the right-angled bracket and auxiliary drivebelt tensioner to the engine.*

49 Lay the wiring harness in position, then reconnect the fuel supply and return hoses.

50 Refit the upper part of the inlet manifold, as described in Chapter 4A.

51 Refill the cooling system as described in Chapter 1A.

52 Refit the engine top cover, and reconnect the battery negative lead.

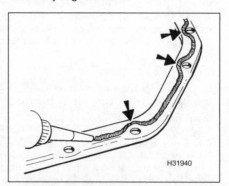

13.9 Apply the sealant around the inside of the bolt holes

13 Sump –
removal and refitting

Note: *VW sealant (D 176404 A2 or equivalent) will be required to seal the sump on refitting.*

Removal

1 Apply the handbrake, then jack up the front of the vehicle and support securely on axle stands (see *Jacking and vehicle support*).

2 Remove the securing screws and withdraw the engine undershield(s).

3 Drain the engine oil as described in Chapter 1A.

4 Where fitted, disconnect the wiring connector from the oil level/temperature sender in the sump **(see illustration)**.

5 Slacken and remove the bolts securing the sump to the cylinder block, and the bolts securing the sump to the transmission casing, then withdraw the sump. If necessary, release the sump by tapping with a soft-faced hammer.

6 If desired, unbolt the oil baffle plate from the cylinder block. **Note:** *There is no oil baffle plate fitted to 2.0 litre AZJ engines.*

Refitting

7 Begin refitting by thoroughly cleaning the mating faces of the sump and cylinder block. Ensure that all traces of old sealant are removed.

8 Where applicable, refit the oil baffle plate, and tighten the securing bolts.

9 Ensure that the cylinder block mating face of the sump is free from all traces of old sealant, oil and grease, and then apply a 2.0 to 3.0 mm thick bead of silicone sealant (VW D 176404 A2 or equivalent) to the sump **(see illustration)**. Note that the sealant should be run around the inside of the bolt holes in the sump. The sump must be fitted within 5 minutes of applying the sealant.

10 Offer the sump up to the cylinder block, then refit the sump-to-cylinder block bolts, and lightly tighten them by hand, working progressively in a diagonal sequence. **Note:** *If the sump is being refitted with the engine and transmission separated, make sure that the sump is flush with the flywheel/driveplate end of the cylinder block.*

11 Refit the sump-to-transmission casing bolts, and tighten them lightly, using a socket.

12 Again working in a diagonal sequence, *lightly* tighten the sump-to-cylinder block bolts, using a socket.

13 Tighten the sump-to-transmission casing bolts to the specified torque.

14 Working in a diagonal sequence, progressively tighten the sump-to-cylinder block bolts to the specified torque.

15 Refit the wiring connector to the oil level/temperature sender (where fitted), then refit the engine undershield(s), and lower the vehicle to the ground.

16 Allow at least 30 minutes from the time of

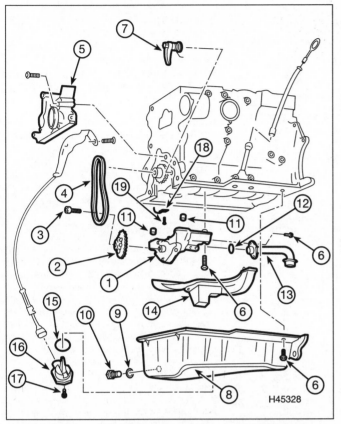

14.3 Sump and oil pump components – except AZJ engine

1 Oil pump
2 Oil pump sprocket
3 Bolt
4 Oil pump drive
  chain
5 Crankshaft oil seal
  housing
6 Bolt

7 Drive chain
  tensioner
8 Sump
9 Seal
10 Sump drain plug
11 Dowels
12 O-ring
13 Oil pick-up pipe

14 Oil baffle
15 Seal
16 Oil level/
  temperature
  sender
17 bolt
18 Oil spray jet
19 bolt

14.5 Sump and oil pump components – AZJ engine

1 Oil pump
2 Oil pump
  sprocket
3 Bolt
4 Oil pump drive
  chain
5 Crankshaft oil seal
  housing

6 Bolt
7 Drive chain
  tensioner
8 Sump
9 Seal
10 Sump drain plug
11 Chain cover
12 Seal

13 Oil level/
  temperature
  sender
14 bolt
15 Oil spray jet
16 bolt
17 Balancer shaft
  unit

refitting the sump for the sealant to dry, then refill the engine with oil, with reference to Chapter 1A.

14 Oil pump, drive chain and sprockets – removal, inspection and refitting

Note: *The oil pump on 2.0 litre AZJ engines is part of the balancer shaft unit, refer to Section 22 for more information.*

Oil pump removal

1 Remove the sump as described in Section 13.
2 Where applicable unscrew the securing bolts, and remove the oil baffle from the cylinder block.

All engines except 2.0 litre AZJ

3 Unscrew and remove the three mounting bolts, and release the oil pump from the dowels in the crankcase **(see illustration)**. Unhook the oil pump drive sprocket from the chain and withdraw the oil pump and oil pick-

up pipe from the engine. Note that the tensioner will attempt to tighten the chain, and it may be necessary to use a screwdriver to hold it in its released position before releasing the oil pump sprocket from the chain.
4 If desired, unscrew the flange bolts and remove the suction pipe from the oil pump. Recover the O-ring seal. Unscrew the bolts and remove the cover from the oil pump. **Note:** *If the oil pick-up pipe is removed from the oil pump, a new O-ring will be required on refitting.*

2.0 litre AZJ engines

5 Release the securing clips and withdraw the protector cover from the oil pump drive chain **(see illustration)**.
6 Slacken the oil pump sprocket retaining bolt, then using a screwdriver carefully release the tension on the chain by pressing the tensioner in and locking it in position with a 3mm Allen key (see Section 22).
7 Remove the retaining bolt and withdraw the oil pump sprocket.

8 Undo the retaining bolts and remove the chain tensioner from the housing.
9 Undo the five retaining bolts from the housing and remove the oil pump inner and outer rotors, noting their fitted position **(see illustration 22.1)**.

Oil pump inspection

10 Clean the pump thoroughly, and inspect the gear teeth/rotors for signs of damage or wear. If evident, renew the oil pump.
11 On all engines except 2.0 litre AZJ engines, to remove the sprocket from the oil pump, unscrew the retaining bolt and slide off the sprocket (note that the sprocket can only be fitted in one position).

Oil pump refitting

All engines except 2.0 litre AZJ

12 Prime the pump with oil by pouring oil into the pick-up pipe aperture while turning the driveshaft.
13 Refit the cover to the oil pump and tighten the bolts securely. Where applicable, refit the

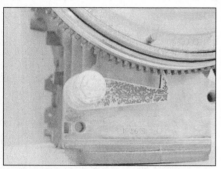

**15.5a Tool used to hold the flywheel/
driveplate stationary – 2.0 litre engine**

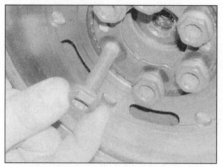

15.5b Unscrew the securing bolts . . .

pick-up pipe to the oil pump, using a new O-ring seal, and tighten the securing bolts.

14 If the drive chain, crankshaft sprocket and tensioner have been removed, delay refitting them until after the oil pump has been mounted on the cylinder block. If they have not been removed, use a screwdriver to press the tensioner against its spring to provide sufficient slack in the chain to refit the oil pump.

15 Engage the oil pump sprocket with the drive chain, then locate the oil pump on the dowels. Refit and tighten the three mounting bolts to the specified torque.

16 Where applicable, refit the drive chain, tensioner and crankshaft sprocket using a reversal of the removal procedure.

17 Refit the oil baffle, and tighten the securing bolts.

18 Refit the sump as described in Section 13.

2.0 litre AZJ engines

19 Lubricate the inner and outer rotors with clean engine oil and refit into the balance shaft housing.

20 Refit the oil pump cover and tighten the five retaining bolts to their specified torque.

21 Refit the chain tensioner and tighten the retaining bolts.

22 Refit the oil pump sprocket making sure the balance shaft is timed correctly as described in Section 22, paragraphs 7 to 13.

23 Refit the sump as described in Section 13.

Oil pump drive chain and sprockets

Note: *VW sealant (D 176404 A2 or equivalent) will be required to seal the crankshaft oil seal housing on refitting, and it is advisable to fit a new crankshaft oil seal.*

Removal

24 Proceed as described in paragraphs 1 and 2.

25 To remove the oil pump sprocket, unscrew the securing bolt, then pull the sprocket from the pump shaft, and unhook it from the drive chain.

26 To remove the chain, remove the timing belt as described in Section 7, then unbolt the crankshaft oil seal housing from the cylinder block. Unbolt the chain tensioner from the cylinder block, then unhook the chain from the sprocket on the end of the crankshaft.

27 The oil pump drive sprocket is a press-fit on the crankshaft, and cannot easily be removed. Consult a VW dealer for advice if the sprocket is worn or damaged.

Inspection

28 Examine the chain for wear and damage. Wear is usually indicated by excessive lateral play between the links, and excessive noise in operation. It is wise to renew the chain in any case if the engine is to be overhauled. Note that the rollers on a very badly worn chain may be slightly grooved. If there is any doubt as to the condition of the chain, renew it.

29 Examine the teeth on the sprockets for wear. Each tooth forms an inverted V. If worn, the side of each tooth under tension will be slightly concave in shape when compared with the other side of the tooth (ie, the teeth will have a hooked appearance). If the teeth appear worn, the sprocket should be renewed (consult a VW dealer for advice if the crankshaft sprocket is worn or damaged).

Refitting

30 If the oil pump has been removed, refit the oil pump as described previously in this Section before refitting the chain and sprocket.

31 Refit the chain tensioner to the cylinder block, and tighten the securing bolt to the specified torque. Make sure that the tensioner spring is correctly positioned to pretension the tensioner arm.

32 Engage the oil pump sprocket with the chain, then engage the chain with the crankshaft sprocket. Use a screwdriver to press the tensioner against its spring to

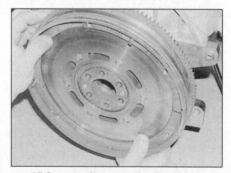

**15.6 . . . and remove the flywheel –
2.0 litre engine**

provide sufficient slack in the chain to engage the sprocket with the oil pump. Note that the sprocket will only fit in one position.

33 Refit the oil pump sprocket bolt, and tighten to the specified torque.

34 Fit a new crankshaft oil seal to the housing, and refit the housing as described in Section 16.

35 Where applicable, refit the oil baffle, and tighten the securing bolts.

36 Refit the sump as described in Section 13.

15 Flywheel/driveplate – removal, inspection and refitting

1.6 litre engines

1 On 1.6 litre engines with manual transmission, the clutch pressure plate is bolted directly to the crankshaft flange, and the dished flywheel is then bolted to the pressure plate. Removal and refitting procedures for the clutch pressure plate and flywheel are given in Chapter 6.

2 On 1.6 litre engines with automatic transmission, removal, inspection and refitting of the driveplate is as described for 2.0 litre engines in the following paragraphs.

2.0 litre engines

Note: *New flywheel/driveplate securing bolts will be required on refitting.*

Removal

3 On manual transmission models, remove the gearbox (see Chapter 7A) and clutch (see Chapter 6).

4 On automatic transmission models, remove the automatic transmission as described in Chapter 7B.

5 The flywheel/driveplate bolts are offset to ensure correct fitment. Unscrew the bolts while holding the flywheel/driveplate stationary. Temporarily insert a bolt in the cylinder block, and use a screwdriver to hold the flywheel/driveplate, or make up a holding tool **(see illustrations)**.

6 Lift the flywheel/driveplate from the crankshaft **(see illustration)**. If removing a driveplate, note the location of the shim (where applicable – between the driveplate and the crankshaft), and the spacer under the securing bolts. Recover the engine-to-transmission plate if it is loose.

Inspection

7 Check the flywheel/driveplate for wear and damage. Examine the starter ring gear for excessive wear to the teeth. If the driveplate or its ring gear are damaged, the complete driveplate must be renewed. The flywheel ring gear, however, may be renewed separately from the flywheel, but the work should be entrusted to a VW dealer. If the clutch friction face is discoloured or scored excessively, it may be possible to regrind it, but this work should also be entrusted to a VW dealer.

Refitting

8 Refitting is a reversal of removal, bearing in mind the following points.

a) *Ensure that the engine-to-transmission plate is in place before fitting the flywheel/driveplate.*

b) *On automatic transmission models temporarily refit the driveplate using the old bolts tightened to 30 Nm, and check that the distance from the rear machined face of the cylinder block to the torque converter mounting face on the driveplate is between 19.5 and 21.1 mm. The measurement is most easily made through one of the holes in the driveplate, using vernier calipers. If necessary, remove the driveplate, and fit a shim between the driveplate and the crankshaft to achieve the correct dimension.*

c) *On automatic transmission models, the raised pip on the spacer under the securing bolts must face the torque converter.*

d) *Use new bolts when refitting the flywheel or driveplate, and coat the threads of the bolts with locking fluid before inserting them. Tighten the securing bolts to the specified torque.*

---

16 Crankshaft oil seals – renewal

Note: *The oil seals are a PTFE (Teflon) type and are fitted dry, without using any grease or oil. These have a wider sealing lip and have been introduced instead of the coil spring type oil seal.*

Timing belt end oil seal

Note: *If the oil seal housing is removed, VW sealant (D 176 404 A2, or equivalent) will be required to seal the housing on refitting.*

1 Remove the timing belt as described in Section 7, and the crankshaft sprocket with reference to Section 8.

2 To remove the seal without removing the housing, drill two small holes diagonally opposite each other, insert self-tapping screws, and pull on the heads of the screws with pliers.

3 Alternatively, to remove the oil seal complete with its housing, proceed as follows.

a) *Remove the sump as described in Section 13. This is necessary to ensure a satisfactory seal between the sump and oil seal housing on refitting.*

b) *Unbolt and remove the oil seal housing.*

c) *Working on the bench, lever the oil seal from the housing using a suitable screwdriver. Take care not to damage the seal seating in the housing.*

4 Thoroughly clean the oil seal seating in the housing.

5 Wind a length of tape around the end of the crankshaft to protect the oil seal lips as the seal (and housing, where applicable) is fitted.

6 Fit a new oil seal to the housing, pressing or driving it into position using a socket or tube of suitable diameter. Ensure that the socket or tube bears only on the hard outer ring of the seal, and take care not to damage the seal lips. Press or drive the seal into position until it is seated on the shoulder in the housing. Make sure that the closed end of the seal is facing outwards.

7 If the oil seal housing has been removed, proceed as follows, otherwise proceed to paragraph 9.

8 Clean all traces of old sealant from the crankshaft oil seal housing and the cylinder block. Apply a bead of VW sealant (D 176 404 A2, or equivalent), 2.0 to 3.0 mm thick along the cylinder block mating face of the oil seal housing **(see illustration)**. Note that the seal housing must be refitted within 5 minutes of applying the sealant.

Caution: DO NOT put excessive amounts of sealant onto the housing as it may get into the sump and block the oil pick-up pipe.

9 Refit the oil seal housing, taking care not to damage the seal (see paragraph 5), then tighten the bolts progressively to the specified torque.

10 Refit the sump as described in Section 13.

11 Refit the crankshaft sprocket with reference to Section 8, and the timing belt as described in Section 7.

Flywheel/driveplate end oil seal

Note: *If the original seal housing was fitted using sealant, VW sealant (D 176 404 A2, or equivalent) will be required to seal the housing on refitting.*

12 Remove the clutch pressure plate/flywheel/driveplate as described in Section 15.

13 Remove the sump as described in Section 13. This is necessary to ensure a satisfactory seal between the sump and oil seal housing on refitting.

14 Unbolt and remove the oil seal housing, complete with the oil seal.

15 The new oil seal will be supplied ready-fitted to a new oil seal housing.

16 Thoroughly clean the oil seal housing mating face on the cylinder block.

17 New oil seal/housing assemblies are supplied with a fitting tool to prevent damage to the oil seal as it is being fitted. Locate the tool over the end of the crankshaft.

18 If the original oil seal housing was fitted using sealant, apply a thin bead of VW sealant (D 176 404 A2, or equivalent) to the cylinder block mating face of the oil seal housing. Note that the seal housing must be refitted within 5 minutes of applying the sealant.

Caution: DO NOT put excessive amounts of sealant onto the housing as it may get into the sump and block the oil pick-up pipe.

19 Carefully fit the oil seal/housing assembly over the rear of the crankshaft, and tighten the bolts progressively, in a diagonal sequence, to the specified torque.

20 Remove the oil seal protector tool from the end of the crankshaft.

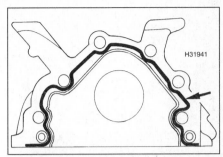

16.8 Apply sealant to the cylinder block mating face of the crankshaft oil seal housing

21 Refit the sump as described in Section 13.

22 Refit the clutch pressure plate/flywheel/driveplate as described in Section 15.

---

17 Engine/transmission mountings – inspection and renewal

Inspection

1 If improved access is required, jack up the front of the vehicle, and support it securely on axle stands (see *Jacking and vehicle support*). Remove the securing screws and remove the engine undershield(s).

2 Check the mounting rubbers to see if they are cracked, hardened or separated from the metal at any point; renew the mounting if any such damage or deterioration is evident.

3 Check that all the mounting fasteners are securely tightened; use a torque wrench to check if possible.

4 Using a large screwdriver or a crowbar, check for wear in the mounting by carefully levering against it to check for free play. Where this is not possible, enlist the aid of an assistant to move the engine/transmission back-and-forth, or from side-to-side, whilst you observe the mounting. While some free play is to be expected, even from new components, excessive wear should be obvious. If excessive free play is found, check first that the fasteners are correctly secured, then renew any worn components as described in the following paragraphs.

Renewal

Right-hand mounting

Note: *New mounting securing bolts will be required on refitting.*

5 Attach a hoist and lifting tackle to the engine lifting brackets on the cylinder head, and raise the hoist to just take the weight of the engine. Alternatively the engine can be supported on a trolley jack under the engine. Use a block of wood between the sump and the head of the jack, to prevent any damage to the sump.

6 Unbolt the power steering fluid reservoir, and move it to one side, leaving the fluid hoses connected.

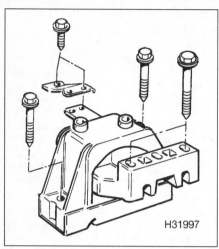

17.9 Engine right-hand mounting components

7 Similarly, unbolt the coolant reservoir and move it to one side, leaving the coolant hoses connected.

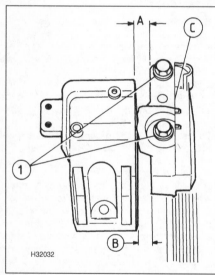

17.11 Engine right-hand mounting alignment details – both bolt heads (1) must be flush with edge (C)

A = 14.0 mm   *B = at least 10.0 mm*

17.14 Removing the battery tray

17.10a View of the engine right-hand mounting – three of the main mounting bolts visible

8 Where applicable, move any wiring harnesses, pipes or hoses to one side to enable removal of the engine mounting. Note that it may be necessary to disconnect certain hoses.
9 Where applicable, unscrew the two securing bolts, and remove the small bracket from the top of the mounting (see illustration).
10 Unscrew the two bolts securing the mounting to the bracket on the engine, and the two bolts securing the mounting to the body, then lift the mounting from the engine compartment (see illustrations).
11 Refitting is a reversal of removal, bearing in mind the following points.
a) Use new bolts when refitting the main mounting assembly.
b) Before fully tightening the mounting securing bolts, ensure that the distance between the mounting and the engine mounting bracket is as shown, and also check the mounting-to-engine mounting bracket bolt heads are flush with the edge of the mounting (see illustration).
c) Tighten all fixings to the specified torque.

Left-hand mounting

Note: *New mounting bolts will be required on refitting (there is no need to renew the smaller mounting-to-body bolts).*
12 Proceed as described in paragraph 5.
13 Remove the battery, as described in Chapter 5A, then disconnect the main starter motor feed cable from the positive battery terminal box.

17.18a View of the engine/transmission left-hand mounting

17.10b Removing the engine right-hand mounting

14 Release any relevant wiring or hoses from the clips on the battery tray, then unscrew the four securing bolts and remove the battery tray (see illustration).
15 Where applicable, to improve access to the engine-transmission mounting, remove the air cleaner assembly as described in Chapter 4A.
16 On some models, it may be necessary to unclip wiring harnesses and/or hoses from brackets close to the engine/transmission mounting to enable the mounting to be removed.
17 Carefully lift the wiring harness housing from the wing panel to improve access to the mounting-to-body bolts. Note that access to the smaller mounting-to-body bolt can be gained by unclipping the cover from the wiring harness housing, and moving the harnesses to one side to expose the bolt.
18 Unscrew the two bolts securing the mounting to the transmission, and the three bolts securing the mounting to the body, then lift the mounting from the engine compartment, noting that it may be necessary to manipulate the mounting out from under the wiring harness housing (see illustrations).

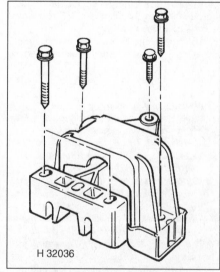

17.18b Engine/transmission left-hand mounting components

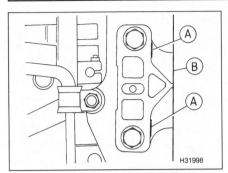

17.19 Engine/transmission left-hand mounting alignment details – edges (A) and (B) must be parallel

19 Refitting is a reversal of removal, bearing in mind the following points:

a) *The edge of the engine/transmission mounting must be parallel with the body (see illustration).*

b) *Use new mounting bolts (there is no need to renew the smaller mounting-to-body bolt).*

c) *Tighten all fixings to the specified torque.*

Rear mounting

Note: *New mounting bolts will be required on refitting.*

20 Apply the handbrake, then jack up the front of the vehicle and support securely on axle stands (see *Jacking and vehicle support*). Remove the engine undershield(s) for access to the rear engine/transmission mounting.

21 Proceed as described in paragraph 5.

22 Working under the vehicle, unscrew and remove the two bolts securing the mounting assembly to the subframe **(see illustration)**.

17.23 Engine/transmission rear mounting seen from underneath

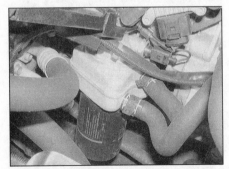

18.1a Oil cooler – 1.6 litre SOHC engine

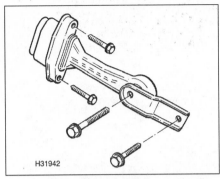

17.22 Engine/transmission rear mounting components

23 Unscrew the two bolts securing the mounting to the transmission **(see illustration)**, then withdraw the mounting from under the vehicle.

24 Refitting is a reversal of removal, but use new mounting securing bolts, and tighten all fixings to the specified torque.

18 Engine oil cooler – removal and refitting

Note: *A new oil filter and a new oil cooler O-ring will be required on refitting.*

Removal

1 The oil cooler is mounted above the oil filter, at the front of the cylinder block **(see illustrations)**.

2 Position a container beneath the oil filter to catch escaping oil and coolant, then remove the oil filter, with reference to Chapter 1A if necessary.

3 Clamp the oil cooler coolant hoses to minimise coolant spillage, then remove the clips, and disconnect the hoses from the oil cooler. Be prepared for coolant spillage.

4 Where applicable, release the oil cooler pipes from any retaining brackets or clips.

5 Unscrew the oil cooler securing nut from

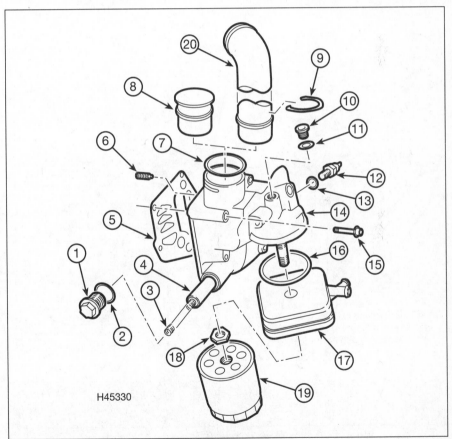

H45330

18.1b Oil cooler details

1 Sealing plug	7 Seal	13 Seal
2 Seal	8 Sealing cap (except AVU and BFQ engines)	14 Oil filter housing
3 Oil pressure relief valve spring	9 Retaining clip	15 Bolt
4 Oil pressure relief valve piston	10 Sealing plug	16 Seal
5 Gasket	11 Seal	17 Oil cooler
6 Non-return valve	12 Oil pressure warning light switch	18 Nut
		19 Oil filter
		20 Connecting pipe

21.1 Oil level/temperature sender (arrowed) – located in the base of the sump

the oil filter mounting threads, then slide off the oil cooler. Recover the O-ring from the top of the oil cooler.

Refitting

6 Refitting is a reversal of removal, bearing in mind the following points.

a) Use a new oil cooler O-ring.
b) Fit a new oil filter.
c) On completion, check and if necessary top up the oil and coolant levels.

19 Oil pressure relief valve – removal, inspection and refitting

Removal

1 The oil pressure relief valve is fitted to the right-hand side of the oil filter housing (**see illustration 18.1b**).
2 Wipe clean the area around the relief valve plug then slacken and remove the plug and sealing ring from the filter housing. Withdraw the valve spring and piston, noting their correct fitted positions. If the valve is to be left removed from the engine for any length of time, plug the hole in the oil filter housing.

Inspection

3 Examine the relief valve piston and spring for signs of wear or damage. At the time of writing it appears that the relief valve spring and piston were not available separately; check with your VW dealer for the latest parts availability. If the spring and piston are worn it will be necessary to renew the complete oil filter housing assembly. The valve plug and sealing ring are listed as separate components.

Refitting

4 Fit the piston to the inner end of the spring then insert the assembly into the oil filter housing. Ensure the sealing ring is correctly fitted to the valve plug then fit the plug to the housing, tightening it to the specified torque.
5 On completion, check and, if necessary, top-up the engine oil as described in *Weekly checks*.

20 Oil pressure warning light switch – removal and refitting

Removal

1 The oil pressure warning light switch is fitted to the left-hand side of the oil filter housing (**see illustration 18.1b**).
2 Disconnect the wiring connector and wipe clean the area around the switch.
3 Unscrew the switch from the filter housing and remove it, along with its sealing washer. If the switch is to be left removed from the engine for any length of time, plug the oil filter housing aperture.

Refitting

4 Examine the sealing washer for signs of damage or deterioration and if necessary renew.
5 Refit the switch, complete with washer, and tighten it to the specified torque.
6 Securely reconnect the wiring connector then check and, if necessary, top-up the engine oil as described in *Weekly checks*.

21 Oil level/temperature sender – removal and refitting

Removal

1 The oil level/temperature sender is fitted to bottom of the sump (**see illustration**).
2 Drain the engine oil as described in Chapter 1A.
3 Disconnect the wiring connector and wipe clean the area around the sender.
4 Undo the three retaining bolts and remove the sender.

Refitting

5 Examine the sealing washer for signs of

H45325

22.1 Layout of balancer shaft unit – 2.0 litre AZJ engines

1 Chain protector cover
2 Chain tensioner
3 Chain
4 Dowels
5 Oil pump/balancer shaft assembly
6 Bolt
7 Cover to prevent oil frothing
8 Oil return element with seal
9 Bolt
10 Bolt
11 Bolt
12 Oil strainer/suction pipe
13 O-ring/seal
14 Sealing bolt
15 O-ring/seal
16 Oil pump outer rotor
17 Dowels
18 Oil pump inner rotor
19 Bolt
20 Bolt
21 Oil pump drive sprocket
22 Oil pump cover
23 Bolt

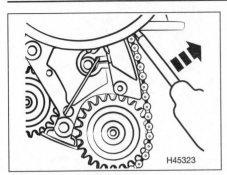

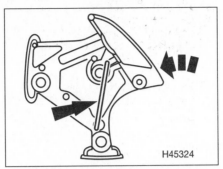

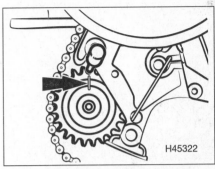

22.4a Press against the tensioner using a screwdriver – in direction of arrow . . .

22.4b . . . then lock the tensioner in position with a 3mm Allen key

22.8 Align timing mark (arrowed) and insert locking pin – VW tool T10060

damage or deterioration and if necessary renew.

6 Refit the sender and tighten the retaining bolts to the specified torque.

7 Securely reconnect the wiring connector then refill the engine with oil, with reference to Chapter 1A.

8 On completion, check and, if necessary, top up the engine oil as described in *Weekly checks*.

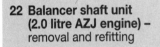

22 Balancer shaft unit (2.0 litre AZJ engine) – removal and refitting

Removal

1 Models fitted with the 2.0 litre AZJ engine are equipped with a balancer unit fitted between the cylinder block and the main sump casting. The unit consists of two counter-rotating balance shafts driven by the crankshaft **(see illustration opposite)**.

2 Remove the sump main casting as described in Section 13.

3 Release the securing clips and withdraw the protector cover from the oil pump drive chain.

4 Slacken the oil pump sprocket retaining bolt, then using a screwdriver carefully release the tension on the chain by pressing the tensioner in and locking it in position with a 3mm Allen key **(see illustrations)**.

5 Remove the retaining bolt and withdraw the oil pump sprocket, then release the chain from the balance shaft sprocket.

6 Working from the outside to the middle, slacken the retaining bolts, noting their fitted position. Remove the balancer unit, releasing it from the drive chain from the crankshaft.

Caution: The balance shaft unit retaining bolts are different lengths, make a note of their position for refitting.

Refitting

7 With reference to Section 3, set the crankshaft at TDC on No 1 cylinder at the end of the compression stroke.

8 Position the balance shafts so that the timing mark on the sprocket is aligned with the hole in the housing and insert a locking pin **(see illustration)**.

9 Fit the balancer unit to the cylinder block, noting the fitted position of the bolts on removal. Insert the retaining bolts and tighten them to the specified torque, starting from the middle and working outwards.

10 With the VW tool T10060 still in position and the 3mm Allen key locking the chain tensioner, refit the drive chain around the balance shaft sprocket.

11 Position the chamfered side of the oil pump shaft upwards and fit the oil pump sprocket, locating it in the drive chain. Tighten the retaining bolt by hand at this moment.

12 With the sprockets aligned, remove the locking keys from the balance shaft sprocket and chain tensioner, then tighten the oil pump sprocket to the specified torque.

13 Refit the protector cover to the oil pump drive chain.

14 Refit the sump as described in Section 13.

Notes

Chapter 2 Part B:
DOHC petrol engine in-car repair procedures

Contents

Camshaft carrier (1.4 and 1.6 litre engines) – removal and refitting . 10
Camshaft cover (1.8 litre engines) – removal and refitting 4
Camshaft oil seals – renewal 14
Camshafts (1.4 and 1.6 litre engines) – removal, inspection and refitting 11
Camshafts and tappets (1.8 litre engines) – removal, inspection and refitting 13
Compression test – description and interpretation 2
Crankshaft oil seals – renewal 20
Crankshaft pulley – removal and refitting 5
Cylinder head – removal, inspection and refitting 15
Engine assembly and valve timing marks – general information and usage 3
Engine oil cooler – removal and refitting 22
Engine/transmission mountings – inspection and renewal 21
Flywheel/driveplate – removal, inspection and refitting 19

General information 1
Inlet camshaft timing components/camshaft adjuster (1.8 litre engines) 9
Oil level/temperature sender – removal and refitting 25
Oil pressure relief valve – removal, inspection and refitting 23
Oil pressure warning light switch – removal and refitting 24
Oil pump (1.4 and 1.6 litre engines) – removal, inspection and refitting 17
Oil pump and drive chain (1.8 litre engines) – removal, inspection and refitting 18
Rockers and tappets (1.4 and 1.6 litre engines) – removal, inspection and refitting 12
Sump – removal and refitting 16
Timing belt covers – removal and refitting 6
Timing belt tensioner and sprockets – removal and refitting 8
Timing belt(s) – removal and refitting 7

Degrees of difficulty

Easy, suitable for novice with little experience	Fairly easy, suitable for beginner with some experience	Fairly difficult, suitable for competent DIY mechanic 	Difficult, suitable for experienced DIY mechanic	Very difficult, suitable for expert DIY or professional

Specifications

General

Manufacturer's engine codes*:
1390 cc	AHW, AXP and BCA
1597 cc	AZD and BCB
1781 cc	AUM and AUQ

Maximum power output:
1.4 litre engines	55 kW at 5000 rpm
1.6 litre engines	77 kW at 5700 rpm
1.8 litre engines:	
AUM	110 kW at 5700 rpm
AUQ	132 kW at 5500 rpm

Maximum torque output:
1.4 litre engines	128 Nm at 3300 rpm
1.6 litre engines	148 Nm at 4500 rpm
1.8 litre engines:	
AUM	210 Nm at 1750 to 4600 rpm
AUQ	235 Nm at 1950 to 5000 rpm

* **Note:** *See 'Vehicle identification' at the end of this manual for the location of engine code markings.*

General (continued)

Bore:
  1.4 and 1.6 litre engines . . . . 76.5 mm
  1.8 litre engines . . . . 81.0 mm
Stroke:
  1.4 litre engines . . . . 75.6 mm
  1.6 litre engines . . . . 86.9 mm
  1.8 litre engines . . . . 86.4 mm
Compression ratio:
  1.4 litre engines . . . . 10.5 : 1
  1.6 litre engine . . . . 11.5 : 1
  1.8 litre engines . . . . 9.5 : 1
Compression pressures:
  Minimum compression pressure . . . . Approximately 7.0 bar
  Maximum difference between cylinders . . . . Approximately 3.0 bar
Firing order . . . . 1 – 3 – 4 – 2
No 1 cylinder location . . . . Timing belt end

Camshafts

Camshaft endfloat:
  1.4 and 1.6 litre engines (maximum) . . . . 0.40 mm
  1.8 litre engines (maximum) . . . . 0.20 mm
Camshaft bearing running clearance:
  1.4 and 1.6 litre engines . . . . No figure specified
  1.8 litre engines (maximum) . . . . 0.10 mm
Camshaft run-out:
  1.4 and 1.6 litre engines . . . . No figure specified
  1.8 litre engines (maximum) . . . . 0.01 mm

Lubrication system

Oil pump type:
  1.4 and 1.6 litre engines . . . . Rotor type, driven directly from crankshaft
  1.8 litre engines . . . . Gear type, chain-driven from crankshaft
Oil pressure (oil temperature 80°C):
  At idling:
    1.4 and 1.6 litre engines . . . . No figure specified
    1.8 litre engines . . . . 2.0 bar
  At 2000 rpm:
    1.4 and 1.6 litre engines . . . . 2.0 bar
    1.8 litre engines . . . . 3.0 to 4.5 bar

Torque wrench settings

	Nm`	lbf ft
Ancillary (alternator, etc) bracket mounting bolts:		
1.4 and 1.6 litre engines	50	37
1.8 litre engines	45	33
Auxiliary drivebelt tensioning pulley bolts:		
1.8 litre engines	25	18
Auxiliary drivebelt tensioner securing bolt:		
1.4 and 1.6 litre engines:		
M8 bolt:		
Stage 1	20	15
Stage 2	Angle-tighten a further 90°	
M10 bolt	45	33
Big-end bearing caps bolt/nuts*:		
Stage 1	30	22
Stage 2	Angle-tighten a further 90°	
Camshaft bearing cap bolts:		
1.8 litre engines	10	7
Camshaft carrier bolts*:		
1.4 and 1.6 litre engines:		
Stage 1	10	7
Stage 2	Angle-tighten a further 90°	
Camshaft cover nuts:		
1.8 litre engines	10	7
Camshaft exhaust sprocket bolt:		
1.8 litre engines	65	48
Camshaft sealing cap bolts:		
1.4 and 1.6 litre engines	10	7

* Note: *Use new bolts*

Torque wrench settings (continued)

	Nm	lbf ft
Camshaft sprocket bolts*:		
1.4 and 1.6 litre engines:		
Stage 1	20	15
Stage 2	Angle-tighten a further 90°	
Camshaft timing chain tensioner/camshaft adjuster mechanism bolts:		
1.8 litre engines	10	7
Clutch pressure plate/driveplate mounting bolts*:		
1.4 and 1.6 litre engines:		
Stage 1	60	44
Stage 2	Angle-tighten a further 90°	
Coolant pump bolts:		
1.4 and 1.6 litre engines	20	15
1.8 litre engines	15	11
Crankcase breather/oil separator bolts	10	7
Crankshaft left-hand oil seal housing bolts:		
1.4 and 1.6 litre engines	10	7
1.8 litre engines	15	11
Crankshaft right-hand oil seal housing bolts:		
1.8 litre engines	15	11
Crankshaft pulley/sprocket bolt*:		
1.4 and 1.6 litre engines:		
Stage 1	90	66
Stage 2	Angle-tighten a further 90°	
Crankshaft pulley bolts:		
1.8 litre engines	25	18
Crankshaft speed/position sensor wheel-to-crankshaft bolts*:		
1.8 litre engines:		
Stage 1	10	7
Stage 2	Angle-tighten a further 90°	
Crankshaft sprocket bolt*:		
1.8 litre engines:		
Stage 1	90	66
Stage 2	Angle-tighten a further 90°	
Cylinder head bolts*:		
1.4 and 1.6 litre engines:		
Stage 1	30	22
Stage 2	Angle-tighten a further 90°	
Stage 3	Angle-tighten a further 90°	
1.8 litre engines:		
Stage 1	40	30
Stage 2	Angle-tighten a further 90°	
Stage 3	Angle-tighten a further 90°	
Engine-to-automatic transmission bolts:		
M12 bolts	80	59
M10 cylinder block-to-transmission bolts	60	44
M10 sump-to-transmission bolts	25	18
Engine-to-manual transmission bolts:		
Cylinder block-to-transmission (M12 bolts)	80	59
Alloy sump-to-transmission bolts (M10 bolts):		
02J transmission	60	44
02K transmission	25	18
02M transmission	40	30
Engine-to-manual transmission cover plate bolts	10	7
Engine mountings:		
Left-hand mounting-to-body bolts:		
Large bolts*:		
Stage 1	40	30
Stage 2	Angle-tighten a further 90°	
Small bolts	25	18
Left-hand mounting-to-engine bracket bolts	100	74
Right-hand mounting-to-body bolts*:		
Stage 1	40	30
Stage 2	Angle-tighten a further 90°	
Right-hand mounting plate bolts (small bolts)	25	18
Right-hand mounting-to-engine bracket bolts	100	74

* **Note:** *Use new bolts*

Torque wrench settings (continued)

	Nm`	lbf ft
Engine mountings (continued):		
Right-hand mounting bracket-to-engine bolts:		
1.4 and 1.6 litre engines	50	37
1.8 litre engines	45	33
Rear engine/transmission mounting:		
Bracket-to-subframe bolts*:		
Stage 1	20	15
Stage 2	Angle-tighten a further 90°	
Bracket-to-transmission bolts*:		
Stage 1	40	30
Stage 2	Angle-tighten a further 90°	
Exhaust camshaft timing belt sprocket bolt:		
1.8 litre engines	65	48
Exhaust manifold nuts	25	18
Exhaust pipe-to-manifold nuts	40	30
Inlet camshaft adjuster valve bolts:		
1.8 litre engines	3	2
Inlet camshaft position sensor bolts:		
1.8 litre engines	10	7
Inlet camshaft position sensor rotor bolt:		
1.8 litre engines	25	18
Main bearing cap bolts:		
1.6 litre engines	65	48
1.8 litre engines*:		
Stage 1	65	48
Stage 2	Angle-tighten a further 90°	
Oil cooler securing nut	25	18
Oil drain plug	30	22
Oil filter housing-to-cylinder block bolts*:		
1.8 litre engines:		
Stage 1	15	11
Stage 2	Angle-tighten a further 90°	
Oil level/temperature sender-to-sump bolts	10	7
Oil pick-up pipe securing bolts:		
1.4 and 1.6 litre engines	10	7
Oil pressure relief valve plug:		
1.8 litre engines	40	30
Oil pressure warning light switch	25	18
Oil pump chain tensioner bolt:		
1.8 litre engines	15	11
Oil pump securing bolts:		
1.4 and 1.6 litre engines*	12	9
1.8 litre engines	15	11
Piston oil spray jet/oil pressure relief valve bolt:		
1.8 litre engines	27	20
Sump:		
Sump-to-cylinder block bolts:		
1.4 and 1.6 litre engines	13	10
1.8 litre engines	15	11
Sump-to-transmission bolts:		
1.4 and 1.6 litre engines	45	33
Sump baffle plate bolts:		
1.8 litre engines	15	11
Thermostat cover bolts:		
1.8 litre engines	15	11
Timing belt idler pulley bolt:		
1.4 and 1.6 litre engines	50	37
1.8 litre engines	20	15
Timing belt outer cover bolts:		
1.4 and 1.6 litre engines:		
Small bolts	10	7
Large bolts	20	15
1.8 litre engines	10	7
Timing belt rear cover bolts:		
1.4 and 1.6 litre engines:		
Small bolts	10	7
Large bolt (coolant pump bolts)	20	15

* **Note:** *Use new bolts*

Torque wrench settings (continued)

	Nm	lbf ft
Timing belt tensioner:		
1.4 and 1.6 litre engines:		
Main timing belt tensioner bolt	20	15
Secondary timing belt tensioner bolt	20	15
1.8 litre engines:		
Tensioner roller securing bolt	27	20
Timing belt tensioner housing bolts:		
Small bolt	15	11
Large bolt	20	15
Turbocharger oil supply pipe-to-oil filter housing banjo bolt:		
1.8 litre engines	30	22

* Note: *Use new bolts*

---

1 General information

Using this Chapter

Chapter 2 is divided into four Parts; A, B, C and D. Repair operations that can be carried out with the engine in the vehicle are described in Part A (SOHC petrol engines), Part B (DOHC petrol engines), and Part C (diesel engines). Part D covers the removal of the engine/transmission as a unit, and describes the engine dismantling and overhaul procedures.

In Parts A, B and C, the assumption is made that the engine is installed in the vehicle, with all ancillaries connected. If the engine has been removed for overhaul, the preliminary dismantling information that precedes each operation may be ignored.

Engine description

Throughout this Chapter, engines are identified and referred to by their capacity and, where necessary, by the manufacturer's code letters. A listing of all engines covered, together with their code letters, is given in the Specifications.

The engines are water-cooled, double overhead camshaft, in-line four-cylinder units. 1.6 and 1.8 litre engines have cast-iron cylinder blocks, whereas 1.4 litre engines have aluminium alloy cylinder blocks. All engines have aluminium-alloy cylinder heads. All engines are mounted transversely at the front of the vehicle, with the transmission bolted to the left-hand end of the engine.

The crankshaft is of five-bearing type, and thrustwashers are fitted to the centre main bearing to control crankshaft endfloat.

On 1.4 litre engines, the crankshaft and main bearings are matched to the alloy cylinder block, and it is not possible to reassemble the crankshaft and cylinder block once the components have been separated. If the crankshaft or bearings are worn, the complete cylinder block/crankshaft assembly must be renewed.

On 1.4 and 1.6 litre engines, the inlet camshaft is driven via a toothed belt from the crankshaft sprocket, and the exhaust camshaft is driven from the inlet camshaft by a second toothed belt.

On 1.8 litre engines, the exhaust camshaft is driven via a toothed timing belt from the crankshaft sprocket, and the inlet camshaft is driven from the left-hand end of the exhaust camshaft via a chain.

The engines covered in this manual, have variable inlet valve timing, and the valve timing is varied by altering the tension on the drive chain using an electronically-actuated mechanical tensioner.

On 1.4 and 1.6 litre engines, the camshafts are located in a camshaft carrier, which is bolted to the top of the cylinder head. On 1.8 litre engines, the cylinder head carries the camshafts.

The valves are closed by coil springs, and run in guides pressed into the cylinder head. On 1.4 and 1.6 litre engines, the camshafts actuate the valves via roller rockers and hydraulic tappets. On 1.8 litre engines, the camshafts actuate the valves directly via hydraulic tappets.

1.4 and 1.6 litre engines have four valves per cylinder; two inlet valves and two exhaust valves, whereas 1.8 litre engines have five valves per cylinder; three inlet valves and two exhaust valves.

On 1.4 and 1.6 litre engines, the oil pump is driven directly from the front of the crankshaft. On 1.8 litre engines, the gear-type oil pump is driven via a chain from a sprocket on the crankshaft. Oil is drawn from the sump through a strainer, and then forced through an externally-mounted, renewable filter. From there, it is distributed to the cylinder head, where it lubricates the camshaft journals and hydraulic tappets, and also to the crankcase, where it lubricates the main bearings, connecting rod big-ends, gudgeon pins and cylinder bores. A coolant-fed oil cooler is fitted to most engines.

On all engines, engine coolant is circulated by a pump, driven by the timing belt (main timing belt on 1.4 and 1.6 litre engines). For details of the cooling system, refer to Chapter 3.

Operations with engine in car

The following operations can be performed without removing the engine:

a) *Compression pressure – testing.*

b) *Camshaft cover (1.8 litre engines) – removal and refitting.*

c) *Camshaft carrier (1.4 and 1.6 litre engines) – removal and refitting.*

d) *Crankshaft pulley – removal and refitting.*

e) *Timing belt covers – removal and refitting.*

f) *Timing belt – removal, refitting and adjustment.*

g) *Timing belt tensioner and sprockets – removal and refitting.*

h) *Inlet camshaft timing belt, sprockets and tensioner (1.4 and 1.6 litre engines) – removal and refitting.*

i) *Inlet camshaft timing chain, sprockets and adjuster mechanism (1.8 litre engines) – removal and refitting.*

j) *Inlet camshaft adjuster mechanism – removal and refitting.*

k) *Camshaft oil seal(s) – renewal.*

l) *Camshaft(s) and hydraulic tappets – removal, inspection and refitting.*

m) *Cylinder head – removal and refitting.*

n) *Cylinder head and pistons – decarbonising.*

o) *Sump – removal and refitting.*

p) *Oil pump – removal, overhaul and refitting.*

q) *Crankshaft oil seals – renewal.*

r) *Engine/transmission mountings – inspection and renewal.*

s) *Flywheel – removal, inspection and refitting.*

Note: *It is possible to remove the pistons and connecting rods (after removing the cylinder head and sump) without removing the engine. However, this is not recommended. Work of this nature is more easily and thoroughly completed with the engine on the bench, as described in Chapter 2D.*

2 Compression test – description and interpretation

Note: *A suitable compression tester will be required for this test.*

1 When engine performance is down, or if misfiring occurs which cannot be attributed to the ignition or fuel systems, a compression test can provide diagnostic clues as to the engine's condition. If the test is performed regularly, it can give warning of trouble before any other symptoms become apparent.

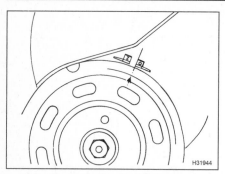

3.4a Crankshaft pulley timing mark aligned with TDC mark on timing belt cover – 1.4 and 1.6 litre engines

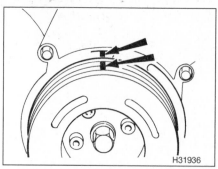

3.4b Crankshaft pulley timing mark aligned with TDC mark on timing belt cover – 1.8 litre engine

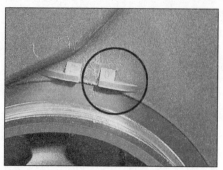

3.4c Timing mark scribed on inner flange of pulley aligned with TDC mark on timing belt cover – 1.4 litre engine

2 The engine must be fully warmed-up to normal operating temperature, the battery must be fully-charged and the spark plugs must be removed. The aid of an assistant will be required.

3 On 1.4 litre engines, disable the ignition system by disconnecting the wiring plug from the DIS ignition module.

4 On 1.6 and 1.8 litre engines, disconnect the wiring plugs from the ignition coils. Remove the ignition HT coils, with reference to Chapter 5B.

5 Fit a compression tester to the No 1 cylinder spark plug hole. The type of tester that screws into the plug thread is preferred.

6 Have the assistant hold the throttle wide open and crank the engine for several seconds on the starter motor. **Note:** *On models fitted with an throttle position sensor instead of a cable, the throttle will not operate until the ignition is switched on.* After one or two revolutions, the compression pressure should build-up to a maximum figure and then stabilise. Record the highest reading obtained.

7 Repeat the test on the remaining cylinders, recording the pressure in each.

8 All cylinders should produce very similar pressures. Any difference greater than that specified indicates the existence of a fault. Note that the compression should build-up quickly in a healthy engine. Low compression on the first stroke, followed by gradually increasing pressure on successive strokes, indicates worn piston rings. A low compression reading on the first stroke, which does not build-up during successive strokes, indicates leaking valves or a blown head gasket (a cracked head could also be the cause). Deposits on the undersides of the valve heads can also cause low compression.

9 If the pressure in any cylinder is reduced to the specified minimum or less, carry out the following test to isolate the cause. Introduce a teaspoonful of clean oil into that cylinder through its spark plug hole and repeat the test.

10 If the addition of oil temporarily improves the compression pressure, this indicates that bore or piston wear is responsible for the pressure loss. No improvement suggests that

leaking or burnt valves, or a blown head gasket, may be to blame.

11 A low reading from two adjacent cylinders is almost certainly due to the head gasket having blown between them and the presence of coolant in the engine oil will confirm this.

12 If one cylinder is about 20 percent lower than the others and the engine has a slightly rough idle, a worn camshaft lobe could be the cause.

13 If the compression reading is unusually high, the combustion chambers are probably coated with carbon deposits. If this is the case, the cylinder head should be removed and decarbonised.

14 On completion of the test, refit the spark plugs. On 1.4 litre engines, reconnect the DIS ignition module wiring. On 1.6 and 1.8 litre engines, refit the ignition coils, then reconnect the coil wiring plugs with reference to Chapter 5B.

3 Engine assembly and valve timing marks – general information and usage

General information

1 TDC is the highest point in the cylinder that each piston reaches as it travels up-and-down when the crankshaft turns. Each piston reaches TDC at the end of the compression stroke and again at the end of the exhaust

3.5 Crankshaft sprocket tooth with chamfered edge aligns with cast arrow on oil pump – 1.4 litre engine

stroke, but TDC generally refers to piston position on the compression stroke. No 1 piston is at the timing belt end of the engine.

2 Positioning No 1 piston at TDC is an essential part of many procedures, such as timing belt removal and camshaft removal.

3 The design of the engines covered in this Chapter is such that piston-to-valve contact may occur if the camshaft or crankshaft is turned with the timing belt removed. For this reason, it is important to ensure that the camshaft and crankshaft do not move in relation to each other once the timing belt has been removed from the engine.

4 The crankshaft pulley has a marking which, when aligned with a corresponding reference marking on the timing belt cover, indicates that No 1 piston (and hence also No 4 piston) is at TDC. Note that on some models, the crankshaft pulley timing mark is located on the outer flange of the pulley. In order to make alignment of the timing marks easier, it is advisable to remove the pulley (see Section 5) and, using a set-square, scribe a corresponding mark on the inner flange of the pulley **(see illustrations)**.

5 Note also that on 1.4 and 1.6 litre engines, there is also a timing mark which can be used with the crankshaft sprocket – this is useful if the crankshaft pulley and timing belt have been removed. When No 1 piston is at TDC, the crankshaft sprocket tooth with the chamfered inner edge aligns with a cast arrow on the oil pump **(see illustration)**.

6 On 1.4 and 1.6 litre engines, the camshaft sprockets are equipped with TDC positioning holes. When the positioning holes are aligned with the corresponding holes in the camshaft carrier, No 1 piston is at TDC on the compression stroke **(see illustration)**.

7 On 1.8 litre engines, the exhaust camshaft sprocket is equipped with a timing mark. When this mark is aligned with a mark on the camshaft cover, No 1 piston is at TDC on the compression stroke **(see illustration)**.

8 Additionally, on some models, the flywheel/driveplate has a TDC marking, which can be observed by unscrewing a protective plastic cover from the transmission bell-housing. The mark takes the form of a notch in the edge of the flywheel on manual trans-

mission models, or an O marking on automatic transmission models. Note that it is not possible to use these marks on all models due to the limited access available to view the marks (see illustrations).

Setting No 1 cylinder to TDC

1.4 and 1.6 litre engines

Note: *Suitable locking pins will be required to lock the camshaft sprockets in position during this procedure. On some engines, it may be necessary to use a small engineer's mirror to view the timing marks from under the wheel arch.*

9 Before starting work, make sure that the ignition is switched off (ideally, the battery negative lead should be disconnected – see *Disconnecting the battery*).

10 Remove the engine top cover, and remove the air cleaner assembly as described in Chapter 4A.

11 If desired, to make the engine easier to turn, remove all of the spark plugs as described in Chapter 1A.

12 Apply the handbrake, then jack up the front of the vehicle and support on axle stands (see *Jacking and vehicle support*). Remove the right-hand front roadwheel, then remove the securing screws and/or clips, and remove the appropriate engine undershields to enable access to the crankshaft pulley.

13 Remove the upper timing belt cover as described in Section 6.

14 Turn the engine clockwise, using a spanner on the crankshaft pulley bolt, until the TDC mark on the crankshaft pulley or flywheel/driveplate is aligned with the corresponding mark on the timing belt cover or transmission casing, and the locking pin holes in the camshaft sprockets are aligned with the corresponding holes in the camshaft carrier.

15 If necessary, to give sufficient clearance for the camshaft locking tool to be engaged with the camshaft sprockets, unbolt the air cleaner support bracket from the engine mounting. Similarly, if necessary, unbolt the power steering fluid reservoir and move it to one side, leaving the fluid hoses connected.

16 A suitable tool will now be required to lock the camshaft sprockets in the TDC position. A special VW tool is available for this purpose, but a suitable tool can be improvised using two M8 bolts and nuts, and a short length of steel bar. With the camshaft sprocket positioned as described in paragraph 14, measure the distance between the locking pin hole centres, and drill two corresponding 8 mm clearance holes in the length of steel bar. Slide the M8 bolts through the holes in the bar, and secure them using the nuts.

17 Slide the tool into position in the holes in the camshaft sprockets, ensuring that the pins (or bolts) engage with the holes in the camshaft carrier (see illustration). The engine is now locked in position, with No 1 piston at TDC on the firing stroke.

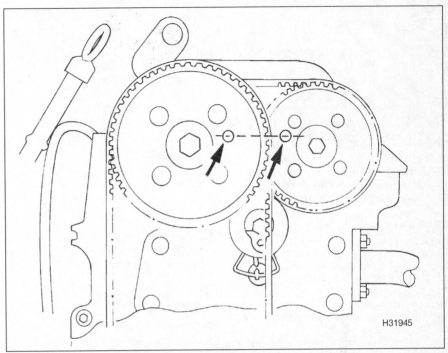

3.6 Camshaft sprocket positioning holes (arrowed) aligned with holes in camshaft carrier (No 1 piston at TDC) – 1.4 and 1.6 litre engines

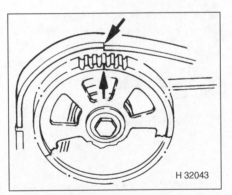

3.7 Camshaft sprocket timing mark (arrowed) aligned with mark on camshaft cover (No 1 piston at TDC) – 1.8 litre engine

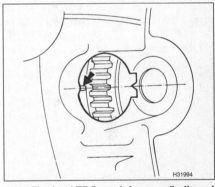

3.8a Flywheel TDC mark (arrowed) aligned with pointer on transmission casing – 1.8 litre engine with manual transmission

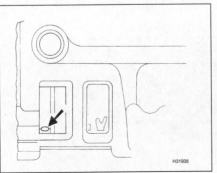

3.8b Driveplate TDC mark (arrowed) aligned with window in transmission casing – 1.8 litre engine with automatic transmission

3.17 Improvised tool used to lock camshaft sprockets in position at TDC (viewed with engine removed, and timing belt removed from engine) – 1.4 litre engine

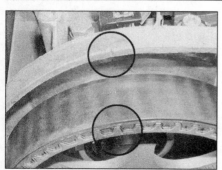

3.20 Exhaust camshaft sprocket timing mark aligned with timing mark on camshaft cover – 1.8 litre engine

4.1a Unbolt the coil earth wiring lead . . .

4.1b . . . then release the coil wiring from the clips on the camshaft cover – 1.8 litre engine

1.8 litre engines

Note: *On some engines, it may be necessary to use a small engineer's mirror to view the timing marks from under the wheel arch.*

18 Proceed as described in paragraphs 9 to 12, but note that there is no need to remove the air cleaner.

19 Remove the upper timing belt cover as described in Section 6.

20 Turn the engine clockwise, using a spanner on the crankshaft sprocket bolt, until the TDC mark on the crankshaft pulley or flywheel/driveplate is aligned with the corresponding mark on the timing belt cover or transmission casing, and the mark on the exhaust camshaft sprocket is aligned with the corresponding mark on the camshaft cover **(see illustration)**.

4 Camshaft cover (1.8 litre engines) – removal and refitting

Note: *Suitable sealant (VW D 454 300 A2 or equivalent) will be required on refitting.*

Removal

1 Remove the ignition HT coils as described in Chapter 5B. Unbolt the coil wiring earth lead from the top of the camshaft cover, then release the coil wiring from the clips on the camshaft cover, and move the wiring clear of the camshaft cover **(see illustrations)**.

2 Release the clips securing the upper timing belt cover to the camshaft cover **(see illustration)**.

3 Where applicable, unscrew the bolt securing the metal pipe to the rear left-hand corner of the camshaft cover **(see illustration)**.

4 Release the three clips, and remove the plastic cover from the front of the engine, above the inlet manifold **(see illustration)**.

5 Slacken the hose clip and disconnect the breather hose from the left-hand end of the camshaft cover. Note that it may be necessary to unscrew the securing bolt and move the breather housing away from the end of the cylinder head to enable the hose to be disconnected **(see illustrations)**.

6 Make a final check to ensure that all relevant pipes, hoses and wires have been disconnected and moved clear of the working area.

7 Unscrew the securing nuts, and carefully lift the camshaft cover from the cylinder head.

4.2 Release the clips securing the upper timing belt cover to the camshaft cover – 1.8 litre engine

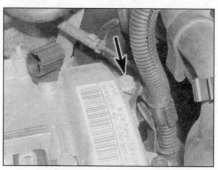

4.3 Where fitted, unscrew the bolt (arrowed) – 1.8 litre engine

4.4 Remove the plastic cover from the front of the engine – 1.8 litre engine

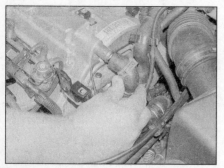

4.5a Disconnect the breather hose from the left-hand end of the camshaft cover . . .

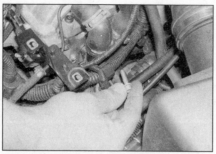

4.5b . . . noting that it may be necessary to unscrew the breather housing bolt – 1.8 litre engine

4.7a Unscrew the securing nuts . . .

Note the locations of any brackets or spacers under the securing nuts. Recover the gaskets, noting that a separate gasket is used to seal the spark plug holes in the centre of the cover **(see illustrations)**.

8 If desired, lift the oil deflectors from the inlet camshaft, noting their locations **(see illustration)**.

Refitting

9 Inspect the camshaft cover gaskets, and renew if worn or damaged.

10 Thoroughly clean the mating surfaces of the camshaft cover and the cylinder head, then lay the oil deflector in position over the camshaft bearing caps.

11 Working at the timing belt end of the cylinder head, apply VW sealant (D 454 300 A2 or equivalent) to the two points where the combined camshaft bearing cap contacts the edge of the cylinder head **(see illustration)**.

12 Similarly, working at the transmission end of the cylinder head, apply sealant to the two points where the camshaft drive chain tensioner/camshaft adjustment mechanism contacts the edge of the cylinder head **(see illustration)**.

13 Carefully fit the camshaft cover gaskets to the cylinder head, then carefully slide the camshaft cover over the studs on the cylinder head. Where applicable, lay the spacer(s) and/or bracket(s) in position, then refit the securing nuts, and tighten them progressively to the specified torque.

14 Refit the ignition coils with reference to Chapter 5B.

15 Further refitting is a reversal of removal.

---

5 Crankshaft pulley – removal and refitting

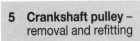

1.4 and 1.6 litre engines

Note: *A new crankshaft pulley bolt will be required on refitting.*

Removal

1 Disconnect the battery negative lead. **Note:** *Before disconnecting the battery, refer to 'Disconnecting the battery' at the rear of this manual.*

2 For improved access, jack up the front of the vehicle, and support securely on axle stands (see *Jacking and vehicle support*). Remove the right-hand front roadwheel.

3 Remove the securing screws and/or release the clips, and withdraw the relevant engine undershield(s) to enable access to the crankshaft pulley.

4 If necessary (for any later work to be carried out), turn the crankshaft using a socket or spanner on the crankshaft pulley bolt, until the relevant timing marks align (see Section 3).

5 Remove the auxiliary drivebelt, as described in Chapter 1A.

6 To prevent the crankshaft from turning as

4.7b . . . and lift the camshaft cover from the cylinder head – 1.8 litre engine

4.8 Lift the oil deflectors from the inlet camshaft – 1.8 litre engine

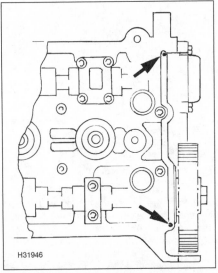

4.11 Apply sealant to the points shown (arrowed) where the combined bearing cap contacts the cylinder head – 1.8 litre engines

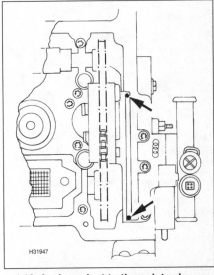

4.12 Apply sealant to the points shown (arrowed) where the camshaft drive chain tensioner/camshaft adjustment mechanism contacts the cylinder head – 1.8 litre engines

the pulley bolt is slackened, a suitable tool can be used. Engage the tool with two of the slots in the pulley **(see illustration)**.

7 Counterhold the pulley, and slacken the pulley bolt (take care – the bolt is very tight) using a socket and a suitable extension.

8 Unscrew the bolt, and remove the pulley **(see illustration)**.

9 Refit the crankshaft pulley securing bolt,

with a spacer washer positioned under its head, to retain the crankshaft sprocket.

Refitting

10 Unscrew the crankshaft pulley/sprocket bolt used to retain the sprocket, and remove the spacer washer, then refit the pulley to the sprocket. Ensure that the locating pin on the sprocket engages with the corresponding hole in the pulley.

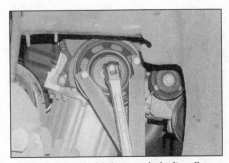

5.6 Counterhold the crankshaft pulley using a tool similar to that shown – 1.4 litre engine

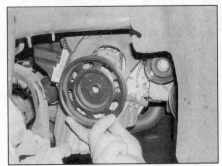

5.8 Removing the crankshaft pulley – 1.4 litre engine

5.15a Slacken the hose clips securing the hoses to the turbocharger-to-intercooler air pipe . . .

5.15b . . . then unscrew the securing bolt . . .

5.15c . . . and remove the pipe – 1.8 litre engine model

5.15d Removing the right-hand engine undershield – 1.8 litre engine model

5.19 Removing the crankshaft pulley – 1.8 litre engine

the pulley securing bolts. Note that the bolts holes are offset, so the pulley can only be fitted in one position.

21 Refit and tension the auxiliary drivebelt as described in Chapter 1A.

22 Prevent the crankshaft from turning as during removal, then tighten the pulley securing bolts to the specified torque.

23 Proceed as described in paragraphs 13 and 14, but additionally, refit the turbocharger-to-intercooler air pipe.

---

6 Timing belt covers – removal and refitting

---

11 Oil the threads of the new crankshaft pulley bolt. Prevent the crankshaft from turning as during removal, then fit the new pulley securing bolt, and tighten it to the specified torque, in the two stages given in the Specifications.

12 Refit and tension the auxiliary drivebelt as described in Chapter 1A.

13 Refit the engine undershield(s).

14 Refit the roadwheel, lower the vehicle to the ground, and reconnect the battery negative lead.

1.8 litre engines

Removal

15 Proceed as described in paragraphs 1 to 3, noting that it will be necessary to remove the turbocharger-to-intercooler air pipe before the right-hand undershield can be removed. To remove the air pipe, slacken the hose clips and

disconnect the hoses from each end of the pipe, then unscrew the bolt securing the pipe to the body **(see illustrations)**.

16 If necessary (for any later work to be carried out), turn the crankshaft using a socket or spanner on the crankshaft sprocket bolt until the relevant timing marks align (see Section 3).

17 Slacken the bolts securing the crankshaft pulley, using an Allen key or a hexagon bit. If necessary, the pulley can be prevented from turning by counterholding with a spanner or socket on the centre crankshaft sprocket bolt.

18 Remove the auxiliary drivebelt, as described in Chapter 1A.

19 Unscrew the bolts securing the pulley to the sprocket, and remove the pulley **(see illustration)**.

Refitting

20 Refit the pulley to the sprocket, and refit

1.4 and 1.6 litre engine

Upper outer cover

1 Remove the air cleaner assembly as described in Chapter 4A.

2 Release the two securing clips, and lift the cover from the engine **(see illustration)**.

3 Refitting is a reversal of removal.

Lower outer cover

4 Remove the crankshaft pulley, as described in Section 5.

5 Release the two cover securing clips, located at the rear of the engine, then unscrew the two lower securing bolts, and the single bolt securing the cover to the engine mounting bracket. Withdraw the cover downwards from the engine **(see illustrations)**.

6 Refitting is a reversal of removal, but refit

6.2 Removing the upper outer timing belt cover – 1.4 litre engine

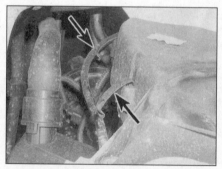

6.5a Release the two securing clips (arrowed) . . .

6.5b . . . then unscrew the two lower securing bolts (arrowed) . . .

6.5c . . . and the single bolt securing the cover to the engine mounting bracket . . .

6.5d . . . and withdraw the lower timing belt cover – 1.4 litre engine

6.8 Removing the idler pulley/bracket assembly (viewed with engine removed) – 1.4 litre engine

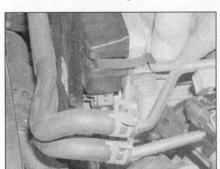

6.9 Unscrew the rear timing belt cover securing bolt located next to the right-hand engine lifting eye – 1.4 litre engine

6.10 Removing the rear timing belt cover (viewed with engine removed) – 1.4 litre engine

6.13a Release the securing clips . . .

the crankshaft pulley with reference to Section 5.

Rear timing belt cover

Note: *As the rear timing belt cover securing bolts also secure the coolant pump, it is advisable to drain the cooling system (see Chapter 1A) before starting this procedure, and to renew the coolant pump seal/gasket (see Chapter 3) before refitting the cover. Refill the cooling system with reference to Chapter 1A.*

7 Remove the timing belt as described in Section 7.

8 Unbolt the timing belt idler pulley/bracket assembly **(see illustration)**.

9 Unscrew the rear timing belt cover securing

bolt located next to the right-hand engine lifting eye **(see illustration)**.

10 Unscrew the two securing bolts, and remove the rear timing belt cover. Note that the bolts also secure the coolant pump **(see illustration)**.

11 Refitting is a reversal of removal, but tighten the timing belt idler pulley/bracket bolt to the specified torque, and refit the timing belt as described in Section 7.

1.8 litre engine

Upper cover

12 Release the securing clips, and remove the engine top cover.

13 Release the two securing clips, and manipulate the timing belt cover from the engine **(see illustrations)**.

14 Refitting is a reversal of removal. Make sure that the securing clips are securely engaged.

Centre cover

15 Remove the upper timing belt cover as described previously in this Section.

16 Remove the auxiliary drivebelt as described in Chapter 1A.

17 Unscrew the three securing bolts, and withdraw the centre cover downwards from the engine **(see illustration)**. Note that the lower two securing bolts also secure the lower timing belt cover.

6.13b . . . and remove the upper timing belt cover – 1.8 litre engine

6.17 Centre timing belt cover securing bolts (arrowed) viewed with right-hand engine mounting removed – 1.8 litre engine

18 Refitting is a reversal of removal.

Lower cover

19 Remove the crankshaft pulley as described in Section 5.
20 If the centre timing belt cover has not been removed, unscrew the two bolts that secure both the centre and lower timing belt covers to the engine.
21 Unscrew the two lower timing belt cover lower securing bolts, and withdraw the cover downwards from the engine **(see illustrations)**.
22 Refitting is a reversal of removal, but refit the crankshaft pulley with reference to Section 5.

---

7 Timing belt(s) – removal and refitting

1.4 and 1.6 litre engines

Main timing belt removal

1 1.4 and 1.6 litre engines have two timing belts; the main timing belt drives the inlet camshaft from the crankshaft, and the secondary timing belt drives the exhaust camshaft from the inlet camshaft.
2 Disconnect the battery negative lead, then unscrew the securing bolts and remove the engine top cover. **Note:** *Before disconnecting the battery, refer to 'Disconnecting the battery' at the rear of this manual.*
3 Remove the air cleaner assembly as described in Chapter 4A.

6.21a Unscrew the lower securing bolts (arrowed) . . .

4 Release the two securing clips and remove the upper outer timing belt cover.
5 Turn the crankshaft to position No 1 piston at TDC on the firing stroke, and lock the camshaft sprockets in position, as described in Section 3.
6 Remove the crankshaft pulley as described in Section 5. Refit the crankshaft pulley securing bolt, with a spacer washer positioned under its head, to retain the crankshaft sprocket.
7 Remove the lower outer timing belt cover, as described in Section 6.
8 Where applicable, on models with air conditioning, unscrew the securing bolt, and remove the auxiliary drivebelt idler pulley.
9 Unscrew the securing screw, and move the power steering fluid reservoir clear of the working area, leaving the fluid hoses connected. Note that it will be necessary to

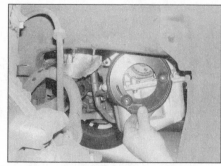

6.21b . . . and withdraw the lower timing belt cover – 1.8 litre engine

unclip the charcoal canister hose from the reservoir **(see illustrations)**.
10 Similarly, unscrew the two securing screws, and move the coolant expansion tank clear of the working area **(see illustrations)**.
11 Attach a hoist and lifting tackle to the right-hand (timing belt end) engine lifting bracket, and raise the hoist to just take the weight of the engine.
12 Remove the complete right-hand engine mounting assembly, as described in Section 21 **(see illustrations)**.
13 Unscrew the four securing bolts, and remove the right-hand engine mounting bracket from the engine **(see illustration)**.
14 If either of the timing belts are to be refitted, mark their running directions to ensure correct refitting.
15 Engage a suitable Allen key with the hole in the main timing belt tensioner plate, then

7.9a Unclip the charcoal canister hose from the power steering fluid reservoir . . .

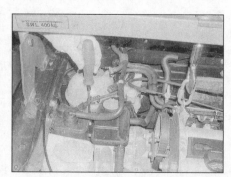

7.9b . . . then unscrew the securing screw . . .

7.9c . . . and move the reservoir clear of the working area – 1.4 litre engine

7.10a Unscrew the securing screws . . .

7.10b . . . and move the coolant expansion tank clear of the working area – 1.4 litre engine

7.12a Remove the small bracket . . .

7.12b ... and the complete right-hand engine mounting assembly – 1.4 litre engine

7.13 Removing the right-hand engine mounting bracket – 1.4 litre engine

7.15 Slacken the tensioner bolt and lever the tensioner anti-clockwise using an Allen key, then retighten the tensioner bolt – 1.4 litre engine

7.16 Removing the main timing belt – 1.4 litre engine

7.19a Slacken the secondary timing belt tensioner bolt, and lever the tensioner clockwise using an Allen key ...

slacken the tensioner bolt, lever the tensioner anti-clockwise using the Allen key (to release the tension on the belt), and retighten the tensioner bolt **(see illustration)**.

16 Temporarily remove the camshaft sprocket locking tool, then slide the main timing belt from the sprockets, noting its routing **(see illustration)**. Refit the camshaft sprocket locking tool once the timing belt has been removed.

17 Turn the crankshaft a quarter-turn (90°) anti-clockwise to position Nos 1 and 4 pistons slightly down their bores from the TDC position. This will eliminate any risk of piston-to-valve contact if a camshaft is turned whilst the timing belt is removed.

Inlet camshaft timing belt removal

18 Once the main timing belt has been

removed, to remove the secondary timing belt, proceed as follows.

19 Engage a suitable Allen key with the hole in the secondary timing belt tensioner plate, then slacken the tensioner bolt, and lever the tensioner clockwise using the Allen key (to release the tension on the belt). Unscrew the securing bolt, and remove the secondary timing belt tensioner **(see illustrations)**.

20 Temporarily remove the camshaft sprocket locking tool, and slide the secondary timing belt from the sprockets **(see illustration)**. Refit the sprocket locking tool once the belt has been removed.

Inlet camshaft timing belt refitting

21 Check that the camshaft sprockets are still locked in position by the locking pins, then turn the crankshaft a quarter-turn (90°)

clockwise to reposition Nos 1 and 4 pistons at TDC. Ensure that the crankshaft sprocket tooth with the chamfered inner edge is aligned with the corresponding mark on the oil pump housing **(see illustration)**.

22 Temporarily remove the camshaft sprocket locking tool, and fit the secondary timing belt around the camshaft sprockets. Make sure that the belt is as tight as possible on its top run between the sprockets (but note that there will be some slack in the belt). If the original belt is being refitted, observe the running direction markings. Refit the camshaft sprocket locking tool once the belt has been fitted to the sprockets.

23 Check that the secondary timing belt tensioner pointer is positioned on the far right of the tensioner backplate.

24 Press the secondary timing belt up using the tensioner, and fit the tensioner securing bolt (if necessary turn the tensioner with an Allen key until the bolt hole in the tensioner aligns with the bolt hole in the cylinder head). Make sure that the lug on the tensioner backplate engages with the core plug hole in the cylinder head **(see illustration)**.

25 Use the Allen key to turn the tensioner anti-clockwise until the tensioner pointer aligns with the lug on the tensioner backplate, with the lug positioned against the left-hand stop in the core plug hole **(see illustration)**. Tighten the tensioner bolt to the specified torque.

7.19b ... then unscrew the securing bolt and remove the tensioner – 1.4 litre engine

7.20 Removing the secondary timing belt – 1.4 litre engine

7.21 Crankshaft sprocket tooth with chamfered edge aligned with cast arrow on oil pump – 1.4 litre engine

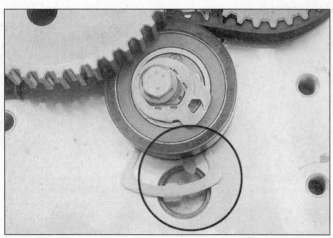

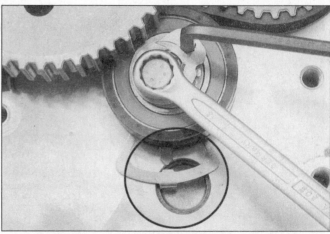

7.24 The secondary timing belt tensioner pointer should be positioned on the far right of the tensioner backplate, and the lug on the backplate should be engaged with the core plug hole – 1.4 and 1.6 litre engines

7.25 Turn the tensioner anti-clockwise until the tensioner pointer aligns with the lug on the tensioner backplate, with the lug positioned against the left-hand stop in the core plug hole – 1.4 and 1.6 litre engines

Main timing belt refitting

26 Where applicable, reposition the crankshaft at TDC (see paragraph 21) and ensure that the secondary drivebelt has been refitted and tensioned. Temporarily remove the camshaft sprocket locking tool, and fit the main timing belt around the sprockets. Work in an anti-clockwise direction, starting at the coolant pump, followed by the tensioner roller, crankshaft sprocket, idler roller, inlet camshaft sprocket and the second idler roller. If the original belt is being refitted, observe the running direction markings. Once the belt has been refitted, refit the camshaft sprocket locking tool.

27 Ensure that the tensioner bolt is slack, then engage an Allen key with the hole in the tensioner plate, and turn the plate clockwise until the tension indicator pointer is aligned with the centre of the cut-out in the backplate. Tighten the tensioner securing bolt to the specified torque.

28 Remove the camshaft sprocket locking tool.

29 Using a spanner or socket on the crankshaft pulley bolt, turn the engine through two complete turns in the normal direction of rotation, until the crankshaft sprocket tooth with the chamfered inner edge is aligned with

the corresponding mark on the oil pump housing **(see illustration 7.21)**. Check that the locking tool can again be fitted to lock the camshaft sprockets in position – if not, one or both of the timing belts may have been incorrectly fitted.

30 With the crankshaft timing marks aligned, and the camshaft sprockets locked in position, check the tension of the timing belts. The secondary and main tension indicators should be positioned as described in paragraphs 25 and 27 respectively – if not, repeat the appropriate tensioning procedure, then recheck the tension.

31 When the belt tension is correct, refit the right-hand engine mounting bracket, and tighten the securing bolts to the specified torque.

32 Refit the complete right-hand engine mounting assembly, as described in Section 21.

33 Disconnect the hoist and lifting tackle from the engine lifting bracket.

34 Refit the power steering reservoir, and clip the charcoal canister hose into position.

35 Refit the coolant reservoir.

36 Where applicable, refit the auxiliary drivebelt idler pulley.

37 Refit the lower outer timing belt cover, with reference to Section 6 if necessary.

38 Refit the crankshaft pulley as described in Section 5.

39 Refit the upper outer timing belt cover.

40 Refit the air cleaner assembly, then refit the engine top cover, and reconnect the battery negative lead.

1.8 litre engine

Note: *A length (approximately 55 mm) of M5 threaded rod will be required to depress the timing belt tensioner piston during this procedure.*

Removal

41 On 1.8 litre engines, the exhaust camshaft is driven via a toothed belt from the crankshaft sprocket, and the inlet camshaft is driven from the left-hand end of the exhaust camshaft via a chain. Refer to Section 9 for details of inlet camshaft timing chain removal, inspection and refitting.

42 Disconnect the battery negative lead.

Note: *Before disconnecting the battery, refer to 'Disconnecting the battery' at the rear of this manual.*

43 For improved access, raise the front right-hand side of the vehicle, and support securely on axle stands (see *Jacking and vehicle support*). Remove the roadwheel.

44 Remove the securing screws and withdraw the front engine undershield **(see illustration)**.

45 Working under the right-hand wheel arch, slacken the hose clips, and disconnect the hoses from the turbocharger-to-intercooler pipe. Unscrew the bolts securing the turbocharger-to-intercooler pipe to the body, then remove the pipe **(see illustrations 5.15a to 5.15c)**.

46 Release the securing clips, and remove the right-hand engine undershield.

47 Remove the auxiliary drivebelt as described in Chapter 1A.

48 Unscrew the three securing bolts, and remove the auxiliary drivebelt tensioner **(see illustration)**. Note that the top two securing

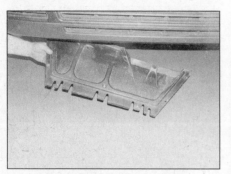

7.44 Removing the front engine undershield – 1.8 litre engine

7.48 Removing the auxiliary drivebelt tensioner – 1.8 litre engine

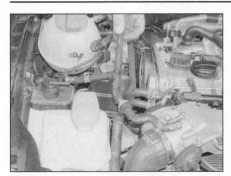

7.50 Move the charcoal canister hose to one side, clear of the working area – 1.8 litre engine

7.51a Remove the upper . . .

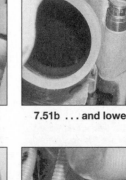

7.51b . . . and lower securing bolts . . .

bolts also secure a wiring/pipe support bracket.

49 Turn the crankshaft to position No 1 piston at TDC on the firing stroke, as described in Section 3.

50 Proceed as described in paragraphs 9 to 12 of this Section, but instead of unclipping the charcoal canister hose from the power steering fluid reservoir, disconnect the hose from the charcoal canister and the throttle body, and move the hose to one side, clear of the working area **(see illustration)**.

51 Unscrew the three securing bolts, and remove the right-hand engine mounting bracket from the engine. One bolt is accessible from above the engine, and two from below. It may be necessary to raise or lower the engine slightly, using the hoist, to enable the bracket to be manipulated out of position from below the vehicle **(see illustrations)**.

52 Remove the crankshaft pulley as described in Section 5.

53 Remove the centre and lower timing belt covers, with reference to Section 6 if necessary.

54 If the original timing belt is to be refitted, mark the running direction to ensure correct refitting.

55 Screw a length (approximately 55 mm) of M5 threaded rod into the threaded hole in the timing belt tensioner. A rod can be made by cutting the head from an M5 bolt of suitable length. Fit a large washer and a nut to the rod **(see illustration)**.

56 The next stage in the procedure is to lock the tensioner piston in position, using a piece of wire, or a twist drill. If necessary, turn the tensioner piston using pointed pliers or a length of wire, until the hole in the piston aligns with the hole in the housing.

57 Turn the nut on the threaded rod to depress the tensioner piston, until the piston can be locked in position using a suitable metal pin, or a twist drill inserted through the hole in the housing **(see illustrations)**.

58 Slide the timing belt from the sprockets, and remove it from the engine **(see illustration)**.

59 If desired, as a safety precaution, turn the crankshaft a quarter-turn (90°) anti-clockwise

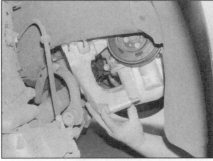

7.51c . . . and remove the right-hand engine mounting bracket from below the vehicle – 1.8 litre engine

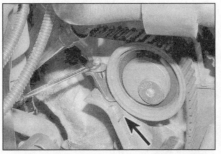

7.57a Turn the nut on the threaded rod until the piston can be locked in position using a metal pin or a twist drill (arrowed) inserted through the hole in the housing – 1.8 litre engine

to position Nos 1 and 4 pistons slightly down their bores from the TDC position. This will eliminate any risk of piston-to-valve contact if a camshaft is turned whilst the timing belt is removed.

Refitting

60 Check that the timing marks on the camshaft sprocket and camshaft cover are still aligned, as described in Section 3.

61 If the crankshaft has been turned anti-clockwise to avoid piston-to-valve contact, turn the crankshaft clockwise back to the TDC position. If desired, the lower timing belt cover and the crankshaft pulley can be temporarily refitted to check that the timing mark on the pulley aligns with the mark on the cover – once the timing marks are aligned, remove the

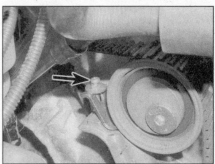

7.55 Screw an M5 threaded rod into the timing belt tensioner, then fit a washer and a nut to the rod (arrowed) – 1.8 litre engine

7.57b View showing twist drill inserted through hole in tensioner piston and housing, with tensioner removed for clarity – 1.8 litre engine

crankshaft pulley and the lower timing belt cover.

7.58 Removing the timing belt – 1.8 litre engine

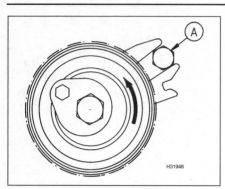

8.3 Turn the tensioner anti-clockwise to the position shown before fitting. Note that the cut-out engages with the bolt (A) on the cylinder block when fitting – 1.4 and 1.6 litre engines

62 Engage the timing belt with the crankshaft sprocket, observing the running direction markings if the original belt is being refitted.

63 Ensure that the timing belt is securely engaged with the crankshaft sprocket, then fit the belt around the coolant pump, tensioner roller and camshaft sprocket.

64 Pull out the metal pin used to lock the tensioner piston in position, and unscrew the nut from the threaded rod in the timing belt tensioner. This will allow the tensioner to automatically tension the belt.

65 Turn the crankshaft clockwise through two complete revolutions, and check that the crankshaft and camshaft timing markings are still aligned as described in Section 3. If the marks do not align, the timing belt has been incorrectly fitted (again, temporarily refit the lower timing belt cover and the crankshaft pulley to view the marks).

66 Fit the lower timing belt cover, and tighten the securing bolts.

67 Refit the centre timing belt cover, and tighten the securing bolts.

68 Refit the crankshaft pulley, and tighten the securing bolts to the specified torque.

69 Refit the right-hand engine mounting bracket, noting that the two lower securing bolts must be in position in the bracket as it is fitted, then tighten the bolts to the specified torque. If necessary, raise or lower the engine slightly, using the hoist, to enable the bracket to be manipulated into position.

70 Refit the right-hand engine mounting assembly, as described in Section 21.

71 Disconnect the hoist and lifting tackle from the engine.

72 Refit the upper timing belt cover.

73 Reconnect the charcoal canister and throttle body hoses, ensuring that they are connected to their correct locations, and correctly routed.

74 Refit the power steering fluid reservoir and the coolant expansion tank, ensuring that the fixings are secure.

75 Refit the auxiliary drivebelt tensioner, then refit the auxiliary drivebelt, with reference to Chapter 1A.

76 Refit the engine undershields and, where applicable, refit the turbocharger-to-intercooler air pipe.

77 Refit the roadwheel, and lower the vehicle to the ground.

8 Timing belt tensioner and sprockets – removal and refitting

1.4 and 1.6 litre engines

Main timing belt tensioner

1 Remove the main timing belt as described in Section 7.

2 Unscrew the main timing belt tensioner bolt, and remove the tensioner from the engine.

3 Engage an Allen key with the hole in the tensioner plate, and turn the tensioner anti-clockwise to the position shown (see illustration).

4 Refit the tensioner to the engine, ensuring that the cut-out in the tensioner backplate engages with the bolt on the cylinder block (see illustration 8.3). Refit the tensioner securing bolt, and tighten by hand.

5 Refit and tension the main timing belt as described in Section 7.

Inlet camshaft timing belt tensioner

6 Removal and refitting of the tensioner is described as part of the timing belt removal procedure in Section 7.

Main timing belt idler pulleys

7 Remove the timing belt as described in Section 7.

8 Unscrew the securing bolt and remove the relevant idler pulley. Note that the smaller pulley (the idler pulley nearest the inlet manifold side of the engine) can be removed complete with its mounting bracket (unbolt the mounting bracket bolt, leaving the pulley attached to the bracket) (see illustrations).

9 Refit the relevant idler pulley and tighten the securing bolt to the specified torque. Note that if the smaller idler pulley has been removed complete with its bracket, ensure that the bracket locates over the rear timing belt cover bolt on refitting.

10 Refit and tension the main timing belt as described in Section 7.

Crankshaft sprocket

11 Remove the main timing belt as described in Section 7.

12 Unscrew the crankshaft pulley bolt, and the washer used to retain the sprocket, and withdraw the sprocket from the crankshaft.

13 Commence refitting by positioning the sprocket on the end of the crankshaft, noting that the pulley locating pin must be outermost (see illustration). Temporarily refit the pulley securing bolt and washer to retain the sprocket.

14 Refit the main timing belt as described in Section 7.

Camshaft sprockets

Note: A new camshaft sprocket securing bolt must be used on refitting.

15 Remove the main and secondary timing belts as described in Section 7. Ensure that the crankshaft has been turned a quarter-turn (90°) anti-clockwise to position Nos 1 and 4 pistons slightly down their bores from the TDC position. This will eliminate any risk of piston-to-valve contact if a camshaft is turned whilst the timing belt is removed.

16 The relevant camshaft sprocket bolt must now be slackened. The camshaft must be prevented from turning as the sprocket bolt is unscrewed – do not rely solely on the sprocket locking tool for this. To hold the sprocket, make up a tool and use it to hold the sprocket stationary by means of the holes in the sprocket (see illustration 8.19).

17 Unscrew the camshaft sprocket bolt, and withdraw the sprocket from the end of the camshaft, noting which way round it is fitted.

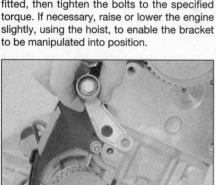

8.8a Removing the smaller . . .

8.8b . . . and larger timing belt idler pulleys – 1.4 litre engine

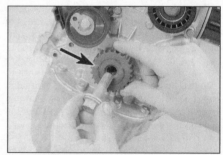

8.13 Refitting the crankshaft sprocket. Pulley locating pin (arrowed) must be outermost – 1.4 litre engine

18 Commence refitting by offering the sprocket up to the camshaft, ensuring that lug on the sprocket engages with the notch in the end of the camshaft. If both camshaft sprockets have been removed, note that the double sprocket (for the main and secondary timing belts) should be fitted to the inlet camshaft, and note that the exhaust camshaft sprocket must be fitted first **(see illustration)**.

19 Fit a new sprocket securing bolt, then use the tool to hold the sprocket stationary, as during removal, and tighten the bolt to the specified torque, in the two stages given in the Specifications **(see illustration)**.

20 Refit the secondary and main timing belts as described in Section 7.

Coolant pump sprocket

21 The coolant pump sprocket is integral with the coolant pump. Refer to Chapter 3 for details of coolant pump removal.

1.8 litre engines

Timing belt tensioner

22 Remove the timing belt as described in Section 7.

23 Unscrew the securing bolt, and remove the tensioner from the engine **(see illustration)**. Recover the washer that fits between the tensioner and the cylinder block. If desired, the threaded locking pin can be removed from the tensioner, and the nut and threaded rod used to retract the tensioner can then be unscrewed. **Do not** remove the nut and threaded rod before removing the locking pin.

24 Refitting is a reversal of removal, but ensure that the washer is in place between the tensioner and the cylinder block, and ensure that the nut, threaded rod, and locking pin are refitted to retract the tensioner before the tensioner is refitted to the engine **(see illustration)**. Refit the timing belt as described in Section 7.

Crankshaft sprocket

Note: *A new crankshaft sprocket bolt must be used on refitting.*

25 Remove the timing belt as described in Section 7.

26 The sprocket securing bolt must now be slackened, and the crankshaft must be prevented from turning as the sprocket bolt is unscrewed. To hold the sprocket, make up a suitable tool similar to that used to counterhold the camshaft sprocket **(see illustration 8.19)**, and screw it to the sprocket using a two suitable bolts.

27 Hold the sprocket using the tool, then slacken the sprocket securing bolt. Take care, as the bolt is very tight. **Do not** allow the crankshaft to turn as the bolt is slackened.

28 Unscrew the bolt, and slide the sprocket from the end of the crankshaft, noting its orientation.

29 Commence refitting by positioning the sprocket on the end of the crankshaft, with the raised boss outermost.

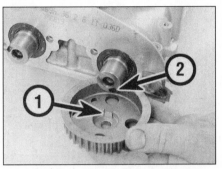

8.18 Refit the sprocket, ensuring that the lug (1) on the sprocket engages with the notch (2) in the end of the camshaft – 1.4 litre engine

30 Fit a new sprocket securing bolt, then counterhold the sprocket using the method employed on removal, and tighten the bolt to the specified torque in the two stages given in the Specifications.

31 Refit the timing belt as described in Section 7.

Exhaust camshaft sprocket

32 Remove the timing belt as described in Section 7. Ensure that the crankshaft has been turned a quarter-turn (90°) anti-clockwise to position Nos 1 and 4 pistons slightly down their bores from the TDC position. This will eliminate any risk of piston-to-valve contact if a camshaft is turned whilst the timing belt is removed.

33 The camshaft sprocket bolt must now be slackened, and the camshaft must be prevented from turning as the sprocket bolt is unscrewed. Make up a tool and use it to hold the sprocket stationary by means of the holes in the sprocket **(see illustration 8.19)**.

34 Unscrew the camshaft sprocket bolt, recover the washer, and withdraw the sprocket from the front of the camshaft, noting which way round it is fitted. Recover the Woodruff key from the end of the camshaft, where applicable.

35 Commence refitting by refitting the Woodruff key to the end of the camshaft (where applicable), then offer the sprocket up to the camshaft, ensuring that it is fitted the correct way round.

8.23 Removing the timing belt tensioner from the engine – 1.8 litre engine

8.19 Tighten the sprocket securing bolt using a suitable tool to hold the sprocket stationary – 1.4 litre engine

36 Refit the sprocket bolt, ensuring that the washer is in place, then counterhold the sprocket using the tool employed on removal, and tighten the bolt to the specified torque.

37 Refit the timing belt as described in Section 7.

Coolant pump sprocket

38 The coolant pump sprocket is integral with the coolant pump. Refer to Chapter 3 for details of coolant pump removal.

Idler pulley

39 Remove the timing belt as described in Section 7.

40 Unscrew the securing bolt, and remove the idler pulley.

41 Refitting is a reversal of removal, but tighten the idler pulley bolt to the specified torque, and refit the timing belt as described in Section 7.

| 9 | Inlet camshaft timing components/camshaft adjuster (1.8 litre engines) |

Removal and refitting of the timing chain and chain tensioner/camshaft adjuster mechanism is described as part of the camshaft removal and refitting procedure in Section 13. The sprockets are integral with the camshafts.

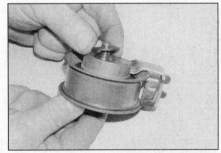

8.24 Ensure that the washer is in place between the tensioner and the cylinder block – 1.8 litre engine

10.3a Use a hooked length of wire to pull the connectors from the spark plugs – 1.4 litre engine

10.3b Unscrew the DIS module securing bolts . . .

10.3c . . . then remove the DIS module and HT leads – 1.4 litre engine

10 Camshaft carrier (1.4 and 1.6 litre engines) – removal and refitting

Note: *New camshaft carrier securing bolts must be used on refitting. Suitable sealant (VW AMV 188 003, or equivalent) will be required, and two M6 studs (approximately 70 mm long) will be required – see text.*

Removal

1 Disconnect the battery negative lead. **Note:** *Before disconnecting the battery, refer to 'Disconnecting the battery' at the rear of this manual.*

2 Remove the main and secondary timing belts, as described in Section 7.

3 On models with engine code AHW and AXP, disconnect the HT leads from the spark plugs. Use a hooked length of stout wire to pull the connectors from the spark plugs. Release the securing lug, and disconnect the wiring plug from the DIS module, then unscrew the securing bolts, and remove the DIS module and HT leads as an assembly **(see illustrations)**.

4 On models with engine code AZD, BCA and BCB, remove the ignition HT coils as described in Chapter 5B. Unbolt the coil wiring earth lead from the top of the camshaft cover, then release the coil wiring from the clips on the camshaft cover, and move the wiring clear of the camshaft cover **(see illustrations 4.1a and 4.1b)**.

5 Disconnect the inlet camshaft position sensor wiring connector **(see illustration)**.

6 Unscrew the bolt securing the exhaust gas recirculation solenoid valve to the end of the camshaft carrier **(see illustration)**. Move the valve to one side.

7 Disconnect the wiring plug from the oil pressure warning light switch, located at the front left-hand corner of the camshaft carrier. Release the wiring harness from the clip on the end of the camshaft carrier, and move the wiring to one side **(see illustrations)**.

8 Remove the rear timing belt cover securing bolt, located next to the right-hand engine lifting eye **(see illustration)**.

9 Working progressively from the centre out, in a diagonal sequence, slacken and remove the camshaft carrier securing bolts **(see illustration)**.

10 Carefully lift the camshaft carrier from the cylinder head **(see illustration)**. The camshafts can be removed from the carrier, as described in Section 11.

Refitting

11 Commence refitting by thoroughly cleaning all traces of old sealant, and all traces of oil and grease, from the mating

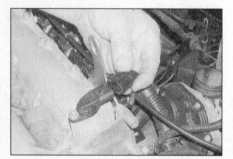

10.5 Disconnect the wiring connector from the inlet camshaft position sensor – 1.4 litre engine

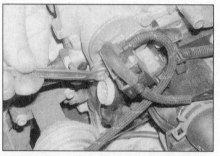

10.6 Unscrew the bolt securing the exhaust gas recirculation solenoid valve to the end of the camshaft carrier – 1.4 litre engine

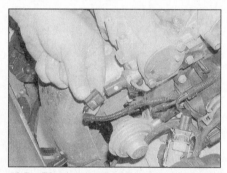

10.7a Disconnect the oil pressure warning light switch wiring plug . . .

10.7b . . . then release the wiring from the clip on the end of the camshaft carrier – 1.4 litre engine

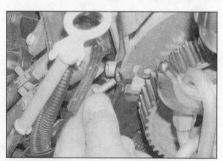

10.8 Remove the rear timing belt cover securing bolt located next to the right-hand engine lifting eye – 1.4 litre engine

10.9 Remove the camshaft carrier securing bolts . . .

10.10 ... then lift the camshaft carrier from the cylinder head – 1.4 litre engine

10.14 Apply a thin, even coat of sealant to the cylinder head mating face of the camshaft carrier – 1.4 litre engine

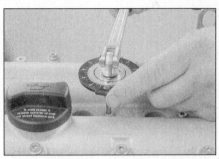

10.17 Tightening a camshaft carrier bolt through the specified Stage 2 angle – 1.4 litre engine

faces of the cylinder head and camshaft carrier. Ensure that no debris enters the cylinder head or camshaft carrier.

12 Ensure that the crankshaft is still positioned a quarter-turn (90°) anti-clockwise from the TDC position, and that the camshafts are locked in position with the locking tool, as described in Section 3.

13 Check that the valve rockers are correctly located on the valves, and securely clipped into position on the hydraulic tappets.

14 Apply a thin, even coat of sealant (VW AMV 188 003, or equivalent) to the cylinder head mating face of the camshaft carrier **(see illustration)**. Do not apply the sealant too thickly, as excess sealant may enter and block the oilways, causing engine damage.

15 Carefully lower the camshaft carrier onto the cylinder head, until the camshafts rest on the rockers. Note that the camshaft carrier locates on dowels in the cylinder head; if desired, to make fitting easier, two guide studs can be made up as follows:

a) Cut the heads off two M6 bolts, then cut slots in the top of each bolt to enable the bolt to be unscrewed using a flat-bladed screwdriver.

b) Screw one bolt into each of the camshaft carrier bolt locations at opposite corners of the cylinder head.

c) Lower the camshaft carrier over the bolts to guide it into position on the cylinder head.

16 Fit new camshaft carrier securing bolts, and tighten them progressively, working from the centre out, in a diagonal sequence (ie, tighten all bolts through one turn, then tighten

all bolts through a further turn, and so on). Ensure that the camshaft carrier sits squarely on the cylinder head as the bolts are tightened, and make sure that the carrier engages with the cylinder head dowels. Where applicable, once the camshaft carrier contacts the surface of the cylinder head, unscrew the two guide studs, and fit the two remaining new camshaft carrier securing bolts in their place.

17 Tighten the camshaft carrier securing bolts to the specified torque, in the two stages given in the Specifications **(see illustration)**.

18 Leave the camshaft carrier sealant to dry for approximately 30 minutes before carrying out any further work on the cylinder head or camshaft carrier.

19 Once the sealant has been allowed to dry, refit the rear timing belt cover bolt.

20 Reconnect the oil pressure warning light switch wiring plug, and clip the wiring into position on the end of the camshaft carrier.

21 Refit the exhaust gas recirculation solenoid valve bracket to the camshaft carrier, and tighten the securing bolt. Make sure that the lug on the camshaft carrier endplate engages with the corresponding hole in the solenoid valve bracket.

22 Reconnect the camshaft position sensor wiring connector.

23 On engines with code AHW and AXP, refit the DIS module and tighten the securing bolts, then reconnect the DIS module wiring connector, and the spark plug HT leads.

24 On engines with code AZD, BCA and BCB, Refit the ignition coils with reference to Chapter 5B.

25 Refit the secondary and main timing belts, as described in Section 7.

26 Reconnect the battery negative lead.

11 Camshafts (1.4 and 1.6 litre engines) – removal, inspection and refitting

Removal

1 Remove the camshaft carrier as described in Section 10.

2 Remove the camshaft sprockets, with reference to Section 8 if necessary.

3 If the inlet camshaft is to be removed, unscrew the securing bolt, and remove the inlet camshaft position sensor **(see illustration)**.

4 Remove the relevant camshaft carrier endplate **(see illustration)**. Note that on engines with code AHW and AXP, the inlet camshaft endplate is secured by the DIS module bolts, which have already been removed, and the exhaust camshaft endplate is secured by three bolts, one of which also secures the exhaust gas recirculation solenoid valve.

5 Carefully withdraw the relevant camshaft from the endplate end of the camshaft carrier, taking care not to damage the bearing surfaces of the camshaft and housing as the camshaft is withdrawn **(see illustration)**.

Inspection

6 Visually inspect the camshafts for evidence of wear on the surfaces of the lobes and journals. Normally their surfaces should be

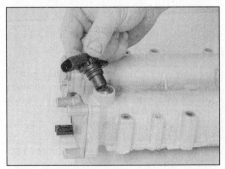

11.3 Remove the inlet camshaft position sensor – 1.4 litre engine

11.4 Remove the camshaft carrier endplate – 1.4 litre engine

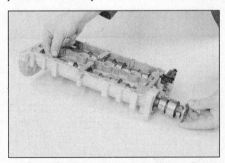

11.5 Withdraw the camshaft from the endplate end of the camshaft carrier – 1.4 litre engine

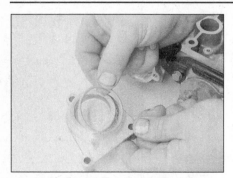

11.10 Renew the camshaft carrier endplate O-ring – 1.4 litre engine

smooth and have a dull shine; look for scoring, erosion or pitting and areas that appear highly polished, indicating excessive wear. Accelerated wear will occur once the hardened exterior of the camshaft has been damaged, so always renew worn items. **Note:** *If these symptoms are visible on the tips of the camshaft lobes, check the corresponding rocker, as it will probably be worn as well.*

7 If the machined surfaces of the camshaft appear discoloured or blued, it is likely that it has been overheated at some point, probably due to inadequate lubrication. This may have distorted the shaft, so check the run-out as follows: place the camshaft between two V-blocks and, using a DTI gauge, measure the run-out at the centre journal. No maximum run-out figure is quoted by the manufacturers, but it should be obvious if the camshaft is excessively distorted.

8 To measure camshaft endfloat, temporarily refit the relevant camshaft to the camshaft carrier, and refit the camshaft sealing plate to the rear of the camshaft carrier. Anchor a DTI gauge to the timing belt end of the camshaft carrier and align the gauge probe with the camshaft axis. Push the camshaft to one end of the camshaft carrier as far as it will travel, then rest the DTI gauge probe on the end of the camshaft, and zero the gauge display. Push the camshaft as far as it will go to the other end of the camshaft carrier, and record the gauge reading. Verify the reading by pushing the camshaft back to its original position and checking that the gauge indicates zero again.

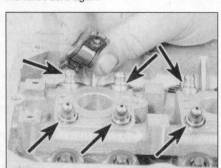

12.3 Removing a rocker (hydraulic tappets arrowed) – 1.4 litre engine

9 Check that the camshaft endfloat measurement is within the limit listed in the Specifications. Wear outside of this limit may be cured by renewing the relevant camshaft carrier endplate, although wear is unlikely to be confined to any one component, so renewal of the camshafts and camshaft carrier must be considered.

Refitting

10 Refitting is a reversal of removal, bearing in mind the following points.
  a) Before refitting the camshaft, renew the camshaft front oil seal, with reference to Section 14.
  b) Lubricate the bearing surfaces in the camshaft carrier, and the camshaft lobes before refitting the camshaft(s).
  c) Renew the sealing O-ring on each camshaft carrier endplate **(see illustration)**.
  d) Refit the camshaft sprocket(s) with reference to Section 8, noting that if both sprockets have been removed, the exhaust camshaft sprocket must be fitted first.
  e) Refit the camshaft carrier as described in Section 10.

12 Rockers and tappets (1.4 and 1.6 litre engines) – removal, inspection and refitting

Removal

1 Remove the camshaft carrier, as described in Section 10.
2 As the components are removed, keep them in strict order, so that they can be refitted in their original locations.
3 Unclip the rockers from the hydraulic tappets, and lift them from the cylinder head **(see illustration)**.
4 Carefully lift the tappets from their bores in the cylinder head. It is advisable to store the tappets (in order) upright in an oil bath whilst they are removed from the engine.

Inspection

5 Check the cylinder head bore contact surfaces of the tappets for signs of scoring or damage. Similarly, check the tappet bores in

12.9 Oil the tappets before fitting – 1.4 litre engine

the cylinder head for signs of scoring or damage. If significant scoring or damage is found, it may be necessary to renew the cylinder head and the complete set of tappets.
6 Inspect the hydraulic tappets for obvious signs of wear or damage, and renew if necessary. Check that the oil holes in the tappets are free from obstructions.
7 Check the valve, tappet, and camshaft contact faces of the rockers for wear or damage, and also check the rockers for any signs of cracking. Renew any worn or damaged rockers.
8 Inspect the camshaft lobes, as described in Section 11.

Refitting

9 Oil the tappet bores in the cylinder head, and the tappets themselves, then carefully slide the tappets into their original bores **(see illustration)**.
10 Oil the rocker contact faces of the tappets, and the tops of the valve stems, then refit the rockers to their original locations, ensuring that the rockers are securely clipped onto the tappets.
11 Check the endfloat of each camshaft, as described in Section 11, then refit the camshaft carrier as described in Section 10.

13 Camshafts and tappets (1.8 litre engines) – removal, inspection and refitting

Note: *A suitable tool will be required to lock the camshaft adjuster, or chain tensioner, in position during this procedure – see text. VW sealant (D 454 300 A2 sealant, or equivalent) will be required on refitting.*

Removal

1 Disconnect the battery negative lead, then remove the engine top cover. **Note:** *Before disconnecting the battery, refer to 'Disconnecting the battery' at the rear of this manual.*
2 Remove the upper timing belt cover, with reference to Section 6.
3 Turn the crankshaft to position No 1 piston at TDC on the firing stroke, as described in Section 3.
4 Remove the camshaft cover as described in Section 4.
5 Remove the timing belt, as described in Section 7. Note that there is no need to remove the timing belt completely – the belt can simply be released from the exhaust camshaft sprocket. Ensure that the crankshaft has been turned a quarter-turn (90°) anti-clockwise to position Nos 1 and 4 pistons slightly down their bores from the TDC position; this will eliminate any risk of piston-to-valve contact if a camshaft is turned whilst the timing belt is removed.
6 Remove the exhaust camshaft sprocket, with reference to Section 8.

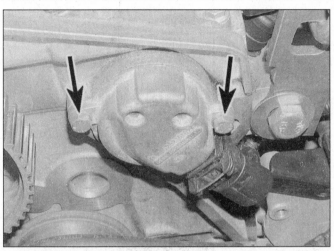

13.7 Inlet camshaft position sensor securing bolts (arrowed) – 1.8 litre engine

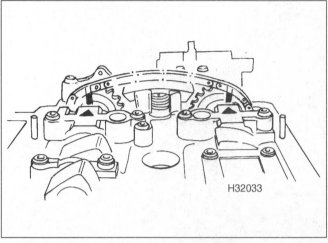

H32033

13.8 Mark the inlet camshaft drive chain and the sprockets in relation to each other (see text) – 1.8 litre engine

7 Disconnect the wiring plug from the inlet camshaft position sensor, then unscrew the securing bolts, and remove the sensor from the front of the cylinder head **(see illustration)**. With the sensor removed, unscrew the securing bolt and remove the washer and sensor rotor from the end of the inlet camshaft.

8 Clean the inlet camshaft drive chain, and the camshaft sprockets, in line with the arrows on the tops of the camshaft rear bearing caps, then mark the chain and sprockets in relation to each other **(see illustration)**. Mark the chain with paint or a scriber – **do not** mark the chain using a punch. Note that the distance between the two marks must be 16 chain rollers, but also note that the mark on the exhaust camshaft side will be slightly offset towards the centre of the cylinder head.

9 The camshaft adjuster or chain tensioner, as applicable, must now be locked in position.

VW special tool 3366 is available for this purpose; alternatively, it is possible to make up a similar tool using a threaded rod, nuts, and a small metal plate to keep the adjuster compressed. As a safety precaution, use a plastic cable-tie to keep the home-made tool in position **(see illustrations)**.

 Warning: Compressing the chain tensioner too far can result in damage to the camshaft adjuster mechanism.

10 Check the camshaft bearing caps for identification markings, and make suitable marks if necessary. The bearing caps should be numbered 1 to 6 from the chain end of the cylinder head, number 6 being the combined cap which straddles both camshafts. Note on which side of the bearing caps the marks are made, to ensure correct refitting **(see illustration overleaf)**.

11 Progressively slacken Nos 3 and 5 bearing cap bolts for both the inlet and exhaust

camshafts, then repeat the process for the double No 6 bearing cap, then the No 1 bearing caps.

12 Slacken and remove the chain adjuster/tensioner securing bolts. Also disconnect the wiring connector from the adjuster/tensioner solenoid valve.

13 Progressively slacken Nos 2 and 4 bearing cap bolts for both the inlet and exhaust camshafts, then lift both camshafts from the cylinder head, complete with the chain tensioner/camshaft adjuster mechanism **(see illustrations)**.

14 Release the chain tensioner/camshaft adjuster mechanism from the chain, and remove the chain from the camshaft sprockets. Remove the oil seal from each camshaft.

15 Lift the hydraulic tappets from their bores, and store them with the valve contact surface facing downwards, to prevent the oil from draining out **(see illustration)**. It is

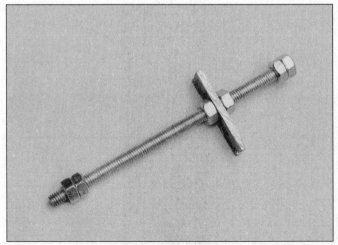

13.9a Home-made tool for locking camshaft adjuster, or chain tensioner, in position – 1.8 litre engine

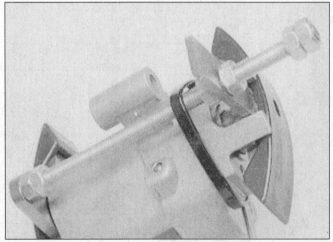

13.9b Home-made tool in position, locking camshaft adjuster in its compressed condition (shown with camshaft adjuster removed for clarity) – 1.8 litre engine

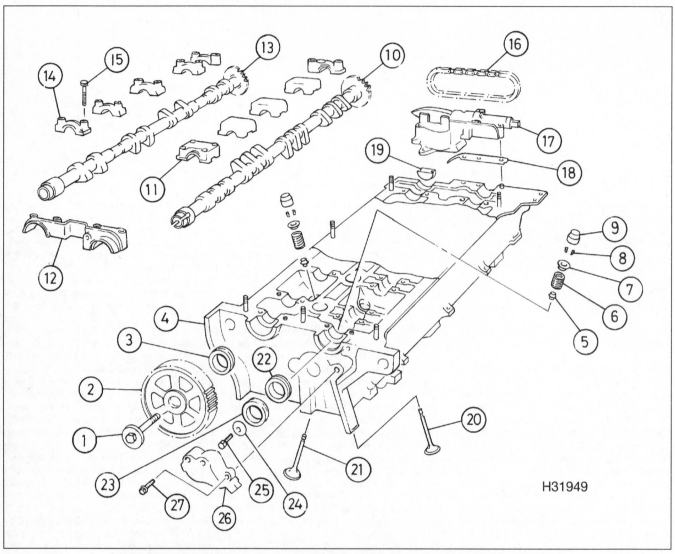

13.10 Cylinder head and camshaft components – 1.8 litre engines with variable valve timing

1 Camshaft sprocket bolt	8 Split collets	14 Bearing cap, exhaust
2 Camshaft sprocket	9 Hydraulic tappet	camshaft
3 Oil seal	10 Inlet camshaft	15 Camshaft bearing cap
4 Cylinder head	11 Bearing cap, inlet	bolt
5 Valve stem oil seal	camshaft	16 Drive chain
6 Valve spring	12 Combined bearing cap	17 Automatic camshaft
7 Valve cap	13 Exhaust camshaft	adjuster

18 Rubber seal	24 Tapered washer
19 Rubber grommet	25 Rotor securing bolt
20 Exhaust valve	26 Camshaft position
21 Inlet valve	sensor
22 Oil seal	27 Camshaft position
23 Camshaft position	sensor securing bolt
sensor rotor	

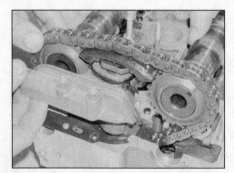

13.13a Removing the camshaft adjuster mechanism – 1.8 litre engine

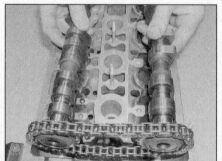

13.13b Lifting the camshafts and drive chain from the cylinder head – 1.8 litre engine

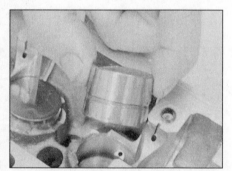

13.15 Lift the hydraulic tappets from their bores – 1.8 litre engine

13.18 Checking camshaft endfloat using a DTI gauge – 1.8 litre engine

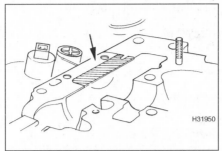

13.22 Apply sealant to the area of the chain tensioner/camshaft adjuster gasket shown – 1.8 litre engine

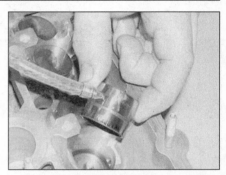

13.23 Oil the tappets before fitting – 1.8 litre engine

recommended that the tappets are kept immersed in oil whilst they are removed from the cylinder head. Keep the tappets in order, as they must be refitted to their original valves – accelerated wear, leading to early failure may result if they are interchanged.

Inspection

16 Visually inspect each camshaft for evidence of wear on the surfaces of the lobes and journals. Normally their surfaces should be smooth and have a dull shine; look for scoring, erosion or pitting and areas that appear highly polished, indicating excessive wear. Accelerated wear will occur once the hardened exterior of the camshaft has been damaged, so always renew worn items. **Note:** *If these symptoms are visible on the tips of the camshaft lobes, check the corresponding tappet, as it will probably be worn as well.*

17 If the machined surfaces of the camshaft appear discoloured or blued, it is likely that it has been overheated at some point, probably due to inadequate lubrication. This may have distorted the shaft, so check the run-out as follows: place the camshaft between two V-blocks and using a DTI gauge, measure the run-out at the centre journal. If it exceeds the figure quoted in the Specifications at the start of this Chapter, renew the camshaft.

18 To measure the camshaft endfloat, temporarily refit the camshafts to the cylinder head, then Nos 2 and 4 bearing caps for both camshafts, and tighten the retaining bolts to the specified torque. Anchor a DTI gauge to the timing belt end of the cylinder head and align the gauge probe with the relevant camshaft axis. Push the camshaft to one end of the cylinder head as far as it will travel, then rest the DTI gauge probe on the end of the camshaft, and zero the gauge display. Push the camshaft as far as it will go to the other end of the cylinder head, and record the gauge reading. Verify the reading by pushing the camshaft back to its original position and checking that the gauge indicates zero again **(see illustration)**. Repeat the checking procedure for the remaining camshaft. **Note:** *The hydraulic tappets must not be fitted whilst this measurement is being taken.*

19 Check that the camshaft endfloat measurement for each camshaft is within the limit given in the Specifications. Wear outside of this limit is unlikely to be confined to any one component, so renewal of the camshafts, cylinder head and bearing caps must be considered.

20 Inspect the hydraulic tappets for obvious signs of wear or damage, and renew if necessary. Check that the oil holes in the tappets are free from obstructions.

Refitting

21 Commence refitting by thoroughly cleaning all traces of old gasket and sealant from the chain tensioner/camshaft adjuster mating faces on the cylinder head.

22 Fit a new chain tensioner/camshaft adjuster gasket to the cylinder head, then coat the area shown with VW D 454 300 A2 sealant, or a suitable equivalent **(see illustration)**.

23 Smear the hydraulic tappets with clean engine oil, then fit them to their original positions in the cylinder head. Push the tappets down until they contact the valves, then lubricate the camshaft contact surfaces **(see illustration)**.

24 Lubricate the camshafts and the cylinder head bearing journals with clean engine oil.

25 Engage the chain with the camshaft sprockets, making sure that the marks made on the chain and sprockets before removal are aligned. Make sure that the distance between the marks is 16 chain rollers **(see illustration 13.8)**. Locate the chain tensioner/camshaft adjuster between the chain runs, then carefully lower the camshafts, chain and chain tensioner/camshaft adjuster into position in the cylinder head. Support the ends of the camshafts as they are fitted, to avoid damaging the lobes and journals.

26 The camshaft oil seals may be fitted at this stage, or alternatively fitted later. Dip the new seals in engine oil, then locate them on each camshaft. Make sure that the closed ends of the seals face outwards from the camshafts, and take care not to damage the seal lips. Locate the seals against the seats in the cylinder head.

27 Refit the chain adjuster/tensioner bolts and tighten them to the specified torque. Reconnect the wiring connector to the adjuster/tensioner solenoid valve.

28 Refit Nos 2 and 4 bearing caps for both camshafts. Ensure that the bearing caps are fitted the correct way round, as noted before removal. Refit the bearing cap securing bolts, and working progressively in a diagonal sequence, tighten the bolts to the specified torque.

29 Refit the No 1 bearing caps for both camshafts (again, ensure that the bearing caps are fitted the correct way round), then refit the bearing cap bolts and tighten progressively to the specified torque.

30 Remove the tool used to lock the camshaft adjuster or chain tensioner (as applicable) in position.

31 Apply a thin film of sealant to the cylinder head contact faces of the combined bearing cap (No 6 bearing cap), then fit the cap, making sure that the oil seals (where fitted) locate against their seatings **(see illustration)**. Progressively tighten the bearing cap securing bolts to the specified torque.

32 Fit Nos 3 and 5 bearing caps for both camshafts (again, ensure that the bearing caps are fitted the correct way round), then refit the bearing cap bolts and tighten progressively to the specified torque.

33 Check that the marks made on the chain and sprockets before removal are still aligned. If not, the components have been incorrectly refitted.

34 Refit the inlet camshaft sensor rotor, and refit the washer and securing bolt. Tighten the securing bolt to the specified torque.

35 Refit the inlet camshaft position sensor to the cylinder head, then refit the securing bolts and tighten to the specified torque.

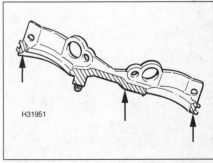

13.31 Apply a thin film of sealant to the contact face of the combined bearing cap in the areas shown – 1.8 litre engine

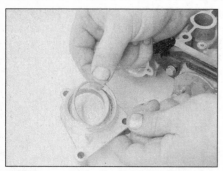

14.12 Locate the new O-ring in the groove in the endplate – 1.4 litre engine

36 Refit the exhaust camshaft sprocket with reference to Section 8, then refit the timing belt as described in Section 7.

37 Refit the camshaft cover as described in Section 4.

38 If not already done, refit the upper outer timing belt cover as described in Section 6.

39 Refit the engine top cover, and reconnect the battery negative lead.

14 Camshaft oil seals – renewal

1.4 and 1.6 litre engines

Right-hand oil seals

1 Remove the main and secondary timing belts as described in Section 7.

2 Remove the relevant camshaft sprocket as described in Section 8.

3 Drill two small holes into the existing oil seal, diagonally opposite each other. Take great care to avoid drilling through into the seal housing or camshaft sealing surface. Thread two self-tapping screws into the holes and, using a pair of pliers, pull on the heads of the screws to extract the oil seal.

4 Clean out the seal housing and the sealing surface of the camshaft by wiping it with a lint-free cloth. Remove any swarf or burrs that may cause the seal to leak.

5 Lubricate the lip and outer edge of the new oil seal with clean engine oil, and push it over

15.5 A suitable engine lifting bracket can be bolted to the cylinder block using a long bolt screwed into the hole located next to the coolant pump – 1.4 litre engine

the camshaft until it is positioned above its housing. To prevent damage to the sealing lips, wrap some adhesive tape around the end of the camshaft.

6 Using a hammer and a socket of suitable diameter, drive the seal squarely into its housing. **Note:** *Select a socket that bears only on the hard outer surface of the seal, not the inner lip which can easily be damaged.*

7 Refit the relevant camshaft sprocket with reference to Section 8.

8 Refit and tension the secondary and main timing belts as described in Section 7.

Left-hand oil seals

9 The camshaft oil seals take the form of O-rings located in the grooves in the camshaft carrier endplates.

10 Unscrew the securing bolts, and remove the relevant camshaft endplate, noting that on engines with code AHW and AXP, the DIS ignition module securing bolts secure the exhaust camshaft endplate.

11 Prise the old O-ring from the groove in the endplate.

12 Lightly oil the new O-ring, and carefully locate it in the groove in the endplate **(see illustration)**.

13 Refit the endplate (and the DIS module, where applicable), and tighten the bolts securely.

1.8 litre engine

Exhaust camshaft oil seal

14 Remove the timing belt as described in Section 7.

15 Remove the camshaft sprocket as described in Section 8.

16 Proceed as described in paragraphs 3 to 6.

17 Refit the camshaft sprocket as described in Section 8.

18 Refit and tension the timing belt as described in Section 7.

Inlet camshaft oil seal

19 Remove the upper timing belt cover, with reference to Section 6.

20 Disconnect the wiring plug from the inlet camshaft position sensor, then unscrew the securing bolts, and remove the sensor from the front of the cylinder head. With the sensor removed, unscrew the securing bolt and

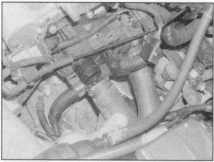

15.6 Disconnect the radiator hoses from the coolant housing at the transmission end of the cylinder head – 1.4 litre engine

remove the washer and sensor rotor from the end of the inlet camshaft.

21 Proceed as described in paragraphs 3 to 6.

22 Refit the inlet camshaft sensor rotor, and refit the washer and securing bolt. Tighten the securing bolt to the specified torque.

23 Refit the inlet camshaft position sensor to the cylinder head, then refit the securing bolts and tighten to the specified torque.

24 Refit the upper timing belt cover, with reference to Section 6.

15 Cylinder head – removal, inspection and refitting

1.4 and 1.6 litre engines

Note: *The cylinder head must be removed with the engine cold. New cylinder head bolts, a new cylinder head gasket, new inlet manifold O-rings, a new exhaust manifold gasket, and a new EGR pipe-to-throttle body gasket will be required on refitting.*

Removal

1 Disconnect the battery negative lead, then remove the engine top cover. **Note:** *Before disconnecting the battery, refer to 'Disconnecting the battery' at the rear of this manual.*

2 Drain the cooling system as described in Chapter 1A.

3 Remove the main and secondary timing belts as described in Section 7.

4 As the engine is currently supported using a hoist attached to the engine lifting brackets bolted to the cylinder head, it is now necessary to attach a suitable bracket to the cylinder block, so that the engine can still be supported as the cylinder head is removed.

5 A suitable bracket can be bolted to the cylinder block using spacers, and a long bolt screwed into the hole located next to the coolant pump **(see illustration)**. Ideally, attach a second set of lifting tackle to the hoist, adjust the lifting tackle to support the engine using the bracket attached to the cylinder block, then disconnect the lifting tackle attached to the bracket on the cylinder head. Alternatively, temporarily support the engine under the sump using a jack and a block of wood, then transfer the lifting tackle from the bracket on the cylinder head to the bracket bolted to the cylinder block.

6 Release the hose clips, and disconnect the two radiator hoses from the coolant housing at the transmission end of the cylinder head **(see illustration)**. Similarly, release the hose clips and disconnect the remaining three small coolant hoses from the rear of the coolant housing.

7 Remove the air cleaner assembly, complete with the air trunking, as described in Chapter 4A.

8 Unscrew the bolt securing the oil level

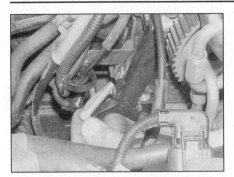

15.8 Unscrew the bolt securing the oil level dipstick tube bracket to the cylinder head – 1.4 litre engine

15.9 Disconnect the EGR pipe from the throttle body and recover the gasket – 1.4 litre engine

15.11 Lift the inlet manifold back from the engine – 1.4 litre engine

dipstick tube bracket to the cylinder head, then lift the dipstick tube, and turn it to one side, to clear the working area **(see illustration)**. Release the wiring harnesses from the clip on the dipstick tube bracket. Note that the dipstick tube bracket bolt also secures the inlet manifold.

9 Unscrew the two securing bolts and disconnect the exhaust gas recirculation (EGR) pipe from the throttle body. Recover the gasket **(see illustration)**.

10 Unscrew the bolt securing the EGR pipe bracket to the coolant housing.

11 Unscrew the six securing bolts (three upper and three lower) and lift the inlet manifold back from the engine **(see illustration)**. Ensure that the inlet manifold is adequately supported in the engine compartment, and take care not to strain any wires,

cables or hoses. Recover the O-rings if they are loose.

12 Unbolt the wiring connector bracket from the right-hand rear corner of the cylinder head **(see illustration)**.

13 Disconnect the wiring plug from the coolant temperature sensor, located in the coolant housing at the transmission end of the cylinder head, then unclip the wiring harnesses from the coolant housing, and move them to one side **(see illustrations)**.

14 Disconnect the vacuum hose from the exhaust gas recirculation (EGR) valve **(see illustration)**.

15 Unclip the wiring from the bracket attached to the exhaust heat shield, then unscrew the securing bolts (two upper bolts and one lower bolt), and remove the heat shield **(see illustrations)**.

16 Disconnect the exhaust front section from the manifold with reference to Chapter 4C. If desired, the exhaust manifold can be removed as follows.

a) *Unscrew the union nut securing the EGR pipe to the exhaust manifold, and remove the EGR pipe.*

b) *Unscrew the exhaust manifold securing nuts, then lift off the manifold and recover the gasket.*

17 Remove the camshaft carrier, with reference to Section 10.

18 Pull out the metal clip securing the plastic coolant pipe to the coolant housing at the left-hand rear corner of the cylinder head **(see illustration)**.

19 Progressively slacken the cylinder head bolts in order, then unscrew and remove the bolts **(see illustrations)**.

15.12 Unbolt the wiring connector bracket from the right-hand rear corner of the cylinder head – 1.4 litre engine

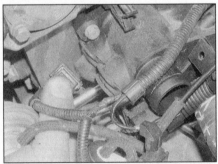

15.13a Disconnect the coolant temperature sensor wiring plug . . .

15.13b . . . then unclip the wiring harnesses and move them to one side – 1.4 litre engine

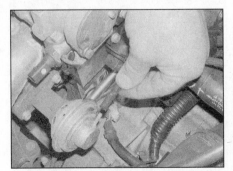

15.14 Disconnect the vacuum hose from the EGR valve – 1.4 litre engine

15.15a Unclip the wiring from the bracket on the exhaust heat shield . . .

15.15b . . . then remove the heat shield – 1.4 litre engine

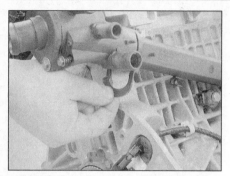

15.18 Pull out the metal clip securing the coolant pipe to the coolant housing (shown with engine removed for clarity) – 1.4 litre engine

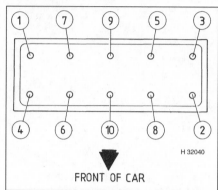

15.19a Cylinder head bolt slackening sequence – 1.4 and 1.6 litre engines

15.19b Slackening the cylinder head bolts – 1.4 litre engine

15.20 Removing the cylinder head – 1.4 litre engine

20 With all the bolts removed, lift the cylinder head from the block **(see illustration)**. If the cylinder head is stuck, tap it with a soft-faced mallet to break the joint. **Do not** insert a lever into the gasket joint. As the cylinder head is lifted off, release the coolant pump pipe from the thermostat housing on the cylinder head.
21 Lift the cylinder head gasket from the block.

Inspection

22 Dismantling and inspection of the cylinder head is covered in Part D of this Chapter. Additionally, check the condition of the coolant pump pipe-to-thermostat housing O-ring, and renew if necessary.

Refitting

23 The mating faces of the cylinder head and block must be perfectly clean before refitting the head. Use a scraper to remove all traces of gasket and carbon, also clean the tops of the pistons. Take particular care with the aluminium surfaces, as the soft metal is easily damaged. Make sure that debris is not allowed to enter the oil and water passages – this is particularly important for the oil circuit, as carbon could block the oil supply to the camshaft and crankshaft bearings. Using adhesive tape and paper, seal the water, oil and bolt holes in the cylinder block. To prevent carbon entering the gap between the pistons and bores, smear a little grease in the

gap. After cleaning a piston, rotate the crankshaft to that the piston moves down the bore, then wipe out the grease and carbon with a cloth rag. Clean the other piston crowns in the same way.
24 Check the head and block for nicks, deep scratches and other damage. If slight, they may be removed carefully with a file. More serious damage may be repaired by machining, but this is a specialist job.
25 If warpage of the cylinder head is suspected, use a straight-edge to check it for distortion, as described in Part D of this Chapter.
26 Ensure that the cylinder head bolt holes in the crankcase are clean and free of oil. Syringe or soak up any oil left in the bolt holes. This is most important in order that the correct bolt tightening torque can be applied, and to prevent the possibility of the block being cracked by hydraulic pressure when the bolts are tightened.
27 Ensure that the crankshaft has been turned to position Nos 1 and 4 pistons slightly down their bores from the TDC position (see Section 7). This will eliminate any risk of piston-to-valve contact as the cylinder head is refitted. Also ensure that the camshaft sprockets are locked in the TDC position using the locking tool, as described in Section 3.
28 Ensure that the cylinder head locating dowels are in place in the cylinder block, then fit a new cylinder head gasket over the dowels, ensuring that the part number is uppermost. Where applicable, the OBEN/TOP marking should also be uppermost **(see illustrations)**. Note that VW recommend that the gasket is only removed from its packaging immediately prior to fitting.
29 Lower the cylinder head into position on the gasket, ensuring that it engages correctly over the dowels. As the cylinder head is lowered into position, ensure that the coolant pump pipe engages with the thermostat housing (use a new O-ring if necessary).
30 Fit the new cylinder head bolts, and screw them in as far as possible by hand.
31 Working progressively, in sequence, tighten all the cylinder head bolts to the specified Stage 1 torque **(see illustration)**.

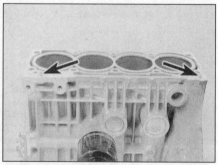

15.28a Ensure that the dowels (arrowed) are in place in the cylinder block – 1.4 litre engine

15.28b Ensure that the part number and OBEN/TOP markings on the cylinder head gasket are uppermost – 1.4 litre engine

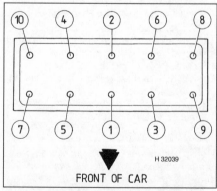

15.31 Cylinder head bolt tightening sequence – 1.4 and 1.6 litre engines

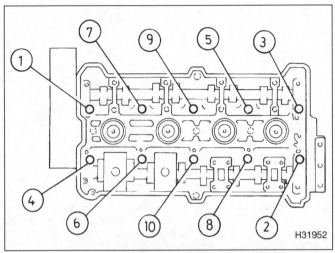

15.49 Cylinder head bolt slackening sequence –
1.8 litre engine

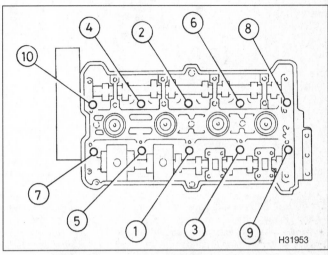

15.57 Cylinder head bolt tightening sequence –
1.8 litre engine

32 Again working progressively, in sequence, tighten all the cylinder head bolts through the specified Stage 2 angle.

33 Finally, tighten all the cylinder head bolts, in sequence, to the specified Stage 3 angle.

34 Reconnect the lifting tackle to the right-hand engine lifting bracket on the cylinder head, then adjust the lifting tackle to support the engine. Once the engine is adequately supported using the cylinder head bracket, disconnect the lifting tackle from the bracket bolted to the cylinder block, and unbolt the improvised engine lifting bracket from the cylinder block. Alternatively, remove the trolley jack and block of wood from under the sump.

35 Refit the clip securing the plastic coolant pipe to the coolant housing.

36 Refit the camshaft carrier as described in Section 10.

37 Further refitting is a reversal of removal, bearing in mind the following points.

a) *Refit the exhaust manifold and reconnect the EGR pipe, and/or reconnect the exhaust front section to the manifold, as described in Section 4C.*

b) *Refit the inlet manifold using new O-rings.*

c) *Reconnect the EGR pipe to the throttle body using a new gasket.*

d) *Refit the secondary and main timing belts as described in Section 7.*

e) *Ensure that all wires, pipes and hoses are correctly reconnected and routed, as noted before removal.*

f) *Tighten all fixings to the specified torque, where applicable.*

g) *On completion, refill the cooling system as described in Chapter 1A.*

1.8 litre engines

Note: *The cylinder head must be removed with the engine cold. New cylinder head bolts and a new cylinder head gasket will be required on refitting. Suitable studs (see text) will be required to guide the cylinder head into position on refitting.*

Removal

38 Proceed as described in paragraphs 1 and 2 of this Section.

39 If the cylinder head is to be removed leaving the inlet manifold in the engine compartment, unscrew the securing bolts and lift the inlet manifold back from the engine. Ensure that the inlet manifold is adequately supported in the engine compartment, and take care not to strain any wires, cables or hoses. Recover the gaskets it they are loose.

40 Alternatively, if the cylinder head is to be removed complete with the inlet manifold, work around the manifold and disconnect all relevant pipes, hoses and wires. When disconnecting the fuel supply and return hoses at the connections on the fuel rail, take care, because the fuel supply hose will be pressurised. Wrap a clean cloth around each connection to absorb escaping fuel, then slacken the hose clip and pull the relevant hose from the connection. Clamp or plug the open ends of the hoses and connections to prevent dirt entry and further fuel spillage.

41 Release the hose clips, and disconnect the coolant hoses from the coolant housing at the transmission end of the cylinder head.

42 Disconnect the wiring plug from the inlet camshaft position sensor.

43 Disconnect the wiring plug from the coolant temperature sensor, located in the coolant housing at the transmission end of the cylinder head.

44 Disconnect the exhaust front section from the manifold or turbocharger, as applicable, as described in Chapter 4C.

45 Remove the timing belt as described in Section 7 then remove the tensioner as described in Section 8.

46 Proceed as described in paragraphs 4 and 5.

47 Remove the camshaft cover as described in Section 4.

48 Work around the cylinder head (and manifolds, where applicable), and disconnect all remaining pipes, wires and hoses to facilitate cylinder head removal. Note the location and routing of all pipes, wires and hoses to aid refitting.

49 Proceed as described in paragraphs 19 to 21, ignoring the reference to the coolant pump pipe, and slackening the cylinder head bolts in order **(see illustration)**.

Inspection

50 Dismantling and inspection of the cylinder head is covered in Part D of this Chapter.

Refitting

51 Proceed as described in paragraphs 23 to 27.

52 To guide the cylinder head into position, screw two long studs (or old cylinder head bolts with the heads cut off, and slots cut in the ends to enable the bolts to be unscrewed) into the end cylinder head bolt locations on the exhaust side of the cylinder block.

53 Ensure that the cylinder head locating dowels are in place in the cylinder block, then fit a new cylinder head gasket over the dowels, ensuring that the part number is uppermost. Where applicable, the OBEN/TOP marking should also be uppermost. Note that VW recommend that the gasket is only removed from its packaging immediately prior to fitting.

54 Lower the cylinder head into position on the gasket, ensuring that it engages correctly over the guide studs and dowels.

55 Fit the new cylinder head bolts to the eight remaining bolt locations, and screw them in as far as possible by hand.

56 Unscrew the two guide studs from the exhaust side of the cylinder block, then screw in the two remaining cylinder head bolts as far as possible by hand.

57 Proceed as described in paragraphs 31 to 34, tightening the cylinder head bolts in order **(see illustration)**.

17.7 Removing the oil pick-up pipe – 1.4 litre engine

17.9 Removing the oil pump – 1.4 litre engine

17.11 Lifting off the oil pump rear cover – 1.4 litre engine

58 Further refitting is a reversal of removal, bearing in mind the following points.
a) *Ensure that all pipes, wires and hoses are correctly reconnected and routed as noted before removal.*
b) *Refit the camshaft cover as described in Section 4.*
c) *Install the tensioner as described in Section 8 then fit the timing belt as described in Section 7.*
d) *Reconnect the exhaust front section to the manifold or turbocharger, as applicable, as described in Chapter 4C.*
e) *Where applicable, refit the inlet manifold using new gaskets.*
f) *Tighten all fixings to the specified torque, where applicable.*
g) *On completion, refill the cooling system as described in Chapter 1A.*

16 Sump –
removal and refitting

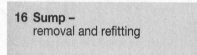

1.4 and 1.6 litre engines

1 Proceed as described in Chapter 2A, Section 13 (Sump – removal and refitting), bearing in mind the following points.
a) *The exhaust front section must be removed as described in Chapter 4C, to allow clearance for removal of the sump.*
b) *When refitting the sump, to guide the sump into position on the cylinder block mating face, two guide studs can be improvised by*

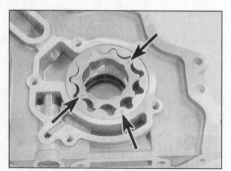

17.12 Note that the rotors fit with the punched dots (arrowed) facing the oil pump cover – 1.4 litre engine

cutting the heads off two M6 bolts, and cutting slots in the ends of the bolts so that they can later by unscrewed using a flat-bladed screwdriver. Screw the guide studs into two diagonally opposite sump securing bolt holes. Offer the sump into position, then fit the remaining sump bolts. Once the sump is held securely in position, unscrew the guide studs, and refit the remaining two sump securing bolts.

1.8 litre engines

2 Proceed as described in Chapter 2A, Section 13 (Sump – removal and refitting), but note that it will be necessary to use a long ratchet extension to reach some of the sump securing bolts.

17 Oil pump
(1.4 and 1.6 litre engines) – removal, inspection and refitting

Note: *New oil pump securing bolts, a new oil pump gasket, a new oil pick-up pipe gasket, and a new crankshaft oil seal will be required on refitting.*

Removal

1 Remove the main timing belt, as described in Section 7.
2 Refit the crankshaft pulley securing bolt, with a spacer washer positioned under its head, to retain the crankshaft sprocket.
3 Turn the crankshaft a quarter-turn (90°) clockwise to reposition Nos 1 and 4 pistons at

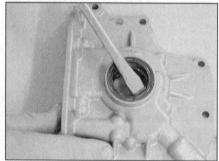

17.16 Prise the crankshaft oil seal from the oil pump – 1.4 litre engine

TDC. Ensure that the crankshaft sprocket tooth with the chamfered inner edge is aligned with the corresponding mark on the oil pump housing (see Section 3).
4 Turn the crankshaft to move the crankshaft sprocket three teeth anti-clockwise away from the TDC position. The third tooth to the right of the tooth with the ground down outer edge must align with the corresponding mark on the oil pump housing. This procedure positions the crankshaft correctly to enable oil pump refitting.
5 Remove the main timing belt tensioner, as described in Section 8.
6 Remove the sump as described in Section 16.
7 Unscrew the securing bolts and remove the oil pick-up pipe from the oil pump and cylinder block **(see illustration)**. Recover the gasket.
8 Remove the crankshaft sprocket, noting which way round it is fitted.
9 Unscrew the securing bolts, noting their locations to ensure correct refitting, and remove the oil pump **(see illustration)**. Recover the gasket.

Inspection

10 No spare parts are available for the oil pump, and if worn or faulty, the complete pump must be renewed.
11 To inspect the oil pump rotors, remove the securing screws, and lift off the oil pump rear cover **(see illustration)**.
12 Note that the rotors fit with the punched dots on the edges of the rotors facing the oil pump cover **(see illustration)**.
13 Lift out the rotors, and inspect them for wear and damage. If there are any signs of wear or damage, the complete oil pump assembly must be renewed.
14 Lubricate the contact faces of the rotors with clean engine oil, then refit the rotors to the pump, ensuring that the punched dots on the edges of the rotors face the pump cover.
15 Refit the pump cover, and tighten the screws securely.
16 Using a flat-bladed screwdriver, prise the crankshaft oil seal from the oil pump, and discard it **(see illustration)**.
17 Thoroughly clean the oil seal seat in the oil pump.

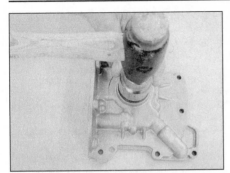

17.18 Driving a new oil seal into the oil pump using a socket – 1.4 litre engine

17.21 Fit a new gasket over the dowels in the cylinder block – 1.4 litre engine

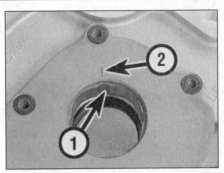

17.22 Align one of the drive cut-outs (1) in the edge of the rotor with the line (2) on the oil pump rear cover – 1.4 litre engine

18 Press or drive a new oil seal into position in the oil pump, using a socket or tube of suitable diameter **(see illustration)**. Ensure that the seal seats squarely in the oil pump. Ensure that the socket or tube bears only on the hard outer ring of the seal, and take care not to damage the seal lips. Press or drive the seal into position until it is seated on the shoulder in the housing. Make sure that the closed end of the seal is facing outwards.

Refitting

19 Commence refitting by cleaning all traces of old gasket and sealant from the mating faces of the cylinder block and oil pump.
20 Wind a length of tape around the front of the crankshaft to protect the oil seal lips as the oil pump is slid into position.
21 Fit a new oil pump gasket over the dowels in the cylinder block **(see illustration)**.
22 Turn the inner oil pump rotor to align one of the drive cut-outs in the edge of the inner rotor with the line on the oil pump rear cover **(see illustration)**.
23 Lightly oil the four tips of the oil pump drive cam on the end of the crankshaft.
24 Coat the lips of the crankshaft oil seal with a thin film of clean engine oil.
25 Slide the oil pump into position over the end of the crankshaft until it engages with the dowels, taking care not to damage the oil seal, and ensuring that the inner rotor engages with the drive cam on the crankshaft **(see illustration)**.
26 Fit new oil pump securing bolts, to the

locations noted before removal, and tighten them to the specified torque **(see illustration)**.
27 Remove the tape from the end of the crankshaft, then refit the crankshaft sprocket, noting that the pulley locating pin must be outermost. Temporarily refit the securing bolt and washer to retain the sprocket.
28 Refit the oil pick-up pipe, using a new gasket, and tighten the securing bolts to the specified torque **(see illustration)**.
29 Refit the sump as described in Section 16.
30 Refit the main timing belt tensioner as described in Section 8.
31 Refit the main timing belt as described in Section 7.

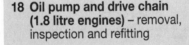

18 Oil pump and drive chain (1.8 litre engines) – removal, inspection and refitting

Proceed as described in Chapter 2A, Section 14 (Oil pump, drive chain and sprockets – removal, inspection and refitting).

19 Flywheel/driveplate – removal, inspection and refitting

1.4 and 1.6 litre engines

1 On 1.4 and 1.6 litre engines with manual transmission, the clutch pressure plate is

bolted directly to the crankshaft flange, and the dished flywheel is then bolted to the pressure plate. Removal and refitting procedures for the clutch pressure plate and flywheel are given in Chapter 6.
2 On 1.4 and 1.6 litre engines with automatic transmission, removal, inspection and refitting of the driveplate is as described for 2.0 litre engines, in Chapter 2A, Section 15.

1.8 litre engines

3 Proceed as described for 2.0 litre engines, in Chapter 2A, Section 15.

20 Crankshaft oil seals – renewal

1.4 and 1.6 litre engines

Timing belt end oil seal

1 Remove the main timing belt as described in Section 7, and the crankshaft sprocket with reference to Section 8.
2 To remove the seal without removing the oil pump, drill two small holes diagonally opposite each other, insert self-tapping screws, and pull on the heads of the screws with pliers.
3 Alternatively, the oil seal can be removed with the oil pump, as described in Section 17.
4 Thoroughly clean the oil seal seating in the oil pump.
5 Wind a length of tape around the end of the

17.25 Slide the oil pump over the end of the crankshaft. Note the tape used to protect the oil seal – 1.4 litre engine

17.26 Fit the new oil pump securing bolts to the locations (arrowed) noted before removal – 1.4 litre engine

17.28 Fit a new oil pick-up pipe gasket – 1.4 litre engine

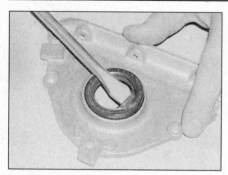

20.11 Using a screwdriver to lever the crankshaft oil seal from its housing – 1.8 litre engine

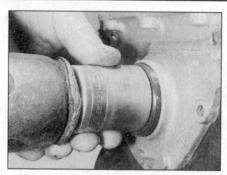

20.14 Driving a new crankshaft oil seal into position using a socket – 1.8 litre engine

crankshaft to protect the oil seal lips as the seal is fitted.

6 Fit a new oil seal to the oil pump, pressing or driving it into position using a socket or tube of suitable diameter. Ensure that the socket or tube bears only on the hard outer ring of the seal, and take care not to damage the seal lips. Press or drive the seal into position until it is seated on the shoulder in the oil pump. Make sure that the closed end of the seal is facing outwards.

7 Refit the crankshaft sprocket with reference to Section 8, and the main timing belt as described in Section 7.

Flywheel/driveplate end oil seal

8 The crankshaft left-hand oil seal is integral with the housing, and must be renewed as an assembly, complete with the crankshaft speed/position sensor wheel. The sensor wheel is attached to the oil seal/housing assembly, and is a press-fit on the crankshaft flange. VW special tool T10017 is required to fit this assembly and, in the workshop, we found that there is no means of accurately aligning the sensor wheel on the crankshaft without the tool (there is no locating key, and there are no alignment marks). If the sensor wheel is not precisely aligned on the

crankshaft, the crankshaft speed/position sensor will send incorrect TDC signals to the engine management ECU, and the engine will not run correctly (the engine may not run at all). As the appropriate special tool is only available to VW dealers, there is no alternative but to have the new assembly fitted by a VW dealer.

1.8 litre engines

Timing belt end oil seal

Note: *If the oil seal housing is removed, suitable sealant (VW D 176 404 A2, or equivalent) will be required on refitting.*

9 Remove the timing belt as described in Section 7, and the crankshaft sprocket with reference to Section 8.

10 To remove the seal without removing the oil seal housing, drill two small holes diagonally opposite each other, insert self-tapping screws, and pull on the heads of the screws with pliers.

11 Alternatively, to remove the oil seal complete with its housing, proceed as follows.

a) *Remove the sump as described in Section 16. This is necessary to ensure a satisfactory seal between the sump and oil seal housing on refitting.*

b) *Unbolt and remove the oil seal housing.*

c) *Working on the bench, lever the oil seal from the housing using a suitable screwdriver (see illustration). Take care not to damage the seal seating in the housing.*

12 Thoroughly clean the oil seal seating in the housing.

13 Wind a length of tape around the end of the crankshaft to protect the oil seal lips as the seal (and housing, where applicable) is fitted.

14 Fit a new oil seal to the housing, pressing or driving it into position using a socket or tube of suitable diameter **(see illustration)**. Ensure that the socket or tube bears only on the hard outer ring of the seal, and take care not to damage the seal lips. Press or drive the seal into position until it is seated on the shoulder in the housing. Make sure that the closed end of the seal is facing outwards.

15 If the oil seal housing has been removed, proceed as follows, otherwise proceed to paragraph 19.

16 Clean all traces of old sealant from the crankshaft oil seal housing and the cylinder block, then coat the cylinder block mating faces of the oil seal housing with a 2.0 to 3.0 mm thick bead of sealant (VW D 176 404 A2, or equivalent). Note that the seal housing must be refitted within 5 minutes of applying the sealant **(see illustration)**.

17 Refit the oil seal housing, and tighten the bolts progressively to the specified torque.

18 Refit the sump as described in Section 16.

19 Refit the crankshaft sprocket with reference to Section 8, and the timing belt as described in Section 7.

Flywheel/driveplate end oil seal

Note: *If the original oil seal housing was fitted using sealant, suitable sealant (VW D 176 404 A2, or equivalent) will be required to seal the housing on refitting.*

20 Remove the flywheel/driveplate as described in Section 19.

21 Remove the sump as described in Section 16. This is necessary to ensure a satisfactory seal between the sump and oil seal housing on refitting.

22 Unbolt and remove the oil seal housing, complete with the oil seal.

23 The new oil seal will be supplied ready-fitted to a new oil seal housing.

24 Thoroughly clean the oil seal housing mating face on the cylinder block.

25 If the original oil seal housing was fitted using sealant, apply a thin bead of suitable sealant (VW D 176 404 A2, or equivalent) to the cylinder block mating face of the oil seal housing. Note that the seal housing must be refitted within 5 minutes of applying the sealant.

26 New oil seal/housing assemblies are supplied with a fitting tools to prevent damage to the oil seal as it is being fitted. Locate the tool over the end of the crankshaft **(see illustration)**.

27 Carefully fit the oil seal/housing assembly

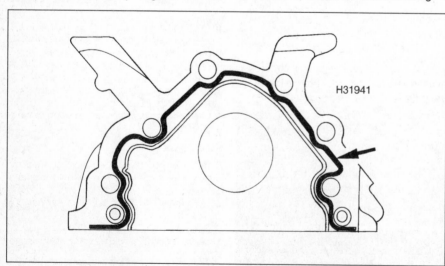

H31941

20.16 Apply sealant as shown to the crankshaft oil seal housing – 1.8 litre engine

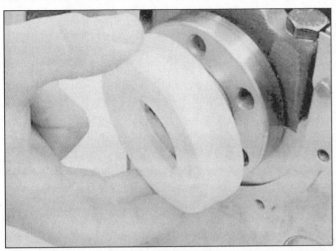

20.26 Locate the oil seal fitting tool over the end of the crankshaft – 1.8 litre engine

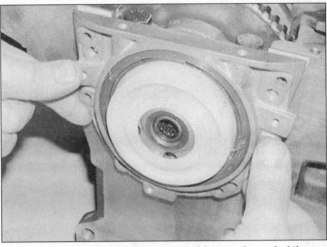

20.27 Fit the oil seal/housing assembly over the end of the crankshaft – 1.8 litre engine

over the end of the crankshaft, and tighten the bolts progressively, in a diagonal sequence, to the specified torque **(see illustration)**.

28 Remove the oil seal protector tool from the end of the crankshaft.

29 Refit the sump as described in Section 16.

30 Refit the flywheel/driveplate as described in Section 19.

21 Engine/transmission mountings – inspection and renewal

Refer to Chapter 2A, Section 17.

22 Engine oil cooler – removal and refitting

Refer to Chapter 2A, Section 18.

23 Oil pressure relief valve – removal, inspection and refitting

1.4 and 1.6 litre engines

1 The oil pressure relief valve is an integral

24.2 Disconnect the oil pressure switch wiring connector – 1.4 litre engine

part of the oil pump. The valve piston and spring are located to the side of the oil pump rotors and can be inspected once the oil pump has been removed from the engine and the rear cover has been removed (see Section 17). If any sign of wear or damage is found the oil pump assembly will have to be renewed; the relief valve piston and spring are not available separately.

1.8 litre engine

2 Refer to Chapter 2A, Section 19.

24 Oil pressure warning light switch – removal and refitting

1.4 and 1.6 litre engines

Removal

1 The oil pressure warning light switch is fitted to the front of the cylinder head, on its left-hand end. To gain access to the switch, undo the securing bolts and remove the engine top cover.

2 Disconnect the wiring connector and wipe clean the area around the switch **(see illustration)**.

25.1 Oil level/temperature sender (arrowed)

3 Unscrew the switch from the cylinder head and remove it along with its sealing washer. If the switch is to be left removed from the engine for any length of time, plug the hole in the cylinder head.

Refitting

4 Examine the sealing washer for signs of damage or deterioration and if necessary renew.

5 Refit the switch, complete with washer, and tighten it to the specified torque.

6 Securely reconnect the wiring connector then refit the engine cover. Check and, if necessary, top up the engine oil as described in *Weekly checks*.

1.8 litre engine

7 Refer to Chapter 2A, Section 20.

25 Oil level/temperature sender – removal and refitting

Removal

1 The oil level/temperature sender is fitted to bottom of the sump **(see illustration)**.

2 Drain the engine oil as described in Chapter 1A.

3 Disconnect the wiring connector and wipe clean the area around the sender.

4 Undo the three retaining bolts and remove the sender.

Refitting

5 Examine the sealing washer for signs of damage or deterioration and if necessary renew.

6 Refit the switch and tighten the retaining bolts to the specified torque.

7 Securely reconnect the wiring connector then refill the engine with oil, with reference to Chapter 1A.

8 On completion, check and, if necessary, top-up the engine oil as described in *Weekly checks*.

Notes

Chapter 2 Part C:
Diesel engine in-car repair procedures

Contents

Camshaft and hydraulic tappets – removal, inspection and refitting 10
Camshaft cover – removal and refitting 4
Camshaft oil seals – renewal 12
Compression and leakdown tests – description and interpretation . 2
Crankshaft oil seals – renewal 17
Crankshaft pulley – removal and refitting 5
Cylinder head – removal, inspection and refitting 13
Engine assembly and valve timing marks – general information and
  usage 3
Engine oil cooler – removal and refitting 19
Engine/transmission mountings – inspection and renewal 18
Flywheel/driveplate/clutch pressure plate – removal, inspection and
  refitting 16
General information 1
Hydraulic tappets – testing 11
Oil pressure relief valve – removal, inspection and refitting 20
Oil pressure warning light switch – removal and refitting 21
Oil pump and drive chain – removal, inspection and refitting 15
Pump injector rocker shaft assembly – removal and refitting 9
Sump – removal and refitting 14
Timing belt – removal, inspection and refitting 7
Timing belt covers – removal and refitting 6
Timing belt tensioner and sprockets – removal and refitting 8

Degrees of difficulty

| Easy, suitable for novice with little experience | | Fairly easy, suitable for beginner with some experience | | Fairly difficult, suitable for competent DIY mechanic | 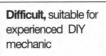 | Difficult, suitable for experienced DIY mechanic | 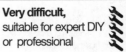 | Very difficult, suitable for expert DIY or professional |

Specifications

General

Manufacturer's engine codes*:	
1896 cc, direct injection, non-turbo	AGP and AQM
1896 cc, direct injection, turbo	AGR, AHF, ALH and ASV
1896 cc, direct injection, unit injectors, turbo	AJM, ARL, ASZ, ATD, AUY and AXR
Maximum power output:	
Engine codes AGP and AQM	50 kW at 4200 rpm
Engine code AGR	66 kW at 4000 rpm
Engine code ALH	66 kW at 3750 rpm
Engine codes AHF and ASV	81 kW at 4150 rpm
Engine codes ATD and AXR	74 kW at 4000 rpm
Engine codes AJM and AUY	85 kW at 4000 rpm
Engine code ASZ	96 kW at 4000 rpm
Engine code ARL	110 kW at 4000 rpm
Maximum torque output:	
Engine codes AGP and AQM	133 Nm at 2200 to 2600 rpm
Engine codes AGR and ALH	210 Nm at 1900 rpm
Engine codes AHF and ASV	235 Nm at 1900 rpm
Engine codes ATD and AXR	240 Nm at 1800 to 2400 rpm
Engine code AJM	285 Nm at 1900 rpm
Engine codes ASZ and AUY	310 Nm at 1900 rpm
Engine code ARL	320 Nm at 1900 rpm
Bore	79.5 mm
Stroke	95.5 mm
Compression ratio:	
AGP, AQM, AGR, AHF, ALH, ASV and ARL	19.5 : 1
ASZ, ATD and AXR	19.0 : 1
AJM and AUY	18.0 : 1
Compression pressures:	
Minimum compression pressure	Approximately 19.0 bar
Maximum difference between cylinders	Approximately 5.0 bar
Firing order	1 – 3 – 4 – 2
No 1 cylinder location	Timing belt end

* **Note:** See 'Vehicle identification' at the end of this manual for the location of engine code markings.

Camshaft

Camshaft endfloat (maximum)	0.15 mm
Camshaft bearing running clearance (maximum)	0.11 mm
Camshaft run-out (maximum)	0.01 mm

Lubrication system

Oil pump type	Gear type, chain-driven from crankshaft
Oil pressure (oil temperature 80°C, at 2000 rpm)	2.0 bar

Torque wrench settings

	Nm	lbf ft
Ancillary (alternator, etc) bracket mounting bolts	45	33
Auxiliary drivebelt tensioner securing bolt:		
All engines except codes AGP and AQM	25	18
Big-end bearing caps bolts*:		
Stage 1	30	22
Stage 2	Angle-tighten a further 90°	
Camshaft bearing cap nuts:		
Engine codes AGP, AQM, AGR, AHF, ALH and ASV	20	15
Camshaft bearing cap bolts*:		
Engine codes AJM, ARL, ASZ, ATD, AUY and AXR:		
Stage 1	8	6
Stage 2	Angle-tighten a further 90°	
Camshaft cover nuts/bolts	10	7
Camshaft sprocket centre bolt:		
Engine codes AGP, AQM, AGR, AHF, ALH and ASV	45	33
Engine codes AJM, ARL, ASZ, ATD, AUY and AXR	100	74
Camshaft sprocket outer bolts:		
Engine codes AJM, ARL, ASZ, ATD, AUY and AXR	25	18
Clutch pressure plate/driveplate mounting bolts*:		
Engine codes AGP and AQM:		
Stage 1	60	44
Stage 2	Angle-tighten a further 90°	
Coolant pump bolts	15	11
Crankshaft oil seal housing bolts	15	11
Crankshaft pulley bolts:		
Stage 1	10	7
Stage 2	Angle-tighten a further 90°	
Crankshaft speed/position sensor wheel-to-crankshaft bolts*:		
Stage 1	10	7
Stage 2	Angle-tighten a further 90°	
Crankshaft sprocket bolt*:		
Stage 1	120	89
Stage 2	Angle-tighten a further 90°	
Cylinder head bolts*:		
Stage 1	40	30
Stage 2	60	44
Stage 3	Angle-tighten a further 90°	
Stage 4	Angle-tighten a further 90°	
Engine mountings:		
Left-hand mounting-to-body bolts:		
Large bolts*:		
Stage 1	40	30
Stage 2	Angle-tighten a further 90°	
Small bolts	25	18
Left-hand mounting-to-transmission bolts	100	74
Right-hand mounting-to-body bolts*:		
Stage 1	40	30
Stage 2	Angle-tighten a further 90°	
Right-hand mounting plate bolts (small bolts)	25	18
Right-hand mounting-to-engine bracket bolts	100	74
Right-hand mounting bracket-to-engine bolts	45	33
Rear engine/transmission mounting:		
Bracket-to-subframe bolts*:		
Stage 1	20	15
Stage 2	Angle-tighten a further 90°	
Bracket-to-transmission bolts*:		
Stage 1	40	30
Stage 2	Angle-tighten a further 90°	

Torque wrench settings (continued)

	Nm	lbf ft
Exhaust manifold nuts	25	18
Exhaust pipe-to-manifold/turbocharger nuts	25	18
Fuel injector pipe union nuts	25	18
Glow plugs	15	11
Injector rocker arm shafts*:		
Engine codes AJM, ARL, ASZ, ATD, AUY and AXR:		
Stage 1	20	15
Stage 2	Angle-tighten a further 90°	
Injection pump sprocket bolts (see illustration 7.24):		
Type 1*:		
Stage 1	20	15
Stage 2	Angle-tighten a further 90°	
Type 2	25	18
Main bearing cap bolts*:		
Stage 1	65	48
Stage 2	Angle-tighten a further 90°	
Oil baffle-to-camshaft cover bolt:		
Engine codes AGR, AHF, ALH and ASV	5	4
Oil cooler securing plate	25	18
Oil drain plug	30	22
Oil filter housing-to-cylinder block bolts*:		
Stage 1	15	11
Stage 2	Angle-tighten a further 90°	
Oil filter cover	25	18
Oil level/temperature sensor-to-sump bolts	10	7
Oil pick-up pipe securing bolts	15	11
Oil pressure relief valve plug	40	30
Oil pressure warning light switch:		
Engine codes AGP, AQM, AGR, AHF, ALH and ASV	25	18
Engine codes AJM, ARL, ASZ, ATD, AUY and AXR	20	15
Oil pump chain tensioner bolt	15	11
Oil pump securing bolts	15	11
Oil pump sprocket securing bolt:		
Engine codes AGP, AQM, AGR, AHF, ALH and ASV	20	15
Engine codes AJM, ATD, AUY and AXR	25	18
Engine codes ARL and ASZ:		
Stage 1	20	15
Stage 2	Angle-tighten a further 90°	
Piston oil spray jet bolt	25	18
Sump:		
Sump-to-cylinder block bolts	15	11
Sump-to-transmission bolts	45	33
Timing belt idler pulley bolt:		
Engine codes AJM, ARL, ASZ, ATD, AUY and AXR	20	15
Timing belt idler pulleys:		
Lower left-hand idler roller nut:		
Engine codes AGR, AHF, ALH and ASV	22	16
Lower right-hand idler roller (below coolant pump sprocket) bolt*:		
Stage 1	40	30
Stage 2	Angle-tighten a further 90°	
Upper idler roller bolt	20	15
Timing belt outer cover bolts	10	7
Timing belt rear cover bolts:		
Cover-to-cylinder head bolt	10	7
Cover-to-injection pump bolts	30	22
Timing belt tensioner roller securing nut:		
Engine codes AGP, AQM, AGR, AHF, ALH and ASV	20	15
Engine codes AJM, ARL, ASZ, ATD, AUY and AXR:		
Stage 1	20	30
Stage 2	Angle-tighten a further 45°	
Turbocharger oil return pipe-to-cylinder block banjo bolt	40	30
Turbocharger oil supply pipe-to-oil filter housing:		
Engine codes AGP, AQM, AGR, AHF, ALH and ASV	20	15
Engine codes AJM, ARL, ASZ, ATD, AUY and AXR:		
Banjo bolt	25	18
Union nut	22	16

*Note: Use new bolts

1 General information

Using this Chapter

Chapter 2 is divided into four Parts; A, B, C and D. Repair operations that can be carried out with the engine in the vehicle are described in Part A (SOHC petrol engines), Part B (DOHC petrol engines), and Part C (diesel engines). Part D covers the removal of the engine/transmission as a unit, and describes the engine dismantling and overhaul procedures.

In Parts A, B and C, the assumption is made that the engine is installed in the vehicle, with all ancillaries connected. If the engine has been removed for overhaul, the preliminary dismantling information which precedes each operation may be ignored.

Engine description

Throughout this Chapter, engines are identified and referred to by the manufacturer's code letters. A listing of all engines covered, together with their code letters, is given in the Specifications at the start of this Chapter.

The engines are water-cooled, single overhead camshaft, in-line four-cylinder units, with cast-iron cylinder blocks and aluminium-alloy cylinder heads. All are mounted transversely at the front of the vehicle, with the transmission bolted to the left-hand end of the engine.

The crankshaft is of five-bearing type, and thrustwashers are fitted to the centre main bearing to control crankshaft endfloat.

The camshaft is driven via a toothed timing belt from the crankshaft; on engines with codes AGP, AQM, AGR, AHF, ALH and ASV the timing belt also drives the fuel injection pump. The camshaft is mounted at the top of the cylinder head, and is secured by bearing caps.

The valves are closed by coil springs, and run in guides pressed into the cylinder head. The camshaft actuates the valves directly, via hydraulic tappets.

The gear-type oil pump is driven via a chain from a sprocket on the crankshaft. Oil is drawn from the sump through a strainer, and then forced through an externally-mounted, renewable filter. From there, it is distributed to the cylinder head, where it lubricates the camshaft journals and hydraulic tappets, and also to the crankcase, where it lubricates the main bearings, connecting rod big-ends, gudgeon pins and cylinder bores. A coolant-fed oil cooler is fitted to the oil filter housing on all engines. Oil jets are fitted to the base of each cylinder – these spray oil onto the underside of the pistons, to improve cooling.

All engines are fitted with a brake servo vacuum pump driven by the camshaft on the transmission end of the cylinder head. On engines with codes AJM, ASZ, ARL, ATD, AUY and AXR a tandem pump is fitted, incorporating a vacuum pump and a fuel pump, driven by the camshaft.

On all engines, engine coolant is circulated by a pump, driven by the timing belt. For details of the cooling system, refer to Chapter 3.

Operations with engine in car

The following operations can be performed without removing the engine:

a) Compression pressure – testing.
b) Camshaft cover – removal and refitting.
c) Crankshaft pulley – removal and refitting.
d) Timing belt covers – removal and refitting.
e) Timing belt – removal, refitting and adjustment.
f) Timing belt tensioner and sprockets – removal and refitting.
g) Camshaft oil seals – renewal.
h) Camshaft and hydraulic tappets – removal, inspection and refitting.
i) Cylinder head – removal and refitting.
j) Cylinder head and pistons – decarbonising.
k) Sump – removal and refitting.
l) Oil pump – removal, overhaul and refitting.
m) Crankshaft oil seals – renewal.
n) Engine/transmission mountings – inspection and renewal.
o) Flywheel/driveplate – removal, inspection and refitting.

Note: It is possible to remove the pistons and connecting rods (after removing the cylinder head and sump) without removing the engine. However, this is not recommended. Work of this nature is more easily and thoroughly completed with the engine on the bench, as described in Chapter 2D.

2 Compression and leakdown tests – description and interpretation

Compression test

Note: A compression tester suitable for use with diesel engines will be required for this test.

1 When engine performance is down, or if misfiring occurs which cannot be attributed to the ignition or fuel systems, a compression test can provide diagnostic clues as to the engine's condition. If the test is performed regularly, it can give warning of trouble before any other symptoms become apparent.

2 The engine must be fully warmed-up to normal operating temperature, the battery must be fully-charged and you will require the aid of an assistant.

3 On non-turbo models, remove the inlet manifold upper section as described in Chapter 4B.

4 On engine codes AGP, AQM, AGR, AHF, ALH and ASV, the stop solenoid and fuel metering control wiring must be disconnected, to prevent the engine from running or fuel from being discharged **(see illustrations)**. **Note:** As a result of the wiring being disconnected, faults will be stored in the ECU memory. These must be erased after the compression test.

5 On engine codes AJM, ASZ, ARL, ATD, AUY and AXR, disconnect the injector solenoids by disconnecting the connector at the end of the cylinder head **(see illustration)**. **Note:** As a result of the wiring being disconnected, faults will be stored in the ECU memory. These must be erased after the compression test.

6 Remove the glow plugs as described in Chapter 5C, then fit a compression tester to the No 1 cylinder glow plug hole. The type of tester which screws into the plug thread is preferred.

2.4a Fuel cut-off solenoid wiring connector is secured by a nut (arrowed)

2.4b Wiring plug for fuel quantity adjuster is behind oil filter housing

2.5 Disconnect the injector solenoids wiring plug connector (arrowed)

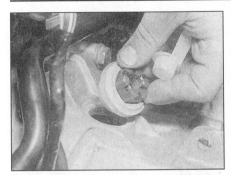

3.7a Using a large nut to unscrew the inspection plug from the transmission bellhousing

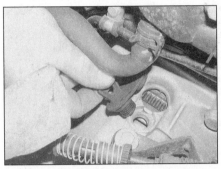

3.7b Removing the rubber bung from the bellhousing – seen with air cleaner removed

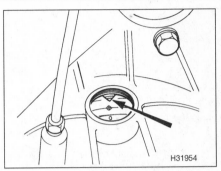

3.7c Timing mark on the edge of the flywheel (arrowed) lined up with the pointer on the bellhousing casing (manual transmission)

7 Have your assistant, crank the engine for several seconds on the starter motor. After one or two revolutions, the compression pressure should build-up to a maximum figure and then stabilise. Record the highest reading obtained.

8 Repeat the test on the remaining cylinders, recording the pressure in each.

9 The cause of poor compression is less easy to establish on a diesel engine than on a petrol engine. The effect of introducing oil into the cylinders (wet testing) is not conclusive, because there is a risk that the oil will sit in the recess on the piston crown, instead of passing to the rings. However, the following can be used as a rough guide to diagnosis.

10 All cylinders should produce very similar pressures. Any difference greater than that specified indicates the existence of a fault. Note that the compression should build-up quickly in a healthy engine. Low compression on the first stroke, followed by gradually increasing pressure on successive strokes, indicates worn piston rings. A low compression reading on the first stroke, which does not build-up during successive strokes, indicates leaking valves or a blown head gasket (a cracked head could also be the cause).

11 A low reading from two adjacent cylinders is almost certainly due to the head gasket having blown between them and the presence of coolant in the engine oil will confirm this.

12 On completion, remove the compression tester, and refit the glow plugs, with reference to Chapter 5C.

13 Reconnect the fuel quantity adjuster and fuel cut-off solenoid wiring connectors, and (where applicable) refit the inlet manifold upper section as described in Chapter 4B.

Leakdown test

14 A leakdown test measures the rate at which compressed air fed into the cylinder is lost. It is an alternative to a compression test, and in many ways it is better, since the escaping air provides easy identification of where pressure loss is occurring (piston rings, valves or head gasket).

15 The equipment required for leakdown testing is unlikely to be available to the home mechanic. If poor compression is suspected,

have the test performed by a suitably-equipped garage.

---

3 Engine assembly and valve timing marks – general information and usage

General information

1 TDC is the highest point in the cylinder that each piston reaches as it travels up-and-down when the crankshaft turns. Each piston reaches TDC at the end of the compression stroke and again at the end of the exhaust stroke, but TDC generally refers to piston position on the compression stroke. No 1 piston is at the timing belt end of the engine.

2 Positioning No 1 piston at TDC is an essential part of many procedures, such as timing belt removal and camshaft removal.

3 The design of the engines covered in this Chapter is such that piston-to-valve contact may occur if the camshaft or crankshaft is turned with the timing belt removed. For this reason, it is important to ensure that the camshaft and crankshaft do not move in relation to each other once the timing belt has been removed from the engine.

Setting TDC on No 1 cylinder

Engine codes
AGP, AQM, AGR, AHF, ALH and ASV

Note: *Suitable tools will be required to lock the camshaft and the fuel injection pump*

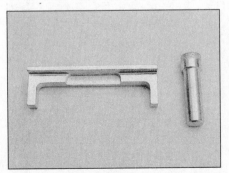

3.9 Camshaft and fuel injection sprocket locking tools

sprocket in position during this procedure – see text.

4 Remove the camshaft cover as described in Section 4.

5 Remove the upper outer timing belt cover as described in Section 6.

6 Remove the glow plugs, as described in Chapter 5C, to allow the engine to turn more easily.

7 Where fitted, remove the inspection plug from the transmission bellhousing, if necessary using a large nut to unscrew it **(see illustrations)**. Access to the inspection plug is greatly improved if the air cleaner is removed first, as described in Chapter 4B.

8 Rotate the crankshaft clockwise, using a socket or spanner on the crankshaft sprocket bolt, until the timing mark machined onto the edge of the flywheel/driveplate lines up with the pointer on the transmission casing **and** the timing hole in the fuel injection sprocket lines up with the hole in the support bracket.

9 To lock the engine in the TDC position, the camshaft (not the sprocket) and fuel injection pump sprocket must be locked in position, using special locking tools. Improvised tools may be fabricated, but due to the exact measurements and machining involved, it is strongly recommended that a kit of locking tools is either borrowed or hired from a VW dealer, or purchased from a reputable tool manufacturer **(see illustration)**.

10 Engage the edge of the locking bar (VW tool 3418) with the slot in the end of the camshaft **(see illustrations)**.

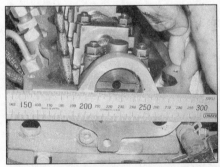

3.10a Using a straight-edge to assess alignment of the camshaft slot with the head

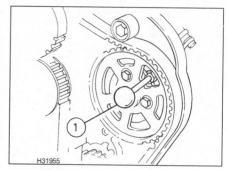

3.10b Engage the locking bar with the slot in the camshaft

3.12 Camshaft centred and locked using the locking bar and feeler blades

3.13 Injection pump sprocket locked using the locking pin (1)

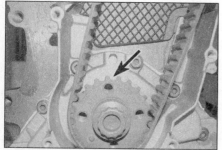
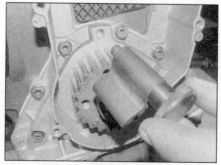

3.19a Position the crankshaft so that the mark on the sprocket is almost vertical (arrowed) . . .

3.19b . . . then insert the VW tool T10050 . . .

3.19c . . . and align the marks (arrowed) on the tool and sprocket

11 With the locking bar still inserted, turn the camshaft slightly (by turning the crankshaft clockwise, as before), so that the locking bar rocks to one side, allowing one end of the bar to contact the cylinder head surface. At the other side of the locking bar, measure the gap between the end of the bar and the cylinder head using a feeler blade.

12 Turn the camshaft back slightly, then pull out the feeler blade. The idea now is to level the locking bar by inserting two feeler blades, each with a thickness equal to *half* the originally measured gap, on either side of the camshaft between each end of the locking bar and the cylinder head. This centres the camshaft, and sets the valve timing in reference condition **(see illustration)**.

13 Insert the locking pin (VW tool 3359) through the fuel injection pump sprocket

timing hole, so that it passes through the timing hole in the injection pump hub, and into the support bracket behind the hub. This locks the fuel injection pump in the TDC reference position **(see illustration)**.

14 The engine is now set to TDC on No 1 cylinder.

Engine codes AJM, ARL, ASZ, ATD, AUY and AXR

Note: VAG special tool (T10050) is required to lock the crankshaft sprocket in the TDC position.

15 Remove the auxiliary drivebelt(s) as described in Chapter 1B.

16 Remove the crankshaft pulley/vibration damper as described in Section 5.

17 Remove the timing belt covers as described in Section 6.

18 Remove the glow plugs, as described in Chapter 5C, to allow the engine to turn more easily.

19 Using a spanner or socket on the crankshaft sprocket bolt, turn the crankshaft in the normal direction of rotation (clockwise) until the alignment mark on the face of the sprocket is almost vertical **(see illustrations)**.

20 The arrow (marked 4Z) on the rear section of the upper timing belt upper cover aligns between the two lugs on the rear of the camshaft hub sender wheel **(see illustration)**.

21 While in this position it should be possible to insert VAG tool T10050 to lock the crankshaft, and 6 mm diameter rod to lock the camshaft **(see illustration)**. *Note: The mark on the crankshaft sprocket and the mark on the VAG tool T10050 must align, whilst at the same time the shaft of tool T10050 must engage in the drilling in the crankshaft oil seal housing.*

22 The engine is now set to TDC on No 1 cylinder.

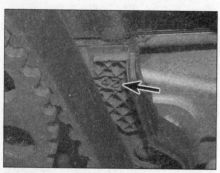

3.20 Align the arrow on the rear of the timing belt cover (arrowed) between the lugs on the rear of the camshaft hub sender wheel

3.21 Insert a 6 mm drill bit (arrowed) through the camshaft hub into the cylinder head to lock the camshaft

4 Camshaft cover – removal and refitting

Removal

Engine codes AGP, AQM, AGR, AHF, ALH and ASV

1 Remove the engine top cover(s). Removal details vary according to model, but the cover retaining nuts are concealed under circular

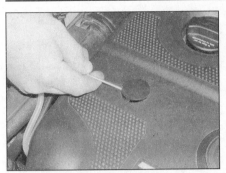

4.1a Prise out the covers . . .

4.1b . . . remove the nuts beneath . . .

4.1c . . . on this engine, the dipstick has to be removed . . .

4.1d . . . before the cover can be lifted off

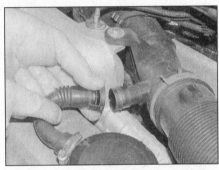

4.3 Disconnecting the pressure-regulating valve breather hose

4.4a Unscrew the retaining bolts . . .

covers, which are prised out of the main cover. Where plastic screws or turn-fasteners are used, these can be removed using a wide-bladed screwdriver. Remove the nuts or screws, and lift the cover from the engine, releasing any wiring or hoses attached **(see illustrations)**.

2 On engines with codes AGP and AQM, remove the upper section of the inlet manifold, as described in Chapter 4B.

3 Disconnect the breather hose from the air inlet duct **(see illustration)**. If wished, the breather valve can be removed from the top of the camshaft cover by carefully pulling upwards, but its removal is not essential.

4 Unscrew the securing nuts/bolts, and lift the camshaft cover from the cylinder head **(see illustrations)**. On most models, the bolts

at the rear are very awkward to reach – a selection of Allen keys/bits and a knuckle joint may well be needed. Recover the gasket if it is loose.

Engine codes
AJM, ARL, ASZ, ATD, AUY and AXR

5 Remove the dipstick and prise off and remove the engine top cover, then disconnect the breather hose from the camshaft cover **(see illustration)**.

6 Unscrew the camshaft cover retaining bolts and lift the cover away. If it sticks, do not attempt to lever it off – instead free it by working around the cover and tapping it lightly with a soft-faced mallet.

7 Recover the camshaft cover gasket **(see illustration)**. Inspect the gasket carefully, and renew it if damage or deterioration is evident.

8 Clean the mating surfaces of the cylinder head and camshaft cover thoroughly, removing all traces of oil and old gasket – take care to avoid damaging the surfaces as you do this.

Refitting

9 Refit the camshaft cover by following the removal procedure in reverse, noting the following points:

a) *On engine codes AGP, AQM, AGR, AHF, ALH and ASV, before refitting the camshaft cover, apply a small amount of sealant at the front and rear of the cylinder head, to the two points where the camshaft bearing caps contact the cylinder head (see illustration). Ensure that the gasket is correctly seated on the cylinder head, and take care to avoid*

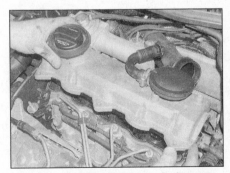

4.4b . . . and lift off the camshaft cover

4.5 One of the cover locating pegs (arrowed) and also breather pipe (arrowed)

4.7 The camshaft cover gasket locates in a groove in the cover

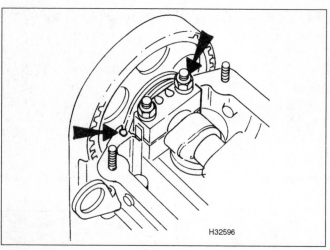

4.9a Apply sealant to the rear and front (arrowed) bearing cap joints

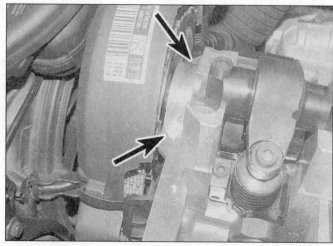

4.9b Apply sealant to the points (arrowed) on the cylinder head

displacing it as the camshaft cover is lowered into position.
b) *On engine codes AJM, ARL, ASZ, ATD, AUY and AXR, apply suitable sealant to the points where the camshaft bearing cap contacts the cylinder head (see illustration).*

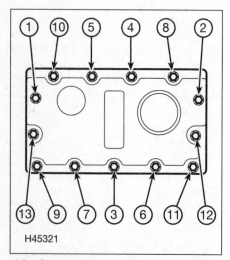

4.9c Camshaft cover tightening sequence

c) *Tighten the camshaft cover retaining nuts/bolts progressively to the specified torque.* **Note:** *On engine codes AJM, ARL, ASZ, ATD, AUY and AXR, tighten the retaining nuts/bolts in sequence (see illustration).*

5 Crankshaft pulley – removal and refitting

Removal

1 Disconnect the battery negative lead. **Note:** *Before disconnecting the battery, refer to 'Disconnecting the battery' at the rear of this manual.*
2 For improved access, raise the front right-hand side of the vehicle, and support securely on axle stands (see *Jacking and vehicle support*). Remove the roadwheel.
3 Remove the securing screws and withdraw the engine undershield(s) and/or wheel arch liner panels. On turbo models, unscrew the nut at the rear, and the washer-type fasteners further forward, then release the air hose clip and manipulate out the plastic air duct for the intercooler **(see illustration)**.

4 Where applicable, prise the cover from the centre of the pulley to expose the securing bolts **(see illustration)**.
5 Slacken the bolts securing the crankshaft pulley to the sprocket **(see illustration)**. If necessary, the pulley can be prevented from turning by counterholding with a spanner or socket on the crankshaft sprocket bolt.
6 Remove the auxiliary drivebelt, as described in Chapter 1B.
7 Unscrew the bolts securing the pulley to the sprocket, and remove the pulley.

Refitting

8 Refit the pulley over the locating peg on the crankshaft sprocket, then refit the pulley securing bolts.
9 Refit and tension the auxiliary drivebelt as described in Chapter 1B.
10 Prevent the crankshaft from turning as during removal, then fit the pulley securing bolts, and tighten to the specified torque.
11 Refit the engine undershield(s), wheel arch liners and the intercooler air duct, as applicable.
12 Refit the roadwheel, lower the vehicle to the ground, and reconnect the battery negative lead.

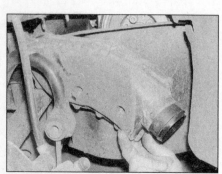

5.3 Removing the intercooler air duct for access to the crankshaft pulley

5.4 Prising out the crankshaft pulley centre cap

5.5 Showing the four crankshaft pulley bolts (arrowed)

6.1 Removing the air intake hose from across the top of the timing belt cover

6.2a Release the retaining clips (one arrowed) . . .

6.2b . . . and withdraw the upper cover

6 Timing belt covers – removal and refitting

Upper outer cover

1 Where applicable, release the retaining clips and remove the air intake hose from across the top of the timing belt cover **(see illustration)**.

2 Release the uppermost part of the timing belt outer cover by prising open the metal spring clips, then withdraw the cover away from the engine **(see illustrations)**.

3 Refitting is a reversal of removal, noting that the lower edge of the upper cover engages with the centre cover.

Centre outer cover

4 Remove the auxiliary drivebelt as described in Chapter 1B.

5 Remove the crankshaft pulley as described in Section 5. It is assumed that, if the centre cover is being removed, the lower cover will be also – if not, simply remove the components described in Section 5 for access to the crankshaft pulley, and leave the pulley in position.

6 With the upper cover removed (paragraphs 1 to 3), unscrew and remove the retaining bolts from the centre cover. Withdraw the centre cover from the engine, noting how it fits over the lower cover.

7 Refitting is a reversal of removal.

Lower outer cover

8 Remove the upper and centre covers as described previously.

9 If not already done, remove the crankshaft pulley as described in Section 5.

10 Unscrew the remaining bolt(s) securing the lower cover, and lift it out.

11 Refitting is a reversal of removal; locate the centre cover in place before fitting the top two bolts.

Rear cover

12 Remove the upper, centre and lower covers as described previously.

13 Remove the timing belt, tensioner and sprockets as described in Sections 7 and 8.

14 Slacken and withdraw the retaining bolts and lift the timing belt inner cover from the studs on the end of the engine, and remove it from the engine compartment.

15 Refitting is a reversal of removal.

7 Timing belt – removal, inspection and refitting

Removal

1 The primary function of the toothed timing belt is to drive the camshaft, but it also drives the coolant pump. On engine codes AGP, AQM, AGR, AHF, ALH and ASV it also drives the fuel injection pump. Should the belt slip or break in service, the valve timing will be disturbed and piston-to-valve contact may occur, resulting in serious engine damage. For this reason, it is important that the timing belt is tensioned correctly, and inspected regularly for signs of wear or deterioration.

2 Disconnect the battery negative lead. **Note:** *Before disconnecting the battery, refer to 'Disconnecting the battery' at the rear of this manual.*

3 On turbo models, remove the right-hand headlight as described in Chapter 12, Section 7, and the inlet manifold-to-intercooler air trunking as described in Chapter 4D.

4 Apply the handbrake, then jack up the front of the vehicle and support securely on axle stands (see *Jacking and vehicle support*).

5 Remove the securing screws and withdraw the engine undershield(s), and the right-hand wheel arch liner.

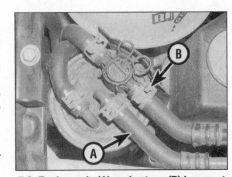

7.8 Fuel supply (A) and return (B) hoses at the fuel filter

6 Remove the complete right-hand engine mounting assembly, with reference to Section 18. Also, unbolt the mounting bracket from the cylinder block.

7 Remove the auxiliary drivebelt as described in Chapter 1B.

8 Disconnect the fuel supply and return hoses from the fuel filter, referring to Chapter 1B if necessary **(see illustration)**. Label the hoses if necessary, to ensure correct refitting.

9 If required, to further improve working room, remove the windscreen washer bottle, as described in Chapter 12.

10 Remove the timing belt covers, as described in Section 6.

Engine codes AGP, AQM, AGR, AHF, ALH and ASV

11 Remove the camshaft cover as described in Section 4.

12 Remove the brake servo vacuum pump as described in Chapter 9.

13 Turn the crankshaft to position No 1 piston at TDC on the firing stroke, and lock the camshaft and the fuel injection sprocket in position, as described in Section 3.

14 If the original timing belt is to be refitted, mark the running direction of the belt, to ensure correct refitting.

Caution: If the belt appears to be in good condition and can be re-used, it is essential that it is refitted the same way around, otherwise accelerated wear will result, leading to premature failure.

15 Slacken the timing belt tensioner nut, and allow the tensioner to rotate anti-clockwise, relieving the tension on the timing belt.

16 Slide the belt from the sprockets, taking care not to twist or kink the belt excessively if it is to be re-used.

Engine codes AJM, ARL, ASZ, ATD, AUY and AXR

Note: *VAG technicians use special tool T10008 to lock the timing belt tensioner in the released position. It is possible to manufacture a home-made alternative – see below.*

17 Set the engine to TDC on No 1 cylinder as described in Section 3.

18 Undo the bolt and remove the idler roller **(see illustration)**.

19 With reference to Section 8, relieve the tension on the timing belt by slackening the

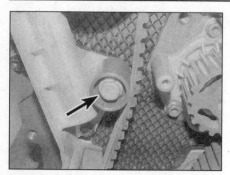

7.18 Undo the retaining bolt (arrowed) and remove the idler roller

7.19b . . . then insert the locking tool through the slot to lock the tensioner . . .

7.19a Turn the tensioner arm anti-clockwise until it contacts the stop (A) . . .

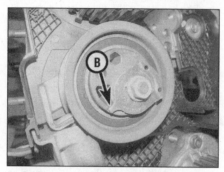

7.19c . . . and turn the tensioner arm clockwise until it contacts the stop (B)

tensioner mounting nut slightly, and turning the tensioner anti-clockwise with circlip pliers until it contacts the stop (A). It may take a few moments for the tensioner plunger to fully compress. Lock the plunger by inserting a locking plate (VAG tool No T10008). If this special tool is not available, an alternative can be manufactured by copying the design **(see illustrations)**. Now turn the tensioner clockwise onto stop (B) **(see illustration)**.

20 Examine the timing belt for manufacturer's markings that indicate the direction of rotation. If none are present, make your own using typist's correction fluid or a dab of paint – do not cut or score the belt in any way.

Caution: If the belt appears to be in good condition and can be re-used, it is essential that it is refitted the same way around, otherwise accelerated wear will result, leading to premature failure.

21 Slide the belt off the sprockets, taking care to avoid twisting or kinking it excessively if it is to be re-used.

Inspection

22 Examine the belt for evidence of contamination by coolant or lubricant. If this is the case, find the source of the contamination before progressing any further. Check the belt for signs of wear or damage, particularly around the leading edges of the belt teeth. Renew the belt if its condition is in doubt; the cost of belt renewal is negligible compared with potential cost of the engine repairs, should the belt fail in service. The belt must be renewed if it has covered the mileage given in Chapter 1B, however, if it has covered less, it is prudent to renew it regardless of condition, as a precautionary measure.

23 If the timing belt is not going to be refitted for some time, it is a wise precaution to hang a warning label on the steering wheel, to remind yourself (and others) not to attempt to start the engine.

24 On engine codes AGP, AQM, AGR, AHF, ALH and ASV, the bolts securing the injection pump sprocket to the hub may have to be renewed. There are two different types of bolts fitted **(see illustration)** the stretch-type of bolt (1), requires angle-tightening and it is for this reason that they cannot be re-used once loosened. VW state that the pump sprocket **must** be reset each time the timing belt is removed – it is not acceptable to simply refit the belt to the sprocket without carrying out the resetting procedure. Where applicable, obtain three new bolts before commencing the refitting procedure.

Refitting

Engine codes
AGP, AQM, AGR, AHF, ALH and ASV

25 Ensure that the crankshaft and camshaft are still set to TDC on No 1 cylinder, as described in Section 3.

26 Refer to Section 8, and slacken the camshaft sprocket bolt by half-a-turn. Do not use the timing locking bar to hold the camshaft stationary; it must be removed before loosening the sprocket bolt. Release the sprocket from the camshaft taper mounting by carefully tapping it with a soft metal drift inserted through the hole provided in the timing belt rear cover **(see illustration)**. Refit the timing locking bar (see Section 3) once the sprocket has been released.

27 Unscrew the three bolts securing the fuel injection pump sprocket to the hub on the injection pump **(see illustration)**, and screw the three bolts into position **(see illustration 7.24)** – **do not** tighten the bolts at this stage. Position the injection pump sprocket so that the securing bolts are central in the elongated holes.

⚠ *Warning: Do not loosen the injection pump sprocket central nut, otherwise the basic setting of*

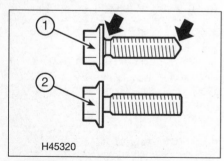

7.24 Different types of injection pump sprocket retaining bolts – Type 1 bolt is a stretch bolt and must always be renewed

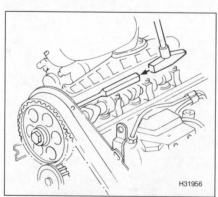

7.26 Releasing the camshaft sprocket from the taper using soft metal drift

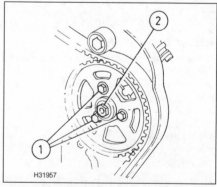

7.27 Unscrew the three bolts (1) securing the fuel injection pump to the injection pump hub

DO NOT unscrew the central nut (2)

7.28 The timing belt must locate under the upper idler pulley

the injection pump will be lost, and it will require resetting by a VW dealer.

28 Fit the timing belt around the crankshaft sprocket, idler pulley, coolant pump sprocket, injection pump sprocket, camshaft sprocket, and tensioner. Where applicable, ensure that the running direction markings made on the belt during removal are observed. Make sure that the belt teeth seat correctly on the sprockets. The upper belt run must be located beneath the small upper idler pulley (it may be necessary to adjust the position of the camshaft sprocket slightly to achieve this), and the belt run between the tensioner and crankshaft sprocket should be located to the right of the lower small idler pulley (when viewed from the timing belt end of the engine) **(see illustration)**.

29 Check that the fuel injection pump sprocket is still positioned centrally in the elongated holes.

30 Ensure that any slack in the belt is in the section which passes over the tensioner.

31 Check that the tensioner is seated correctly, with the lug on the backplate positioned in the slot in the rear timing belt cover.

32 On engines with codes AGR, AHF, ALH and ASV, engage a suitable tool, such as a pair of angled circlip pliers, with the two holes in the belt tensioner hub, then turn the tensioner clockwise until the notch on the hub is aligned with the raised tab on the backplate **(see illustration)**. **Note:** *If the tensioner is turned too far clockwise, it must be completely slackened off before retensioning.* With the tensioner marks aligned, tighten the tensioner nut to the specified torque.

33 On engines with codes AGP and AQM, engage a suitable Allen key or hexagon bit with the hole in the tensioner hub, and turn the tensioner clockwise until the indicator is aligned with the centre of the notch in the backplate **(see illustration)**. **Note:** *If the tensioner is turned too far clockwise, it must be completely slackened off before retensioning.* With the tensioner marks aligned, tighten the tensioner nut to the specified torque.

34 Check that the crankshaft is still set to TDC on No 1 cylinder, as described in Section 3.

35 Refer to Section 8, and tighten the camshaft sprocket bolt to the specified torque. Do not use the timing locking bar to

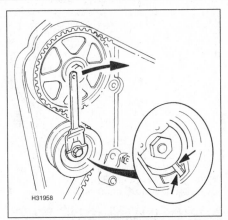

7.32 Turn the tensioner clockwise until the notch on the hub is aligned with the raised tab on the backplate – engine codes AGR, AHF, ALH and ASV

hold the camshaft stationary; it must be removed before tightening the sprocket bolt. Refit the timing locking bar (see Section 3) once the sprocket bolt has been tightened.

36 Tighten the fuel injection pump sprocket bolts to the specified torque. On models with stretch type bolts (see paragraph 24) tighten the bolts to Stage 1 torque setting, whilst holding the sprocket stationary. Volkswagen recommend that the bolts are tightened to the final Stage 2 setting only after checking the dynamic timing of the injection pump (see Chapter 4B, Section 7) – however, this requires the use of special VW equipment. If the dynamic timing will be checked later, tighten the bolts securely, but not to the full Stage 2 angle (the engine *can* be run with the bolts tightened to the Stage 1 setting only).

37 Remove the timing locking bar from the camshaft, and remove the timing pin from the fuel injection pump sprocket.

38 Turn the engine through two complete turns in the normal direction of rotation, until the timing locking bar and timing pin can be re-inserted to set the engine at TDC on No 1 cylinder (see Section 3).

39 Check that the timing belt tensioner notch and raised tab (engine codes AGR, AHF, ALH and ASV) or indicator and notch (engine codes AGP and AQM) are aligned as described in paragraphs 32 and 33 respectively. If the tensioner marks align, proceed to paragraph 41.

40 If the timing belt tensioner marks are not aligned, repeat the tensioning procedure described in paragraphs 31 to 33, then repeat the checking procedure in paragraphs 38 and 39.

41 Refit the right-hand engine mounting bracket to the cylinder block and tighten the bolts to the specified torque. Refit the right-hand engine mounting assembly , with reference to Section 18, then disconnect the hoist and lifting tackle from the engine.

42 Refit the centre and lower outer timing belt covers, with reference to Section 6.

43 Refit the crankshaft pulley, with reference to Section 5.

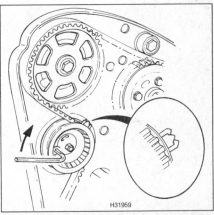

7.33 Turn the tensioner clockwise until the indicator is aligned with the centre of the notch in the backplate – engine codes AGP and AQM

44 If not already done, remove the tools used to lock the camshaft and fuel injection pump sprocket in position with No 1 piston at TDC.

45 Further refitting is a reversal of the removal procedure. On completion, Volkswagen recommend that the dynamic injection timing is checked using their dedicated test equipment. Once the dynamic timing has been checked, the fuel injection pump sprocket bolts can be tightened fully to their Stage 2 torque setting, where applicable, and the upper outer timing belt cover can be refitted.

46 Refit the splash guard under the engine compartment, then lower the vehicle to the ground. Also refit the engine top cover.

47 Reconnect the battery negative (earth) lead (see Chapter 5A).

Engine codes AJM, ARL, ASZ, ATD, AUY and AXR

48 Ensure that the crankshaft and camshaft are still set to TDC on No 1 cylinder, as described in Section 3.

49 Carefully turn the crankshaft anti-clockwise 90°, to eliminate the possibility of accidental piston-to-valve contact. Refer to Section 5 and slacken the camshaft sprocket bolts by half a turn.

50 Position the camshaft sprocket so that the securing bolts are in the centre part of the elongated holes **(see illustration)**. Turn the crankshaft clockwise, back to the TDC position.

7.50 Position the camshaft sprocket so that the securing bolts are in the centre part of the elongated holes

7.53 Refit the idler roller

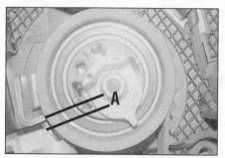

7.55 The gap between the top edge of the tensioner housing and the tensioner back plate arm (A) must be 4 mm

51 Loop the timing belt loosely under the crankshaft sprocket. **Note:** *Observe any direction of rotation markings on the belt.*

52 Engage the timing belt teeth with the camshaft sprocket, then manoeuvre it into position around the tensioning roller, crankshaft sprocket, and finally around the coolant pump sprocket. Make sure that the belt teeth seat correctly on the sprockets. **Note:** *Slight adjustment to the position of the camshaft sprocket may be necessary to achieve this.* Avoid bending the belt back on itself or twisting it excessively as you do this.

53 Refit the idler roller and tighten the bolt to the specified torque **(see illustration)**.

54 Ensure that any slack in the belt is in the section of belt that passes over the tensioner roller.

55 Using a suitable tool (eg, circlip pliers) engaged with the two holes in the tensioner hub, turn the tensioner pulley anti-clockwise until the locking plate (T10008) is no longer under tension and can be removed. Turn the tensioner in a clockwise direction until gap of 4 mm exists between the tensioner backplate arm and the top edge of the tensioner housing **(see illustration)**.

56 With the tensioner held in this position, tighten the locknut to the specified torque.

57 Tighten the camshaft sprocket bolts to the specified torque, remove the sprocket locking pin and the crankshaft locking tool.

58 Using a spanner or wrench and socket on the crankshaft pulley centre bolt, rotate the crankshaft through two complete revolutions. Reset the engine to TDC on No 1 cylinder, with reference to Section 3 and check that the

8.2 Timing belt tensioner nut (arrowed)

camshaft sprocket locking pin (3359 or 6 mm rod) can still be inserted, and that the correct gap still exists between the tensioner backplate arm and top edge of the tensioner housing **(see illustration 7.55)**. If the tensioner gap is incorrect, carry out the tensioning procedure again (paragraphs 55 and 56). If the camshaft sprocket locking pin cannot be inserted, slacken the retaining bolts, turn the **hub** until the pin fits, and tighten the sprocket retaining bolts to the specified torque.

59 Refit the lower timing belt cover and the auxiliary drivebelt drive pulley. Note that the offset of the pulley mounting holes allows only one fitting position – tighten the bolts to the specified torque.

60 Install the centre timing belt cover, and where applicable, refit the bolts/nuts securing the fuel coolant pipes.

61 Refit the auxiliary drivebelt tensioner, and the timing belt upper cover.

62 With reference to Chapter 1B, refit the auxiliary drivebelt.

63 Refit the splash guard under the engine compartment, then lower the vehicle to the ground. Also refit the engine top cover.

64 Reconnect the battery negative (earth) lead.

8 Timing belt tensioner and sprockets – removal, inspection and refitting

Timing belt tensioner removal

1 Remove the timing belt as described in Section 7.

Engine codes
AGP, AQM, AGR, AHF, ALH and ASV

2 Unscrew the timing belt tensioner nut, and remove the tensioner from the engine **(see illustration)**.

3 When refitting the tensioner to the engine, ensure that the lug on the tensioner backplate engages with the corresponding cut-out in the rear timing belt cover, then refit the tensioner nut **(see illustration)**.

Engine codes
AJM, ARL, ASZ, ATD, AUY and AXR

4 Relieve the tension on the timing belt by

slackening the tensioner mounting nut slightly, and turning the tensioner anti-clockwise with circlip pliers until it contacts the stop (A). It may take a few moments for the tensioner plunger to fully compress. Lock the plunger by inserting a locking plate (VAG tool No T10008). If this special tool is not available, an alternative can be manufactured by copying the design. Now turn the tensioner clockwise onto stop (B) **(see illustrations 7.19a, 7.19b and 7.19c)**.

5 Undo the retaining nut fully, and remove the tensioner pulley.

6 To remove the tensioner plunger and housing assembly, remove the right-hand cover, and the tensioner housing retaining bolts.

Timing belt tensioner refitting

7 Refit and tension the timing belt as described in Section 7.

Idler pulleys

Note: *On engine codes AGP, AQM, AGR, AHF, ALH and ASV, if the lower right-hand idler pulley is removed, a new securing bolt will be required on refitting.*

8 Remove the timing belt as described in Section 7.

9 Unscrew the relevant idler pulley securing bolt/nut, then withdraw the pulley.

10 Refit the pulley and tighten the securing bolt (where applicable, use a new bolt when refitting the lower right-hand pulley) or nut to the specified torque.

11 Refit and tension the timing belt as described in Section 7.

Crankshaft sprocket

Note: *A new crankshaft sprocket securing bolt must be used on refitting.*

12 Remove the timing belt as described in Section 7.

13 The sprocket securing bolt must now be slackened, and the crankshaft must be prevented from turning as the sprocket bolt is unscrewed. To hold the sprocket, make up a suitable tool, and screw it to the sprocket using a two bolts screwed into two of the crankshaft pulley bolt holes.

14 Hold the sprocket using the tool, then slacken the sprocket securing bolt. Take care,

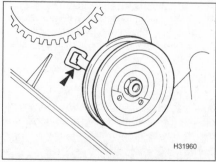

8.3 Ensure that the lug on the tensioner backplate engages with the cut-out in the rear timing belt cover

8.17 Fitting a new crankshaft sprocket securing bolt

8.22 Removing the camshaft sprocket

8.28 Using a fabricated tool to counterhold the camshaft hub

as the bolt is very tight. **Do not** allow the crankshaft to turn as the bolt is slackened.

15 Unscrew the bolt, and slide the sprocket from the end of the crankshaft, noting which way round the sprocket's raised boss is fitted.

16 Commence refitting by positioning the sprocket on the end of the crankshaft, with the raised boss fitted as noted on removal.

17 Fit a new sprocket securing bolt, then counterhold the sprocket using the method employed on removal, and tighten the bolt to the specified torque in the two stages given in the Specifications **(see illustration)**.

18 Refit the timing belt as described in Section 7.

Camshaft sprocket removal

19 Remove the timing belt as described in Section 7.

20 The camshaft sprocket bolt(s) must now be slackened. Do not use the timing locking bar to hold the camshaft stationary; it must be removed before loosening the sprocket bolt. In order to eliminate any possibility of accidental piston-to-valve contact, turn the crankshaft 90° anti-clockwise so that all the pistons are halfway up the cylinder bore.

Engine codes
AGP, AQM, AGR, AHF, ALH and ASV

21 With the sprocket bolt loosened, release the sprocket from the camshaft taper mounting by carefully tapping it with a soft metal drift inserted through the hole provided in the timing belt rear cover. Refit the timing locking bar (see Section 3) once the sprocket has been released.

22 Unscrew the sprocket bolt and withdraw it, then withdraw the sprocket from the end of the camshaft, noting which way round it is fitted **(see illustration)**.

Engine codes
AJM, ARL, ASZ, ATD, AUY and AXR

23 Unscrew and remove the three retaining bolts and remove the camshaft sprocket from the camshaft hub.

Camshaft sprocket refitting

24 Refit the sprocket ensuring that it is fitted the correct way round, as noted before removal.

25 Refit the sprocket bolt(s), and tighten by hand only at this stage.

26 If the crankshaft has been turned (see paragraph 20) turn the crankshaft clockwise 90° back to TDC. Refit and tension the timing belt as described in Section 7.

Camshaft hub

Engine codes
AJM, ARL, ASZ, ATD, AUY and AXR

Note: *VAG technicians use special tool T10051 to counterhold the hub, however it is possible to fabricate a suitable alternative – see below.*

27 Remove the camshaft sprocket as described in this Section.

28 Engage special tool T10051 with the three locating holes in the face of the hub to prevent the hub from turning. If this tool is not available, fabricate a suitable alternative. Whilst holding the tool, undo the central hub retaining bolt about two turns **(see illustration)**.

29 Leaving the central hub retaining bolt in place, attach VW tool T10052 (or a similar three-legged puller) to the hub, and evenly tighten the puller until the hub is free of the camshaft taper **(see illustration)**.

30 Ensure that the camshaft taper and the hub centre is clean and dry, locate the hub on the taper, noting that the built-in key in the hub taper must align with the key way in the camshaft taper **(see illustration)**.

31 Hold the hub in this position with tool T10051 (or similar home-made tool), and tighten the central bolt to the specified torque.

32 The remainder of refitting is a reversal of removal.

Fuel injection pump sprocket

Engine codes
AGP, AQM, AGR, AHF, ALH and ASV

Note: *New fuel injection pump sprocket securing bolts will be required on refitting.*

33 Remove the timing belt as described in Section 7.

34 Unscrew and remove the three bolts securing the fuel injection pump sprocket to the hub on the injection pump. The bolts can be discarded, as new bolts must be used on refitting.

⚠ **Warning: Do not loosen the injection pump sprocket central nut, otherwise the basic setting of the injection pump will be lost, and it will require resetting by a VW dealer.**

35 Temporarily remove the tool used to lock the fuel injection pump sprocket and hub in the TDC position, then slide the sprocket from the hub, noting which way round it is fitted. Refit the locking tool to the pump hub once the sprocket has been removed.

36 To refit the sprocket, again temporarily remove the locking tool from the hub, then refit the sprocket, ensuring that it is fitted the correct way round, as noted before removal.

37 If necessary turn the sprocket until the locking tool can be inserted through the sprocket and hub to engage with the pump support bracket.

38 Fit the new sprocket securing bolts, then turn the sprocket to that the bolts are positioned centrally in the elongated holes. Tighten the sprocket bolts by hand only at this stage.

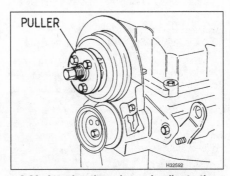

8.29 Attach a three-legged puller to the hub, and evenly tighten the puller until the hub is free of the camshaft taper

8.30 The built in key in the hub taper must align with the key way in the camshaft taper (arrowed)

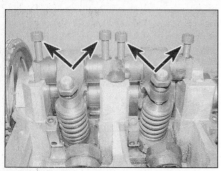

9.2 Starting with the outer bolts first, carefully and evenly slacken the rocker shaft retaining bolts (arrowed)

39 Refit and tension the timing belt as described in Section 7.

Coolant pump sprocket

40 The coolant pump sprocket is integral with the coolant pump. Refer to Chapter 3 for details of coolant pump removal.

9 Pump injector rocker shaft assembly – removal and refitting

Note: *The injector rocker shafts are only fitted to engine codes AJM, ARL, ASZ, ATD, AUY and AXR.*

Removal

1 Remove the camshaft cover as described in Section 4. In order to ensure that the rocker arms are refitted to their original locations, use a marker pen or paint and number the arms 1 to 4, with No 1 nearest the timing belt end of the engine. If the arms are not fitted to their original locations the injector basic clearance setting procedure must be carried out as described in Chapter 4B, Section 5.

2 Starting with the outer bolts first, carefully and evenly slacken the rocker shaft retaining bolts. Discard the rocker shaft bolts, new ones must be fitted **(see illustration)**.

Refitting

3 Carefully check the rocker shaft, rocker arms and camshaft bearing cap seating surface for any signs of excessive wear or damage.

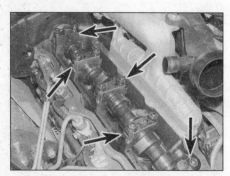

10.6 Check the camshaft bearing caps (arrowed) for markings

4 Ensure that the shaft seating surface is clean and position the rocker shaft assembly in the camshaft bearing caps, making sure that, if reusing the original rocker arms, they are in their original locations.

5 Insert the new rocker shaft retaining bolts, and starting from the inner bolts, gradually and evenly tighten the bolts to the Stage 1 torque setting.

6 Again, starting with the inner retaining bolts, tighten the bolts to the Stage 2 angle as listed in this Chapter's Specifications.

7 Refit the camshaft cover as described in Section 4.

10 Camshaft and hydraulic tappets – removal, inspection and refitting

Note: *A new camshaft oil seal will be required on refitting.*

Removal

1 Turn the crankshaft to position No 1 piston at TDC on the firing stroke, and lock the camshaft and the fuel injection sprocket in position, as described in Section 3.

2 Remove the timing belt as described in Section 7.

3 Remove the camshaft sprocket as described in Section 8.

4 Remove the brake vacuum pump as described in Chapter 9.

5 On engine codes AJM, ARL, ASZ, ATD, AUY and AXR remove the injector rocker arms as described in Section 9.

6 Check the camshaft bearing caps for identification markings **(see illustration)**. The bearing caps are normally stamped with their respective cylinder numbers. If no marks are present, make suitable marks using a scriber or punch. The caps should be numbered from 1 to 5, with No 1 at the timing belt end of the engine. Note on which side of the bearing caps the marks are made to ensure that they are refitted the correct way round.

7 On engine codes AJM, ARL, ASZ, ATD, AUY and AXR, the camshaft rotates in shell bearings. As the camshaft bearing caps are removed, recover the shell bearing halves from the camshaft. Number the back of the

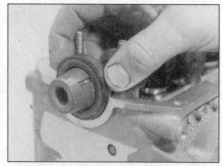

10.11 Remove the camshaft oil seal

bearings with a felt pen to ensure that, if re-used, the bearings are fitted to their original locations. **Note:** *Fitted into the cylinder head, under each camshaft bearing cap, is a washer for each cylinder head bolt.*

8 Unscrew the securing nuts, and remove Nos 1, 3 and 5 bearing caps.

9 Working progressively, in a diagonal sequence, slacken the nuts securing Nos 2 and 4 bearing caps. Note that as the nuts are slackened, the valve springs will push the camshaft up.

10 Once the nuts securing Nos 2 and 4 bearing caps have been fully slackened, lift off the bearing caps.

11 Carefully lift the camshaft from the cylinder head, keeping it level and supported at both ends as it is removed so that the journals and lobes are not damaged. Remove the oil seal from the end of the camshaft and discard it – a new one will be required for refitting **(see illustration)**.

12 Lift the hydraulic tappets from their bores in the cylinder head, and store them with the valve contact surfaces facing downwards, to prevent the oil from draining out. It is recommended that the tappets are kept immersed in oil for the period they are removed from the cylinder head. Make a note of the position of each tappet, as they must be refitted in their original locations on reassembly – accelerated wear leading to early failure will result if the tappets are interchanged.

13 On engine codes AJM, ARL, ASZ, ATD, AUY and AXR, recover the lower shell bearing halves from the cylinder head; number the back of the shells with a felt pen to ensure that, if re-used, the bearings are fitted to their original locations.

Inspection

14 With the camshaft removed, examine the bearing caps and the bearing locations in the cylinder head for signs of obvious wear or pitting. If evident, a new cylinder head will probably be required. Also check that the oil supply holes in the cylinder head are free from obstructions.

15 Visually inspect the camshaft for evidence of wear on the surfaces of the lobes and journals. Normally their surfaces should be smooth and have a dull shine; look for scoring, erosion or pitting and areas that appear highly polished, indicating excessive wear. Accelerated wear will occur once the hardened exterior of the camshaft has been damaged, so always renew worn items. **Note:** *If these symptoms are visible on the tips of the camshaft lobes, check the corresponding tappet, as it will probably be worn as well.*

16 If the machined surfaces of the camshaft appear discoloured or blued, it is likely that it has been overheated at some point, probably due to inadequate lubrication. This may have distorted the shaft, so check the run-out as follows: place the camshaft between two V-blocks and using a DTI gauge, measure the run-out at the centre journal. If it exceeds the figure quoted in the Specifications at the start of this Chapter, renew the camshaft.

17 To measure the camshaft endfloat, temporarily refit the camshaft to the cylinder head, then fit Nos 1 and 5 bearing caps and tighten the retaining nuts to the specified torque setting. Anchor a DTI gauge to the timing belt end of the cylinder head **(see illustration)**. Push the camshaft to one end of the cylinder head as far as it will travel, then rest the DTI gauge probe on the end face of the camshaft, and zero the gauge. Push the camshaft as far as it will go to the other end of the cylinder head, and record the gauge reading. Verify the reading by pushing the camshaft back to its original position and checking that the gauge indicates zero again. **Note:** *The hydraulic tappets must **not** be fitted whilst this measurement is being taken.*

18 Check that the camshaft endfloat measurement is within the limit listed in the Specifications. If the measurement is outside the specified limit, wear is unlikely to be confined to any one component, so renewal of the camshaft, cylinder head and bearing caps must be considered.

19 The camshaft bearing running clearance should now be measured. This will be difficult to achieve without a range of micrometers or internal/external expanding calipers, measure the outside diameters of the camshaft bearing surfaces and the internal diameters formed by the bearing caps (and shell bearings where applicable) and the bearing locations in the cylinder head. The difference between these two measurements is the running clearance.

20 Compare the camshaft running clearance measurements with the figure given in the Specifications; if any are outside the specified tolerance, the camshaft, cylinder head and bearing caps (and shell bearings where applicable) should be renewed.

21 Inspect the hydraulic tappets for obvious signs of wear or damage, and renew if necessary. Check that the oil holes in the tappets are free from obstructions.

Refitting

22 Smear some clean engine oil onto the sides of the hydraulic tappets, and offer them into position in their original bores in the cylinder head. Push them down until they contact the valves, then lubricate the camshaft lobe contact surfaces.

23 Lubricate the camshaft and cylinder head bearing journals (and shell bearings where applicable) with clean engine oil.

24 Carefully lower the camshaft into position in the cylinder head making sure that the cam lobes for No 1 cylinder are pointing upwards.

25 Refit a new camshaft oil seal on the front of the camshaft. Make sure that the closed end of the seal faces the camshaft sprocket end of the camshaft, and take care not to damage the seal lip. Locate the seal against the seat in the cylinder head.

26 Oil the upper surfaces of the camshaft

10.17 Checking camshaft endfloat using a DTI gauge

bearing journals (and shell bearings where applicable), then fit Nos 2 and 4 bearing caps. Ensure that they are fitted the right way round and in the correct locations (see paragraph 6), then progressively tighten the retaining nuts in a diagonal sequence to the specified torque. Note that as the nuts are tightened, the camshaft will be forced down against the pressure of the valve springs.

27 Fit bearing caps 1, 3 and 5 over the camshaft and progressively tighten the nuts to the specified torque. Note that it may be necessary to locate No 5 bearing cap by tapping lightly on the end of the camshaft.

28 Refit the camshaft sprocket as described in Section 8.

29 Refit and tension the timing belt as described in Section 7.

30 Refit the brake vacuum pump as described in Chapter 9.

11 Hydraulic tappets – testing

⚠ *Warning: After fitting hydraulic tappets, wait a minimum of 30 minutes (or preferably, leave overnight) before starting the engine, to allow the tappets time to settle, otherwise the valve heads will strike the pistons.*

1 The hydraulic tappets are self-adjusting, and require no attention whilst in service.

2 If the hydraulic tappets become excessively noisy, their operation can be checked as described below.

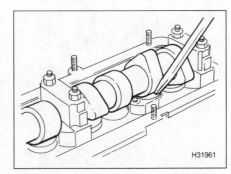

11.8 Press down on the tappet using a wooden or plastic instrument

3 Start the engine, and run it until it reaches normal operating temperature, increase the engine speed to approximately 2500 rpm for 2 minutes.

4 If any hydraulic tappets are heard to be noisy, carry out the following checks.

5 Remove the camshaft cover as described in Section 4.

6 Using a socket or spanner on the crankshaft sprocket bolt, turn the crankshaft until the tip of the camshaft lobe above the tappet to be checked is pointing vertically upwards.

7 Using feeler blades, check the clearance between the top of the tappet, and the cam lobe. If the play is in excess of 0.1 mm, renew the relevant tappet. If the play is less than 0.1 mm, or there is no play, proceed as follows.

8 Press down on the tappet using a wooden or plastic instrument **(see illustration)**. If free play in excess of 1.0 mm is present before the tappet contacts the valve stem, renew the relevant tappet.

9 On completion, refit the camshaft cover as described in Section 4.

12 Camshaft oil seals – renewal

Right-hand oil seal

1 Remove the timing belt as described in Section 7.

2 Remove the camshaft sprocket and hub, as described in Section 8.

3 Drill two small holes into the existing oil seal, diagonally opposite each other. Take great care to avoid drilling through into the seal housing or camshaft sealing surface. Thread two self-tapping screws into the holes, and using a pair of pliers, pull on the heads of the screws to extract the oil seal.

4 Clean out the seal housing and the sealing surface of the camshaft by wiping it with a lint-free cloth. Remove any swarf or burrs that may cause the seal to leak.

5 Do **not** lubricate the lip and outer edge of the new oil seal, push it over the camshaft until it is positioned in place above its housing. To prevent damage to the sealing lips, wrap some adhesive tape around the end of the camshaft.

6 Using a hammer and a socket of suitable diameter, drive the seal squarely into its housing. **Note:** *Select a socket that bears only on the hard outer surface of the seal, not the inner lip which can easily be damaged.*

7 Refit the camshaft sprocket and its hub, as described in Section 8.

8 Refit and tension the timing belt as described in Section 7.

Left-hand oil seal

9 The left-hand camshaft oil seal is formed by the brake vacuum pump seal. Refer to Chapter 9 for details of brake vacuum pump removal and refitting.

13.6a Where applicable, undo the bolt (arrowed) from the inner cover . . .

13.6b . . . and the one (arrowed) on the side of the cover

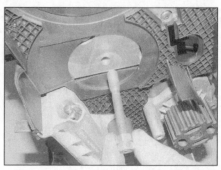

13.7 Using two nuts locked together to unscrew the tensioner mounting stud

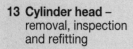

13 Cylinder head –
removal, inspection and refitting

Note: *The cylinder head must be removed with the engine cold. New cylinder head bolts and a new cylinder head gasket will be required on refitting, and suitable studs will be required to guide the cylinder head into position – see text.*

Removal

1 Disconnect the battery negative lead and remove the engine top cover. **Note:** *Before disconnecting the battery, refer to 'Disconnecting the battery' at the rear of this manual.*

2 Drain the cooling system and engine oil as described in Chapter 1B.

3 Remove the camshaft cover as described in Section 4.

4 Remove the timing belt as described in Section 7.

5 Remove the camshaft sprocket and timing belt tensioner as described in Section 8.

6 Where applicable, unscrew the bolt(s) securing the rear timing belt cover to the cylinder head **(see illustrations)**.

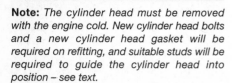

7 Using two suitable nuts locked together, unscrew the timing belt tensioner mounting stud from the cylinder head **(see illustration)**.

8 If the engine is currently supported using a hoist and lifting tackle attached to the engine lifting brackets on the cylinder head, it is now necessary to attach a suitable bracket to the

cylinder block, so that the engine can still be supported as the cylinder head is removed. Alternatively, the engine can be supported using a trolley jack and a block of wood positioned under the engine sump.

Engine codes
AGP, AQM, AGR, AHF, ALH and ASV

9 Slacken the clip and disconnect the radiator top hose from the front of the coolant housing on the left-hand side of the cylinder head. Similarly, disconnect the heater hose from the rear of the housing, and the smaller oil cooler hose from the bottom of the housing. Move the hoses to one side.

10 Slacken the clip, and disconnect the coolant purge hose from the rear left-hand side of the cylinder head.

11 Disconnect the exhaust front section from the exhaust manifold or the turbocharger, as applicable, as described in Chapter 4D.

12 On turbo models, proceed as follows:

a) *Disconnect the vacuum hose from the turbocharger wastegate actuator.*

b) *Where applicable, disconnect the boost pressure solenoid valve hose from the turbocharger.*

c) *Slacken the hose clips, and disconnect the air inlet trunking from the turbocharger.*

d) *Slacken the hose clips, and remove the turbocharger-to-intercooler air trunking.*

e) *Where applicable, unbolt and remove the turbocharger support bracket.*

f) *Unscrew the union bolt, and disconnect the turbocharger oil return pipe from the cylinder block. Recover the sealing rings.*

g) *Slacken the union nut and disconnect the oil supply pipe from the turbocharger. Release the pipe from any brackets on the exhaust manifold and cylinder head.*

13 Disconnect the wiring from the following components, noting the routing of the wiring:

a) *Fuel injection pump fuel cut-off solenoid (on top of injection pump – loosen securing nut).*

b) *Fuel injection pump start-of-injection valve (see illustration).*

c) *Inlet manifold flap adjuster valve (turbo engines) – at rear of inlet manifold.*

d) *Coolant temperature sensor/temperature gauge sender (left-hand end of cylinder head).*

e) *Fuel injector needle lift sensor (behind oil filter housing).*

f) *Main glow plug feed wiring.*

14 Disconnect the main fuel leak-off hose from the fuel injectors.

15 Slacken the union nuts, whilst counter-holding the unions with a second spanner, and remove the fuel injector pipes as an assembly.

16 Disconnect the vacuum hoses from the brake vacuum pump and EGR valve **(see illustrations)**.

17 On models fitted with an inlet manifold flap vacuum damper (see Chapter 4D, Section 3), either remove the damper reservoir from the bracket on the cylinder head, or remove the reservoir *with* its bracket.

18 Make a final check to ensure that all relevant pipes, hoses and wires have been disconnected and moved clear of the working area to enable removal of the cylinder head.

13.13 Disconnect the injection system wiring plug (arrowed) behind the oil filter housing

13.16a Disconnect the vacuum hose (arrowed) from the brake vacuum pump

13.16b EGR valve and vacuum hose (arrowed) – turbo models

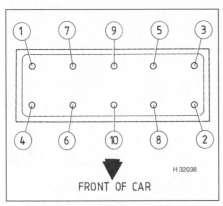

13.19 Cylinder head bolt slackening sequence

19 Progressively slacken the cylinder head bolts, by one turn at a time, in order **(see illustration)**. Remove the cylinder head bolts.

20 With all the bolts removed, lift the cylinder head from the block, together with the manifolds (and turbocharger, where applicable). If the cylinder head is stuck, tap it with a soft-faced mallet to break the joint. **Do not** insert a lever into the gasket joint.

21 Lift the cylinder head gasket from the block. Do not discard the gasket at this stage, as it will be required when determining the thickness of the new gasket required.

22 If desired, the manifolds can be removed from the cylinder head with reference to Chapter 4B (inlet manifold) or 4D (exhaust manifold).

Engine codes
AJM, ARL, ASZ, ATD, AUY and AXR

Note: *It is necessary to unplug the central connector for the unit injectors – this may cause a fault code to be logged by the engine management ECU. This code can only be erased by a VW dealer or suitably-equipped specialist.*

23 Remove the bolt securing the camshaft position sensor to the cylinder head. There is no need to disconnect the wiring at this stage **(see illustration)**.

24 Disconnect the charge air pipe from the inlet manifold to the intercooler and place to one side.

25 Disconnect the central connector for the unit injectors **(see illustration)**.

26 Undo the two bolts securing the coolant junction to the end of the cylinder head **(see illustration)**. There is no need to disconnect the pipes or wiring plugs at this stage.

27 Unscrew the four retaining bolts and pull the tandem pump away from the cylinder head without disconnecting the fuel or vacuum hoses **(see illustration)**.

28 Disconnect and remove the hose connecting the upper coolant pipe to the pipe at the end of the cylinder head **(see illustration)**.

29 Remove the turbocharger as described in Chapter 4D.

13.23 Unscrew the bolt and remove the camshaft position sensor

13.26 Undo the two bolts (arrowed) and remove the coolant outlet from the end of the cylinder head

30 Slacken and remove the bolt securing the upper metal coolant pipe to the cylinder head.

31 Disconnect the wiring connectors from the glow plugs – if necessary, refer to Chapter 5C.

32 Disconnect vacuum pipes to the EGR valve and the manifold flap actuator **(see illustration)**.

33 Using a multi-splined tool, undo the cylinder head bolts, working from the outside-in, evenly and gradually. Check that nothing remains connected, and lift the cylinder head from the engine block. Seek assistance if possible, as it is a heavy assembly, especially as it is being removed complete with the manifolds.

34 Remove the gasket from the top of the block, noting the locating dowels. If the dowels are a loose fit, remove them and store them with the head for safe-keeping. Do not discard the gasket yet – it will be needed for identification purposes.

13.28 Disconnect the coolant hose from the end of the cylinder head

13.25 Disconnect the central connector for the injectors

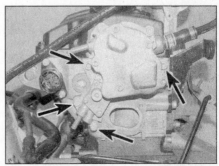

13.27 Undo the four tandem pump retaining bolts (arrowed)

Inspection

35 Dismantling and inspection of the cylinder head is covered in Part Chapter 2D.

Cylinder head gasket selection

Note: *A dial test indicator (DTI) will be required for this operation.*

36 Examine the old cylinder head gasket for manufacturer's identification markings **(see illustration)**. These will be in the form of holes or notches, and a part number on the edge of the gasket. Unless new pistons have been fitted, the new cylinder head gasket must be of the same type as the old one. In this case, purchase a new gasket, and proceed to paragraph 43.

37 If new piston assemblies have been fitted as part of an engine overhaul, or if a new short engine is to be fitted, the projection of the piston crowns above the cylinder head mating face of the cylinder block at TDC must be

13.32 Disconnect the vacuum pipes (arrowed)

13.36 The thickness of the cylinder head gasket can be identified by notches or holes

13.39 Measuring the piston projection at TDC using a dial gauge

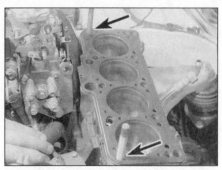

13.51 Two of the old head bolts (arrowed) can be used as cylinder head alignment guides

measured. This measurement is used to determine the thickness of the new cylinder head gasket required.

38 Anchor a dial test indicator (DTI) to the top face (cylinder head gasket mating face) of the cylinder block, and zero the gauge on the gasket mating face.

39 Rest the gauge probe on No 1 piston crown, and turn the crankshaft slowly by hand until the piston reaches TDC. Measure and record the maximum piston projection at TDC **(see illustration)**.

40 Repeat the measurement for the remaining pistons, and record the results.

41 If the measurements differ from piston-to-piston, take the highest figure, and use this to determine the thickness of the head gasket required as follows.

Piston projection	Gasket identification (number of holes/notches)
0.91 to 1.00 mm	1
0.01 to 1.10 mm	2
1.11 to 1.20 mm	3

42 Purchase a new gasket according to the results of the measurements.

Refitting

Note: *If a VW exchange cylinder head, complete with camshaft, is to be fitted, the manufacturers recommend the following:*

a) *Lubricate the contact surfaces between the tappets and the cam lobes before fitting the camshaft cover.*

b) *Do not remove the plastic protectors from the open valves until immediately before fitting the cylinder head.*

c) *Additionally, if a new cylinder head is fitted, VW recommend that the coolant is renewed.*

43 The mating faces of the cylinder head and block must be perfectly clean before refitting the head. Use a scraper to remove all traces of gasket and carbon, also clean the tops of the pistons. Take particular care with the aluminium surfaces, as the soft metal is easily damaged.

44 Make sure that debris is not allowed to enter the oil and water passages – this is particularly important for the oil circuit, as carbon could block the oil supply to the camshaft and crankshaft bearings. Using adhesive tape and paper, seal the water, oil and bolt holes in the cylinder block.

45 To prevent carbon entering the gap between the pistons and bores, smear a little grease in the gap. After cleaning a piston, rotate the crankshaft to that the piston moves down the bore, then wipe out the grease and carbon with a cloth rag. Clean the other piston crowns in the same way.

46 Check the head and block for nicks, deep scratches and other damage. If slight, they may be removed carefully with a file. More serious damage may be repaired by machining, but this is a specialist job.

47 If warpage of the cylinder head is suspected, use a straight-edge to check it for distortion, as described in Chapter 2D.

48 Ensure that the cylinder head bolt holes in the crankcase are clean and free of oil. Syringe or soak up any oil left in the bolt holes. This is most important in order that the correct bolt tightening torque can be applied, and to prevent the possibility of the block being cracked by hydraulic pressure when the bolts are tightened.

49 Turn the crankshaft anti-clockwise all the pistons at an equal height, approximately halfway down their bores from the TDC position (see Section 3). This will eliminate any risk of piston-to-valve contact as the cylinder head is refitted.

50 Where applicable, refit the manifolds with reference to Chapters 4B and/or 4D.

51 To guide the cylinder head into position, screw two long studs (or old cylinder head bolts with the heads cut off, and slots cut in the ends to enable the bolts to be unscrewed) into the cylinder block **(see illustration)**.

52 Ensure that the cylinder head locating dowels are in place in the cylinder block, then fit the new cylinder head gasket over the dowels, ensuring that the part number is uppermost. Where applicable, the OBEN/TOP marking should also be uppermost. Note that VW recommend that the gasket is only removed from its packaging immediately prior to fitting.

53 Lower the cylinder head into position on the gasket, ensuring that it engages correctly over the guide studs and dowels.

54 Fit the new cylinder head bolts to the eight remaining bolt locations, and screw them in as far as possible by hand.

55 Unscrew the two guide studs from the exhaust side of the cylinder block, then screw in the two remaining new cylinder head bolts as far as possible by hand.

56 Working progressively, in sequence, tighten all the cylinder head bolts to the specified Stage 1 torque **(see illustrations)**.

57 Again working progressively, in sequence, tighten all the cylinder head bolts to the specified Stage 2 torque.

58 Tighten all the cylinder head bolts, in sequence, through the specified Stage 3 angle **(see illustration)**.

59 Finally, tighten all the cylinder head bolts, in sequence, through the specified Stage 4 angle.

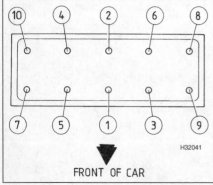

13.56a Cylinder head bolt tightening sequence

13.56b Using a torque wrench to tighten the cylinder head bolts

13.58 Angle-tighten the cylinder head bolts

60 After finally tightening the cylinder head bolts, turn the camshaft so that the cam lobes for No 1 cylinder are pointing upwards.

61 Where applicable, reconnect the lifting tackle to the engine lifting brackets on the cylinder head, then adjust the lifting tackle to support the engine. Once the engine is adequately supported using the cylinder head brackets, disconnect the lifting tackle from the bracket bolted to the cylinder block, and unbolt the improvised engine lifting bracket from the cylinder block. Alternatively, remove the trolley jack and block of wood from under the sump.

62 The remainder of the refitting procedure is a reversal of the removal procedure, bearing in mind the following points.

a) Refit the camshaft cover with reference to Section 4.

b) On turbo models, use new sealing rings when reconnecting the turbocharger oil return pipe to the cylinder block.

c) Reconnect the exhaust front section to the exhaust manifold or turbocharger, as applicable, with reference to Chapter 4D.

d) Refit the timing belt tensioner with reference to Section 8.

e) Refit the camshaft sprocket as described in Section 8, and refit the timing belt as described in Section 7.

f) On non-turbo engines, refit the upper section of the inlet manifold as described in Chapter 4B.

g) Refill the cooling system and engine oil as described in Chapter 1B.

14 Sump – removal and refitting

Proceed as described in Section 13, in Chapter 2A.

15 Oil pump and drive chain – removal, inspection and refitting

Proceed as described in Section 14 in Chapter 2A.

16 Flywheel/driveplate/clutch pressure plate – removal, inspection and refitting

Non-turbo engines

1 The clutch pressure plate is bolted directly to the crankshaft flange, and the dished flywheel is then bolted to the pressure plate. Removal and refitting procedures for the clutch pressure plate and flywheel are given in Chapter 6.

Turbo engines

2 Proceed as described for 2.0 litre engines, in Section 15, Chapter 2A.

17 Crankshaft oil seals – renewal

Note 1: *The oil seals are a PTFE (Teflon) type and are fitted dry, without using any grease or oil. These have a wider sealing lip and have been introduced instead of the coil spring type oil seal.*

Note 2: *If the oil seal housing is removed, suitable sealant (VW D 176 404 A2, or equivalent) will be required to seal the housing on refitting.*

Right-hand oil seal

1 Remove the timing belt as described in Section 7, and the crankshaft sprocket with reference to Section 8.

2 To remove the seal without removing the housing, drill two small holes diagonally opposite each other, insert self-tapping screws, and pull on the heads of the screws with pliers **(see illustration)**.

3 Alternatively, to remove the oil seal complete with its housing, proceed as follows.

a) Remove the sump as described in Section 14. This is necessary to ensure a satisfactory seal between the sump and oil seal housing on refitting.

b) Unbolt and remove the oil seal housing.

c) Working on the bench, lever the oil seal from the housing using a suitable screwdriver. Take care not to damage the seal seating in the housing **(see illustration)**.

4 Thoroughly clean the oil seal seating in the housing.

5 Wind a length of tape around the end of the crankshaft to protect the oil seal lips as the seal (and housing, where applicable) is fitted.

6 Fit a new oil seal to the housing, pressing or driving it into position using a socket or tube of suitable diameter. Ensure that the socket or tube bears only on the hard outer ring of the seal, and take care not to damage the seal lips. Press or drive the seal into position until it is seated on the shoulder in the housing. Make sure that the closed end of the seal is facing outwards.

7 If the oil seal housing has been removed, proceed as follows, otherwise proceed to paragraph 11.

8 Clean all traces of old sealant from the crankshaft oil seal housing and the cylinder block, then coat the cylinder block mating faces of the oil seal housing with a 2.0 to 3.0 mm thick bead of sealant (VW D 176 404 A2, or equivalent). Note that the seal housing must be refitted within 5 minutes of applying the sealant. **Caution: DO NOT put excessive amounts of sealant onto the housing as it may get into the sump and block the oil pick-up pipe.**

9 Refit the oil seal housing, and tighten the bolts progressively to the specified torque **(see illustration)**.

10 Refit the sump as described in Section 14.

11 Refit the crankshaft sprocket with reference to Section 8, and the timing belt as described in Section 7.

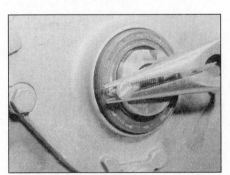

17.2 Removing the crankshaft oil seal using self-tapping screws

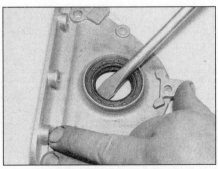

17.3 Prising the oil seal from the crankshaft oil seal housing

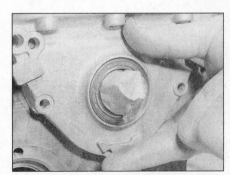

17.9 Slide the oil seal housing over the end of the crankshaft

17.17 Locate the crankshaft oil seal fitting tool over the end of the crankshaft

Left-hand oil seal

12 Remove the flywheel/driveplate as described in Section 16.

13 Remove the sump as described in Section 14. This is necessary to ensure a satisfactory seal between the sump and oil seal housing on refitting.

14 Unbolt and remove the oil seal housing, complete with the oil seal.

15 The new oil seal will be supplied ready-fitted to a new oil seal housing.

16 Thoroughly clean the oil seal housing mating face on the cylinder block.

17 New oil seal/housing assemblies are supplied with a fitting tool to prevent damage to the oil seal as it is being fitted. Locate the tool over the end of the crankshaft **(see illustration)**.

18 If the original oil seal housing was fitted using sealant, apply a thin bead of suitable sealant (VW D 176 404 A2, or equivalent) to the cylinder block mating face of the oil seal housing. Note that the seal housing must be refitted within 5 minutes of applying the sealant.

Caution: DO NOT put excessive amounts of sealant onto the housing as it may get into the sump and block the oil pick-up pipe.

19 Carefully fit the oil seal/housing assembly over the end of the crankshaft, then refit the securing bolts and tighten the bolts progressively, in a diagonal sequence, to the specified torque **(see illustrations)**.

20 Remove the oil seal protector tool from the end of the crankshaft.

21 Refit the sump as described in Section 14.

22 Refit the flywheel/driveplate as described in Section 16.

17.19a Fit the oil seal/housing assembly over the end of the crankshaft . . .

18 Engine/transmission mountings – inspection and renewal

Refer to Section 17 in Chapter 2A for the basic procedure, however, note that the right-hand engine mounting is different.

19 Engine oil cooler – removal and refitting

Note: *New sealing rings will be required on refitting.*

Removal

1 The oil cooler is mounted under the oil filter housing on the front of the cylinder block **(see illustration opposite)**.

2 Position a container beneath the oil filter to catch escaping oil and coolant.

3 Clamp the oil cooler coolant hoses to minimise coolant spillage, then remove the clips, and disconnect the hoses from the oil cooler. Be prepared for coolant spillage.

4 Unscrew the oil cooler securing plate from the bottom of the oil filter housing, then slide off the oil cooler. Recover the O-rings from the top and bottom of the oil cooler.

Refitting

5 Refitting is a reversal of removal, bearing in mind the following points:

a) *Use new oil cooler O-rings.*

b) *Tighten the oil cooler securing plate to the specified torque.*

c) *On completion, check and if necessary top up the oil and coolant levels.*

20 Oil pressure relief valve – removal, inspection and refitting

Note: *On engine codes AJM, ARL, ASZ, ATD, AUY and AXR, the pressure relief valve is part of the oil filter housing and cannot be removed, DO NOT loosen the sealing plug on these models.*

17.19b . . . then tighten the securing bolts to the specified torque

Removal

1 The oil pressure relief valve is fitted to the right-hand side of the oil filter housing **(see illustration 19.1)**. Remove the engine top cover(s) to gain access to the switch (see Section 4).

2 Wipe clean the area around the relief valve plug then slacken and remove the plug and sealing ring from the filter housing. Withdraw the valve spring and piston, noting their correct fitted positions. If the valve is to be left removed from the engine for any length of time, plug the oil filter housing aperture.

Inspection

3 Examine the relief valve piston and spring for signs of wear or damage. At the time of writing it appears that the relief valve components were not available separately; check with your VW dealer for the latest parts availability. If wear or damage is present it will be necessary to renew the complete oil filter housing assembly.

Refitting

4 Fit the piston to the inner end of the spring then insert the assembly into the oil filter housing. Ensure the sealing ring is correctly fitted to the valve plug then fit the plug to the housing tightening it to the specified torque.

5 On completion, check and, if necessary, top-up the engine oil as described in *Weekly checks*. On completion, refit the engine top cover(s).

21 Oil pressure warning light switch – removal and refitting

Removal

1 The oil pressure warning light switch is fitted to the right-hand side of the oil filter housing **(see illustration 19.1)**. Remove the engine top cover(s) to gain access to the switch (see Section 4).

2 Disconnect the wiring connector and wipe clean the area around the switch.

3 Unscrew the switch from the filter housing and remove it, along with its sealing washer. If the switch is to be left removed from the engine for any length of time, plug the oil filter housing aperture.

Refitting

4 Examine the sealing washer for signs of damage or deterioration and if necessary renew.

5 Refit the switch, complete with washer, and tighten it to the specified torque.

6 Securely reconnect the wiring connector then check and, if necessary, top-up the engine oil as described in *Weekly checks*. On completion, refit the engine top cover(s).

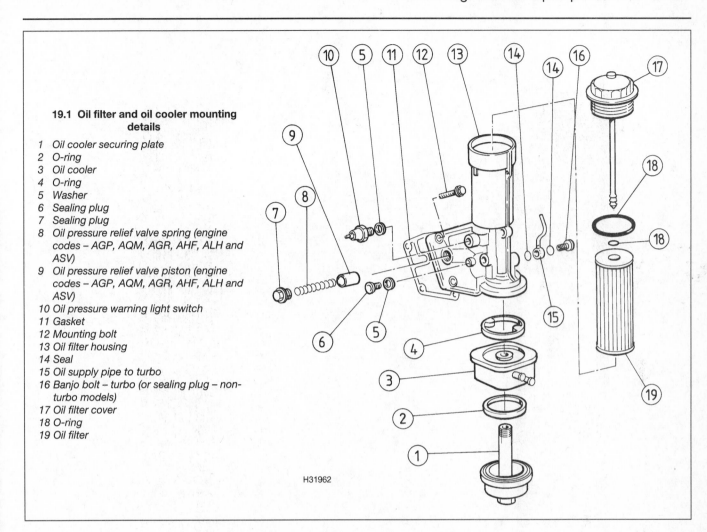

19.1 Oil filter and oil cooler mounting details

1 Oil cooler securing plate
2 O-ring
3 Oil cooler
4 O-ring
5 Washer
6 Sealing plug
7 Sealing plug
8 Oil pressure relief valve spring (engine codes – AGP, AQM, AGR, AHF, ALH and ASV)
9 Oil pressure relief valve piston (engine codes – AGP, AQM, AGR, AHF, ALH and ASV)
10 Oil pressure warning light switch
11 Gasket
12 Mounting bolt
13 Oil filter housing
14 Seal
15 Oil supply pipe to turbo
16 Banjo bolt – turbo (or sealing plug – non-turbo models)
17 Oil filter cover
18 O-ring
19 Oil filter

H31962

Notes

Chapter 2 Part D:
Engine removal and overhaul procedures

Contents

Crankshaft – checking endfloat and inspection 15
Crankshaft – refitting and main bearing clearance check 19
Crankshaft – removal 12
Cylinder block/crankcase – cleaning and inspection 13
Cylinder head – dismantling 8
Cylinder head – reassembly 10
Cylinder head and valves – cleaning and inspection 9
Engine – initial start-up after overhaul and reassembly 21
Engine and transmission (diesel engines) – removal and refitting . . . 6
Engine and transmission (DOHC petrol engines) – removal and
　refitting 5
Engine and transmission (SOHC petrol engines) – removal and
　refitting 4

Engine overhaul – general information 2
Engine overhaul – preliminary information 7
Engine overhaul – reassembly sequence 17
Engine/transmission removal – preparation and precautions 3
General information 1
Main and big-end bearings – inspection 16
Piston rings – refitting 18
Piston/connecting rod assemblies – cleaning and inspection 14
Piston/connecting rod assemblies – refitting and big-end bearing
　clearance check 20
Piston/connecting rod assemblies – removal 11

Degrees of difficulty

Easy, suitable for novice with little experience	**Fairly easy,** suitable for beginner with some experience	**Fairly difficult,** suitable for competent DIY mechanic
Difficult, suitable for experienced DIY mechanic	**Very difficult,** suitable for expert DIY or professional 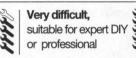	

Specifications

Cylinder head

Minimum permissible dimension between top of valve stem and top surface of cylinder head:

1.6 SOHC engines:
　Except BFQ and AVU engines:
　　Inlet valves . . . . 33.8 mm
　　Exhaust valves . . . . 34.1 mm
　BFQ and AVU engines:
　　Inlet valves . . . . 31.7 mm
　　Exhaust valves . . . . 31.7 mm
2.0 SOHC engines:
　Inlet valves . . . . 33.8 mm
　Exhaust valves . . . . 34.1 mm
1.4 and 1.6 litre DOHC petrol engines:
　Inlet valves . . . . 7.6 mm
　Exhaust valves . . . . 7.6 mm
1.8 litre DOHC petrol engines:
　Outer inlet valves . . . . 31.0 mm
　Centre inlet valves . . . . 32.3 mm
　Exhaust valve . . . . 31.9 mm
Diesel engines:
　Inlet valves . . . . 35.8 mm
　Exhaust valves . . . . 36.1 mm
Minimum cylinder head height:
　1.6 SOHC petrol engines:
　　Except BFQ and AVU . . . . 132.6 mm
　　BFQ and AVU . . . . 132.9 mm
　2.0 SOHC petrol engines . . . . 132.6 mm
　1.4 and 1.6 litre DOHC petrol engines . . . . 108.25 mm
　1.8 litre DOHC petrol engines . . . . 139.2 mm
　Diesel engines . . . . No reworking permitted
Maximum cylinder head gasket face distortion:
　All engines except 1.4 and 1.6 litre DOHC engines . . . . 0.1 mm
　1.4 and 1.6 litre DOHC engines . . . . 0.05 mm

Valves

Valve stem diameter:	Inlet valves	Exhaust valves
1.6 SOHC engines:		
Except BFQ and AVU engines	6.92 ± 0.02 mm	6.92 ± 0.02 mm
BFQ and AVU engines	5.98 ± 0.007 mm	5.96 ± 0.007 mm
2.0 litre SOHC engines	6.98 ± 0.007 mm	6.96 ± 0.007 mm
1.4 and 1.6 litre DOHC engines	5.973 mm	5.953 mm
1.8 litre DOHC engines	5.963 mm	5.943 mm
Diesel engine	6.963 mm	6.943 mm
Valve head diameter:		
SOHC engines	39.5 ± 0.15 mm	32.9 ± 0.15 mm
1.4 and 1.6 litre DOHC engines	29.5 mm	26.0 mm
1.8 litre DOHC engines	26.9 mm	29.9 mm
Diesel engine:		
AGP, AQM, AGR, ALH, AHF and ASV engines	6.963 mm	6.943 mm
AJM, ASZ, ARL, ATD, AUY and AXR engines	6.980 mm	6.956 mm
Valve length:		
1.6 SOHC engines:		
Except BFQ and AVU engines	91.85 mm	91.15 mm
BFQ and AVU engines	93.85 mm	93.85 mm
2.0 SOHC engines	91.85 mm	91.15 mm
1.4 and 1.6 litre DOHC engines	100.9 mm	100.5 mm
1.8 litre DOHC engines	104.84 to 105.34 mm	103.64 to 104.14 mm
Diesel engine:		
AGR, AHF, ALH and ASV engines	96.85 mm	96.85 mm
AGP and AQM engines	96.55 mm	96.35 mm
AJM, ASZ, ARL, ATD, AUY and AXR engines	89.95 mm	89.95 mm
Valve seat angle (all engines)	45°	

Crankshaft

See Note in Section 2 about 1.4 litre engines

1.6 and 2.0 litre SOHC engines:
  Main journal diameter:
    Basic dimension:
      All except 1.6 litre BFQ engines .... 54.00 mm (Nominal)
      1.6 litre BFQ engine .... 48.00 mm (Nominal)
  Big-end journal diameter:
    Basic dimension:
      All except 1.6 litre BFQ engines .... 47.80 mm (Nominal)
      1.6 litre BFQ engine .... 42.00 mm (Nominal)
  Endfloat:
    New .... 0.07 to 0.23 mm
    Wear limit .... 0.30 mm
1.6 litre DOHC engines:
  Main journal diameter:
    Basic dimension .... 54.00 mm (Nominal)
  Big-end journal diameter:
    Basic dimension .... 47.80 mm (Nominal)
  Endfloat:
    New .... 0.07 to 0.18 mm
    Wear limit .... 0.20 mm
1.8 litre DOHC engines:
  Main journal diameter:
    Basic dimension .... 54.00 mm (Nominal)
  Big-end journal diameter:
    Basic dimension .... 47.80 mm (Nominal)
  Endfloat:
    New .... 0.07 to 0.23 mm
    Wear limit .... 0.30 mm
Diesel engines:
  Main journal diameter:
    Basic dimension .... 54.00 mm (Nominal)
  Big-end journal diameter:
    Basic dimension .... 47.80 mm (Nominal)
  Endfloat:
    New .... 0.07 to 0.17 mm
    Wear limit .... 0.37 mm

Bearing running clearances

See Note in Section 2 about 1.4 litre engines

1.6 litre SOHC engines:	New	Wear limit
Main bearings:		
Except for BFQ engines	0.01 to 0.04 mm	0.15 mm
BFQ engines	0.01 to 0.04 mm	0.07 mm
Big-end bearings:		
Except for BFQ engines	0.01 to 0.06 mm	0.12 mm
BFQ engines	0.01 to 0.05 mm	0.09 mm
2.0 litre SOHC engines:		
Main bearings:		
Except for AZJ engines	0.01 to 0.04 mm	0.15 mm
AZJ engines	0.01 to 0.04 mm	0.07 mm
Big-end bearings:		
Except for AZJ engines	0.01 to 0.06 mm	0.12 mm
AZJ engines	0.01 to 0.05 mm	0.09 mm
1.4 DOHC engines:		
Big-end bearings	0.020 to 0.061 mm	0.091 mm
1.6 litre DOHC engines:		
Main bearings	0.03 to 0.08 mm	0.17 mm
Big-end bearings	0.020 to 0.061 mm	0.091 mm
1.8 litre DOHC engines:		
Main bearings	0.01 to 0.04 mm	0.07 mm
Big-end bearings	0.01 to 0.05 mm	0.09 mm
Diesel engines:		
Main bearings	0.03 to 0.08 mm	0.17 mm
Big-end bearings		0.08 mm

Pistons/connecting rods

Connecting rod side-play on crankshaft journal:	New	Wear limit
1.6 litre SOHC engines	0.05 to 0.31 mm	0.37 mm
2.0 litre SOHC engines:		
All except AZJ engine	0.05 to 0.31 mm	0.37 mm
AZJ engine	0.10 to 0.35 mm	0.40 mm
1.4 and 1.6 litre DOHC engines	No figure specified	
1.8 litre DOHC engines	0.10 to 0.31 mm	0.40 mm
Diesel engines		0.37 mm

Piston rings

End gaps:	New	Wear limit
1.6 and 2.0 SOHC engines:		
Compression rings	0.20 to 0.40 mm	0.80 mm
Oil scraper ring	0.25 to 0.50 mm	0.80 mm
1.4 and 1.6 litre DOHC engines:		
Top compression ring	0.20 to 0.50 mm	1.0 mm
Lower compression ring	0.40 to 0.70 mm	1.0 mm
Oil scraper ring	0.40 to 1.40 mm	
1.8 litre DOHC engines:		
Compression rings	0.20 to 0.40 mm	0.8 mm
Oil scraper ring	0.25 to 0.50 mm	0.8 mm
Diesel engines:		
Compression rings	0.20 to 0.40 mm	1.0 mm
Oil scraper ring:	0.25 to 0.50 mm	1.0 mm
Ring-to-groove clearance:		
1.6 and 2.0 litre SOHC engines:		
Compression rings	0.06 to 0.09 mm	0.20 mm
Oil scraper ring:	0.03 to 0.06 mm	0.15 mm
1.4 and 1.6 litre DOHC engines:		
Compression rings	0.04 to 0.08 mm	0.15 mm
Oil scraper ring	Cannot be measured	
1.8 litre DOHC engines:		
Common conrods:		
Compression rings	0.02 to 0.07 mm	0.12 mm
Oil scraper ring	0.02 to 0.06 mm	0.12 mm
Cracked conrods:		
Compression rings	0.06 to 0.09 mm	0.20 mm
Oil scraper ring	0.03 to 0.06 mm	0.15 mm

Piston rings (continued)

Ring-to-groove clearance (continued):	New	Wear limit
Diesel engines:		
1st compression ring	0.06 to 0.09 mm	0.25 mm
2nd compression ring	0.05 to 0.08 mm	0.25 mm
Oil scraper ring	0.03 to 0.06 mm	0.15 mm

Piston and cylinder bore diameters

	Piston	Cylinder bore
1.6 litre SOHC engines	80.965 mm	81.010 mm
2.0 litre SOHC engines:		
Standard	82.465 mm	82.510 mm
1st oversize	82.965 mm	83.010 mm
1.4 and 1.6 litre DOHC engines:		
Standard	76.470 mm	76.510 mm
1st oversize	76.720 mm	76.760 mm
2nd oversize	76.970 mm	77.010 mm
1.8 litre DOHC engines:		
Standard	80.965 mm	81.010 mm
1st oversize	81.465 mm	81.510 mm
Diesel engines:		
Standard	79.470 mm	79.510 mm
1st oversize	79.720 mm	79.760 mm
2nd oversize	79.970 mm	80.010 mm

Torque wrench settings

Refer to Chapter 2A, 2B or 2C, as applicable.

---

1 General information

Included in this Part of Chapter 2 are details of removing the engine from the car and general overhaul procedures for the cylinder head, cylinder block and all other engine internal components.

The information given ranges from advice concerning preparation for an overhaul and the purchase of new parts, to detailed step-by-step procedures covering removal, inspection, renovation and refitting of engine internal components.

After Section 7, all instructions are based on the assumption that the engine has been removed from the car. For information concerning in-car engine repair, as well as the removal and refitting of those external components necessary for full overhaul, refer to the relevant in-car repair procedure section (Chapters 2A, 2B and 2C) and to Section 7 of this Chapter. Ignore any preliminary dismantling operations described in the relevant in-car repair sections that are no longer relevant once the engine has been removed from the car.

Apart from torque wrench settings, which are given at the beginning of the relevant in-car repair procedure in Chapters 2A, 2B or 2C, all specifications relating to engine overhaul are given at the beginning of this Part of Chapter 2.

2 Engine overhaul – general information

Note: *On 1.4 litre engines, the crankshaft must not be removed. Loosening the main bearing cap bolts will cause deformation of the cylinder block. On 1.4 litre engines, if the crankshaft or main bearing surfaces are worn or damaged, the complete crankshaft/cylinder block assembly must be renewed.*

1 It is not always easy to determine when, or if, an engine should be completely overhauled, as a number of factors must be considered.

2 High mileage is not necessarily an indication that an overhaul is needed, while low mileage does not preclude the need for an overhaul. Frequency of servicing is probably the most important consideration. An engine which has had regular and frequent oil and filter changes, as well as other required maintenance, should give many thousands of miles of reliable service. Conversely, a neglected engine may require an overhaul very early in its life.

3 Excessive oil consumption is an indication that piston rings, valve seals and/or valve guides are in need of attention. Make sure that oil leaks are not responsible before deciding that the rings and/or guides are worn. Perform a compression (or leakdown) test, as described in Part A, B or C of this Chapter (as applicable), to determine the likely cause of the problem.

4 Check the oil pressure with a gauge fitted in place of the oil pressure switch, and compare it with that specified (see Specifications in Chapter 2A, 2B and 2C). If it is extremely low, the main and big-end bearings, and/or the oil pump, are probably worn.

5 Loss of power, rough running, knocking or metallic engine noises, excessive valve gear noise, and high fuel consumption may also point to the need for an overhaul, especially if they are all present at the same time. If a complete service does not remedy the situation, major mechanical work is the only solution.

6 An engine overhaul involves restoring all internal parts to the specification of a new engine. During an overhaul, the pistons and the piston rings are renewed. New main and big-end bearings are generally fitted (where possible); if necessary, the crankshaft may be renewed to restore the journals. The valves are also serviced as well, since they are usually in less-than-perfect condition at this point. While the engine is being overhauled, other components, such as the starter and alternator, can be overhauled as well. The end result should be an as-new engine that will give many trouble-free miles. **Note:** *Critical cooling system components such as the hoses, thermostat and coolant pump should be renewed when an engine is overhauled. The radiator should be checked carefully, to ensure that it is not clogged or leaking. Also, it is a good idea to renew the oil pump whenever the engine is overhauled.*

7 Before beginning the engine overhaul, read through the entire procedure, to familiarise yourself with the scope and requirements of the job. Overhauling an engine is not difficult if you follow carefully all of the instructions, have the necessary tools and equipment, and pay close attention to all specifications. It can, however, be time-consuming. Plan on the car being off the road for a minimum of two weeks, especially if parts must be taken to an engineering works for repair or reconditioning. Check on the availability of parts and make sure that any necessary special tools and equipment are obtained in advance. Most work can be done with typical hand tools, although a number of precision measuring tools are required for inspecting parts to determine if they must be renewed. Often the engineering works will handle the inspection of parts and offer advice concerning reconditioning and renewal. Note: *Always wait until the engine has been completely dismantled, and until all components (especially the cylinder block and the crankshaft) have been inspected, before deciding what service and repair operations must be performed by an engineering works. The condition of these components will be the major factor to consider when determining whether to overhaul the original engine, or to buy a reconditioned unit. Do not, therefore, purchase parts or have overhaul work done on other components until they have been thoroughly inspected.* As a general rule, time is the primary cost of an overhaul, so it does not pay to fit worn or sub-standard parts.

8 As a final note, to ensure maximum life and minimum trouble from a reconditioned engine, everything must be assembled with care, in a spotlessly-clean environment.

3 Engine/transmission removal – preparation and precautions

If you have decided that the engine must be removed for overhaul or major repair work, several preliminary steps should be taken.

Locating a suitable place to work is extremely important. Adequate work space, along with storage space for the vehicle, will be needed. If a workshop or garage is not available, at the very least a solid, level, clean work surface is required.

If possible, clear some shelving close to the work area and use it to store the engine components and ancillaries as they are removed and dismantled. In this manner, the components stand a better chance of staying clean and undamaged during the overhaul. Laying out components in groups together with their fixings bolts, screws, etc, will save time and avoid confusion when the engine is refitted.

Clean the engine compartment and engine before beginning the removal procedure; this will help visibility and help to keep tools clean.

The help of an assistant is essential; there are certain instances when one person cannot

safely perform all of the operations required to remove the engine from the vehicle. Safety is of primary importance, considering the potential hazards involved in this kind of operation. A second person should always be in attendance to offer help in an emergency. If this is the first time you have removed an engine, advice and aid from someone more experienced would also be beneficial.

Plan the operation ahead of time. Before starting work, obtain (or arrange for the hire of) all of the tools and equipment you will need. Access to the following items will allow the task of removing and refitting the engine to be completed safely and with relative ease: a hoist and lifting tackle – rated in excess of the weight of the engine, complete sets of spanners and sockets as described at the rear of this manual, wooden blocks, and plenty of rags and cleaning solvent for mopping up spilled oil, coolant and fuel. A selection of different-sized plastic storage bins will also prove useful for keeping dismantled components grouped together. If any of the equipment must be hired, make sure that you arrange for it in advance, and perform all of the operations possible without it beforehand; this may save you time and money.

Plan on the vehicle being out of use for quite a while, especially if you intend to carry out an engine overhaul. Read through the whole of this Section and work out a strategy based on your own experience, and the tools, time and workspace available to you. Some of the overhaul processes may have to be carried out by a VW dealer or an engineering works – these establishments often have busy schedules, so it would be prudent to consult them before removing or dismantling the engine, to get an idea of the amount of time required to carry out the work.

When removing the engine from the vehicle, be methodical about the disconnection of external components. Labelling cables and hoses as they are removed will greatly assist the refitting process.

Always be extremely careful when lifting the engine from the engine compartment. Serious injury can result from careless actions. If help is required, it is better to wait until it is available rather than risk personal injury and/or damage to components by continuing

alone. By planning ahead and taking your time, a job of this nature, although major, can be accomplished successfully and without incident.

4 Engine and transmission (SOHC petrol engines) – removal and refitting

Removal

1 The engine and transmission are removed by lowering them out as a unit from underneath the engine compartment.

2 Disconnect the battery negative lead. Note: *Before disconnecting the battery, refer to 'Disconnecting the battery' at the rear of this manual.*

3 Release the securing clips, and remove the engine top cover.

4 Drain the cooling system as described in Chapter 1A.

5 To allow improved access and clearance for removal of the engine/transmission, it is useful to unbolt and remove the body front panel as follows:

a) *Remove the front bumper as described in Chapter 11.*

b) *Disconnect the bonnet release cable from the bonnet lock, with reference to Chapter 11.*

c) *Unscrew the four bolts (two on each side) securing the front bumper carrier to the brackets on the body.*

d) *Disconnect the cooling fan switch wiring plug.*

e) *Release the cooling fan wiring connector from the clips on the rear of the cooling fan shroud, then separate the two halves of the connector.*

f) *Disconnect the headlight wiring connectors (one connector for each headlight).*

g) *Unscrew the two upper bolts securing the body front panel to the front wing panels.*

h) *Make a final check to ensure that all relevant wiring, hoses and pipes have been disconnected, then pull the front body panel forwards, and withdraw it from the vehicle.*

6 Remove the battery as described in Chapter 5A, then remove the battery tray.

7 Depressurise the fuel system as described in Chapter 4A. Place a wad of clean cloth around the fuel supply and return hose connections on the right-hand side of the engine compartment, then depress the connector locking tabs, and disconnect the fuel line connectors. Be prepared for fuel spillage, and take adequate fire precautions.

8 Disconnect the vacuum hose from the valve on the charcoal canister at the right-hand side of the engine compartment.

9 Disconnect the wiring connectors from the following components, depending on model and equipment fitted:

a) *DIS ignition module.*

b) *Camshaft position sensor (see illustration).*

4.9a Disconnecting the camshaft position sensor wiring plug

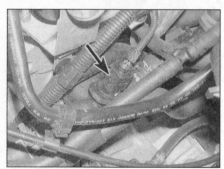

4.9b Coolant temperature sensor wiring plug (arrowed)

4.9c Wiring plugs for knock sensor (black) and engine speed sensor (grey)

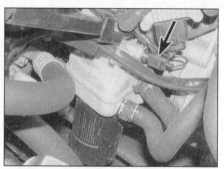

4.9d Oil pressure warning light switch wiring plug (arrowed)

c) *Fuel injectors.*
d) *Coolant temperature sensor (see illustration).*
e) *Crankshaft speed/position sensor (see illustration).*
f) *Knock sensor.*
g) *EGR valve.*
h) *Secondary air injection motor.*
i) *Oil pressure warning light switch (see illustration).*
j) *Air mass meter.*
k) *Throttle valve control assembly.*
l) *Air conditioning system thermostatic cut-out switch (where applicable).*

10 Slacken the hose clips and remove the intake air hose connecting the air mass meter to the throttle housing.
11 Remove the air cleaner as described in Chapter 4A.
12 Remove the upper section of the inlet manifold as described in Chapter 4A.
13 On models with manual transmission, disconnect the gear selector mechanism from the transmission as described in Chapter 7A, Section 2, and remove the clutch slave cylinder as described in Chapter 6. **Note:** *Do not depress the clutch pedal once the slave cylinder has been removed.*
14 On models with automatic transmission, disconnect the gear selector cable from the transmission, as described in Chapter 7B.
15 Remove the auxiliary drivebelt as described in Chapter 1A.
16 Remove the clamps securing the power steering fluid pressure pipe. This will allow the power steering pump to be removed from the engine without disconnecting the fluid lines.
17 Unbolt the power steering pump from the engine, with reference to Chapter 10, but leave the fluid lines connected, and support the pump clear of the working area.
18 On models with air conditioning, remove the air conditioning compressor as described in Chapter 3.

⚠️ *Warning: Have the air conditioning system discharged by a suitably-qualified specialist before attempting to remove the compressor.*

19 Work around the engine and transmission, and disconnect any remaining hoses, pipes and wires to allow removal of the engine/transmission assembly, noting their location and routing to aid refitting.
20 If necessary, remove the secondary air injection pump and its mounting bracket, as described in Chapter 4C.
21 Remove the rear engine mounting with reference to Chapter 2A.
22 Remove the right-hand driveshaft as described in Chapter 8, and disconnect the left-hand driveshaft from the transmission.
23 Remove the exhaust front section as described in Chapter 4C.
24 If not already done, connect a hoist and lifting tackle to the engine lifting brackets on the cylinder head, and raise the hoist to just take the weight of the engine.
25 Remove the right-hand and left-hand engine/transmission mountings, with reference to Chapter 2A.
26 Carefully lower the engine/transmission assembly out from under the vehicle. Support the assembly on a trolley, or on wooden blocks. Manipulate the assembly out from underneath the vehicle.

Engine and transmission separation

Manual transmission

27 Unscrew the two securing bolts, and remove the starter motor.
28 Where applicable, unscrew the bolt securing the small engine-to-transmission plate to the transmission.
29 Ensure that both engine and transmission are adequately supported, then unscrew the remaining engine-to-transmission bolts, noting the location of each bolt, and the locations of any brackets secured by the bolts.
30 Carefully withdraw the transmission from the engine, ensuring that the weight of the transmission is not allowed to hang on the input shaft while it is engaged with the clutch friction disc. Recover the engine-to-transmission plate.

Automatic transmission

31 Unscrew the two securing bolts, and remove the starter motor.
32 Prise out the torque converter nuts cover from the transmission casing. The cover is located behind the left-hand driveshaft flange. Turn the crankshaft to position one of the torque converter-to-driveplate nuts in the access aperture. Unscrew and remove the nut whilst preventing the engine from turning using a wide-bladed screwdriver engaged with the ring gear teeth on the driveplate.
33 Using the same method described in the previous paragraph, unscrew the remaining two torque converter-to-driveplate nuts, turning the crankshaft a third-of-a-turn at a time to locate them.
34 Ensure that both engine and transmission are adequately supported, then unscrew the engine-to-transmission bolts, noting the location of each bolt, and the locations of any brackets secured by the bolts.
35 Carefully withdraw the transmission from the engine (take care – the transmission is heavy), making sure that the torque converter remains fully engaged with the transmission input shaft. If necessary, use a lever to release the torque converter from the driveplate. Recover the engine-to-transmission plate.
36 Once the transmission has been separated from the engine, strap a restraining bar across the front of the bellhousing to keep the torque converter in position.

Reconnection and refitting

Engine and manual transmission

37 Reconnection and refitting are a reversal of removal, bearing in mind the following points:
a) *Smear the splines of the transmission input shaft with a little high-melting-point grease.*
b) *Ensure that any brackets noted before removal are in place on the engine-to-transmission bolts.*
c) *Tighten all fixings to the specified torque, where given.*
d) *Refit the engine mountings with reference to Chapter 2A.*
e) *Reconnect the driveshafts to the transmission with reference to Chapter 8.*
f) *Where applicable, refit the secondary air injection pump and its mounting bracket, with reference to Chapter 4C.*
g) *Where applicable, refit the air conditioning compressor, with reference to Chapter 3, and have the system recharged with refrigerant by a suitably-qualified professional.*

h) *Refit the auxiliary drivebelt with reference to Chapter 1A.*

i) *Refit the upper section of the inlet manifold as described in Chapter 4A.*

j) *Reconnect that all wiring, hoses and pipes are correctly reconnected and routed as noted before removal.*

k) *Ensure that the fuel lines are correctly reconnected. The lines are colour-coded, white for supply, and blue for return.*

l) *On completion, refill the cooling system as described in Chapter 1A.*

Engine and automatic transmission

38 Proceed as described in paragraph 37, but note the following additional points:

a) *When fitting the torque converter, make sure that both the drive pins engage with the transmission fluid pump.*

b) *Reconnect and if necessary adjust the gear selector cable, as described in Chapter 7B.*

c) *On completion, check and if necessary top-up the automatic transmission fluid level as described in Chapter 1A.*

5 Engine and transmission (DOHC petrol engines) – removal and refitting

1.4 and 1.6 litre engines removal

1 The engine and transmission are removed by lifting them out as a unit from the top of the engine compartment.

2 To improve access, jack up the front of the vehicle and support securely on axle stands (see *Jacking and vehicle support*). Remove the roadwheels.

3 Working under the front of the vehicle, remove the securing screws and withdraw the engine undershield(s).

4 Drain the cooling system as described in Chapter 1A.

5 Slacken the hose clips, and disconnect the radiator top and bottom hoses, and the three smaller coolant hoses from the thermostat housing **(see illustration)**.

6 Disconnect the radiator top hose from the radiator, and move the hose assembly towards the rear of the engine compartment, clear of the engine.

7 Disconnect the battery negative lead. **Note:** *Before disconnecting the battery, refer to 'Disconnecting the battery' at the rear of this manual.*

8 To allow improved access and clearance for removal of the engine/transmission, it is now necessary to unbolt and remove the body front panel as follows:

a) *Remove the front bumper as described in Chapter 11.*

b) *Disconnect the bonnet release cable from the bonnet lock (see illustration), with reference to Chapter 11.*

c) *Unscrew the four bolts (two on each side)*

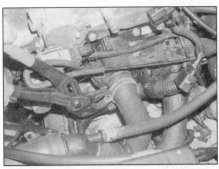

5.5 Disconnecting the radiator top hose from the thermostat housing

5.8b Unscrew the two bolts on each side securing the bumper carrier to the brackets on the body

*securing the front bumper carrier to the brackets on the body **(see illustration)**.*

d) *Disconnect the cooling fan switch wiring plug.*

e) *Release the cooling fan wiring connector from the clips on the rear of the cooling fan shroud, then separate the two halves of the connector.*

f) *Disconnect the headlight wiring connectors (one connector for each headlight).*

g) *Unscrew the two upper bolts securing the body front panel to the front wing panels **(see illustration)**.*

h) *Make a final check to ensure that all relevant wiring, hoses and pipes have been disconnected, then pull the front body panel forwards, and withdraw it from the vehicle.*

9 Remove the battery, as described in

5.8a Disconnect the bonnet release cable from the lock

5.8c Unscrew the upper bolt (arrowed) on each side securing the body front panel to the wing panels

Chapter 5A, then disconnect the main starter motor feed cable from the positive battery terminal box.

10 Release any relevant wiring or hoses from the clips on the battery tray, then unscrew the four securing bolts and remove the battery tray **(see illustrations)**.

11 Where applicable, unclip the accelerator cable from the top of the air cleaner assembly, then release the cable from the support bracket and the throttle linkage, with reference to Chapter 4A.

12 Remove the air cleaner as described in Chapter 4A.

13 Depressurise the fuel system as described in Chapter 4A. Place a wad of clean cloth around the fuel supply and return hose connections on the right-hand side of the engine compartment, then depress the connector locking tabs, and disconnect the

5.10a Unscrew the four securing bolts . . .

5.10b . . . and remove the battery tray

5.13 Disconnect the fuel line connectors

5.14 Disconnect the charcoal canister hose from the inlet manifold

5.15a Disconnect the brake servo vacuum hose from the inlet manifold . . .

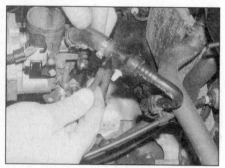

5.15b . . . then disconnect the EGR vacuum pipe from the servo vacuum hose

5.17a Disconnect the throttle valve control assembly wiring connector . . .

5.17b . . . the oil pressure warning light wiring connector . . .

fuel line connectors **(see illustration)**. Be prepared for fuel spillage, and take adequate fire precautions.

14 Disconnect the charcoal canister hose from the inlet manifold **(see illustration)**.

15 Disconnect the brake servo vacuum hose from the inlet manifold, then disconnect the EGR vacuum pipe from the servo vacuum hose, and move the servo vacuum hose to one side, clear of the engine **(see illustrations)**.

16 Release the crankshaft speed/position sensor wiring connector from the bracket located below the engine oil dipstick tube bracket, then separate the two halves of the connector. Release the sensor wiring from the bracket at the rear of the engine.

17 Disconnect the following wiring connectors:

a) *DIS ignition module.*
b) *Camshaft position sensor.*
c) *Throttle valve control assembly* **(see illustration)**.
d) *Coolant temperature sensor.*
e) *Oil pressure warning light switch* **(see illustration)**.
f) *Exhaust gas recirculation solenoid valve.*
g) *Fuel injectors* **(see illustration)**.

18 Prise up the covers, and release the fuel injector wiring harness from the harness housing **(see illustration)**.

19 On models with manual transmission, disconnect the gear selector mechanism from the transmission, as follows:

a) *Unscrew and remove the pinch-nut and bolt securing the gear selector rod to the linkage clamp sleeve* **(see illustration)**.
b) *Prise off the rubber cover, then prise off the clip securing the gear linkage to the pivot mounted on the subframe* **(see illustrations)**.
c) *Carefully slide the linkage from the pivot on the subframe, then unhook and remove the pivot sleeve and counterbalance weight, noting its fitted position* **(see illustration)**.

20 On models with automatic transmission,

5.17c . . . and the fuel injector wiring connectors

5.18 Release the fuel injector wiring harness from the harness housing

5.19a Remove the pinch-nut and bolt (arrowed) securing the gear selector rod to the linkage clamp sleeve

5.19b Prise off the rubber cover . . .

5.19c ... then prise off the clip securing the gear linkage to the pivot ...

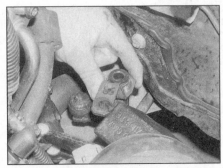

5.19d ... and slide the linkage from the pivot on the subframe

5.21 Disconnect the inlet manifold pressure sensor wiring connector (viewed from underneath vehicle)

5.22 Separate the two halves of the oxygen sensor wiring connector

5.23 Disconnect the reversing light switch wiring connector ...

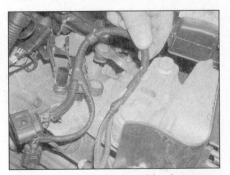

5.24 ... then unclip the wiring harness from the engine/transmission mounting

disconnect the gear selector cable from the transmission, as described in Chapter 7B.

21 Working under the vehicle, disconnect the inlet manifold pressure sensor wiring connector (located at the front right underside of the inlet manifold) **(see illustration)**.

22 Release the oxygen sensor wiring connector from the bracket on the top of the transmission, and separate the two halves of the connector **(see illustration)**.

23 Disconnect the reversing light switch wiring connector **(see illustration)**.

24 Unclip the oxygen sensor and reversing light switch wiring harness from the left-hand engine/transmission mounting **(see illustration)**.

25 Disconnect the speedometer sensor wiring plug (located at the rear of the transmission), and unclip the sensor wiring harness from the left-hand engine/transmission mounting **(see illustration)**.

26 Working under the vehicle, disconnect the knock sensor wiring connector. Note that access is difficult, and can be improved by unbolting the coolant/thermostat housing from the left-hand side of the cylinder head, and removing the plastic coolant pipe which connects the coolant pump to the coolant/thermostat housing (pull the plastic pipe from the coolant pump). If the wiring connector proves particularly difficult to release, it may be necessary to remove the inlet manifold for access, with reference to Chapter 4A.

27 Slacken the power steering pump pulley securing bolts, then remove the power steering pump drivebelt as described in Chapter 1A.

28 Unbolt the power steering fluid pipe from the bracket at the front of the engine.

29 Unbolt the power steering pump pulley, then remove the power steering pump from

the engine, with reference to Chapter 10, and secure the pump to the body using wire or cable-ties, etc **(see illustration)**. Note that there is no need to disconnect the fluid hoses from the pump.

30 On models fitted with air conditioning, remove the air conditioning compressor, with reference to Chapter 3.

⚠ *Warning: The air conditioning system must be discharged by a suitably-qualified professional before attempting to remove the compressor.*

31 Release the alternator wiring connector from the bracket on the top of the transmission, then separate the two halves of the connector **(see illustration)**.

32 Slide the wiring harness housing from the bracket attached to the upper starter motor securing bolt **(see illustration)**.

5.25 Disconnect the speedometer sensor wiring plug

5.29 Unbolt the power steering pump from the engine

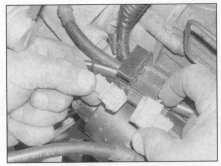

5.31 Separate the two halves of the alternator wiring connector

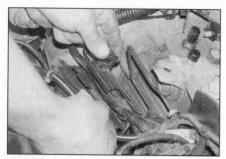

5.32 Slide the wiring harness housing from the bracket attached to the starter motor securing bolt

5.33 Disconnect the starter motor wiring connector

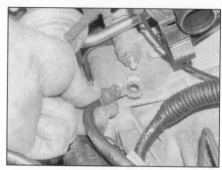

5.34 Disconnect the earth cable from the transmission

33 Disconnect the starter motor wiring connector **(see illustration)**.

34 Unscrew the securing nut, and disconnect the earth cable from the transmission **(see illustration)**.

35 Disconnect the alternator wiring plug, then unscrew the securing nuts, and disconnect the remaining two cables from the alternator **(see illustration)**.

36 On models with manual transmission, unbolt the clutch slave cylinder from the transmission, with reference to Chapter 6 if necessary, and move the slave cylinder to one side, clear of the engine. Use cable-ties, or a strong rubber band to retain the piston in the slave cylinder.

 Warning: Do not depress the clutch pedal once the clutch slave cylinder has been removed.

37 Release the coolant reservoir hose from the bracket at the rear of the engine.

38 Connect a suitable hoist and lifting tackle to the engine lifting brackets on the cylinder head, then raise the hoist to just take the weight of the engine and transmission. Depending on the type of hoist and lifting tackle to be used, it may be necessary to remove the bonnet – refer to Chapter 11 for details.

39 Work around the engine and transmission, and make a final check to ensure that all relevant wiring, hoses and pipes have been disconnected and released to enable removal of the engine/transmission assembly.

40 Remove the engine rear mounting, with reference to Chapter 2B.

41 Disconnect the exhaust front section from the manifold as described in Chapter 4C.

42 Unbolt the inner ends of both driveshafts from the flanges on the transmission, with reference to Chapter 8 **(see illustration)**. Support the free ends of the driveshafts using

wire or string – do not allow them to hang down under their own weight.

43 Unscrew the two securing screws, and move the coolant reservoir to one side, clear of the working area.

44 Similarly, unscrew the securing screw, and move the power steering reservoir to one side, clear of the working area.

45 Unbolt the power steering fluid pipe from the bracket on the left-hand end of the transmission.

46 Remove the right-hand engine mounting, as described in Chapter 2B.

47 Unscrew the three bolts securing the left-hand engine/transmission mounting to the transmission **(see illustration)**. The mounting can be left attached to the body.

48 With the aid of an assistant, manipulate the engine/transmission assembly clear of the surrounding components in the engine compartment, and raise the hoist to lift the assembly clear of the vehicle **(see illustration)**.

49 Once the assembly has been lifted clear of the vehicle, lower it onto a bench, or onto wooden blocks on the workshop floor.

50 To separate the engine and transmission, proceed as follows.

Engine and manual transmission separation

51 Unscrew the two securing bolts, and remove the starter motor.

52 Unscrew the bolt securing the small engine-to-transmission plate to the transmission **(see illustration)**.

5.35 Disconnect the alternator wiring plug

5.42 Unbolt the driveshafts from the transmission flanges

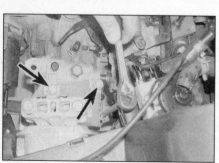

5.47 Unscrew the three bolts securing the engine/transmission mounting to the transmission

5.48 Lift the engine/transmission assembly clear of the vehicle

5.52 Remove the small engine-to-transmission plate

53 Ensure that both engine and transmission are adequately supported, then unscrew the remaining engine-to-transmission bolts, noting the location of each bolt, and the locations of any brackets secured by the bolts.

54 Carefully withdraw the transmission from the engine, ensuring that the weight of the transmission is not allowed to hang on the input shaft while it is engaged with the clutch friction disc.

Engine and automatic transmission separation

55 Unscrew the two securing bolts, and remove the starter motor.

56 Prise out the torque converter nuts cover from the transmission casing. On 1.4 litre engine models, the cover is located above the right-hand driveshaft flange, and on 1.6 litre engines, the cover is located behind the left-hand driveshaft flange. Turn the crankshaft to position one of the torque converter-to-driveplate nuts in the access aperture. Unscrew and remove the nut whilst preventing the engine from turning using a wide-bladed screwdriver engaged with the ring gear teeth on the driveplate.

57 Using the same method described in the previous paragraph, unscrew the remaining two torque converter-to-driveplate nuts, turning the crankshaft a third-of-a-turn at a time to locate them.

58 Ensure that both engine and transmission are adequately supported, then unscrew the engine-to-transmission bolts, noting the location of each bolt, and the locations of any brackets secured by the bolts.

59 Carefully withdraw the transmission from the engine (take care – the transmission is heavy), making sure that the torque converter remains fully engaged with the transmission input shaft. If necessary, use a lever to release the torque converter from the driveplate. Recover the engine-to-transmission plate.

60 Once the transmission has been separated from the engine, strap a restraining bar across the front of the bellhousing to keep the torque converter in position.

1.4 and 1.6 litre engines reconnection and refitting

Engine and manual transmission

61 Reconnection and refitting are a reversal of removal, bearing in mind the following points:
  a) Smear the splines of the transmission input shaft with a little high-melting-point grease.
  b) Note that the lug at the top of the engine-to-transmission plate locates behind the crankshaft oil seal housing.
  c) Ensure that any brackets noted before removal are in place on the engine-to-transmission bolts.
  d) Tighten all fixings to the specified torque, where given.
  e) Refit the engine mountings with reference to Chapter 2B.

5.66a Removing one of the engine cover fasteners

  f) Reconnect the driveshafts to the transmission with reference to Chapter 8.
  g) Where applicable, refit the air conditioning compressor, with reference to Chapter 3, and have the system recharged with refrigerant by a suitably-qualified professional.
  h) Refit the auxiliary drivebelt with reference to Chapter 1A.
  i) Ensure that all wiring, hoses and pipes are correctly reconnected and routed as noted before removal.
  j) Where applicable, use new O-rings when refitting the coolant pump-to-coolant housing plastic pipe.
  k) Ensure that the fuel lines are correctly reconnected. The lines are colour-coded, white for supply, and blue for return.
  l) On completion, refill the cooling system as described in Chapter 1A.

Engine and automatic transmission

62 Proceed as described in paragraph 61, but note the following additional points:
  a) When fitting the torque converter, make sure that both the drive pins engage with the transmission fluid pump.
  b) Reconnect and if necessary adjust the gear selector cable, as described in Chapter 7B.
  c) On completion, check and if necessary top-up the automatic transmission fluid level as described in Chapter 1A.

1.8 litre engines removal

63 The engine and transmission are removed by lowering them out as a unit from underneath the engine compartment.

64 Disconnect the battery negative lead.
Note: *Before disconnecting the battery, refer to 'Disconnecting the battery' at the rear of this manual.*

65 To allow improved access and clearance for removal of the engine/transmission, it is useful to unbolt and remove the body front panel as follows:
  a) Remove the front bumper as described in Chapter 11.
  b) Disconnect the bonnet release cable from the bonnet lock, with reference to Chapter 11.
  c) Unscrew the four bolts (two on each side)

5.66b Removing the front section of the engine cover

securing the front bumper carrier to the brackets on the body.
  d) Disconnect the cooling fan switch wiring plug.
  e) Release the cooling fan wiring connector from the clips on the rear of the cooling fan shroud, then separate the two halves of the connector.
  f) Disconnect the headlight wiring connectors (one connector for each headlight).
  g) Unscrew the two upper bolts securing the body front panel to the front wing panels.
  h) Make a final check to ensure that all relevant wiring, hoses and pipes have been disconnected, then pull the front body panel forwards, and withdraw it from the vehicle.

66 Remove the engine top cover(s). Removal details vary according to model, but the cover retaining nuts are concealed under circular covers, which are prised out of the main cover. Where plastic screws or turn-fasteners are used, these can be removed using a wide-bladed screwdriver. Remove the nuts or screws, and lift the cover from the engine, releasing any wiring or hoses attached **(see illustrations)**.

67 Remove the air cleaner assembly as described in Chapter 4A.

68 Work around the engine and transmission, and disconnect all relevant vacuum and breather hoses to facilitate engine removal **(see illustration)**. Note the location and routing of the hoses to aid refitting.

69 Depressurise the fuel system as described in Chapter 4A. Place a wad of clean cloth around the fuel supply and return hose

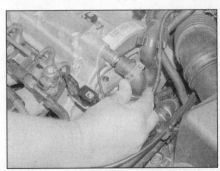

5.68 Disconnecting the breather hose from the camshaft cover

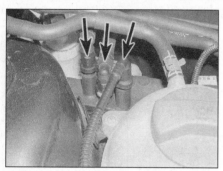

5.69 Fuel supply, return and breather hose connections (arrowed)

connections on the right-hand side of the engine compartment, then depress the connector locking tabs, and disconnect the fuel line connectors **(see illustration)**. Be prepared for fuel spillage, and take adequate fire precautions.

70 Disconnect the vacuum hose from the valve on the charcoal canister at the right-hand side of the engine compartment **(see illustration)**.

71 Remove the air intake trunking connecting the air mass meter to the throttle housing on non-turbo models, or the air intake trunking connecting the air mass meter to the turbocharger on turbocharged engines.

72 On turbocharged models, remove the air intake trunking which connects the intercooler to the throttle housing.

73 On models with manual transmission, disconnect the gear selector mechanism from the transmission, as described in paragraph 19, and remove the clutch slave cylinder as described in Chapter 6. **Note:** *Do not depress the clutch pedal once the slave cylinder has been removed.*

74 Apply the handbrake, then jack up the front of the vehicle and support securely on axle stands (see *Jacking and vehicle support*). Note that the vehicle must be raised to give sufficient clearance to allow removal of the engine/transmission assembly from underneath the vehicle.

75 Remove the securing screws and/or clips, and remove the engine undershield(s).

76 On models with automatic transmission, disconnect the gear selector cable from the transmission as described in Chapter 7B.

5.70 Disconnecting the charcoal canister hose from the throttle housing

77 Drain the cooling system as described in Chapter 1A.

78 Slacken the hose clips and disconnect the radiator top and bottom hoses from the engine.

79 Disconnect the wiring plug from the coolant temperature sensor.

80 Remove the engine rear mounting with reference to Chapter 2B.

81 Disconnect all relevant wiring from the transmission, alternator and starter motor, noting the location and routing of the wiring to aid refitting.

82 Remove the exhaust front section as described in Chapter 4C.

83 Remove the auxiliary drivebelt as described in Chapter 1A.

84 Remove the clamps securing the power steering fluid pressure pipe. This will allow the power steering pump to be removed from the engine without disconnecting the fluid lines.

85 Unbolt the power steering pump from the engine, with reference to Chapter 10, but leave the fluid lines connected, and support the pump clear of the working area.

86 Work around the engine and transmission, and disconnect any remaining hoses, pipes and wires to allow removal of the engine/transmission assembly, noting their location and routing to aid refitting.

87 Remove the right-hand driveshaft as described in Chapter 8, and disconnect the left-hand driveshaft from the transmission.

88 On models with air conditioning, remove the air conditioning compressor as described in Chapter 3.

⚠ **Warning: Have the air conditioning system discharged by a suitably-qualified specialist before attempting to remove the compressor.**

89 If not already done, connect a hoist and lifting tackle to the engine lifting brackets on the cylinder head, and raise the hoist to just take the weight of the engine.

90 Remove the right-hand and left-hand engine/transmission mountings, with reference to Chapter 2B.

91 Carefully lower the engine/transmission assembly out from under the vehicle. Support the assembly on a trolley, or on wooden blocks. Manipulate the assembly out from underneath the vehicle.

Engine and manual transmission separation

92 Unscrew the two securing bolts, and remove the starter motor.

93 Where applicable, unscrew the bolt securing the small engine-to-transmission plate to the transmission.

94 Ensure that both engine and transmission are adequately supported, then unscrew the remaining engine-to-transmission bolts, noting the location of each bolt, and the locations of any brackets secured by the bolts.

95 Carefully withdraw the transmission from

the engine, ensuring that the weight of the transmission is not allowed to hang on the input shaft while it is engaged with the clutch friction disc. Recover the engine-to-transmission plate.

Engine and automatic transmission separation

96 Unscrew the two securing bolts, and remove the starter motor.

97 Prise out the torque converter nuts cover from the transmission casing. The cover is located behind the left-hand driveshaft flange. Turn the crankshaft to position one of the torque converter-to-driveplate nuts in the access aperture. Unscrew and remove the nut whilst preventing the engine from turning using a wide-bladed screwdriver engaged with the ring gear teeth on the driveplate.

98 Using the same method described in the previous paragraph, unscrew the remaining two torque converter-to-driveplate nuts, turning the crankshaft a third-of-a-turn at a time to locate them.

99 Ensure that both engine and transmission are adequately supported, then unscrew the engine-to-transmission bolts, noting the location of each bolt, and the locations of any brackets secured by the bolts.

100 Carefully withdraw the transmission from the engine (take care – the transmission is heavy), making sure that the torque converter remains fully engaged with the transmission input shaft. If necessary, use a lever to release the torque converter from the driveplate. Recover the engine-to-transmission plate.

101 Once the transmission has been separated from the engine, strap a restraining bar across the front of the bellhousing to keep the torque converter in position.

1.8 litre engines reconnection and refitting

Engine and manual transmission

102 Reconnection and refitting are a reversal of removal, bearing in mind the following points:

a) *Smear the splines of the transmission input shaft with a little high-melting-point grease.*

b) *Ensure that any brackets noted before removal are in place on the engine-to-transmission bolts.*

c) *Tighten all fixings to the specified torque, where given.*

d) *Refit the engine mountings with reference to Chapter 2B.*

e) *Reconnect the driveshafts to the transmission with reference to Chapter 8.*

f) *Where applicable, refit the air conditioning compressor, with reference to Chapter 3, and have the system recharged with refrigerant by a suitably-qualified professional.*

g) *Refit the auxiliary drivebelt with reference to Chapter 1A.*

h) *Refit the exhaust front section as described in Chapter 4C.*

i) Ensure that all wiring, hoses and pipes are correctly reconnected and routed as noted before removal.

j) Ensure that the fuel lines are correctly reconnected. The lines are colour-coded, white for supply, and blue for return.

k) On completion, refill the cooling system as described in Chapter 1A.

Engine and automatic transmission

103 Proceed as described in paragraph 102, but note the following additional points:

a) When fitting the torque converter, make sure that both the drive pins engage with the transmission fluid pump.

b) Reconnect and if necessary adjust the gear selector cable, as described in Chapter 7B.

c) On completion, check and if necessary top-up the automatic transmission fluid level as described in Chapter 1A.

---

6 Engine and transmission (diesel engines) – removal and refitting

Removal

1 The engine and transmission are removed by lowering them out as a unit from underneath the engine compartment.

2 Disconnect the battery negative lead. **Note:** *Before disconnecting the battery, refer to 'Disconnecting the battery' at the rear of this manual.*

3 Remove the engine top cover(s) – see Chapter 2C. Removal details vary according to model, on some models the cover retaining nuts are concealed under circular covers, which are prised out of the main cover. Where plastic screws or turn-fasteners are used, these can be removed using a wide-bladed screwdriver. Remove the nuts or screws, and lift the cover from the engine, releasing any wiring or hoses attached.

4 Remove the battery as described in Chapter 5A, then remove the battery tray.

5 To allow improved access and clearance for removal of the engine/transmission, it is useful to unbolt and remove the body front panel as follows:

a) Remove the front bumper as described in Chapter 11.

b) Disconnect the bonnet release cable from the bonnet lock, with reference to Chapter 11.

c) Unscrew the four bolts (two on each side) securing the front bumper carrier to the brackets on the body.

d) Disconnect the cooling fan switch wiring plug.

e) Release the cooling fan wiring connector from the clips on the rear of the cooling fan shroud, then separate the two halves of the connector.

f) Disconnect the headlight wiring connectors (one connector for each headlight).

g) Unscrew the two upper bolts securing the body front panel to the front wing panels.

h) Make a final check to ensure that all relevant wiring, hoses and pipes have been disconnected, then pull the front body panel forwards, and withdraw it from the vehicle.

6 Remove the air cleaner assembly as described in Chapter 4B.

7 On turbocharged models, disconnect the intercooler-to-inlet manifold air trunking at the inlet manifold.

8 Disconnect the fuel supply and return hoses at the fuel filter. Be prepared for fuel spillage, and plug the open ends of the hoses and connections to prevent dirt entry and further fuel loss.

9 On models with manual transmission, disconnect the gear selector mechanism from the transmission as described in Chapter 7A, Section 2, and remove the clutch slave cylinder as described in Chapter 6. **Note:** *Do not depress the clutch pedal once the slave cylinder has been removed.*

10 On models with automatic transmission, disconnect the gear selector cable from the transmission, as described in Chapter 7B.

11 Apply the handbrake, then jack up the front of the vehicle and support securely on axle stands (see *Jacking and vehicle support*).

12 Remove the securing screws and/or clips, and withdraw the engine undershield(s).

13 Drain the cooling system as described in Chapter 1B.

14 If not already done, disconnect the wiring connectors from the cooling fan and the cooling fan switch (located in the radiator).

15 Slacken the hose clips, and disconnect the radiator top and bottom hoses from the engine **(see illustration)**.

16 Remove the rear engine mounting with reference to Chapter 2C.

17 Work around the engine and transmission, and disconnect any remaining hoses, pipes and wires to allow removal of the engine/transmission assembly, noting their location and routing to aid refitting **(see illustrations)**.

18 Remove the exhaust front section as described in Chapter 4D.

19 Remove the auxiliary drivebelt as described in Chapter 1B.

20 Remove the clamps securing the power

6.15 Coolant hoses at the inlet elbow on the left-hand end of the engine

steering fluid pressure pipe. This will allow the power steering pump to be removed from the engine without disconnecting the fluid lines.

21 Unbolt the power steering pump from the engine, with reference to Chapter 10, but leave the fluid lines connected, and support the pump clear of the working area.

22 Remove the right-hand driveshaft as described in Chapter 8, and disconnect the left-hand driveshaft from the transmission.

23 On models with air conditioning, remove the air conditioning compressor as described in Chapter 3.

⚠ *Warning: Have the air conditioning system discharged by a suitably-qualified specialist before attempting to remove the compressor.*

24 If not already done, connect a hoist and lifting tackle to the engine lifting brackets on the cylinder head, and raise the hoist to just take the weight of the engine.

25 Remove the right-hand and left-hand engine/transmission mountings, with reference to Chapter 2C.

26 Carefully lower the engine/transmission assembly out from under the vehicle. Support the assembly on a trolley, or on wooden blocks. Manipulate the assembly out from underneath the vehicle.

Engine and transmission separation

Manual transmission

27 Unscrew the two securing bolts, and remove the starter motor.

6.17a Coolant temperature sensor wiring plug (arrowed)

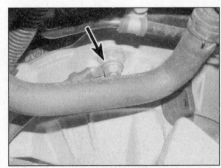

6.17b Earth strap attachment point on transmission bellhousing

28 Where applicable, unscrew the bolt securing the small engine-to-transmission plate to the transmission.

29 Ensure that both engine and transmission are adequately supported, then unscrew the remaining engine-to-transmission bolts, noting the location of each bolt, and the locations of any brackets secured by the bolts.

30 Carefully withdraw the transmission from the engine, ensuring that the weight of the transmission is not allowed to hang on the input shaft while it is engaged with the clutch friction disc. Recover the engine-to-transmission plate.

Automatic transmission

31 Unscrew the two securing bolts, and remove the starter motor.

32 Prise out the torque converter nuts cover from the transmission casing. The cover is located behind the left-hand driveshaft flange. Turn the crankshaft to position one of the torque converter-to-driveplate nuts in the access aperture. Unscrew and remove the nut whilst preventing the engine from turning using a wide-bladed screwdriver engaged with the ring gear teeth on the driveplate.

33 Using the same method described in the previous paragraph, unscrew the remaining two torque converter-to-driveplate nuts, turning the crankshaft a third-of-a-turn at a time to locate them.

34 Ensure that both engine and transmission are adequately supported, then unscrew the engine-to-transmission bolts, noting the location of each bolt, and the locations of any brackets secured by the bolts.

35 Carefully withdraw the transmission from the engine (take care – the transmission is heavy), making sure that the torque converter remains fully engaged with the transmission input shaft. If necessary, use a lever to release the torque converter from the driveplate. Recover the engine-to-transmission plate.

36 Once the transmission has been separated from the engine, strap a restraining bar across the front of the bellhousing to keep the torque converter in position.

Engine and transmission reconnection and refitting

Manual transmission

37 Reconnection and refitting are a reversal of removal, bearing in mind the following points:
a) Smear the splines of the transmission input shaft with a little high melting points grease.
b) Ensure that any brackets noted before removal are in place on the engine-to-transmission bolts.
c) Tighten all fixings to the specified torque, where given.
d) Refit the engine mountings with reference to Chapter 2C.
e) Refit the right-hand driveshaft, and reconnect the driveshafts to the transmission with reference to Chapter 8.

f) Where applicable, refit the air conditioning compressor, with reference to Chapter 3, and have the system recharged with refrigerant by a suitably-qualified professional.
g) Refit the auxiliary drivebelt with reference to Chapter 1B.
h) Refit the exhaust front section with reference to Chapter 4D.
i) Ensure that all wiring, hoses and pipes are correctly reconnected and routed as noted before removal.
j) Ensure that the fuel lines are correctly reconnected. The lines are colour-coded, white for supply, and blue for return.
k) Refit the clutch slave cylinder as described in Chapter 6, and reconnect the gear selector mechanism to the transmission as described in Chapter 7A.
l) On completion, refill the cooling system as described in Chapter 1B.

Automatic transmission

38 Proceed as described in paragraph 37, but note the following additional points:
a) When fitting the torque converter, make sure that both the drive pins engage with the transmission fluid pump.
b) Reconnect and if necessary adjust the gear selector cable, as described in Chapter 7B.
c) On completion, check and if necessary top-up the automatic transmission fluid level as described in Chapter 1B.

7 Engine overhaul – preliminary information

1 It is much easier to dismantle and work on the engine if it is mounted on a portable engine stand. These stands can often be hired from a tool hire shop. Before the engine is mounted on a stand, the flywheel should be removed, so that the stand bolts can be tightened into the end of the cylinder block/crankcase. **Note:** Do not measure cylinder bore dimensions with the engine mounted on this type of stand.

2 If a stand is not available, it is possible to dismantle the engine with it blocked up on a sturdy workbench, or on the floor. Be very careful not to tip or drop the engine when working without a stand.

3 If you intend to obtain a reconditioned engine, all ancillaries must be removed first, to be transferred to the new engine (just as they will if you are doing a complete engine overhaul yourself). These components include the following (it may be necessary to transfer additional components, such as the oil level dipstick/tube assembly, oil filter housing, etc, depending on which components are supplied with the reconditioned engine):

Petrol engines

a) Alternator (including mounting brackets) and starter motor (Chapter 5A).

b) The ignition system components including all sensors, HT leads and spark plugs (Chapters 1A and 5B).
c) The fuel injection system components (Chapter 4A).
d) All electrical switches, actuators and sensors, and the engine wiring harness (Chapters 3, 4A and 5B).
e) Inlet and exhaust manifolds, and turbo-charger (where applicable) (Chapter 4C).
f) Engine mountings (Chapter 2A or 2B).
g) Clutch components (Chapter 6).
h) Oil separator (where applicable).

Diesel engines

a) Alternator (including mounting brackets) and starter motor (Chapter 5A).
b) The glow plug/preheating system components (Chapter 5C).
c) All fuel system components, including the fuel injection pump, fuel injectors, all sensors and actuators (Chapter 4B).
d) The brake vacuum pump (Chapter 9).
e) All electrical switches, actuators and sensors, and the engine wiring harness (Chapter 3, 4B and 5C).
f) Inlet and exhaust manifolds, and turbo-charger (where applicable) (Chapter 4B).
g) Engine mountings (Chapter 2B).
h) Clutch components (Chapter 6).

All engines

Note: When removing the external components from the engine, pay close attention to details that may be helpful or important during refitting. Note the fitted position of gaskets, seals, spacers, pins, washers, bolts, and other small components.

4 If you are obtaining a short engine (the engine cylinder block/crankcase, crankshaft, pistons and connecting rods, all fully assembled), then the cylinder head, sump, oil pump, timing belt(s) and chain (as applicable – together with tensioner(s) and covers), auxiliary drivebelt (together with its tensioner), coolant pump, thermostat housing, coolant outlet elbows, oil filter housing and where applicable oil cooler will also have to be removed.

5 If you are planning a full overhaul, the engine can be dismantled in the order given below:
a) Inlet and exhaust manifolds (see the relevant part of Chapter 4).
b) Timing belt(s), sprockets and tensioner(s) (see Chapter 2A, 2B or 2C).
c) Inlet camshaft timing chain and tensioner/camshaft adjuster mechanism – 1.8 litre engines (see Chapter 2B).
d) Cylinder head (see Chapter 2A, 2B or 2C).
e) Flywheel/driveplate (see Chapter 2A, 2B or 2C).
f) Sump (see Chapter 2A, 2B or 2C).
g) Oil pump (see Chapter 2A, 2B or 2C).
h) Piston/connecting rod assemblies (see Section 11).
i) Crankshaft (see Section 12).

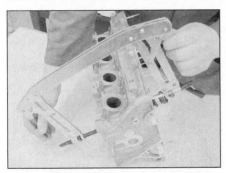

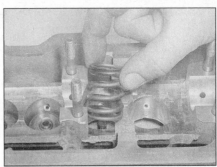

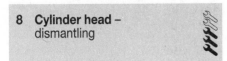

8.9a Compressing a valve spring with a compressor tool

8.9b Removing the spring cap . . .

8.9c . . . and valve spring – SOHC engine

8 Cylinder head – dismantling

Note: *A valve spring compressor tool will be required for this operation.*

SOHC petrol engines

1 With the cylinder head removed as described in Chapter 2A, proceed as follows.
2 Remove the inlet and exhaust manifolds as described in Chapter 4A and 4C respectively.
3 Remove the camshaft and hydraulic tappets/roller rocker fingers, as described in Chapter 2A.
4 If desired, unbolt the coolant housing from the rear of the cylinder head, and recover the seal.
5 If not already done, remove the camshaft position sensor, with reference to Chapter 4A, Section 5.
6 Unscrew the securing nut, and recover the washer, and remove the timing belt tensioner pulley from the stud on the cylinder head.
7 Unbolt any remaining auxiliary brackets and/or engine lifting brackets from the cylinder head as necessary, noting their locations to aid refitting.
8 Turn the cylinder head over, and rest it on one side.
9 Using a valve spring compressor, compress each valve spring in turn, until the split collets can be removed. Release the compressor, and lift off the spring cap and spring. If, when the valve spring compressor is screwed

down, the spring cap refuses to free and expose the split collets, gently tap the top of the tool, directly over the spring cap, with a light hammer. This will free the retainer **(see illustrations)**.
10 Using a pair of pliers, or a removal tool, carefully extract the valve stem oil seal from the top of the valve guide **(see illustration)**.
11 Withdraw the valve from the gasket side of the cylinder head **(see illustration)**.
12 It is essential that each valve is stored together with its collets, cap, spring and spring seat. The valves should be kept in their correct sequences, unless they are so badly worn that they are to be renewed.

 HAYNES HINT *If they are going to be kept and used again, place each valve assembly in a labelled polythene bag or similar small container. Label each bag from 1 to 8, noting that No 1 valve is nearest to the timing belt end of the cylinder head.*

DOHC petrol engines

1.4 and 1.6 litre

13 With the cylinder head removed as described in Chapter 2B, proceed as follows.
14 Remove the inlet and exhaust manifolds as described in Chapter 4A and 4C respectively.
15 Unscrew the securing bolt and remove the secondary timing belt tensioner from the timing belt end of the cylinder head.
16 Unbolt any remaining auxiliary brackets

and/or engine lifting brackets from the cylinder head as necessary, noting their locations to aid refitting.
17 Proceed as described in paragraphs 8 to 12, but when labelling the valve components, make sure that the valves are identified as inlet and exhaust, as well as numbered.

1.8 litre

18 With the cylinder head removed as described in Chapter 2B, proceed as follows.
19 Remove the inlet and exhaust manifolds (and turbocharger, where applicable) as described in Chapters 4A and 4C.
20 Remove the camshafts and hydraulic tappets as described in Chapter 2B.
21 Unbolt any remaining auxiliary brackets and/or engine lifting brackets from the cylinder head as necessary, noting their locations to aid refitting.
22 Proceed as described in paragraphs 8 to 12, but when labelling the valve components, make sure that the valves are identified as inlet and exhaust, as well as numbered.

Diesel engines

23 With the cylinder head removed as described in Chapter 2C, proceed as follows.
24 Remove the inlet and exhaust manifolds (and turbocharger, where applicable) as described in Chapters 4B and 4D.
25 Remove the camshaft and hydraulic tappets, as described in Chapter 2C.
26 Remove the glow plugs, with reference to Chapter 5C.
27 Remove the fuel injectors, with reference to Chapter 4B.

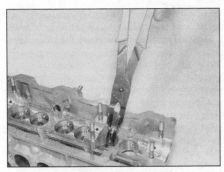

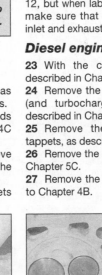

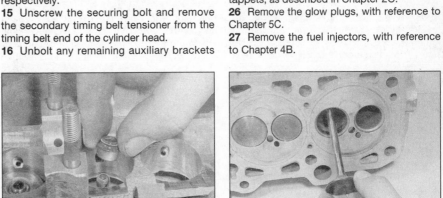

8.10a Using a removal tool . . .

8.10b . . . to remove the valve stem oil seals – SOHC engine

8.11 Removing a valve – SOHC engine

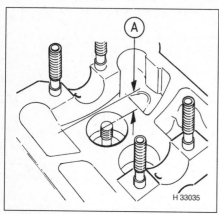

9.6 Measure the distance (A) between the top face of the valve stem and the top surface of the cylinder head

28 Unscrew the nut and remove the timing belt tensioner pulley from the stud on the timing belt end of the cylinder head.

29 Unbolt any remaining auxiliary brackets and/or engine lifting brackets from the cylinder head as necessary, noting their locations to aid refitting.

30 Proceed as described in paragraphs 8 to 12.

9 Cylinder head and valves – cleaning and inspection

1 Thorough cleaning of the cylinder head and valve components, followed by a detailed inspection, will enable you to decide how much valve service work must be carried out during engine overhaul. **Note:** *If the engine has been severely overheated, it is best to assume that the cylinder head is warped – check carefully for signs of this.*

Cleaning

2 Using a suitable degreasing agent, remove all traces of oil deposits from the cylinder head, paying particular attention to the camshaft bearing surfaces, hydraulic tappet bores, valve guides and oilways. Scrape off any traces of old gasket from the mating surfaces, taking care not to score or gouge them. If using emery paper, do not use a

grade of less than 100. Turn the head over and, using a blunt blade, scrape any carbon deposits from the combustion chambers and ports. Finally, wash the entire head casting with a suitable solvent to remove the remaining debris.

3 Clean the valve heads and stems using a fine wire brush (or a power-operated wire brush). If the valve is covered with heavy carbon deposits, scrape off the majority of the deposits with a blunt blade first, then use the wire brush.

4 Thoroughly clean the remainder of the components using solvent and allow them to dry completely. Discard the oil seals, as new ones must be fitted when the cylinder head is reassembled.

Inspection

Cylinder head

Note: *If the valve seats are to be recut, ensure that the maximum permissible reworking dimension is not exceeded (the maximum dimension will only allow minimal reworking to produce a perfect seal between valve and seat). If the maximum dimension is exceeded, the function of the hydraulic tappets cannot be guaranteed, and the cylinder head must be renewed. Refer to paragraph 6 for details of how to calculate the maximum permissible reworking dimension.*

5 Examine the head casting closely to identify any damage or cracks that may have developed. Cracks can often be identified from evidence of coolant or oil leakage. Pay particular attention to the areas around the valve seats and spark plug/fuel injector holes. If cracking is discovered in this area, VW state that on diesel engines and SOHC petrol engines, the cylinder head may be re-used, provided the cracks are no larger than 0.5 mm wide on diesel engines, or 0.3 mm wide on SOHC petrol engines. More serious damage will mean the renewal of the cylinder head casting.

6 Moderately pitted and scorched valve seats can be repaired by lapping the valves in during reassembly, as described later in this Chapter. Badly worn or damaged valve seats may be restored by recutting, however the maximum permissible reworking dimension **must** not be exceeded, which will only allow

minimal reworking (see note at beginning of paragraph 5). To calculate the maximum permissible reworking dimension, proceed as follows **(see illustration)**:

a) *If a new valve is to be fitted, use the new valve for the following calculation.*

b) *Insert the valve into its guide in the cylinder head, and push the valve firmly on to its seat.*

c) *Using a flat edge placed across the top surface of the cylinder head, measure the distance between the top face of the valve stem, and the top surface of the cylinder head. Record the measurement obtained.*

d) *Consult the Specifications, and look up the value for the minimum permissible dimension between the top face of the valve stem and the top surface of the cylinder head.*

e) *Now take the measured distance and subtract the minimum permissible dimension, to give the maximum permissible reworking dimension; eg, Measured distance (34.4 mm) minus Minimum permissible dimension (34.0 mm) = Maximum permissible reworking dimension (0.4 mm).*

7 Measure any distortion of the gasket surfaces using a straight-edge and a set of feeler blades. Take one measurement longitudinally on the manifold mating surface(s). Take several measurements across the head gasket surface, to assess the level of distortion in all planes **(see illustration)**. Compare the measurements with the figures in the Specifications.

8 On petrol engines, if the head is distorted beyond the specified limit, it may be possible to have it machined by an engineering works, provided that the minimum permissible cylinder head height is maintained.

9 On diesel engines, if the head is distorted beyond the specified limit, the head must be renewed.

Camshaft

10 Inspection of the camshaft is covered in Part A, B or C of this Chapter, as applicable.

Valves and associated components

Note: *On all engines, the valve heads cannot be recut, although they may be lapped in. On 1.8 litre petrol engines, if new valves are to be fitted, the old valves must be disposed of carefully (do not dispose of them as normal scrap), as the valve stems are filled with sodium. Consult your local scrap or recycling centre for advice.*

11 Examine each valve closely for signs of wear. Inspect the valve stems for wear ridges, scoring or variations in diameter; measure their diameters at several points along their lengths with a micrometer, and compare with the figures given in the Specifications **(see illustration)**.

12 The valve heads should not be cracked, badly pitted or charred. Note that light pitting of the valve head can be rectified by lapping-

9.7 Measuring the distortion of the cylinder head gasket surface

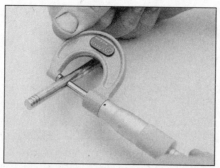

9.11 Measure the diameter of the valve stems using a micrometer

in the valves during reassembly, as described in Section 10.

13 Check that the valve stem end face is free from excessive pitting or indentation; this could be caused by defective hydraulic tappets.

14 Using vernier calipers, measure the free length of each of the valve springs. As a manufacturer's figure is not quoted, the only way to check the length of the springs is by comparison with a new component. Note that valve springs are usually renewed during a major engine overhaul **(see illustration)**.

15 Stand each spring on its end on a flat surface, against an engineer's square **(see illustration)**. Check the squareness of the spring visually, and renew it if it appears distorted.

16 Renew the valve stem oil seals regardless of their apparent condition.

---

10 Cylinder head – reassembly

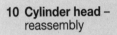

Note: *A valve spring compressor tool will be required for this operation.*

SOHC petrol engines

1 To achieve a gas-tight seal between the valves and their seats, it will be necessary to lap-in (or grind-in) the valves. To complete this process you will need a quantity of fine/coarse grinding paste and a grinding tool – this can either be of the rubber sucker type, or the automatic type which is driven by a rotary power tool.

2 Smear a small quantity of *fine* grinding paste on the sealing face of the valve head. Turn the cylinder head over so that the combustion chambers are facing upwards and insert the valve into the correct guide. Attach the grinding tool to the valve head and using a backward/forward rotary action, grind the valve head into its seat. Periodically lift the valve and rotate it to redistribute the grinding paste **(see illustration)**.

3 Continue this process until the contact between valve and seat produces an unbroken, matt grey ring of uniform width, on both faces. Repeat the operation on the remaining valves.

4 If the valves and seats are so badly pitted

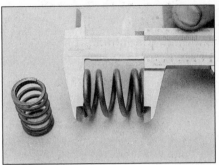

9.14 Measure the free length of each valve spring

that coarse grinding paste must be used, bear in that there is a maximum permissible reworking dimension for the valves and seats. Refer to the Specifications at the beginning of this Chapter for the minimum dimension from the end of the valve stem to the top face of the cylinder head (see Section 9, paragraph 6). If this minimum dimension is exceeded due to excessive lapping-in, the hydraulic tappets may not operate correctly, and the cylinder head must be renewed.

5 Assuming the repair is feasible, work as described previously, but use coarse grinding paste initially, to achieve a dull finish on the valve face and seat. Wash off the coarse paste with solvent and repeat the process using fine grinding paste to obtain the correct finish.

6 When all the valves have been ground in, remove all traces of grinding paste from the cylinder head and valves using solvent, and allow the head and valves to dry completely.

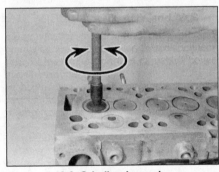

10.2 Grinding-in a valve

9.15 Checking the squareness of a valve spring

7 Turn the cylinder head on its side.

8 Working on one valve at a time, lubricate the valve stem with clean engine oil, and insert the valve into its guide. Fit one of the protective plastic sleeves supplied with the new valve stem oil seals over the end of the valve stem – this will protect the oil seal as it is being fitted **(see illustrations)**.

9 Dip a new valve stem seal in clean engine oil, and carefully push it over the valve stem and onto the top of the valve guide – take care not to damage the stem seal as it is fitted. Use a suitable long-reach socket or a suitable valve stem seal fitting tool to press the seal firmly into position **(see illustration)**. Remove the protective sleeve from the valve stem.

10 Locate the valve spring over the valve stem, ensuring that the lower end of the spring seats correctly on the cylinder head **(see illustration)**.

11 Fit the upper spring seat over the top of

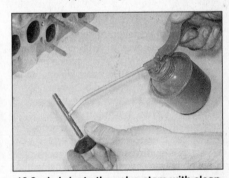

10.8a Lubricate the valve stem with clean engine oil – SOHC engine

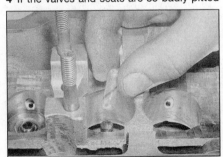

10.8b Fitting a protective sleeve over the valve stem before fitting the stem seal – SOHC engine

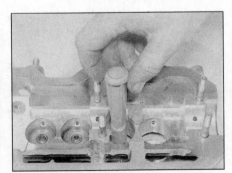

10.9 Using a special installer to fit a valve stem oil seal – SOHC engine

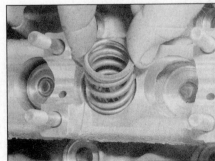

10.10 Fitting a valve spring – SOHC engine

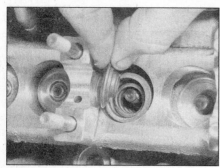

10.11a Fitting the upper spring seat – SOHC engine

10.11b Use grease to hold the split collets in the groove – SOHC engine

the spring, then using a valve spring compressor, compress the spring until the upper seat is pushed beyond the collet grooves in the valve stem. Refit the split collets. Gradually release the spring compressor, checking that the collets remain correctly seated as the spring extends. When correctly seated, the upper spring seat should force the collets securely into the grooves in the end of the valve stem **(see illustrations)**.

 HAYNES HiNT *Use a little dab of grease to hold the collets in position on the valve stem while the spring compressor is released.*

12 Repeat this process for the remaining sets of valve components, ensuring that all components are refitted to their original locations. To settle the components after

installation, strike the end of each valve stem with a mallet, using a block of wood to protect the stem from damage. Check before progressing any further that the split collets remain firmly seated in the grooves in the end of the valve stem.

13 Refit any auxiliary brackets and/or engine lifting brackets to their original locations, as noted before removal.

14 Refit the timing belt tensioner pulley, and secure with the nut and washer.

15 Where applicable, refit the camshaft position sensor, with reference to Chapter 4A, Section 5.

16 Where applicable, refit the coolant housing to the rear of the cylinder head, using a new seal.

17 Refit the camshaft and hydraulic tappets as described in Chapter 2A.

18 Refit the inlet and exhaust manifolds as described in Chapter 4A and 4C.

1.4 and 1.6 litre DOHC petrol engines

19 Proceed as described in paragraphs 1 to 13 **(see illustrations)**.
20 Refit the secondary timing belt tensioner, then refit the securing bolt.
21 Refit the inlet and exhaust manifolds as described in Chapter 4A and 4C.

1.8 litre DOHC petrol engines

22 Proceed as described in paragraphs 1 to 13.
23 Refit the hydraulic tappets and camshafts as described in Chapter 2B.
24 Refit the inlet and exhaust manifolds as described in Chapter 4A and 4C.

Diesel engines

25 Proceed as described in paragraphs 1 to 13.
26 Refit the timing belt tensioner pulley to the stud on the cylinder head, and refit the securing nut.
27 Refit the fuel injectors, with reference to Chapter 4B.
28 Refit the glow plugs, with reference to Chapter 5C.
29 Refit the hydraulic tappets and camshaft, as described in Chapter 2C.
30 Refit the inlet and exhaust manifolds (and turbocharger, where applicable), as described in Chapter 4B.

11 Piston/connecting rod assemblies – removal

1 Proceed as follows according to engine type:
a) On SOHC petrol engines, remove the cylinder head, sump and oil baffle plate, and oil pump and pick-up pipe, as described in Chapter 2A. **Note:** On 2.0 litre AZJ engines, it will necessary to remove the balance shaft assembly.
b) On 1.4 and 1.6 litre DOHC petrol engines, remove the cylinder head, sump, and oil pick-up pipe, as described in Chapter 2B.
c) On 1.8 litre DOHC engines, remove the cylinder head, sump and oil baffle plate, and oil pump and pick-up pipe, as described in Chapter 2B.
d) On diesel engines, remove the cylinder head, sump and oil baffle plate, and oil pump and pick-up pipe, as described in Chapter 2C.

2 Inspect the tops of the cylinder bores for ridges at the point where the pistons reach top dead centre. These must be removed otherwise the pistons may be damaged when they are pushed out of their bores. Use a scraper or ridge reamer to remove the ridges. Such a ridge indicates excessive wear of the cylinder bore.

3 Check the connecting rods and big-end caps for identification markings. Both connecting rods and caps should be marked with the cylinder number on one side of each

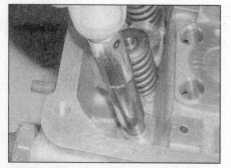

10.19a Using a long-reach socket to fit a valve stem oil seal – 1.4 litre DOHC engine

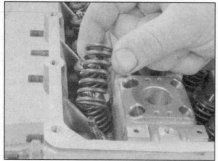

10.19b Fitting a valve spring . . .

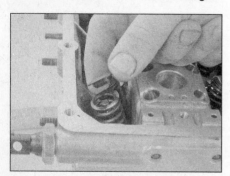

10.19c . . . and upper spring seat – 1.4 litre DOHC engine

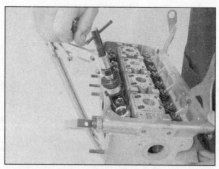

10.19d Compressing a valve spring using a compressor tool – 1.4 litre DOHC engine

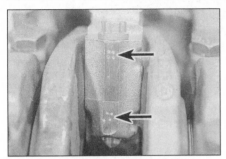

11.3 Mark the big-end caps and connecting rods with their cylinder numbers (arrowed)

11.6a Unscrew the big-end bearing cap bolts . . .

11.6b . . . and remove the cap

assembly. Note that No 1 cylinder is at the timing belt end of the engine. If no marks are present, using a hammer and centre-punch, paint or similar, mark each connecting rod and big-end bearing cap with its respective cylinder number – note on which side of the connecting rods and caps the marks are made **(see illustration)**.

4 Similarly, check the piston crowns for direction markings. An arrow on each piston crown should point towards the timing belt end of the engine. On some engines, this mark may be obscured by carbon build-up, in which case the piston crown should be cleaned to check for a mark. In some cases, the direction arrow may have worn off, in which case a suitable mark should be made on the piston crown using a scriber – do not deeply score the piston crown, but ensure that the mark is easily visible.

5 Turn the crankshaft to bring Nos 1 and 4 pistons to bottom dead centre.

6 Unscrew the bolts or nuts, as applicable, from No 1 piston big-end bearing cap. Lift off the cap, and recover the bottom half bearing shell. If the bearing shells are to be re-used, tape the cap and bearing shell together. Note that if the bearing shells are to be re-used, they must be fitted to the original connecting rod and cap **(see illustrations)**.

7 Where the bearing caps are secured with nuts, wrap the threaded ends of the bolts with insulating tape to prevent them scratching the crankpins and bores when the pistons are removed **(see illustration)**.

8 Using a hammer handle, push the piston up through the bore, and remove it from the top of the cylinder block. Where applicable, take care not to damage the piston cooling oil spray jets in the cylinder block as the piston/connecting rod assembly is removed. Recover the upper bearing shell, and tape it to the connecting rod for safe-keeping.

9 Loosely refit the big-end cap to the connecting rod, and secure with the bolts or nuts, as applicable – this will help to keep the components in their correct order.

10 Remove No 4 piston assembly in the same way.

11 Turn the crankshaft as necessary to bring Nos 2 and 3 pistons to bottom dead centre, and remove them in the same way.

12 Where applicable, remove the securing bolts, and withdraw the piston cooling oil spray jets from the bottom of the cylinder block **(see illustrations)**.

12 Crankshaft – removal

> ⚠ **Warning: On 1.4 litre engines, the crankshaft must not be removed. Loosening the main bearing cap bolts will cause deformation of the cylinder block. On these engines, if the crankshaft or main bearing surfaces are worn or damaged, the complete crankshaft/ cylinder block assembly must be renewed. The following procedure applies to all engines except 1.4 litre engines.**

Note: *If no work is to be done on the pistons and connecting rods, there is no need to push the pistons out of the cylinder bores. The pistons should just be pushed far enough up the bores so that they are positioned clear of the crankshaft journals.*

1 Proceed as follows according to engine type:

a) *On SOHC petrol engines, remove the timing belt and crankshaft sprocket, sump and oil baffle plate, oil pump and pick-up pipe, flywheel/driveplate, and the crankshaft oil seal housings, as described in Chapter 2A.* **Note:** *On 2.0 litre AZJ engines, it will necessary to remove the balance shaft assembly.*

b) *On 1.6 litre DOHC petrol engines, remove the main timing belt, sump, oil pump and pick-up pipe, flywheel/driveplate, and the crankshaft oil seal housing, as described in Chapter 2B.*

c) *On 1.8 litre DOHC petrol engines, remove*

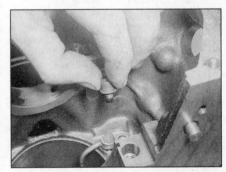

11.7 Wrap the threaded ends of the bolts with tape

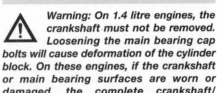

11.12a Remove the securing bolts . . .

11.12b . . . and withdraw the piston cooling oil spray jets

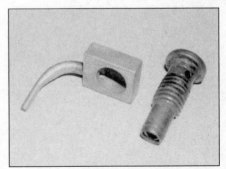

11.12c Piston cooling spray jet and retainer

12.5 Slacken and remove the main bearing cap bolts

the timing belt and crankshaft sprocket, sump and oil baffle plate, oil pump and pick-up pipe, flywheel/driveplate, and the crankshaft oil seal housings, as described in Chapter 2B.

d) On diesel engines, remove the timing belt and crankshaft sprocket, sump and oil baffle plate, oil pump and pick-up pipe, flywheel/driveplate, and the crankshaft oil seal housings, as described in Chapter 2C.

2 Remove the pistons and connecting rods, or disconnect them from the crankshaft, as described in Section 11 (see Note at the beginning of this Section).

3 Check the crankshaft endfloat as described in Section 15, then proceed as follows.

4 The main bearing caps should be numbered 1 to 5 from the timing belt end of the engine. If the bearing caps are not marked, mark them accordingly using a centre-punch. Note the orientation of the markings to ensure correct refitting.

5 Slacken and remove the main bearing cap bolts, and lift off each cap. If the caps appear to be stuck, tap them with a soft-faced mallet to free them from the cylinder block **(see illustration)**. Recover the lower bearing shells, and tape them to their caps for safe-keeping.

6 On 1.6 litre DOHC petrol engines and diesel engines, recover the lower crankshaft endfloat control thrustwasher halves from either side of the No 3 main bearing cap, noting their orientation.

7 Lift the crankshaft from the cylinder block **(see illustration)**. Take care, as the crankshaft is heavy. On engines with a

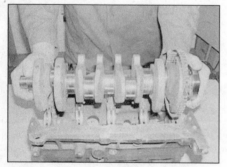

12.7 Lifting the crankshaft from the cylinder block

crankshaft speed/position sensor fitted, lay the crankshaft on wooden blocks – **do not** rest the crankshaft on the sensor wheel.

8 Recover the upper bearing shells from the cylinder block, and tape them to their respective caps for safe-keeping. Similarly, recover the upper crankshaft endfloat control thrustwasher halves, noting their orientation.

9 On engines with a crankshaft speed/position sensor wheel fitted, unscrew the securing bolts, and remove the sensor wheel, noting which way round it is fitted.

13 Cylinder block/crankcase – cleaning and inspection

Cleaning

1 Remove all external components and electrical switches/sensors from the block, including mounting brackets, the coolant pump, the oil filter/cooler housing, etc. For complete cleaning, the core plugs should ideally be removed. Drill a small hole in the plugs, then insert a self-tapping screw into the hole. Extract the plugs by pulling on the screw with a pair of grips, or by using a slide hammer.

2 Scrape all traces of gasket and sealant from the cylinder block/crankcase, taking care not to damage the sealing surfaces.

3 Remove all oil gallery plugs (where fitted). The plugs are usually very tight – they may have to be drilled out, and the holes *re*tapped. Use new plugs when the engine is reassembled.

4 If the casting is extremely dirty, it should be steam-cleaned. After this, clean all oil holes and galleries one more time. Flush all internal passages with warm water until the water runs clear. Dry thoroughly, and apply a light film of oil to all mating surfaces and cylinder bores, to prevent rusting. If you have access to compressed air, use it to speed up the drying process, and to blow out all the oil holes and galleries.

 Warning: Wear eye protection when using compressed air.

5 If the castings are not very dirty, you can do an adequate cleaning job with hot, soapy water and a stiff brush. Take plenty of time, and do a thorough job. Regardless of the cleaning method used, be sure to clean all oil holes and galleries very thoroughly, and to dry all components well. Protect the cylinder bores as described above, to prevent rusting.

6 Where applicable, check the piston cooling oil spray jets **(see illustrations 11.12a and 11.12b)** for damage, and renew if necessary. Check the oil spray hole and the oil passages for blockage.

7 All threaded holes must be clean, to ensure accurate torque readings during reassembly. To clean the threads, run the correct-size tap into each of the holes to remove rust,

corrosion, thread sealant or sludge, and to restore damaged threads **(see illustration)**. If possible, use compressed air to clear the holes free of debris produced by this operation. **Note:** *Take extra care to exclude all cleaning liquid from blind tapped holes, as the casting may be cracked by hydraulic action if a bolt is threaded into a hole containing liquid.*

HAYNES HiNT *A good alternative is to inject aerosol-applied water dispersant lubricant into each hole, using the long spout usually supplied.*
Warning: Wear eye protection when cleaning out these holes in this way.

8 After coating the mating surfaces of the new core plugs with suitable sealant, fit them to the cylinder block. Make sure that they are driven in straight and seated correctly, or leakage could result.

HAYNES HiNT *A large socket with an outside diameter which will just fit into the core plug can be used to the drive core plug into position.*

9 Apply suitable sealant to the new oil gallery plugs, and insert them into the holes in the block. Tighten them securely.

10 If the engine is not going to be reassembled immediately, cover it with a large plastic bag to keep it clean; protect all mating surfaces and the cylinder bores, to prevent rusting.

Inspection

11 Visually check the castings for cracks and corrosion. Look for stripped threads in the threaded holes. If there has been any history of internal coolant leakage, it may be worthwhile having an engine overhaul specialist check the cylinder block/crankcase for cracks with special equipment. If defects are found, have them repaired, if possible, or renew the assembly.

12 Check each cylinder bore for scuffing and scoring.

13.7 To clean the cylinder block threads, run a correct-size tap into the holes

13 If in any doubt as the condition of the cylinder block have the block/bores inspected and measured by an engine reconditioning specialist. They will be able to advise on whether the block is serviceable, whether a rebore is necessary, and supply the appropriate pistons and rings.

14 If the bores are in reasonably good condition and not excessively worn, then it may only be necessary to renew the piston rings.

15 If this is the case, the bores should be honed, to allow the new rings to bed-in correctly and provide the best possible seal. Consult an engine reconditioning specialist

16 On diesel engines, if the oil/water pump housing was removed, it can be refitted at this stage if wished. Use a new gasket, and before fully tightening the bolts, align the housing faces with those of the engine block.

17 The cylinder block/crankcase should now be completely clean and dry, with all components checked for wear or damage, and repaired or overhauled as necessary.

18 Apply a light coating of engine oil to the mating surfaces and cylinder bores to prevent rust forming.

19 Refit as many ancillary components as possible, for safe-keeping. If reassembly is not to start immediately, cover the block with a large plastic bag to keep it clean, and protect the machined surfaces as described above to prevent rusting.

14 Piston/connecting rod assemblies – cleaning and inspection

Cleaning

1 Before the inspection process can begin, the piston/connecting rod assemblies must be cleaned, and the original piston rings removed from the pistons.

2 The rings should have smooth, polished working surfaces, with no dull or carbon-coated sections (showing that the ring is not sealing correctly against the bore wall, so allowing combustion gases to blow by) and no traces of wear on their top and bottom surfaces. The end gaps should be clear of carbon, but not polished (indicating a too-small end gap), and all the rings (including the elements of the oil control ring) should be free to rotate in their grooves, but without excessive up-and-down movement. If the rings appear to be in good condition, they are probably fit for further use; check the end gaps (in an unworn part of the bore) as described in Section 18.

3 If any of the rings appears to be worn or damaged, or has an end gap significantly different from the specified value, the usual course of action is to renew all of them as a set. **Note:** *While it is usual to renew piston rings when an engine is overhauled, they may be re-used if in acceptable condition. If re-using the rings, make sure that each ring is marked during removal to ensure that it is refitted correctly.*

4 Carefully expand the old rings over the top of the pistons. The use of two or three old feeler blades will be helpful in preventing the rings dropping into empty grooves **(see illustration)**. Be careful not to scratch the piston with the ends of the ring. The rings are brittle, and will snap if they are spread too far. They are also very sharp – protect your hands and fingers. Note that the third ring incorporates an expander. Keep each set of rings with its piston if the old rings are to be re-used. Note which way up each ring is fitted to ensure correct refitting.

5 Scrape away all traces of carbon from the top of the piston. A hand-held wire brush (or a piece of fine emery cloth) can be used, once the majority of the deposits have been scraped away.

6 Remove the carbon from the ring grooves in the piston, using an old ring. Break the ring in half to do this (be careful not to cut your fingers – piston rings are sharp). Be careful to remove only the carbon deposits – do not remove any metal, and do not nick or scratch the sides of the ring grooves.

7 Once the deposits have been removed, clean the piston/connecting rod assembly with paraffin or a suitable solvent, and dry thoroughly. Make sure that the oil return holes in the ring grooves are clear.

Inspection

8 If the pistons and cylinder bores are not damaged or worn excessively, and if the cylinder block does not need to be rebored, the original pistons can be refitted.

9 Using a micrometer, measure the diameter of all four pistons at a point 10 mm from the bottom of the skirt, at right-angles to the gudgeon pin axis **(see illustration)**. Compare the measurements with those listed in the Specifications. Note that the piston size grades are stamped on the piston crowns.

10 If the piston diameter is incorrect for its particular size, then it must be renewed. **Note:** *If the cylinder block was rebored during a previous overhaul, oversize pistons may already have been fitted.* Record all of the measurements and use them to check the piston clearances against the cylinder bore measurements made in Section 13.

11 Normal piston wear shows up as even vertical wear on the piston thrust surfaces, and slight looseness of the top ring in its groove. New piston rings should always be used when the engine is reassembled.

12 Carefully inspect each piston for cracks around the skirt, around the gudgeon pin holes, and at the piston ring 'lands' (between the ring grooves).

13 Look for scoring and scuffing on the piston skirt, holes in the piston crown, and burned areas at the edge of the crown. If the skirt is scored or scuffed, the engine may have been suffering from overheating, and/or

14.4 Old feeler blades can be used to prevent piston rings from dropping into empty grooves

abnormal combustion which caused excessively high operating temperatures. The cooling and lubrication systems should be checked thoroughly.

14 Scorch marks on the sides of the pistons show that blow-by has occurred.

15 A hole in the piston crown, or burned areas at the edge of the piston crown, indicates that abnormal combustion (pre-ignition, knocking, or detonation) has been occurring.

16 If any of the above problems exist, the causes must be investigated and corrected, or the damage will occur again. The causes may include incorrect ignition/injection pump timing, inlet air leaks or incorrect air/fuel mixture (petrol engines), or a faulty fuel injector (diesel engines).

17 Corrosion of the piston, in the form of pitting, indicates that coolant has been leaking into the combustion chamber and/or the crankcase. Again, the cause must be corrected, or the problem may persist in the rebuilt engine.

18 Locate a new piston ring in the appropriate groove and measure the ring-to-groove clearance using a feeler blade **(see illustration)**. Note that the rings are of different widths, so use the correct ring for the groove. Compare the measurements with those listed; if the clearances are outside of the tolerance band, then the piston must be renewed. Confirm this by checking the width of the piston ring with a micrometer.

19 New pistons can be purchased from a VW dealer.

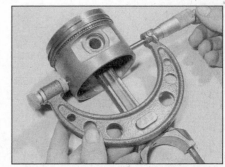

14.9 Using a micrometer to measure the diameter of a piston

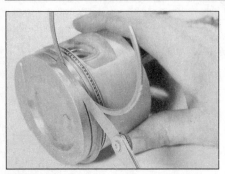

14.18 Measuring the piston ring-to-groove clearance using a feeler blade

14.22a Use a small flat-bladed screwdriver to prise out the circlip . . .

14.22b . . . then push out the gudgeon pin and separate the piston and connecting rod

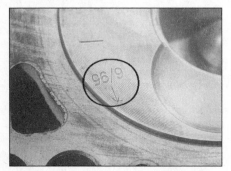

14.25a The piston crown is marked with an arrow which must point towards the timing belt end of the engine

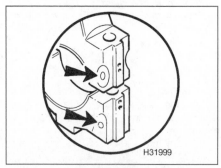

14.25b The recesses (arrowed) in the connecting rod and bearing cap must face towards the timing belt end of the engine

20 Examine each connecting rod carefully for signs of damage, such as cracks around the big-end and small-end bearings. Check that the rod is not bent or distorted. Damage is highly unlikely, unless the engine has been seized or badly overheated. Detailed checking of the connecting rod assembly can only be carried out by a VW dealer or engine repair specialist with the necessary equipment.

21 The gudgeon pins are of the floating type, secured in position by two circlips. The pistons and connecting rods can be separated as follows.

22 Using a small flat-bladed screwdriver, prise out the circlips, and push out the gudgeon pin **(see illustrations)**. Hand pressure should be sufficient to remove the pin. Identify the piston and rod to ensure correct reassembly. Discard the circlips – new ones *must* be used on refitting. If the

gudgeon pin proves difficult to remove, heat the piston to 60°C with hot water – the resulting expansion will then allow the two components to be separated.

23 Examine the gudgeon pin and connecting rod small-end bearing for signs of wear or damage. It should be possible to push the gudgeon pin through the connecting rod bush by hand, without noticeable play. Wear can be cured by renewing both the pin and bush. Bush renewal, however, is a specialist job – press facilities are required, and the new bush must be reamed accurately.

24 Examine all components, and obtain any new parts from your VW dealer. If new pistons are purchased, they will be supplied complete with gudgeon pins and circlips. Circlips can also be purchased individually.

25 The orientation of the piston with respect to the connecting rod must be correct when

the two are reassembled. The piston crown is marked with an arrow (which may be obscured by carbon deposits); this must point towards the timing belt end of the engine when the piston is installed. The connecting rod and its bearing cap both have recesses machined into them on one side, close to their mating surfaces – these recesses must both face the same way as the arrow on the piston crown (ie, towards the timing belt end of the engine) when correctly installed. Reassemble the two components to satisfy this requirement **(see illustrations)**.

26 Apply a smear of clean engine oil to the gudgeon pin. Slide it into the piston and through the connecting rod small-end. Check that the piston pivots freely on the rod, then secure the gudgeon pin in position with two new circlips. Ensure that each circlip is correctly located in its groove in the piston.

27 Repeat the cleaning and inspection process for the remaining pistons and connecting rods.

15 Crankshaft –
checking endfloat
and inspection

Checking endfloat

1 If the crankshaft endfloat is to be checked, this must be done when the crankshaft is still installed in the cylinder block/crankcase, but is free to move (see Section 12).

2 Check the endfloat using a dial gauge in contact with the end of the crankshaft. Push the crankshaft fully one way, and then zero the gauge. Push the crankshaft fully the other way, and check the endfloat. The result can be compared with the specified amount, and will give an indication as to whether new thrustwasher halves are required **(see illustration)**. Note that all thrustwashers must be of the same thickness.

3 If a dial gauge is not available, feeler blades can be used. First push the crankshaft fully towards the flywheel end of the engine, then use feeler blades to measure the gap between the web of No 3 crankpin and the thrustwasher halves **(see illustration)**.

15.2 Measuring crankshaft endfloat using a dial gauge

15.3 Measuring crankshaft endfloat using feeler blades

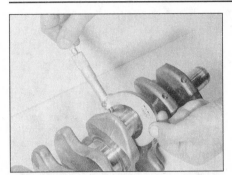

15.10 Use a micrometer to measure the diameter of each crankshaft bearing journal

Inspection

4 Clean the crankshaft using paraffin or a suitable solvent, and dry it, preferably with compressed air if available. Be sure to clean the oil holes with a pipe cleaner or similar probe, to ensure that they are not obstructed.

 Warning: Wear eye protection when using compressed air.

5 Check the main and big-end bearing journals for uneven wear, scoring, pitting and cracking.
6 Big-end bearing wear is accompanied by distinct metallic knocking when the engine is running (particularly noticeable when the engine is pulling from low speed) and some loss of oil pressure.
7 Main bearing wear is accompanied by severe engine vibration and rumble – getting progressively worse as engine speed increases – and again by loss of oil pressure.
8 Check the bearing journal for roughness by running a finger lightly over the bearing surface. Any roughness (which will be accompanied by obvious bearing wear) indicates that the crankshaft requires regrinding (where possible) or renewal.
9 If the crankshaft has been reground, check for burrs around the crankshaft oil holes (the holes are usually chamfered, so burrs should not be a problem unless regrinding has been carried out carelessly). Remove any burrs with a fine file or scraper, and thoroughly clean the oil holes as described previously.
10 Using a micrometer, measure the diameter of the main and big-end bearing journals, and compare the results with the Specifications **(see illustration)**. By measuring the diameter at a number of points around each journal's circumference, you will be able to determine whether or not the journal is out-of-round. Take the measurement at each end of the journal, near the webs, to determine if the journal is tapered.
11 Check the oil seal contact surfaces at each end of the crankshaft for wear and damage. If the seal has worn a deep groove in the surface of the crankshaft, consult an engine overhaul specialist; repair may be possible, but otherwise a new crankshaft will be required.
12 If the crankshaft journals have not already

been reground, it may be possible to have the crankshaft reconditioned, and to fit oversize shells (see Section 19). If no oversize shells are available and the crankshaft has worn beyond the specified limits, it will have to be renewed. Consult your VW dealer or engine specialist for further information on parts availability.

16 Main and big-end bearings – inspection

Inspection

1 Even though the main and big-end bearings should be renewed during the engine overhaul, the old bearings should be retained for close examination, as they may reveal valuable information about the condition of the engine **(see illustration)**.
2 Bearing failure can occur due to lack of lubrication, the presence of dirt or other foreign particles, overloading the engine, or corrosion. Regardless of the cause of bearing failure, the cause must be corrected before the engine is reassembled, to prevent it from happening again.
3 When examining the bearing shells, remove them from the cylinder block/crankcase, the main bearing caps, the connecting rods and the connecting rod big-end bearing caps. Lay them out on a clean surface in the same general position as their location in the engine. This will enable you to match any bearing problems with the corresponding crankshaft journal. *Do not* touch any shell's internal bearing surface with your fingers while checking it, or the delicate surface may be scratched.
4 Dirt and other foreign matter gets into the engine in a variety of ways. It may be left in the engine during assembly, or it may pass through filters or the crankcase ventilation system. It may get into the oil, and from there into the bearings. Metal chips from machining operations and normal engine wear are often present. Abrasives are sometimes left in engine components after reconditioning, especially when parts are not thoroughly cleaned using the proper cleaning methods. Whatever the source, these foreign objects often end up embedded in the soft bearing material, and are easily recognised. Large particles will not embed in the bearing, but will score or gouge the bearing and journal. The best prevention for this cause of bearing failure is to clean all parts thoroughly, and keep everything spotlessly-clean during engine assembly. Frequent and regular engine oil and filter changes are also recommended.
5 Lack of lubrication (or lubrication breakdown) has a number of interrelated causes. Excessive heat (which thins the oil), overloading (which squeezes the oil from the bearing face) and oil leakage (from excessive bearing clearances, worn oil pump or high

engine speeds) all contribute to lubrication breakdown. Blocked oil passages, which usually are the result of misaligned oil holes in a bearing shell, will also oil-starve a bearing, and destroy it. When lack of lubrication is the cause of bearing failure, the bearing material is wiped or extruded from the steel backing of the bearing. Temperatures may increase to the point where the steel backing turns blue from overheating.
6 Driving habits can have a definite effect on bearing life. Full-throttle, low-speed operation (labouring the engine) puts very high loads on bearings, tending to squeeze out the oil film. These loads cause the bearings to flex, which produces fine cracks in the bearing face (fatigue failure). Eventually, the bearing material will loosen in pieces, and tear away from the steel backing.
7 Short-distance driving leads to corrosion of bearings, because insufficient engine heat is produced to drive off the condensed water and corrosive gases. These products collect in the engine oil, forming acid and sludge. As the oil is carried to the engine bearings, the acid attacks and corrodes the bearing material.
8 Incorrect bearing installation during engine assembly will lead to bearing failure as well. Tight-fitting bearings leave insufficient bearing running clearance, and will result in oil starvation. Dirt or foreign particles trapped behind a bearing shell result in high spots on the bearing, which lead to failure.
9 *Do not* touch any shell's internal bearing surface with your fingers during reassembly as there is a risk of scratching the delicate surface, or of depositing particles of dirt on it.
10 As mentioned at the beginning of this Section, the bearing shells should be renewed as a matter of course during engine overhaul. To do otherwise is false economy.

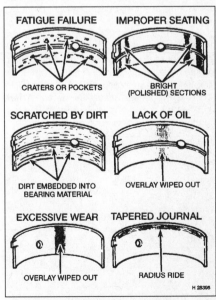

16.1 Typical bearing failures

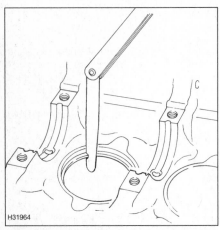

18.4 Checking a piston ring end gap using a feeler blade

Main and big-end bearings selection

11 Main and big-end bearings for the engines described in this Chapter are available in standard sizes and a range of undersizes to suit reground crankshafts.

12 The running clearances will need to be checked when the crankshaft is refitted with its new bearings (see Sections 19 and 20).

17 Engine overhaul –
reassembly sequence

1 Before reassembly begins, ensure that all new parts have been obtained, and that all necessary tools are available. Read through the entire procedure to familiarise yourself with the work involved, and to ensure that all items necessary for reassembly of the engine are at hand. In addition to all normal tools and materials, thread-locking compound will be needed. A suitable tube of liquid sealant will also be required for the joint faces that are fitted without gaskets.

2 In order to save time and avoid problems, engine reassembly can be carried out in the following order, referring to Part A, B, or C of this Chapter unless otherwise stated. Where applicable, use new gaskets and seals when refitting the various components.

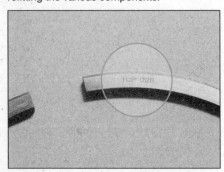

18.9 Piston ring TOP marking

a) Crankshaft (Section 19).
b) Piston/connecting rod assemblies (Section 20).
c) Oil pump.
d) Sump.
e) Flywheel/driveplate.
f) Cylinder head.
g) Timing belt(s), tensioner and sprockets.
h) Engine external components.

3 At this stage, all engine components should be absolutely clean and dry, with all faults repaired. The components should be laid out (or in individual containers) on a completely clean work surface.

18 Piston rings –
refitting

1 Before fitting new piston rings, the ring end gaps must be checked as follows.

2 Lay out the piston/connecting rod assemblies and the new piston ring sets, so that the ring sets will be matched with the same piston and cylinder during the end gap measurement and subsequent engine reassembly.

3 Insert the top ring into the first cylinder, and push it down the bore using the top of the piston. This will ensure that the ring remains square with the cylinder walls. Position the ring approximately 15.0 mm the bottom of the cylinder bore, at the lower limit of ring travel. Note that the top and second compression rings are different.

4 Measure the end gap using feeler blades, and compare the measurements with the figures given in the Specifications **(see illustration)**.

5 If the gap is too small (unlikely if genuine VW parts are used), it must be enlarged, or the ring ends may contact each other during engine operation, causing serious damage. Ideally, new piston rings providing the correct end gap should be fitted. As a last resort, the end gap can be increased by filing the ring ends very carefully with a fine file. Mount the file in a vice equipped with soft jaws, slip the ring over the file with the ends contacting the file face, and slowly move the ring to remove material from the ends. Take care, as piston rings are sharp, and are easily broken.

6 With new piston rings, it is unlikely that the end gap will be too large. If the gaps are too large, check that you have the correct rings for your engine and for the particular cylinder bore size.

7 Repeat the checking procedure for each ring in the first cylinder, and then for the rings in the remaining cylinders. Remember to keep rings, pistons and cylinders matched up.

8 Once the ring end gaps have been checked and if necessary corrected, the rings can be fitted to the pistons.

9 Fit the piston rings using the same technique as for removal. Fit the bottom (oil control) ring first, and work up. Note that a two- or three-

section oil control ring may be fitted; where a two-section ring is fitted, first insert the wire expander, then fit the ring. Ensure that the rings are fitted the correct way up – the top surface of the rings is normally marked TOP **(see illustration)**. Offset the piston ring gaps by 120° from each other. **Note:** *Always follow any instructions supplied with the new piston ring sets – different manufacturers may specify different procedures. Do not mix up the top and second compression rings, as they have different cross-sections.*

19 Crankshaft –
refitting and main bearing clearance check

Main bearing clearance check

1 The running clearance check can be carried out using the original bearing shells. However, it is preferable to use a new set, since the results obtained will be more conclusive. If new shells are being fitted, ensure that all traces of the protective grease are cleaned off using paraffin.

2 Clean the backs of the bearing shells, and the bearing locations in both the cylinder block/crankcase and the main bearing caps.

3 With the cylinder block positioned on a clean work surface, with the crankcase uppermost, press the bearing shells into their locations, ensuring that the tab on each shell engages in the notch in the cylinder block or bearing cap, and that the oil holes in the cylinder block and bearing shell are aligned **(see illustration)**. Take care not to touch any shell's bearing surface with your fingers. If the original bearing shells are being used for the check, ensure that they are refitted in their original locations.

4 Fit the crankshaft endfloat control thrustwasher halves either side of the No 3 bearing location. Use a small quantity of grease to hold them in place. Ensure that the thrustwashers are seated correctly in the machined recesses, with the oil grooves facing outwards.

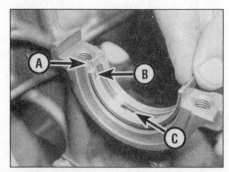

19.3 Bearing shell correctly refitted

A Recess in cylinder block
B Lug on bearing shell
C Oil hole

5 The running clearance can be checked, although this will be difficult to achieve without a range of internal micrometers or internal/external expanding calipers. Refit the main bearing caps to the cylinder block/crankcase, with bearing shells in place. With the original cap retaining bolts tightened to the specified torque, measure the internal diameter of each assembled pair of bearing shells. If the diameter of each corresponding crankshaft journal is measured and then subtracted from the bearing internal diameter, the result will be the main bearing running clearance.

Final crankshaft refitting

6 Carefully lift the crankshaft out of the cylinder block once more, and wipe off the surfaces of the bearing shells in the crankcase and bearing caps.

7 Where applicable, refit the crankshaft speed/position sensor wheel, and tighten the securing bolts to the specified torque. Make sure that the sensor wheel is correctly orientated as noted before removal.

8 Liberally coat the bearing shells in the crankcase with clean engine oil of the appropriate grade **(see illustration)**. Make sure that the bearing shells are still correctly seated in their locations.

9 Lower the crankshaft into position so that No 1 cylinder crankpin is at BDC, ready for fitting No 1 piston. Ensure that the crankshaft endfloat control thrustwasher halves, either side of the No 3 main bearing location, remain in position. Where applicable, take care not to damage the crankshaft speed/position sensor wheel as the crankshaft is lowered into position.

10 Lubricate the lower bearing shells in the main bearing caps with clean engine oil. On 1.6 litre DOHC petrol engines and diesel engines, make sure that the crankshaft endfloat control thrustwasher halves are still correctly seated either side of No 3 bearing cap **(see illustrations)**.

11 Fit the main bearing caps in the correct order and orientation – No 1 bearing cap must be at the timing belt end of the engine and the bearing shell tab locating recesses in the crankcase and bearing caps must be adjacent to each other **(see illustration)**. Insert the bearing cap bolts (using new bolts where necessary – see Torque wrench settings in the Specifications), and hand-tighten them only.

12 Working from the centre bearing cap outwards, tighten the bearing cap bolts to their specified torque. On engines where two Stages are given for the torque, tighten all bolts to the Stage 1 torque, then go round again, and tighten all bolts through the Stage 2 angle **(see illustrations)**.

13 Check that the crankshaft rotates freely by turning it by hand. If resistance is felt, recheck the bearing running clearances, as described previously.

14 Check the crankshaft endfloat as described at the beginning of Section 15. If the thrust surfaces of the crankshaft have

19.8 Lubricate the upper bearing shells

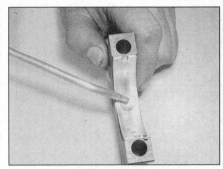
19.10a Lubricate the lower bearing shells . . .

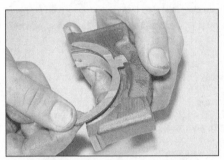
19.10b . . . and make sure that the thrustwashers are correctly seated – 1.6 litre DOHC petrol engines and diesel engines

19.11 Fitting No 1 main bearing cap

been checked and new thrustwashers have been fitted, then the endfloat should be within specification.

15 Refit the pistons and connecting rods or reconnect them to the crankshaft as described in Section 20.

16 Proceed as follows according to engine type:

a) *On SOHC petrol engines, refit the crankshaft oil seal housings, flywheel/driveplate, oil pump and pick-up pipe, sump and oil baffle plate, and the crankshaft sprocket and timing belt, as described in Chapter 2A.* **Note:** *On 2.0 litre AZJ engines, it will necessary to refit the balance shaft assembly.*

b) *On 1.6 litre DOHC petrol engines, refit the crankshaft oil seal housing, flywheel/driveplate, oil pump and pick-up pipe, sump, and main timing belt, as described in Chapter 2B.*

c) *On 1.8 litre DOHC petrol engines, refit the crankshaft oil seal housings, flywheel/driveplate, oil pump and pick-up pipe, sump and oil baffle plate, and the crankshaft sprocket and timing belt, as described in Chapter 2B.*

d) *On diesel engines, refit the crankshaft oil seal housings, flywheel/driveplate, oil pump and pick-up pipe, sump and oil baffle plate, and the crankshaft sprocket and timing belt, as described in Chapter 2C.*

20 Piston/connecting rod assemblies – refitting and big-end bearing clearance check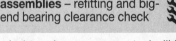

Note: *A piston ring compressor tool will be required for this operation.*

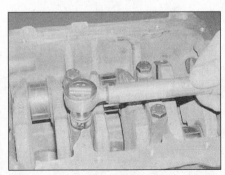
19.12a Tighten the main bearing cap bolts to the specified torque . . .

19.12b . . . then through the specified angle

20.9a Lubricate the pistons . . .

20.9b . . . and big-end upper bearing shells with clean engine oil

Big-end bearing clearance check

1 The running clearance check can be carried out using the original bearing shells. However, it is preferable to use a new set, since the results obtained will be more conclusive.

2 Clean the backs of the bearing shells, and the bearing locations in both the connecting rods and the big-end bearing caps.

3 Press the bearing shells into their locations, ensuring that the tab on each shell engages in the notch in the connecting rod or cap. Take care not to touch any shell's bearing surface with your fingers. If the original bearing shells are being used for the check, ensure that they are refitted in their original locations.

4 The running clearance can be checked, although this will be difficult to achieve without a range of internal micrometers or internal/external expanding calipers. Refit the big-end bearing cap to the connecting rod, using the marks made or noted on removal to ensure that they are fitted the correct way around, with the bearing shells in place. With the original cap retaining bolts or nuts (as applicable) correctly tightened, use an internal micrometer or vernier caliper to measure the internal diameter of each assembled pair of bearing shells. If the diameter of each corresponding crankshaft journal is measured, and then subtracted from the bearing internal diameter, the result will be the big-end bearing running clearance.

Piston/connecting rods refitting

5 Note that the following procedure assumes that the crankshaft main bearing caps are in place.

6 Where applicable, refit the piston cooling oil spray jets to the bottom of the cylinder block, and tighten the securing bolts to the specified torque.

7 On engines where the big-end bearing caps are secured by nuts, fit new bolts to the connecting rods. Tap the old bolts out of the connecting rods using a soft-faced mallet, and tap the new bolts into position.

8 Ensure that the bearing shells are correctly fitted, as described at the beginning of this Section. If new shells are being fitted, ensure that all traces of the protective grease are cleaned off using paraffin. Wipe dry the shells and connecting rods with a lint-free cloth.

9 Lubricate the cylinder bores, the pistons, piston rings and upper bearing shells with clean engine oil **(see illustrations)**. Lay out each piston/connecting rod assembly in order on a clean work surface. Where the bearing caps are secured with nuts, pad the threaded ends of the bolts with insulating tape to prevent them scratching the crankpins and bores when the pistons are refitted.

10 Start with piston/connecting rod assembly No 1. Make sure that the piston rings are still spaced as described in Section 18, then clamp

them in position with a piston ring compressor tool.

11 Insert the piston/connecting rod assembly into the top of cylinder No 1. Lower the big-end in first, guiding it to protect the cylinder bores. Where oil jets are located at the bottoms of the bores, take particular care not to damage them when guiding the connecting rods onto the crankpins.

12 Ensure that the orientation of the piston in its cylinder is correct – the piston crown, connecting rod and big-end bearing cap have markings, which must point towards the timing belt end of the engine when the piston is installed in the bore – refer to Section 14 for details. On diesel engines, the piston crowns are specially shaped to improve the engine's combustion characteristics. Because of this, pistons 1 and 2 are different to pistons 3 and 4. When correctly fitted, the larger inlet valve chambers on pistons 1 and 2 must face the flywheel/driveplate end of the engine, and the larger inlet valve chambers on the remaining pistons must face the timing belt end of the engine. New pistons have number markings on their crowns to indicate their type – 1/2 denotes piston 1 or 2, 3/4 indicates piston 3 or 4 **(see illustration)**.

13 Using a block of wood or hammer handle against the piston crown, tap the assembly into the cylinder until the piston crown is flush with the top of the cylinder **(see illustration)**.

14 Ensure that the bearing shell is still correctly installed in the connecting rod, then liberally lubricate the crankpin and both bearing shells with clean engine oil.

15 Taking care not to mark the cylinder bores, tap the piston/connecting rod assembly down the bore and onto the crankpin. On engines where the big-end caps are secured by nuts, remove the insulating tape from the threaded ends of the connecting rod bolts. Oil the bolt threads, and on engines where the big-end caps are secured by bolts, oil the undersides of the bolt heads.

16 Fit the big-end bearing cap, tightening its retaining nuts or bolts (as applicable) finger-tight at first. The connecting rod and its bearing cap both have recesses machined into them on one side, close to their mating surfaces – these recesses must both face the same way as the arrow on the

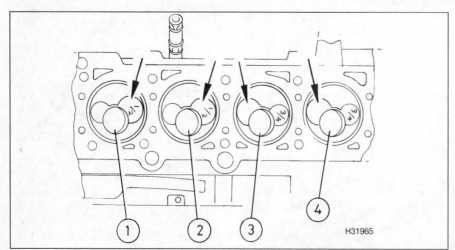

20.12 Piston orientation and coding on diesel engines

20.13 Using a hammer handle to tap the piston into its bore

piston crown (ie, towards the timing belt end of the engine) when correctly installed **(see illustration 14.25b)**. Reassemble the two components to satisfy this requirement.

17 Tighten the retaining bolts or nuts (as applicable) to the specified torque and angle, in the two stages given in the Specifications **(see illustrations)**.

18 Refit the remaining three piston/connecting rod assemblies in the same way.

19 Rotate the crankshaft by hand. Check that it turns freely; some stiffness is to be expected if new parts have been fitted, but there should be no binding or tight spots.

20 On diesel engines, if new pistons have been fitted, or if a new short engine has been fitted, the projection of the piston crowns above the cylinder head mating face of the cylinder block at TDC must be measured. This measurement is used to determine the thickness of the new cylinder head gasket required. This procedure is described as part of the Cylinder head – removal, inspection and refitting procedure in Chapter 2C.

21 Proceed as follows according to engine type:

a) On SOHC petrol engines, refit the oil pump and pick-up pipe, sump and oil baffle plate, and cylinder head, as described in Chapter 2A. **Note:** On 2.0 litre AZJ engines, it will necessary to refit the balance shaft assembly.

b) On 1.4 and 1.6 litre DOHC petrol engines, refit the oil pick-up pipe, sump, and cylinder head, as described in Chapter 2B.

c) On 1.8 litre DOHC engines, refit the oil pump and pick-up pipe, sump and oil baffle plate, and cylinder head, as described in Chapter 2B.

d) On diesel engines, refit the oil pump and pick-up pipe, sump and oil baffle plate, and cylinder head, as described in Chapter 2C.

21 Engine –
initial start-up after overhaul and reassembly

1 Refit the remainder of the engine components in the order listed in Section 7 of this Chapter. Refit the engine to the vehicle as described in the relevant Section of this Chapter. Double-check the engine oil and coolant levels, and make a final check that everything has been reconnected. Make sure that there are no tools or rags left in the engine compartment.

20.17a Tighten the big-end bearing cap bolts/nuts to the specified torque . . .

2 Reconnect the battery leads, with reference to *Disconnecting the battery* at the rear of this manual.

Petrol models

3 Remove the spark plugs, referring to Chapter 1A for details.

4 The engine must be immobilised such that it can be turned over using the starter motor, without starting – disable the fuel pump by unplugging the fuel pump power relay from the relay board with reference to Chapter 12, and also disable the ignition system by disconnecting the wiring from the DIS module or coils, as applicable.

Caution: To prevent damage to the catalytic converter, it is important to disable the fuel system.

5 Turn the engine using the starter motor until the oil pressure warning lamp goes out. If the lamp fails to extinguish after several seconds of cranking, check the engine oil level and oil filter security. Assuming these are correct, check the security of the oil pressure switch wiring – do not progress any further until you are satisfied that oil is being pumped around the engine at sufficient pressure.

6 Refit the spark plugs, and reconnect the wiring to the fuel pump relay and DIS module or coils, as applicable.

Diesel models

7 On engine codes AGP, AQM, AGR, AHF, ALH and ASV, disconnect the electrical cable from the fuel cut-off valve at the fuel injection pump. On engine codes AJM, ARL, ASZ, ATD, AUY and AXR disconnect the injector harness wiring plug at the end of the cylinder head – refer to Chapter 4B for details.

8 Turn the engine using the starter motor until the oil pressure warning lamp goes out.

20.17b . . . then through the specified angle

9 If the lamp fails to extinguish after several seconds of cranking, check the engine oil level and oil filter security. Assuming these are correct, check the security of the oil pressure switch cabling – do not progress any further until you are satisfied that oil is being pumped around the engine at sufficient pressure.

10 Reconnect the fuel cut-off valve cable or the injector wiring plug as applicable.

All models

11 Start the engine, but be aware that as fuel system components have been disturbed, the cranking time may be a little longer than usual.

12 While the engine is idling, check for fuel, water and oil leaks. Don't be alarmed if there are some odd smells and the occasional plume of smoke as components heat up and burn off oil deposits.

13 Assuming all is well, keep the engine idling until hot water is felt circulating through the top hose.

14 On diesel engine codes AGP, AQM, AGR, AHF, ALH and ASV, check the fuel injection pump timing and engine idle speed, as described in Chapter 4B.

15 After a few minutes, recheck the oil and coolant levels, and top-up as necessary.

16 There is no need to retighten the cylinder head bolts once the engine has been run following reassembly.

17 If new pistons, rings or crankshaft bearings have been fitted, the engine must be treated as new, and run-in for the first 600 miles (1000 km). *Do not* operate the engine at full-throttle, or allow it to labour at low engine speeds in any gear. It is recommended that the engine oil and filter are changed at the end of this period.

Notes

Chapter 3
Cooling, heating and air conditioning systems

Contents

Air conditioning system – general information and precautions 11
Air conditioning system components – removal and refitting 12
Antifreeze mixture . . . . .See Chapter 1A or 1B
Auxiliary drivebelt checking and renewal . . . . .See Chapter 1A or 1B
Climatronic system components – removal and refitting 13
Coolant level check . . . . .See *Weekly checks*
Coolant pump – removal and refitting 7
Cooling system – draining . . . . .See Chapter 1A or 1B
Cooling system – filling . . . . .See Chapter 1A or 1B
Cooling system – flushing . . . . .See Chapter 1A or 1B

Cooling system electrical switches and sensors – testing, removal and
  refitting 6
Cooling system hoses – disconnection and renewal 2
Electric cooling fan – testing, removal and refitting 5
General information and precautions 1
Heating and ventilation system – general information 8
Heating/ventilation system components – removal and refitting . . . 9
Heating/ventilation system vents – removal and refitting 10
Radiator – removal, inspection and refitting 3
Thermostat – removal, testing and refitting 4

Degrees of difficulty

Easy, suitable for novice with little experience 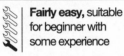	Fairly easy, suitable for beginner with some experience	Fairly difficult, suitable for competent DIY mechanic 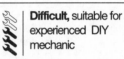	Difficult, suitable for experienced DIY mechanic	Very difficult, suitable for expert DIY or professional

Specifications

Cooling system pressure cap

Opening pressure . . . . 1.4 to 1.6 bar

Thermostat

1.4 litre engines:
  Begins to open . . . . 86°C
  Fully open . . . . 98°C
1.6 litre engines:
  SOHC engines:
    Begins to open . . . . 84°C
    Minimum opening lift 7mm
  DOHC engines:
    Begins to open . . . . 86°C
    Fully open . . . . 98°C
1.8 litre engine:
  Begins to open . . . . 87°C
  Fully open . . . . 102°C
2.0 litre engines:
  Begins to open . . . . 86°C
  Fully open . . . . 102°C
1.9 litre diesel engines:
  Begins to open . . . . 85°C
  Fully open . . . . 105°C

Cooling fan

Fan speeds:
  1st speed cut-in . . . . 92 to 97°C
  1st speed cut-out . . . . 91 to 84°C
  2nd speed cut-in . . . . 99 to 105°C
  2nd speed cut-out . . . . 98 to 91°C

Torque wrench settings

	Nm	lbf ft
Coolant pump housing/coolant pump-to-engine bolts:		
1.4 litre and 1.6 litre DOHC engines	20	15
All other engines	15	11
Facia crossmember retaining bolts	25	18
Radiator cooling fan shroud bolts	10	7
Radiator mounting bolts	10	7
Thermostat cover bolts	10	7
Thermostat housing-to-engine bolts:		
1.4 litre and 1.6 litre DOHC engines	10	7

1 General information and precautions

A pressurised cooling system is used, comprising a pump, an aluminium crossflow radiator, an electric cooling fan, a thermostat and a heater matrix, as well as the interconnecting hoses. The system functions as follows. Cold coolant from the radiator passes through the hose to the coolant pump where it is pumped around the cylinder block and head passages. After cooling the cylinder bores, combustion surfaces and valve seats, the coolant reaches the underside of the thermostat, which is initially closed. The coolant passes through the heater and is returned through the cylinder block to the timing belt driven coolant pump.

When the engine is cold the coolant circulates only through the cylinder block, cylinder head, expansion tank and heater. When the coolant reaches a predetermined temperature, the thermostat opens and the coolant passes through to the radiator. As the coolant circulates through the radiator it is cooled by the inrush of air when the car is in forward motion. Airflow is supplemented by the action of the electric cooling fan(s) when necessary. Upon leaving the radiator, the coolant is has cooled and the cycle is repeated.

A thermostatic switch controls the electric cooling fan(s) mounted on the rear of the radiator. At a preset coolant temperature, the switch actuates the fan(s).

Refer to Section 11 for information on the air conditioning system fitted to certain models.

Coolant temperature information for the gauge mounted in the instrument panel, and for the fuel system, is provided by a single temperature sensor, mounted in the coolant hose connector on the left-hand end of the cylinder head (1.6 litre SOHC engines, 1.8 and 2.0 litre petrol engines & diesel engines), or on the underside of the thermostat housing (1.4 litre and 1.6 litre DOHC engine).

Precautions

⚠️ *Warning: Do not attempt to remove the expansion tank filler cap or disturb any part of the cooling system while the engine is hot, as there is a high risk of scalding. If the expansion tank filler cap must be removed before the engine and radiator have fully cooled (even though this is not recommended) the pressure in the cooling system must first be relieved. Cover the cap with a thick layer of cloth, to avoid scalding, and slowly unscrew the filler cap until a hissing sound can be heard. When the hissing has stopped, indicating that the pressure has reduced, slowly unscrew the filler cap until it can be removed; if more hissing sounds are heard, wait until they have stopped before unscrewing the cap completely. At all times keep well away from the filler cap opening.*

• *Do not allow antifreeze to come into contact with skin or painted surfaces of the vehicle. Rinse off spills immediately with plenty of water. Never leave antifreeze lying around in an open container or in a puddle in the driveway or on the garage floor. Children and pets are attracted by its sweet smell. Antifreeze can be fatal if ingested.*

• *If the engine is hot, the electric cooling fan may start rotating even if the engine is not running, so be careful to keep hands, hair and loose clothing well clear when working in the engine compartment.*

• *Refer to Section 12 for additional precautions to be observed when working on models with air conditioning.*

2 Cooling system hoses – disconnection and renewal

Note: *Refer to the warnings given in Section 1 of this Chapter before proceeding.*

1 If the checks described in the relevant part of Chapter 1 reveal a faulty hose, it must be renewed as follows.

2 First drain the cooling system as described in Chapter 1A or 1B. If the coolant is not due for renewal, it may be re-used if it is collected in a clean container.

3 To disconnect a hose, release its retaining clips, then move them along the hose, clear of the relevant inlet/outlet union. Carefully work the hose free.

4 In order to disconnect the radiator inlet and outlet hoses, apply pressure to hold the hose on to the relevant union, pull out the spring clip and pull the hose from the union **(see illustration)**. Note that the radiator inlet and outlet unions are fragile; do not use excessive force when attempting to remove the hoses. If a hose proves to be difficult to remove, try to release it by rotating the hose ends before attempting to free it.

> **HAYNES HiNT**
>
> *If all else fails, cut the hose with a sharp knife, then slit it so that it can be peeled off in two pieces. Although this may prove expensive if the hose is otherwise undamaged, it is preferable to buying a new radiator.*

5 When fitting a hose, first slide the clips onto the hose, then work the hose into position. If clamp type clips were originally fitted, it is a good idea to use screw type clips when refitting the hose. If the hose is stiff, use a little soapy water as a lubricant, or soften the hose by soaking it in hot water.

6 Work the hose into position, checking that it is correctly routed, then slide each clip along the hose until it passes over the flared end of the relevant union, before securing it in position with the retaining clip.

7 Prior to refitting a radiator inlet or outlet hose, renew the connection O-ring regardless of condition. The connections are a push-fit over the radiator unions.

8 Refill the cooling system as described in Chapter 1A or 1B.

9 Check thoroughly for leaks as soon as possible after disturbing any part of the cooling system.

2.4 Pull out the retaining clip

3 Radiator –
removal, inspection and refitting

Models without air conditioning

Removal

1 Disconnect the battery negative lead. **Note:** *Before disconnecting the battery, refer to 'Disconnecting the battery' in the reference section at the rear of this manual.*

2 Drain the cooling system as described in the relevant part of Chapter 1.

3 Remove the front bumper cover as described in Chapter 11.

4 Prise out the sealing caps where fitted, undo the retaining screws/nuts and remove the engine cover(s). Disconnect the upper and lower hoses from the radiator, with reference to Section 2 if necessary.

5 Disconnect the electric cooling fan wiring connector, and release the wiring from the cooling fan shroud.

6 Disconnect the wiring plug from the cooling fan switch mounted in the radiator.

7 Remove the front panel complete with headlamps, radiator and cooling fan (see Chapter 2D, Section 4, 5 or 6).

8 Unscrew the four Torx screws securing the shroud to the radiator, and if necessary undo the three screws and remove the cooling fan from the shroud **(see illustrations)**.

9 From the outside of the front panel, undo the four Torx screws and lift the radiator from the inside of the panel. Note the location of the four radiator mounting rubbers **(see illustrations)**.

Inspection

10 If the radiator has been removed due to suspected blockage, reverse flush it as described in the relevant part of Chapter 1.

11 Clean dirt and debris from the radiator fins, using an air line (in which case, wear eye protection) or a soft brush. Be careful, as the fins are sharp and easily damaged.

12 If necessary, a radiator specialist can perform a 'flow test' on the radiator, to establish whether an internal blockage exists.

13 A leaking radiator must be referred to a specialist for permanent repair. Do not attempt to weld or solder a leaking radiator, as damage may result.

14 If the radiator is to be sent for repair or renewed, remove the cooling fan switch.

Refitting

15 Refitting is a reversal of removal. On completion, refill the cooling system using the correct type of antifreeze as described in the relevant part of Chapter 1.

Models with air conditioning

Warning: Do not attempt to disconnect the refrigerant lines – refer to the warnings given in Section 11.

3.8a Undo the cooling fan screws (arrowed)

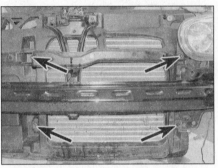

3.9a Undo the radiator mounting screws (arrowed)

Removal

16 Proceed as described in paragraphs 1 to 6.

17 Unscrew the four bolts securing the radiator to the front panel, then remove the front panel complete with headlamps (see Chapter 2D, Section 4, 5 or 6).

18 Remove the four screws securing the condenser to the radiator. Remove the retaining clamps from the refrigerant pipes, and remove the condenser from the radiator.

19 Using cable ties (or similar) secure the condenser to the inner wing or convenient support. Take care not to stretch, kink or bend the refrigerant pipes/hoses.

20 Carefully remove the radiator downwards and out from the engine compartment, complete with cooling fan(s) and shroud. Take care not to damage the radiator on surrounding components.

21 If required, unscrew the four cooling fan shroud securing bolts, and remove the shroud.

Inspection

22 Proceed as described in paragraphs 10 to 14.

Refitting

23 Refitting is a reversal of the removal procedure; ensure all the hose and wiring are correctly and securely reconnected. On completion, refill the cooling system with the correct type of coolant as described in the relevant part of Chapter 1.

3.8b Remove the radiator shroud screw (arrowed)

3.9b Radiator mounting rubbers

4 Thermostat –
removal, testing and refitting

1.4 and 1.6 litre DOHC engines

Removal

1 The thermostat is located in a housing at the left-hand end of the cylinder head.

2 Drain the cooling system as described in Chapter 1A.

3 Undo the four Allen screws and remove the engine cover. Release the securing clip and disconnect the coolant hose from the thermostat cover **(see illustration)**.

4 Unscrew the two retaining screws, and remove the thermostat cover, noting the locations of any brackets secured by the

4.3 Disconnect the hose

4.4a Remove the thermostat . . .

4.4b . . . and recover the seal

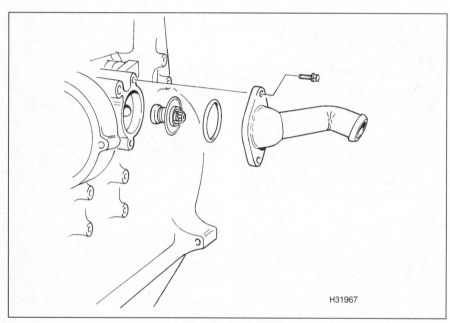

**4.11 Thermostat assembly –
1.6 litre SOHC, 1.8 and 2.0 litre engines**

screws, then lift out the thermostat. Recover the O-ring if it is loose **(see illustrations)**.

Testing

5 A rough test of the thermostat may be made by suspending it with a piece of string in a container full of water, but not touching the container. Heat the water to bring it to the boil – the thermostat must open by the time the water boils. If not, renew it.

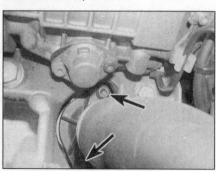

4.18a Thermostat cover screws (arrowed)

6 If a thermometer is available, the precise opening temperature of the thermostat may be determined, and compared with the figures given in the Specifications. The opening temperature is also marked on the thermostat.
7 A thermostat which fails to close as the water cools must also be renewed.

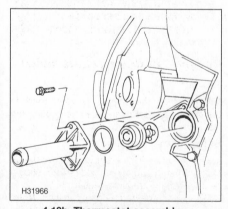

**4.18b Thermostat assembly –
diesel engines**

Refitting

8 Refitting is a reversal of removal, bearing in mind the following points.
  a) *Refit the thermostat using a new O-ring.*
  b) *Refill the cooling system with the correct type and quantity of coolant as described in Chapter 1A.*

1.6 litre SOHC, 1.8 and 2.0 litre engines

Removal

9 The thermostat is located behind a connection flange in the front side of the engine block.
10 Drain the cooling system as described in Chapter 1A.
11 Prise out the sealing caps, undo the retaining nuts and remove the engine cover(s). Release the securing clip and disconnect the coolant hose from the thermostat cover/connection flange **(see illustration)**.
12 Unscrew the two securing bolts, and remove the thermostat cover/connection flange, noting the locations of any brackets secured by the bolts, then lift out the thermostat. Recover the O-ring if it is loose.

Testing

13 Proceed as described in paragraphs 5 to 7.

Refitting

14 Refitting is a reversal of removal, bearing in mind the following points.
  a) *Refit the thermostat using a new O-ring.*
  b) *The thermostat should be fitted with the brace almost vertical.*
  c) *Ensure that any brackets are in place on the thermostat cover bolts as noted before removal.*
  d) *Refill the cooling system with the correct type and quantity of coolant as described in Chapter 1A.*

Diesel engines

Removal

15 The thermostat is located behind a connection flange in the front side of the engine block, at the timing belt end.
16 Drain the cooling system as described in Chapter 1B. Prise out the sealing caps, undo the retaining nuts and remove the engine covers.
17 Release the securing clip and disconnect the coolant hose from the thermostat cover/connection flange.
18 Unscrew the two securing bolts, and remove the thermostat cover/connection flange complete with the thermostat. Note the locations of any brackets secured by the bolts. Recover the O-ring if it is loose **(see illustrations)**.
19 To remove the thermostat from the cover, twist the thermostat 90° anti-clockwise, and pull it from the cover.

Testing

20 Proceed as described in paragraphs 5 to 7.

Refitting

21 Refitting is a reversal of removal, bearing in mind the following points.

  a) *Refit the thermostat using a new O-ring.*
  b) *Insert the thermostat into the cover and twist 90° clockwise.*
  c) *The thermostat should be fitted with the brace almost vertical.*
  d) *Ensure that any brackets are in place on the thermostat cover bolts as noted before removal.*
  e) *Refill the cooling system with the correct type and quantity of coolant as described in Chapter 1B.*

5 Electric cooling fan – testing, removal and refitting

Models without air conditioning

Testing

1 Vehicles may be fitted with one or two cooling fans, depending on model. The cooling fan is supplied with current through the ignition switch, cooling fan control unit (where applicable), the relay(s) and fuses/fusible link (see Chapter 12). The circuit is completed by the cooling fan thermostatic switch, which is mounted in the left-hand end of the radiator. The cooling fan has two speed settings; the thermostatic switch actually contains two switches, one for the stage 1 fan speed setting and another for the stage 2 fan speed setting. Testing of the cooling fan circuit is as follows, noting that the following check should be carried out on both the stage 1 speed circuit and speed 2 circuit (see wiring diagrams at the end of Chapter 12).

2 If a fan does not appear to work, first check the fuses/fusible links. If they are good, run the engine until normal operating temperature is reached, then allow it to idle. If the fan does not cut in within a few minutes, switch off the ignition and disconnect the wiring plug from the cooling fan switch. Bridge the relevant two contacts in the wiring plug using a length of spare wire, and switch on the ignition. If the fan now operates, the switch is probably faulty and should be renewed.

3 If the switch appears to work, the motor can be checked by disconnecting the motor wiring connector and connecting a 12 volt supply directly to the motor terminals. If the motor is faulty, it must be renewed, as no spares are available.

4 If the fan still fails to operate, check the cooling fan circuit wiring (Chapter 12). Check each wire for continuity and ensure that all connections are clean and free of corrosion.

5 On models with a cooling fan control unit, if no fault can be found with the fuses/fusible links, wiring, fan switch, or fan motor, then it is likely that the cooling fan control unit is faulty. Testing of the unit should be entrusted to a

VW dealer or specialist; if the unit is faulty it must be renewed.

Removal

6 Disconnect the battery negative lead. **Note:** *Before disconnecting the battery, refer to 'Disconnecting the battery' in the reference section at the rear of this manual.*

7 Prise out the sealing caps (where fitted), undo the retaining screws/nuts and remove the engine cover(s).

8 Disconnect the wiring plug from the cooling fan motor, and slide the connector from the retaining bracket.

9 Undo the three Torx screws securing the fan to the radiator shroud, and manoeuvre the cooling fan up and out of the engine compartment. Take care not to damage the radiator **(see illustration 3.8a)**.

Refitting

10 Refitting is a reversal of removal.

Models with air conditioning

Testing

11 Proceed as described in paragraphs 1 to 5. **Note:** *On models equipped with air conditioning, there is also a second switch (fitted into one of the coolant outlet housings/hoses on the cylinder head). This switch controls the cooling fan stage 3 speed setting.*

Removal

12 Remove the radiator as described in Section 3.

13 Disconnect the wiring connector from the rear of the cooling fan motor.

14 Slacken and remove the motor retaining nuts, and remove the cooling fan assembly from the radiator shroud.

Refitting

15 Refitting is a reversal of removal, but refit the radiator as described in Section 3, and refill the cooling system with the correct type of coolant as described in the relevant part of Chapter 1. On completion, check the operation of the cooling fan(s).

6 Cooling system electrical switches and sensors – testing, removal and refitting

Cooling fan thermostatic switch

Testing

1 Testing of the switch is described in Section 5, as part of the electric cooling fan test procedure.

Removal and refitting

2 The switch is located in the left-hand side of the radiator. The engine and radiator should be cold before removing the switch.

3 Disconnect the battery negative lead. **Note:** *Before disconnecting the battery, refer to 'Disconnecting the battery' in the reference*

section at the rear of this manual. Where necessary, prise out the sealing caps, undo the retaining screws/nuts and remove the engine cover(s).

4 Either drain the radiator to below the level of the switch (as described in Chapter 1A or 1B), or have ready a suitable plug which can be used to plug the switch aperture in the radiator whilst the switch is removed. If a plug is used, take great care not to damage the radiator, and do not use anything which will allow foreign matter to enter the radiator.

5 Disconnect the wiring plug from the switch.

6 Carefully unscrew the switch from the radiator **(see illustration)**.

7 Refitting is a reversal of removal, applying a smear of suitable grease to the threads of the switch and tightening it securely. On completion, refill the cooling system with the correct type and quantity of coolant as described in Chapter 1A or 1B, or top up as described in *Weekly checks*.

8 Start the engine and run it until it reaches normal operating temperature, then continue to run the engine and check that the cooling fan cuts in and functions correctly.

Coolant temperature sensor – 1.4 and 1.6 litre DOHC engines

Testing

9 The sensor is clipped into the underside of the thermostat housing at the left-hand end of the cylinder head.

10 The sensor contains a thermistor, which consists of an electronic component whose electrical resistance decreases at a predetermined rate as its temperature rises. When the coolant is cold, the sensor resistance is high, current flow through the gauge is reduced, and the gauge needle points towards the 'cold' end of the scale. No resistance-to-temperature values are available. Therefore the only method of accurately checking the sensor is with dedicated diagnostic equipment, and should be entrusted to a VW dealer or specialist. If the sensor is faulty, it must be renewed.

Removal and refitting

11 Disconnect the battery negative lead. **Note:** *Before disconnecting the battery, refer to 'Disconnecting the battery' in the reference*

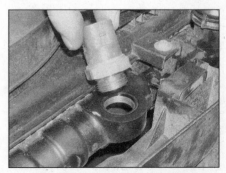

6.6 Unscrew the thermoswitch

6.18 Disconnect the sensor

6.23 Coolant temperature sensor – diesel engines

Refitting

5 Refitting is a reversal of removal, bearing in mind the following points.

  a) *Refit the pump using a new gasket (refer to note above).*

  b) *Refill the cooling system as described in Chapter 1A.*

1.6 litre SOHC, 1.8 and 2.0 litre engines

Removal

6 Drain the cooling system as described in Chapter 1A.

7 Remove the camshaft timing belt as described in Chapter 2A or 2B, noting the following points.

  a) *The lower part of the timing belt guard need not be removed.*

  b) *The timing belt should be left in position on the crankshaft sprocket.*

  c) *Cover the timing belt with a cloth to protect it from coolant.*

8 Remove the two securing bolts, and remove the rear timing belt guard.

9 Remove the remaining retaining bolts, and withdraw the coolant pump from the engine block. If the pump is faulty, it must be renewed.

Refitting

10 Refitting is a reversal of removal, bearing in mind the following points.

  a) *Fit the coolant pump with a new O-ring.*

  b) *Lubricate the O-ring with coolant.*

  c) *Install the pump with the cast lug facing down.*

  d) *Refill the cooling system as described in Chapter 1A.*

Diesel engines

Removal

11 Drain the cooling system as described in Chapter 1B.

12 Remove the camshaft timing belt as described in Chapter 2C, noting the following points.

  a) *The lower part of the timing belt guard need not be removed.*

  b) *The timing belt should be left in position on the crankshaft sprocket.*

  c) *Cover the timing belt with a cloth to protect it from coolant.*

13 Unscrew the timing belt idler pulley, and push the pulley downwards approximately 30 mm.

14 Unscrew the coolant pump retaining bolts, and remove the pump from the engine block. If the pump is faulty, it must be renewed **(see illustration opposite)**.

Refitting

15 Refitting is a reversal of removal, bearing in mind the following points.

  a) *Fit the coolant pump with a new O-ring.*

  b) *Lubricate the O-ring with coolant.*

  c) *Install the pump with the cast lug facing down.*

  d) *Refill the cooling system as described in Chapter 1B.*

---

section at the rear of this manual. Undo the four Allen screws and remove the engine cover.

12 Disconnect the wiring plug from the sensor, located on the underside of the thermostat housing at the left-hand end of the cylinder head. Partially drain the cooling system to below the level of the sensor (as described in Chapter 1A).

13 Carefully withdraw the retaining clip and pull the sensor from the housing. Recover the O-ring.

14 Refitting is a reversal of removal. Bearing in mind the following points.

  a) *Refit the sensor with a new O-ring.*

  b) *Refill the cooling system as described in Chapter 1A, or top-up as described in 'Weekly checks'.*

Coolant temperature sensor – 1.6 litre SOHC, 1.8 and 2.0 litre engines

Testing

15 Proceed as outlined in paragraph 10. Note that the sensor is clipped into the top of the hose connector, bolted to the left-hand end of the cylinder head.

Removal and refitting

16 Disconnect the battery negative lead. **Note:** *Before disconnecting the battery, refer to 'Disconnecting the battery' in the reference section at the rear of this manual.*

17 Prise out the sealing caps, undo the retaining nuts and remove the engine cover(s).

18 Disconnect the wiring plug from the sensor **(see illustration)**.

7.4 Withdraw the coolant pump

19 Partially drain the cooling system to below the level of the sensor (as described in Chapter 1A).

20 Carefully withdraw the retaining clip and pull the sensor from the housing. Recover the O-ring.

21 Refitting is a reversal of removal. Bearing in mind the following points.

  a) *Refit the sensor with a new O-ring.*

  b) *Refill the cooling system as described in Chapter 1A, or top-up as described in 'Weekly checks'.*

Coolant temperature sensor – diesel engines

Testing

22 Proceed as described in paragraph 10, but note that the sensor is clipped into the rear of the hose connector bolted to the left-hand end of the cylinder head.

Removal and refitting

23 Proceed as described in paragraphs 16 to 21, but note that the sensor is clipped in to the rear of the hose connector bolted to the left-hand end of the cylinder head **(see illustration)**. Refill the system as described in Chapter 1B or *Weekly checks*.

---

7 Coolant pump – removal and refitting

Note: *New coolant pumps may be of a modified design, which do not require gaskets. Use a suitable sealer.*

1.4 and 1.6 litre DOHC engines

Removal

1 Drain the cooling system as described in Chapter 1A.

2 Remove the camshaft timing belt as described in Chapter 2B. If the belt is to be re-used, note the direction of rotation.

3 Remove the camshaft timing belt idler roller, and rear timing belt cover.

4 Unscrew the coolant pump retaining bolts, and withdraw the pump from the engine block. If faulty, the pump must be renewed **(see illustration)**.

8 Heating and ventilation system – general information

1 The heating/ventilation system consists of a four-speed blower motor (housed in the passenger compartment), face-level vents in the centre and at each end of the facia, and air ducts to the front and rear footwells.

2 The control unit is located in the facia, and the controls operate flap valves to deflect and mix the air flowing through the various parts of the heating/ventilation system. The flap valves are contained in the air distribution housing, which acts as a central distribution unit, passing air to the various ducts and vents.

3 Cold air enters the system through the grille at the rear of the engine compartment. On some models (depending on specification) a pollen filter is fitted to the ventilation inlet to filter out dust, soot, pollen and spores from the air entering the vehicle.

4 The airflow, which can be boosted by the blower, then flows through the various ducts, according to the settings of the controls. Stale air is expelled through ducts below the rear window. If warm air is required, the cold air is passed through the heater matrix, which is heated by the engine coolant.

5 If necessary, the outside air supply can be closed off, allowing the air inside the vehicle to be recirculated. This can be useful to prevent unpleasant odours entering from outside the vehicle, but should only be used briefly, as the recirculated air inside the vehicle will soon deteriorate.

9 Heating/ventilation system components – removal and refitting

Models without air conditioning

Heater/ventilation control unit

1 Switch off the ignition and all electrical consumers.

2 Carefully prise off the heater control panel trim plate **(see illustration)**.

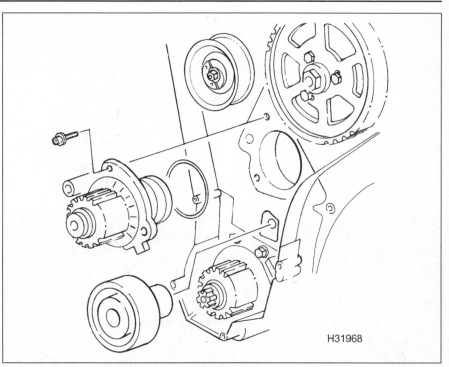

7.14 Coolant pump – diesel engines

3 Remove the passenger side lower facia trim panel and centre console as described in Chapter 11, Sections 28 and 29.

4 Undo the four Torx screws and push the control unit back into the facia. Manoeuvre the control unit down and out of the facia **(see illustration)**.

5 Unclip the control cables and release each cable from the control unit, noting each cable's correct fitted location and routing; to avoid confusion on refitting, label each cable as it is disconnected. The outer cables are released by simply pressing the locking tab and lifting the retaining clips **(see illustration)**.

6 Refitting is reversal of removal. Ensure that the control cables are correctly routed and reconnected to the control panel, as noted before removal. Clip the outer cables in position and check the operation of each knob/lever before refitting the switch mounting plate and the trim plate.

Heater/ventilation control cables

7 Remove the heater/ventilation control unit from the facia as described previously, detaching the relevant cable from the control unit.

8 Remove the right-hand lower facia trim panel for access to the heater control cable connections on the heater/ventilation distribution unit.

9 Follow the run of the cable behind the facia, taking note of its routing, and disconnect the cable from the lever on the air distribution/blower motor housing. Note that the method of fastening is the same as that used at the control unit **(see illustration)**.

10 Fit the new cable, ensuring that it is correctly routed and free from kinks and obstructions. The outer cable sleeves are colour-coded to assist correct reassembly.

a) *Central flap to rotary control: Grey (right-hand drive), Yellow (left-hand drive).*

9.2 Prise off the panel trim

9.4 Undo the Torx screws

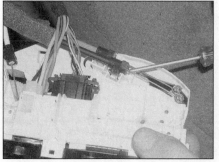

9.5 Press the lock tab, and lift the retaining clip

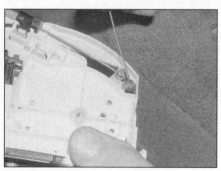

9.9 Disconnect the cable

9.15 Prise out the retaining clip

9.17 Remove the centre bracket

9.18 Manoeuvre the air duct to the right

9.19 Undo the Torx screw

9.21 Undo the retaining nuts (arrowed)

b) *Footwell/Defrost flap to rotary control: Black (right-hand drive), Green (left-hand drive).*

c) *Temperature flap to rotary control: White (right-hand drive), Beige (left-hand drive).*

11 Connect the cable to the control unit and air distribution/blower motor housing making sure the outer cable is clipped securely in position.

12 Check the operation of the control knob then refit the control unit as described previously in this Section. Finally refit the facia trim panel.

Heater matrix

13 Unscrew the expansion tank cap (referring to the Warning note in Section 1) to release any pressure present in the cooling system, then securely refit the cap.

14 Remove the engine cover(s). Clamp both heater hoses as close to the bulkhead as possible to minimise coolant loss. Alternatively, drain the cooling system as described in the relevant part of Chapter 1.

15 Disconnect both hoses from the heater matrix unions, located in the centre of the engine compartment bulkhead, by prising out the retaining clips until they lock in the open position, and pulling the hoses from the connections **(see illustration)**.

16 Remove the facia assembly as described in Chapter 11.

17 Undo the three securing bolts, and remove the facia crossmember-to-centre tunnel bracket **(see illustration)**.

18 Remove the lower air duct connecting piece by manoeuvring it to the right under the steering column **(see illustration)**.

19 Undo the two wiring loom support brackets either side of the steering column, secured by Torx screws **(see illustration)**.

20 Note the location of the various wiring loom retaining clips, and disengage the looms from the facia crossmember.

21 Undo the relay plate retaining nuts and carefully remove the plate from the studs **(see illustration)**.

22 Unscrew and remove the central locking ECU retaining screws **(see illustration)**.

23 Disconnect the passenger airbag. The airbag should have already been rendered safe during the facia removal procedure.

24 Remove the wiper motor and linkage assembly as described in Chapter 12.

25 Working in the wiper motor aperture, unscrew and remove the facia crossmember retaining bolt **(see illustration)**.

26 Unscrew and remove the two Torx screws securing the upper support bracket to the facia crossmember **(see illustration)**.

27 Unclip and remove the central air vent from the facia crossmember.

9.22 Remove the ECU retaining screws (arrowed)

9.25 Undo the crossmember bolt (arrowed)

9.26 Unscrew the two Torx screws

9.28 Unbolt the earth connections

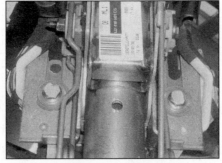

9.30a Remove the column vertical mounting bolts . . .

9.30b . . . and the horizontal bolt

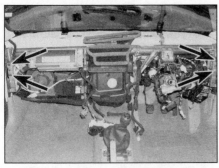

9.31 Undo the crossmember bolts (arrowed)

9.32 Tie the column to the bracket

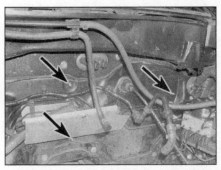

9.33 Heater retaining nuts (arrowed)

28 Undo the wiring earth connections from the crossmember **(see illustration)**.

29 Where the crossmember is secured to its support brackets, make alignment marks to aid refitting.

30 Undo and remove the three steering column mounting bolts. Have an assistant support the steering column whilst the crossmember is being removed **(see illustrations)**.

31 Remove the four crossmember retaining bolts, two at each end, and manoeuvre the crossmember out of the cabin **(see illustration)**.

32 Suspend the steering column by tying it to the upper crossmember support bracket **(see illustration)**.

33 Working in the engine compartment, remove the three heater assembly retaining nuts. Recover the washers **(see illustration)**.

34 Open the wiring loom retaining guide, and release the loom from the top of the heater assembly.

35 Disconnect the wiring plug from the connector on the heater trunking.

36 With reference to Chapter 11, Section 28, remove the lower door post trim on the passenger side.

37 Disconnect the wiring earth connection from the lower door post area **(see illustration)**.

38 Carefully pull the heater assembly from the bulkhead, disengaging the airbag ECU wiring loom from the retaining guide at the front of the heater assembly as the unit is withdrawn **(see illustration)**. Be prepared for

coolant spillage as the assembly is removed from the cabin.

39 With the heater unit on the bench, undo the two retaining screws, and carefully lift the heater matrix from the housing **(see illustrations)**.

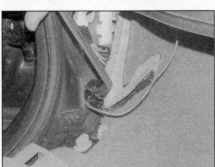

9.37 Unbolt the earth connection

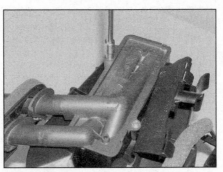

9.39a Undo the screws . . .

40 Refitting is reversal of removal, noting the following points:

a) Check the condition of the gasket which fits between the matrix pipes and the bulkhead, and renew if necessary.

9.38 Release the cable from the guide

9.39b . . . and lift out the matrix

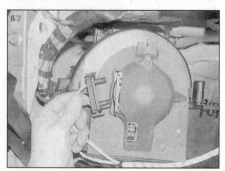

9.43a Disconnect the blower motor . . .

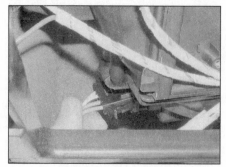

9.43b . . . and resistor

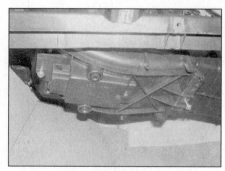

9.44 Remove the resistor screws

b) Take care to avoid damage to the matrix fins when sliding the matrix into its housing.
c) Ensure that the airbag ECU wiring loom is refitted into the retainer on the front of the heater as the assembly is refitted.
d) Make sure that all wiring is correctly reconnected and routed.
e) Make sure that the air ducts are securely clipped into position.
f) Ensure that the pedal support bracket engages correctly as the crossmember is refitted.
g) Align the previously made marks to ensure that the facia crossmember is refitted correctly.
h) Tighten the facia crossmember retaining bolts to the specified torque.
i) Refit the facia assembly as described in Chapter 11.
j) On completion, check the coolant level and top-up if necessary as described in 'Weekly checks'.

Heater blower motor

41 Switch off the ignition and all electrical consumers.
42 Remove the passenger side glovebox as described in Chapter 11, Section 28.
43 Reach under the facia and disconnect the blower motor wiring plug, and the series resistor wiring plug located under the blower motor housing **(see illustrations)**.
44 Unscrew the two series resistor retaining screws, and remove the resistor **(see illustration)**.
45 Unscrew the three retaining screws and remove the blower motor cover.

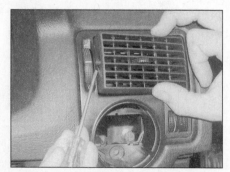

10.1 Carefully prise out the vent

46 Pull the blower motor downwards and withdraw it from the housing.
47 Refitting is a reversal of removal.

Heater blower motor resistor

48 Disconnect the battery negative lead.
Note: Before disconnecting the battery, refer to 'Disconnecting the battery' in the reference section at the rear of this manual.
49 Undo the two retaining screws and remove the passenger side lower facia trim in the footwell.
50 Reach up under the facia and disconnect the wiring connector from the resistor.
51 Remove the two retaining screws, and withdraw the resistor from its housing **(see illustration 9.44)**.
52 Refitting is the reverse of removal.

Fresh/recirculating air flap positioning motor

53 Remove the passenger side glovebox as described in Chapter 11, Section 28.
54 Disconnect the wiring plug from the motor located at the end of the heater unit next to the blower motor.
55 Reaching underneath the motor, remove the retaining screw.
56 Swivel the motor down and separate it from the air flap lever.
57 Refitting is a reversal of removal.

Models with air conditioning

Heater control unit

58 The procedure is as described previously in this Section for models without air conditioning.

Heater matrix

59 On models equipped with air conditioning it is not possible to remove the heater matrix without opening the refrigerant circuit. Therefore this task must be entrusted to a VW dealer or an air conditioning specialist.

Heater blower motor

60 The procedure is as described previously in this Section for models without air conditioning.

Heater blower motor resistor

61 The procedure is as described previously in this Section for models without air conditioning.

10 Heating/ventilation system vents – removal and refitting

Side vents

1 To remove a vent, carefully prise it from the housing using a small flat-bladed screwdriver **(see illustration)**. Take care not to damage the surrounding trim.
2 To refit, carefully push the vent into position until the locating clips engage.

Central facia vents

3 Proceed as described previously for the side vents, but note that each vent must be prised progressively from both sides to release it from the housing.

11 Air conditioning system – general information and precautions

General information

An air conditioning system is available on certain models. It enables the temperature of incoming air to be lowered, and dehumidifies the air, which makes for rapid demisting and increased comfort.

The cooling side of the system works in the same way as a domestic refrigerator. Refrigerant gas is drawn into a belt-driven compressor and passes into a condenser mounted in front of the radiator, where it loses heat and becomes liquid. The liquid passes through an expansion valve to an evaporator, where it changes from liquid under high pressure to gas under low pressure. This change is accompanied by a drop in temperature, which cools the evaporator. The refrigerant returns to the compressor and the cycle begins again.

Air blown through the evaporator passes to the air distribution unit, where it is mixed with hot air blown through the heater matrix to achieve the desired temperature in the passenger compartment.

The heating side of the system works in the same way as on models without air conditioning.

The operation of the system is controlled electronically by coolant temperature switches, and pressure switches which are screwed into the compressor high-pressure line. Any problems with the system should be referred to a VW dealer or an air conditioning specialist.

Precautions

• *When an air conditioning system is fitted, it is necessary to observe special precautions whenever dealing with any part of the system, its associated components and any items which require disconnection of the system. If for any reason the system must be disconnected, entrust this task to your VW dealer or an air conditioning specialist.*

Warning: The refrigeration circuit contains a refrigerant and it is therefore dangerous to disconnect any part of the system without specialised knowledge and equipment. The refrigerant is potentially dangerous and should only be handled by qualified persons. If it is splashed onto the skin it can cause frostbite. It is not itself poisonous, but in the presence of a naked flame (including a cigarette) it forms a poisonous gas. Uncontrolled discharging of the refrigerant is dangerous and potentially damaging to the environment.

• *Do not operate the air conditioning system if it is known to be short of refrigerant, as this may damage the compressor.*

12 Air conditioning system components – removal and refitting

Warning: Do not attempt to open the refrigerant circuit. Refer to the precautions given in Section 11.

1 The only operation which can be carried out easily without discharging the refrigerant is the renewal of the compressor drivebelt, which is covered in the relevant part of Chapter 1. All other operations must be referred to a VW dealer or an air conditioning specialist.

2 If necessary the compressor can be unbolted and moved aside, without disconnecting its flexible hoses, after removing the drivebelt.

13.12a Use a small screwdriver to release the trim plate . . .

13.12b . . . then withdraw it

13.13 Undo the mounting screws . . .

13.14 . . . withdraw the display unit and disconnect the wiring

13 Climatronic system components – removal and refitting

General information

1 The Climatronic system, fitted to some models, works in conjunction with the heating and air conditioning systems to maintain a selected vehicle interior temperature fully automatically. The only components which can be removed easily without discharging the refrigerant, are as follows:

Sunlight penetration sensor

2 Switch off the ignition and all electrical consumers.

3 Using a small screwdriver, gently prise the sensor from the central defrosting vent.

4 Disconnect the wiring plug and withdraw the sensor.

5 Refitting is a reversal of removal.

Footwell vent temperature sender

6 Switch off the ignition and all electrical consumers.

7 Remove the trim under the steering column.

8 Disconnect the wiring plug from the sender.

9 Turn the sender through 90°, and withdraw it from the housing.

10 Refitting is a reversal of removal.

Control and display unit

11 Switch off the ignition and all electrical consumers.

12 Carefully prise off the trim plate (see illustrations).

13 Undo the mounting screws located at each corner of the display unit (see illustration).

14 Pull out the display unit and disconnect the wiring (see illustration).

15 Refitting is a reversal of removal.

Notes

Chapter 4 Part A:
Petrol engine fuel systems

Contents

Accelerator cable – removal, refitting and adjustment 4
Air cleaner and inlet system – removal and refitting 2
Air cleaner filter element – renewal . . . . .See Chapter 1A
Cruise control system – general information 13
Fuel filter – renewal 6
Fuel injection system – depressurisation 9
Fuel injection system – testing and adjustment 11
Fuel pump and gauge sender unit – removal and refitting 7
Fuel system components – removal and refitting 5
Fuel tank – removal and refitting 8
General information and precautions 1
Inlet air temperature control system – general information 3
Inlet manifold and associated components – removal and refitting . 10
Intercooler – removal and refitting . . . . .See Chapter 4C
Turbocharger – removal and refitting . . . . .See Chapter 4C
Unleaded petrol – general information and usage 12

Degrees of difficulty

Easy, suitable for novice with little experience		Fairly easy, suitable for beginner with some experience		Fairly difficult, suitable for competent DIY mechanic	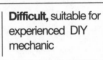	Difficult, suitable for experienced DIY mechanic		Very difficult, suitable for expert DIY or professional	

Specifications

System type*

1.4 litre engines:	
Engine code AHW	Magneti-Marelli 4AV
Engine codes AXP and BCA	Bosch Motronic ME7.5.10
1.6 litre:	
SOHC engines:	
Codes AEH and AKL:	
Vehicles with cruise control	Simos 2.2
Vehicles without cruise control	Simos 2.1
Codes AVU and BFQ	Simos 3.3
DOHC engines, codes AZD and BCB	Magneti-Marelli 4MV
1.8 litre engines, codes AUM and AUQ	Bosch Motronic ME7.5
2.0 litre engines:	
Codes APK and AQY	Bosch Motronic M5.9.2
Codes AZJ and AZH	Bosch Motronic ME7.5

* Refer to Chapter 2A or 2B for engine code listings.

Recommended fuel

Minimum octane rating:	
All models except engine codes AZD, BCB and AUQ	95 RON unleaded (91 RON unleaded may be used, but with reduced performance)
Engine codes AZD, BCB and AUQ	98 RON unleaded (95 RON unleaded may be used, but with reduced performance)

Fuel system data

Fuel pump type	Electric, immersed in fuel tank
Fuel pump delivery rate	400 cc/min (battery voltage of 12.5 V)
Regulated fuel pressure	2.5 bar
Engine idle speed (non-adjustable, electronically controlled):	
Engine codes:	
AHW	700 to 800 rpm
AXP and BCA	650 to 850 rpm
AEH and AKL	760 to 880 rpm
AVU and BFQ	640 to 900 rpm
AZD and BCB	630 to 730 rpm
AUM and AUQ:	
Manual transmission	700 to 820 rpm
Automatic transmission	640 to 760 rpm
APK and AQY	740 to 820 rpm
AZJ and AZH	790 to 890 rpm
Idle CO content (non-adjustable, electronically controlled)	0.5 % max
Injector electrical resistance (typical)	12 to 17 ohms

Torque wrench settings

	Nm	lbf ft
All models		
Fuel tank strap retaining bolts	25	18
Knock sensor(s)	20	15
Oxygen sensor(s)	50	37
1.4 and 1.6 litre DOHC engines		
Fuel rail mounting bolts	10	7
Inlet manifold to cylinder head	20	15
Thermostat housing bolts	10	7
Throttle housing mounting bolts	10	7
1.6 litre SOHC engine		
Air cleaner mounting 'bolts'	10	7
Inlet manifold support:		
To cylinder head	15	11
To inlet manifold	8	6
Inlet manifold upper part-to-lower part screws	3	2
Inlet manifold-to-cylinder head nuts/bolts	15	11
Throttle housing mounting bolts	8	6
1.8 litre non-turbo engine		
Air cleaner mounting 'bolts'	10	7
Camshaft position sensor inner element mounting bolt	25	18
Fuel rail mounting bolts	10	7
Inlet air temperature sensor mounting bolt	10	7
Inlet manifold upper part to lower part	10	7
Inlet manifold upper part to mounting bracket	20	15
Inlet manifold-to-cylinder head nuts/bolts	20	15
Throttle housing mounting bolts	10	7
1.8 litre turbo engine		
Air cleaner mounting 'bolts'	10	7
Camshaft position sensor inner element mounting bolt	25	18
Fuel rail mounting bolts	10	7
Inlet air temperature sensor mounting bolt	10	7
Inlet manifold support bracket:		
To cylinder block	45	33
To inlet manifold	20	15
Inlet manifold-to-cylinder head nuts/bolts	10	7
Throttle housing mounting bolts	10	7
2.0 litre engine		
Fuel rail mounting bolts	10	7
Inlet manifold upper part to lower part	10	7
Inlet manifold-to-cylinder head nuts/bolts	10	7
Throttle housing mounting bolts	10	7

1 General information and precautions

General information

The systems described in this Chapter are all self-contained engine management systems, which control both the fuel injection and ignition. This Chapter deals with the fuel system components only – see Chapter 4C for information on the turbocharger, exhaust and emission control systems, and to Chapter 5B for details of the ignition system.

The fuel injection system comprises a fuel tank, an electric fuel pump/level sender unit, a fuel filter, fuel supply and return lines, a throttle housing, a fuel rail, a fuel pressure regulator, four electronic fuel injectors, and an Electronic Control Unit (ECU) together with its associated sensors, actuators and wiring. The fuel systems used are essentially very similar, but there are significant detail differences, particularly in the sensors used and in the inlet manifold arrangements.

The fuel pump is immersed in the fuel inside the tank, and delivers a constant supply of fuel through a cartridge filter to the fuel rail, at a slightly higher pressure than required – the fuel pressure regulator maintains a constant fuel pressure to the fuel injectors, and returns excess fuel to the tank via the return line. This constant flow system also helps to reduce fuel temperature, and prevents vaporisation.

The fuel injectors are opened and closed by an Electronic Control Unit (ECU), which calculates the injection timing and duration according to engine speed, crankshaft/camshaft position, throttle position and rate of opening, inlet manifold depression, inlet air temperature, coolant temperature, road speed and exhaust gas oxygen content information, received from sensors mounted on and around the engine.

Some models are equipped with a secondary air injection system, which feeds air into the exhaust gases, to promote combustion of any unburnt fuel during engine warm-up; this process also helps to heat the catalytic converter more quickly to its effective operating temperature. Refer to Chapter 4C for more information.

Inlet air is drawn into the engine through the air cleaner, which contains a renewable paper filter element. On some non-turbo models, the inlet air temperature is regulated by a valve mounted in the air cleaner inlet trunking, which blends air at ambient temperature with hot air, drawn from over the exhaust manifold.

The temperature and pressure of the air entering the throttle housing is measured either by a sensor mounted on the inlet manifold, or by the air mass meter attached to the air cleaner. This information is used by the ECU to fine-tune the fuelling requirements for different operating conditions. Turbocharged engines have an additional air temperature sensor mounted downstream of the throttle housing, which monitors the (compressed) air temperature after it has been through the turbocharger and intercooler.

On 1.6 litre SOHC engines, a variable-length inlet manifold is fitted. A vacuum-controlled flap is fitted inside the manifold assembly, which is used to divert the inlet air into one of two paths through the manifold, the paths being of different lengths. Controlling the inlet air in this way has the effect of altering the engine's torque characteristics at different engine speeds and loads.

Idle speed control is achieved partly by an electronic throttle valve positioning module, which is part of the throttle housing, and partly by the ignition system, which gives fine control of the idle speed by altering the ignition timing. As a result, manual adjustment of the engine idle speed is not necessary or possible.

The exhaust gas oxygen content is constantly monitored by the ECU via an oxygen sensor (also known as a lambda sensor), which is mounted in the front section of the exhaust pipe. On all engines except the earliest 1.4 and 1.6 litre units, two oxygen sensors are fitted, one before the catalytic converter, and one after – this improves sensor response time and accuracy, and the ECU compares the signals from each sensor to confirm that the converter is working correctly. The ECU uses the information from the sensor(s) to modify the injection timing and duration to maintain the optimum air/fuel ratio – a result of this is that manual adjustment of the idle exhaust CO content is not necessary or possible. All models are fitted with a catalytic converter – see Chapter 4C.

Where fitted, the ECU controls the operation of the activated charcoal filter evaporative loss system – refer to Chapter 4C for further details.

It should be noted that fault diagnosis of all the engine management systems described in this Chapter is only possible with dedicated electronic test equipment. Problems with the systems operation should therefore be referred to a VW dealer for assessment. Once the fault has been identified, the removal/refitting sequences detailed in the following Sections will then allow the appropriate component(s) to be renewed as required.

Precautions

 Warning: Petrol is extremely flammable – great care must be taken when working on any part of the fuel system.

• *Do not smoke, or allow any naked flames or uncovered light bulbs near the work area. Note that gas-powered domestic appliances with pilot flames, such as*

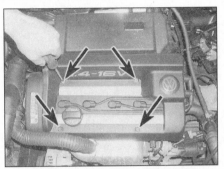

2.1a Unscrew the fasteners (arrowed) . . .

heaters boilers and tumble-dryers, also present a fire hazard – bear this in mind if you are working in an area where such appliances are present. Always keep a suitable fire extinguisher close to the work area, and familiarise yourself with its operation before starting work. Wear eye protection when working on fuel systems, and wash off any fuel spilt on bare skin immediately with soap and water. Note that fuel vapour is just as dangerous as liquid fuel – possibly more so; a vessel that has been emptied of liquid fuel will still contain vapour, and can be potentially explosive.

• *Many of the operations described in this Chapter involve the disconnection of fuel lines, which may cause an amount of fuel spillage. Before commencing work, refer to the above 'Warning' and the information in 'Safety first!' at the beginning of this manual.*

• *Residual fuel pressure always remains in the fuel system, long after the engine has been switched off. This pressure must be relieved in a controlled manner before work can commence on any component in the fuel system – refer to Section 9 for details.*

• *When working with fuel system components, pay particular attention to cleanliness – dirt entering the fuel system may cause blockages, which will lead to poor running.*

• *In the interests of personal safety and equipment protection, many of the procedures in this Chapter suggest that the negative lead be removed from the battery terminal. This firstly eliminates the possibility of accidental short-circuits being caused as the vehicle is being worked upon,*

2.2 Disconnect the breather hose from the air cleaner

2.1b . . . and remove the engine top cover – 1.4 litre engine

and secondly prevents damage to electronic components (eg, sensors, actuators, ECUs) which are particularly sensitive to the power surges caused by disconnection or reconnection of the wiring harness whilst they are still 'live'. Refer to 'Disconnecting the battery' at the rear of this manual.

2 Air cleaner and inlet system – removal and refitting

Removal

1 Where applicable and/or necessary for access, remove the engine top cover(s). Removal details vary according to model, but the cover retaining nuts are concealed under circular covers, which are prised out of the main cover. Where plastic screws or turn-fasteners are used, these can be removed using a wide-bladed screwdriver. Remove the nuts or screws, and lift the cover from the engine, releasing any wiring or hoses attached **(see illustrations)**.

1.4 and 1.6 litre DOHC engines

Note: *On 1.4 litre and 1.6 litre DOHC engine codes AZD, BCA and BCB, the air filter is incorporated in the engine top cover. Refer to Chapter 1A, Section 24 for details.*

2 Disconnect the breather pipe from the right-hand side of the air cleaner **(see illustration)**.
3 Where applicable, unclip the accelerator cable from the front and rear of the air cleaner **(see illustration)**.

2.3 Unclipping the accelerator cable from the air cleaner

2.4a Prise out and remove the rectangular cover . . .

2.4b . . . and remove the screw beneath it

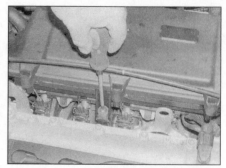

2.5 Remove the screw at the front of the air cleaner

2.6a Remove the screws securing the inlet trunking

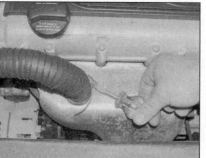

2.6b Release the hot-air hose clip . . .

2.6c . . . and remove the hose from the manifold shroud

4 Prise out the rectangular cover from the top of the air cleaner, and remove the securing screw beneath (**see illustrations**).

5 Unscrew the central screw at the front of the air cleaner (**see illustration**).

6 On early 1.4 litre engines, remove the two screws securing the inlet trunking to the bracket on the engine mounting, and release the hose clip securing the hot-air hose to the exhaust manifold (**see illustrations**).

7 Pull the air cleaner up to release it from the right-hand rear mounting, then release the air inlet spout from the hot-air hose, and lift the assembly from the engine (**see illustration**). Recover the seal which fits over the throttle housing air inlet, and check its condition – renew if it is split or otherwise damaged.

8 The inlet trunking can be removed from the engine mounting by removing the securing screws and releasing the hot-air hose from the manifold shroud.

All other engines

9 Disconnect the wiring plug from the air mass meter.

10 On turbo models, disconnect the two wiring plugs from the ignition power stage at the rear of the air cleaner (**see illustration**).

11 On 1.6 litre models (engine code AVU and BFQ), disconnect the small-bore EGR hose from the air cleaner.

12 Where applicable, detach the large-diameter air inlet hose which leads to the secondary air pump – the hose end fitting is released by squeezing the lugs together.

13 On non-turbo models, release the hose clip securing the hot-air hose to the air cleaner lid, and disconnect the hose.

14 Loosen the hose clip securing the air mass meter to the air inlet trunking (**see illustration**).

15 Unclip any hoses, wiring, etc, which may be clipped to the air cleaner, noting their routing for refitting.

16 Remove the two screws securing the air cleaner lid, and unhook it from the front clips, complete with the air mass meter (**see illustrations**). Lift out the air filter element.

2.7 Removing the air cleaner assembly – 1.4 litre model

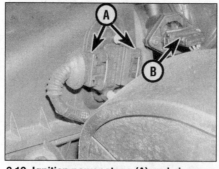

2.10 Ignition power stage (A) and air mass meter (B) wiring plugs

2.14 Disconnecting the air inlet trunking from the air mass meter

2.16a Unscrew the retaining screws . . .

17 The lower half of the air cleaner is secured by two screws – one in front, one behind. Remove the screws and lift out the air cleaner, releasing the air inlet spout from its location.

18 On turbo models, if required, the rest of the inlet trunking can be removed by releasing the hose clips and disconnecting the wiring plug from the boost pressure limitation solenoid. Note the fitted locations of all the hoses prior to disconnection – label the hoses if necessary, to aid refitting.

Refitting

19 Refitting is a reversal of removal, noting the following points:

a) Where applicable, ensure that the air filter element is correctly refitted, referring to Chapter 1A if necessary.

b) It is most important that an airtight seal is made between the air cleaner and the throttle housing (1.4 and 1.6 litre DOHC engines) or between the air mass meter and the air inlet trunking (all other engines). Either check the condition of the seal as described in paragraph 7, or tighten the hose clip securely.

---

3 Inlet air temperature control system – general information

Note: This system may not be fitted to all models.

1 Where fitted, the inlet air temperature control system consists of a temperature-controlled flap valve, mounted in its own housing in the air cleaner inlet trunking or in the air cleaner lid, and a duct to the warm-air collector plate over the exhaust manifold.

2 The temperature sensor in the flap valve housing senses the temperature of the inlet air, and opens the valve when a preset lower limit is reached. As the flap valve opens, warm air drawn from around the exhaust manifold blends with the inlet air.

3 As the temperature of the inlet air rises, the sensor closes the flap progressively, until the warm-air supply from the exhaust manifold is completely closed off, and only air at ambient temperature is admitted to the air cleaner.

4 With the ducting removed from the temperature control flap valve housing, the sensor is visible. If a hairdryer and suitable freeze spray is available, the action of the sensor can be tested.

---

4 Accelerator cable – removal, refitting and adjustment

Note: Most models do not have an accelerator cable, and instead have an electronically-controlled arrangement known variously as Electronic Power Control (EPC), E-Gas or, alternatively, a 'fly-by-wire' throttle. The throttle position sensor at the accelerator

2.16b . . . and remove the air cleaner lid

pedal is linked via the ECU to a motor (positioner) which opens and closes the throttle valve.

Removal

1 Where applicable and/or necessary for access, remove the engine top cover(s). Removal details vary according to model, but the cover retaining nuts are concealed under circular covers, which are prised out of the main cover. Where plastic screws or turn-fasteners are used, these can be removed using a wide-bladed screwdriver. Remove the nuts or screws, and lift the cover from the engine, releasing any wiring or hoses attached.

2 At the throttle housing, hold the throttle valve open and disconnect the accelerator cable inner from the throttle valve spindle **(see illustrations)**.

3 Remove the metal clip and extract the

4.2a Hold the throttle valve open by hand . . .

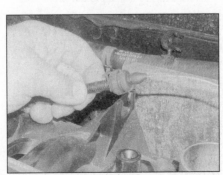

4.3 Unclip the accelerator cable from the mounting bracket

cable outer from the mounting bracket next to the throttle housing **(see illustration)**.

4 On right-hand-drive models, remove the glovebox as described in Chapter 11, Section 28. The accelerator pedal has an extension rod attached which extends across the car, and is accessible by reaching in over the heater housing – have an assistant operate the pedal to identify its location if necessary **(see illustration)**

5 On left-hand-drive models, refer to Chapter 11, Section 28, and remove the facia trim panels from underneath the steering column.

6 Depress the accelerator pedal slightly, then unclip the accelerator cable end from the pedal extension lever. Where applicable, unclip the balance weight from the top of the pedal to improve access.

7 At the point where the cable passes through the bulkhead, unscrew the cap from the two-piece grommet so that the cable can move freely.

8 Release the cable from its securing clips and guide it out through the bulkhead grommet.

Refitting

9 Refit the accelerator cable by following the removal procedure in reverse.

Adjustment

10 At the throttle housing, fix the position of the cable outer in its mounting bracket by inserting the metal clip in one of the locating slots, such that when the accelerator is depressed fully, the throttle valve is just touching its end stop **(see illustration overleaf)**.

4.2b . . . and detach the accelerator cable inner

4.4 Accelerator cable end fitting (arrowed) – seen with glovebox removed

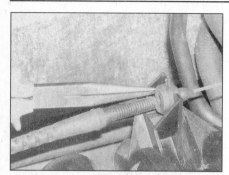

4.10 Using pliers to set the metal clip in position

5 Fuel system components – removal and refitting

Note: *Observe the precautions in Section 1 before working on any component in the fuel system. Information on the engine management system sensors which are more directly related to the ignition system will be found in Chapter 5B.*

Throttle housing

1 On some models, the throttle housing is coolant-heated, so removing it entails disconnecting two coolant pipes. Even if the cooling system is drained as described in Chapter 1A, it is likely that the throttle housing supply pipes will not be drained, and spillage will result. If the coolant is not due for renewal,

it may be preferable not to drain the system, but be prepared to plug the pipes once they have been disconnected.

2 On non-turbo models, remove the air cleaner as described in Section 2.

3 On turbo models, remove the engine top cover(s). Removal details vary according to model, but the cover retaining nuts are concealed under circular covers, which are prised out of the main cover. Where plastic screws or turn-fasteners are used, these can be removed using a wide-bladed screwdriver. Remove the nuts or screws, and lift the cover from the engine, releasing any wiring or hoses attached.

4 Where applicable, refer to Section 4 and detach the accelerator cable from the throttle valve lever.

5 Disconnect the battery negative lead and position it away from the terminal. **Note:** *Refer to 'Disconnecting the battery' at the rear of this manual first.*

6 Disconnect the hose for the charcoal canister from the port on the throttle housing. Also disconnect the brake servo vacuum supply hose, where applicable **(see illustrations)**.

7 Unplug the wiring connector from the throttle potentiometer **(see illustration)**.

8 Where applicable, disconnect the coolant pipes from the throttle housing, noting their positions carefully for refitting. Be prepared for coolant spillage, and plug the pipe ends to prevent too much coolant loss.

9 On 1.4 litre engines and 1.6 litre engine codes AVU and BFQ, unscrew the two bolts securing the metal pipe for the EGR system.

Separate the pipe flange from the throttle housing, and recover the gasket – a new gasket must be used when refitting **(see illustration)**.

10 On turbo models, loosen the hose clip and remove the large-diameter air inlet trunking from the throttle housing **(see illustration)**.

11 Slacken and withdraw the through-bolts, then lift the throttle housing away from the inlet manifold. On 1.4 litre engines, recover the mounting flange to which the EGR pipe is bolted, noting its orientation. Recover and discard the gasket(s). Note that, on some models, one of the bolts secures the throttle housing earth strap.

12 Refitting is a reversal of removal, noting the following:
   a) Use a new throttle housing-to-inlet manifold gasket.
   b) Tighten the throttle housing through-bolts evenly to the specified torque, to prevent air leaks.
   c) Ensure that all hoses and electrical connectors are refitted securely.
   d) Where applicable, with reference to Section 4, check and if necessary adjust the accelerator cable.

Fuel injectors and fuel rail

Note: *Observe the precautions in Section 1 before working on any component in the fuel system. If a faulty injector is suspected, before removing the injectors, it is worth trying the effect of one of the proprietary injector-cleaning treatments. These can be added to the petrol in the tank, and are intended to clean the injectors as you drive.*

13 Disconnect the battery negative lead, and position it away from the terminal. **Note:** *Refer to 'Disconnecting the battery' at the rear of this manual first.*

14 Where applicable, remove the engine top cover(s). Removal details vary according to model, but the cover retaining nuts are concealed under circular covers, which are prised out of the main cover. Where plastic screws or turn-fasteners are used, these can be removed using a wide-bladed screwdriver. Remove the nuts or screws, and lift the cover from the engine, releasing any wiring or hoses attached **(see illustrations)**.

5.6a Disconnect the vacuum hose for the charcoal canister . . .

5.6b . . . and for the brake servo

5.7 Disconnect the wiring plug from the throttle housing

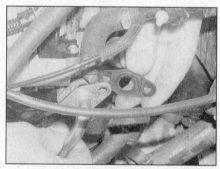

5.9 Unscrew the EGR pipe flange bolts, separate the joint, and recover the gasket

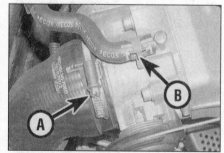

5.10 Throttle housing – turbo models. Air inlet hose clip (A) and charcoal canister hose (B)

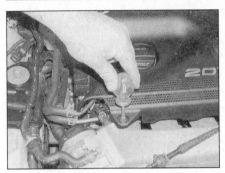

5.14a Release the fasteners . . .

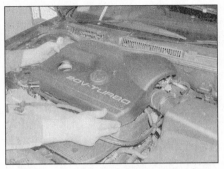

5.14b . . . and remove the main engine cover . . .

5.14c . . . and the front engine cover – turbo model

15 On 1.6 and 2.0 litre SOHC engines, remove the upper part of the inlet manifold as described in Section 10.
16 Unplug the injector harness connectors, labelling them to aid correct refitting later. Release the wiring harness clips from the top of the fuel rail, and lay the harness to one side **(see illustrations)**.
17 Refer to Section 9 and depressurise the fuel system.
18 Disconnect the vacuum hose from the port on the fuel pressure regulator **(see illustration)**.
19 On models with secondary air injection, disconnect the air supply hose for the injector air shrouds.
20 Squeeze the catches on the quick-release fittings, and disconnect the fuel supply and return hoses from the entry points at the bulkhead. Alternatively, release the spring clips securing the hoses to the fuel rail **(see**

illustrations). *Carefully* note the fitted positions of the hoses – the supply hose is marked with a black or white arrow, and the return hose is marked with a blue arrow.
21 Slacken and withdraw the fuel rail mounting bolts **(see illustration)**, then carefully lift the rail away from the inlet manifold, together with the injectors. Recover the injector lower O-ring seals as they emerge from the manifold.
22 The injectors can be removed individually from the fuel rail by extracting the relevant metal clip and easing the injector out of the rail. Recover the injector upper O-ring seals.
23 If required, remove the fuel pressure regulator, referring to the relevant sub-Section for guidance.
24 Check the electrical resistance of the injectors using a multimeter, and compare it with the Specifications.
25 Refit the injectors and fuel rail by following

the removal procedure in reverse, noting the following points:
a) *Renew the injector O-ring seals if they appear worn or damaged.*
b) *Ensure that the injector retaining clips are securely seated.*
c) *Check that the fuel supply and return hoses are reconnected correctly – refer to the colour coding described in removal.*
d) *Check that all vacuum and electrical connections are remade correctly and securely.*
e) *On completion, check exhaustively for fuel leaks before bringing the vehicle back into service.*

Fuel pressure regulator

Note: *Observe the precautions in Section 1 before working on any component in the fuel system.*
26 Disconnect the battery negative lead, and

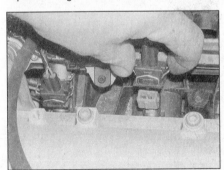

5.16a Disconnect the wiring plugs from the injectors . . .

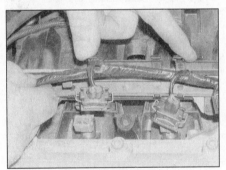

5.16b . . . then release the injector wiring harness from the fuel rail

5.18 Disconnecting the pressure regulator vacuum hose

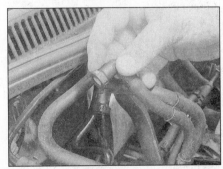

5.20a Press the catches to disconnect the fuel hose quick-release fittings . . .

5.20b . . . or release the spring clips securing the hoses at the fuel rail

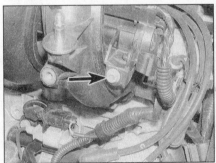

5.21 One of the fuel rail mounting bolts

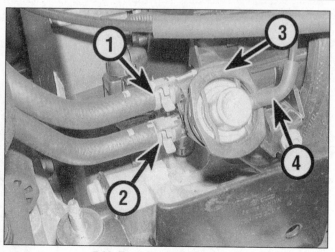

**5.29 Fuel pressure regulator –
1.6 litre SOHC engine**

1 *Fuel supply hose*
2 *Fuel return hose*
3 *Spring clip*
4 *Vacuum hose*

5.36 Accelerator pedal and throttle position sensor

1 *Bracket*
2 *Position sensor wiring
   connector*
3 *Mounting nuts*
4 *Position sensor*
5 *Retainer for footwell cover*

position it away from the terminal. **Note:** *Refer to 'Disconnecting the battery' at the rear of this manual first.*

27 Refer to Section 9 and depressurise the fuel system.

28 Where applicable, remove the engine top cover(s). Removal details vary according to model, but the cover retaining nuts are concealed under circular covers, which are prised out of the main cover. Where plastic screws or turn-fasteners are used, these can be removed using a wide-bladed screwdriver. Remove the nuts or screws, and lift the cover from the engine, releasing any wiring or hoses attached.

29 Disconnect the vacuum hose from the port on the bottom (or side) of the fuel pressure regulator **(see illustration)**.

30 Release the spring clip and temporarily disconnect the fuel supply hose from the end of the fuel rail. This will allow the majority of fuel in the regulator to drain out. Be prepared for an amount of fuel loss – position a small container and some old rags underneath the fuel regulator housing. Reconnect the hose once the fuel has drained. **Note:** *The supply hose is marked with a black or white arrow.*

31 On 1.4 and 1.6 litre DOHC engines, remove the regulator collar securing screw, and lift off the collar. Lift out the regulator, and recover the O-ring seals.

32 On all other engines, extract the retaining spring clip from the top of the regulator housing and lift out the regulator body, recovering the O-ring seals.

33 Refit the fuel pressure regulator by following the removal procedure in reverse, noting the following points:

a) *Renew the O-ring seals if they appear worn or damaged.*

b) *Ensure that the regulator retaining clip is securely seated, or that the collar is correctly fitted and the screw securely tightened.*

c) *Refit the regulator vacuum hose securely.*

Throttle valve potentiometer/positioner

34 The potentiometer (or motor/positioner, on models with a 'fly-by-wire' throttle) is matched to the throttle housing during manufacture, and is not available separately – if defective, a complete throttle housing assembly will be required. Although the unit can be removed from the housing by removing the retaining screws, doing so will damage the seal between the two, and it does not appear that a new seal is available as a new part.

Throttle position sensor

35 On models with a conventional accelerator cable, the throttle position sensor function is performed by the potentiometer attached to the throttle housing. As described above, the potentiometer is not available separately.

36 On models with the 'fly-by-wire' throttle, the position sensor is integral with the accelerator pedal. The pedal assembly can be removed (once access has been gained by removing the driver's lower facia panel –

5.39 Disconnect the inlet manifold pressure sensor wiring connector (viewed from underneath vehicle)

Chapter 11, Section 28) by disconnecting the sensor wiring plug and unscrewing the nuts securing the pedal to its mounting bracket **(see illustration)**.

Inlet air temperature/ pressure sensors

37 All models except those with the 1.4 and 1.6 litre DOHC engines have an air temperature sensor built into the air mass meter. This sensor is an integral part of the air mass meter, and cannot be renewed separately. On 1.8 litre engines, an additional air temperature sensor is fitted to the inlet manifold, and this can be renewed as described below.

1.4 and 1.6 litre DOHC engines

38 The sensor is attached to the right-hand side of the inlet manifold (right as seen from the driver's seat) **(refer to illustration 10.6)**.

39 Disconnect the battery negative lead, and position it away from the terminal. **Note:** *Refer to 'Disconnecting the battery' at the rear of this manual first.* Unplug the wiring connector from the sensor **(see illustration)**.

40 Remove the two securing screws, and pull the sensor from the manifold. Recover the O-ring seals and the guide plate if it is loose – note how the plate is fitted.

41 Refitting is a reversal of removal, noting the following point:

a) *Fit the guide plate and renew the O-ring seal(s) if necessary. Tighten the sensor retaining screws securely.*

1.8 litre engines

42 The sensor is located on the inlet manifold, next to the throttle housing. Disconnect the battery negative lead, and position it away from the terminal. **Note:** *Refer to 'Disconnecting the battery' at the rear of this manual first.* Unplug the wiring connector from the sensor **(see illustration)**.

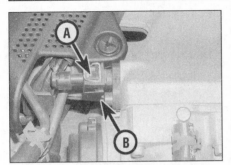

5.42 Inlet air temperature sensor – 1.8 litre turbo engine

Wiring connector (A) and retaining bolt (B)

5.49 Separate the two halves of the oxygen sensor wiring plug – above the transmission on this model

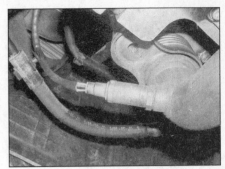

5.50 Oxygen sensor location – 1.4 litre engine

43 Unscrew the sensor retaining bolt, then pull the sensor out of its location in the inlet manifold. Recover the O-ring seal.

44 Refitting is a reversal of removal, noting the following point:

a) *Renew the O-ring seal if it shows signs of damage. Tighten the sensor bolt to the specified torque.*

Roadspeed sensor

45 The roadspeed sensor is mounted on the transmission, next to the gearchange linkage – refer to Chapter 7A. Do not confuse the sensor with the reversing light switch, which has a smaller wiring connector.

Coolant temperature sensor

46 Refer to Chapter 3, Section 6.

Oxygen (lambda) sensor(s)

47 All models have a sensor threaded into the exhaust downpipe or manifold, ahead of the catalytic converter. Most models have an additional oxygen sensor, mounted downstream of the converter. Refer to Chapter 4C for more details.

48 Disconnect the battery negative lead and position it away from the terminal. **Note:** *Refer to 'Disconnecting the battery' at the rear of this manual first.*

⚠ **Warning: Working on the sensor(s) is only advisable with the engine (and therefore the exhaust system) completely cold. The catalytic converter in particular will be very hot for some time after the engine has been switched off.**

49 Working from the sensor, trace the wiring harness from the oxygen sensor back to the connector, and disconnect it **(see illustration)**. Typically, the wiring plug is coloured black for the front sensor, and brown for the rear sensor. Unclip the sensor wiring from any retaining clips, noting how it is routed.

50 Access to the front sensor is possible on some models from above, while the rear sensor (where fitted) is only accessible from below **(see illustration)**. On some models, access to a front pipe-mounted sensor is improved by unbolting and removing the cover from the right-hand driveshaft inner CV joint.

51 Slacken and withdraw the sensor, taking care to avoid damaging the sensor probe as it is removed. **Note:** *As a flying lead remains connected to the sensor after it has been disconnected, if the correct-size spanner is not available, a slotted socket will be required to remove the sensor.*

52 Apply a little high-temperature anti-seize grease to the sensor threads – avoid contaminating the probe tip.

53 Refit the sensor, tightening it to the correct torque. Restore the harness connection.

Engine speed sensor

54 On 1.4 and 1.6 litre DOHC engines, the engine speed sensor is mounted at the left-hand rear of the cylinder block, next to the transmission bellhousing, and access is very difficult. Prise out the rubber bung for access to the sensor **(see illustration)**.

55 On all other engines, the engine speed sensor is mounted on the front, left-hand side of the cylinder block, adjacent to the mating surface of the block and transmission bellhousing, next to the oil filter. If necessary, drain the engine oil and remove the oil filter and cooler to improve access, with reference to Chapter 1A.

56 Trace the wiring back from the sensor, and unplug the harness connector **(see illustration)**.

57 Unscrew the retaining bolt and withdraw the sensor from the cylinder block.

58 Refitting is a reversal of removal.

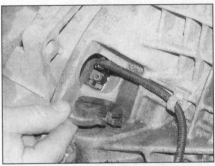

5.54 Prise out the rubber bung for access to the speed sensor

Camshaft position sensor

1.4 and 1.6 litre DOHC engines

59 Where applicable, remove the engine top cover(s). Removal details vary according to model, but the cover retaining nuts are concealed under circular covers, which are prised out of the main cover. Where plastic screws or turn-fasteners are used, these can be removed using a wide-bladed screwdriver. Remove the nuts or screws, and lift the cover from the engine, releasing any wiring or hoses attached.

60 Remove the oil filler cap.

61 Remove the four screws securing the cover over the camshaft housings, and lift the cover off the engine.

62 Pull the wiring connector upwards off the sensor, which is located next to the engine lifting eye **(see illustration)**.

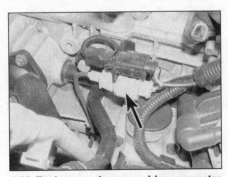

5.56 Engine speed sensor wiring connector (arrowed) – 1.6 litre SOHC engine

5.62 Disconnecting the camshaft position sensor – 1.4 litre engine

5.70 Disconnecting the camshaft position sensor – 1.6 litre SOHC engine

5.85 Disconnecting one of the two ECU wiring plugs

63 Unscrew the sensor mounting bolt, and pull the sensor out of the camshaft housing.
64 Refitting is a reversal of removal.

1.8 litre engines

65 Remove the timing belt outer cover with reference to Chapter 2B.
66 Release the clip and disconnect the wiring multiplug from the sensor.
67 Unscrew the mounting bolts and withdraw the sensor from the cylinder head. If required, unscrew the central bolt and remove the inner element and hood, noting how they are fitted.
68 Refitting is a reversal of removal; tighten the mounting bolts securely.

1.6 and 2.0 litre SOHC engines

69 Remove the camshaft sprocket with reference to Chapter 2A.
70 Note the location of the sensor and if necessary mark it in relation to the cylinder head. Disconnect the wiring from the sensor **(see illustration)**.
71 Unbolt the timing belt inner cover from the cylinder head.
72 Unscrew the remaining bolts and remove the sensor from the cylinder head.
73 Refitting is a reversal of removal, but make sure that the sensor base plate is central before tightening the retaining bolts.

Clutch pedal switch

74 Fitted to 1.6, 1.8 and 2.0 litre engines, the clutch switch is mounted on the clutch pedal, and sends a signal to the ECU. The purpose of the switch is to disable the throttle closing damper during gearchanges, allowing the engine revs to die down more quickly than

would otherwise happen when the accelerator is released. The switch also deactivates the cruise control system (where fitted) when the pedal is pressed.
75 To remove the switch, first remove the facia lower trim panel on the driver's side, as described in Chapter 11, Section 28.
76 Locate the switch wiring plug in front of the clutch pedal, and disconnect it.
77 Release the switch retaining lugs, and withdraw it from the pedal.
78 When refitting the switch, first extend the switch plunger to its fullest extent, then hold the clutch pedal depressed when offering it into position. Once the switch has been clipped into place, release the pedal – this sets the switch adjustment. Further refitting is a reversal of removal.

Power steering pressure switch

79 When the steering is at or near full left or right lock, this places a greater load on the power steering pump. Since the pump is driven by the engine, this could result in the engine idle speed dropping, risking the engine stalling. The pressure switch fitted to the pump detects the rise in system fluid pressure, and signals the ECU, which raises the idle speed temporarily to compensate for the extra load.
80 The pressure switch is screwed into the top of the steering pump fluid supply union, and is most easily accessed from below.
81 Disconnect the wiring plug from the top of the switch.
82 Hold the (slim) union nut against rotation with one spanner, and use another to unscrew

the pressure switch from the union. Recover the sealing washer, where fitted. Anticipate some fluid spillage as the switch is unscrewed. Once the switch has been removed, cover the open connection to prevent dirt from entering.
83 Refitting is a reversal of removal, noting the following points:
a) Use a new sealing washer, where applicable. Tighten the switch securely, holding the union nut as for removal.
b) Top-up the power steering system as described in 'Weekly checks'. If a large amount of fluid was lost, bleed the system as described in Chapter 10.
c) On completion, start the engine and have an assistant turn the steering wheel from lock-to-lock, while you check around the switch for leaks.

Electronic control unit (ECU)

Caution: Always wait at least 30 seconds after switching off the ignition before disconnecting the wiring from the ECU. When the wiring is disconnected, all the learned values are erased, although any contents of the fault memory are retained. After reconnecting the wiring, the basic settings must be reinstated by a VW dealer using a special test instrument. Note also that if the ECU is renewed, the identification of the new ECU must be transferred to the immobiliser control unit by a VW dealer.

84 The ECU is located centrally behind the engine compartment bulkhead, under one of the windscreen cowl panels. Remove the wiper arms and cowl panel as for windscreen wiper motor removal and refitting, described in Chapter 12.
85 Release the locking clip or lever on each ECU wiring connector, and disconnect the plug. On most models, there are two separate plugs to be disconnected **(see illustration)**.
86 Press the control unit to the right, to release its retaining clip, and pull it from its location. Alternatively, the clip on the right-hand side of the unit can be released using a screwdriver **(see illustrations)**.
87 Refitting is a reversal of removal. Press the unit to the left, once in position, to secure it. Bear in mind the comments made in the Caution above – the ECU will not work correctly until it has been electronically coded.

Camshaft chain adjuster solenoid valve

1.8 litre engines

88 The solenoid valve is an integral part of the inlet camshaft drive chain adjuster/tensioner. At the time of writing it was unclear if the solenoid valve was available separately or whether it is an integral part of the adjuster/tensioner assembly. Refer to your VW dealer for solenoid valve availability. The chain adjuster/tensioner assembly is removed with the camshafts (see Chapter 2B for details).

5.86a We found that releasing this locking clip on the right made ECU removal easier

5.86b Removing the ECU from its location

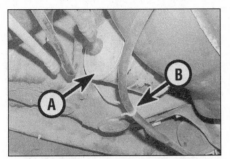

6.2 Fuel filter (A) is located in front of the fuel tank. Note the handbrake cable wire clip (B)

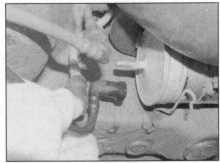

6.5 Disconnecting the fuel hose at the front of the filter

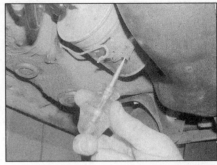

6.7 Loosening the filter securing clip

6 Fuel filter – renewal

Note: *Observe the precautions in Section 1 before working on any component in the fuel system.*

1 Depressurise the fuel system as described in Section 9. Remember, however, that this procedure merely relieves the fuel pressure, reducing the risk of fuel spraying when the connections are disturbed – fuel will still be spilt during filter renewal, so take precautions accordingly.

2 The fuel filter is located in front of the fuel tank, on the right-hand underside of the car **(see illustration)**.

3 Jack up the right-hand rear of the car, and support it on an axle stand (see *Jacking and vehicle support*). When positioning the axle stand, ensure that it will not inhibit access to the filter.

4 To further improve access, unhook the handbrake cable from the adjacent wire clip.

5 Disconnect the fuel hoses at either end of the filter, noting their locations for refitting. The connections are of quick-release type, disconnected by squeezing the catch on each **(see illustration)**. It may be necessary to release the hoses from the clips on the underside of the car, to allow greater movement. Both filter hoses should be black.

6 The filter is held in position by a large-diameter worm-drive clip. Before removing the filter, look for an arrow marking, which

points in the direction of fuel flow – in this case, towards the front of the car. The new filter must be fitted the same way round.

7 Loosen the worm-drive clip, and slide the filter out of position **(see illustration)**. Try to keep it as level as possible, to reduce fuel spillage. Dispose of the old filter carefully – even if the fuel inside is tipped out, the filter element will still be soaked in fuel, and will be highly flammable.

8 Offer the new filter into position, ensuring that the direction-of-flow arrow is pointing towards the front of the car. Tighten the worm-drive clip securely, but without risking crushing the filter body.

9 Connect the fuel hoses to each end of the filter, in the same positions as noted on removal. Push the hoses fully onto the filter stubs, and if necessary, clip them back to the underside of the car. Hook the handbrake cable back in place, if it was disturbed.

10 Lower the car to the ground, then start the engine and check for signs of fuel leakage at both ends of the filter.

7 Fuel pump and gauge sender unit – removal and refitting

Note: *Observe the precautions in Section 1 before working on any component in the fuel system.*

⚠ **Warning: Avoid direct skin contact with fuel – wear protective clothing and gloves**

when handling fuel system components. Ensure that the work area is well-ventilated to prevent the build-up of fuel vapour.

General information

1 The fuel pump and gauge sender unit are combined in one assembly, which is mounted on the top of the fuel tank. Access is via a hatch provided in the load space floor. The unit protrudes into the fuel tank, and its removal involves exposing the contents of the tank to the atmosphere.

Removal

2 Depressurise the fuel system (Section 9).

3 Ensure that the vehicle is parked on a level surface, then disconnect the battery negative lead and position it away from the terminal. **Note:** *Refer to 'Disconnecting the battery' at the rear of this manual first.*

4 Fold the rear seat forwards, and lift the carpet section from the load space floor.

5 Slacken and withdraw the access hatch screws, and lift the hatch away from the floorpan **(see illustrations)**.

6 Unplug the wiring harness connector from the pump/sender unit **(see illustration)**.

7 Pad the area around the supply and return fuel hoses with rags to absorb any spilt fuel, then squeeze the catch to release the hose clips and disconnect them from the ports at the sender unit **(see illustration)**. Observe the supply and return arrow markings on the ports – label the fuel hoses accordingly to ensure correct refitting later. The supply pipe is black, and may have white markings, while the return pipe is blue, or has blue markings.

7.5a Loosen and remove the screws . . .

7.5b . . . then lift out the access hatch

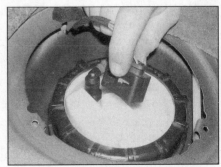

7.6 Unplug the pump/sender unit wiring connector

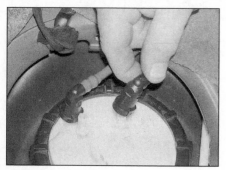

7.7 Disconnecting the fuel supply hose

7.8 Unscrew and remove the securing ring

7.9 Lift out the unit, and let the fuel drain into the tank

8 Note the position of the alignment marks, then unscrew the plastic securing ring and lift it out **(see illustration)**. Use a pair of water pump pliers to grip and rotate the plastic securing ring, if possible. Recover the flange and seal.

9 Lift out the pump/sender unit, holding it above the level of the fuel in the tank until the excess fuel has drained out **(see illustration)**.

10 Remove the pump/sender unit from the car, and lay it on an absorbent card or rag. Inspect the float at the end of the sender unit swinging arm for punctures and fuel ingress – renew the unit if it appears damaged.

11 The fuel pick-up incorporated in the assembly is spring-loaded to ensure that it always draws fuel from the lowest part of the tank. Check that the pick-up is free to move under spring tension with respect to the sender unit body.

12 Inspect the rubber seal from the fuel tank aperture for signs of fatigue – renew it if necessary **(see illustration)**.

13 Inspect the sender unit wiper and track; clean off any dirt and debris that may have accumulated, and look for breaks in the track.

14 If required, the sender unit can be separated from the assembly, as follows. Disconnect the two small wires (note their positions), then remove the four screws and slide the unit downwards to remove **(see illustrations)**.

15 The unit top plate can be removed by releasing the plastic tags at either side; recover the large spring which fits onto a peg on the plate underside **(see illustrations)**.

Refitting

16 Refit the pump/sender unit by following the removal procedure in reverse, noting the following points:

a) Take care not to bend the float arm as the unit is refitted.

b) Smear the outside of tank aperture rubber seal with clean fuel or lubricating spray, to ease fitting. Unless a new seal is required, the seal should be left on the pump unit before fitting. When the unit is almost fully in place, slide the seal down and locate it on the rim of the tank aperture, then slide the unit fully home.

c) The arrow markings on the sender unit body and the access aperture must be aligned **(see illustration)**.

d) Reconnect the fuel hoses to the correct ports – observe the direction-of-flow arrow markings, and refer to paragraph 7. The return port is marked R, while the supply port is marked V; on some models, there may be arrow markings indicating fuel flow. Ensure that the fuel hose fittings click fully into place.

e) On completion, check that all associated pipes are securely clipped to the tank.

7.12 If not removed with the unit, recover the rubber seal and check its condition

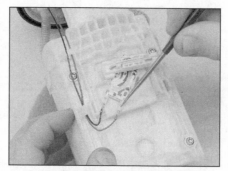

7.14a Carefully separate the wiring connections . . .

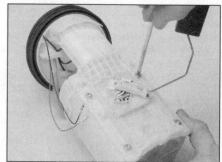

7.14b . . . then remove the four screws and take off the sender unit

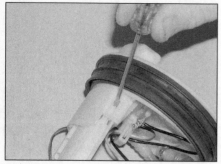

7.15a Prise up the retaining tags . . .

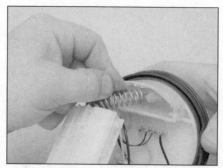

7.15b . . . and recover the spring fitted under the top plate

7.16 Arrow markings on pump/sender unit and access aperture aligned

f) *Before refitting the access hatch and rear seat, run the engine and check for fuel leaks.*

8 Fuel tank – removal and refitting

Note: *Observe the precautions in Section 1 before working on any component in the fuel system.*

Removal

1 Before the tank can be removed, it must be drained of as much fuel as possible. As no drain plug is provided, it is preferable to carry out this operation with the tank almost empty.
2 Open the fuel filler flap, and unscrew the fuel filler cap – leave the cap loosely in place.
3 Disconnect the battery negative lead and position it away from the terminal. **Note:** *Refer to 'Disconnecting the battery' at the rear of this manual first.* Using a hand pump or syphon, remove any remaining fuel from the bottom of the tank.
4 Loosen the right-hand rear wheel bolts, then jack up the rear of the car and remove the right-hand rear wheel.
5 Remove the right-hand rear wheel arch liner as described in Chapter 11, Section 24.
6 Gain access to the top of the fuel pump/sender unit as described in Section 7, and disconnect the wiring harness from the top of the pump/sender unit at the multiway connector.
7 Unscrew the fuel filler flap unit retaining screw (on the side opposite the flap hinge), and ease the flap unit out of position. Recover the rubber seal which fits around the filler neck.
8 The fuel tank is protected from below by one or more plastic covers – our project car had one in front of, and one behind, the rear axle. These covers are secured either by washer-type fasteners (which can be unscrewed using a screwdriver blade between the 'washer' tangs), or ordinary nuts. Remove the fasteners securing the fuel tank cover, noting that the 'ordinary' nuts have a **left-hand thread** – ie, they unscrew in a **clockwise** direction. Remove the covers from the tank strap studs, and withdraw them from under the car **(see illustrations)**.
9 Referring to Chapter 4C if necessary, unbolt the exhaust rear silencer mounting, and carefully lower the rear section of the exhaust system. Given that the rear axle assembly has to be removed (or at least lowered) to allow the tank to be removed, it is preferable to remove the rear section of the exhaust system completely.
10 Remove the nuts or washer-type fasteners securing the fuel tank exhaust heat shield, and withdraw the shield from around the exhaust pipe.
11 At the front of the tank, disconnect the fuel return hose, and the breather pipe, noting

8.8a Removing the fuel tank covers behind . . .

8.8b . . . and in front of the rear axle

their locations for refitting. The connections are of quick-release type, disconnected by squeezing the catch on each. The return hose is blue, and the breather pipe is white **(see illustration)**. Similarly, disconnect the fuel supply hose from the tank side of the fuel filter.
12 Refer to Chapter 10 and remove the rear axle assembly. In order to remove the tank, it is possible to just lower the axle out of position, rather than completely removing it.
13 Position a trolley jack under the centre of the tank. Insert a block of wood between the jack head and the tank to prevent damage to the tank surface. Raise the jack until it just takes the weight of the tank.
14 Loosen and remove the retaining bolts and detach the tank straps at the front and rear of the tank **(see illustration)**. Note that the straps are of different lengths, so do not confuse them when they are finally removed.
15 Lower the jack and tank away from the underside of the vehicle; detach the filler pipes and the outlet pipe from the fuel filter as the tank is lowered. Disconnect the charcoal canister vent pipe from the port on the filler neck as it is exposed. Locate the earthing strap and disconnect it from the terminal at the filler neck.
16 If the tank is contaminated with sediment or water, remove the fuel pump/sender unit (see Section 7) and swill the tank out with clean fuel. The tank is injection-moulded from a synthetic material, and if damaged, it should be renewed. However, in certain cases it may be possible to have small leaks or minor damage repaired. Seek the advice of a

suitable specialist before attempting to repair the fuel tank.

Refitting

17 Refitting is the reverse of the removal procedure, noting the following points:
  a) *When lifting the tank back into position, make sure the mounting rubbers are correctly positioned, and take care to ensure none of the hoses get trapped between the tank and vehicle body.*
  b) *Ensure that all pipes and hoses are correctly routed, are not kinked, and are securely held in position with their retaining clips.*
  c) *Reconnect the earth strap to its terminal on the filler neck.*
  d) *Tighten the tank strap retaining bolts to the specified torque.*
  e) *On completion, refill the tank with fuel, and exhaustively check for signs of leakage prior to taking the vehicle out on the road.*

9 Fuel injection system – depressurisation

Note: *Observe the precautions in Section 1 before working on any component in the fuel system.*

⚠️ **Warning: The following procedure will merely relieve the pressure in the fuel system – remember that fuel will still be present in the system components and take precautions**

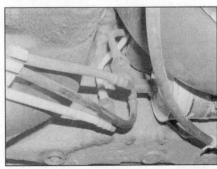

8.11 Fuel hose connections at the front of the fuel tank

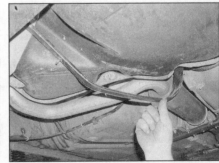

8.14 Removing one of the fuel tank straps

accordingly before disconnecting any of them.

1 The fuel system referred to in this Section is defined as the tank-mounted fuel pump, the fuel filter, the fuel injectors, the fuel pressure regulator, and the metal pipes and flexible hoses of the fuel lines between these components. All these contain fuel, which will be under pressure while the engine is running and/or while the ignition is switched on. The pressure will remain for some time after the ignition has been switched off, and must be relieved before any of these components are disturbed for servicing work. Ideally, the engine should be allowed to cool completely before work commences.

2 Referring to Chapter 12, locate and remove the fuel pump relay. Alternatively, identify and remove the fuel pump fuse from the fusebox.

3 With the fuel pump disabled, crank the engine for about ten seconds. The engine may fire and run for a while, but let it continue running until it stops. The fuel injectors should have opened enough times during cranking to considerably reduce the line fuel pressure, and reduce the risk of fuel spraying out when a fuel line is disturbed.

4 Disconnect the battery negative lead and position it away from the terminal. **Note:** *Refer to 'Disconnecting the battery' at the rear of this manual first.*

5 Place a suitable container beneath the relevant connection/union to be disconnected, and have a large rag ready to soak up any escaping fuel not being caught by the container.

6 Slowly open the connection to avoid a sudden release of pressure, and position the rag around the connection to catch any fuel spray which may be expelled. Once the pressure has been released, disconnect the fuel line. Insert plugs to minimise fuel loss and prevent the entry of dirt into the fuel system.

10 Inlet manifold and associated components – removal and refitting

Note: *Observe the precautions in Section 1 before working on any component in the fuel system.*

1 The design of the inlet manifold varies considerably depending on engine type. On models with the 1.6 SOHC and 2.0 litre engines, the inlet manifold is in two sections – the upper part has to be removed for various routine servicing tasks. All other engines have a one-piece manifold. Refer to the appropriate sub-section below.

One-piece manifold

Removal

2 Disconnect the battery negative lead and position it away from the terminal. **Note:** *Refer to 'Disconnecting the battery' at the rear of this manual first.*

3 With reference to Section 5, remove the throttle housing from the inlet manifold. If preferred, the housing need not be unbolted from the manifold, and can be removed with it, but all the services to the housing must be disconnected.

4 Disconnect the vacuum hoses for the fuel pressure regulator, and (if not already removed) for the brake servo. Note how the hoses are routed, for use when refitting.

5 To allow the manifold to be removed completely, and to improve access to the manifold mounting bolts, remove the fuel rail and injectors as described in Section 5. However, if the manifold is being removed as part of another procedure (such as cylinder head or engine removal), the fuel rail can be left in place.

6 Disconnect the wiring plug from the inlet air temperature/pressure sensor, referring if necessary to Section 5 for more details **(see illustration)**.

7 On 1.8 litre engines, unbolt and remove the manifold support bracket from the engine block, then unbolt the mounting bracket for the secondary air inlet valve from the front of the manifold (refer to Chapter 4C, Section 5, if necessary).

8 Progressively loosen the bolts (nuts and bolts, on 1.8 litre engines) and withdraw the manifold from the cylinder head **(see illustrations)**. Recover the gasket on 1.6 and 1.8 litre engines, or the four seals on 1.4 litre engines – all should be renewed when refitting the manifold.

Refitting

9 Refitting is a reversal of removal. Use a new gasket or seals, as applicable, and tighten the retaining bolts (and nuts) to the specified torque. It is most important that there are no air leaks at the joint.

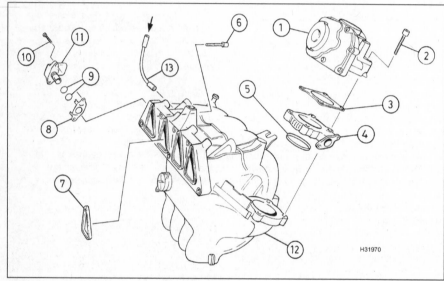

10.6 One-piece inlet manifold – 1.4 litre DOHC engine

1 Throttle housing	6 Inlet manifold bolt	11 Inlet air temperature/pressure sensor
2 Throttle housing bolt	7 Manifold seal	
3 Gasket	8 Guide plate	12 Inlet manifold
4 EGR pipe flange	9 O-rings	13 Fuel pressure regulator vacuum hose
5 Seal	10 Screw	

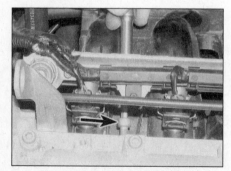

10.8a Loosening an inlet manifold mounting bolt (arrowed)

10.8b Removing the inlet manifold from the cylinder head – 1.4 litre DOHC engine

10.12 Disconnecting the brake servo vacuum hose – 1.6 litre SOHC engine

Two-piece manifold – upper part

Removal

10 Disconnect the battery negative lead and position it away from the terminal. **Note:** *Refer to 'Disconnecting the battery' at the rear of this manual first.*

11 With reference to Section 5, remove the throttle housing from the inlet manifold. If preferred, the housing need not be unbolted from the manifold, and can be removed with it, but all the services to the housing must be disconnected. Where applicable, unclip the accelerator cable completely from the manifold, and lay it to one side.

12 Release the hose clip and disconnect the brake servo vacuum hose from the side of the manifold (1.6 litre) or from the rear (2.0 litre) **(see illustration)**.

13 On 2.0 litre engines, unscrew and remove the bolt securing the clip at the rear of the manifold for the charcoal canister hose **(see illustration)**.

14 On 1.6 litre engines, disconnect the wiring plug from the manifold changeover valve on the right-hand side **(see illustration)**.

15 On early 1.6 litre models, remove the two bolts and washers from the mounting bracket located below the throttle housing mounting flange. Recover the rubber mountings from the mounting bracket if they are loose **(see illustrations)**.

16 On later 1.6 litre engines, unscrew the nut from the support bracket at the rear of the manifold; recover the bolt and washer. Alternatively, unscrew the two bolts securing the support bracket to the engine block.

17 Trace the fuel pressure regulator vacuum hose back, and unclip it from the base of the inlet manifold. Disconnect the vacuum hose from the fuel pressure regulator **(see illustrations)**.

18 Check around the upper part of the manifold, and unclip any hoses or wiring which may still be attached **(see illustration)**.

19 Remove the screws securing the upper part of the manifold to the lower part. On 1.6 litre engines, also remove the plastic spreader rivet from the flanges at either end of the manifold; prise the rivets out – do not push the centre part inwards, or it may fall into the manifold itself **(see illustrations)**.

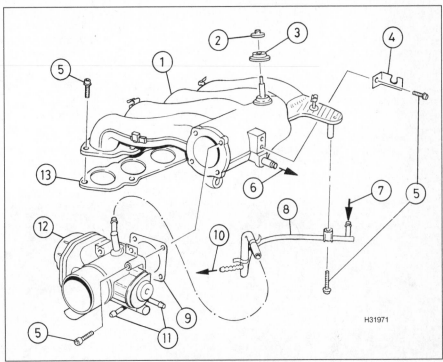

10.13 Inlet manifold upper section – 2.0 litre APK and AQY engines

1 Inlet manifold upper section	4 Accelerator cable support bracket	9 Throttle housing gasket
2 Screw-on washer	5 Support bracket bolt	10 To inlet duct
3 Rubber bush (for engine top cover)	6 Brake servo connection	11 Coolant hose connections
	7 From charcoal canister	12 Throttle housing
	8 Charcoal canister hose	13 Manifold gasket

10.14 Inlet manifold changeover valve wiring plug (arrowed)

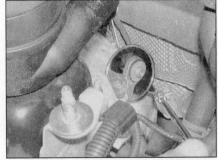

10.15a One of the inlet manifold mounting bracket bolts – seen using a circular mirror

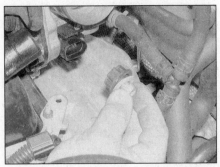

10.15b One of the mounting bracket bolts removed, with washer and rubber mounting

10.17a Unclip the vacuum hose from the base of the manifold . . .

10.17b ... and disconnect it at the fuel pressure regulator

10.18 On this 1.6 litre model, unclip the charcoal canister hose from the top of the manifold

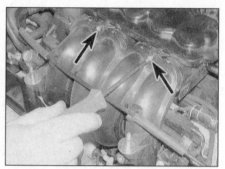

10.19a Unscrew the two screws (arrowed) securing the two manifold sections ...

10.19b ... and prise out the plastic rivets – 1.6 litre engine

10.20a Prise the flanges outwards over the locating pegs ...

10.20b ... then withdraw the upper section rearwards, and remove it

20 On 1.6 litre engines, carefully prise the plastic flanges (into which the rivets were fitted) outwards to release them from the locating pegs. As this is done, move the upper part of the manifold rearwards to disengage the four ports on the lower part – recover the four seals. Lift the manifold upwards, and remove it from the engine compartment **(see illustrations)**.

21 On 2.0 litre engines, lift the upper part of the manifold off the lower part, and remove it from the engine compartment. Recover the gasket.

Refitting

22 Refitting is a reversal of removal. Use new seals or gaskets as necessary, and tighten the upper-to-lower part bolts to the specified torque. It is most important that there are no air leaks at the joint.

Two-piece manifold – lower part

Removal

23 Remove the upper part of the manifold as described previously in this Section.

24 To allow the manifold to be removed completely, and to improve access to the manifold mounting bolts, remove the fuel rail and injectors as described in Section 5. If the lower part is to be removed with the fuel rail, at least the fuel lines and injector wiring must be disconnected.

25 On 1.6 litre models, disconnect the wiring plug from the camshaft position sensor on the right-hand side of the engine **(refer to illustration 5.70)**.

26 Where applicable, the secondary air injection pump must be removed from the front of the manifold – refer to Chapter 4C.

27 Check around the manifold, and unclip any hoses or wiring which may still be attached **(see illustration)**.

28 Progressively loosen the nuts and bolts and withdraw the manifold from the cylinder head **(see illustrations)**. Recover the seals/gaskets – all should be renewed when refitting the manifold.

Refitting

29 Refitting is a reversal of removal. Use new seals or gaskets as necessary, and tighten the manifold-to-head nuts and bolts to the specified torque. It is most important that there are no air leaks at the joint.

Changeover valve and diaphragm unit

30 Models with the 1.6 litre SOHC engine have a variable-length inlet manifold, described

10.27 Unclipping the accelerator cable – 1.6 litre SOHC engine

10.28a Unscrew the (nuts and) bolts ...

10.28b ... and withdraw the lower section of inlet manifold

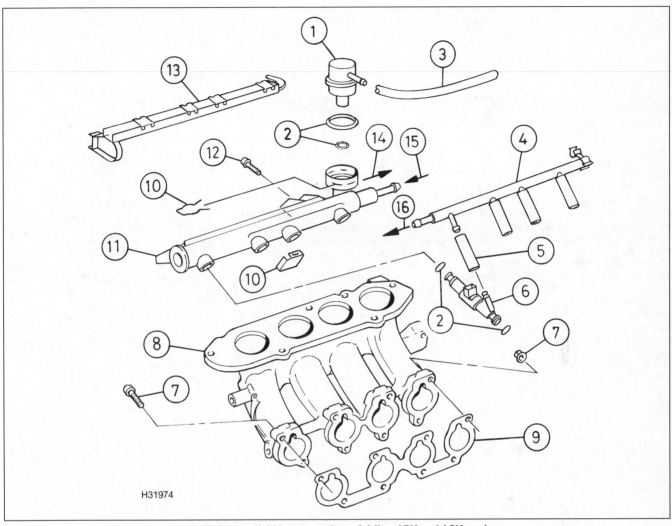

10.28c Inlet manifold lower section – 2.0 litre APK and AQY engines

1 *Fuel pressure regulator*	5 *Air shrouds*	9 *Gasket*
2 *O-ring*	6 *Fuel injector*	10 *Injector retaining clip*
3 *Vacuum hose*	7 *Manifold nuts/bolts*	11 *Fuel rail*
4 *Air supply pipe*	8 *Inlet manifold lower section*	12 *Fuel rail mounting bolt*
13 *Wiring harness guide channel*	14 *Fuel return hose connection*	15 *Fuel supply hose connection*
16 *To air inlet duct/air cleaner*		

in Section 1. Removal of the changeover valve and diaphragm unit are described below – further dismantling is not possible. In the event of apparent failure of the system, check the vacuum hoses for damage, and ensure that the operating rod is free to move – lubricate if necessary. In-depth testing of the system must be left to a VW dealer.

Removal

31 Disconnect the vacuum hose from the valve or diaphragm unit, as applicable.
32 The diaphragm unit operating rod has a ball-end fitting which is clipped into the operating rod on the left-hand side of the manifold. Prise the end fitting out of the operating rod, and unclip the unit from its location.
33 To remove the changeover valve, first disconnect the wiring plug from it **(refer to illustration 10.14)**.

34 Unclip the valve from the underside of the inlet manifold, and disconnect the vacuum hose as the valve is removed.

Refitting

35 Refitting is a reversal of removal.

11 Fuel injection system – testing and adjustment

1 If a fault appears in the fuel injection system, first ensure that all the system wiring connectors are securely connected and free of corrosion. Then ensure that the fault is not due to poor maintenance; ie, check that the air cleaner filter element is clean, the spark plugs are in good condition and correctly gapped, the cylinder compression pressures are correct, the

ignition system wiring is in good condition and securely connected, and the engine breather hoses are clear and undamaged, referring to Chapter 1A, Chapter 2A or 2B and Chapter 5B.
2 If these checks fail to reveal the cause of the problem, the vehicle should be taken to a suitably-equipped VW dealer for testing. A diagnostic connector is incorporated in the engine management system wiring harness, into which dedicated electronic test equipment can be plugged (the connector is located behind a trim panel above the front ashtray – unclip and remove the panel for access). The test equipment is capable of 'interrogating' the engine management system ECU electronically and accessing its internal fault log (reading fault codes).
3 Fault codes can only be extracted from the ECU using a dedicated fault code reader. A

VW dealer will obviously have such a reader, but they are also available from other suppliers. It is unlikely to be cost-effective for the private owner to purchase a fault code reader, but a well-equipped local garage or auto-electrical specialist will have one.

4 Using this equipment, faults can be pinpointed quickly and simply, even if their occurrence is intermittent. Testing all the system components individually in an attempt to locate the fault by elimination is a time-consuming operation that is unlikely to be fruitful (particularly if the fault occurs dynamically), and carries a high risk of damage to the ECU's internal components.

5 Experienced home mechanics equipped with an accurate tachometer and a carefully-calibrated exhaust gas analyser may be able to check the exhaust gas CO content and the engine idle speed; if these are found to be out of specification, then the vehicle must be taken to a suitably-equipped VW dealer for assessment. Neither the air/fuel mixture (exhaust gas CO content) nor the engine idle speed are manually adjustable; incorrect test results indicate the need for maintenance (possibly, injector cleaning) or a fault within the fuel injection system.

12 Unleaded petrol – general information and usage

Note: *The information given in this Chapter is correct at the time of writing, and applies only to petrol's currently available in the UK. Check with a VW dealer as more up-to-date information may be available. If travelling abroad, consult one of the motoring organisations (or a similar authority) for advice on the petrol's available and their suitability for your vehicle.*

1 The fuel recommended by VW is given in the Specifications of this Chapter.

2 RON and MON are different testing standards; RON stands for Research Octane Number (also written as RM), while MON stands for Motor Octane Number (also written as MM).

13 Cruise control system – general information

1 Certain models may be equipped with a cruise control system, in which the driver can set a chosen speed, which the system will then try to maintain regardless of gradients, etc.

2 Once the desired speed has been set, the system is entirely under the control of the engine management ECU, which regulates the speed via the throttle housing.

3 The system refers to signals from the engine speed sensor (see Section 5) and roadspeed sensor (on the transmission).

4 The system is deactivated if the clutch or brake pedals are pressed, signalled by the clutch pedal switch (Section 5) or the brake stop-light switch (Chapter 9).

5 The cruise control switch is part of the steering column combination switch assembly, which can be removed as described in Chapter 12, Section 4.

6 Any problems with the system which are not caused by wiring faults or failure of the components mentioned in this Section should be referred to a VW dealer. In the event of a problem occurring, it is advisable to first take the car to a suitably-equipped dealer for electronic fault diagnosis, using a fault code reader – refer to Section 11.

Chapter 4 Part B:
Diesel engine fuel system

Contents

Accelerator cable – general information 3
Air cleaner assembly – removal and refitting 2
Diesel engine management system – component removal and
   refitting 4
Fuel cut-off solenoid valve – removal and refitting 8
Fuel filter – renewal 10
Fuel gauge sender unit – removal and refitting 11
Fuel injection pump timing – checking and adjustment 7
Fuel tank – removal and refitting 12

General information and precautions 1
Injection pump – removal and refitting 6
Injectors – general information, removal and refitting 5
Inlet manifold – removal and refitting 9
Inlet manifold changeover flap and valve – removal and refitting .. 14
Intercooler – removal and refitting ....See Chapter 4D
Tandem fuel pump – removal and refitting 13
Turbocharger – removal and refitting ....See Chapter 4D

Degrees of difficulty

Easy, suitable for novice with little experience		Fairly easy, suitable for beginner with some experience		Fairly difficult, suitable for competent DIY mechanic		Difficult, suitable for experienced DIY mechanic		Very difficult, suitable for expert DIY or professional	

Specifications

General

Engine code by type*:
Electronic direct injection, non-turbocharged .... AGP and AQM
Electronic direct injection, turbocharged .... AGR, ALH, AHF and ASV
Electronic direct injection, unit injectors, turbocharged .... AJM, ASZ, ARL, ATD, AUY and AXR
Firing order 1-3-4-2
Maximum engine speed .... N/A (ECU controlled)
Engine idle speed:
Codes AGP, AQM, AGR, ALH, AHF and ASV .... 900 ± 30 rpm (ECU controlled)
Codes AJM, ASZ, ARL, ATD, AUY and AXR:
   Manual transmission .... 860 to 940 rpm
   Automatic transmission .... 790 to 870 rpm
Engine fast idle speed .... N/A (ECU controlled)

* Note: *See 'Vehicle identification' for the location of the code marking on the engine.*

Fuel injectors

Injection pressure:
Engine codes AGP, AQM, AGR, and AHF .... 170 bar minimum
Engine codes ALH and ASV .... 200 bar minimum
Engine codes AJM, ASZ, ARL, ATD, AUY and AXR .... 180 to 2050 bar

Tandem pump

Fuel pressure at 1500 rpm .... 3.5 bar

Turbocharger

Type .... Garrett or KKK

Torque wrench settings

	Nm	lbf ft
EGR pipe flange bolts	25	18
EGR valve (non-turbo) clamp bolt	10	7
EGR valve mounting bolts:		
Engine codes AGR, ALH, AHF and ASV	25	18
Engine codes AJM, ASZ, ARL, ATD, AUY and AXR	10	7
Fuel cut-off solenoid valve	40	30
Fuel pump return pipe cap nut	25	18
Injection pump head fuel union stubs	45	33
Injection pump sprocket:		
Stage 1	20	15
Stage 2	Angle-tighten a further 90°	
Injector clamp bolt:		
Engine codes AGP, AQM, AGR, ALH, AHF and ASV	20	15
Engine codes AJM, ASZ, ARL, ATD, AUY and AXR*:		
Stage 1	12	8
Stage 2	Angle-tighten a further 270°	
Injection pump-to-support bracket bolts	25	18
Injector pipe union nut	25	18
Inlet manifold flap housing to manifold	10	7
Inlet manifold to cylinder head	25	18
Inlet manifold upper section (engine codes AQM, AGP):		
To front mounting bracket	20	15
To lower section	15	11
Pump injector rocker shaft bolts*:		
Stage 1	20	15
Stage 2	Angle-tighten a further 90°	
Tandem pump bolts:		
Upper	20	15
Lower	10	7
Turbocharger oil return pipe to cylinder block		
Engine codes AGR, ALH, AHF and ASV	30	22
Engine codes AJM, ASZ, ARL, ATD, AUY and AXR	40	30
Turbocharger to catalytic converter	25	18
Turbocharger to exhaust manifold*	25	18

* Use new fasteners

---

1 General information and precautions

General information

Two different fuel injection systems are fitted to the range of engines covered by this manual. Whilst both are direct injection systems, the difference lies in how the fuel is delivered to the injectors. Both systems comprise of a fuel tank, an engine-bay mounted fuel filter with an integral water separator, fuel supply and return lines and four fuel injectors.

On engine codes AGP, AQM, AGR, AHF, ALH and ASV, the fuel is pressurised by an injection pump, and commencement of injection is controlled by the engine management ECU and a solenoid valve on the injection pump. The pump is driven at half crankshaft speed by the camshaft timing belt. Fuel is drawn from the fuel tank and through the filter by the injection pump, which then distributes the fuel under very high pressure to the injectors via separate delivery pipes. On engine codes AJM, ARL, ASZ, ATD, AUY and AXR, the fuel is delivered by a camshaft driven 'tandem pump' at low pressure to the

injectors (known as 'Unit injectors'). A 'roller rocker' assembly, mounted above the camshaft bearing caps, uses an extra set of camshaft lobes to compress the top of each injector once per firing cycle. This arrangement creates far higher injection pressures. The precise timing of the pre-injection and main injection is controlled by the engine management ECU and a solenoid on each injector. The resultant effect of this system is improved engine torque and power output, greater combustion efficiency, and lower exhaust emissions. All engines except for AGP and AQM are fitted with a turbocharger.

The direct-injection fuelling system is controlled electronically by a diesel engine management system, comprising an Electronic Control Unit (ECU) and its associated sensors, actuators and wiring.

On engine codes AGP, AQM, AGR, AHF, ALH and ASV, basic injection timing is set mechanically by the position of the pump on its mounting bracket. Dynamic timing and injection duration are controlled by the ECU and are dependant on engine speed, throttle position and rate of opening, inlet air flow, inlet air temperature, coolant temperature, fuel temperature, ambient pressure (altitude) and manifold depression information,

received from sensors mounted on and around the engine. Closed loop control of the injection timing is achieved by means of an injector needle lift sensor. Note that injector No 3 is fitted with the needle lift sensor. Two-stage injectors are used, which improve the engine's combustion characteristics, leading to quieter running and better exhaust emissions.

In addition, the ECU manages the operation of the Exhaust Gas Recirculation (EGR) emission control system (Chapter 4D), the turbocharger boost pressure control system (Chapter 4D) and the glow plug control system (Chapter 5C).

On non-turbo models, an electrically-operated flap valve is fitted to the inlet manifold to increase the vacuum when the engine speed is less than 2200 rpm; this is necessary to operate the EGR system efficiently.

On turbo models, the flap valve fitted to the inlet manifold is closed by the ECU for 3 seconds as the engine is switched off, to minimise the air intake as the engine shuts down. This minimises the vibration felt as the pistons come up against the volume of highly compressed air present in the combustion chambers. A vacuum reservoir mounted on the front of the engine provides the vacuum supply to a vacuum capsule which operates the flap (see illustrations).

It should be noted that fault diagnosis of the diesel engine management system is only possible with dedicated electronic test equipment. Problems with the system's operation should therefore be referred to a VW dealer or suitably-equipped specialist for assessment. Once the fault has been identified, the removal/refitting sequences detailed in the following Sections will then allow the appropriate component(s) to be renewed as required. Note: *Throughout this Chapter, vehicles are frequently referred to by their engine code, rather than by engine capacity – refer to Chapter 2C for engine code listings.*

Precautions

Many of the operations described in this Chapter involve the disconnection of fuel lines, which may cause an amount of fuel spillage. Before commencing work, refer to the warnings below and the information in *Safety first!* at the beginning of this manual.

⚠️ *Warning: When working on any part of the fuel system, avoid direct contact skin contact with diesel fuel – wear protective clothing and gloves when handling fuel system components. Ensure that the work area is well ventilated to prevent the build-up of diesel fuel vapour.*

• *Fuel injectors operate at extremely high pressures and the jet of fuel produced at the nozzle is capable of piercing skin, with potentially fatal results. When working with pressurised injectors, take care to avoid exposing any part of the body to the fuel spray. It is recommended that a diesel fuel systems specialist should carry out any pressure testing of the fuel system components.*

• *Under no circumstances should diesel fuel be allowed to come into contact with coolant hoses – wipe off accidental spillage immediately. Hoses that have been contaminated with fuel for an extended period should be renewed.*

• *Diesel fuel systems are particularly sensitive to contamination from dirt, air and water. Pay particular attention to*

1.7a Vacuum reservoir for inlet manifold flap valve

cleanliness when working on any part of the fuel system, to prevent the ingress of dirt. Thoroughly clean the area around fuel unions before disconnecting them. Only use lint-free cloths and clean fuel for component cleansing.

• *Store dismantled components in sealed containers to prevent contamination and the formation of condensation.*

2	Air cleaner assembly – removal and refitting

Removal

1 Loosen the clips (or release the spring clips) and disconnect the air ducting from the air cleaner assembly or air mass meter (as applicable) (see illustration).

2.1 Using a pair of pliers to release the spring clip from the air inlet duct

1.7b Vacuum capsule on inlet manifold below EGR valve

2 On non-turbo models, disconnect the wiring plug from the inlet air temperature sensor at the rear of the air cleaner lid.
3 On turbo models, disconnect the wiring plug from the air mass meter. Also disconnect the vacuum hose below the air mass meter wiring connector (see illustrations).
4 Unclip any hoses, wiring, etc, which may be clipped to the air cleaner, noting their routing for refitting.
5 Remove the two screws securing the air cleaner lid, and unhook it from the front clips, complete with the air mass meter on turbo models. Lift out the air filter element.
6 The lower half of the air cleaner is secured by two screws – one in front, one behind. Remove the screws and lift out the air cleaner, releasing the air inlet spout from its location (see illustrations).
7 If required, the rest of the air inlet ducting can be removed by releasing the retaining

2.3a Disconnect the air mass meter wiring plug . . .

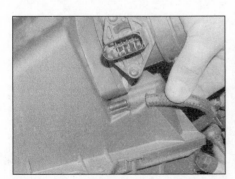

2.3b . . . and the vacuum hose below it

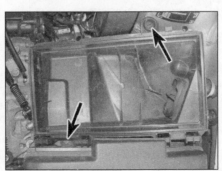

2.6a Remove the screws (arrowed) . . .

2.6b . . . and lift out the lower part of the air cleaner housing

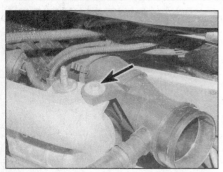

**2.7 Air inlet duct securing bolt (arrowed) –
depending on model**

clips; however, some sections of the inlet duct are bolted in place **(see illustration)**. For details of removing the intercooler-related ducting on turbo models, refer to Chapter 4D.

Refitting

8 Refit the air cleaner by following the removal procedure in reverse.

3 Accelerator cable – general information

Diesel models do not have an accelerator cable, and instead have an electronically-controlled arrangement known as a 'fly-by-wire' throttle. The throttle position sensor at the accelerator pedal is linked to the engine management ECU, which adjusts the quantity of fuel injected, thus controlling the engine speed. Various sensors are used to enable the ECU to set the quantity of fuel to inject, and the pump timing (commencement of injection).

4 Diesel engine management system – component removal and refitting

Throttle position sensor

1 The position sensor is integral with the accelerator pedal. The pedal assembly can be removed (once access has been gained by removing the driver's lower facia panel – Chapter 11, Section 28) by disconnecting the sensor wiring plug and unscrewing the nuts securing the pedal to its mounting bracket – refer to Chapter 4A, Section 5. Depending on the transmission fitted, a separate sensor may be fitted above the pedal bracket, secured by two screws **(see illustration)**.

Coolant temperature sensor

Removal

2 Refer to Chapter 1B and drain approximately one quarter of the coolant from the engine. Alternatively, be prepared for coolant spillage as the sensor is removed.
3 Where necessary for access, remove the engine top cover(s). Removal details vary according to model, but the cover retaining nuts are concealed under circular covers, which are prised out of the main cover. Remove the nuts, and lift the cover from the engine, releasing any wiring or hoses attached.
4 The sensor is at the top coolant outlet elbow, at the front of the cylinder head. Unplug the wiring from it at the connector **(see illustration)**.
5 Remove the securing clip, then extract the sensor from its housing and recover the O-ring seal.

Refitting

6 Refit the coolant temperature sensor by reversing the removal procedure, using a new O-ring seal. Refer to Chapter 1B or *Weekly checks* and top-up the cooling system.

Fuel temperature sensor

7 The fuel temperature sensor is incorporated into the fuel quantity adjuster, which is fitted to the top of the injection pump. It appears from the information available at time of

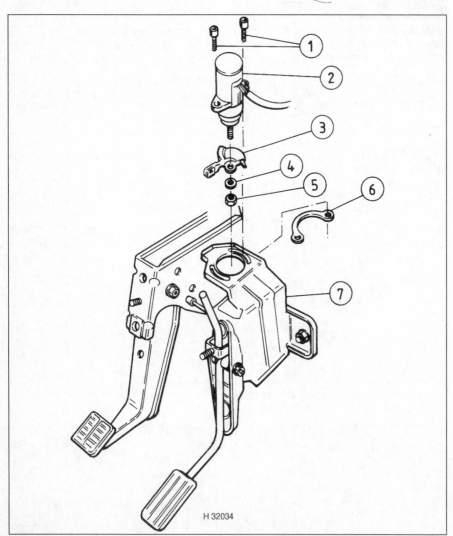

4.1 One type of throttle position sensor fitted to diesel models

Note: *For alternative type of sensor, refer to Chapter 4A, illustration 5.36*

1	Securing screws	3	Cable cam	6	Threaded retainer
2	Throttle position sensor	4	Spring washer	7	Mounting bracket
		5	Locknut		

4.4 Coolant temperature sensor wiring connector (arrowed)

writing that the sensor is not available separately.

Inlet air temperature sensor

Removal – non-turbo models

8 The sensor is mounted on the rear of the air cleaner top cover.

9 Disconnect the sensor wiring plug, then remove the securing clip and extract the sensor. Recover the O-ring seal.

Removal – turbo models

10 All models have an air temperature sensor built into the air mass meter. This sensor is an integral part of the air mass meter, and cannot be renewed separately. An additional air temperature/pressure sensor is fitted, either on top of the intercooler, or on the air hose from the intercooler to the inlet manifold, and this can be renewed as described below.

11 Trace the air hose back from the inlet manifold to the point where it passes through the inner wing.

12 If the sensor is mounted on the hose, disconnect the wiring plug, then remove the two retaining screws and withdraw the sensor. Recover the O-ring seal.

13 If the sensor is mounted on the intercooler, remove the right-hand headlight as described in Chapter 12, Section 7. The sensor can then be removed in the same way as the pipe-mounted type.

Refitting

14 Refit the inlet air temperature sensor by reversing the removal procedure, using a new O-ring seal.

Engine speed sensor

Removal

15 The engine speed sensor is mounted on the front cylinder block, adjacent to the

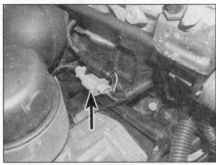

4.17a Wiring connector (arrowed) for speed sensor

mating surface of the block and transmission bellhousing.

16 Where necessary for access, remove the engine top cover(s). Removal details vary according to model, but the cover retaining nuts are concealed under circular covers, which are prised out of the main cover. Remove the nuts, and lift the cover from the engine, releasing any wiring or hoses attached.

17 Trace the wiring back from the sensor, and disconnect it at the plug behind the oil filter housing (see illustrations).

18 Remove the retaining screw and withdraw the sensor from the cylinder block.

Refitting

19 Refit the sensor by reversing the removal procedure.

Air mass meter (turbo models)

Removal

20 With reference to Section 2 , slacken the clips and disconnect the air ducting from the air mass meter, at the rear of the air cleaner housing.

21 Disconnect the wiring from the air mass meter, and the vacuum hose beneath the wiring connector (see Section 2).

22 Remove the retaining screws and extract the meter from the air cleaner housing. Recover the O-ring seal.

Caution: Handle the air mass meter carefully – its internal components are easily damaged.

Refitting

23 Refitting is a reversal of removal. Renew the O-ring seal if it appears damaged.

Absolute pressure (altitude) sensor

24 The absolute pressure sensor is an integral part of the ECU, and hence cannot be renewed separately.

Inlet manifold flap housing

Removal – all models

25 Where necessary for access, remove the engine top cover(s). Removal details vary according to model, but the cover retaining nuts are concealed under circular covers, which are prised out of the main cover. Remove the nuts, and lift the cover from the engine, releasing any wiring or hoses attached.

26 Loosen the clip (or release the spring clip) and disconnect the air trunking from the flap housing.

27 Disconnect the hose from the top of the housing.

Removal – non-turbo models

28 Disconnect the flap control motor wiring plug from the front of the housing.

29 Unscrew the four housing retaining bolts, and withdraw the housing from the inlet manifold. Recover the O-ring seal.

Removal – turbo models

30 Unscrew the two bolts securing the EGR pipe flange to the base of the housing. Separate the flange from the housing slightly, and recover the gasket – do not strain the EGR pipe.

31 Trace the hose back from the flap vacuum unit to the solenoid valve, and disconnect the pipe from the valve (see illustration). The vacuum unit can be removed with the housing.

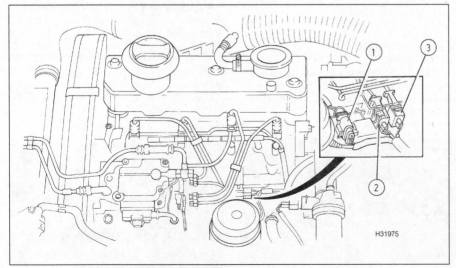

4.17b Wiring connectors behind oil filter housing

1 Fuel temperature sensor, quantity adjuster, shut-off valve and commencement of injection valve

2 Engine speed sensor
3 Needle lift sensor

4.31 EGR solenoid valve location on engine compartment bulkhead

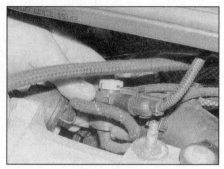

4.32a Unclip the inlet manifold flap solenoid valve . . .

32 Unclip the solenoid valve for the inlet manifold flap operating vacuum capsule; disconnect the wiring plug and vacuum hose from the solenoid, and remove it **(see illustrations)**.
33 Unscrew and remove the three housing retaining bolts, and withdraw the housing from the inlet manifold. Recover the O-ring seal.

Refitting

34 Refitting is a reversal of removal. Renew the O-ring seal if it appears damaged.

Clutch and brake pedal switches

Removal

35 The clutch and brake pedal switches are clipped to mounting brackets directly above their respective pedals.
36 The brake pedal switch operates as a safety device, in the event of a problem with the accelerator position sensor. If the brake pedal switch is depressed while the accelerator pedal is held at a constant position, the engine speed will drop to idle. Thus, a faulty or incorrectly-adjusted brake pedal switch may result in a running problem.
37 The clutch pedal switch operation causes the injection pump to momentarily reduce its output while the clutch is disengaged, to permit smoother gearchanging.
38 To remove either switch, refer to Chapter 11, Section 28, and remove the trim panels from under the steering column area of the facia, to gain access to the pedal cluster.
39 The switches can be removed by unclipping them from their mountings and disconnecting the wiring plugs.

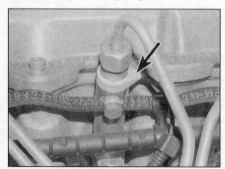

4.41 View of No 3 injector – needle lift sensor arrowed

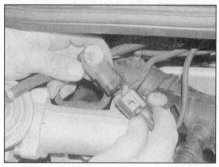

4.32b . . . and disconnect the wiring plug

Refitting

40 Refitting is a reversal of removal. On completion, the adjustment of the switches must be verified electronically, using dedicated test equipment – refer to a VW dealer for advice.

Needle lift sender

Note: *Engine codes AGP, AQM, AGR, AHF, ALH and ASV only.*
41 The needle lift sender is integral with No 3 injector **(see illustration)**. Refer to Section 5 for the removal and refitting procedure.

Electronic control unit (ECU)

Caution: Always wait at least 30 seconds after switching off the ignition before disconnecting the wiring from the ECU. When the wiring is disconnected, all the learned values are erased, however any contents of the fault memory are retained. After reconnecting the wiring, the basic settings must be reinstated by a VW dealer using a special test instrument. Note also that if the ECU is renewed, the identification of the new ECU must be transferred to the immobiliser control unit by a VW dealer.

Removal

42 The ECU is located centrally behind the engine compartment bulkhead, under one of the windscreen cowl panels **(see illustration)**. Remove the wiper arms and cowl panel as for windscreen wiper motor removal and refitting, described in Chapter 12.
43 Release the locking clip or lever on the

4.42 ECU (arrowed) located under windscreen cowling

ECU wiring connector, and disconnect the plug. On most models, there are two separate plugs to be disconnected.
44 Press the control unit to the right, to release its retaining clip, and pull it from its location.

Refitting

45 Refitting is a reversal of removal. Press the unit to the left, once in position, to secure it. Bear in mind the comments made in the Caution above – the ECU will not work correctly until it has been electronically coded.

5	Injectors – general information, removal and refitting

⚠️ *Warning: Exercise extreme caution when working on the fuel injectors. Never expose the hands or any part of the body to injector spray, as the high working pressure can cause the fuel to penetrate the skin, with possibly fatal results. You are strongly advised to have any work which involves testing the injectors under pressure carried out by a dealer or fuel injection specialist. Refer to the precautions given in Section 1 of this Chapter before proceeding.*

General information

1 Injectors do deteriorate with prolonged use, and it is reasonable to expect them to need reconditioning or renewal after 60 000 miles (100 000 km) or so. Accurate testing, overhaul and calibration of the injectors must be left to a specialist.
2 A defective injector which is causing knocking or smoking can be located without dismantling as follows.
3 Run the engine at a fast idle. Slacken each injector union in turn, placing rag around the union to catch spilt fuel and being careful not to expose the skin to any spray. When the union on the defective injector is slackened, the knocking or smoking will stop. **Note:** *This test is not possible on engines fitted with unit injectors (engine codes AJM, ARL, ASZ, ATD, AUY and AXR).*

Removal

Note: *Take care not to allow dirt into the injectors or fuel pipes during this procedure. Do not drop the injectors or allow the needles at their tips to become damaged. The injectors are precision-made to fine limits, and must not be handled roughly.*

Engine codes
AGP, AQM, AGR, AHF, ALH and ASV

4 On non-turbo models, remove the upper section of the inlet manifold as described in Section 9.
5 Cover the alternator with a clean cloth or plastic bag, to protect it from any fuel being spilt onto it.

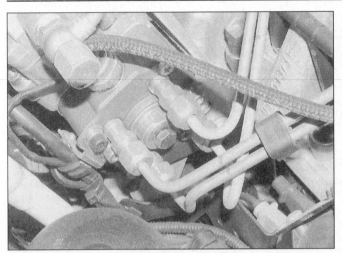

5.7 View of injector pipe union nuts at injection pump

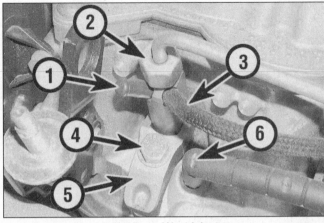

5.10 View of No 1 injector

1	End cap	4	Retaining bolt
2	Union nut	5	Retaining plate
3	Leak-off pipe	6	Glow plug wiring connector

6 Carefully clean around the injectors and pipe union nuts, and disconnect the return pipe from the injector.

7 Wipe clean the pipe unions, then slacken the union nut securing the relevant injector pipes to each injector and the relevant union nuts securing the pipes to the rear of the injection pump (the pipes are removed as one assembly); as each pump union nut is slackened, retain the adapter with a suitable open-ended spanner to prevent it being unscrewed from the pump (see illustration).

8 With the union nuts undone, remove the injector pipes from the engine. Cover the injector and pipe unions to prevent the entry of dirt into the system.

 HAYNES HiNT *Cut the fingertips from an old rubber glove and secure them over the open unions with elastic bands to prevent dirt ingress.*

9 Disconnect the wiring for the needle lift sender from injector No 3.

10 Unscrew and remove the retaining nut or bolt, and recover the washer, retaining plate and mounting collar (see illustration). Note the fitted position of all components, for use when refitting. Withdraw the injector from the cylinder head, and recover the heat shield washer – new washers must be obtained for refitting.

Engine codes
AJM, ARL, ASZ, ATD, AUY and AXR

11 With reference to Chapter 2C, remove the upper timing belt cover and camshaft cover.

12 Using a spanner or socket, turn the crankshaft pulley until the rocker arm for the injector which is to be removed, is at its highest, ie, the injector plunger spring is under the least amount of tension.

13 Slacken the locknut of the adjustment screw on the end of the rocker arm above the injector, and undo the adjustment screw until

the rocker arm lies against the plunger pin of the injector (see illustration).

14 Starting at the outside and working in, gradually and evenly slacken and remove the rocker shaft retaining bolts. Lift off the rocker shaft. Check the contact face of each adjustment screw, and renew any that show signs of wear.

15 Undo the clamping block securing bolt and remove the block from the side of the injector (see illustration).

16 Using a small screwdriver, carefully prise the wiring connector from the injector.

17 VW technicians use a slide hammer (tool

No T10055) to pull the injector from the cylinder head. This is a slide hammer which engages in the side of the injector. If this tool is not available, it is possible to fabricate an equivalent using a short section of angle-iron, a length of threaded rod, a cylindrical weight, and two locknuts. Weld/braze the rod to the angle-iron, slide the weight over the rod, and lock the two nuts together at the end of the rod to provide the stop for the weight (see illustration). Seat the slide hammer/tool in the slot on the side on the injector, and pull the injector out using a few gently taps. Recover circlip, the heat shield and O-rings and

5.13 Undo the adjustment screw until the rocker arm lies against the plunger pin of the injector

5.15 Remove the clamping block securing bolt (arrowed)

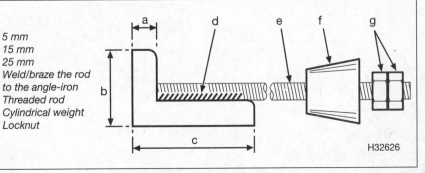

a	5 mm
b	15 mm
c	25 mm
d	Weld/braze the rod to the angle-iron
e	Threaded rod
f	Cylindrical weight
g	Locknut

H32626

5.17a Unit injector removal tool

5.17b Seat the slide hammer/tool in the slot on the side on the injector, and pull the injector out

5.26 Care must be used to ensure that the injector O-rings are fitted without being twisted

5.18a Undo the two nuts at the back of the head and slide the injector loom/rail out

discard. New ones must be used for refitting **(see illustration)**.

18 If required, the injector wiring loom/rail can be removed from the cylinder head by undoing the two retaining nuts/bolts at the back of the head. To prevent the wiring connectors fouling the cylinder head casting as the assembly is withdrawn, insert the connectors into the storage slots in the plastic wiring rail. Carefully push the assembly to the rear, and out of the casting **(see illustrations)**.

5.18b The injector connectors will slide into the loom/rail to prevent them from being damaged as the assembly is withdrawn/inserted into the cylinder head

Refitting

Engine codes AGP, AQM, AGR, AHF, ALH and ASV

19 Insert the injector into position, using a new heat shield washer. Make sure that the injector with the needle lift sender is located in No 3 position (No 1 is at the timing belt end of the engine).

20 Fit the mounting collar and retaining plate then refit the retaining nut or bolt (as applicable) and tighten it to the specified torque.

21 Reconnect the wiring for the needle lift sender on injector No 3.

22 Refit the injector pipes and tighten the union nuts to the specified torque setting. Position any clips attached to the pipes as noted before removal.

23 Reconnect the return pipe to the injector.

24 On non-turbo models, refit the upper section of the inlet manifold as described in Section 9.

25 Reconnect the battery negative (earth) lead, then start the engine and check that it runs correctly.

Engine codes AJM, ARL, ASZ, ATD, AUY and AXR

26 Prior to refitting the injectors, the three O-rings, heat insulation washer and clip must be renewed. Due to the high injection pressures, it is essential that the O-rings are fitted without being twisted. VW recommend the use of three special assembly sleeves to install the O-rings squarely. It may be prudent to entrust O-ring renewal to a VW dealer or suitably-equipped injection specialist, rather than risk subsequent leaks **(see illustration)**.

27 After renewing the O-rings, fit the heat shield and secure it in place with the circlip **(see illustration)**.

28 Smear clean engine oil onto the O-rings, and push the injector evenly down into the cylinder head onto its stop.

29 Fit the clamping block alongside the injector, but only hand-tighten the new retaining bolt at this stage.

30 It is essential that the injectors are fitted at right-angles to the clamping block. In order to achieve this, measure the distance from the rear face of the cylinder head to the rounded

1 Bolt
2 Clamping block
3 Cylinder head
4 Bolt
5 Rocker arm
6 Nut
7 Adjuster
8 Unit injector
9 O-ring
10 O-ring
11 O-ring
12 Heat shield
13 Circlip

H32627

5.27 Unit injector – engine codes AJM, ARL, ASZ, ATD, AUY and AXR

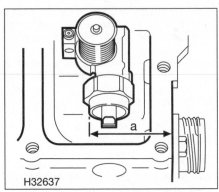

5.30a **Measure the distance (a) from the rear of the cylinder head to the rounded section of the injector (see text)**

section of the injector **(see illustrations)**. The dimensions (a) are as follows:

Cylinder 1 = 332.2 ± 0.08 mm
Cylinder 2 = 244.2 ± 0.08 mm
Cylinder 3 = 152.8 ± 0.08 mm
Cylinder 4 = 64.8 ± 0.08 mm

31 Once the injector(s) are aligned correctly, tighten the clamping bolt to the specified Stage one torque setting, and the Stage two angle tightening setting. **Note:** *If an injector has been renewed, it is essential that the adjustment screw, locknut of the corresponding rocker and ball-pin are renewed at the same time. The ball-pins simply pull out of the injector spring cap. There is an O-ring in each spring cap to stop the ball-pins from falling out.*

32 Smear some grease (VW No G000 100) onto the contact face of each rocker arm adjustment screw, and refit the rocker shaft assembly to the camshaft bearing caps, tightening the retaining bolts as follows. Starting from the inside out, hand-tighten the bolts. Again, from the inside out, tighten the bolts to the Stage one torque setting. Finally, from the inside out, tighten the bolts to the Stage two angle tightening setting.

33 The following procedure is only necessary if an injector has been removed and refitted/renewed. Attach a DTI (Dial Test Indicator) gauge to the cylinder head upper surface, and position the DTI probe against the top of the adjustment screw **(see illustration)**. Turn the crankshaft until the rocker arm roller is on the highest point of its corresponding camshaft lobe, and the adjustment screw is at its lowest. Once this position has been established, remove the DTI gauge, screw the adjustment screw in until firm resistance is felt, and the injector spring cannot be compressed further. Turn the adjustment screw **anti-clockwise** 225°, and tighten the locknut to the specified torque. Repeat this procedure for any other injectors that have been refitted.

34 Reconnect the wiring plug to the injector.
35 Refit the camshaft cover and upper timing belt cover, as described in Chapter 2C.
36 Start the engine and check that it runs correctly.

5.30b **Use a set square against the edge of the injector . . .**

6 Injection pump – removal and refitting

Note: *Engine codes AGP, AQM, AGR, AHF, ALH and ASV only.*
Note: *The injection pump commencement of injection setting must be checked and if necessary adjusted after refitting the injection pump. The commencement of injection is controlled by the ECU, and is influenced by several other engine parameters, including coolant temperature, engine speed and position. Although the adjustment is a mechanical operation, checking can only be carried out by a VW dealer, as dedicated electronic test equipment is needed to interface with the ECU.*

Removal

1 Disconnect the battery negative lead and position it away from the terminal. **Note:** *Refer to 'Disconnecting the battery' at the rear of this manual first.*
2 Remove the air cleaner and the associated ducting as described in Section 2.
3 Remove the engine top cover(s). Removal details vary according to model, but the cover retaining nuts are concealed under circular covers, which are prised out of the main cover. Remove the nuts, and lift the cover from the engine, releasing any wiring or hoses attached.
4 On non-turbo models, remove the upper section of the inlet manifold as described in Section 9.
5 On turbo models, disconnect the intercooler air hose from the inlet manifold.
6 Remove the brake servo vacuum pump as described in Chapter 9.
7 With reference to Chapter 2C, carry out the following:
 a) *Remove the camshaft cover and timing belt outer cover(s).*
 b) *Set the engine to TDC on cylinder No 1.*
 c) *Remove the timing belt from the camshaft and fuel injection pump sprockets.*
 d) *Remove the injection pump sprocket.*
8 Wipe around the pipe unions at the pump and the injectors **(see illustration)**.
9 Using a pair of spanners, slacken the rigid

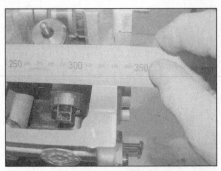

5.30c **. . . and measure the distance to the rear of the cylinder head**

5.33 **Attach a DTI (Dial Test Indicator) gauge to the cylinder head upper surface, and position the DTI probe against the top of the adjustment screw**

fuel pipe unions at the rear of the injection pump and at the injectors, then lift the fuel pipe assembly away from the engine.
Caution: Be prepared for some fuel leakage during this operation by placing cloth rags beneath the unions. Take care to avoid stressing the rigid fuel pipes as they are removed.
10 Cover the open pipes and ports to prevent the ingress of dirt and excess fuel leakage **(see Haynes Hint 1 overleaf)**.
11 Slacken the fuel supply and return banjo bolts at the injection pump ports, again taking precautions to minimise fuel spillage. Cover the open pipes and ports to prevent the ingress of dirt and excess fuel leakage **(see Haynes Hint 2 overleaf)**.
12 Disconnect the three wiring connectors behind the oil filter housing **(refer to**

6.8 **Fuel return union at rear of injection pump**

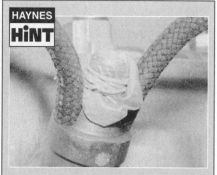

Haynes Hint 1 Cut the fingertips from an old pair of rubber gloves and secure them over the fuel ports with elastic bands.

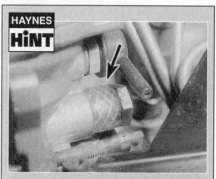

Haynes Hint 2 Fit a short length of hose over the banjo bolt (arrowed) so that the drillings are covered, then thread the bolt back into its injection pump port.

Caution: Do not slacken the pump distributor head bolts, as this could cause serious internal damage to the injection pump.

14 Slacken and withdraw the three nuts/bolts that secure the injection pump to the front mounting bracket. Note that where fixing bolts are used, the two outer bolts are held captive with metal brackets. Support the pump body as the last fixing is removed. Check that nothing remains connected to the injection pump, then lift it away from the engine.

Refitting

15 Offer up the injection pump to the engine, then insert the mounting nuts/bolts and tighten to the specified torque.
16 Prime the injection pump by fitting a small funnel to the fuel return pipe union and filling the cavity with clean diesel. Pad the area around the union with clean dry rags to absorb any spillage.
17 Reconnect the fuel injector delivery pipes to the injectors and injection pump head, then tighten the unions to the correct torque using a pair of spanners.

illustration 4.17). Two of these serve the needle lift sender and engine speed sensor, with the largest being for the fuel cut-off valve/commencement of injection valve and the quantity adjuster module. Unclip the wiring plugs from the mounting bracket – label the wiring plugs to aid refitting later.
13 Unscrew and remove the bolt that secures the injection pump to the rear mounting bracket **(see illustration)**.

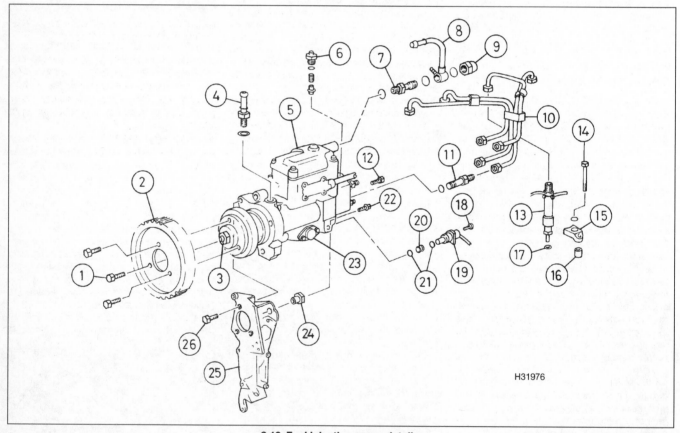

6.13 Fuel injection pump details

1 Sprocket bolts	8 Fuel return pipe	14 Injector retaining bolt	20 Strainer
2 Injection pump sprocket	9 Union nut	15 Retainer plate	21 O-ring
3 Hub nut (do not loosen)	10 Injector pipe assembly	16 Mounting sleeve	22 Injection pump bracket bolt
4 Fuel supply connection	11 Injector pipe connection	17 Heat shield	23 Timing control cover
5 Injection pump	12 Injection pump bracket bolt	18 Mounting bolt	24 Sleeve nut
6 Fuel shut-off solenoid valve	13 No 3 injector (with needle lift sensor)	19 Commencement of injection valve	25 Mounting bracket
7 Fuel return connection			26 Mounting bolt

H31976

18 Reconnect the fuel supply and return pipes using new sealing washers, then tighten the banjo bolts to the specified torque. **Note:** *The inside diameter of the banjo bolt for the fuel return pipe is smaller than that of the fuel supply line, and is marked* **OUT**.

19 The rest of the refitting procedure is a direct reversal of removal. On completion, the commencement of injection must now be dynamically checked and if necessary adjusted by a VW dealer.

7 Fuel injection pump timing – checking and adjustment

Note: *Engine codes AGP, AQM, AGR, AHF, ALH and ASV only.*

The fuel injection pump timing can only be tested and adjusted using dedicated test equipment. Refer to a VW dealer for advice.

8 Fuel cut-off solenoid valve – removal and refitting

Note: *Engine codes AGP, AQM, AGR, AHF, ALH and ASV only.*

General information

1 The fuel cut-off solenoid valve (or 'stop solenoid') provides an electro-mechanical means of switching off the engine. When the 'ignition' switch is turned off, the current supply to the solenoid is interrupted – this causes the valve plunger to drop, closing off the main fuel supply passage in the pump, and stopping the engine.

2 If the cut-off solenoid fails in the open position, this means that, in theory, it will not be possible to switch off the engine. Should this happen, apply the footbrake and handbrake firmly, engage top gear, and slowly let out the clutch until the engine stalls.

3 If the cut-off solenoid fails in the closed position, the engine will not start.

4 Note that the solenoid is linked to the anti-theft immobiliser system, preventing the engine from being started until the immobiliser is correctly deactivated by the driver.

Removal

5 The fuel cut-off valve is located at the upper, rear of the injection pump.

6 Unscrew the securing nut and disconnect the wiring from the top of the valve (**see illustration**).

7 Unscrew and withdraw the valve body from the injection pump. Recover the seal and the plunger.

Refitting

8 Refitting is a reversal of removal, using a new seal.

9 Inlet manifold – removal and refitting

Engine codes AGP and AQM

Upper section removal

1 Remove the engine top cover(s). Removal details vary according to model, but the cover retaining nuts are concealed under circular covers, which are prised out of the main cover. Remove the nuts, and lift the cover from the engine, releasing any wiring or hoses attached.

2 Referring to Section 4, remove the inlet manifold flap housing from the inlet manifold. If preferred, however, the manifold upper section can be removed with the flap housing – in this case, all services must be disconnected from the housing as described in Section 4, but the housing retaining bolts can be left in place.

3 Unscrew and remove the three bolts securing the manifold upper section to the front mounting bracket (**see illustration**). Note that the rear bolt is longer than the other two, and has a washer.

4 Unscrew and remove the five bolts securing the manifold upper section to the lower part, at the rear of the engine. The central bolt is longer than the other four.

5 Check around the manifold to ensure that there are no hoses or wiring still attached, then carefully lift it from its location. Recover the four large O-ring seals from the manifold ports.

8.6 Fuel cut-off solenoid wiring connector is secured by a nut (arrowed)

6 If required, the manifold front mounting bracket can also be removed; it is secured to the cylinder head by two bolts. Access to the bolts, however, is extremely limited with the oil filter housing and injection pipes in place.

Upper section refitting

7 Refitting is a reversal of removal, using four new O-ring seals on the manifold ports. Tighten all bolts to the specified torque.

Lower section removal

8 Remove the upper section of the manifold as described previously in this Section.

9 Unscrew the two EGR valve mounting bolts from the left-hand side of the manifold, then separate the joint and move the valve away from the manifold slightly, without straining the EGR pipe. Recover the EGR valve gasket, and discard it – a new one must be used when refitting.

10 Support the manifold, then unscrew and

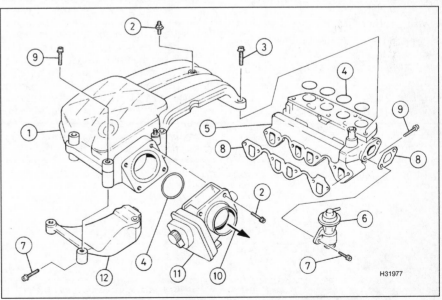

9.3 Inlet manifold details – non-turbo engine

1 Inlet manifold upper section	4 Seal	9 Upper section to mounting bracket
2 Engine cover mounting stud	5 Inlet manifold lower section	10 To air cleaner
3 Upper-to-lower section bolt	6 EGR valve	11 Inlet manifold flap housing
	7 Mounting bolt	12 Front mounting bracket
	8 Gasket	

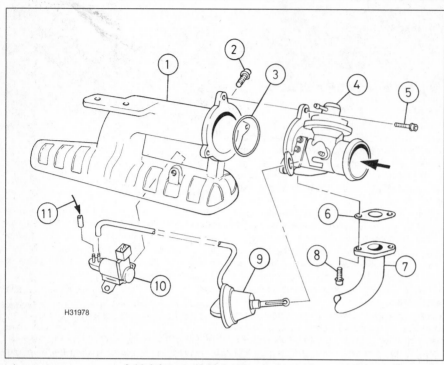

9.14 Inlet manifold details – turbo engine

1 Inlet manifold	5 Housing mounting	9 Manifold flap vacuum
2 Manifold mounting bolt	bolt	capsule
3 Seal	6 Gasket	10 Vacuum solenoid
4 Inlet manifold flap	7 EGR pipe	11 From vacuum
housing	8 Pipe flange bolt	pump/reservoir

remove the six retaining bolts. Separate the manifold lower section from the cylinder head, and recover the gasket.

Lower section refitting

11 Refitting is a reversal of removal. Ensure that the mating surfaces are clean. Use new gaskets and tighten all bolts to the specified torque.

Engine codes AGR, ALH, AHF and ASV

Removal

12 Remove the engine top cover(s). Removal details vary according to model, but the cover retaining nuts are concealed under circular

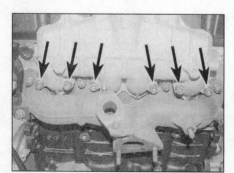

9.21 Unscrew the inlet manifold mounting bolts (arrowed)

covers, which are prised out of the main cover. Remove the nuts, and lift the cover from the engine, releasing any wiring or hoses attached.
13 Referring to Section 4, remove the inlet manifold flap housing from the inlet manifold. If preferred, however, the manifold can be removed with the flap housing – in this case, all services must be disconnected from the housing as described in Section 4, but the housing retaining bolts can be left in place.
14 Disconnect the wiring plug from the vacuum unit solenoid valve, and unclip the wiring from the manifold **(see illustration)**.
15 Support the manifold, then unscrew and remove the six retaining bolts. Separate manifold from the cylinder head, and recover the gasket.

Refitting

16 Refitting is a reversal of removal. Ensure that the mating surfaces are clean. Use a new gasket and tighten the manifold bolts to the specified torque.

Engine codes AJM, ARL, ASZ, ATD, AUY and AXR

Removal

17 Unclip and remove the engine top cover.
18 Undo the bolts securing the EGR pipe to the inlet manifold flap assembly.
19 Undo the retaining screws and separate

the inlet manifold flap assembly from the inlet manifold (see Section 14). Recover the O-ring.
20 Unbolt the EGR pipe from the exhaust manifold. On automatic transmission models, also release the three retaining bolts and manoeuvre the EGR cooler away from the inlet manifold.
21 Remove the heat shield from the manifold, then unscrew the mounting nuts/bolts and remove the inlet manifold from the cylinder head. Recover the gaskets from the inlet manifold **(see illustration)**.

Refitting

22 Refitting is a reversal of removal, using new manifold, EGR pipe and manifold flap assembly gaskets.

10 Fuel filter – renewal

Note: Observe the precautions in Section 1 before working on any component in the fuel system.
Refer to Chapter 1B.

11 Fuel gauge sender unit – removal and refitting

Note: Observe the precautions in Section 1 before working on any component in the fuel system.

⚠ **Warning: Avoid direct skin contact with fuel – wear protective clothing and gloves when handling fuel system components. Ensure that the work area is well-ventilated to prevent the build-up of fuel vapour.**

1 The fuel gauge sender unit is mounted on the top of the fuel tank. Access is via a hatch provided in the load space floor. The unit protrudes into the fuel tank, and its removal involves exposing the contents of the tank to the atmosphere.
2 Refer to the procedures in Chapter 4A, Section 7, for removal and refitting. On petrol models, the gauge sender unit is combined with the fuel pump, so ignore references to the fuel pump.

12 Fuel tank – removal and refitting

Note: Observe the precautions in Section 1 before working on any component in the fuel system.
1 Refer to the procedures in Chapter 4A, Section 8. There is no breather pipe to disconnect at the front of the tank – instead, the fuel supply pipe (coloured black) should be disconnected, with the return pipe (coloured blue).

13.2 Disconnect the injector connectors

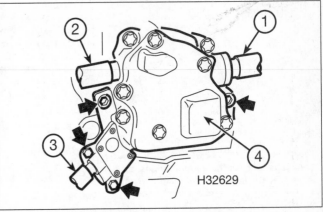

H32629

13.3 Fuel tandem pump securing bolts (arrowed)

1 *Brake servo hose*
2 *Fuel supply hose*
3 *Fuel return hose*
4 *Tandem pump*

13 Tandem fuel pump – removal and refitting

Note: *Only engine codes AJM, ARL, ASZ, ATD, AUY and AXRII-pi are fitted with a tandem fuel pump.*
Note: *Disconnecting the central connector for the unit injectors may cause a fault code to be logged by the engine management ECU. This code can only be erased by a VW dealer or suitably-equipped specialist.*

Removal

1 Unclip and remove the engine top cover.
2 Disconnect the charge air pipe, and place it to one side. Disconnect the central connector for the unit injectors (see illustration).
3 Release the retaining clip (where fitted) and disconnect the brake servo pipe from the tandem pump (see illustration).
4 Disconnect the fuel supply hose (marked white) from the tandem pump (see illustration 13.3). Be prepared for fuel spillage.
5 Unscrew the four retaining bolts and move the tandem pump away from the cylinder head (see illustration 13.3). As the pump is lifted up, disconnect the fuel return hose (marked blue). Be prepared for fuel spillage. There are no serviceable parts within the tandem pump. If the pump is faulty, it must be renewed.

Refitting

6 Reconnect the fuel return hose to the pump and refit the pump to the cylinder head, using new rubber seals, and ensuring that the pump pinion engages correctly with the drive slot in the camshaft (see illustration).
7 Refit the pump retaining bolts, and tighten them to the specified torque.
8 Re-attach the fuel supply hose and brake servo hose to the pump.

9 Reconnect the central connector for the unit injectors.
10 Refit the charge air pipe.
11 Disconnect the fuel filter return hose (marked blue), and connect the hose to a hand vacuum pump. Operate the vacuum pump until fuel comes out of the return hose. This primes the tandem pump. Take care not to suck any fuel into the vacuum pump. Reconnect the return hose to the fuel filter.
12 Refit the engine top cover.
13 Have the engine management ECU's fault memory interrogated and erased by a VW dealer or suitably-equipped specialist.

14 Inlet manifold changeover flap and valve – removal and refitting

Note: *Engine codes AJM, ARL, ASZ, ATD, AUY and AXR only.*

Changeover flap housing and vacuum control element

Removal

1 As diesel engines have a very high compression ratio, when the engine is turned off, the pistons still compress a large

quantity of air for a few revolutions and cause the engine unit to shudder. The inlet manifold changeover flap is located in the inlet flange housing bolted to the inlet manifold. When the ignition switch is turned to the 'off' position, the engine management ECU-controlled valve actuates the flap, which shuts off the air supply to the cylinders. This allows the pistons to compress very little air, and the engine runs softly to a halt. The flap must open again approximately 3 seconds after switching off the ignition switch. The EGR (Exhaust Gas Recirculation) valve is also incorporated into the flap housing.
2 Where fitted, unclip and remove the engine top cover.
3 Release the retaining clips, and disconnect the air inlet trucking from the inlet manifold flange housing.
4 Undo the two retaining bolts and disconnect the EGR pipe from the underside of the inlet flange. Recover the gasket.
5 Disconnect the vacuum pipe to the actuator. Disconnect the vacuum pipe for the EGR valve.
6 Unscrew the three retaining bolts and remove the inlet manifold flange housing. Discard the sealing O-ring, a new one must be used (see illustration).

13.6 Ensure that the tandem pump pinion engages correctly with the drive slot in the camshaft

14.6 Unscrew the three retaining bolts and remove the inlet manifold flange housing

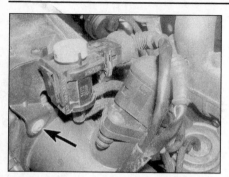

14.10 Disconnect the vacuum pipes, and unscrew the inlet manifold flap control valve mounting screw (arrowed)

7 Although it is possible to remove the vacuum actuator from the inlet flange housing, by unscrewing the two bracket retaining bolts and disengaging the actuating arm from the flap spindle, at the time of writing the inlet manifold flange was only available as a unit complete with the vacuum actuator and EGR valve. Consult your VW dealer.

Refitting

8 Refitting is a reversal of removal. Tighten the inlet manifold flap housing bolts to the specified torque.

Changeover valve

Removal

9 The changeover valve controls the supply of vacuum to the changeover flap. The electrical supply to the valve is controlled by the engine management ECU. When the ignition key is turned to the 'off' position, the ECU signals the valve, which allows vacuum to pull the flap shut. Approximately three seconds later, the power supply to the valve is cut, the vacuum to the actuator collapses, and the flap opens.

10 The valve is located on the right-hand side of the engine compartment, on the top of the air filter housing. Note their fitted positions and disconnect the vacuum pipes from the valve **(see illustration)**.

11 Disconnect the wiring plug from the valve.

12 Undo the retaining screw and remove the valve.

Refitting

13 Refitting is a reversal of removal.

Chapter 4 Part C:
Emission control and exhaust systems – petrol engines

Contents

Catalytic converter – general information and precautions 10
Crankcase emission system – general information 3
Evaporative loss emission control system – information and
    component renewal 2
Exhaust Gas Recirculation (EGR) system – component removal . . 4
Exhaust manifold – removal and refitting 8
Exhaust system – component renewal 9

General information 1
Intercooler – general information, removal and refitting 7
Secondary air injection system – information and component
    renewal 5
Turbocharger – general information, precautions, removal and
    refitting 6

Degrees of difficulty

Easy, suitable for novice with little experience	Fairly easy, suitable for beginner with some experience	Fairly difficult, suitable for competent DIY mechanic	Difficult, suitable for experienced DIY mechanic	Very difficult, suitable for expert DIY or professional

Specifications

Torque wrench settings	Nm	lbf ft
Coolant pipe banjo bolts	35	26
EGR pipe flange bolts to throttle housing	10	7
EGR pipe flange nuts:		
1.6 litre SOHC engine codes AVU and BFQ	25	18
EGR pipe mounting bolts:		
1.6 litre SOHC engine codes AVU and BFQ	25	18
All other engines	10	7
EGR pipe union nut:		
1.4 litre engine codes AHW, AXP and BCA	35	26
1.6 litre SOHC engine codes AVU and BFQ	60	44
EGR valve mounting/through-bolts:		
1.4 litre engines:		
Engine code AHW	10	7
Engine codes AXP and BCA	20	15
1.6 litre DOHC engine	20	15
Exhaust clamp nuts	40	30
Exhaust manifold nuts*	25	18
Exhaust manifold support bracket to engine	25	18
Exhaust manifold-to-downpipe nuts*	40	30
Exhaust mounting bracket nuts and bolts	25	18
Intercooler mounting bolts	10	7
Oil supply pipe banjo bolts	30	22
Oxygen sensor	50	37
Secondary air adaptor plate mounting bolts	10	7
Secondary air combi-valve mounting bolts	10	7
Secondary air pipe union nuts	25	18
Turbocharger support bracket to engine	25	18
Turbocharger-to-downpipe nuts**	40	30
Turbocharger-to-manifold bolts**	30	22
Turbocharger-to-support bracket bolt	30	22

* Use new nuts

** Use thread-locking compound

1 General information

Emission control systems

All petrol models are designed to use unleaded petrol, and are controlled by engine management systems that are programmed to give the best compromise between driveability, fuel consumption and exhaust emission production. In addition, a number of systems are fitted that help to minimise other harmful emissions. A crankcase emission control system is fitted, which reduces the release of pollutants from the engine's lubrication system, and a catalytic converter is fitted which reduces exhaust gas pollutant. An evaporative loss emission control system is fitted which reduces the release of gaseous hydrocarbons from the fuel tank.

Crankcase emission control

To reduce the emission of unburned hydrocarbons from the crankcase into the atmosphere, the engine is sealed and the blow-by gases and oil vapour are drawn from inside the crankcase, through a wire-mesh oil separator, into the inlet tract to be burned by the engine during normal combustion.

Under conditions of high manifold depression, the gases will be sucked positively out of the crankcase. Under conditions of low manifold depression, the gases are forced out of the crankcase by the (relatively) higher crankcase pressure. If the engine is worn, the raised crankcase pressure (due to increased blow-by) will cause some of the flow to return under all manifold conditions.

Exhaust emission control

To minimise the amount of pollutants which escape into the atmosphere, all petrol models are fitted with a three-way catalytic converter in the exhaust system. The fuelling system is of the closed-loop type, in which an oxygen (lambda) sensor in the exhaust system provides the engine management system ECU with constant feedback, enabling the ECU to adjust the air/fuel mixture to optimise combustion.

All 1.4 and 1.6 litre DOHC models (except code AHW) have two catalysts – while some later models have a pre-catalyst built into the exhaust manifold, and can be identified by having the (first) oxygen sensor screwed into the manifold.

The oxygen sensor has a built-in heating element, controlled by the ECU through the oxygen sensor relay, to quickly bring the sensor's tip to its optimum operating temperature. The sensor's tip is sensitive to oxygen, and sends a voltage signal to the ECU that varies according on the amount of oxygen in the exhaust gas. If the inlet air/fuel mixture is too rich, the exhaust gases are low in oxygen so the sensor sends a low-voltage signal, the voltage rising as the mixture weakens and the amount of oxygen rises in the exhaust gases.

2.2 Charcoal canister location on right-hand inner wing – mounting bolt arrowed

Peak conversion efficiency of all major pollutants occurs if the inlet air/fuel mixture is maintained at the chemically-correct ratio for the complete combustion of petrol of 14.7 parts (by weight) of air to 1 part of fuel (the stoichiometric ratio). The sensor output voltage alters in a large step at this point, the ECU using the signal change as a reference point and correcting the inlet air/fuel mixture accordingly by altering the fuel injector pulse width.

Most later models have two sensors – one before and one after the main catalytic converter. This enables more efficient monitoring of the exhaust gas, allowing a faster response time. The overall efficiency of the converter itself can also be checked. Details of the oxygen sensor removal and refitting are given in Chapter 4A, Section 5.

An Exhaust Gas Recirculation (EGR) system is also fitted to most models. This reduces the level of nitrogen oxides produced during combustion by introducing a proportion of the exhaust gas back into the inlet manifold, under certain engine operating conditions, via a plunger valve. The system is controlled electronically by the engine management ECU.

Some engines are equipped with a secondary air system, to reduce cold-start emissions when the catalytic converter is still warming-up. The system comprises an electric air pump, fed with air from the air cleaner, and a system of valves. When the engine is cold, air is pumped into additional pipework on the exhaust manifold, and mixes with the exhaust gas – this has the effect of raising the temperature of the exhaust, which helps to 'burn' the pollutants. The extra heat

2.3 Disconnect the purge valve wiring connector

produced also helps to bring the catalytic converter to its working temperature more quickly. When the engine coolant temperature is high enough, and the converter is operating normally, the system is switched off by the engine management ECU.

Evaporative emission control

To minimise the escape of unburned hydrocarbons into the atmosphere, an evaporative loss emission control system is fitted to all petrol models. The fuel tank filler cap is sealed and a charcoal canister is mounted underneath the right-hand wing to collect the petrol vapours released from the fuel contained in the fuel tank. It stores them until they can be drawn from the canister (under the control of the fuel injection/ignition system ECU) via the purge valve(s) into the inlet tract, where they are then burned by the engine during normal combustion.

To ensure that the engine runs correctly when it is cold and/or idling and to protect the catalytic converter from the effects of an over-rich mixture, the purge control valve(s) are not opened by the ECU until the engine has warmed-up, and the engine is under load; the valve solenoid is then modulated on and off to allow the stored vapour to pass into the inlet tract.

Exhaust systems

On most models, the exhaust system comprises the exhaust manifold (with oxygen sensor), front pipe, catalytic converter (with second oxygen sensor on most models), intermediate pipe and silencer, and tailpipe and silencer. The systems fitted differ in detail depending on the engine fitted – for example, in how the catalytic converter is incorporated into the system. The majority of models have the converter integral with the front pipe, but some 1.4 litre engines have the converter integral with the manifold; others have a separate front pipe and converter. On turbocharged models, the turbocharger is mounted on the exhaust manifold, and is driven by the exhaust gases.

The system is supported by various metal brackets screwed to the vehicle floor, with rubber vibration dampers fitted to suppress noise.

2 Evaporative loss emission control system – information and component renewal

1 The evaporative loss emission control system consists of the purge valve, the activated charcoal filter canister and a series of connecting vacuum hoses.

2 The purge valve and canister are located on the right-hand side of the engine compartment, in front of the coolant expansion tank **(see illustration)**.

3 Ensure that the ignition is switched off, then unplug the wiring harness from the purge valve at the connector **(see illustration)**.

4 Pull off the larger hose (which leads to the throttle housing); if required, the purge valve can now be prised out from the top of the canister. Prise out the round end fitting to which the smaller (tank breather) hose is attached **(see illustrations)**.

5 Unscrew the mounting bolt, then lift the charcoal canister out of its lower mounting, noting how it is fitted, and remove it from the engine compartment **(see illustration)**.

6 Refitting is a reversal of removal.

3 Crankcase emission system – general information

1 The crankcase emission control system consists of hoses connecting the crankcase to the air cleaner or inlet manifold. Oil separator units are fitted to some petrol engines, usually at the back of the engine **(see illustration)**.

2 The system requires no attention other than to check at regular intervals that the hoses, valve and oil separator are free of blockages and in good condition.

4 Exhaust Gas Recirculation (EGR) system – component removal

1 The EGR system consists of the EGR valve, the modulator (solenoid) valve and a series of connecting vacuum hoses.

2.4a Pull off the larger hose from the purge valve . . .

2.4b . . . if required, the purge valve can be prised out and removed

2.4c Prise out the tank breather hose end fitting

2.5 Removing the charcoal canister

2 The EGR valve is mounted on a flange joint at the exhaust manifold and is connected to a second flange joint at the throttle housing by a metal pipe.

3 To improve access, remove the engine top cover(s). Removal details vary according to model, but the cover retaining nuts are concealed under circular covers, which are prised out of the main cover. Where plastic screws or turn-fasteners are used, these can be removed using a wide-bladed screwdriver. Remove the nuts or screws, and lift the cover from the engine, releasing any wiring or hoses attached.

EGR solenoid

1.4 litre code AHW

4 Locate the EGR valve at the front left-hand side of the engine, on the exhaust manifold. The solenoid valve is located next to the EGR valve, on a bracket bolted to the end of the camshaft carrier.

5 Disconnect the wiring plug from the solenoid valve.

6 Disconnect the vacuum hose which leads to the EGR valve, and the other vacuum hose on the base of the solenoid valve – the smaller interconnecting hoses need not be removed.

7 Unscrew the solenoid valve mounting bolt, and remove the valve from the engine **(see illustrations)**.

8 Refitting is a reversal of removal. Ensure that the hoses and wiring plug are reconnected securely and correctly.

EGR valve

1.4 litre code AHW

9 Disconnect the vacuum hose from the port on the EGR valve **(see illustration)**.

3.1 Oil separator box on rear of engine (seen with engine removed)

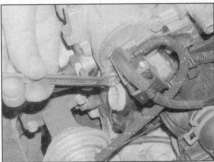

4.7a Unscrew the mounting bolt . . .

4.7b . . . and remove the EGR solenoid from the engine

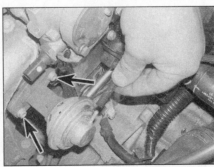

4.9 Disconnect the vacuum hose from the EGR valve – mounting bolts arrowed

4.10 Separate the EGR pipe at the throttle housing, and recover the gasket

4.11a Unscrew the union nut at the EGR valve . . .

4.11b . . . and remove the EGR pipe (engine removed for clarity)

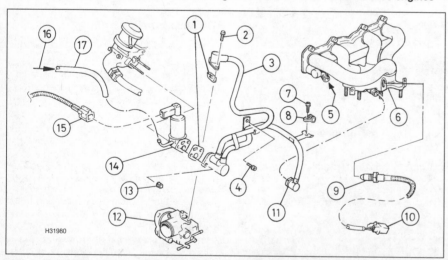

1	Throttle housing bolt
2	Throttle housing
3	Gasket
4	Mounting flange
5	Seal
6	EGR valve
7	Adaptor elbow bolt
8	Adaptor elbow
9	EGR pipe bolts
10	Through-bolt
11	Vacuum hose
12	EGR pipe

4.15 EGR valve components – 1.4 litre engine codes AXP and 1.6 litre DOHC engines

4.20 EGR valve components – 1.6 litre SOHC engine codes AVU and BFQ

1	Gasket	6	Oxygen sensor connection	12	Throttle housing
2	EGR pipe flange bolt	7	Mounting bolt	13	EGR pipe flange nut
3	EGR pipework	8	Oxygen sensor wiring clip	14	EGR valve
4	Mounting bolt	9	Oxygen sensor	15	EGR wiring connector
5	Exhaust manifold EGR pipe connection	10	Oxygen sensor wiring plug	16	From air filter
		11	EGR pipe union	17	Air hose

10 Trace the metal pipe from the valve to the throttle housing, and unscrew the pipe mounting bolt(s) and the two flange bolts at the throttle housing **(see illustration)**.

11 Unscrew the large union nut securing the metal pipe to the EGR valve **(see illustrations)**. If the nut will not loosen easily, it is preferable to remove the two bolts securing the valve to the manifold, then unscrew the valve from the metal pipe.

12 Unscrew and remove the two EGR valve mounting bolts, and remove the valve from the manifold. Recover the gasket – a new one must be used when refitting.

13 Refitting is a reversal of removal. Use a new gasket, and tighten the mounting bolts and union nut to the specified torque. On completion, run the engine and check for signs of gas leakage at the valve.

1.4 litre codes AXP

14 Disconnect the vacuum hose from the port on the EGR valve.

15 Support the EGR valve, then unscrew and remove the two through-bolts which secure the EGR pipe flange and the valve **(see illustration)**. Withdraw the valve, and recover the gaskets fitted either side of it.

16 If required, unscrew the two bolts securing the adaptor elbow to the exhaust manifold. Withdraw the adaptor from the manifold, and recover the gasket.

17 Refitting is a reversal of removal. Use new gaskets, and tighten the mounting and through-bolts to the specified torque. On completion, run the engine and check for signs of gas leakage.

1.6 litre SOHC codes AVU and BFQ

18 Disconnect the air hose and wiring plug from the EGR valve.

19 Unscrew the two nuts from the EGR pipe flange at the EGR valve.

20 Trace the EGR pipework back from the valve, and unscrew the pipe mounting bolt **(see illustration)**. Unscrew the union nut at the exhaust manifold, and disconnect the EGR pipe from the manifold. Unscrew the two bolts at the throttle housing flange, and separate the joint. Apart from the oxygen sensor wiring harness clipped to it, the EGR pipework is now sufficiently free to move it aside without risking damage.

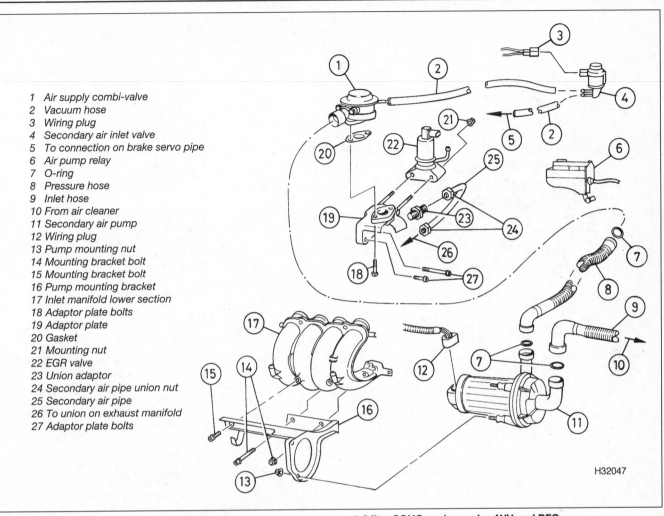

1   Air supply combi-valve
2   Vacuum hose
3   Wiring plug
4   Secondary air inlet valve
5   To connection on brake servo pipe
6   Air pump relay
7   O-ring
8   Pressure hose
9   Inlet hose
10 From air cleaner
11 Secondary air pump
12 Wiring plug
13 Pump mounting nut
14 Mounting bracket bolt
15 Mounting bracket bolt
16 Pump mounting bracket
17 Inlet manifold lower section
18 Adaptor plate bolts
19 Adaptor plate
20 Gasket
21 Mounting nut
22 EGR valve
23 Union adaptor
24 Secondary air pipe union nut
25 Secondary air pipe
26 To union on exhaust manifold
27 Adaptor plate bolts

5.1a Secondary air injection system components – 1.6 litre SOHC engine codes AVU and BFQ

21 Move the EGR pipe flange at the EGR valve aside, off the two studs; recover the gasket. Slide the EGR valve off the mounting studs, and remove it.

22 Refitting is a reversal of removal. Use new gaskets, and tighten the EGR pipe mountings to the specified torque. On completion, run the engine and check for signs of gas leakage.

1.6 litre DOHC

23 Disconnect the vacuum hose from the port on the EGR valve.

24 Support the EGR valve, then unscrew and remove the two through-bolts which secure the EGR pipe flange and the valve **(see illustration 4.15)**. Withdraw the valve, and recover the gaskets fitted either side of it.

25 If required, unscrew the two bolts securing the adaptor elbow to the exhaust manifold. Withdraw the adaptor from the manifold, and recover the gasket.

26 Refitting is a reversal of removal. Use new gaskets, and tighten the mounting and through-bolts to the specified torque. On completion, run the engine and check for signs of gas leakage.

5   Secondary air injection system – information and component renewal

1 The secondary air injection system (also known as a 'pulse-air' system) comprises an electrically-operated air pump (fed with air from the air cleaner), a relay for the air pump, a vacuum-operated air supply combi-valve, a solenoid valve to regulate the vacuum supply, and pipework to feed the air into the exhaust manifold. For more information on the principles of operation, refer to Section 1 **(see illustrations)**.

Air pump

2 The air pump is mounted on a bracket attached to the lower section of the inlet manifold. To improve access to the pump, remove the engine top cover.

3 Disconnect the air hoses on top of the pump by squeezing together the lugs on the hose end fittings, and pulling the hoses upwards. Recover the O-ring seal from each

hose – new seals should be used when refitting. The hoses are of different sizes, and so cannot be refitted incorrectly.

4 Disconnect the wiring plug from the air pump.

5 Unscrew the pump-to-mounting bracket nuts/nuts and bolts (as applicable) and slide the pump out of the mounting bracket.

6 If required, the mounting bracket can be removed from the inlet manifold. The bracket is secured by two bolts and a nut, or by three bolts, depending on model. Where three bolts are used, they are of different lengths, so note their locations.

7 Refitting is a reversal of removal.

Air pump relay

8 The relay is among those in the engine compartment fuse and relay box – refer to Chapter 12 for more details.

Air supply combi-valve

9 The combi-valve is mounted on top of the exhaust manifold. To improve access to the valve, remove the engine top cover.

10 On 2.0 litre (AQY) engines, loosen and

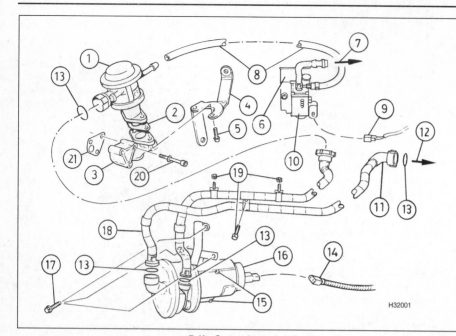

1 Air supply combi-valve
2 Gasket
3 Adaptor plate
4 Mounting flange
5 Mounting flange bolts
6 Mounting bracket (on inlet manifold)
7 To vacuum reservoir
8 Vacuum hose
9 Wiring connector
10 Secondary air inlet valve
11 Inlet hose
12 To air cleaner
13 O-ring
14 Wiring connector
15 Pump mounting nuts
16 Secondary air pump
17 Mounting bracket bolts
18 Pressure hose
19 Mounting nuts/bolts
20 Adaptor plate bolts
21 Gasket

H32001

5.1b Secondary air injection system components – 1.8 litre engine

remove the nuts securing the heat shield over the exhaust manifold; this will allow the shield to be moved for access to the combi-valve mounting bolts.

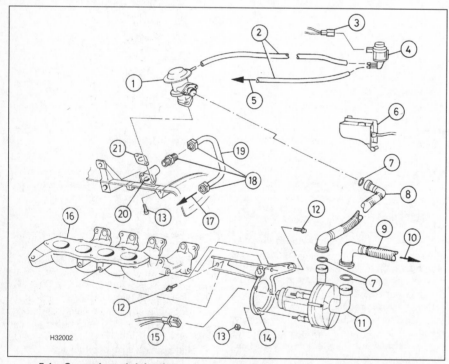

H32002

5.1c Secondary air injection system components – 2.0 litre engine code AQY

1 Air supply combi-valve	8 Pressure hose	16 Inlet manifold lower section
2 Vacuum hose	9 Inlet hose	
3 Wiring connector	10 To air cleaner	17 To union on exhaust manifold
4 Secondary air inlet valve	11 Secondary air pump	
5 To connection on brake servo vacuum pipe	12 Mounting bracket bolts	18 Union nut
	13 Mounting bolt	19 Secondary air pipe
6 Secondary air pump relay	14 Air pump mounting bracket	20 Warm-air collector plate
7 O-ring	15 Wiring connector	21 Gasket

11 Disconnect the vacuum hose and the large-diameter air hose from the valve – the air hose is released by squeezing together the lugs on the hose end fitting.

12 Remove the two valve mounting bolts from below the valve, and lift the valve off its mounting flange. Recover the gasket.

13 Refitting is a reversal of removal. Use a new gasket, and tighten the mounting bolts to the specified torque.

Vacuum solenoid valve

14 The solenoid valve is mounted at the rear of the engine compartment, near the combi-valve.

15 Disconnect the wiring plug and vacuum pipes from the valve – note which ports the pipes are fitted to, to avoid confusion when refitting.

16 Unscrew the bolts, or unclip the valve, and remove it from its mounting bracket.

17 Refitting is a reversal of removal.

Other components

18 On 1.6 litre SOHC (AVU and BFQ) engines and 2.0 litre (AQY) engines, the air supply from the combi-valve passes to the exhaust manifold via a metal pipe. Removing the pipe entails unscrewing the union nuts at either end, and withdrawing it. The union nuts should be tightened to the specified torque when refitting.

19 On 1.6 litre SOHC (AVU and BFQ) engines and 1.8 litre (AUM and AUQ) engines, the combi-valve is mounted on an adaptor elbow, which is screwed onto the exhaust manifold. This elbow can be removed if required (after removing the combi-valve as described above) by unscrewing the adaptor mounting bolts; recover the gasket. When refitting, use a new gasket, and tighten the adaptor elbow mounting bolts to the specified torque.

6 Turbocharger – general information, precautions, removal and refitting

General information

1 A turbocharger is fitted to the 1.8 litre engines, and is mounted directly on the exhaust manifold. Lubrication is provided by an oil supply pipe that runs from the engine oil filter mounting. Oil is returned to the sump via a return pipe that connects to the sump. The turbocharger unit has a separate wastegate valve and vacuum actuator diaphragm, which is used to control the boost pressure applied to the inlet manifold.

2 The turbocharger's internal components rotate at a very high speed, and as such are sensitive to contamination; a great deal of damage can be caused by small particles of dirt, particularly if they strike the delicate turbine blades.

Precautions

The turbocharger operates at extremely high speeds and temperatures. Certain precautions must be observed to avoid premature failure of the turbo, or injury to the operator.

• *Do not operate the turbo with any parts exposed. Foreign objects falling onto the rotating vanes could cause excessive damage and (if ejected) personal injury.*

• *Cover the turbocharger air inlet ducts to prevent debris entering, and clean using lint-free cloths only.*

• *Do not race the engine immediately after start-up, especially if it is cold. Give the oil a few seconds to circulate.*

• *Always allow the engine to return to idle speed before switching it off – do not blip the throttle and switch off, as this will leave the turbo spinning without lubrication.*

• *Allow the engine to idle for several minutes before switching off after a high-speed run.*

• *Observe the recommended intervals for oil and filter changing, and use a reputable oil of the specified quality. Neglect of oil changing, or use of inferior oil, can cause carbon formation on the turbo shaft and subsequent failure. Thoroughly clean the area around all oil pipe unions before disconnecting them, to prevent the ingress of dirt. Store dismantled components in a sealed container to prevent contamination.*

Removal

Caution: Thoroughly clean the area around all oil pipe unions before disconnecting them, to prevent the ingress of dirt. Store dismantled components in a sealed container to prevent contamination. Cover the turbocharger air inlet ducts to prevent debris entering, and clean using lint-free cloths only.

3 Apply the handbrake, then jack up the front of the vehicle and support it on axle stands (see *Jacking and vehicle support*). Remove the engine compartment undershield.

4 Where applicable, remove the engine top cover(s). Removal details vary according to model, but the cover retaining nuts are concealed under circular covers, which are prised out of the main cover. Where plastic screws or turn-fasteners are used, these can be removed using a wide-bladed screwdriver. Remove the nuts or screws, and lift the cover from the engine, releasing any wiring or hoses attached.

5 Loosen the clips and disconnect the air hoses leading to and from the turbocharger.

6 Unscrew the two bolts securing the heat shield above the turbocharger, and remove the shield (**see illustration**).

1 Exhaust downpipe nuts
2 Exhaust downpipe gasket
3 Wastegate bracket bolt
4 Wastegate
5 Circlip
6 Turbocharger
7 O-ring
8 Mounting bolt
9 Air inlet pipe stub
10 Gasket
11 Heat shield mounting bolt
12 Heat shield
13 Mounting bolt
14 Banjo bolt
15 Oil supply pipe
16 Turbocharger mounting bolts
17 Exhaust manifold
18 Manifold gasket
19 Mounting bolt
20 Banjo bolt
21 Manifold mounting nuts
22 Banjo bolt
23 Coolant return pipe
24 Mounting bolt
25 Spacer sleeve
26 Banjo bolt
27 Mounting bolt
28 Coolant supply pipe
29 Banjo bolt
30 Turbocharger-to-support bracket bolt
31 Turbocharger support bracket
32 Support bracket bolt
33 Gasket
34 Gasket
35 Oil return pipe flange bolt
36 Oil return pipe
37 Oil return pipe flange bolt
38 Wastegate setting/locknuts

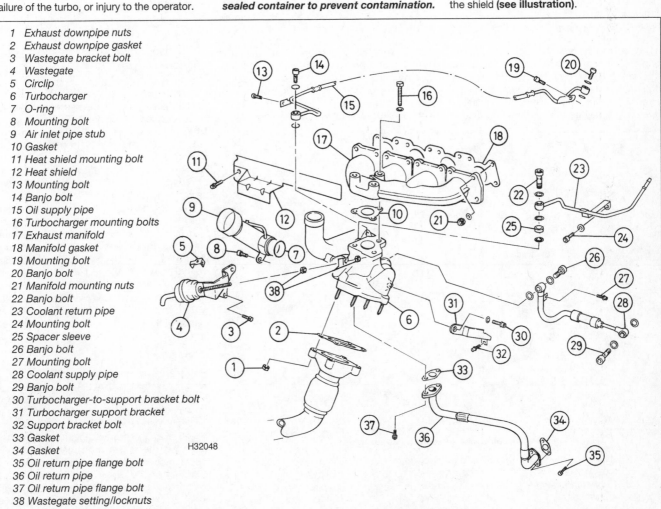

H32048

6.6 Turbocharger and associated components

7 Remove the screw securing the air inlet pipe stub to the turbocharger. Ease the pipe stub out of the turbocharger, and recover the O-ring seal (a new seal must be used when refitting).

8 Unscrew the union bolt and disconnect the oil supply pipe from the top of the turbocharger; recover the sealing washers, noting their order of fitting. Anticipate some oil spillage as the pipe is removed. Plug or cover the pipe and aperture to prevent entry of dust and dirt. Remove the small bolt securing the pipe mounting bracket, and move the pipe to one side.

9 The turbocharger housing is water-cooled, so removing it entails disconnecting two coolant pipes. Even if the cooling system is drained as described in Chapter 1A, it is likely that the pipes will not be drained, and spillage will result. If the coolant is not due for renewal therefore, it may be preferable not to drain the system, but be prepared to plug the pipes once they have been disconnected.

10 Unscrew the union bolts and disconnect the coolant supply and return pipe unions from the front and top of the turbocharger. Recover the sealing washers, noting their order of fitting. Remove the small bolt securing the supply pipe mounting bracket, and move the pipe aside.

11 Access to the coolant supply pipe union is particularly poor – it may be found easier to unscrew the pipe union bolt at the other end, and remove the turbocharger with the supply pipe. Depending on the extent of dismantling required, it may be advisable in any case to

unscrew the other pipe union bolt (supply pipe) or pipe mounting bolt (return pipe), and move the pipes aside (or remove them completely).

12 Note the location of the two vacuum hoses, then disconnect them from the wastegate vacuum control unit.

13 Unscrew and remove the four nuts securing the exhaust downpipe to the base of the turbocharger. Separate the downpipe, and recover the gasket (a new one should be obtained for refitting). If the nuts are in poor condition, it is advisable to obtain new ones for refitting.

14 Unscrew the two bolts securing the oil return pipe to the base of the turbocharger. Anticipate some oil spillage as the pipe is disconnected, and recover the gasket (obtain a new one for refitting).

15 Unscrew the nut and bolt securing the turbocharger to the cylinder block support bracket.

16 The turbocharger is secured to the exhaust manifold by three bolts, removed from above. Supporting the turbocharger (which is a heavy assembly), loosen and remove the three bolts (new bolts should be fitted on reassembly). Manoeuvre the turbocharger and wastegate assembly out from behind the engine, and remove it from the engine compartment. Recover the manifold-to-turbocharger gasket, and discard it – a new one must be used when refitting.

17 It is not advisable to separate the wastegate assembly from the turbocharger without first consulting a VW dealer or

turbocharger specialist, as the setting may be lost. Interfering with the wastegate setting may lead to a reduction in performance, or could result in engine damage.

Refitting

18 Refit the turbocharger by following the removal procedure in reverse, noting the following points:
a) Renew all gaskets, sealing washers and O-rings.
b) Renew the three turbocharger mounting bolts, and any self-locking nuts ('stiffnuts' with a nylon insert).
c) Before reconnecting the oil supply pipe, fill the turbocharger with fresh oil using an oil can.
d) Tighten all nuts and bolts to the specified torque, where given.
e) Ensure that the air hose clips are securely tightened, to prevent air leaks.
f) When the engine is started after refitting, allow it to idle for approximately one minute to give the oil time to circulate around the turbine shaft bearings. Check for signs of oil or coolant leakage from the relevant unions.

---

7 Intercooler –
general information, removal and refitting

1 The intercooler is effectively an 'air radiator', used to cool the pressurised inlet air before it enters the engine.

2 When the turbocharger compresses the inlet air, one side-effect is that the air is heated, causing the air to expand. If the inlet air can be cooled, a greater effective volume of air will be inducted, and the engine will produce more power.

3 The compressed air from the turbocharger, which would normally be fed straight into the inlet manifold, is instead ducted around the engine to the base of the intercooler (see illustration). The intercooler is mounted at the front of the car, in the air flow. The heated air entering the base of the unit rises upwards, and is cooled by the air flow over the intercooler fins, much as with the radiator. When it reaches the top of the intercooler, the cooled air is then ducted into the throttle housing.

Removal

4 The intercooler is located under the right-hand front wheel arch, at the front.

5 To gain access to the intercooler, remove the bumper as described in Chapter 11, and the right-hand headlight as described in Chapter 12, Section 7. Although not essential, removing the wheel arch inner panel will further improve access (see illustrations).

6 Working in the engine compartment, loosen the hose clips from the air hoses leading to and from the intercooler, and disconnect the hoses at the point where they disappear under the inner wing (see illustration). On

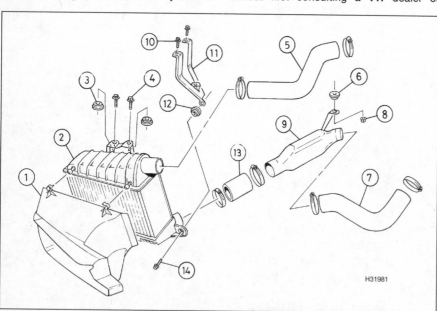

7.3 Intercooler and associated components

1 Air inlet duct	6 Rubber mounting	11 Mounting bracket
2 Intercooler	7 Hose to turbocharger	12 Rubber mounting
3 Rubber mounting	8 Mounting nut	13 Connecting hose
4 Mounting bolt	9 Plastic duct	14 Mounting bolt
5 Intercooler-to-throttle housing hose	10 Mounting bolt	

7.5a Removing the wheel arch liner

7.5b Intercooler viewed under right-hand front wheel arch

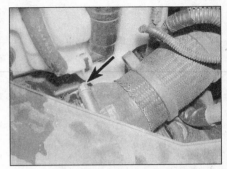

7.6 Intercooler hose clip (arrowed) – viewed from above

7.7 Unclip the air duct from the front of the intercooler

7.8 Intercooler upper retaining bolts (arrowed)

7.9 Using slip-joint pliers to release one of the intercooler hoses

some models, large spring clips are used, which must be released by compressing the spring ends – slip-joint ('water pump') pliers are ideal for this.

7 Working under the wheel arch, unclip the air duct from the two locating pegs at the front of the intercooler, and remove it from under the wheel arch **(see illustration)**.

8 Locate the intercooler mounting bolts on the inner wing. There are two at the top, and a further two at the side **(see illustration)**. Loosen the top two bolts, and remove the two at the side.

9 Release the hose clips, and disconnect the intercooler hoses under the wheel arch as necessary **(see illustration)**.

10 Unscrew the nut at the rear, and the washer-type fasteners further forward, and release the plastic air duct from under the wheel arch **(see illustrations)**.

11 Reach inside the wheel arch, and remove

the mounting bolt securing the intercooler to the lower bracket **(see illustration)**.

12 Support the intercooler from below, then remove the two top mounting bolts. Manoeuvre the intercooler out from under the

wheel arch, taking care not to damage the cooling fins. Recover the rubber grommets from the three mounting bolts.

13 Examine the intercooler for any damage, and check the air hoses for splits.

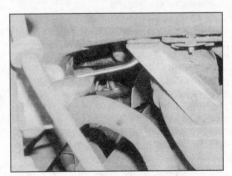

7.10a Unscrew the nut at the rear . . .

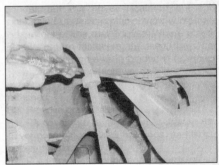

7.10b . . . and the washer-type fasteners further forward . . .

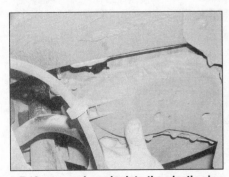

7.10c . . . and manipulate the plastic air duct . . .

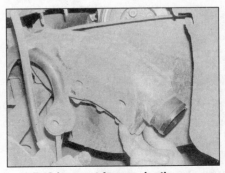

7.10d . . . out from under the car

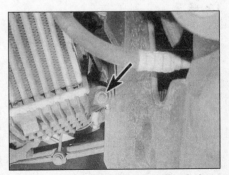

7.11 Intercooler lower mounting bolt (arrowed)

8.3 Pull off the warm-air hose from the manifold heat shield

Refitting

14 Refitting is a reversal of removal. Ensure that the air hose clips are securely tightened/refitted, to prevent air leaks.

8 Exhaust manifold – removal and refitting

Removal

1 Where applicable, remove the engine top cover(s). Removal details vary according to model, but the cover retaining nuts are concealed under circular covers, which are prised out of the main cover. Where plastic screws or turn-fasteners are used, these can be removed using a wide-bladed screwdriver. Remove the nuts or screws, and lift the cover from the engine, releasing any wiring or hoses attached.

1.4 and 1.6 litre DOHC engines

2 Apply the handbrake, then jack up the front of the car and support it on axle stands (see *Jacking and vehicle support*).
3 Pull off the warm-air hose (for the air cleaner) from the heat shield over the manifold, and place the hose end to one side **(see illustration)**.
4 Unscrew the two top bolts securing the heat shield to the manifold **(see illustration)**. Some models may have an additional pair of bolts securing the heat shield to the engine top cover – these should also be removed.
5 Unscrew and remove the two bolts at the

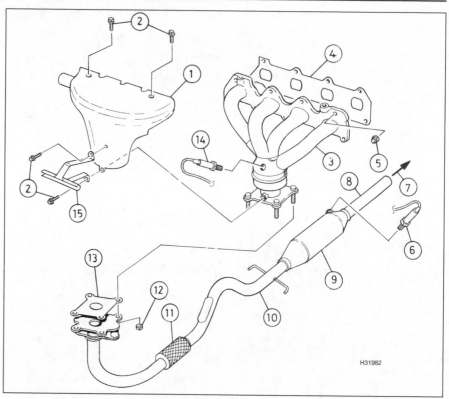

H31982

8.4 Exhaust manifold and downpipe – 1.4 and 1.6 litre DOHC engines

1 Heat shield	6 Oxygen sensor 2	11 Flexible section
2 Heat shield bolts	7 To centre silencer	12 Manifold-to-downpipe nut
3 Exhaust manifold	8 Clamp position marking	13 Downpipe gasket
4 Manifold gasket	9 Catalytic converter	14 Oxygen sensor 1
5 Manifold mounting nut	10 Front pipe	15 Wiring harness guide tube

front of the manifold heat shield which secure a small tubular wiring bracket. Access to these bolts may be easier from below. Take off the bracket, unclipping the oxygen sensor wiring from it (where applicable) **(see illustration)**.
6 Remove the heat shield from the manifold, and remove it from the engine compartment **(see illustration)**.
7 On models with an oxygen sensor screwed into the manifold, trace the wiring from the sensor around the front of the engine to the connector plug, which should be above the transmission. Disconnect the wiring plug, and free the wiring from any retaining clips or ties

(see illustration). It is preferable to remove the manifold with the sensor in place, but care must be taken not to damage the sensor if this is done.
8 Unscrew the two bolts securing the EGR pipe and valve to the manifold. Separate the joint(s), and recover the gasket(s). Take care that the EGR pipe is not strained as the manifold is removed – it may be preferable to remove the pipe mounting bolt, and the two bolts securing the pipe flange to the throttle housing.
9 Working from below, unscrew and remove the four nuts securing the manifold to the front

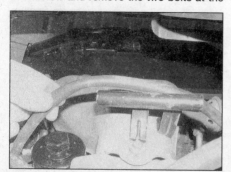

8.5 Unclip the oxygen sensor wiring from the tubular bracket

8.6 Removing the manifold heat shield

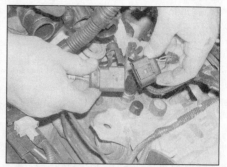

8.7 Disconnect the oxygen sensor wiring plug

section of the exhaust **(see illustration)**. Use a wire brush and plenty of penetrating oil if the studs are rusty. If a nut appears to be sticking, do not try to force it; tighten the nut back half a turn, apply some more penetrating oil to the stud threads, wait several seconds for it to soak in, then gradually unscrew the nut by one turn. Repeat this process until the nut is free.

10 Separate the front pipe from the manifold, and recover the gasket (a new gasket must be used on reassembly). Once this is done, it is advisable to support the front pipe on an axle stand, to avoid placing strain on the exhaust system or second oxygen sensor wiring (for preference, remove the exhaust front section entirely, as described in Section 9).

11 Unscrew and remove the manifold retaining nuts, noting the advice given in paragraph 9. In some cases, the manifold studs will come out with the nuts – this poses no great problem, and the studs can be refitted if they are in good condition. For preference, however, a complete set of manifold studs and nuts (and manifold-to-front pipe nuts) should be obtained, as the old ones are likely to be in less-than-perfect condition.

12 Remove the washers, then withdraw the manifold from the cylinder head, and recover the gasket from the studs.

1.8 litre turbocharged engines

13 Loosen the clips and disconnect the air inlet hoses leading to and from the turbocharger.

14 Unscrew the two bolts securing the heat shield above the turbocharger, and remove the shield **(refer to illustration 6.6)**.

15 Unscrew and remove the three bolts from above which secure the turbocharger to the exhaust manifold; recover the washers. Note that new bolts must be used when refitting.

16 Where applicable, disconnect the secondary air hose and vacuum hose from the valve mounted above the manifold heat shield. The larger hose fitting is released by squeezing the lugs together; recover the sealing O-ring, which must be renewed when refitting. Unscrew and remove the two bolts from below securing the secondary air valve to its mounting bracket on the exhaust manifold, and lift the valve clear. Recover the gasket – a new one must be used when refitting.

17 Unscrew and remove the manifold retaining nuts. Use plenty of penetrating oil if the studs are rusty. If a nut appears to be sticking, do not try to force it; tighten the nut back half a turn, apply some more penetrating oil to the stud threads, wait several seconds for it to soak in, then gradually unscrew the nut by one turn. Repeat this process until the nut is free.

18 In some cases, the manifold studs will come out with the nuts – this poses no great problem, and the studs can be refitted if they are in good condition. For preference, however, a complete set of manifold studs

8.9 Two of the manifold-to-exhaust downpipe nuts

and nuts should be obtained, as the old ones are likely to be in less-than-perfect condition.

19 Remove the washers, then withdraw the manifold from the cylinder head, separating it from the turbocharger, and recover the gaskets from the studs and turbocharger mating face.

20 If the proximity of the turbocharger prevents the manifold from being withdrawn, unscrew the nut and bolt securing the turbocharger to the cylinder block mounting bracket, and lower the turbocharger slightly. If this is done, note that the weight of the turbocharger will be taken by the exhaust

front pipe – also note that no great strain should be placed on the turbocharger oil and coolant pipes. If absolutely necessary, refer to Section 6 and remove the turbocharger completely.

1.6 litre SOHC codes AVU and BFQ and 2.0 litre

21 To improve access to the exhaust manifold, remove the upper part of the inlet manifold as described in Chapter 4A.

22 Apply the handbrake, then jack up the front of the car and support it on axle stands (see *Jacking and vehicle support*).

23 Disconnect the secondary air hose and vacuum hose from the valve mounted above the manifold heat shield. The larger hose fitting is released by squeezing the lugs together; recover the sealing O-ring, which must be renewed when refitting.

24 Unscrew and remove the two bolts securing the secondary air valve to the exhaust manifold flange, and lift the valve clear. Recover the gasket – a new one must be used when refitting.

25 Unscrew the large union nuts from each end of the secondary air pipe at the top of the manifold, and separate the pipe from the joints **(see illustration)**.

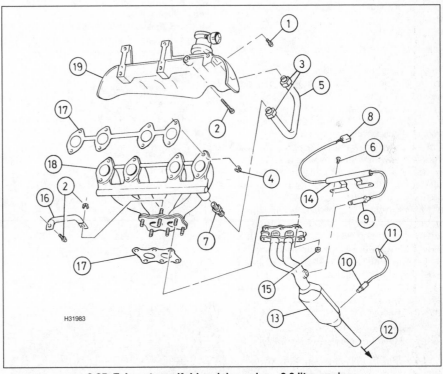

H31983

8.25 Exhaust manifold and downpipe – 2.0 litre engines

1 Heat shield bolt	7 Secondary air pipe union	13 Catalytic converter
2 Mounting nut/bolt	8 Oxygen sensor wiring	14 Wiring guide tube
3 Union nut	plug	15 Manifold-to-downpipe
4 Exhaust manifold	9 Oxygen sensor 1	nut
mounting nut	10 Oxygen sensor wiring	16 Manifold support bracket
5 Secondary air pipe	plug	17 Gasket
6 Wiring mounting bracket	11 Oxygen sensor 2	18 Exhaust manifold
bolt	12 To centre silencer	19 Heat shield

26 Unscrew the bolts used to secure the heat shield over the exhaust manifold, and remove the shield from the manifold.

27 Trace the wiring from the oxygen sensor around the front of the engine to the connector plug, which should be accessible from below on the right-hand side.

28 As necessary, remove the cover for the right-hand driveshaft inner CV joint, then open the square access panel at the rear of the wheel arch (into which the wiring loom disappears) and disconnect the sensor wiring plug. On some models, note that it may be necessary to remove the right-hand driveshaft as described in Chapter 8. Free the sensor wiring from any retaining clips or ties. On models where the oxygen sensor is screwed into the manifold, care must be taken not to damage the sensor as the manifold is removed.

29 On the 1.6 litre engine, unscrew the large union nut from the EGR pipe at the base of the manifold. It is preferable to unbolt the pipe mounting bolt and the two flange bolts at the throttle housing, and move the EGR pipe and valve to one side. To remove the assembly completely, also disconnect the wiring plug and vacuum hose from the EGR valve.

30 Working from below, unscrew and remove the six nuts securing the exhaust downpipe to the manifold (note the advice given in paragraphs 17 and 18).

31 Lower the downpipe sufficiently to clear the manifold studs, and recover the gasket. Once this is done, it is advisable to support the front pipe on an axle stand, to avoid placing strain on the exhaust system or second oxygen sensor wiring (for preference, remove the exhaust front section entirely, as described in Section 9).

32 To remove the manifold support bracket, either unscrew the nut above the manifold-to-downpipe flange, or (more easily) remove the bolt securing the bracket to the back of the engine.

33 Progressively unscrew the manifold retaining nuts, again noting the advice in paragraphs 17 and 18. Note that two of the nuts also retain a wiring support bracket – remove the bracket from the cylinder head studs, noting how it is fitted.

34 Recover the washers, then ease the manifold from the cylinder head studs, and remove it. Recover the manifold gasket, which must of course be renewed.

1.6 litre SOHC codes AEH and AKL

35 To improve access to the exhaust manifold, remove the upper part of the inlet manifold as described in Chapter 4A.

36 Apply the handbrake, then jack up the front of the car and support it on axle stands (see *Jacking and vehicle support*).

37 Unscrew the nuts used to secure the heat shield over the exhaust manifold, and remove the shield from the manifold.

38 Working from below, unscrew and remove the six nuts securing the exhaust downpipe to the manifold (note the advice given in paragraphs 17 and 18). To improve access, remove the cover from the right-hand driveshaft inner CV joint.

39 Lower the downpipe sufficiently to clear the manifold studs, and recover the gasket. Once this is done, it is advisable to support the front pipe on an axle stand, to avoid placing strain on the exhaust system or second oxygen sensor wiring (for preference, remove the exhaust front section entirely, as described in Section 9).

40 Progressively unscrew the manifold retaining nuts, again noting the advice in paragraphs 17 and 18. Note that two of the nuts also retain a wiring support bracket – remove the bracket from the cylinder head studs, noting how it is fitted.

41 Recover the washers, then ease the manifold from the cylinder head studs, and remove it. Recover the manifold gasket, which must of course be renewed.

Refitting

42 Refitting is a reversal of the removal procedure, noting the following points:

a) *Always fit new gaskets and seals, as applicable.*

b) *If any studs were broken when removing, drill out the remains of the stud, and fit new studs and nuts.*

c) *It is recommended that new studs and nuts are used as a matter of course – even if the old ones came off without difficulty, they may not stand being retightened. New components will be much easier to remove in future, should this be necessary.*

d) *If the old studs are re-used, clean the threads thoroughly to remove all traces of rust.*

e) *Tighten the manifold securing nuts to the specified torque.*

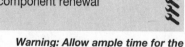

9 Exhaust system – component renewal

> ⚠ **Warning: Allow ample time for the exhaust system to cool before starting work. In particular, note**

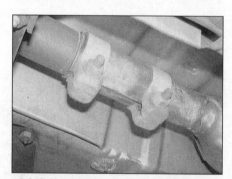

9.6 Exhaust front-to-rear section clamp

that the catalytic converter runs at very high temperatures. If there is any chance that the system may still be hot, wear suitable gloves. When removing the exhaust front section, take care not to damage the oxygen sensor(s) if they are not removed from their locations.

Removal

1 The original VW system fitted in the factory is in two sections. The front section includes the catalytic converter (or 'catalyst'), and can be removed complete. The original rear section cannot be removed in one piece, as it passes over the rear axle – the pipe must be cut through between the centre and rear silencers, at a point marked on the pipe.

2 To remove part of the system, first jack up the front or rear of the car and support it on axle stands (see *Jacking and vehicle support*). Alternatively, position the car over an inspection pit or on car ramps.

Front pipe and catalytic converter

Note: *Where applicable, handle the flexible, braided section of the front pipe carefully, and do not bend it excessively.*

3 Before removing the front section of the exhaust, establish how many oxygen sensors are fitted – most models have two. Trace the wiring back from each sensor, and disconnect the wiring connector. On some models, the sensor wiring disappears behind an access panel behind the right-hand driveshaft, and it will be necessary to remove the cover fitted over the right-hand inner CV joint (or even the complete driveshaft, as described in Chapter 8) for access.

4 Unclip the oxygen sensor wiring from any clips or brackets, noting how it is routed for refitting.

5 If a new front section and catalyst are being fitted, unscrew the oxygen sensor(s) from the pipe. If two sensors are fitted, note which fits where, as they should not be interchanged.

6 Loosen the two nuts on the clamp behind the catalyst, and free the clamp so that it can be moved relative to the front and rear pipes **(see illustration)**.

7 Loosen and remove the nuts securing the front flange to the exhaust manifold or turbocharger. On some models, the shield over the right-hand driveshaft inner CV joint must be removed to improve access. Separate the front joint, and move it down sufficiently to clear the mounting studs.

8 Support the front of the pipe, then slide the clamp behind the catalyst either forwards or backwards to separate the joint. Twist the front pipe slightly from side-to-side, while pulling towards the front to release it from the rear section. When the pipe is free, lower it to the ground and remove it from under the car.

Rear pipe and silencers

9 If the factory-fitted VW rear section is being worked on, examine the pipe between the two silencers for three pairs of punch marks, or three line markings. The centre marking indicates the point at which to cut the pipe, while the outer marks indicate the position for the ends of the new clamp required when refitting. Cut through the pipe using the centre mark as a guide, making the cut as square to the pipe as possible if either resulting section is to be re-used **(see illustration)**.

10 If the factory-fitted rear section has already been renewed, loosen the nuts securing the clamp between the silencers so that the clamp can be moved.

Centre silencer

11 To remove the centre silencer, first loosen the nuts on the clamp behind the catalyst. Remove the four bolts securing the two mounting brackets to the centre cradle under the car **(see illustration)**. To improve access, also remove the nuts securing the cradle to the underside of the car, and lower the cradle completely.

12 Slide the clamps at either end of the silencer section to release the pipe ends, and lower the silencer out of position.

Rear silencer

13 Depending on model, the rear silencer is supported either just at the very back, or in front and behind, by a rubber mounting which is bolted to the underside of the car **(see illustrations)**. The silencer is attached to these mountings by metal pegs which push into the rubber section of each mounting.

14 Unscrew the bolts, and release the mounting(s) from the underside of the car. On models with two silencer mountings, it may prove sufficient to unbolt only one, and to prise the silencer from the remaining mounting, but for preference, both should be removed, where applicable.

15 Where applicable, slide the clamp at the front end of the silencer section to release the pipe ends, and lower the silencer out of position.

Refitting

16 Each section is refitted by a reversal of the removal sequence, noting the following points:

a) *Ensure that all traces of corrosion have been removed from the flanges or pipe ends, and renew all necessary gaskets.*

b) *The design of the clamps used between the exhaust sections means that they play a greater role in ensuring a gas-tight seal – fit new clamps if they are in less than perfect condition.*

c) *When fitting the clamps, use the markings on the pipes as a guide to the clamp's correct fitted position.*

d) *Inspect the mountings for signs of damage or deterioration, and renew as necessary.*

e) *If using exhaust assembly paste, make sure this is only applied to joints downstream of the catalyst.*

f) *Prior to tightening the exhaust system mountings and clamps, ensure that all rubber mountings are correctly located and that there is adequate clearance*

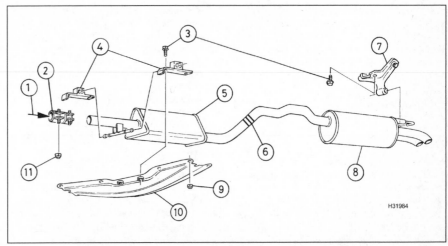

9.9 Exhaust rear section and mountings – 1.6 litre SOHC model

1 From front section	5 Centre silencer	8 Rear silencer
2 Exhaust clamp	6 Centre marking for	9 Cradle-to-floor nut
3 Mounting bolts	cutting point	10 Cradle
4 Front mounting-to-cradle	7 Rear mounting	11 Clamp nut

9.11 Exhaust centre cradle – four mounting bracket bolts arrowed

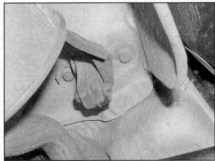

9.13a Rear silencer mounting

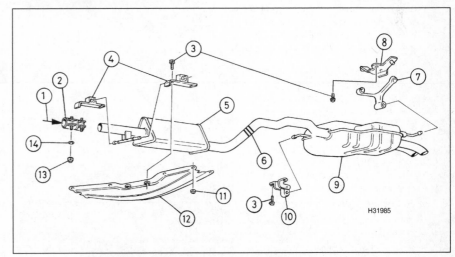

9.13b Exhaust rear section and mountings – 2.0 litre model

1 From front section	6 Centre marking for	10 Rear silencer front
2 Exhaust clamp	cutting point	mounting
3 Mounting bolts	7 Rear silencer rear	11 Cradle-to-floor nut
4 Front mounting to	mounting	12 Cradle
cradle	8 Bracket	13 Clamp nut
5 Centre silencer	9 Rear silencer	14 Washer

between the exhaust system and vehicle underbody. Try to ensure that no unnecessary twisting stresses are applied to the pipes – move the pipes relative to each other at the clamps to relieve this.

10 Catalytic converter – general information and precautions

1 The catalytic converter is a reliable and simple device which needs no maintenance in itself, but there are some facts of which an owner should be aware if the converter is to function properly for its full service life:

a) DO NOT use leaded or lead-replacement petrol in a car equipped with a catalytic converter – the lead (or other additives) will coat the precious metals, reducing their converting efficiency and will eventually destroy the converter.

b) Always keep the ignition and fuel systems well-maintained in accordance with the manufacturer's schedule (see Chapter 1A).

c) If the engine develops a misfire, do not drive the car at all (or at least as little as possible) until the fault is cured.

d) DO NOT push- or tow-start the car – this will soak the catalytic converter in unburned fuel, causing it to overheat when the engine does start.

e) DO NOT switch off the ignition at high engine speeds – ie do not 'blip' the throttle immediately before switching off the engine.

f) DO NOT use fuel or engine oil additives – these may contain substances harmful to the catalytic converter.

g) DO NOT continue to use the car if the engine burns oil to the extent of leaving a visible trail of blue smoke.

h) Remember that the catalytic converter operates at very high temperatures. DO NOT, therefore, park the car in dry undergrowth, over long grass or piles of dead leaves after a long run.

i) Remember that the catalytic converter is FRAGILE – do not strike it with tools during servicing work, and take care handling it when removing it from the car for any reason.

j) In some cases, a sulphurous smell (like that of rotten eggs) may be noticed from the exhaust. This is common to many catalytic converter-equipped cars, and has more to do with the sulphur content of the brand of fuel being used than the converter itself.

k) The catalytic converter, used on a well-maintained and well-driven car, should last for between 50 000 and 100 000 miles – if the converter is no longer effective, it must be renewed.

Chapter 4 Part D:
Emission control and exhaust systems – diesel engines

Contents

Catalytic converter – general information and precautions 10
Crankcase emission system – general information 2
Exhaust Gas Recirculation (EGR) system – component removal . . . 3
Exhaust manifold – removal and refitting 8
Exhaust system – component renewal 9
General information 1

Intercooler – general information, removal and refitting 7
Turbocharger – general information and precautions 4
Turbocharger – removal and refitting 5
Turbocharger boost control system components – removal and
    refitting 6

Degrees of difficulty

Easy, suitable for novice with little experience	**Fairly easy,** suitable for beginner with some experience	**Fairly difficult,** suitable for competent DIY mechanic	**Difficult,** suitable for experienced DIY mechanic	**Very difficult,** suitable for expert DIY or professional

Specifications

Torque wrench settings	Nm	lbf ft
EGR pipe nuts/bolts	25	18
EGR valve (non-turbo) clamp bolt	10	7
EGR valve mounting bolts:		
Engine codes AGR, ALH, AHF and ASV	25	18
Engine codes AJM, ASZ, ARL, ATD, AUY and AXR	10	7
Exhaust clamp nuts	40	30
Exhaust manifold nuts*	25	18
Exhaust manifold-to-downpipe nuts*	25	18
Exhaust mounting bracket nuts and bolts	25	18
Intercooler mounting bolts	10	7
Turbocharger oil return pipe flange bolts	15	11
Turbocharger oil return union bolt	40	30
Turbocharger support bracket to engine	40	30
Turbocharger-to-downpipe nuts**	25	18
Turbocharger-to-manifold bolts (renew)**	30	22
Turbocharger-to-mounting bracket bolt	25	18
Wastegate flange bolts (engine code AGR)**	10	7

Use new nuts/bolts
** *Use thread-locking compound*

1 General information

Emission control systems

All diesel-engined models have a crankcase emission control system, and in addition, are fitted with a catalytic converter. All diesel engines are fitted with an Exhaust Gas Recirculation (EGR) system to reduce exhaust emissions.

Crankcase emission control

To reduce the emission of unburned hydrocarbons from the crankcase into the atmosphere, the engine is sealed and the blow-by gases and oil vapour are drawn from inside the crankcase, through a wire mesh oil separator, into the inlet tract to be burned by the engine during normal combustion.

Under conditions of high manifold depression, the gases will be sucked positively out of the crankcase. Under conditions of low manifold depression, the gases are forced out of the crankcase by the (relatively) higher crankcase pressure. If the engine is worn, the raised crankcase pressure (due to increased blow-by) will cause some of the flow to return under all manifold conditions. All diesel engines have a pressure-regulating valve on the camshaft cover, to control the flow of gases from the crankcase.

Exhaust emission control

An oxidation catalyst is fitted in the exhaust system of all diesel-engined models. This has the effect of removing a large proportion of the gaseous hydrocarbons, carbon monoxide and particulates present in the exhaust gas.

An Exhaust Gas Recirculation (EGR) system is fitted to all diesel-engined models. This reduces the level of nitrogen oxides produced during combustion by introducing a proportion of the exhaust gas back into the inlet manifold, under certain engine operating conditions, via a plunger valve. The system is controlled electronically by the diesel engine management ECU.

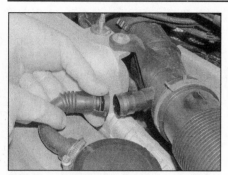

2.1 Disconnecting the pressure-regulating valve breather hose

3.4a EGR solenoid valve location on engine compartment bulkhead – engine codes AGP, AQM, AGR, ALH, AHF and ASV

3.4b EGR valve (1), changeover valve (2) and charge pressure solenoid valve (3) – engine codes AJM, ASZ, ARL, ATD, AUY and AXR

Exhaust systems

The exhaust system comprises the exhaust manifold, front pipe with catalytic converter, intermediate pipe and silencer (non-turbo models), and tailpipe and silencer. On turbo models, the turbocharger is mounted on the exhaust manifold, and is driven by the exhaust gases.

The system is supported by various metal brackets screwed to the vehicle floor, with rubber vibration dampers fitted to suppress noise.

2 Crankcase emission system – general information

1 The crankcase emission control system consists of hoses connecting the crankcase to the air cleaner or inlet manifold. In addition, a pressure-regulating valve is fitted to the camshaft cover **(see illustration)**.

2 The system requires no attention other than to check at regular intervals that the hoses and pressure-regulating valve are free of blockages and in good condition.

3 Exhaust Gas Recirculation (EGR) system – component removal

1 The EGR system consists of the EGR (mechanical) valve, the modulator (solenoid) valve and a series of connecting vacuum hoses.

2 On non-turbo models, the EGR valve is mounted on a flange joint at the inlet manifold and is connected to a second flange joint at the exhaust manifold by a short metal pipe.

3 On turbo models, the EGR valve is part of the inlet manifold flap housing, and is joined to the exhaust manifold by a flanged pipe.

EGR solenoid

4 The EGR solenoid valve/modulator valve is mounted on the bulkhead at the rear of the engine compartment **(see illustrations)**. On some models, do not confuse the EGR solenoid with the turbo boost pressure solenoid, which is mounted further to the left (left as seen from the driver's seat).

5 Disconnect the wiring plug from the solenoid valve.

6 Disconnect the vacuum hose which leads to the EGR valve, and the other vacuum hose on the base of the solenoid valve.

7 Unscrew the solenoid valve mounting bolt, and remove the valve from the engine.

8 Refitting is a reversal of removal. Ensure that the hoses and wiring plug are reconnected securely and correctly.

EGR valve

9 To improve access, remove the engine top cover(s). Removal details vary according to model, but the cover retaining nuts are concealed under circular covers, which are prised out of the main cover. Where plastic screws or turn-fasteners are used, these can be removed using a wide-bladed screwdriver. Remove the nuts or screws, and lift the cover from the engine, releasing any wiring or hoses attached.

Non-turbo models

10 Disconnect the vacuum hose from the port on the EGR valve.

11 Loosen the clamp bolt which secures the valve to the short connecting pipe.

12 Unscrew and remove the two EGR valve mounting bolts **(see illustration)**.

13 Separate the valve from the lower section of the inlet manifold, and recover the gasket. Ease the valve upwards out of the clamp and connecting pipe, and remove it.

14 The connecting pipe can also be removed if required. Unscrew the pipe flange nuts, and separate the pipe from the exhaust manifold. Recover the gasket.

15 Refitting is a reversal of removal. Use new gaskets as required, and tighten the nuts and bolts to the specified torques.

Turbo models

16 The EGR valve is part of the inlet manifold flap housing, and cannot be removed separately.

17 If required, the pipe from the housing to the exhaust manifold can be removed, after unscrewing the flange nuts and bolts. Recover the gasket from each end of the pipe **(see illustration)**.

18 Refitting the pipe is a reversal of removal.

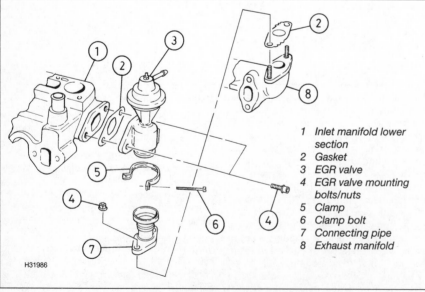

1 Inlet manifold lower section
2 Gasket
3 EGR valve
4 EGR valve mounting bolts/nuts
5 Clamp
6 Clamp bolt
7 Connecting pipe
8 Exhaust manifold

H31986

3.12 EGR valve details – non-turbo models

Use new gaskets, and tighten the flange nuts and bolts to the specified torque.

EGR damper

19 To improve access, remove the engine top cover(s). Removal details vary according to model, but the cover retaining nuts are concealed under circular covers, which are prised out of the main cover. Where plastic screws or turn-fasteners are used, these can be removed using a wide-bladed screwdriver. Remove the nuts or screws, and lift the cover from the engine, releasing any wiring or hoses attached.
20 Disconnect the vacuum pipe from the damper reservoir at the front of the engine.
21 Unbolt the damper from the mounting bracket, and remove it front he engine compartment.
22 Refitting is a reversal of removal.

4 Turbocharger – general information and precautions

General information

A turbocharger is fitted to all engines (except engine codes AQM and AGP), and is mounted directly on the exhaust manifold.

The turbocharger increases engine efficiency by raising the pressure in the inlet manifold above atmospheric pressure. Instead of the air simply being sucked into the cylinders, it is forced in. Additional fuel is supplied by the injection pump, in proportion to the increased amount of air.

Energy for the operation of the turbocharger comes from the exhaust gas. The gas flows through a specially-shaped housing (the turbine housing) and in so doing, spins the turbine wheel. The turbine wheel is attached to a shaft, at the end of which is another vaned wheel, known as the compressor wheel. The compressor wheel spins in its own housing, and compresses the inducted air on the way to the inlet manifold.

Between the turbocharger and the inlet manifold, the compressed air passes through an intercooler (see Section 7 for details). The purpose of the intercooler is to remove from the inducted air some of the heat gained in being compressed. Because cooler air is denser, removal of this heat further increases engine efficiency.

Boost pressure (the pressure in the inlet manifold) is limited by a wastegate, which diverts the exhaust gas away from the turbine wheel in response to a pressure-sensitive actuator.

The turbo shaft is pressure-lubricated by an oil feed pipe from the engine oil filter mounting. The shaft 'floats' on a cushion of oil. Oil is returned to the sump via a return pipe that connects to the sump.

Some engines have a so-called 'adjustable' turbocharger, which further boosts the engine's power output compared with a normal turbo installation. At low engine speeds, vanes are used to restrict the exhaust gas supply passage before the gases hit the turbine wheel – this has the effect of increasing the gas flow through the restriction, and the wheel reaches optimum speed faster (reducing turbo 'lag'). At higher engine speeds, the vanes open up the supply passage, which lowers the exhaust back-pressure and reduces fuel consumption.

Precautions

The turbocharger operates at extremely high speeds and temperatures. Certain precautions must be observed to avoid premature failure of the turbo, or injury to the operator.
• *Do not operate the turbo with any parts exposed. Foreign objects falling onto the rotating vanes could cause excessive damage and (if ejected) personal injury.*
• *Cover the turbocharger air inlet ducts to prevent debris entering, and clean using lint-free cloths only.*
• *Do not race the engine immediately after start-up, especially if it is cold. Give the oil a few seconds to circulate.*
• *Always allow the engine to return to idle speed before switching it off – do not blip the throttle and switch off, as this will leave the turbo spinning without lubrication.*

• *Allow the engine to idle for several minutes before switching off after a high-speed run.*
• *Observe the recommended intervals for oil and filter changing, and use a reputable oil of the specified quality. Neglect of oil changing, or use of inferior oil, can cause carbon formation on the turbo shaft and subsequent failure. Thoroughly clean the area around all oil pipe unions before disconnecting them, to prevent the ingress of dirt. Store dismantled components in a sealed container to prevent contamination.*

5 Turbocharger – removal and refitting

Note: *On all engines except engine code AGR, the turbocharger is part of the exhaust manifold assembly.*

Removal

1 Apply the handbrake, then jack up the front of the vehicle and support it on axle stands (see *Jacking and vehicle support*). Remove the engine compartment undershield.
2 Remove the engine top cover(s). Removal details vary according to model, but the cover retaining nuts are concealed under circular covers, which are prised out of the main

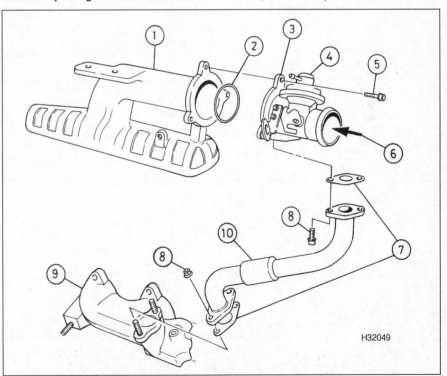

3.17 EGR pipe mounting details – turbo models

1 Inlet manifold	4 EGR valve	8 Flange nut/bolt
2 O-ring	5 Mounting bolt	9 Exhaust
3 Inlet manifold flap housing	6 From intercooler	manifold
	7 Gasket	10 EGR pipe

cover. Where plastic screws or turn-fasteners are used, these can be removed using a wide-bladed screwdriver. Remove the nuts or screws, and lift the cover from the engine, releasing any wiring or hoses attached.

3 Access to the turbocharger may be improved by removing the inlet manifold as described in Part B of this Chapter, although this is not essential.

4 Remove the EGR pipe from the exhaust manifold and inlet manifold flap housing, using the information in Section 3.

5 Unscrew the two nuts and washers securing the heat shield above the turbocharger, and remove the shield.

6 Unscrew the union bolt and disconnect the oil supply pipe from the top of the turbocharger; recover the sealing washers, noting their order of fitting. Anticipate some oil spillage as the pipe is removed. Plug or cover the pipe and aperture to prevent entry of dust and dirt. Remove the small bolt securing the pipe mounting bracket, and move the pipe to one side.

7 Loosen the clips and disconnect the air hoses leading to and from the turbocharger.

8 Disconnect the vacuum hose(s) from the wastegate vacuum control unit.

9 Unscrew and remove the nuts securing the exhaust downpipe to the side of the turbocharger. Separate the downpipe, and recover the gasket (a new one should be obtained for refitting). If the nuts are in poor condition, it is advisable to obtain new ones for refitting. On some models, the shield over the right-hand driveshaft inner CV joint must be removed to improve access.

10 Unscrew the two bolts securing the oil return pipe to the base of the turbocharger. Anticipate some oil spillage as the pipe is disconnected, and recover the gasket (obtain a new one for refitting).

Engine code AGR

11 Unscrew the union bolt, recover the washers, and disconnect the turbo boost solenoid valve hose from the side of the turbocharger **(see illustration)**.

12 The turbocharger is secured to the exhaust manifold by three bolts, removed from above. Supporting the turbocharger (which is a heavy assembly), loosen and remove the three bolts (new bolts should be fitted on reassembly). Manoeuvre the turbocharger and wastegate assembly out from behind the engine, and remove it from the engine compartment. Recover the manifold-to-turbocharger gasket, and discard it – a new one must be used when refitting.

13 It is not advisable to separate the wastegate assembly from the turbocharger without first consulting a VW dealer or turbocharger specialist, as the setting may be lost. Interfering with the wastegate setting may lead to a reduction in performance, or could result in engine damage.

All other engine codes

14 Unscrew the bolt securing the turbocharger to the cylinder block support bracket. Alternatively, unscrew the bolt securing the bracket to the cylinder block, and

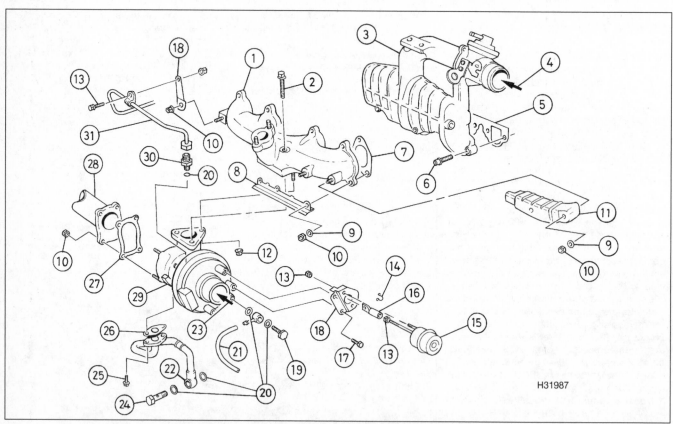

5.11 Turbocharger and associated components – engine code AGR

1 Exhaust manifold	9 Washer	17 Mounting bracket bolt	24 Banjo bolt
2 Turbocharger mounting bolt	10 Nut	18 Mounting bracket	25 Flange bolt
3 Inlet manifold	11 Heat shield	19 Banjo bolt	26 Gasket
4 From intercooler	12 Turbocharger mounting nut	20 Seal	27 Exhaust gasket
5 Inlet manifold gasket	13 Mounting nut/bolt	21 Boost solenoid valve	28 Exhaust front pipe
6 Inlet manifold mounting bolt	14 Circlip	hose	29 Turbocharger
7 Exhaust manifold gasket	15 Wastegate	22 Oil return pipe	30 Connection
8 Heat shield mounting bracket	16 Operating rod	23 From air cleaner	31 Oil supply pipe

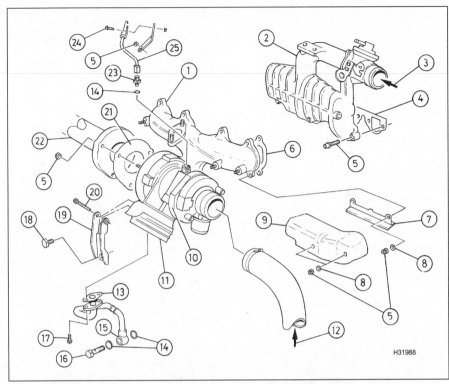

5.14 Turbocharger and associated components – except engine code AGR

1 Exhaust manifold	*10 Turbocharger*	*19 Turbo support bracket*
2 Inlet manifold	*11 Wastegate*	*20 Turbo support bracket*
3 From intercooler	*12 From air cleaner*	*bolt*
4 Inlet manifold gasket	*13 Gasket*	*21 Exhaust pipe gasket*
5 Mounting nut/bolt	*14 Seal*	*22 Exhaust front pipe*
6 Exhaust manifold gasket	*15 Oil return pipe*	*23 Connection*
7 Heat shield mounting	*16 Banjo bolt*	*24 Oil supply pipe mounting*
bracket	*17 Flange bolt*	*bolt*
8 Washer	*18 Turbo support bracket*	*25 Oil supply pipe*
9 Heat shield	*bolt to engine*	

remove the turbocharger with its support bracket **(see illustration)**.

15 The turbocharger cannot be separated from the exhaust manifold, and so the two must be removed together. This makes a bulky assembly – in order to gain the necessary clearance to remove it, the right-hand driveshaft must first be removed as described in Chapter 8.

16 Support the manifold and turbocharger – it is a heavy assembly. Unscrew and remove the eight exhaust manifold retaining nuts, noting that the heat shield mounting bracket is secured by one of the nuts. Use plenty of penetrating oil if the studs are rusty. If a nut appears to be sticking, do not try to force it; tighten the nut back half a turn, apply some more penetrating oil to the stud threads, wait several seconds for it to soak in, then gradually unscrew the nut by one turn. Repeat this process until the nut is free.

17 In some cases, the manifold studs will come out with the nuts – this poses no great problem, and the studs can be refitted if they are in good condition. For preference, however, a complete set of manifold studs

and nuts should be obtained, as the old ones are likely to be in less-than-perfect condition.

18 Carefully separate the manifold from the cylinder head, and slide the manifold off the mounting studs. Manoeuvre the manifold and turbocharger out from below. Recover the manifold gaskets from the cylinder head studs, and discard them.

Refitting

19 Refit the turbocharger by following the removal procedure in reverse, noting the following points:

a) *Renew all gaskets, sealing washers and O-rings.*
b) *On engine code AGR, renew the three turbocharger mounting bolts.*
c) *Before reconnecting the oil supply pipe, fill the turbocharger with fresh oil using an oil can.*
d) *Tighten all nuts and bolts to the specified torque, where given.*
e) *Ensure that the air hose clips are securely tightened, to prevent air leaks.*
f) *When the engine is started after refitting, allow it to idle for approximately one*

6.1 Boost pressure solenoid valve – engine codes AGR, ALH, AHF and ASV

minute to give the oil time to circulate around the turbine shaft bearings. Check for signs of oil or coolant leakage from the relevant unions.

6 Turbocharger boost control system components – removal and refitting

Boost pressure solenoid valve

1 The boost pressure solenoid valve is mounted on the left-hand side of the bulkhead **(see illustration)**.
2 Disconnect the wiring from the boost pressure valve.
3 Remove the vacuum hoses from the ports on the boost control valve, noting their order of connection carefully to aid correct refitting **(see illustrations)**.
4 Remove the retaining screw and withdraw the valve.
5 Refitting is a reversal of removal.

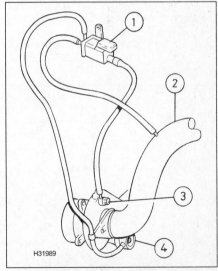

6.3a Hose connections to boost pressure solenoid valve – engine code AGR

1 Boost pressure solenoid valve
2 Air hose from air cleaner
3 Turbocharger hose connection
4 Wastegate

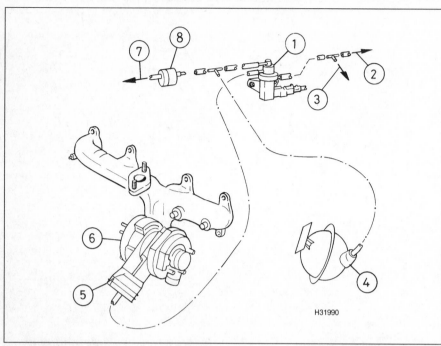

6.3b Hose connections to boost pressure solenoid valve – other turbo engines

1 Boost pressure solenoid valve
2 To EGR valve
3 To air cleaner
4 Vacuum reservoir
5 Wastegate
6 Turbocharger
7 To inlet manifold flap valve
8 Non-return valve

Boost pressure valve (wastegate)

Engine code AGR

6 Remove the turbocharger (see Section 5).
7 Remove the circlip securing the wastegate operating rod to the valve lever on the turbo **(see illustration)**.
8 Unscrew and remove the three small bolts securing the wastegate flange to the turbo, and remove the wastegate.
9 Clean the threads of the wastegate flange

bolts, coat them with a suitable thread-locking compound, then fit and tighten them to the specified torque.
10 If the original wastegate is being refitted, proceed to paragraph 15.
11 Loosen the operating rod locknut.
12 Turn the valve lever on the turbo towards the wastegate, and hold it on its stop.
13 Adjust the length of the operating rod along its threaded section, so that the rod eye fits easily over the valve lever, when the valve lever is held on its stop.

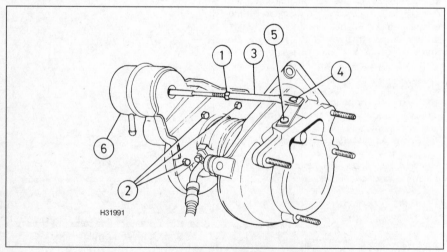

6.7 Wastegate mounting details – engine code AGR

1 Locknut
2 Flange bolt
3 Operating rod
4 Circlip
5 Valve lever
6 Wastegate

14 Separate the rod from the valve lever, and turn the rod inwards by eight full turns, so that the rod length effectively shortens, and tighten the rod locknut.
15 Refit the operating rod to the valve lever, and secure with the circlip.
16 Refit the turbocharger as described in Section 5.

All other engine codes

17 The boost pressure valve is an integral part of the turbocharger, and cannot be renewed separately.

7 Intercooler – general information, removal and refitting

Refer to Chapter 4C, Section 7 – the intercooler installation for petrol and diesel models is all but identical. The only difference of note is the air temperature sensor, fitted either on top of the intercooler, or on the air hose from the intercooler to the inlet manifold. In either case, disconnect the wiring plug from the sensor as required. **Note:** On engine codes AJM, ASZ, ARL, ATD, AUY and AXR, the intercooler is attached to the cooling system radiator, see Chapter 3 for the removal and refitting procedure of the radiator, then unbolt intercooler.

8 Exhaust manifold – removal and refitting

Note: On all engine codes, except AGR, the turbocharger cannot be separated from the exhaust manifold. Therefore, manifold removal is covered as part of the turbocharger removal procedure in Section 5.

Removal

1 Remove the engine top cover(s). Removal details vary according to model, but the cover retaining nuts are concealed under circular covers, which are prised out of the main cover. Where plastic screws or turn-fasteners are used, these can be removed using a wide-bladed screwdriver. Remove the nuts or screws, and lift the cover from the engine, releasing any wiring or hoses attached.
2 Access to the exhaust manifold (at least from above) is greatly improved if the inlet manifold is removed first, as described in Part B of this Chapter.
3 On engine code AGR, if not already done, release the clips and remove the hose between the air mass meter and the turbocharger. Similarly, disconnect and remove the intercooler air hose from the inlet manifold.
4 Referring to Section 3, remove the EGR connecting pipe from the exhaust manifold. On non-turbo models, if the inlet manifold has not been removed, unbolt the EGR valve from

1   Manifold gasket
2   Washer
3   Mounting nut
4   Exhaust manifold
5   Catalytic converter
6   To exhaust rear section
7   Front mounting
8   Downpipe gasket

H31992

8.5 Exhaust manifold and front pipe – non-turbo models

the inlet manifold, so that the connecting pipe can be removed.

5 Unscrew the retaining nuts, and separate the exhaust downpipe from the manifold or turbocharger **(see illustration)**. There should be sufficient movement in the pipe to free it from the studs – if not, loosen the bolts securing the exhaust front mounting. On some models, the shield over the right-hand driveshaft inner CV joint must be removed to improve access.

6 On engine code AGR, it is advisable to remove the turbocharger from the exhaust manifold, as described in Section 5. If left in place, the turbocharger limits access to the manifold nuts, and the assembly may be too bulky to remove without further dismantling.

7 Support the manifold, then unscrew and remove the manifold retaining nuts and recover the washers. Use plenty of penetrating oil if the studs are rusty. If a nut appears to be sticking, do not try to force it; tighten the nut back half a turn, apply some more penetrating oil to the stud threads, wait several seconds for it to soak in, then gradually unscrew the nut by one turn. Repeat this process until the nut is free.

8 In some cases, the manifold studs will come out with the nuts – this poses no great problem, and the studs can be refitted if they are in good condition. For preference, however, a complete set of manifold studs and nuts should be obtained, as the old ones are likely to be in less-than-perfect condition.

9 Carefully separate the manifold from the

cylinder head, and slide the manifold off the mounting studs. Manoeuvre the manifold out from below. Recover the manifold gaskets from the cylinder head studs, and discard them.

Refitting

10 Refitting is a reversal of the removal procedure, noting the following points:
a) *Always fit new gaskets and seals, as applicable.*
b) *If any studs were broken when removing, drill out the remains of the stud, and fit new studs and nuts.*
c) *It is recommended that new studs and nuts are used as a matter of course – even if the old ones came off without difficulty, they may not stand being retightened. New components will be much easier to remove in future, should this be necessary.*
d) *If the old studs are re-used, clean the threads thoroughly to remove all traces of rust.*
e) *Tighten the manifold securing nuts to the specified torque.*

9   Exhaust system – component renewal

⚠ *Warning: Allow ample time for the exhaust system to cool before starting work. In particular, note*

that the catalytic converter runs at very high temperatures. If there is any chance that the system may still be hot, wear suitable gloves.

Removal

1 The original VW system fitted in the factory is in two sections. The front section includes the catalytic converter (or 'catalyst'), and can be removed complete. The original rear section cannot be removed in one piece, as it passes over the rear axle – the pipe must be cut through between the centre pipe (or centre silencer) and rear silencers, at a point marked on the pipe.

2 Only non-turbo models have a centre silencer; turbo models have a centre pipe between the catalyst and rear silencer.

3 To remove part of the system, first jack up the front or rear of the car and support it on axle stands (see *Jacking and vehicle support*). Alternatively, position the car over an inspection pit or on car ramps.

Front pipe and catalytic converter

Note: *Where applicable, handle the flexible, braided section of the front pipe carefully, and do not bend it excessively.*

4 Loosen the two nuts on the clamp behind the catalyst, and free the clamp so that it can be moved relative to the front and rear pipes.

5 Remove the bolts securing the exhaust front mounting (below the pipe) to the crossmember

6 Loosen and remove the nuts securing the

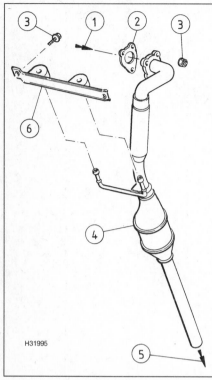

H31995

9.6 Exhaust front pipe – turbo models

1 *From turbocharger*
2 *Front pipe gasket*
3 *Mounting nut/bolt*
4 *Catalytic converter*
5 *To exhaust rear section*
6 *Front mounting*

front flange to the exhaust manifold or turbocharger **(see illustration)**. On some models, the shield over the right-hand driveshaft inner CV joint must be removed to improve access. Separate the front joint, and move it down (or to the side) sufficiently to clear the mounting studs.

7 Support the front of the pipe, then slide the clamp behind the catalyst either forwards or backwards to separate the joint. Twist the front pipe slightly from side-to-side, while pulling towards the front to release it from the rear section. When the pipe is free, lower it to the ground and remove it from under the car.

Rear pipe and silencers

Note: *Refer to the illustrations in Chapter 4C, Section 9.*

8 If the factory-fitted VW rear section is being

worked on, examine the pipe between the two silencers for three pairs of punch marks, or three line markings. The centre marking indicates the point at which to cut the pipe, while the outer marks indicate the position for the ends of the new clamp required when refitting. Cut through the pipe using the centre mark as a guide, making the cut as square to the pipe as possible if either resulting section is to be re-used.

9 If the factory-fitted rear section has already been renewed, loosen the nuts securing the clamp between the silencers so that the clamp can be moved.

Centre silencer

10 To remove the centre silencer, first loosen the nuts on the clamp behind the catalyst. Remove the four bolts securing the two mounting brackets to the centre cradle under the car. To improve access, also remove the nuts securing the cradle to the underside of the car, and lower the cradle completely.

11 Slide the clamps at either end of the silencer section to release the pipe ends, and lower the silencer out of position.

Rear silencer

12 Depending on model, the rear silencer is supported either just at the very back, or in front and behind, by a rubber mounting which is bolted to the underside of the car. The silencer is attached to these mountings by metal pegs which push into the rubber section of each mounting.

13 Unscrew the bolts, and release the mounting(s) from the underside of the car. On models with two silencer mountings, it may prove sufficient to unbolt only one, and to prise the silencer from the remaining mounting, but for preference, both should be removed, where applicable.

14 Where applicable, slide the clamp at the front end of the silencer section to release the pipe ends, and lower the silencer out of position.

Refitting

15 Each section is refitted by a reversal of the removal sequence, noting the following points:

a) *Ensure that all traces of corrosion have been removed from the flanges or pipe ends, and renew all necessary gaskets.*

b) *The design of the clamps used between the exhaust sections means that they play a greater role in ensuring a gas-tight seal*

– *fit new clamps if they are in less than perfect condition.*

c) *When fitting the clamps, use the markings on the pipes as a guide to the clamp's correct fitted position.*

d) *Inspect the mountings for signs of damage or deterioration, and renew as necessary.*

e) *If using exhaust assembly paste, make sure this is only applied to joints downstream of the catalyst.*

f) *Prior to tightening the exhaust system mountings and clamps, ensure that all rubber mountings are correctly located and that there is adequate clearance between the exhaust system and vehicle underbody. Try to ensure that no unnecessary twisting stresses are applied to the pipes – move the pipes relative to each other at the clamps to relieve this.*

10 Catalytic converter – general information and precautions

1 The catalytic converter fitted to diesel models is simpler than that fitted to petrol models, but it still needs to be treated with respect to avoid problems. The converter is a reliable and simple device which needs no maintenance in itself, but there are some facts of which an owner should be aware if the converter is to function properly for its full service life:

a) *DO NOT use fuel or engine oil additives – these may contain substances harmful to the catalytic converter.*

b) *DO NOT continue to use the car if the engine burns (engine) oil to the extent of leaving a visible trail of blue smoke.*

c) *Remember that the catalytic converter operates at very high temperatures. DO NOT, therefore, park the car in dry undergrowth, over long grass or piles of dead leaves after a long run.*

d) *Remember that the catalytic converter is FRAGILE – do not strike it with tools during servicing work, and take care handling it when removing it from the car for any reason.*

e) *The catalytic converter, used on a well-maintained and well-driven car, should last for between 50 000 and 100 000 miles – if the converter is no longer effective, it must be renewed.*

Chapter 5 Part A:
Starting and charging systems

Contents

Alternator – brush holder/regulator module renewal 6
Alternator – removal and refitting 5
Alternator/charging system – testing in vehicle 4
Battery – removal and refitting 3
Battery – testing and charging 2
Battery check . . . . .See *Weekly checks*
Electrical system check . . . . .See *Weekly checks*
General information and precautions 1
Starter motor – removal and refitting 8
Starter motor – testing and overhaul 9
Starting system – testing 7

Degrees of difficulty

Easy, suitable for novice with little experience	**Fairly easy,** suitable for beginner with some experience	**Fairly difficult,** suitable for competent DIY mechanic 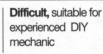	**Difficult,** suitable for experienced DIY mechanic	**Very difficult,** suitable for expert DIY or professional

Specifications

General
System type . . . . 12 volt, negative earth

Starter motor
Rating:
    Petrol engines . . . . 12V, 1.1 kW
    Diesel engines . . . . 12V, 2.0 kW

Battery
Ratings . . . . 36 to 72 Ah (depending on model and market)

Alternator
Rating . . . . 55, 60, 70 or 90 amp
Minimum brush length . . . . 5.0 mm

Torque wrench settings

	Nm	lbf ft
Alternator mounting bolts	25	18
Alternator mounting bracket:		
1.4 litre engines	55	41
1.6, 1.8 and 2.0 litre engines	45	33
Diesel engines	45	33
Battery clamping plate bolt	22	16
Starter mounting bolts	65	48

1 General information and precautions

General information

The engine electrical system consists mainly of the charging and starting systems. Because of their engine-related functions, these are covered separately from the body electrical devices such as the lights, instruments, etc (which are covered in Chapter 12). On petrol engine models refer to Part B of this Chapter for information on the ignition system, and on diesel models refer to Part C.

The electrical system is of the 12 volt negative earth type.

The battery may be of the low maintenance or maintenance-free (sealed for life) type and is charged by the alternator, which is belt-driven from the crankshaft pulley.

The starter motor is of the pre-engaged type, with an integral solenoid. On starting, the solenoid moves the drive pinion into engagement with the flywheel ring gear before the starter motor is energised. Once the engine has started, a one-way clutch prevents the motor armature being driven by the engine until the pinion disengages from the flywheel.

Further details of the various systems are given in the relevant Sections of this Chapter.

While some repair procedures are given, the usual course of action is to renew the component concerned. The owner whose interest extends beyond mere component renewal should obtain a copy of the *Automotive Electrical & Electronic Systems Manual*, available from the publishers of this manual.

Precautions

⚠ *Warning: It is necessary to take extra care when working on the electrical system to avoid damage to semi-conductor devices (diodes and transistors), and to avoid the risk of personal injury. In addition to the precautions given in 'Safety first!', observe the following when working on the system:*

• *Always remove rings, watches, etc, before working on the electrical system.* Even with the battery disconnected, capacitive discharge could occur if a component's live terminal is earthed through a metal object. This could cause a shock or nasty burn.

• *Do not reverse the battery connections.* Components such as the alternator, electronic control units, or any other components having semi-conductor circuitry could be irreparably damaged.

• *Never disconnect the battery terminals, the alternator, any electrical wiring or any test instruments when the engine is running.*

• *Do not allow the engine to turn the alternator when the alternator is not connected.*

• *Never test for alternator output by flashing the output lead to earth.*

• *Always ensure that the battery negative lead is disconnected when working on the electrical system.*

• If the engine is being started using jump leads and a slave battery, connect the batteries *positive-to-positive* and *negative-to-negative* (see *Jump starting* at the beginning of the manual). This also applies when connecting a battery charger.

• Before using electric-arc welding equipment on the car, *disconnect the battery, alternator and components such as the electronic control units* (where applicable) to protect them from the risk of damage.

Caution: Certain radio/cassettes fitted as standard equipment by VW have a built-in security code to deter thieves. If the power source to the unit is cut, the anti-theft system will activate. Even if the power source is immediately reconnected, the radio/cassette unit will not function until the correct security code has been entered. Therefore, if you do not know the correct security code for the radio/cassette unit do not disconnect the battery negative terminal or remove the radio/cassette unit from the vehicle. Refer to your VW dealer for further information on whether the unit fitted to your car has a security code. Refer to 'Disconnecting the battery' in the Reference section at the rear of this manual.

2 Battery – testing and charging

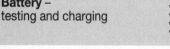

Testing

Standard and low-maintenance battery

1 If the vehicle covers a small annual mileage, it is worthwhile checking the specific gravity of the electrolyte every three months to determine the state of charge of the battery. Remove the battery (see Section 3) then remove the cell caps/cover (as applicable) and use a hydrometer to make the check, comparing the results with the following table. Note that the specific gravity readings assume an electrolyte temperature of 15°C (60°F); for every 10°C (18°F) below 15°C (60°F) subtract 0.007. For every 10°C (18°F) above 15°C (60°F) add 0.007. If the electrolyte level of any cell is low, top it up to the MAX level mark with distilled water.

	Above 25°C	Below 25°C
Fully-charged	1.210 to 1.230	1.270 to 1.290
70% charged	1.170 to 1.190	1.230 to 1.250
Discharged	1.050 to 1.070	1.110 to 1.130

2 If the battery condition is suspect, first check the specific gravity of electrolyte in each cell. A variation of 0.040 or more between any cells indicates loss of electrolyte or deterioration of the internal plates.

3 If the specific gravity variation is 0.040 or more, the battery should be renewed. If the cell variation is satisfactory but the battery is discharged, it should be charged as described later in this Section.

Maintenance-free battery

4 In cases where a sealed for life maintenance-free battery is fitted, topping-up and testing of the electrolyte in each cell is not possible. The condition of the battery can therefore only be tested using a battery condition indicator or a voltmeter.

5 Certain models may be fitted with a maintenance-free battery with a built-in charge condition indicator. The indicator is located in the top of the battery casing, and indicates the condition of the battery from its colour. If the indicator shows green, then the battery is in a good state of charge. If the indicator turns darker, eventually to black, then the battery requires charging, as described later in this Section. If the indicator shows clear/yellow, then the electrolyte level in the battery is too low to allow further use, and the battery should be renewed. **Do not** attempt to charge, load or jump start a battery when the indicator shows clear/yellow.

6 If testing the battery using a voltmeter, connect the voltmeter across the battery and note the voltage. The test is only accurate if the battery has not been subjected to any kind of charge for the previous six hours. If this is not the case, switch on the headlights for 30 seconds, then wait four to five minutes before testing the battery after switching off the headlights. All other electrical circuits must be switched off, so check that the doors and tailgate are fully shut when making the test.

7 If the voltage reading is less than 12.2 volts, then the battery is discharged, whilst a reading of 12.2 to 12.4 volts indicates a partially-discharged condition.

8 If the battery is to be charged, remove it from the vehicle and charge it as described later in this Section.

Charging

Note: *The following is intended as a guide only. Always refer to the manufacturer's recommendations (often printed on a label attached to the battery) before charging a battery.*

Standard and low maintenance battery

9 Charge the battery at a rate equivalent to 10% of the battery capacity (eg, for a 45 Ah battery charge at 4.5 A) and continue to charge the battery at this rate until no further rise in specific gravity is noted over a four-hour period.

10 Alternatively, a trickle charger charging at the rate of 1.5 amps can safely be used overnight.

11 Specially rapid boost charges which are claimed to restore the power of the battery in 1 to 2 hours are not recommended, as they can cause serious damage to the battery plates through overheating.

12 While charging the battery, note that the temperature of the electrolyte should never exceed 37.8°C (100°F).

Maintenance-free battery

13 This battery type takes considerably longer to fully recharge than the standard type, the time taken being dependent on the extent of discharge, but it can take anything up to three days.

14 A constant voltage type charger is required, to be set, when connected, to 13.9 to 14.9 volts with a charger current below 25 amps. Using this method, the battery should be useable within three hours, giving a voltage reading of 12.5 volts, but this is for a partially-discharged battery and, as mentioned, full charging can take far longer.

15 If the battery is to be charged from a fully-discharged state (condition reading less than 12.2 volts), have it recharged by your local automotive electrician, as the charge rate is higher and constant supervision during charging is necessary.

3 Battery – removal and refitting

Note: *If the vehicle has a security-coded radio, make sure that you have the code number before disconnecting the battery. If necessary, a 'code-saver' or 'memory-saver' can be used to preserve the radio code and any other relevant memory values whilst the battery is disconnected (see 'Disconnecting the battery' in the Reference Section).*

Removal

1 The battery is located in the front, left-hand corner of the engine compartment. Where an insulator cover is fitted, open the cover to gain access to the battery.

2 Loosen the clamp nut and disconnect the battery negative (–) lead from the terminal.

3 Lift the plastic cover from the fuse holder on top of the battery, by squeezing together the locking lugs.

4 To remove the fuse holder, undo the retaining nut, push the retaining bracket down onto the battery, and the bracket should unclip from the battery case **(see illustrations)**.

5 Slacken the clamp nut and disconnect the positive (+) lead from the battery terminal **(see illustration)**.

6 Remove the insulator cover (where fitted) then unscrew the bolt and remove the battery clamp **(see illustration)**. The battery can then be lifted out of position.

Refitting

7 Refit the battery by following the removal procedure in reverse. Tighten the clamp bolt to the correct torque.

3.4a Undo the retaining nuts   **3.4b Unclip the bracket**

3.5 Disconnect the positive terminal   **3.6 Unscrew the clamp bolt**

| 4 | Alternator/charging system – testing in vehicle |

Note: *Refer to Section 1 of this Chapter before starting work.*

1 If the charge warning light fails to illuminate when the ignition is switched on, first check the alternator wiring connections for security. If the light still fails to illuminate, check the continuity of the warning light feed wire from the alternator to the bulbholder. If all is satisfactory, the alternator is at fault and should be renewed or taken to an auto-electrician for testing and repair.

2 Similarly, if the charge warning light comes on with the ignition, but is then slow to go out when the engine is started, this may indicate an impending alternator problem. Check all the items listed in the preceding paragraph, and refer to an auto-electrical specialist if no obvious faults are found.

3 If the charge warning light illuminates when the engine is running, stop the engine and check that the drivebelt is correctly tensioned (see Chapter 1A or 1B) and that the alternator

connections are secure. If all is so far satisfactory, check the alternator brushes and slip-rings as described in Section 6. If the fault persists, the alternator should be renewed, or taken to an auto-electrician for testing and repair.

4 If the alternator output is suspect even though the warning light functions correctly, the regulated voltage may be checked as follows.

5 Connect a voltmeter across the battery terminals, and start the engine.

6 Increase the engine speed until the voltmeter reading remains steady; the reading should be approximately 12 to 13 volts, and no more than 14 volts.

7 Switch on as many electrical accessories (eg, the headlights, heated rear window and heater blower) as possible, and check that the alternator maintains the regulated voltage at around 13 to 14 volts.

8 If the regulated voltage is not as stated, this may be due to worn brushes, weak brush springs, a faulty voltage regulator, a faulty diode, a severed phase winding or worn or damaged slip-rings. The brushes and slip-rings may be checked (see Section 6), but if the fault persists, the alternator should be renewed or taken to an auto-electrician.

| 5 | Alternator – removal and refitting |

Removal

1 Disconnect the battery negative lead and position it away from the terminal. **Note:** *Before disconnecting the battery, refer to 'Disconnecting the battery' in the reference section at the rear of this manual.*

2 Remove the auxiliary drivebelt from the alternator pulley (see Chapter 1A or 1B). Mark the drivebelt for direction to ensure it is refitted in the same position.

3 Pull the 2-pin push-in connector from the alternator **(see illustration)**.

4 Unscrew the nut and disconnect earth wiring from the alternator.

5 Remove the protective cap (where fitted), unscrew and remove the nut and washers, then disconnect the battery positive cable from the alternator terminal. Where applicable, unscrew the nut and remove the cable guide **(see illustration)**.

6 Unscrew and remove the lower, then upper bolts, then lift the alternator away from its

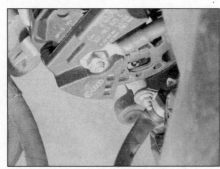

5.3 Unplug the 2-pin connector   **5.5 Disconnect the positive lead**

5.6 Undo the mounting bolts (arrowed)

6.3 Remove the outer cover

bracket **(see illustration)**. If necessary, remove the power steering pump to improve access, as described in Chapter 10.

Refitting

7 Refitting is a reversal of removal. Refer to Chapter 1A or 1B as applicable for details of refitting and tensioning the auxiliary drivebelt. Tighten the alternator mounting bolts to the specified torque.

6 Alternator – brush holder/regulator module renewal

1 Remove the alternator, as described in Section 5.
2 Place the alternator on a clean work surface, with the pulley facing down.
3 Where fitted, undo the screw and the two retaining nuts, and lift away the outer plastic cover **(see illustration)**.
4 Unscrew the three securing screws, and remove the voltage regulator **(see illustrations)**.
5 Measure the free length of the brush contacts **(see illustration)**. Check the measurement with the Specifications; renew the module if the brushes are worn below the minimum limit.

6 Clean and inspect the surfaces of the slip-rings, at the end of the alternator shaft. If they are excessively worn, or damaged, the alternator must be renewed.
7 Reassemble the alternator by following the dismantling procedure in reverse. On completion, refer to Section 5 and refit the alternator.

7 Starting system – testing

Note: *Refer to Section 1 of this Chapter before starting work.*
1 If the starter motor fails to operate when the ignition key is turned to the appropriate position, the following possible causes may be to blame:
a) *The battery is faulty.*
b) *The electrical connections between the switch, solenoid, battery and starter motor are somewhere failing to pass the necessary current from the battery through the starter to earth.*
c) *The solenoid is faulty.*
d) *The starter motor is mechanically or electrically defective.*

2 To check the battery, switch on the headlights. If they dim after a few seconds, this indicates that the battery is discharged – recharge (see Section 2) or renew the battery. If the headlights glow brightly, operate the ignition switch and observe the lights. If they dim, then this indicates that current is reaching the starter motor, therefore the fault must lie in the starter motor. If the lights continue to glow brightly (and no clicking sound can be heard from the starter motor solenoid), this indicates that there is a fault in the circuit or solenoid – see following paragraphs. If the starter motor turns slowly when operated, but the battery is in good condition, then this indicates that either the starter motor is faulty, or there is considerable resistance somewhere in the circuit.
3 If a fault in the circuit is suspected, disconnect the battery leads (including the earth connection to the body), the starter/solenoid wiring and the engine/transmission earth strap. **Note:** *Before disconnecting the battery, refer to 'Disconnecting the battery' in the Reference section at the rear of this manual.* Thoroughly clean the connections, and reconnect the leads and wiring, then use a voltmeter or test light to check that full battery voltage is

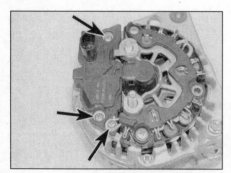

6.4a Undo the screws (arrowed) . . .

6.4b . . . and remove the brush holder/regulator

6.5 Measure the brush length

8.2 Undo the four bolts

8.3 Disconnect the wiring plug

8.4a Solenoid connections (arrowed)

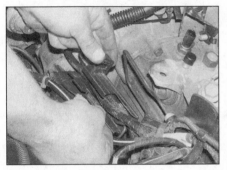

8.4b Release the cables

8.5 Remove the starter top bolt

8.9 Remove the starter lower bolt

available at the battery positive lead connection to the solenoid, and that the earth is sound.

4 If the battery and all connections are in good condition, check the circuit by disconnecting the wire from the solenoid blade terminal. Connect a voltmeter or test light between the wire end and a good earth (such as the battery negative terminal), and check that the wire is live when the ignition switch is turned to the start position. If it is, then the circuit is sound – if not the circuit wiring can be checked as described in Chapter 12.

5 The solenoid contacts can be checked by connecting a voltmeter or test light between the battery positive feed connection on the starter side of the solenoid, and earth. When the ignition switch is turned to the start position, there should be a reading or lighted bulb, as applicable. If there is no reading or lighted bulb, the solenoid is faulty and should be renewed.

6 If the circuit and solenoid are proved sound, the fault must lie in the starter motor. It may be possible to have the starter motor overhauled by a specialist, but check on the availability and cost of spares before

proceeding, as it may prove more economical to obtain a new or exchange motor.

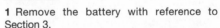

8 Starter motor – removal and refitting

Removal

1 Remove the battery with reference to Section 3.

2 Unscrew the four retaining bolts, and remove the battery tray **(see illustration)**.

3 Unplug the connector above the solenoid, and pull it out from the retainer **(see illustration)**.

4 Note their locations, and disconnect the wiring from the rear of the solenoid. Remove the cables from the guides, then remove the cable guides **(see illustrations)**.

5 Remove the upper starter motor-to-bellhousing bolt and earth connection **(see illustration)**.

6 In order to gain access to the underside of the vehicle, apply the handbrake, then jack up the front of the vehicle and support it on axle stands.

7 Unscrew the retaining bolts, and remove

the engine undertray centre and left-hand sections.

8 Remove the power steering pipe brackets/retainers, and move them to one side.

9 Unscrew and remove the lower starter motor-to-bellhousing bolt, and guide the starter and solenoid assembly out of the bellhousing aperture and downwards out of the engine compartment **(see illustration)**.

Refitting

10 Refit the starter motor by following the removal procedure in reverse. Tighten the mounting bolts to the specified torque.

9 Starter motor – testing and overhaul

If the starter motor is thought to be defective, it should be removed from the vehicle and taken to an auto-electrician for assessment. In the majority of cases, new starter motor brushes can be fitted at a reasonable cost. However, check the cost of repairs first as it may prove more economical to purchase a new or exchange motor.

Notes

Chapter 5 Part B:
Ignition system – petrol engines

Contents

General information 1
Spark plug renewal ....See Chapter 1A
Ignition system – testing 2
HT coil(s) – removal and refitting 3
Ignition timing – checking and adjusting 4
Knock sensor(s) – removal and refitting 5
Ignition switch removal and refitting ....See Chapter 10

Degrees of difficulty

Easy, suitable for novice with little experience		Fairly easy, suitable for beginner with some experience		Fairly difficult, suitable for competent DIY mechanic		Difficult, suitable for experienced DIY mechanic		Very difficult, suitable for expert DIY or professional	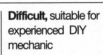

Specifications

System type*

1.4 litre engines:
Engine code AHW	Magneti-Marelli 4AV
Engine codes AXP and BCA	Bosch Motronic ME7.5.10

1.6 litre:
SOHC engines:
Codes AEH and AKL:	
Vehicles with cruise control	Simos 2.2
Vehicles without cruise control	Simos 2.1
Codes AVU and BFQ	Simos 3.3
DOHC engines, codes AZD and BCB	Magneti-Marelli 4MV

1.8 litre engines, codes AUM and AUQ	Bosch Motronic ME7.5

2.0 litre engines:
Codes APK and AQY	Bosch Motronic M5.9.2
Codes AZJ and AZH	Bosch Motronic ME7.5

* Refer to Chapter 2A or 2B for engine code listings.

Ignition coil

Type:
Engine codes:
AHW, AXP, AEH, AKL, AVU, BFQ, APK, AQY AZJ and AZH	Single DIS coil with four HT lead outputs
BCA, AZD, BCB, AUM and AUQ	One coil per spark plug
Primary winding resistance	N/A
Secondary resistance:	
Single DIS coil (four HT lead outputs)	4000 to 6000 ohms
One coil per spark plug	N/A

Spark plugs
See Chapter 1A Specifications

Torque wrench settings

Torque wrench settings	Nm	lbf ft
Ignition coil mounting bolts (single DIS coil)	10	7
Knock sensor mounting bolt	20	15
Spark plugs	30	22

1 General information

The Bosch Motronic, Magneti-Marelli, and Simos systems are self-contained engine management systems, which control both the fuel injection and ignition. This Chapter deals with the ignition system components only – refer to Chapter 4A for details of the fuel system components.

The ignition system fitted to all models is of the increasingly popular 'distributorless' (DIS – Distributorless Ignition System) or 'static' type (there are no moving parts). Despite the many different system names and designations, as far as the ignition systems fitted to the Golf and Bora are concerned, there are essentially only two types of system used – AHW, AXP, AEH, AKL, AVU, BFQ, APK, AQY AZJ and AZH engine codes have a single ignition coil unit with four HT lead terminals, while BCA, AZD, BCB, AUM and AUQ engine codes have four separate coils, one fitted to each spark plug. Therefore, these systems have no distributor cap, rotor arm, or (in the case of BCA, AZD, BCB, AUM and AUQ engine codes) even HT leads, resulting in a simpler, more reliable system requiring even less maintenance.

Because there is no distributor to adjust, the ignition timing cannot be adjusted by conventional means, and the advance and retard functions are carried out by the Electronic Control Unit (ECU).

The ignition system comprises the spark plugs, HT leads (where applicable), electronic ignition coil unit (or four separate coils), and the ECU together with its associated sensors and wiring.

The component layout varies from system to system, but the basic operation is the same for all models: the ECU supplies a voltage to the input stage of the ignition coil, which causes the primary windings in the coil to be energised. The supply voltage is periodically interrupted by the ECU and this results in the collapse of primary magnetic field, which then induces a much larger voltage in the secondary coil, called the HT voltage. This voltage is directed (via the HT leads, where fitted) to the spark plug in the cylinder currently on its ignition stroke. The spark plug electrodes form a gap small enough for the HT voltage to arc across, and the resulting spark ignites the fuel/air mixture in the cylinder. The timing of this sequence of events is critical, and is regulated solely by the ECU.

The ECU calculates and controls the ignition timing primarily according to engine speed, crankshaft position, camshaft position, and inlet air flow rate information, received from sensors mounted on and around the engine. Other parameters that affect ignition timing are throttle position, rate of opening, inlet air temperature, coolant temperature and engine knock, monitored via sensors mounted on the engine. Note that most of these sensors have a dual role, in that the information they provide is equally useful in determining the fuelling requirements as in deciding the optimum ignition or firing point – therefore, removal of some of the sensors mentioned below is described in Chapter 4A.

The ECU computes engine speed and crankshaft position from toothed impulse rotor attached to the engine flywheel, with an engine speed sensor whose inductive head runs just above rotor. As the crankshaft (and flywheel) rotate, the rotor 'teeth' pass the engine speed sensor, which transmits a pulse to the ECU every time a tooth passes it. At the top dead centre (TDC) position, there is one missing tooth in the rotor periphery, which results in a longer pause between signals from the sensor. The ECU recognises the absence of a pulse from the engine speed sensor at this point, and uses it to establish the TDC position for No 1 piston. The time interval between pulses, and the location of the missing pulse, allow the ECU to accurately determine the position of the crankshaft and its speed. The camshaft position sensor enhances this information by detecting whether a particular piston is on an inlet or an exhaust cycle.

Information on engine load is supplied to the ECU via the air mass meter (or via the inlet manifold pressure sensor, as applicable), and from the throttle position sensor. The engine load is determined by computation based on the quantity of air being drawn into the engine. Further engine load information is sent to the ECU from the knock sensor(s). These sensors are sensitive to vibration, and detect the knocking which occurs when the engine starts to 'pink' (pre-ignite). If pre-ignition occurs, the ECU retards the ignition timing of the cylinder that is pre-igniting in steps until the pre-ignition ceases. The ECU then advances the ignition timing of that cylinder in steps until it is restored to normal, or until pre-ignition occurs again.

Sensors monitoring coolant temperature, throttle position, roadspeed, and (where applicable) automatic transmission gear position and air conditioning system operation, provide additional input signals to the ECU on vehicle operating conditions. From all this constantly-changing data, the ECU selects, and if necessary modifies, a particular ignition advance setting from a map of ignition characteristics stored in its memory.

The ECU also uses the ignition timing to finely adjust the engine idle speed, in response to signals from the power steering switch or air conditioning switch (to prevent stalling), or if the alternator output voltage falls too low.

In the event of a fault in the system due to loss of a signal from one of the sensors, the ECU reverts to an emergency ('limp-home') program. This will allow the car to be driven, although engine operation and performance will be limited. A warning light on the instrument panel will illuminate if the fault is likely to cause an increase in harmful exhaust emissions.

It should be noted that comprehensive fault diagnosis of all the engine management systems described in this Chapter is only possible with dedicated electronic test equipment. In the event of a sensor failing or other fault occurring, a fault code will be stored in the ECU's fault log, which can only be extracted from the ECU using a dedicated fault code reader. A VW dealer will obviously have such a reader, but they are also available from other suppliers. It is unlikely to be cost-effective for the private owner to purchase a fault code reader, but a well-equipped local garage or auto-electrical specialist will have one. Once the fault has been identified, the removal/refitting sequences detailed in the following Sections will then allow the appropriate component(s) to be renewed as required.

Ignition coil(s)

The single coil fitted to AHW, AXP, AEH, AKL, AVU, BFQ, APK, AQY AZJ and AZH engine codes operates on the 'wasted spark' principle. The coil unit in fact contains two separate coils – one for cylinders 1 and 4, the other for cylinders 2 and 3. Each of the two coils produces an HT voltage at both outputs every time its primary coil voltage is interrupted – ie, cylinders 1 and 4 always 'fire' together, then 2 and 3 'fire' together. When this happens, one of the two cylinders concerned will be on the compression stroke (and will ignite the fuel/air mixture), while the other one is on the exhaust stroke – because the spark on the exhaust stroke has no effect, it is effectively wasted, hence the term 'wasted spark'.

On BCA, AZD, BCB, AUM and AUQ engine codes, each spark plug has its own dedicated 'plug-top' HT coil which fits directly onto the spark plug (no HT leads are therefore needed). Unlike the 'wasted spark' system, on these models a spark is only generated at each plug once every engine cycle.

2 Ignition system – testing

⚠️ **Warning: Extreme care must be taken when working on the system with the ignition switched on; it is possible to get a substantial electric shock from a vehicle's ignition system. Persons with cardiac pacemaker devices should keep well clear of the ignition circuits, components and test equipment. Always switch off the ignition before disconnecting or connecting any component and when using a multimeter to check resistances.**

3.1a On some models, the coil is mounted on the top/end of the engine ...

3.1b ... while on others, the coil is at the front, above the oil filter housing

3.4 Disconnect the LT wiring plug from the ignition coil

Engines with one coil per plug

1 If a fault appears in the engine management (fuel injection/ignition) system which is thought to ignition related, first ensure that the fault is not due to a poor electrical connection or poor maintenance; ie, check that the air cleaner filter element is clean, the spark plugs are in good condition and correctly gapped, that the engine breather hoses are clear and undamaged, referring to Chapter 1A for further information. Also check that the accelerator cable (where fitted) is correctly adjusted as described in Chapter 4A. If the engine is running very roughly, check the compression pressures as described in Chapter 2A or 2B (as applicable).

2 If these checks fail to reveal the cause of the problem the vehicle should be taken to a suitably-equipped VW dealer for testing. A diagnostic connector is incorporated in the engine management circuit into which a special electronic diagnostic tester can be plugged (see Chapter 4A). The tester will locate the fault quickly and simply, alleviating the need to test all the system components individually which is a time consuming operation that carries a high risk of damaging the ECU.

3 The only ignition system checks which can be carried out by the home mechanic are those described in Chapter 1A, relating to the spark plugs. If necessary, the system wiring and wiring connectors can be checked as described in Chapter 12 ensuring that the ECU wiring connector(s) have first been disconnected.

Engines with single DIS coil

4 Refer to the information given in paragraphs 1 to 3. The only other likely cause of ignition trouble is the HT leads, linking the HT coil to the spark plugs. Check the leads as follows. Never disconnect more than one HT lead at a time to avoid possible confusion.

5 Pull the first lead from the plug by gripping the end fitting, not the lead, otherwise the lead connection may be fractured. Check inside the end fitting for signs of corrosion, which will look like a white crusty powder. Push the end fitting back onto the spark plug, ensuring that it is a tight fit on the plug. If not, remove the lead again and use pliers to carefully crimp

the metal connector inside the end fitting until it fits securely on the end of the spark plug.

6 Using a clean rag, wipe the entire length of the lead to remove any built-up dirt and grease. Once the lead is clean, check for burns, cracks and other damage. Do not bend the lead excessively, nor pull the lead lengthwise – the conductor inside is quite fragile, and might break.

7 Disconnect the other end of the lead from the HT coil. Again, pull only on the end fitting. Check for corrosion and a tight fit in the same manner as the spark plug end.

8 If an ohmmeter is available, check for continuity between the HT lead terminals. If there is no continuity the lead is faulty and must be renewed (as a guide, the resistance of each lead should be in the region of 4 to 8 kΩ).

9 Refit the lead securely on completion of the check then check the remaining leads one at a time, in the same way. If there is any doubt about the condition of any HT leads, renew them as a complete set.

---

3 HT coil(s) – removal and refitting

Removal

Engines with single DIS coil

1 On all models, the ignition coil unit is mounted on the top or front of the engine (see illustrations).

3.6a Note their positions, then disconnect the HT leads ...

2 Make sure the ignition is switched off (take out the key).

3 Where applicable and/or necessary for access, remove the engine top cover(s). Removal details vary according to model, but the cover retaining nuts are concealed under circular covers, which are prised out of the main cover. Where plastic screws or turn-fasteners are used, these can be removed using a wide-bladed screwdriver. Remove the nuts or screws, and lift the cover from the engine, releasing any wiring or hoses attached.

4 Unplug the main wiring plug (LT connector) at the base (or side) of the ignition coil (see illustration).

5 The original HT leads should be marked from 1 to 4, corresponding to the cylinder/spark plug they serve (No 1 is at the timing belt end of the engine). Some leads are also marked from A to D, and corresponding markings are found on the ignition coil HT terminals – in this case, cylinder A corresponds to No 1, B to No 2, and so on. If there are no markings present, label the HT leads before disconnecting, and either paint a marking on the ignition coil terminals or make a sketch of the lead positions for use when reconnecting.

6 Disconnect the HT leads from the ignition coil terminals, then unscrew the three mounting bolts and remove the coil unit from the engine (see illustrations).

Engines with one coil per plug

7 Removal of the ignition coils is covered in the spark plug renewal procedure in Chapter 1A,

3.6b ... unscrew the three Allen bolts, and remove the coil

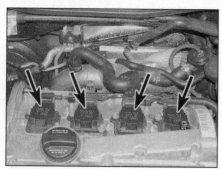

3.7 Ignition coils (arrowed) – engine codes BCA, AZD, BCB, AUM and AUQ

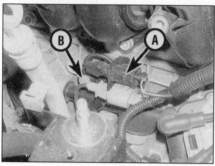

5.3 Knock sensor wiring plug (black, A) and mounting bolt (B) – 1.6 litre engine

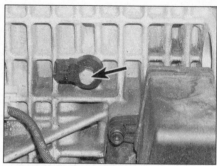

5.4 Knock sensor and mounting bolt – 1.4 litre engine (seen with engine removed)

since the coils must be removed for access to the plugs **(see illustration)**.

Refitting

8 Refitting is a reversal of the relevant removal procedure.

9 Securely tighten the coil mounting bolts. Use the marks noted before disconnecting when refitting the HT leads – if wished, spray a little water-dispersant (such as WD-40) onto each connector as it is refitted (this can also be used on the LT wiring connector).

4 Ignition timing – checking and adjusting

The ignition timing is under the control of the engine management system ECU and is not manually adjustable without access to dedicated electronic test equipment. A basic

setting cannot be quoted because the ignition timing is constantly being altered to control engine idle speed (see Section 1 for details).

The vehicle must be taken to a VW dealer if the timing requires checking or adjustment.

5 Knock sensor(s) – removal and refitting

Removal

1 The knock sensor(s) is/are located on the inlet manifold side of the cylinder block. **Note:** *Some models, have two knock sensors.*

2 Remove the engine top cover(s) to gain access to the sensor from above. If access from above is not sufficient, firmly apply the handbrake then jack up the front of the vehicle and support it on axle stands (see *Jacking and vehicle support*). Undo the

retaining screws and remove the engine undershield(s) so access to the knock sensor can be gained form underneath. Access to the knock sensor(s) is very awkward but it can only be improved by removing the inlet manifold (see Chapter 4A).

3 Disconnect the wiring connector from the sensor or trace the wiring back from the sensor and disconnect its wiring connector (as applicable) **(see illustration)**.

4 Unscrew the mounting bolt and remove the sensor from the cylinder block **(see illustration)**.

Refitting

5 Refitting is the reverse of removal. Ensure the mating surfaces of the sensor and cylinder block are clean and dry and ensure the mounting bolt is tightened to the specified torque to ensure correct operation.

Chapter 5 Part C:
Preheating system – diesel engines

Contents

General description 1   Glow plugs – testing, removal and refitting 2

Degrees of difficulty

Easy, suitable for novice with little experience	**Fairly easy,** suitable for beginner with some experience	**Fairly difficult,** suitable for competent DIY mechanic	**Difficult,** suitable for experienced DIY mechanic	**Very difficult,** suitable for expert DIY or professional

Specifications

Glow plugs
Type .... Bosch 0 250 202 022
Electrical resistance (typical – no value quoted by VW) .... 1.5 ohms
Current consumption (typical – no value quoted by VW) .... 8 amps (per plug)

Torque wrench setting	Nm	lbf ft
Glow plug to cylinder head	15	11

---

1 General information

To assist cold starting, diesel engined models are fitted with a preheating system, which comprises four glow plugs, a glow plug control unit (incorporated in the ECU), a facia-mounted warning light and the associated electrical wiring.

The glow plugs are miniature electric heating elements, encapsulated in a metal case with a probe at one end and electrical connection at the other. Each inlet tract has a glow plug threaded into it, which is positioned directly in line with the incoming spray of fuel. When the glow plug is energised, the fuel passing over it is heated, allowing its optimum combustion temperature to be achieved more readily in the combustion chamber.

The duration of the preheating period is governed by the ECU, which monitors the temperature of the engine via the coolant temperature sensor and alters the preheating time to suit the conditions.

A facia-mounted warning light informs the driver that preheating is taking place. The light extinguishes when sufficient preheating has taken place to allow the engine to be started, but power will still be supplied to the glow plugs for a further period until the engine is started. If no attempt is made to start the engine, the power supply to the glow plugs is switched off to prevent battery drain and glow plug burn-out. If the warning light flashes, or comes on during normal driving, this indicates a fault with the diesel engine management system, which should be investigated by a VW dealer as soon as possible.

After the engine has been started, the glow plugs continue to operate for a further period of time. This helps to improve fuel combustion whilst the engine is warming-up, resulting in quieter, smoother running and reduced exhaust emissions.

2 Glow plugs – testing, removal and refitting

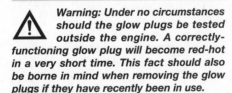

> **Warning: Under no circumstances should the glow plugs be tested outside the engine. A correctly-functioning glow plug will become red-hot in a very short time. This fact should also be borne in mind when removing the glow plugs if they have recently been in use.**

Testing

1 If the system malfunctions, testing is ultimately by substitution of known good units, but some preliminary checks may be made as described in the following paragraphs.

2 Before testing the system, check that the battery voltage is at least 11.5 volts, using a multimeter. Switch off the ignition.

3 Where necessary for access, remove the engine top cover(s). Removal details vary according to model, but the cover retaining nuts are concealed under circular covers, which are prised out of the main cover. Remove the nuts, and lift the cover from the engine, releasing any wiring or hoses attached.

4 Disconnect the wiring plug from the coolant temperature sender at the left-hand end of the engine (left as seen from the driver's seat) – refer to Chapter 3, Section 6, if necessary. Disconnecting the sender in this way simulates a cold engine, which is a requirement for the glow plug system to activate.

5 Disconnect the wiring connector from the most convenient glow plug, and connect a suitable multimeter between the wiring connector and a good earth.

6 Have an assistant switch on the ignition for approximately 20 seconds.

7 Battery voltage should be displayed – note that the voltage will drop to zero when the preheating period ends.

8 If no supply voltage can be detected at the glow plug, then either the glow plug relay (where applicable) or the supply wiring must be faulty. Also check that the glow plug fuse or fusible link (usually located on top of the battery) has not blown – if it has, this may indicate a serious wiring fault; consult a VW dealer for advice.

9 To locate a faulty glow plug, first disconnect the battery negative cable and position it away from the terminal.

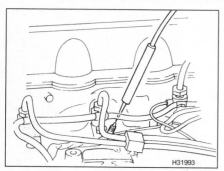

2.10 Testing the glow plugs using a multimeter

2.14a Glow plug wiring connector (arrowed) for No 1 injector

2.14b Removing the wiring loom/rail from the glow plugs

10 Disconnect the wiring plug from the glow plug terminal. Measure the electrical resistance between the glow plug terminal and the engine earth **(see illustration)**. At the time of writing, this information is not available – as a guide, a resistance of more than a few ohms indicates that the plug is defective.

11 If a suitable ammeter is available, connect it between the glow plug and its wiring connector, and measure the steady-state current consumption (ignore the initial current surge, which will be about 50% higher). As a guide, high current consumption (or no current draw at all) indicates a faulty glow plug.

12 As a final check, remove the glow plugs and inspect them visually, as described in the next sub-Section.

Removal

Note: *Refer to the Warning at the start of this Section before proceeding.*

13 Disconnect the battery negative (earth) lead (see *Disconnecting the battery*).

14 Disconnect the wiring connectors/rail from the glow plugs, where necessary label the wiring to make refitting easier **(see illustrations)**. On some models, the glow plug wiring is clipped to the injector leak-off hoses

– make sure that the clips are not lost as the wiring is pulled away.

15 Unscrew and remove the glow plug(s). On AGP, AQM, AGR, ALH, AHF and ASV engine codes, access to the plugs is not easy with the injector pipes in place – an extension handle and universal joint will probably be needed.

16 Inspect the glow plug stems for signs of damage. A badly burned or charred stem may be an indication of a faulty fuel injector.

Refitting

17 Refitting is a reversal of removal, but tighten the glow plug to the specified torque.

Chapter 6
Clutch

Contents

Clutch friction disc and pressure plate – removal, inspection and
   refitting 6
Clutch pedal – removal and refitting 3
General information 1

Hydraulic system – bleeding 2
Master cylinder – removal, overhaul and refitting 4
Release bearing and lever – removal, inspection and refitting 7
Slave cylinder – removal, overhaul and refitting 5

Degrees of difficulty

Easy, suitable for novice with little experience	**Fairly easy,** suitable for beginner with some experience	**Fairly difficult,** suitable for competent DIY mechanic 	**Difficult,** suitable for experienced DIY mechanic	**Very difficult,** suitable for expert DIY or professional

Specifications

General

Type	Single dry plate, diaphragm spring
Operation	Hydraulic with master and slave cylinders

Application:
1.4 and 1.6 litre petrol and non-turbo diesel models	Transmission 02K
1.8 and 2.0 litre petrol	Transmission 02J

Turbo diesel models:
Except AJM, AUY, ASZ and ARL engine codes	Transmission 02J
AJM, AUY, ASZ and ARL engine codes	Transmission 02M

Friction disc diameter:
02J transmission:
1.8 litre engine code AGN	215 mm
2.0 litre engine codes APK and AQY	215 mm
All other engines	219 mm

02K transmission:
1.4 litre engines	190 mm
1.6 litre engines	210 mm
Diesel engines	200 mm
02M transmission	Diameter not stated

Torque wrench settings

	Nm	lbf ft
Clutch master cylinder mounting nuts*	25	18
Clutch pedal mounting bracket nuts*	25	18
Clutch pedal pivot nut*	25	18
Clutch pressure plate-to-crankshaft bolts (02K transmission)*:		
Stage 1	60	44
Stage 2	Angle-tighten a further 90°	
Clutch pressure plate-to-flywheel bolts:		
02J transmission:		
Single-piece flywheel	20	15
Two-piece flywheel	13	10
02K transmission	20	15
02M transmission	22	16
Clutch release bearing/slave cylinder mounting bolts:		
02M transmission	12	9
Clutch slave cylinder mounting bolts:		
02J and 02K transmissions	25	18

Use new bolts/nuts.

1 General information

The clutch is of single dry plate type, incorporating a diaphragm spring pressure plate, and is hydraulically-operated.

02K transmission

Unlike a conventional clutch, the clutch pressure plate is bolted to the flange on the rear of the crankshaft. The flywheel, which is dish-shaped, is bolted to the pressure plate, with the friction disc held between them. This is, in effect, the reverse of the more conventional arrangement where the flywheel is bolted to the crankshaft flange and the clutch pressure plate is bolted to the flywheel.

The release mechanism consists of a metal disc, called the release plate, which is clamped in the centre of the pressure plate by a retaining spring clip. In the centre of the release plate is a boss into which the clutch pushrod is fitted. The pushrod passes through the centre of the transmission input shaft and is actuated by a release bearing located in the transmission end housing. A single finger lever presses on this bearing when the shaft to which it is splined is turned by operation of the clutch slave cylinder. In effect the clutch lever pushes the clutch pushrod, which in turn pushes the centre of the release plate inwards towards the crankshaft. The outer edge of the release plate presses on the pressure plate fingers forcing them back towards the engine and removing the pressure plate friction face from the friction disc, thus disconnecting the drive. When the clutch pedal is released, the pressure plate clamps the friction disc firmly against the flywheel, restoring the drive.

As the linings wear on the friction disc, the quantity of hydraulic fluid in the circuit automatically compensates for wear every time the clutch pedal is operated. No adjustment of the clutch release system is therefore necessary.

02J and 02M transmissions

The pressure plate is bolted to the rear face of the flywheel, and the friction disc is located between the pressure plate and the flywheel friction surface. The friction disc hub is splined to the transmission input shaft and is free to slide along the splines. Friction lining material is riveted to each side of the disc, and the disc hub incorporates cushioning springs to absorb transmission shocks and ensure a smooth take-up of drive.

On 02J transmissions, when the clutch pedal is depressed, the slave cylinder pushrod moves the release lever forwards. On 02M transmissions, the slave cylinder is part of the release bearing and comes as a complete assembly (see illustration 7.29). The release bearing is forced onto the pressure plate diaphragm spring fingers. As

2.3 Bleed screw (arrowed) – 02M transmission

the centre of the diaphragm spring is pushed in, the outer part of the spring moves out and releases the pressure plate from the friction disc. Drive then ceases to be transmitted to the transmission.

When the clutch pedal is released, the diaphragm spring forces the pressure plate into contact with the linings on the friction disc, and at the same time pushes the disc slightly forward along the input shaft splines into engagement with the flywheel. The friction disc is now firmly sandwiched between the pressure plate and flywheel. This causes drive to be taken up.

As the linings wear on the friction disc, the pressure plate rest position moves closer to the flywheel resulting in the 'rest' position of the diaphragm spring fingers being raised. The hydraulic system requires no adjustment since the quantity of hydraulic fluid in the circuit automatically compensates for wear every time the clutch pedal is operated.

2 Hydraulic system – bleeding

⚠️ **Warning:** Hydraulic fluid is poisonous; thoroughly wash off spills from bare skin without delay. Seek immediate medical advice if any fluid is swallowed or gets into the eyes. Certain types of hydraulic fluid are inflammable and may ignite when brought into contact with hot components. Hydraulic fluid is also an effective paint

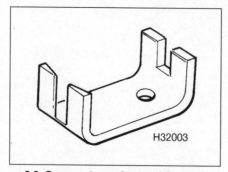

3.2 Over-centre spring retaining tool

stripper. If spillage occurs onto painted bodywork or fittings, it should be washed off immediately, using copious quantities of cold water. It is also hygroscopic (ie, it can absorb moisture from the air) which then renders it useless. Old fluid may have suffered contamination, and should never be re-used.

Note: Suitable pressure-bleeding equipment will be required for this operation.

1 If any part of the hydraulic system is dismantled, or if air has accidentally entered the system, the system will need to be bled. The presence of air is characterised by the pedal having a spongy feel and it results in difficulty in changing gear.

2 The design of the clutch hydraulic system does not allow bleeding to be carried out using the conventional method of pumping the clutch pedal. In order to remove all air present in the system, it is necessary to use pressure bleeding equipment. This is available from auto accessory shops at relatively low cost.

3 The pressure bleeding equipment should be connected to the brake/clutch hydraulic fluid reservoir in accordance with the manufacturer's instructions. The system is bled through the bleed screw of the clutch slave cylinder, which is located at the top of the transmission housing (see illustration). Access is best achieved by jacking up the front of the vehicle and supporting it on axle stands (see Jacking and vehicle support). Where necessary, remove the undershield for access to the transmission.

4 Bleed the system until the fluid being ejected is free from air bubbles. Close the bleed screw, then disconnect and remove the bleeding equipment.

5 Check the operation of the clutch to see that it is satisfactory. If air still remains in the system, repeat the bleeding operation.

6 Discard any fluid which is bled from the system, even if it looks clean. Hydraulic fluid absorbs water and its re-use can cause internal corrosion of the master and slave cylinders, leading to excessive wear and failure of the seals.

3 Clutch pedal – removal and refitting

Removal

1 Remove the driver's side lower facia trim panel, with reference to Chapter 11, Section 28.

2 Make up a tool similar to that shown, press it into position over the spring to hold the clutch pedal over-centre spring in the compressed position (see illustration).

3 Fully depress the clutch pedal until the tool can be fitted to the over-centre spring to retain it in the compressed position.

4 Release the clutch pedal, and lift out the tool, complete with the over-centre spring.

5 Squeeze together the tabs of the pushrod retaining clip, and separate the pedal from the pushrod.

6 Unscrew the nut from the pedal pivot bolt.

7 Pull out the pivot bolt until the pedal can be removed from the bracket assembly into the driver's footwell.

Refitting

8 Refitting is a reversal of removal, bearing in mind the following points:

a) *Before commencing refitting, make sure that the pedal retaining clip is fitted to the master cylinder pushrod.*

b) *Use a new pedal pivot bolt nut, and tighten the nut to the specified torque.*

c) *Make sure that the pedal-to-master cylinder pushrod retaining clip is fitted to the master cylinder pushrod before attempting to reconnect the pushrod to the pedal.*

d) *Push the pedal onto the pushrod to engage the retaining clip. Make sure that the clip is securely engaged.*

e) *On completion, check the brake/clutch fluid level, and top-up if necessary.*

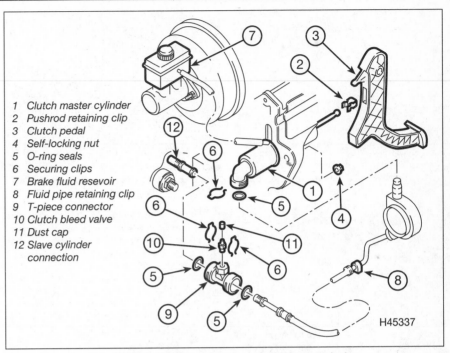

1 Clutch master cylinder
2 Pushrod retaining clip
3 Clutch pedal
4 Self-locking nut
5 O-ring seals
6 Securing clips
7 Brake fluid resevoir
8 Fluid pipe retaining clip
9 T-piece connector
10 Clutch bleed valve
11 Dust cap
12 Slave cylinder connection

4.1 Clutch hydraulic system layout – 02M transmission

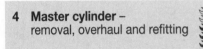

4 Master cylinder –
removal, overhaul and refitting

Note: *Refer to the warning at the beginning of Section 2 regarding the hazards of working with hydraulic fluid.*

Removal

1 The clutch master cylinder is located inside the car on the clutch and brake pedal mounting bracket. Hydraulic fluid for the unit is supplied from the brake master cylinder reservoir **(see illustration)**.

2 Before proceeding, place cloth rags on the carpet inside the car to prevent damage from spilt hydraulic fluid.

3 Working in the engine compartment, clamp the hydraulic fluid hose leading from the brake fluid reservoir to the clutch master cylinder using a brake hose clamp.

4 Similarly, clamp the rubber section of the hydraulic hose leading from the master cylinder to the slave cylinder using a brake hose clamp, to prevent loss of hydraulic fluid.

5 Position a suitable container, or a wad of clean cloth, beneath the master cylinder to catch escaping hydraulic fluid.

6 Pull the hydraulic supply hose from the clutch master cylinder on the bulkhead.

7 Pull the fluid outlet hose retaining clip from the union on the master cylinder, then pull the pipe from the union. Again, be prepared for fluid spillage.

8 Remove the driver's side lower facia trim panel, with reference to Chapter 11, Section 28.

9 Where fitted, unscrew the securing bolts, and remove the plate connecting the clutch

pedal mounting bracket to the brake pedal mounting bracket.

10 Unscrew the three nuts securing the clutch pedal mounting bracket to the bulkhead, then release the mounting bracket from the bulkhead **(see illustration)**.

11 The pedal must now be disconnected from the master cylinder pushrod by squeezing together the tabs of the retaining clip, and moving the pushrod away from the pedal.

12 Twist the clutch pedal stop anti-clockwise, and remove it from the bulkhead.

13 Push the master cylinder downwards until it covers the pedal stop mounting. Make sure that the upper end of the master cylinder flange is not covered by the pedal over-centre spring mounting.

14 Tilt the pushrod end of the master cylinder downwards, and manipulate the master cylinder out from the pedal mounting bracket. Lift the master cylinder out from the footwell, taking care to minimise fluid spillage.

Overhaul

15 No spare parts are available from VW for the master cylinder. If the master cylinder is faulty or worn, the complete assembly must be renewed.

Refitting

16 Refitting is a reversal of removal, bearing in mind the following points:

a) *Ensure that the pedal-to-master cylinder pushrod retaining clip is fitted to the master cylinder pushrod before attempting to reconnect the pushrod to the pedal.*

d) *Push the pedal onto the pushrod to engage the retaining clip. Make sure that the clip is securely engaged.*

c) *When refitting the pedal stop, ensure that the stop is positioned with the lug nearest the master cylinder **(see illustration)**.*

d) *On completion, bleed the clutch hydraulic system as described in Section 2.*

4.10 Undo the pedal bracket nuts (arrowed)

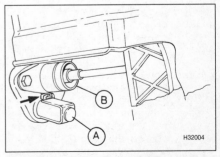

4.16 When refitting the pedal stop, ensure that the stop (A) is positioned with the lug (arrowed) nearest the master cylinder (B)

5.11 Unscrew the cylinder mounting bolts (arrowed)

5.13 Ensure the locating pins are aligned (arrowed)

5 Slave cylinder – removal, overhaul and refitting

Note: *Refer to the warning at the beginning of Section 2 regarding the hazards of working with hydraulic fluid.*

02J transmission

Removal

1 The slave cylinder is located on the top of the transmission casing. Access is gained from the engine compartment.
2 Disconnect the gear selector cable from the gear selector lever, as described in Chapter 7A, Section 3.
3 Place a wad of clean rag beneath the fluid line connection on the slave cylinder to catch escaping fluid.
4 Pull the fluid pipe retaining clip from the union on the slave cylinder, then pull the pipe from the union. Release the fluid line from the bracket, and position it clear of the slave cylinder. Be prepared for fluid spillage.
5 Unscrew the two bolts securing the slave cylinder to the transmission casing, and withdraw the slave cylinder from the transmission.

Overhaul

6 No spare parts are available from VW for the slave cylinder. If the slave cylinder is faulty or worn, the complete assembly must be renewed.

Refitting

7 Refitting is a reversal of removal, bearing in mind the following points:
a) *Tighten the slave cylinder securing bolts to the specified torque.*
b) *Reconnect the gear selector cable to the gear selector lever as described in Chapter 7A.*
c) *On completion, bleed the clutch hydraulic system as described in Section 2.*

02K transmission

Removal

8 The slave cylinder is located at the front of the transmission, towards the top of the casing. Access is gained from the engine compartment.
9 Place a suitable container beneath the fluid pipe connection on the slave cylinder to catch escaping fluid.
10 Pull the fluid pipe retaining clip from the union on the slave cylinder, then pull the pipe from the union. Release the fluid line from the bracket, and position it clear of the slave cylinder. Be prepared for fluid spillage.
11 Unscrew the two bolts securing the slave cylinder to the transmission casing, noting that one of the bolts also secures the hydraulic fluid line bracket, and withdraw the slave cylinder from the transmission **(see illustration)**.

Overhaul

12 No spare parts are available from VW for

the slave cylinder. If the slave cylinder is faulty or worn, the complete assembly must be renewed.

Refitting

13 Refitting is a reversal of removal, bearing in mind the following points:
a) *Ensure that the fluid line bracket is in place on the right-hand slave cylinder securing bolt.*
b) *Engage the locating pins on the cylinder pushrod with the corresponding holes in the clutch actuating lever (see illustration).*
c) *Tighten the slave cylinder securing bolts to the specified torque.*
d) *On completion, bleed the clutch hydraulic system as described in Section 2.*

02M transmission

Removal

14 The slave cylinder is part of the release bearing unit and is located inside the transmission bellhousing. For the removal and refitting procedure of the clutch release bearing/slave cylinder, see Section 7 in this Chapter.

6 Clutch friction disc and pressure plate – removal, inspection and refitting

Warning: Dust created by clutch wear and deposited on the clutch components may contain asbestos, which is a health hazard. DO NOT blow it out with compressed air or inhale any of it. DO NOT use petrol or petroleum-based solvents to clean off the dust. Brake system cleaner or methylated spirit should be used to flush the dust into a suitable receptacle. After the clutch components are wiped clean with clean rags, dispose of the contaminated rags and cleaner in a sealed container.

02K transmission

Note: *New clutch pressure plate securing bolts and new flywheel securing bolts will be required on refitting.*

Removal

1 Remove the transmission as described in Chapter 7A.
2 Slacken the flywheel bolts progressively, then lift the flywheel away from the clutch pressure plate and recover the friction disc **(see illustrations)**.
3 Prise out the spring clip and lift out the clutch release plate **(see illustrations)**.
4 Lock the pressure plate in position using a suitable tool similar to that shown **(see illustration)**.
5 Progressively slacken the pressure plate bolts until they can be removed by hand. Recover the intermediate plate **(see illustration)**.

6.2a Slacken the flywheel bolts . . .

6.2b . . . then lift off the flywheel . . .

6.2c ... and recover the friction disc –
02K transmission

6.3a Prise out the spring clip . . .

6.3b ... and lift out the clutch release
plate – 02K transmission

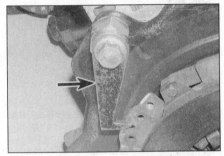

6.4 Lock the pressure plate in position
using a suitable tool (arrowed) –
02K transmission

6.5 Recover the intermediate plate . . .

6.6 ... then lift the pressure plate away
from the crankshaft – 02K transmission

6 Lift the pressure plate away from the crankshaft flange **(see illustration)**. Recover the engine-to-transmission plate if it is loose.

Inspection

7 Clean the pressure plate, disc and flywheel. Do not inhale the dust, as it may contain asbestos which is dangerous to health.

8 Examine the fingers of the diaphragm spring for wear or scoring. If the depth of wear exceeds half the thickness of the fingers, a new pressure plate assembly must be fitted.

9 Examine the pressure plate for scoring, cracking and discoloration. Light scoring is acceptable, but if excessive, a new pressure plate assembly must be fitted.

10 Examine the friction disc linings for wear and cracking, and for contamination with oil or grease. The linings are worn excessively if they are worn down to, or near, the rivets. Check the disc hub and splines for wear, by

temporarily fitting it on the transmission input shaft. Renew the friction disc as necessary.

11 Examine the flywheel friction surface for scoring, cracking and discoloration (caused by overheating). If excessive, it may be possible to have the flywheel machined by an engineering works, otherwise it should be renewed.

12 Check the clutch release plate for damage and distortion, and renew if necessary.

13 Ensure that all parts are clean, and free of oil or grease, before reassembling. Apply just a small amount of high-melting-point grease to the splines of the friction disc hub. Note that new pressure plates and clutch covers may be coated with protective grease. It is only permissible to clean the grease away from the friction disc lining contact area. Removal of the grease from other areas will shorten the service life of the clutch.

Refitting

14 If a new pressure plate is to be fitted, first wipe the protective grease from the friction surface only. Ensure that the engine-to-transmission plate is in place, then offer the pressure plate up to the crankshaft flange together with the intermediate plate. Fit new retaining bolts. Note that the bolt holes are offset, so the pressure plate can only be fitted in one position. Coat the bolt threads with a suitable locking compound, if they are not supplied already coated **(see illustrations)**.

15 Hold the pressure plate still, using the method described during removal, and tighten the retaining bolts progressively to the specified torque **(see illustration)**.

16 Fit the release plate and secure it in position with the spring clip. Apply a smear of high temperature grease to the centre of the release plate.

6.14a Make sure that the intermediate
plate is in place . . .

6.14b ... then fit new pressure plate
securing bolts – 02K transmission

6.15 Hold the pressure plate stationary
using the tool used during removal
(arrowed) – 02K transmission

6.18a Offer up the flywheel . . .

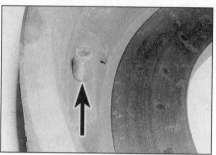

6.18b . . . making sure that the locating dowels (arrowed) engage with the pressure plate – 02K transmission

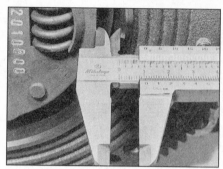

6.19 Centre the friction plate using vernier calipers . . .

17 Smear high temperature grease on the splines at the centre of the friction disc – take care to avoid contaminating the friction surfaces.

18 Hold the friction disc up to the pressure plate, with the spring-loaded boss facing outwards (away from the crankshaft), then offer up the flywheel, ensuring that the locating dowels engage with the recesses on the edge of the pressure plate **(see illustrations)**. Fit a new set of flywheel retaining bolts – hand-tighten them only at this stage.

19 Centre the friction disc using vernier calipers; ensure that there is a uniform gap between outer edge of the friction disc and the inner edge of the flywheel, around the whole circumference **(see illustration)**.

20 Tighten the flywheel retaining bolts diagonally and progressively to the specified torque **(see illustration)**. Recheck the friction disc centralisation.

21 Refit the transmission as described in Chapter 7A.

02J and 02M transmissions

Removal

22 Access to the clutch is obtained by removing the transmission as described in Chapter 7A.

23 Mark the clutch pressure plate and flywheel in relation to each other.

24 Hold the flywheel stationary, then unscrew the clutch pressure plate bolts progressively in diagonal sequence using an Allen key **(see illustration)**. With the bolts unscrewed two or three turns, check that the pressure plate is not binding on the dowel pins. If necessary, use a screwdriver to release the pressure plate.

25 Remove all the bolts, then lift the clutch

pressure plate and friction disc from the flywheel **(see illustration)**.

Inspection

26 Proceed as described in paragraphs 7 to 13, ignoring the reference to the clutch release plate.

Refitting

27 Commence reassembly by locating the friction disc on the flywheel, with the raised, torsion spring side of the hub facing outwards. If necessary, the centralising tool (see paragraph 30) may be used to hold the disc on the flywheel at this stage **(see illustration)**.

28 Locate the clutch pressure plate on the disc, and fit it onto the location dowels **(see illustration)**. If refitting the original pressure plate, make sure that the previously-made marks are aligned.

29 Insert the bolts finger-tight to hold the pressure plate in position.

30 The friction disc must now be centralised, to ensure correct alignment of the transmission input shaft with the spigot bearing in the crankshaft. To do this, a proprietary tool may be used, or alternatively, use a wooden mandrel made to fit inside the friction disc and flywheel spigot bearing. Insert the tool through the friction disc into the spigot bearing, and make sure that it is central.

31 Tighten the pressure plate bolts progressively and in diagonal sequence, until the specified torque setting is achieved, then remove the centralising tool **(see illustration)**.

6.20 . . . then tighten the flywheel retaining bolts to the specified torque – 02K transmission

6.24 Unscrew the pressure plate bolts . . .

6.25 . . . then lift the pressure plate and friction disc away from the flywheel – 02J and 02M transmissions

6.27 Locating the friction disc on the flywheel – 02J and 02M transmissions

6.28 Locating the clutch pressure plate over the friction disc – 02J and 02M transmissions

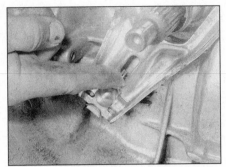

6.31 Tightening the clutch pressure plate bolts – 02J and 02M transmissions

7.2 Push the spring clip to release the arm from the ball-stud – 02J transmission

7.3 Release lever and bearing removed from transmission – 02J transmission

32 Check the release bearing in the transmission bellhousing for smooth operation, and if necessary renew it with reference to Section 7.

33 Refit the transmission with reference to Chapter 7A.

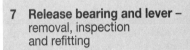

7 Release bearing and lever – removal, inspection and refitting

02J transmission

Removal

1 Remove the transmission as described in Chapter 7A.

2 Using a screwdriver, prise the release lever from the ball-stud on the transmission housing. If this proves difficult, push the

retaining spring from the release lever first **(see illustration)**. Where applicable, remove the plastic pad from the stud.

3 Slide the release bearing, together with the lever, from the guide sleeve, and withdraw it over the transmission input shaft **(see illustration)**.

4 Separate the release bearing from the lever **(see illustrations)**.

Inspection

5 Spin the release bearing by hand, and check it for smooth running. Any tendency to seize or run rough will necessitate renewal of the bearing. If the bearing is to be re-used, wipe it clean with a dry cloth; the bearing should not be washed in a liquid solvent, as this will remove the internal grease.

6 Clean the release lever, ball-stud and guide sleeve.

Refitting

7 Lubricate the ball-stud in the transmission bellhousing with molybdenum sulphide-based grease **(see illustration)**. Also smear a little grease on the release bearing surface which contacts the diaphragm spring fingers in the clutch cover.

8 Push the release bearing into position on the release lever.

9 Fit the retaining spring onto the release lever, then press the release lever onto the ball-stud until the retaining spring holds it in position **(see illustrations)**.

10 Refit the transmission as described in Chapter 7A.

02K transmission

Removal

11 If the transmission has not been removed,

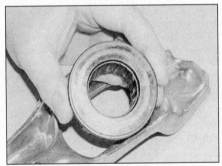

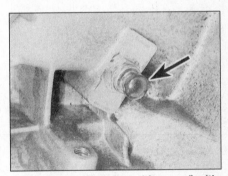

7.4a Use a screwdriver to depress the retaining tags . . .

7.4b . . . then remove the release bearing from the arm – 02J transmission

7.7 Lubricate the ball-stud (arrowed) with a little grease – 02J transmission

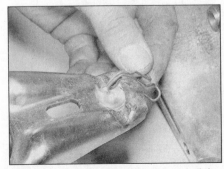

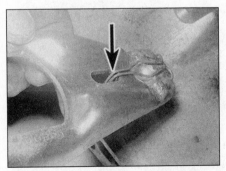

7.9a Locate the spring over the end of the release lever . . .

7.9b . . . and press the spring into the hole . . .

7.9c . . . then press the release lever onto the ball-stud until the spring clip holds it in position – 02J transmission

7.15a **Using a hammer and cold chisel . . .**

7.15b **. . . lever the transmission end cap from the transmission housing – 02K transmission**

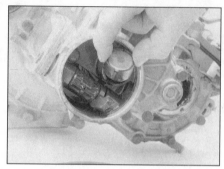

7.16 **Withdrawing the clutch release bearing – 02K transmission**

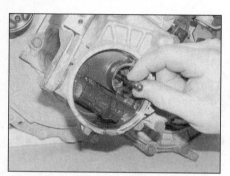

7.17 **Withdrawing the clutch release pushrod – 02K transmission**

7.23 **Driving a new transmission end cap into position – 02K transmission**

apply the handbrake then jack up the front of the vehicle and support securely on axle stands (see *Jacking and vehicle support*). Remove the left-hand roadwheel.

12 Unscrew the securing screws and/or release the clips, and remove the lower and left-hand engine/transmission undershields for access to the transmission end cap.

13 Unbolt the clutch slave cylinder as described in Section 5, and move it clear of the clutch release lever, taking care not to strain the hydraulic fluid line. Do not depress the clutch pedal whilst the slave cylinder is removed, and use a cable-tie or a strong

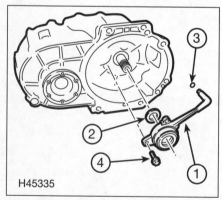

H45335

7.29 **Release bearing/slave cylinder unit – 02M transmission**

1 *Release*
   bearing/slave
   cylinder unit
2 *Input shaft seal*
3 *O-ring seal*
4 *Bolt*
5 *Transmission*
   housing

rubber band to retain the piston in the slave cylinder.

14 Place a suitable container beneath the end of the transmission to catch any oil which may escape when the end cap is removed.

15 Using a hammer and cold chisel, or a similar tool, lever the transmission end cap from its location in the end of the transmission housing. Discard the end cap – a new one must be used on refitting **(see illustrations)**.

16 Pivot the clutch release lever back sufficiently to allow the release bearing to be withdrawn from the transmission housing **(see illustration)**.

17 If desired, the clutch release pushrod can now be withdrawn through the input shaft **(see illustration)**.

Inspection

18 Spin the release bearing by hand, and check it for smooth running. Any tendency to seize or run rough will necessitate renewal of the bearing. If the bearing is to be re-used, wipe it clean with a dry cloth; the bearing should not be washed in a liquid solvent, as this will remove the internal grease.

19 Examine the clutch release pushrod for wear and damage, and wipe the pushrod clean using a clean, lint-free cloth.

Refitting

20 Where applicable, slide the clutch release pushrod back into position in the input shaft.

21 Slide the clutch release bearing into position in the housing, making sure that it is fitted the correct way round.

22 Move the release lever back into position.

23 Fit a new transmission end cap, and drive it into position using a block of wood **(see illustration)**. Ensure that the cap is kept square as it is driven into position.

24 Refit the clutch slave cylinder, with reference to Section 5 if necessary.

25 Refit the roadwheel and lower the vehicle to the ground.

26 Before refitting the undershields, check and if necessary top-up the transmission oil level as described in Chapter 1A or 1B.

02M transmission

Note: *The release bearing and slave cylinder are one unit which cannot be renewed separately.*

Removal

27 Remove the transmission as described in Chapter 7A.

28 Undo the three retaining bolts from the release bearing/slave cylinder unit.

29 Withdraw the release bearing/slave cylinder unit from the transmission housing, and remove it over the input shaft **(see illustration)**.

30 Remove the O-ring and input shaft seal and discard, new ones will be required for refitting.

Inspection

31 Spin the release bearing by hand, and check it for smooth running. Any tendency to seize or run rough will necessitate renewal of the bearing. If the bearing is to be re-used, wipe it clean with a dry cloth; the bearing should not be washed in a liquid solvent, as this will remove the internal grease.

32 Check for fluid leaks around the slave cylinder and hose connection.

Refitting

33 Lubricate slave cylinder hose connection o-ring with some clean brake fluid for refitting.

34 Press the new input shaft seal into position, making sure it sits squarely in the housing.

35 Refit the release bearing/slave cylinder and tighten the retaining bolts to the specified torque setting.

36 Refit the transmission as described in Chapter 7A.

Chapter 7 Part A:
Manual transmission

Contents

Gearchange linkage (02J and 02M transmissions) – adjustment . . . 2
General information 1
Manual transmission – removal and refitting 3
Manual transmission overhaul – general information 4
Reversing light switch – testing, removal and refitting 5
Roadspeed sensor/speedometer drive – removal and refitting 6

Degrees of difficulty

Easy, suitable for novice with little experience		Fairly easy, suitable for beginner with some experience		Fairly difficult, suitable for competent DIY mechanic		Difficult, suitable for experienced DIY mechanic		Very difficult, suitable for expert DIY or professional	

Specifications

General

Type	Transversely-mounted, front-wheel-drive layout with integral transaxle differential/final drive. 5 or 6 forward speeds, 1 reverse.

Application:
1.4 and 1.6 litre petrol and non-turbo diesel models	Transmission 02K
1.8 and 2.0 litre petrol	Transmission 02J
Turbo diesel models:	
Except AJM, AUY, ASZ and ARL engine codes	Transmission 02J
AJM, AUY, ASZ and ARL engine codes	Transmission 02M

Torque wrench settings	Nm	lbf ft
Gearchange rod to selector rod (02K transmission)	20	15
Release bearing guide to transmission	20	15
Reversing light switch	20	15
Transmission to engine:		
M12 bolts	80	59
M10 bolts:		
Except 02K transmission	40	30
02K transmission	25	18
M7 bolts	10	7

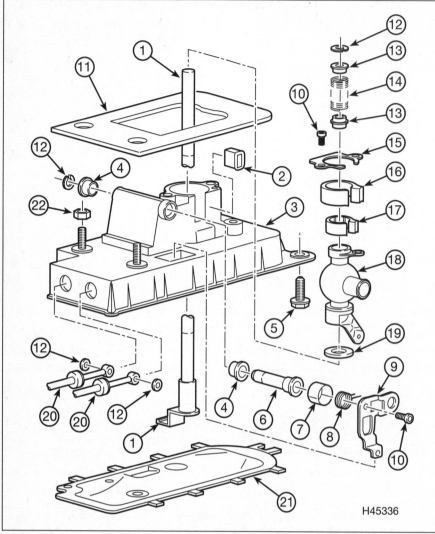

1.3 Gear linkage layout

1 Selector lever	8 Spring	16 Damper collar
2 Damper	9 Selector lever gate	17 Bearing
3 Selector lever	10 Retaining screw	18 Selector lever ball/
housing	11 Housing seal	guide
4 Bush – bearing	12 Securing clip	19 Damping washer
5 Bolt	13 Bush	20 Gear selector cable
6 Fulcrum pin	14 Spring	21 Baseplate
7 Bush – guide	15 Cover plate	22 Securing nut

2.2 Push the collar down and lock in position

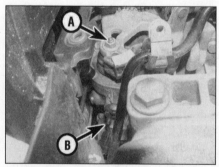

2.3 Press down on (A), then push in locking pin (B)

1 General information

The manual transmission is bolted directly to the left-hand end of the engine. This layout has the advantage of providing the shortest possible drive path to the front wheels, as well as locating the transmission in the airflow through engine bay, optimising cooling. The unit is cased in aluminium alloy.

Drive from the crankshaft is transmitted via the clutch to the gearbox input shaft, which is splined to accept the clutch friction disc.

All forward gears are fitted with synchromesh. The floor-mounted gear lever is connected to the gearbox either by a selector rod, or selector and shift cables, depending on the transmission type **(see illustration)**. This in turn actuates selector forks inside the gearbox which are slotted onto the synchromesh sleeves. The sleeves, which are locked to the gearbox shafts but can slide axially by means of splined hubs, press baulk rings into contact with the respective gear/pinion. The coned surfaces between the baulk rings and the pinion/gear act as a friction clutch, that progressively matches the speed of the synchromesh sleeve (and hence the gearbox shaft) with that of the gear/pinion. This allows gear changes to be carried out smoothly.

Drive is transmitted to the differential crownwheel, which rotates the differential case and planetary gears, thus driving the sun gears and driveshafts. The rotation of the differential planetary gears on their shaft allows the inner roadwheel to rotate at a slower speed than the outer roadwheel during cornering.

2 Gearchange linkage (02J and 02M transmissions) – adjustment

Note: *To accurately adjust the operation of the gear selector rod and shift cables on 02K transmissions, precisely machined jigs are required to set the gearchange lever in a reference position. It is recommended, therefore, that this operation be entrusted to a VW dealer.*

1 Remove the air cleaner assembly as described in Section 2 of Chapter 4A (petrol engines) or 4B (diesel engines).
2 With the gearchange set in the neutral position, push the two locking collars (one on each cable) forwards to compress the springs, turn them clockwise (looking from the driver's seat) to lock into position **(see illustration)**.
3 Press down on the selector shaft in the top of the transmission and push the locking pin into the transmission until it engages and the selector shaft cannot move **(see illustration)**.
Note: *On models with transmissions from*

H45336

2.4 Locking the gear lever in position using a drill bit (arrowed)

date 19/05/03, the locking pin has a bend of 90° at the end of the rod. This locking pin must also be turned clockwise while being pushed into the transmission until it engages.

4 Working inside the vehicle, carefully unclip the gear lever gaiter from the centre console. Still in the neutral position, move the gear lever as far to the left as possible and insert the locking pin (or drill bit – take care of sharp edges if using drill bit) through the hole in the base of the gear lever and into the hole in the housing **(see illustration)**.

5 Working back in the engine bay, turn the two locking collars on the cables anti-clockwise so that the springs will release them back into position and lock the cables **(see illustration)**.

6 With the cable adjustment set, the locking pin can now be pulled back out of the transmission into its original position. **Note:** On models with transmissions from date 19/05/03,

the locking pin must also be turned anti-clockwise while being pulled out, until it disengages.

7 Inside the vehicle, remove the locking pin from the gear lever, then check the operation of the selector mechanism. When the gear lever is at rest in neutral, it should be central ready to select 3rd or 4th. The gear lever gaiter can now be refitted to the centre console.

8 Refit the air cleaner assembly with reference to the relevant Chapter 4A or 4B.

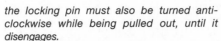

3 Manual transmission – removal and refitting

Removal

1 Select a solid, level surface to park the vehicle upon. Give yourself enough space to move around it easily. Apply the handbrake and chock the rear wheels.

2 Raise the front of the vehicle and support it securely on axle stands (see Jacking and vehicle support). Where fitted, remove the engine/transmission undertray centre and right-hand sections. Position a suitable container beneath the transmission, then unscrew the drain plug and drain the transmission oil.

3 Undo the retaining nuts/screws, and remove the engine cover(s).

4 Disconnect the battery negative (earth) lead. **Note:** Before disconnecting the battery,

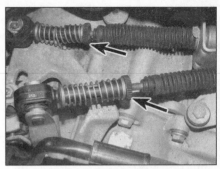

2.5 Release the two locking collars (arrowed) back into position

refer to 'Disconnecting the battery' in the Reference section at the rear of this manual.

5 Refer to the relevant part of Chapter 4 and remove the air cleaner housing and intake hose.

6 Separate the oxygen sensor connector, and slide it out of the retaining bracket **(see illustration)**. Disconnect the reversing light switch **(see illustration 5.7)**.

02K transmission

7 Disconnect the front gear selector rod from the selector lever.

8 Remove the circlip and withdraw the intermediate lever and selector rod **(see illustrations)**.

9 Using a flat-bladed screwdriver, lever off both coupling rods, and the left-hand selector rod **(see illustrations)**.

10 Unbolt the selector bracket from the gearbox casing, and withdraw it complete with the coupling rods **(see illustration)**.

3.6 Disconnect the oxygen sensor

3.8a Remove the circlip . . .

3.8b . . . and the intermediate lever

3.9a Lever off the coupling rods . . .

3.9b . . . and the left-hand selector rod

3.10 Withdraw the bracket complete with the selector rods

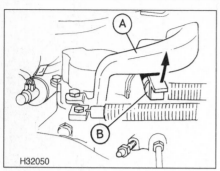

3.12 Gate selector cable (B) and balance weight (A)

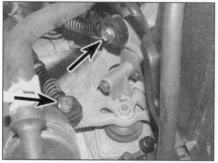

3.15 Release the two securing clips (arrowed)

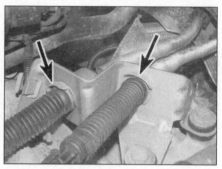

3.16 Withdraw the two securing clips (arrowed)

11 Undo the two retaining bolts and, with reference to Chapter 6, withdraw the clutch slave cylinder without disconnecting the hydraulic pipe.

02J transmission

12 Note the location of the gear selector cable ends and disconnect them, along with the balance weight. Note that the gate selector cable is disconnected by lifting the retaining lug up **(see illustration)**.
13 Unscrew the two selector cable support bracket retaining bolts, and lift the cables clear of the transmission.
14 Undo the two retaining bolts and, with reference to Chapter 6, withdraw the clutch slave cylinder without disconnecting the hydraulic pipe.

02M transmission

15 Release the locking clips **(see illus-** tration), and disconnect the gear selector cables from the selector lever.
16 Remove the retaining clips and withdraw the selector cables from the mounting bracket **(see illustration)**.

All models

17 With reference to Chapter 5A, remove the starter motor.
18 Note the location of the earth cable on the transmission-to-engine mounting bolt, then unscrew and remove the bolt.
19 Unscrew and remove the upper transmission-to-engine mounting bolts.
20 Using a suitable hoist, support the weight of the engine.
21 Unbolt the power steering retaining bracket **(see illustration)**.
22 On models with 02K and 02M transmissions, unscrew the five retaining bolts and withdraw the left-hand mounting bracket

from the transmission **(see illustration)**. On models with 02J transmissions, unscrew the bolts retaining the left-hand transmission mounting support bracket, and the two transmission mounting bolts **(see illustration)**.
23 Disconnect the electronic speedometer sender from the rear of the gearbox **(see illustration 6.5)**.
24 Remove the right-hand constant velocity joint protective cover from the engine, if fitted.
25 Using a multi-spline key, unscrew and remove the bolts securing the driveshafts to the transmission output flanges. Tie the right-hand driveshaft to one side. Tie the left-hand driveshaft to the anti-roll bar, so that the shaft is as high as possible. Alternatively, completely remove the left-hand driveshaft as described in Chapter 8.
26 If fitted, unscrew the retaining bolt and withdraw the small flywheel cover plate by the right-hand output shaft flange **(see illustration)**.
27 With reference to Chapter 4C or 4D, loosen the clamp securing the exhaust intermediate pipe to the rear section. This will allow the engine to be move forwards and backwards during the transmission removal and alignment procedures. Consequently, there is no need to separate the exhaust pipe sections.
28 Unscrew the four retaining bolts, and remove the lower transmission support bracket **(see illustration)**.
29 Lower the engine/transmission assembly slightly and, using a trolley jack, support the

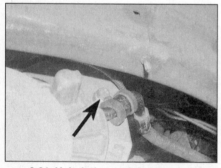

3.21 Unbolt the retaining bracket (arrowed)

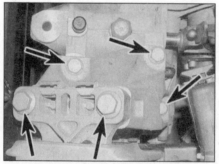

3.22a Undo the five bolts (arrowed)

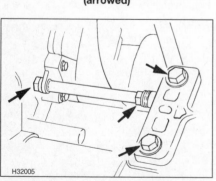

3.22b Remove the mounting and support bracket bolts (arrowed)

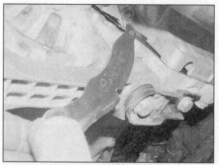

3.26 Remove the cover plate

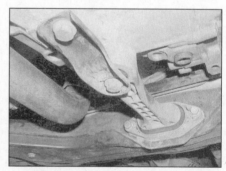

3.28 Undo the lower support bracket

transmission. Position the jack so that it can be withdrawn from the left-hand side of the car.

30 Unscrew and remove the remaining lower transmission-to-engine mounting bolts.

31 Carefully pull the transmission directly away from the engine, taking care not to allow its weight to rest on the clutch friction disc hub.

> ⚠️ *Warning: Support the transmission to ensure that it remains steady on the jack head. Keep the transmission level until the input shaft is fully withdrawn from the clutch friction disc.*

32 When the transmission is clear of the locating dowels and clutch components, lower the transmission to the ground and withdraw from under the car.

Refitting

33 Refitting the transmission is essentially a reversal of the removal procedure, but note the following points:

a) *On models with 02J transmission, before refitting the gearbox, insert a M8x35 bolt into the hole above the slave cylinder aperture with the clutch release lever pressed towards the gearbox housing, to lock the lever in position. Remove the bolt once the gearbox has been fitted.*

b) *Apply a smear of high-melting-point grease to the clutch friction disc hub splines; take care to avoid contaminating the friction surfaces.*

c) *In order align the transmission with the flywheel, gently pull the engine forward as the transmission is manoeuvred into place.*

d) *Tighten the transmission-to-engine bolts to the specified torque.*

e) *Refer to Chapter 2A, 2B or 2C (as applicable) and tighten the engine mounting bolts to the correct torque.*

f) *Refer to Chapter 8 and tighten the driveshaft bolts to the specified torque.*

g) *On models with 02J and 02K transmissions, refer to Chapter 6 and refit the slave cylinder.*

h) *On completion, refer to Section 2 and check the gearchange linkage/cable adjustment (where possible).*

i) *Refill the transmission with the correct grade and quantity of oil. Refer to 'Recommended lubricants and fluids' and Chapter 1A or 1B, as appropriate.*

4 Manual transmission overhaul – general information

The overhaul of a manual transmission is a complex (and often expensive) task for the DIY home mechanic to undertake, which requires access to specialist equipment. It involves dismantling and reassembly of many small components, measuring clearances precisely and. if necessary, adjusting them by selecting shims and spacers. Internal transmission components are also often difficult to obtain and in many instances, extremely expensive. Because of this, if the transmission develops a fault or becomes noisy, the best course of action is to have the unit overhauled by a specialist repairer or to obtain an exchange reconditioned unit.

Nevertheless, it is not impossible for the more experienced mechanic to overhaul the transmission if the special tools are available and the job is carried out in a deliberate step-by-step manner, to ensure nothing is overlooked.

The tools necessary for an overhaul include internal and external circlip pliers, bearing pullers, a slide hammer, a set of pin punches, a dial test indicator and possibly a hydraulic press. In addition, a large, sturdy workbench and a vice will be required.

During dismantling of the transmission, make careful notes of how each component is fitted to make reassembly easier and accurate.

Before dismantling the transmission, it will help if you have some idea of where the problem lies. Certain problems can be closely related to specific areas in the transmission, which can make component examination and renewal easier. Refer to the *Fault finding* Section in this manual for more information.

5 Reversing light switch – testing, removal and refitting

Testing

1 Ensure that the ignition switch is turned to the OFF position.

2 Unplug the wiring harness from the reversing light switch at the connector. The switch is located on the top of the casing on 02K and 02J transmissions. On 02M transmissions it is on the front of the casing.

3 Connect the probes of a continuity tester, or multimeter set to the resistance measurement function, across the terminals of the reversing light switch.

4 The switch contacts are normally open, so with any gear other than reverse selected, the tester/meter should indicate an open circuit or infinite resistance. When reverse gear is selected, the switch contacts should close, causing the tester/meter to indicate continuity or zero resistance.

5 If the switch does not operate correctly, it should be renewed.

Removal

6 Ensure that the ignition switch is turned to the OFF position.

7 Unplug the wiring harness from the reversing light switch at the connector **(see illustration)**.

8 On models with 02K and 02M transmissions, unscrew the switch from the transmission casing, and recover the sealing

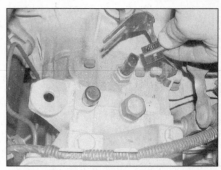

5.7 Disconnect the reversing light switch – 02K transmission

ring. On 02J-equipped models, unscrew the two retaining bolts and lift the switch from the top of the selector mechanism housing **(see illustration)**.

Refitting

9 Refitting is a reversal of removal.

6 Roadspeed sensor/speedometer drive – removal and refitting

General information

1 All transmissions are fitted with an electronic speedometer transducer. This device measures the rotational speed of the transmission final drive and converts the information into an electronic signal, which is then sent to the speedometer module in the instrument panel. On certain models, the signal is also used as an input by the engine management system ECU.

Removal

2 Ensure that the ignition switch is turned to the OFF position.

3 Locate the speed transducer, at the top rear of the transmission casing and unplug the wiring harness from the transducer at the connector.

4 On the 02J transmission, the roadspeed sensor is fitted directly on top of the drive pinion. If required, hold the housing with a spanner, then unscrew the transducer from the top of the pinion housing and recover the

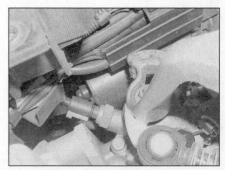

5.8 Reversing light switch – 02J transmission

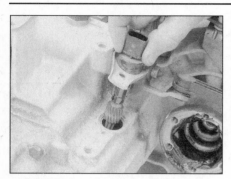

6.5 Withdraw the roadspeed sensor – 02K transmission

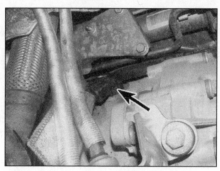

6.6 Speed sensor – 02M transmission

washer. If necessary, unscrew the pinion housing and withdraw it together with the pinion.

5 On the 02K transmission, the transducer and pinion unit is retained by a single screw. Undo the retaining screw using an Allen key and withdraw the unit from the transmission casing. Recover the gasket where applicable **(see illustration)**.

6 On the 02M transmission, the transducer is in the rear of the transmission **(see illustration)**.

Refitting

7 Refitting is a reversal of removal.

Chapter 7 Part B:
Automatic transmission

Contents

Automatic transmission – removal and refitting 2
Automatic transmission overhaul – general information 3
General information 1
Ignition key Park Lock system – description and cable renewal 5
Selector cable – removal, refitting and adjustment 4

Degrees of difficulty

Easy, suitable for novice with little experience		Fairly easy, suitable for beginner with some experience		Fairly difficult, suitable for competent DIY mechanic		Difficult, suitable for experienced DIY mechanic		Very difficult, suitable for expert DIY or professional	

Specifications

General

Description . . . . Electro-hydraulically controlled planetary gearbox providing four/five forward speeds and one reverse speed. Drive transmitted through hydrokinetic torque converter. Lock-up clutch on all four forward speeds, controlled by electronic control unit (ECU). Shift points controlled by the ECU using 'Fuzzy logic'

Transmission type number:
Four speed	01M
Five speed	09A

Ratios (typical – 4 speed)
1st	2.714:1
2nd	1.441:1
3rd	1.000:1
4th	0.742:1
Reverse	2.884:1

Torque wrench settings

	Nm	lbf ft
Fluid pan bolts	12	9
Roadspeed sensor mounting bolt	10	7
Selector cable locking bolt	8	6
Torque converter-to-driveplate nuts	60	44
Transmission bellhousing-to-engine bolts:		
M10 bolts	60	44
M12 bolts	80	59
Transmission bellhousing-to-engine sump M10 bolts	25	18
Transmission mounting spacer-to-casing bolts	40 plus 90°	30 plus 90°
Transmission speed sensor mounting bolt	10	7

1 General information

The VW type 09A automatic transmission has five forward speeds (and one reverse). The automatic gearchanges are electro-hydraulically controlled and the electronic control has a 'self diagnosis' facility. The engine control unit gives information to the transmission control unit and exchanges signals with other control units. Some of the signals exchanged are engine speed, engine torque, throttle position, kickdown, ignition timing and cruise control. On diesel engined vehicles, when the engine is at idle, the vehicle is not moving and the brake pedal is depressed, the control unit for the transmission shifts into neutral (with the selector lever in position D) for more comfort. Any faults are stored in the memory and the transmission will remain in an emergency running mode. If a problem occurs, consult a VW dealer or transmission specialist to test the electrical/electronic controls.

The VW type 01M automatic transmission has four forward speeds (and one reverse). The automatic gearchanges are electronically-controlled, rather than hydraulically as with previous conventional types. The advantage of electronic management is to provide a faster gearchange response. The ECU employs 'Fuzzy logic' to determine the gear up-shift and down-shift points. Instead of having predetermined points for up-shift and down-shift, the ECU takes into account several influencing factors before deciding to shift up or down. These factors include engine speed, driving 'resistance' (engine load), brake pedal position, throttle position, and the rate at which the throttle pedal position is changed. This results in an almost infinite number of shift points, which the ECU can tailor to match the driving style, be that sporty or economic. A kickdown facility is also provided, to enable a faster acceleration response when required.

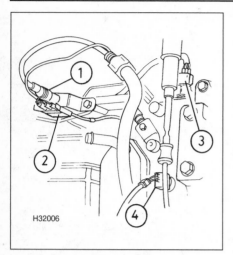

2.8 Gearbox electrical connections

1 *Solenoid valves*
2 *Roadspeed sensor*
3 *Multi-function switch*
4 *Gearbox speed sensor*

The transmission consists of three main assemblies, these being the torque converter, which is directly coupled to the engine; the final drive unit, which incorporates the differential unit; and the planetary gearbox, with its multi-disc clutches and brake bands. The transmission is lubricated with automatic transmission fluid (ATF), and is regarded by the manufacturers as being 'filled for life', with no requirement for the fluid to be changed at regular intervals. No provision is made for easy DIY checking of the fluid level, either – this must be carried out by a VW dealer, using special equipment capable of monitoring the fluid temperature (see Chapter 1A or 1B).

The torque converter incorporates an automatic lock-up feature, which eliminates any possibility of converter slip in all four forward gears; this aids performance and economy.

Another feature of this transmission is the selector lever lock, with which the selector lever can be set in the P or N position when the engine is running, below about 3 mph. Under these conditions, selection from P or N can only be made by depressing the brake pedal. Correct functioning of the brake stop-light switch is therefore vital for this system to work correctly – see Chapter 9.

The kickdown function of the transmission, which acts to select a lower gear (where possible) on full-throttle acceleration, is operated either by the throttle pedal position sensor (models without an accelerator cable) or by a switch incorporated into the accelerator cable (models with an accelerator cable) (see Chapter 4A or 4B for details). On models with an accelerator cable, no adjustment of the kickdown switch is possible other than to ensure the accelerator cable is correctly adjusted.

A starter inhibitor relay is fitted, to prevent starter motor operation unless the transmission is in P or N. The relay is located above the main fuse/relay panel (see Chapter 12), and marked with 175.

Some models also feature a security/safety device which locks the transmission in P when the ignition key is removed (see Section 5).

The transmission is fitted with an electronic roadspeed sensor. This device measures the rotational speed of the transmission final drive, and converts the information into an electronic signal, which is then sent to the speedometer module in the instrument panel. The signal is also used as an input by the engine management system ECU.

A fault diagnosis system is integrated into the control unit, but analysis can only be undertaken with specialised equipment. There is also an emergency running mode, in which only 1st, 3rd and Reverse gears can be selected. In any event, it is important that any transmission fault be identified and rectified at the earliest possible opportunity. Delay in doing so will only cause further problems. A VW dealer can 'interrogate' the ECU fault memory for stored fault codes, enabling him to pinpoint the fault quickly. Once the fault has been corrected and any fault codes have been cleared, normal transmission operation should be restored.

Because of the need for special test equipment, the complexity of some of the parts, and the need for scrupulous cleanliness when servicing automatic transmissions, the amount which the owner can do is limited. Repairs to the final drive differential are also not recommended. Most major repairs and overhaul operations should be left to a VW dealer, who will be equipped with the necessary equipment for fault diagnosis and repair. The information in this Chapter is therefore limited to a description of the removal and refitting of the transmission as a complete unit. The removal, refitting and adjustment of the selector cable is also described.

In the event of a transmission problem occurring, consult a VW dealer or transmission specialist before removing the transmission from the vehicle, since the majority of fault diagnosis is carried out with the transmission *in situ*.

2   Automatic transmission – removal and refitting

Removal

1 Select a solid, level surface to park the vehicle upon. Give yourself enough space to move around it easily. Apply the handbrake and chock the rear wheels.

2 Loosen the front wheel bolts, and the left-hand driveshaft hub nut/bolt, then raise the front of the vehicle and rest it securely on axle stands (see *Jacking and vehicle support*). Remove the front wheels. Allow a suitable working clearance underneath for the eventual withdrawal of the transmission.

3 Refer to Chapter 11 and remove the bonnet from its hinges.

4 Where fitted, remove the engine acoustic cover.

5 Disconnect the battery negative lead and position it away from the terminal. **Note:** *Before disconnecting the battery, refer to 'Disconnecting the battery' in the Reference section at the rear of this manual.*

6 Remove the battery as described in Chapter 5A, then remove the battery tray.

7 On models with the air filter housing on the left-hand side of the engine compartment, remove the complete air filter housing and air inlet trunking with reference to the relevant part of Chapter 4.

8 Disconnect the wiring connectors from the solenoid valves, roadspeed sensor, multi-function switch and gearbox speed sensor **(see illustration)**.

9 Remove the wiring loom from the retainer on the gearbox and place to one side.

10 Remove the power steering bracket complete with the wiring loom retainer.

11 Position the selector lever in P and, using a screwdriver, lever off the end of the selector cable from the selector shaft lever, and unbolt the support bracket **(see illustration)**. Position the cable to one side.

12 Remove the earth cable from the upper transmission-to-engine bolt.

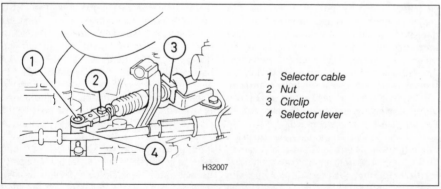

1 *Selector cable*
2 *Nut*
3 *Circlip*
4 *Selector lever*

2.11 Selector cable

13 Refer to Chapter 5A and remove the starter motor.

14 Clamp off the automatic transmission fluid cooler hoses with brake hose type clamps. Release the retaining clips and detach the hoses from the cooler.

15 Remove the upper engine-to-transmission mounting bolts.

16 Support the engine with a hoist or support bar located on the front wing inner channels. Depending on the engine, temporarily remove components as necessary to attach the hoist.

17 Where fitted, remove the left, right and centre sections of the engine undershield. On turbo diesel models, remove the pipe between the intercooler and turbocharger with reference to Chapter 4D.

18 Unscrew the four retaining bolts and remove the gearbox sump protective plate.

19 On 1.4 litre models, free the oxygen sensor connector from its retaining bracket on the front of the gearbox, and remove the bracket.

20 If fitted, remove the right-hand inner constant velocity joint protective cover using an Allen key.

21 With reference to Chapter 8, detach both driveshafts from the transmission flanges. Although not strictly necessary, we found it much easier to remove the transmission with the left-hand driveshaft completely removed.

22 With reference to the relevant part of Chapter 2, undo the four retaining bolts, and remove the rear mounting from under the vehicle.

23 Unclip the blanking cap, located next to the right-hand transmission flange, and turn the engine to locate one of the torque converter-to-driveplate nuts. Unscrew and remove the nut whilst preventing the engine from turning by using a wide-bladed screwdriver engaged with the ring gear teeth on the driveplate visible through the starter aperture. Unscrew the remaining two nuts, turning the engine a third of a turn at a time to locate them.

24 With reference to the relevant part of Chapter 4, separate the exhaust downpipe from the intermediate pipe.

25 Position a trolley jack underneath the transmission, and raise it to just take the weight of the unit.

26 Undo and remove the two bolts securing the left-hand gearbox mounting to the triangular mounting spacer. By controlling both the engine hoist/support bar and the trolley jack, lower the transmission approximately 60 mm. Unscrew the two remaining bolts and one nut, and remove the transmission mounting spacer.

27 Unscrew and remove the lower bolts securing the transmission bellhousing to the engine, noting the bolt locations, as they are of different sizes and lengths.

28 Check that all the fixings and attachments are clear of the transmission. Enlist the aid of an assistant to help in guiding and supporting the transmission during its removal.

29 The transmission is located on engine alignment dowels, and if stuck on them, it may be necessary to carefully tap and prise the transmission free of the dowels to allow separation. Once the transmission is disconnected from the location dowels, swivel the unit out and lower it out of the vehicle.

> ⚠ **Warning: Support the transmission to ensure that it remains steady on the jack head. Ensure that the torque converter remains in position on its shaft in the torque converter housing.**

30 With the transmission removed, bolt a suitable bar and spacer across the front face of the torque converter housing, to retain the torque converter in position.

Refitting

31 Refitting is a reversal of the removal procedure, but note the following special points:

a) *When reconnecting the transmission to the engine, ensure that the location dowels are in position, and that the transmission is correctly aligned with them before pushing it fully into engagement with the engine. As the torque converter is refitted, ensure that the drive pins at the centre of the torque converter hub engage with the recesses in the automatic transmission fluid pump inner wheel.*

b) *Tighten all retaining bolts to their specified torque wrench settings.*

c) *Reconnect and adjust the selector cable, as described in Section 4.*

d) *On completion, check transmission fluid level (see Chapter 1A or 1B).*

e) *If a new transmission unit has been fitted, it may be necessary to have the transmission ECU 'matched' to the engine management ECU electronically, to ensure correct operation – seek the advice of your VW dealer.*

---

3 Automatic transmission overhaul – general information

In the event of a fault occurring, it will be necessary to establish whether the fault is electrical, mechanical or hydraulic in nature, before repair work can be contemplated. Diagnosis requires detailed knowledge of the transmission's operation and construction, as well as access to specialised test equipment, and so is deemed to be beyond the scope of this manual. It is therefore essential that problems with the automatic transmission are referred to a VW dealer for assessment.

Note that a faulty transmission should not be removed before the vehicle has been assessed by a dealer, as fault diagnosis is carried out with the transmission *in situ*.

---

4 Selector cable – removal, refitting and adjustment

Removal

1 Disconnect the battery negative lead and position It away from the terminal. **Note:** *Before disconnecting the battery, refer to 'Disconnecting the battery' in the Reference section at the rear of this manual.*

2 Raise and support the vehicle at the front end on axle stands (see *Jacking and vehicle support*). Allow a suitable working clearance underneath the vehicle.

3 Move the selector lever to the P position.

4 Using a wide-bladed screwdriver, prise the end of the selector cable from the selector lever on the transmission, and remove the circlip securing the outer cable to the support bracket.

5 Separate the exhaust downpipe from the intermediate pipe with reference to the relevant part of Chapter 4.

6 Remove the centre tunnel heat shield from the underside of the vehicle to gain access to the selector lever housing.

7 Undo the securing bolts and remove the cover from the selector lever housing **(see illustration overleaf)**.

8 Prise the end of the cable from the lever with a screwdriver.

9 Remove the circlip securing the outer cable to the selector lever housing, and withdraw the cable from the housing.

Refitting

10 Refit the selector cable by reversing the removal procedure, noting the following points:

a) *Lightly grease the cable end fittings before refitting the cable.*

b) *Ensure that the cable is correctly routed, as noted on removal, and that it is securely held by its retaining clips.*

c) *Take care not to bend or kink the cable.*

d) *Carry out the cable adjustment procedure described below before reconnecting the cable at the transmission end.*

e) *When refitting the outer cable to the selector lever housing and the support bracket, use new circlips.*

f) *Always renew the selector lever housing cover seal.*

Adjustment

11 Inside the car, move the selector lever to the P position.

12 At the transmission, slacken the cable locking bolt at the ball socket. Push the cable ball socket on to the selector lever. Tighten the cable locking bolt to the specified torque.

13 Verify the operation of the selector lever by shifting through all gear positions and checking that every gear can be selected smoothly and without delay.

5 Ignition key Park Lock system – description and cable renewal

Description

1 This system is a security/safety device, intended to prevent the vehicle from being left with the transmission in any position other than P. The ignition key cannot be removed from the lock unless P is selected, and once the key has been removed, no other position than P can be selected.

2 This function is provided by means of a cable fitted to the selector linkage at the selector lever, and to the ignition switch assembly **(see illustration 4.7)**.

Lock cable

Removal

3 Disconnect the battery negative lead and position it away from the terminal. **Note:** *Before disconnecting the battery, refer to 'Disconnecting the battery' in the Reference section at the rear of this manual.*

4 With reference to Chapter 11, Section 28, remove the trim under the dash panel to the right of the steering column.

5 Referring to Chapter 10, remove the steering wheel and the upper and lower steering column shrouds for access to the ignition switch

6 Turn the ignition switch to the On position, and move the selector lever to the P position.

7 Prise the cable retaining clip from the ignition switch, and pull the cable from the housing.

8 At the selector lever, press down the selector lever sleeve with two screwdrivers, and pull the handle from the lever.

9 With reference to Chapter 11 remove the centre console.

10 Slide the cable end fitting from the lever, and withdraw the outer cable by squeezing together the lugs at the outer cable end fitting.

11 The lock cable is now free to be removed from the vehicle. Take careful note of the cable routing, and remove any further trim as necessary to facilitate removal of the cable.

Refitting

12 Refitting is a reversal of removal. Check for the correct operation of the locking mechanism.

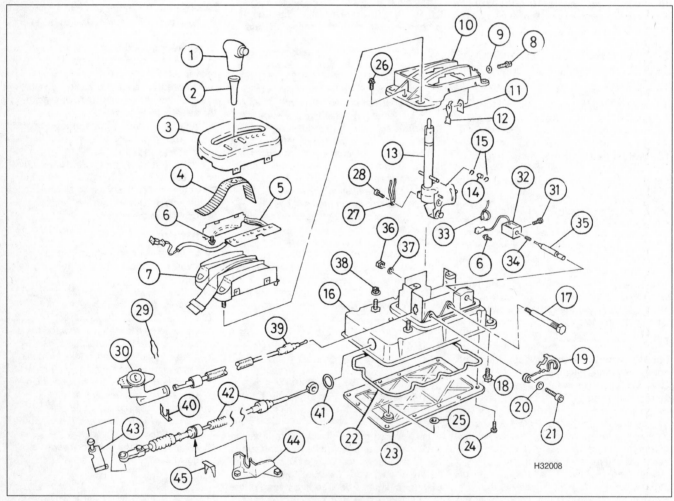

4.7 Selector lever assembly

1 Selector lever handle	7 Frame	14 Roller	22 Gasket	30 Steering lock	38 Nut
2 Sleeve	8 Bolt	15 Circlip	23 Cover	31 Bolt	39 Locking cable
3 Cover	9 Shim	16 Lever housing	24 Bolt	32 Lock solenoid	40 Circlip
4 Cover strip	10 Locking segment	17 Pivot pin	25 O-ring	33 Cable tie	41 Gasket
5 Lever position display	11 Plate	18 Bolt	26 Bolt	34 Spring	42 Selector cable
6 Retaining clip	12 Locating spring with roller	19 Locking lever	27 Contact spring	35 Locking pin	43 Lever
	13 Selector lever	20 Washer	28 Bolt	36 Nut	44 Support bracket
		21 Bolt	29 Clip	37 Washer	45 Circlip

H32008

Chapter 8
Driveshafts

Contents

Driveshaft overhaul – general information 4
Driveshaft rubber gaiters – renewal 3
Driveshafts – removal and refitting 2
General information 1

Degrees of difficulty

| **Easy,** suitable for novice with little experience | | **Fairly easy,** suitable for beginner with some experience | | **Fairly difficult,** suitable for competent DIY mechanic | 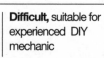 | **Difficult,** suitable for experienced DIY mechanic | | **Very difficult,** suitable for expert DIY or professional | 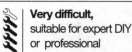 |

Specifications

Lubrication

Type of grease	VAG G 000 603 grease
Quantity of grease per joint:	
Outer joint:	
Joint diameter 81.0 mm	80 g
Joint diameter 90.0 mm	120 g
Inner joint:	
Tripod type CV joint:	
Models with press-fit metal cover (see text)	180 g
Models with metal cover secured by tabs (see text)	120 g
Ball-and-cage type CV joint:	
Joint diameter 94.0 mm	90 g
Joint diameter 100.0 mm	120 g

Torque wrench settings

	Nm	lbf ft
Driveshaft-to-transmission flange bolts:		
M8	40	30
M10	70	52
Hub bolt*:		
Stage 1	250	185
Stage 2	Angle-tighten through 90°	
Stage 3	Slacken by one-half turn (180°)	
Stage 4	Rotate wheel one-half turn (180°)	
Stage 5	250	185
Stage 6	Angle-tighten through 90°	
Hub nut*:		
Stage 1	200	148
Stage 2	Slacken by one-half turn (180°)	
Stage 3	Rotate wheel one-half turn (180°)	
Stage 4	50	37
Stage 5	Angle-tighten through 60° (equivalent to 2 spaces on 12-point nut)	
Lower arm-to-balljoint bolts:		
Stage 1	20	15
Stage 2	Tighten through a further 90°	

Use new nut/bolt

1 General information

Drive is transmitted from the differential to the front wheels by means of two steel driveshafts of either solid or hollow construction (depending on model). Both driveshafts are splined at their outer ends, to accept the wheel hubs, and are secured to the hub by a large nut/bolt. The inner end of each driveshaft is bolted to the transmission drive flange.

Constant velocity (CV) joints are fitted to each end of the driveshafts, to ensure the smooth and efficient transmission of drive at all the angles possible as the roadwheels move up-and-down with the suspension, and as they turn from side to side under steering. On all models with manual transmission, except for models with 1.6 litre DOHC engines, both inner and outer constant velocity joints are of the ball-and-cage type. On 1.6 litre DOHC engine models, and all models with automatic transmission, the outer joint is of the ball-and-cage type, but the inner joint is of the tripod type.

Rubber or plastic gaiters are secured over both CV joints with steel clips. The gaiters contain the grease which lubricates the joints, and also protect the joints from the entry of dirt and debris.

2 Driveshafts – removal and refitting

Note: *A new hub nut/bolt will be required on refitting.*

Note: *On automatic transmission models, in order to gain the necessary clearance required to withdraw the left-hand driveshaft, it may be necessary to unbolt the rear engine transmission mounting from the subframe, and lift the engine slightly.*

Removal

1 Remove the wheel trim/hub cap (as applicable) then apply the handbrake, and partially slacken the relevant hub nut/bolt with the vehicle resting on its wheels – note that the nut/bolt is very tight, and a suitable extension bar will probably be required to aid slackening. Also slacken the roadwheel securing bolts.

2 Apply the handbrake, then jack up the front of the vehicle and support it on axle stands (see *Jacking and vehicle support*). Remove the appropriate front roadwheel.

3 Remove the retaining screws and/or clips, and remove the undershields from beneath the engine/transmission unit to gain access to the driveshafts. Where necessary, also unbolt the heat shield from the transmission housing to improve access to the driveshaft inner joint **(see illustration)**.

2.3 Remove the heat shield

4 Using a multi-splined tool, slacken and remove the bolts securing the inner driveshaft joint to the transmission flange and, where applicable, recover the retaining plates from underneath the bolts **(see illustration)**.

Caution: Support the driveshaft by suspending it with wire or string – do not allow it to hang under its own weight, or the joint may be damaged.

5 Using a suitable marker pen or scriber, draw around the outline of the end of the suspension lower arm on the lower arm balljoint, marking the correct fitted position of the balljoint.

6 Unscrew the lower arm balljoint securing bolts, and remove the retaining plate/hub assembly from the top of the lower arm. **Note:** *On some models, the balljoint inner securing bolt hole is slotted; on these models the inner securing bolt can be slackened, leaving the retaining plate and bolt in position in the arm, and the balljoint disengaged from the bolt.*

7 Unscrew and remove the hub nut/bolt.

8 Carefully pull the hub carrier outwards, and withdraw the driveshaft outer constant velocity joint from the hub. The joint may be a very tight fit in the hub; tap the joint out of the hub using a soft-faced mallet (refit the hub nut to the end of the driveshaft to protect the threads). If this fails to free the driveshaft from the hub, the joint will have to be pressed out using a suitable tool bolted to the hub.

9 Manoeuvre the driveshaft out from underneath the vehicle and (where fitted) recover the gasket from the end of the inner constant velocity joint. Discard the gasket – a new one should be used on refitting.

2.4 Slackening a driveshaft-to-transmission flange bolt

Caution: Do not allow the vehicle to rest on its wheels with one or both driveshaft(s) removed, as damage to the wheel bearings may result.

10 If moving the vehicle is unavoidable, temporarily insert the outer end of the driveshaft(s) in the hub(s), and tighten the driveshaft retaining nut(s)/bolt(s); in this case, the inner end(s) of the driveshaft(s) must be supported, for example by suspending with string from the vehicle underbody.

Refitting

11 Ensure that the transmission flange and inner joint mating surfaces are clean and dry. Where necessary, fit a new gasket to the joint by peeling off its backing foil and sticking it in position.

12 Ensure that the outer joint and hub splines are clean and dry. Coat the splines of the outer constant velocity joint, the threads on the end of the outer joint, the splines in the hub, and the contact face of the hub nut/bolt with a thin layer of oil.

13 Manoeuvre the driveshaft into position, and engage the outer joint with the hub. Fit the new hub nut/bolt and use it to draw the joint fully into position.

14 Align the suspension lower arm balljoint, lower arm, and retaining plate/hub assembly, then fit new lower arm balljoint securing bolts, and tighten them to the specified torque setting, using the marks made on removal to ensure that the balljoint is correctly positioned.

15 Align the driveshaft inner joint with the transmission flange, and refit the retaining bolts and (where necessary) plates. Tighten the retaining bolts to the specified torque.

16 Where applicable (see Note at the beginning of this Section), fit new rear engine/transmission mounting-to-subframe bolts, and tighten the bolts to the specified torque (see relevant part of Chapter 2).

17 Ensure that the outer joint is drawn fully into position, then refit the roadwheel and lower the vehicle to the ground.

18 Tighten the driveshaft nut/bolt in the Stages given in the Specifications.

19 Once the driveshaft nut/bolt is correctly tightened, tighten the wheel bolts to the specified torque (see relevant part of Chapter 1) and refit the wheel trim/hub cap.

3 Driveshaft rubber gaiters – renewal

1 Remove the driveshaft from the car, as described in Section 2. Continue as described under the relevant sub-heading. Driveshafts with a tripod type inner joint can be identified by the shape of the inner CV joint; the driveshaft retaining bolt holes are in tabs extending from the joint, giving it a six-pointed star-shaped exterior, in contrast to the smooth, circular shape of the ball-and-cage joint **(see illustrations)**.

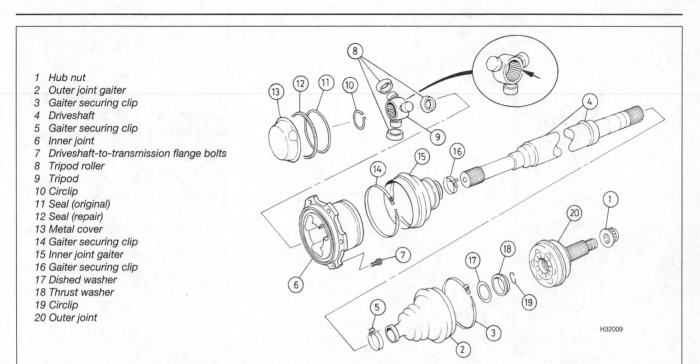

1 Hub nut
2 Outer joint gaiter
3 Gaiter securing clip
4 Driveshaft
5 Gaiter securing clip
6 Inner joint
7 Driveshaft-to-transmission flange bolts
8 Tripod roller
9 Tripod
10 Circlip
11 Seal (original)
12 Seal (repair)
13 Metal cover
14 Gaiter securing clip
15 Inner joint gaiter
16 Gaiter securing clip
17 Dished washer
18 Thrust washer
19 Circlip
20 Outer joint

3.1a Driveshaft components – models with press-fit metal cover on inner end of inner CV joint

Outer CV joint gaiter

2 Secure the driveshaft in a vice equipped with soft jaws, and release the two outer joint gaiter retaining clips. If necessary, the retaining clips can be cut to release them.

3 Slide the rubber gaiter down the shaft to expose the constant velocity joint, and scoop out excess grease.

4 Using a soft-faced mallet, tap the joint off the end of the driveshaft.

5 Remove the circlip from the driveshaft groove, and slide off the thrust washer and dished washer, noting which way around it is fitted.

6 Slide the rubber gaiter off the driveshaft and discard it.

7 Thoroughly clean the constant velocity joint(s) using paraffin, or a suitable solvent, and dry thoroughly. Carry out a visual inspection as follows.

8 Move the inner splined driving member from side-to-side to expose each ball in turn at the top of its track. Examine the balls for cracks, flat spots or signs of surface pitting.

9 Inspect the ball tracks on the inner and outer members. If the tracks have widened, the balls will no longer be a tight fit. At the same time, check the ball cage windows for wear or cracking between the windows.

10 If on inspection any of the constant velocity joint components are found to be worn or damaged, it will be necessary to renew the complete joint assembly. If the joint is in satisfactory condition, obtain a new gaiter and retaining clips, a constant velocity joint circlip and the correct type of grease. Grease is often supplied with the joint repair kit – if

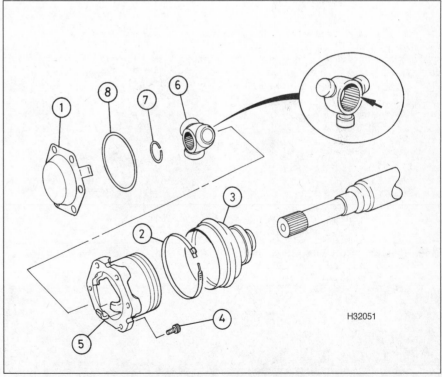

3.1b Inner driveshaft joint components – models with cover on inner end of inner CV joint secured by tabs

1 Metal cover
2 Gaiter securing clip
3 Inner joint gaiter
4 Driveshaft-to-transmission flange bolts
5 Inner joint
6 Tripod/roller assembly (chamfer arrowed faces towards driveshaft)
7 Circlip
8 Seal

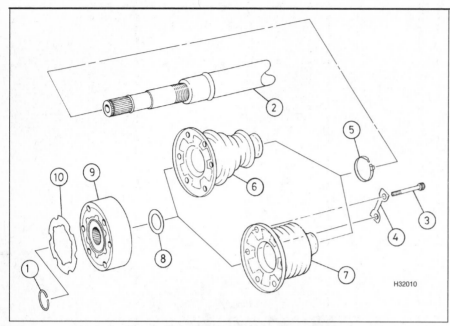

3.11 Tape over the driveshaft splines, then slide the new gaiter along the shaft

3.1c Inner driveshaft components – manual transmission models (except for models with 1.6 litre DOHC engines)

1 Circlip
2 Driveshaft
3 Driveshaft-to-transmission flange bolts
4 Bolt retaining plate
5 Gaiter securing clip
6 Inner joint gaiter
7 Inner joint gaiter (alternative type)
8 Dished washer
9 Inner joint
10 Gasket

not, use a good-quality molybdenum disulphide grease.

11 Tape over the splines on the end of the driveshaft, to protect the new gaiter as it is slid into place **(see illustration)**.

12 Slide the new gaiter onto the end of the driveshaft, then remove the protective tape from the driveshaft splines.

13 Slide on the dished washer, making sure its convex side is innermost, followed by the thrustwasher **(see illustrations)**.
14 Fit a new circlip to the driveshaft, then tap the joint onto the driveshaft until the circlip engages in its groove **(see illustrations)**. Make sure that the joint is securely retained by the circlip.
15 Pack the joint with the specified type of grease. Work the grease well into the bearing tracks whilst twisting the joint, and fill the rubber gaiter with any excess.
16 Ease the gaiter over the joint, and ensure that the gaiter lips are correctly located on both the driveshaft and constant velocity joint. Lift the outer sealing lip of the gaiter to equalise air pressure within the gaiter **(see illustration)**.
17 Fit the large metal retaining clip to the gaiter. Pull the clip as tight as possible, and locate the hooks on the clip in their slots.

3.13a Slide on the dished washer, with its convex side innermost . . .

3.13b . . . then slide on the thrustwasher

3.14a Fit the new circlip to the driveshaft groove . . .

3.14b . . . then locate the joint on the driveshaft splines . . .

3.14c . . . and tap the joint onto the driveshaft

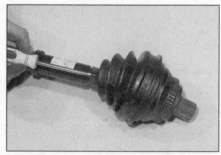

3.16 Seat the gaiter on the outer joint and driveshaft, then lift its inner lip to equalise the air pressure

Remove any slack in the gaiter retaining clip by carefully compressing the raised section of the clip. In the absence of the special tool, a pair of side-cutters may be used, taking care not to cut the clip (see illustrations). Secure the small retaining clip using the same procedure.

18 Check the constant velocity joint moves freely in all directions, then refit the driveshaft to the vehicle, as described in Section 2.

Tripod inner CV joint gaiter

Press-fit metal cover

19 This type of joint can be recognised from the press-fit metal cover fitted to the end of the CV joint outer member (see illustration 3.1a). The cover is round. On models where the inner CV joint gaiter has been renewed previously, a metal cover will not be fitted, in which case this type of joint can be recognised during dismantling by the fact that the tripod rollers are a loose fit on the tripod, and will slide off easily (if the rollers are secured to the tripod, proceed as described in paragraphs 45 to 61).

20 Release the two outer joint gaiter retaining clips. If necessary, the retaining clips can be cut to release them. Slide the rubber gaiter down the shaft, away from the joint outer member.

21 Carefully secure the joint outer member in a vice equipped with soft jaws.

22 Drive a screwdriver through the side of the metal cap over the end of the joint outer member, and use the screwdriver to lever the cap off the outer member. If the cap cannot be levered off, drive a second screwdriver through the opposite side of the cap, and use the two screwdrivers to lever off the cap.

23 Scoop out excess grease from the joint, then remove the O-ring from the groove in the end of the joint outer member.

24 Using a suitable marker pen or a scriber, make alignment marks between the end of the driveshaft, the tripod roller assembly, and the outer member.

25 Support the driveshaft and the joint, and withdraw the outer member from the vice. As the assembly is removed from the vice, make sure that the rollers do not fall off the tripod.

26 Slowly slide the joint outer member down the driveshaft, away from the joint, making sure that the rollers stay on the tripod.

27 Mark the rollers and the arms of the tripod, so that the rollers can be refitted in their original positions, then lift off the rollers and place them to one side on a dry, clean surface.

28 Remove the circlip from the end of the driveshaft.

29 Press or drive the driveshaft from the tripod, taking great care not to damage the surfaces of the roller locating arms.

30 Slide the outer member and the rubber gaiter from the end of the driveshaft.

31 Thoroughly clean the joint components using paraffin, or a suitable solvent, and dry

3.17a Compress the raised section of the gaiter securing clip . . .

3.17b . . . taking great care not to cut through the clip

thoroughly. Carry out a visual inspection as follows.

32 Inspect the tripod rollers and the joint outer member for signs of wear, pitting or scuffing on their mating surfaces. Check that the joint rollers rotate smoothly, with no traces of roughness (see illustration).

33 If the rollers or outer member shown signs of wear or damage, it will be necessary to renew the complete driveshaft, since the joint is not available separately. If the joint is in satisfactory condition, obtain a repair kit, consisting of a new gaiter, retaining clips, circlip, and the correct type and quantity of grease.

34 Tape over the splines on the end of the driveshaft, to protect the new gaiter as it is slid into place, then slide the new gaiter and securing clips, and the joint outer member over the end of the driveshaft (see illustrations). Remove the protective tape from the driveshaft splines.

3.32 Check the tripod rollers and outer member for signs of wear

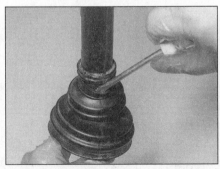

3.34b . . . then lever the gaiter carefully over the ridge on the driveshaft

35 Press or drive the tripod onto the end of the driveshaft until it contacts the stop, ensuring that the marks made on the end of the driveshaft and the tripod before dismantling are aligned. Note that the chamfered edge of the internal splines on the tripod should face towards the driveshaft.

36 Fit the new circlip to retain the tripod on the end of the driveshaft.

37 Refit the rollers to the tripod, ensuring that they are refitted in their original locations, as noted before removal.

38 Work 90 grammes (half) of the grease supplied with the repair kit into the inner end of the joint outer member, then slide the outer member over the tripod, ensuring that the marks made during dismantling are aligned, and clamp the outer member in the vice.

39 Work the rest of the grease supplied with the repair kit into the rear of the joint outer member (see illustration).

3.34a Tape over the driveshaft splines to protect the new gaiter . . .

3.39 Work the grease into the joint outer member

40 Slide the rubber gaiter up the driveshaft onto the joint outer member, and secure with the large clip, as described in paragraph 17.

41 Lift the gaiter outer end to equalise the air pressure in the gaiter, then secure the outer gaiter securing clip in position using the same method used previously **(see illustration)**.

42 Check that the grease in the joint outer member is evenly distributed around the tripod rollers.

43 Wipe any excess grease from the inner face of the joint outer member, then fit the rectangular profile O-ring provided in the repair kit into the groove in the inner face of the joint outer member. The rectangular profile of the seal acts as a grease seal, and takes the place of the metal cover prised off during dismantling.

44 Check the driveshaft joint moves freely in all directions, then refit the driveshaft to the vehicle, as described in Section 2. To prevent the tripod joint from being pushed back down the driveshaft during refitting, temporarily stick adhesive tape over the open end of the joint outer member **(see illustration)**. Remove the tape just before reconnecting the inner end of the driveshaft to the transmission.

Metal cover secured by tabs

45 This type of joint can be recognised from the metal cover fitted to the end of the CV joint outer member **(see illustration 3.1b)**. The cover fits over the end of the outer member flange, and the driveshaft-to-transmission flange bolts pass through the cover. The cover is secured to the outer member flange by three tabs. If the cover is a press-fit, or if no cover is fitted, proceed as described in paragraphs 19 to 44.

46 Proceed as described in paragraphs 20 and 21.

47 Using a screwdriver, prise up the tabs of the metal cap over the end of the joint outer member. Lever the cover from the joint outer member.

48 Proceed as described in paragraphs 23 and 24.

49 Support the driveshaft and the joint, and withdraw the outer member from the vice. Slide the joint outer member down the driveshaft, away from the joint.

50 Remove the circlip from the end of the driveshaft.

51 Press or drive the driveshaft from the tripod, taking great care not to damage the rollers.

52 Proceed as described in paragraphs 30 to 36, taking care not to damage the rollers as the tripod is refitted.

53 Work 60 grammes (half) of the grease supplied with the repair kit into the inner end of the joint outer member, then slide the outer member over the tripod, ensuring that the marks made during dismantling are aligned, and clamp the outer member in the vice.

54 Work the rest of the grease supplied with the repair kit into the rear of the joint outer member.

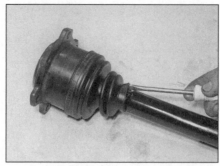

3.41 Lift the gaiter outer end to equalise the air pressure

55 Slide the rubber gaiter up the driveshaft onto the joint outer member, ensuring that the end of the gaiter seats in the groove in the joint outer member, and secure with the large clip as described in paragraph 17.

56 Lift the gaiter outer end to equalise the air pressure in the gaiter, then secure the outer gaiter securing clip in position using the same method used previously.

57 Check that the grease in the joint outer member is evenly distributed around the tripod rollers.

58 Wipe any excess grease from the inner face of the joint outer member, then fit the O-ring provided in the repair kit into the groove in the inner face of the joint outer member.

59 Fit the new cover supplied in the repair kit to the inner end of the joint outer member, ensuring that the bolt holes in the outer member and cover are aligned.

60 Secure the cover by bending the securing tabs around the edge of the outer member flange.

61 Check the driveshaft joint moves freely in all directions, then refit the driveshaft to the vehicle, as described in Section 2.

Ball-and-cage type inner CV joint

62 Secure the driveshaft in a vice equipped with soft jaws, then release the gaiter outer

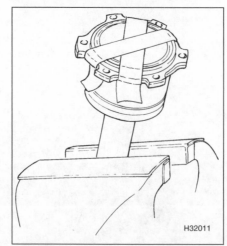

3.44 Tape over the end of the driveshaft joint

securing clip, securing the gaiter to the driveshaft. If necessary, the clip can be cut to release it.

63 Using a hammer and a small drift, carefully drive the inner end of the gaiter from the joint outer member.

64 Slide the gaiter down the driveshaft to expose the constant velocity joint, and scoop out excess grease.

65 Remove the circlip from the end of the driveshaft.

66 Press or drive the driveshaft from the joint, taking great care not to damage the joint. Recover the dished washer fitted between the constant velocity joint and the gaiter.

67 Slide the gaiter from the end of the driveshaft.

68 Proceed as described previously in paragraphs 7 to 12.

69 Slide the dished washer onto the driveshaft, making sure its convex side is innermost.

70 Fit the joint to the end of the driveshaft, noting that the chamfered edge of the internal splines on the joint should face towards the driveshaft. Drive or press the joint into position until it contacts the shoulder on the driveshaft.

71 Fit a new circlip to retain the joint on the end of the driveshaft.

72 It the left-hand driveshaft is being worked on, mark the final installation position of the gaiter outboard end on the driveshaft using tape, or paint – do not scratch the surface of the driveshaft **(see illustration)**.

73 Pack the joint with the recommended quantity of grease (see Specifications), then pack the gaiter with the recommended quantity of grease.

74 Slide the gaiter up the driveshaft, and push or drive the inner end of the gaiter onto the joint outer member.

75 If the left-hand driveshaft is being worked on, slide the outboard end of the gaiter into position using the mark made previously (see paragraph 72), then secure the outer gaiter securing clip in position as described in paragraph 17.

76 If the right-hand driveshaft is being

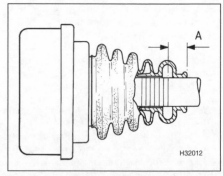

3.72 Installation position of inner joint gaiter on left-hand driveshaft

A = 17.0 mm

worked on, slide the outboard end of the gaiter into position on the driveshaft, then secure the outer gaiter securing clip in position as described in paragraph 17 **(see illustration)**.

77 Check the driveshaft joint moves freely in all directions, then refit the driveshaft to the vehicle, as described in Section 2.

4 Driveshaft overhaul – general information

If any of the checks described in Chapter 1A or 1B reveal wear in any driveshaft joint, first remove the roadwheel trim or centre cap (as applicable) and check that the hub nut/bolt is tight. If the nut/bolt is loose, obtain a new nut/bolt, and tighten it to the specified torque (see Section 2). If the nut/bolt is tight, refit the centre cap/trim, and repeat the check on the other hub nut/bolt.

Road test the vehicle, and listen for a metallic clicking from the front of the vehicle as the vehicle is driven slowly in a circle on full-lock. If a clicking noise is heard, this indicates wear in the outer constant velocity joint; this means that the joint must be renewed.

If vibration consistent with roadspeed is felt through the car when accelerating, there is a possibility of wear in the inner constant velocity joints.

To check the joints for wear, remove the driveshafts, then dismantle them as described in Section 3. If any wear or free play is found, the affected joint must be renewed. Refer to a VW dealer for information on the availability of driveshaft components.

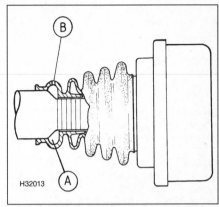

3.76 Installation position of inner joint gaiter on right-hand driveshaft

A Vent chamber in gaiter
B Vent hole

Chapter 9
Braking system

Contents

Anti-lock braking system (ABS) – general information and
  precautions 19
Anti-lock braking system (ABS) components – removal and refitting 20
Brake disc – inspection, removal and refitting 6
Brake fluid level check ....See *Weekly checks*
Brake fluid renewal ....See Chapter 1A or 1B
Brake light switch – removal and refitting 18
Brake pad check ....See Chapter 1A or 1B
Brake pedal – removal and refitting 10
Front brake caliper – removal, overhaul and refitting 5
Front brake disc shield – removal and refitting 7
Front brake pads – removal, inspection and refitting 4
General information and precautions 1
Handbrake – adjustment 14

Handbrake 'on' warning light switch – removal and refitting 17
Handbrake cables – removal and refitting 16
Handbrake lever – removal and refitting 15
Hydraulic pipes and hoses – renewal 3
Hydraulic system – bleeding 2
Master cylinder – removal, overhaul and refitting 13
Rear brake caliper – removal, overhaul and refitting 9
Rear brake pads – removal, inspection and refitting 8
Servo non-return valve – testing, removal and refitting 12
Servo unit – testing, removal and refitting 11
Servo unit electric vacuum pump (diesel models) – testing, removal
  and refitting 22
Servo unit mechanical vacuum pump (diesel models) – testing,
  removal and refitting 21

Degrees of difficulty

Easy, suitable for novice with little experience
Fairly easy, suitable for beginner with some experience
Fairly difficult, suitable for competent DIY mechanic
Difficult, suitable for experienced DIY mechanic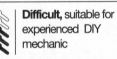
Very difficult, suitable for expert DIY or professional

Specifications

Front brakes
Calipers:
  All models except 1.8 litre petrol and ASZ & ARL diesels .... FSIII
  1.8 litre petrol and ASZ & ARL diesels FN3
Disc diameter:
  All models except 1.8 litre petrol and ASZ & ARL diesels .... 256 or 280 mm
  1.8 litre petrol and ASZ & ARL diesels .... 288 or 312 mm
Disc thickness.
  New:
    All models except 1.8 litre petrol and ASZ & ARL diesels .... 22.0 mm
    1.8 litre petrol and ASZ & ARL diesels .... 25.0 mm
  Minimum permissible thickness:
    All models except 1.8 litre petrol and ASZ & ARL diesels .... 19.0 mm
    1.8 litre petrol and ASZ & ARL diesels .... 22.0 mm
Maximum disc run-out .... 0.1 mm
Brake pad thickness (all models):
  New .... 14.0 mm
  Minimum .... 7.0 mm (including backing plate)
ABS sensor-to-rotor clearance .... 0.3 mm

Rear disc brakes
Disc diameter .... 232 mm
Disc thickness:
  New .... 9.0 mm
  Minimum thickness .... 7.0 mm
Maximum disc run-out .... 0.1 mm
Brake pad thickness (all models):
  New .... 11.5 mm
  Minimum .... 7.5 mm (including backing plate)

Torque wrench settings

	Nm	lbf ft
ABS control unit bracket-to-wing nuts	20	15
ABS control unit retaining bolts	8	6
ABS wheel sensor retaining bolts	8	6
Brake pedal pivot shaft nut	20	15
Front brake caliper:		
Guide pins	30	22
Mounting bracket bolts (FN3)	125	92
Front brake disc shield	10	7
Master cylinder mounting nuts	20	15
Rear brake caliper:		
Guide pin bolts*	35	26
Mounting bracket bolts	65	48
Roadwheel bolts	120	89
Servo unit mounting nuts	20	15
Servo unit mechanical vacuum pump (diesel models)	20	15
Servo unit electric vacuum pump (diesel models)	8	6

* Use new bolts

1 General information and precautions

General information

The braking system is of servo-assisted, diagonal dual-circuit hydraulic type. The arrangement of the hydraulic system is such that each circuit operates one front and one rear brake from a tandem master cylinder. Under normal circumstances, both circuits operate in unison. However, if there is hydraulic failure in one circuit, full braking force will still be available at two wheels.

All models of Golf and Bora covered by this manual are equipped with disc brakes at the front and rear. ABS is fitted as standard to all models (refer to Section 19 for further information on ABS operation).

The front disc brakes are actuated by single-piston sliding type calipers, which ensure that equal pressure is applied to each disc pad.

The rear brakes are also actuated by single-piston sliding calipers, which incorporate independent mechanical handbrake mechanisms as well.

Precautions

• *When servicing any part of the system, work carefully and methodically; also observe scrupulous cleanliness when overhauling any part of the hydraulic system. Always renew components in axle sets (where applicable) if in doubt about their condition, and use only genuine VW replacement parts, or at least those of known good quality. Note the warnings given in 'Safety first!' and at relevant points in this Chapter concerning the dangers of asbestos dust and hydraulic fluid.*

2 Hydraulic system – bleeding

⚠ *Warning: Hydraulic fluid is poisonous; wash off immediately and thoroughly in the case of skin contact, and seek immediate medical advice if any fluid is swallowed or gets into the eyes. Certain types of hydraulic fluid are flammable, and may ignite when allowed into contact with hot components; when servicing any hydraulic system, it is safest to assume that the fluid is flammable, and to take precautions against the risk of fire as though it is petrol that is being handled. Hydraulic fluid is also an effective paint stripper, and will attack plastics; if any is spilt, it should be washed off immediately, using copious quantities of fresh water. Finally, it is hygroscopic (it absorbs moisture from the air) – old fluid may be contaminated and unfit for further use. When topping-up or renewing the fluid, always use the recommended type, and ensure that it comes from a freshly-opened sealed container.*

Note: *VW specify that at least 0.25 litre of brake fluid should be expelled from each caliper.*

General

1 The correct operation of any hydraulic system is only possible after removing all air from the components and circuit; this is achieved by bleeding the system. Since the clutch hydraulic system also uses fluid from the brake system reservoir, it should also be bled at the same time by referring to Chapter 6, Section 2.

2 During the bleeding procedure, add only clean, unused hydraulic fluid of the recommended type; never re-use fluid that has already been bled from the system. Ensure that sufficient fluid is available before starting work.

3 If there is any possibility of incorrect fluid being already in the system, the brake components and circuit must be flushed completely with uncontaminated, correct fluid, and new seals should be fitted to the various components.

4 If hydraulic fluid has been lost from the system, or air has entered because of a leak, ensure that the fault is cured before continuing further.

5 Park the vehicle on level ground, then chock the wheels and release the handbrake.

6 Check that all pipes and hoses are secure, unions tight and bleed screws closed. Clean any dirt from around the bleed screws.

7 Unscrew the master cylinder reservoir cap, and top the reservoir up to the MAX level line; refit the cap loosely, and remember to maintain the fluid level at least above the MIN level line throughout the procedure, or there is a risk of further air entering the system.

8 There is a number of one-man, do-it-yourself brake bleeding kits currently available from motor accessory shops. It is recommended that one of these kits is used whenever possible, as they greatly simplify the bleeding operation, and reduce the risk of expelled air and fluid being drawn back into the system. If such a kit is not available, the basic (two-man) method must be used, which is described in detail below.

9 If a kit is to be used, prepare the vehicle as described previously, and follow the kit manufacturer's instructions, as the procedure may vary slightly according to the type being used; generally, they are as outlined below in the relevant sub-section.

10 Whichever method is used, the same sequence must be followed (paragraphs 11 and 12) to ensure the removal of all air from the system.

Bleeding sequence

11 If the system has been only partially disconnected, and suitable precautions were taken to minimise fluid loss, it should be necessary only to bleed that part of the system.

12 If the complete system is to be bled, then it should be done working in the following sequence:

Mark 20 IE system (see Section 19)

a) Right-hand rear brake.
b) Left-hand rear brake.
c) Right-hand front brake.
d) Left-hand front brake.

Mark 60 system (see Section 19)

a) Left-hand front brake.
b) Right-hand front brake.
c) Left-hand rear brake.
d) Right-hand rear brake.

If the hydraulic fluid has run dry in either chamber of the reservoir, the system must be pre-bled as follows, **before** carrying out the bleeding sequence described above:

a) On RHD models, bleed the primary and secondary circuit bleed screws on the brake master cylinder.
b) On RHD and LHD models, bleed the front left and right brakes simultaneously.
c) On RHD and LHD models, bleed the rear left and right brakes simultaneously.

Bleeding

Basic (two-man) method

13 Collect together a clean glass jar of reasonable size, a suitable length of plastic or rubber tubing which is a tight fit over the bleed screw, and a ring spanner to fit the screw. The help of an assistant will also be required.

14 Remove the dust cap from the first screw in the sequence **(see illustration)**. Fit the spanner and tube to the screw, place the other end of the tube in the jar, and pour in sufficient fluid to cover the end of the tube.

15 Ensure that the master cylinder reservoir fluid level is maintained at least above the MIN level line throughout the procedure.

16 Have the assistant fully depress the brake pedal several times to build-up pressure, then maintain it on the final downstroke.

17 While pedal pressure is maintained, unscrew the bleed screw (approximately one turn) and allow the compressed fluid and air to flow into the jar. The assistant should maintain pedal pressure, following it down to the floor if necessary, and should not release it until instructed to do so. When the flow stops, tighten the bleed screw again, have the assistant release the pedal slowly, and recheck the reservoir fluid level.

18 Repeat the steps given in paragraphs 16 and 17 until the fluid emerging from the bleed screw is free from air bubbles. If the master cylinder has been drained and refilled, and air is being bled from the first screw in the sequence, allow approximately five seconds between cycles for the master cylinder passages to refill.

19 When no more air bubbles appear, tighten the bleed screw securely, remove the tube and spanner, and refit the dust cap. Do not overtighten the bleed screw.

20 Repeat the procedure on the remaining screws in the sequence, until all air is removed from the system and the brake pedal feels firm again.

Using a one-way valve kit

21 As their name implies, these kits consist of a length of tubing with a one-way valve fitted, to prevent expelled air and fluid being drawn back into the system; some kits include a translucent container, which can be positioned so that the air bubbles can be more easily seen flowing from the end of the tube.

22 The kit is connected to the bleed screw, which is then opened. The user returns to the driver's seat, depresses the brake pedal with a smooth, steady stroke, and slowly releases it; this is repeated until the expelled fluid is clear of air bubbles **(see illustration)**.

23 Note that these kits simplify work so much that it is easy to forget the master cylinder reservoir fluid level; ensure that this is maintained at least above the MIN level line at all times.

Using a pressure-bleeding kit

24 These kits are usually operated by the reservoir of pressurised air contained in the spare tyre. However, note that it will be probably necessary to reduce the pressure to less than 1.0 bar (14.5 psi); refer to the instructions supplied with the kit.

25 By connecting a pressurised, fluid-filled container to the master cylinder reservoir, bleeding can be carried out simply by opening each screw in turn (in the specified sequence), and allowing the fluid to flow out until no more air bubbles can be seen in the expelled fluid.

26 This method has the advantage that the large reservoir of fluid provides an additional safeguard against air being drawn into the system during bleeding.

27 Pressure-bleeding is particularly effective when bleeding 'difficult' systems, or when bleeding the complete system at the time of routine fluid renewal.

All methods

28 When bleeding is complete, and firm pedal feel is restored, wash off any spilt fluid, tighten the bleed screws securely, and refit their dust caps.

29 Check the hydraulic fluid level in the master cylinder reservoir, and top-up if necessary (see *Weekly checks*).

30 Discard any hydraulic fluid that has been bled from the system; it will not be fit for re-use.

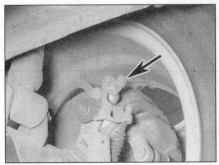

2.14 Remove the dust cap (arrowed) from the first screw in the sequence

31 Check the feel of the brake pedal. If it feels at all spongy, air must still be present in the system, and further bleeding is required. Failure to bleed satisfactorily after a reasonable repetition of the bleeding procedure may be due to worn master cylinder seals.

3 Hydraulic pipes and hoses – renewal

Note: *Refer to the note in Section 2 concerning the dangers of hydraulic fluid.*

1 If any pipe or hose is to be renewed, minimise fluid loss by first removing the master cylinder reservoir cap, then tightening it down onto a piece of polythene to obtain an airtight seal. Alternatively, flexible hoses can be sealed, if required, using a proprietary brake hose clamp; metal brake pipe unions can be plugged (if care is taken not to allow dirt into the system) or capped immediately they are disconnected. Place a wad of rag under any union that is to be disconnected, to catch any spilt fluid.

2 If a flexible hose is to be disconnected, where applicable unscrew the brake pipe union nut before removing the spring clip which secures the hose to its mounting bracket.

3 To unscrew the union nuts, it is preferable to obtain a brake pipe spanner of the correct size; these are available from most large motor accessory shops. Failing this, a close-fitting open-ended spanner will be required,

2.22 Bleeding a brake using a one-way valve kit

4.4 Remove the caliper guide pins

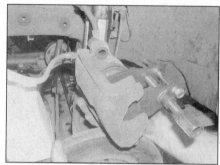

4.9 Open the bleed nipple as the piston is pushed back into the caliper

4.10 The inboard pad is labelled 'Piston side'

though if the nuts are tight or corroded, their flats may be rounded-off if the spanner slips. In such a case, a self-locking wrench is often the only way to unscrew a stubborn union, but it follows that the pipe and the damaged nuts must be renewed on reassembly. Always clean a union and surrounding area before disconnecting it. If disconnecting a component with more than one union, make a careful note of the connections before disturbing any of them.

4 If a brake pipe is to be renewed, it can be obtained, cut to length and with the union nuts and end flares in place, from VW dealers. All that is then necessary is to bend it to shape, following the line of the original, before fitting it to the car. Alternatively, most motor accessory shops can make up brake pipes from kits, but this requires very careful measurement of the original, to ensure that the new pipe is of the correct length. The safest answer is usually to take the original to the shop as a pattern.

5 On refitting, do not overtighten the union nuts. It is not necessary to exercise brute force to obtain a sound joint.

6 Ensure that the pipes and hoses are correctly routed, with no kinks, and that they are secured in the clips or brackets provided. After fitting, remove the polythene from the reservoir, and bleed the hydraulic system as described in Section 2. Wash off any spilt fluid, and check carefully for fluid leaks.

---

4 Front brake pads –
removal, inspection
and refitting

⚠️ *Warning: Renew both sets of brake pads at the same time – never renew the pads on only one wheel, as uneven braking may result. Note that the dust created by wear of the pads may contain asbestos, which is a health hazard. Never blow it out with compressed air, and do not inhale any of it. An approved filtering mask should be worn when working on the brakes. DO NOT use petrol or petroleum-based solvents to clean brake parts; use brake cleaner or methylated spirit only.*

FSIII calipers

Removal

1 Apply the handbrake, then jack up the front of the vehicle and support it on axle stands (see *Jacking and vehicle support*). Remove the front roadwheels.

2 Trace the brake pad wear sensor wiring (where fitted) back from the pads, and disconnect it from the wiring connector. Note the routing of the wiring, and free it from any relevant retaining clips.

3 Where applicable, to improve access, undo the retaining bolts and remove the air deflector shield from the caliper.

4 Remove the two protective rubber caps and, using a suitable hexagon key, loosen and remove the two caliper guide pins from the caliper, then lift the caliper together with pads away from the hub carrier **(see illustration)**.

5 Remove the two brake pads from the caliper, noting their correct fitted locations. The inner pad is retained in the caliper piston by a white clip, and the outer pad is also retained in the caliper cut-out by a black clip. If the original pads are to be refitted, mark them so that they can be refitted in their original positions. Tie the caliper to the suspension strut using a piece of wire. Do not allow the caliper to hang unsupported on the flexible brake hose.

Inspection

6 First measure the thickness of each brake pad (including the backing plate). If either pad is worn at any point to the specified minimum thickness or less, all four pads must be renewed. Also, the pads should be renewed if

4.11 Ensure the pads and caliper are correctly located on the carrier

any are fouled with oil or grease; there is no satisfactory way of degreasing friction material, once contaminated. If any of the brake pads are worn unevenly, or are fouled with oil or grease, trace and rectify the cause before reassembly. New brake pad kits are available from VW dealers.

7 If the brake pads are still serviceable, carefully clean them using a clean, fine wire brush or similar, paying particular attention to the sides and back of the metal backing. Clean out the grooves in the friction material (where applicable), and pick out any large embedded particles of dirt or debris. Carefully clean the pad locations in the caliper body/mounting bracket.

8 Prior to fitting the pads, check that the guide pins are free to slide easily in the caliper body bushes, and are a reasonably tight fit. Brush the dust and dirt from the caliper and piston, but *do not* inhale it, as it is injurious to health. Inspect the dust seal around the piston for damage, and the piston for evidence of fluid leaks, corrosion or damage. If attention to any of these components is necessary, refer to Section 5.

Refitting

9 If new brake pads are to be fitted, the caliper piston must be pushed back into the cylinder to make room for them. Either use a G-clamp or similar tool, or use suitable pieces of wood as levers. To avoid any dirt entering the ABS solenoid valves, connect a pipe to the bleed nipple and, as the piston is pushed back, open the nipple and allow the displaced fluid to flow through the pipe into a suitable container **(see illustration)**.

10 Fit the new pads to the caliper. The inboard pad is marked 'Piston side' with a white clip which must be located in the piston **(see illustration)**. The outboard pad has a black clip which must be located in the outer cut-out of the caliper.

11 Position the caliper and pads over the disc and onto the hub carrier, ensuring that the lower lug engages correctly **(see illustration)**. Pass the pad warning sensor wiring (where fitted) through the caliper aperture.

12 Press the caliper into position sufficiently until it is possible to install the caliper guide pins. Tighten the guide pins to the specified

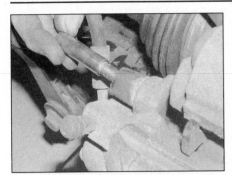

4.12 Insert the guide pins

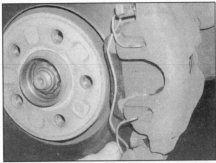

4.19 Lever the spring from the caliper housing

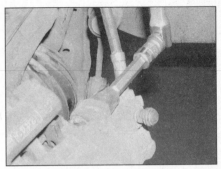

4.20 Undo the caliper pins

torque **(see illustration)**. **Note:** *Do not exert excess pressure on the caliper, as this will deform the pad springs, resulting in noisy operation of the brakes.*

13 Where applicable, reconnect the brake pad wear sensor wiring connectors, ensuring that the wiring is correctly routed. Where applicable, refit the air deflector shield to the caliper.

14 Depress the brake pedal repeatedly, until the pads are pressed into firm contact with the brake disc, and normal (non-assisted) pedal pressure is restored.

15 Repeat the above procedure on the remaining front brake caliper.

16 Refit the roadwheels, then lower the vehicle to the ground and tighten the roadwheel bolts to the specified torque.

17 New pads will not give full braking efficiency until they have bedded-in. Be prepared for this, and avoid hard braking as far as possible for the first hundred miles or so after pad renewal.

FN3 calipers

Removal

18 Proceed as described in paragraphs 1 and 2.

19 Using a screwdriver, lever the brake pad retaining spring from the caliper housing **(see illustration)**.

20 Remove the two protective rubber caps and using a suitable hexagon key, slacken and remove the two caliper guide pins from the caliper **(see illustration)**. Then lift the caliper away from the brake pads and hub, and tie it to the suspension strut using a suitable piece of wire. Do not allow the caliper to hang unsupported on the flexible brake hose.

21 Withdraw the two brake pads from the caliper-mounting bracket. If the original pads are to be refitted, identify them so that they can be refitted in their original locations. Where applicable, disconnect the pad wear sensor wiring connector.

Inspection

22 Examine the pads and caliper as described previously in paragraphs 6 to 8. If new pads are to be refitted, refer to paragraph 9 before attempting to push the piston back into the caliper.

Refitting

23 Where applicable, remove the protect-ive foil from the outer pad backplate. Install the outer pad in the caliper-mounting bracket, ensuring that the friction material of the pad is against the brake disc. Install the inner (piston side) pad into the caliper. If the original pads are being refitted, ensure that they are refitted to their original locations as noted before removal. The inner pad is fitted with a retaining clip, which engages with the recess in the piston. Where applicable, note that the pad with the wear sensor wiring should be installed as the inner pad. New pads are marked with an arrow on the backing plate, which identifies the direction of rotation. Consequently, the pads should be fitted with the arrows pointing to the ground **(see illustrations)**.

24 Press the caliper into position. Install and tighten the guide pins to the specified torque **(see illustration)**.

4.23a Fit the outer pad to the caliper mounting bracket

4.23b Refit the inner pad

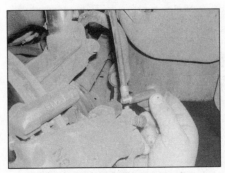

4.24 Install the caliper guide pins

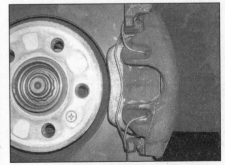

4.25 Refit the retaining spring

25 Refit the brake pad retaining spring to the caliper housing **(see illustration)**.

26 Where applicable, reconnect the brake pad wear sensor wiring connectors, ensuring that the wiring is correctly routed.

27 Depress the brake pedal repeatedly, until the pads are pressed into firm contact with the brake disc, and normal (non-assisted) pedal pressure is restored.

28 Repeat the above procedure on the remaining front brake caliper.

29 Refit the roadwheels, then lower the vehicle to the ground and tighten the roadwheel bolts to the specified torque.

30 Check the hydraulic fluid level as described in *Weekly checks*.

31 New pads will not give full braking efficiency until they have bedded-in. Be prepared for this and avoid hard braking (where possible) in the first hundred miles or so after pad renewal.

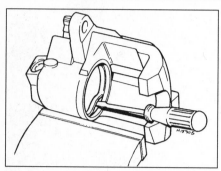

5.8 Use a small screwdriver to extract the caliper piston hydraulic seal

5 Front brake caliper –
removal, overhaul and refitting

Note: *Before starting work, refer to the note at the beginning of Section 2 concerning the dangers of hydraulic fluid, and to the warning at the beginning of Section 4 concerning the dangers of asbestos dust.*

Removal

1 Apply the handbrake, then jack up the front of the vehicle and support it on axle stands (see *Jacking and vehicle support*). Remove the appropriate roadwheel.
2 Minimise fluid loss by first removing the master cylinder reservoir cap, and then tightening it down onto a piece of polythene, to obtain an airtight seal. Alternatively, use a brake hose clamp, a G-clamp or a similar tool to clamp the flexible hose.
3 Clean the area around the union, then loosen the brake hose union nut.
4 Remove the brake pads as described in Section 4.
5 Unscrew the caliper from the end of the brake hose and remove it from the vehicle.

Overhaul

6 With the caliper on the bench, wipe away all traces of dust and dirt, but *avoid inhaling the dust, as it is injurious to health.*

If the piston cannot be withdrawn by hand, it can be pushed out by applying compressed air to the brake hose union hole. Only low pressure should be required, such as is generated by a foot pump. As the piston is expelled, take great care not to trap your fingers between the piston and caliper.

7 Withdraw the partially-ejected piston from the caliper body, and remove the dust seal.
8 Using a small screwdriver, extract the piston hydraulic seal, taking great care not to damage the caliper bore (see illustration).
9 Thoroughly clean all components, using only methylated spirit, isopropyl alcohol or

clean hydraulic fluid as a cleaning medium. Never use mineral-based solvents such as petrol or paraffin, as they will attack the hydraulic system rubber components. Dry the components immediately, using compressed air or a clean, lint-free cloth. Use compressed air to blow clear the fluid passages.
10 Check all components, and renew any that are worn or damaged. Check particularly the cylinder bore and piston; these should be renewed if they are scratched, worn or corroded in any way (note that this means the renewal of the complete caliper body assembly). Similarly check the condition of the spacers/guide pins and their bushes/bores (as applicable); both spacers/pins should be undamaged and (when cleaned) a reasonably tight sliding fit in their bores. If there is any doubt about the condition of any component, renew it.
11 If the assembly is fit for further use, obtain the appropriate repair kit; the components are available from VW dealers in various combinations.
12 Renew all rubber seals, dust covers and caps disturbed on dismantling as a matter of course; these should never be re-used.
13 On reassembly, ensure that all components are clean and dry.
14 Thinly coat the piston and piston seal with brake fitting paste (VW part no G 052 150 A2). This should be included in the VW caliper overhaul/repair kit.
15 Fit the new piston (fluid) seal, using only your fingers (no tools) to manipulate it into the cylinder bore groove. Fit the new dust seal to the piston, and refit the piston to the cylinder bore using a twisting motion; ensure that the piston enters squarely into the bore. Press the piston fully into the bore, then press the dust seal into the caliper body.

Refitting

16 Screw the caliper fully onto the flexible hose union.
17 Refit the brake pads as described in Section 4.
18 Securely tighten the brake pipe union nut.
19 Remove the brake hose clamp or polythene, as applicable, and bleed the hydraulic system as described in Section 2. Note that, providing the precautions described were

6.4 Using a DTI gauge to measure disc run-out

taken to minimise brake fluid loss, it should only be necessary to bleed the relevant front brake.
20 Refit the roadwheel, then lower the vehicle to the ground and tighten the roadwheel bolts to the specified torque.

6 Brake disc –
inspection, removal and refitting

Note: *Before starting work, refer to the note at the beginning of Section 4 concerning the dangers of asbestos dust.*
Note: *If either disc requires renewal, BOTH should be renewed at the same time, to ensure even and consistent braking. New brake pads should also be fitted.*

Front brake disc

Inspection

1 Apply the handbrake, then jack up the front of the car and support it on axle stands (see *Jacking and vehicle support*). Remove the appropriate front roadwheel.
2 Slowly rotate the brake disc so that the full area of both sides can be checked; remove the brake pads if better access is required to the inboard surface. Light scoring is normal in the area swept by the brake pads, but if heavy scoring or cracks are found, the disc must be renewed.
3 It is normal to find a lip of rust and brake dust around the perimeter of the disc; this can be scraped off if required. If, however, a lip has formed due to excessive wear of the brake pad swept area, then the disc thickness must be measured using a micrometer. Take measurements at several places around the disc, at the inside and outside of the pad swept area; if the disc has worn at any point to the specified minimum thickness or less, the disc must be renewed.
4 If the disc is thought to be warped, it can be checked for run-out. Either use a dial gauge mounted on any convenient fixed point, while the disc is slowly rotated, or use feeler blades to measure (at several points all around the disc) the clearance between the disc and a fixed point, such as the caliper mounting bracket. If the measurements obtained are at the specified maximum or beyond, the disc is excessively warped, and must be renewed; however, it is worth checking first that the hub bearing is in good condition (Chapter 1A, Section 16 or Chapter 1B, Section 19, as appropriate). If the run-out is excessive, the disc must be renewed **(see illustration)**.
5 Check the disc for cracks, especially around the wheel bolt holes, and any other wear or damage, and renew if necessary.

Removal

6 Remove the brake pads as described in Section 4.
7 On models with FN3 front brake calipers, unscrew the two bolts securing the brake

caliper mounting bracket to the hub carrier, then slide the caliper assembly off the disc. Using a piece of wire or string, tie the caliper to the front suspension coil spring, to avoid placing any strain on the brake hose.

8 Use chalk or paint to mark the relationship of the disc to the hub, then remove the screw securing the brake disc to the hub, and remove the disc **(see illustration)**. If it is tight, apply penetrating fluid, and tap its rear face gently with a hide or plastic mallet. The use of excessive force could cause the disc to be damaged.

Refitting

9 Refitting is the reverse of the removal procedure, noting the following points:
  a) *Ensure that the mating surfaces of the disc and hub are clean and flat.*
  b) *Align (if applicable) the marks made on removal, and securely tighten the disc retaining screw.*
  c) *If a new disc has been fitted, use a suitable solvent to wipe any preservative coating from the disc, before refitting the caliper.*
  d) *On models with FN3 brake calipers, slide the caliper into position over the disc, making sure the pads pass either side of the disc. Tighten the caliper bracket mounting bolts to the specified torque.*
  e) *Fit the pads as described in Section 4.*
  f) *Refit the roadwheel, then lower the vehicle to the ground and tighten the roadwheel bolts to the specified torque. On completion, repeatedly depress the brake pedal until normal (non-assisted) pedal pressure returns.*

Rear brake disc

Inspection

10 Firmly chock the front wheels, then jack up the rear of the car and support it on axle stands. Remove the appropriate rear road-wheel.
11 Inspect the disc as described in paragraphs 2 to 5.

Removal

12 Unscrew the two bolts securing the brake caliper mounting bracket in position, then slide the caliper assembly off the disc. Using a piece of wire or string, tie the caliper to the rear suspension coil spring, to avoid placing any strain on the hydraulic brake hose.
13 Use chalk or paint to mark the relationship of the disc to the hub, then remove the screw securing the brake disc to the hub, and remove the disc **(see illustration)**. If it is tight, apply penetrating fluid, and tap its rear face gently with a hide or plastic mallet. The use of excessive force could cause the disc to be damaged.

Refitting

14 Refitting is a reversal of the removal procedure, noting the following points:

6.8 Undo the disc retaining screw

  a) *Ensure that the mating surfaces of the disc and hub are clean and flat.*
  b) *Align (if applicable) the marks made on removal, and securely tighten the disc retaining screw.*
  c) *If a new disc has been fitted, use a suitable solvent to wipe any preservative coating from the disc, before refitting the caliper.*
  d) *Slide the caliper into position over the disc, making sure the pads pass either side of the disc. Tighten the caliper bracket mounting bolts to the specified torque. If new discs have been fitted and there is insufficient clearance between the pads to accommodate the new, thicker disc, it may be necessary to push the piston back into the caliper body as described in Section 8.*
  e) *Refit the roadwheel, then lower the vehicle to the ground and tighten the roadwheel bolts to the specified torque. On completion, repeatedly depress the brake pedal until normal (non-assisted) pedal pressure returns.*

7 Front brake disc shield – removal and refitting

Removal

1 Remove the brake disc as described in Section 6.
2 Unscrew the securing bolts, and remove the brake disc shield.

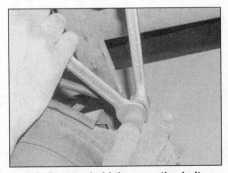

8.3 Counter-hold the mounting bolts

6.13 Lift away the disc

Refitting

3 Refitting is a reversal of removal. Tighten the shield retaining bolts to the specified torque. Refit the brake disc with reference to Section 6.

8 Rear brake pads – removal, inspection and refitting

Note: *Before starting work, refer to the note at the beginning of Section 4 concerning the dangers of asbestos dust. New caliper mounting bolts will be required on refitting.*

Removal

1 Chock the front wheels, then jack up the rear of the vehicle and support it on axle stands (see *Jacking and vehicle support*). Remove the rear wheels.
2 Slacken the handbrake cable and detach it from the caliper as described in Section 16.
3 Slacken and remove the guide pin bolts, using a slim open-ended spanner to prevent the guide pins from rotating **(see illustration)**. Discard the bolts – new ones must be used on refitting.
4 Lift the caliper away from the brake pads, and tie it to the suspension strut using a suitable piece of wire **(see illustration)**. Do not allow the caliper to hang unsupported on the flexible brake hose.
5 Withdraw the two brake pads from the caliper mounting bracket and recover the pad anti-rattle shims from the mounting bracket, noting their correct fitted locations.

8.4 Remove the caliper

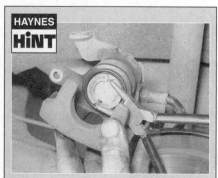

In the absence of the special tool, the piston can be screwed back into the caliper using a pair of circlip pliers.

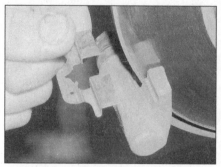

8.10a Refit the anti-rattle shims

8.10b Install the brake pads

Inspection

6 First measure the thickness of each brake pad (including the backing plate). If either pad is worn at any point to the specified minimum thickness or less, **all four** pads must be renewed. Also, the pads should be renewed if any are fouled with oil or grease; there is no satisfactory way of degreasing friction material, once contaminated. If any of the brake pads are worn unevenly, or fouled with oil or grease, trace and rectify the cause before reassembly. New brake pads are available from VW dealers.

7 If the brake pads are still serviceable, carefully clean them using a clean, fine wire brush or similar, paying particular attention to the sides and back of the metal backing. Clean out the grooves in the friction material (where applicable), and pick out any large embedded particles of dirt or debris. Carefully clean the pad locations in the caliper body/mounting bracket.

8 Prior to fitting the pads, check that the guide pins are free to slide easily in the caliper bracket, and check that the rubber guide pin gaiters are undamaged. Brush the dust and dirt from the caliper and piston, but **do not** inhale it, as it is injurious to health. Inspect the dust seal around the piston for damage, and the piston for evidence of fluid leaks, corrosion or damage. If attention to any of these components is necessary, refer to Section 9.

Refitting

9 If new brake pads are to be fitted, it will be necessary to retract the piston fully, by rotating it in a clockwise direction as it is pushed into the caliper bore **(see Haynes Hint above)**. To avoid any dirt entering the ABS solenoid valves, connect a pipe to the bleed nipple, and as the piston is pushed back open the nipple and allow the displaced fluid to flow through the pipe into a suitable container.

10 Fit the pad anti-rattle shims to the caliper mounting bracket, ensuring that they are correctly located. Install the pads in the mounting bracket, ensuring that each pad's friction material is against the brake disc.

Remove the protective foil from the outer pad backing plate **(see illustrations)**.

11 Slide the caliper back into position over the pads.

12 Press the caliper into position, then install the new guide pin bolts, tightening them to the specified torque setting while retaining the guide pin with an open-ended spanner **(see illustration)**.

13 Depress the brake pedal repeatedly, until the pads are pressed into firm contact with the brake disc, and normal (non-assisted) pedal pressure is restored.

14 Repeat the above procedure on the remaining rear brake caliper.

15 Reconnect the handbrake cables to the calipers, and adjust the handbrake as described in Section 14.

16 Refit the roadwheels, then lower the vehicle to the ground and tighten the road-wheel bolts to the specified torque setting.

17 Check the hydraulic fluid level as described in *Weekly checks*.

18 New pads will not give full braking efficiency until they have bedded-in. Be prepared for this, and avoid hard braking as far as possible for the first hundred miles or so after pad renewal.

9 Rear brake caliper – removal, overhaul and refitting

Note: *Before starting work, refer to the note at the beginning of Section 2 concerning the*

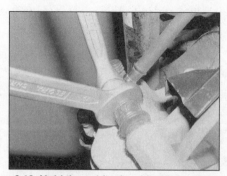

8.12 Hold the guide pin whilst tightening the retaining bolt

dangers of hydraulic fluid, and to the warning at the beginning of Section 4 concerning the dangers of asbestos dust.

Removal

1 Chock the front wheels, then jack up the rear of the vehicle and support on axle stands (see *Jacking and vehicle support*). Remove the relevant rear wheel.

2 Minimise fluid loss by first removing the master cylinder reservoir cap, and then tightening it down onto a piece of polythene, to obtain an airtight seal. Alternatively, use a brake hose clamp, a G-clamp or a similar tool to clamp the flexible hose.

3 Clean the area around the union on the caliper, then loosen the brake hose union nut.

4 Remove the brake pads as described in Section 8.

5 Unscrew the caliper from the end of the flexible hose and remove it from the vehicle.

Overhaul

Note: *It is not possible to overhaul the brake caliper handbrake mechanism. If the mechanism is faulty, or fluid is leaking from the handbrake lever seal the caliper assembly must be renewed.*

6 With the caliper on the bench, wipe away all traces of dust and dirt, but avoid inhaling the dust, as it is injurious to health.

7 Using a small screwdriver, carefully prise out the dust seal from the caliper, taking care not to damage the piston.

8 Remove the piston from the caliper bore by rotating it in an anti-clockwise direction. This can be achieved using a suitable pair of circlip pliers engaged in the caliper piston slots. Once the piston turns freely but does not come out any further, the piston can be withdrawn by hand.

HAYNES HiNT *If the piston cannot be withdrawn by hand, it can be pushed out by applying compressed air to the brake hose union hole. Only low pressure should be required, such as is generated by a foot pump. As the piston is expelled, take care not to trap your fingers between the piston and caliper.*

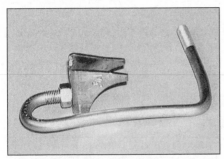

10.5a Improvised special tool constructed from a modified exhaust clamp, used to release the brake pedal from the servo pushrod

10.5b Using the tool to release the brake pedal from the servo pushrod

10.5c Rear view of the brake pedal (pedal removed) showing plastic lugs (arrowed) securing pedal to servo pushrod

9 Using a small screwdriver, extract the piston hydraulic seal(s), taking care not to damage the caliper bore.

10 Withdraw the guide pins from the caliper, and remove the guide sleeve gaiters.

11 Thoroughly clean all components, using only methylated spirit, isopropyl alcohol or clean hydraulic fluid as a cleaning medium. Never use mineral-based solvents such as petrol or paraffin, as they will attack the hydraulic system rubber components. Dry the components immediately, using compressed air or a clean, lint-free cloth. Use compressed air to blow clear the fluid passages.

12 Check all components, and renew any that are worn or damaged. Check particularly the cylinder bore and piston; these should be renewed (note that this means the renewal of the complete caliper body assembly) if they are scratched, worn or corroded in any way. Similarly check the condition of the spacers/guide pins and their bushes/bores (as applicable); both spacers/pins should be undamaged and (when cleaned) a reasonably tight sliding fit in their bores. If there is any doubt about the condition of any component, renew it.

13 If the assembly is fit for further use, obtain the appropriate repair kit; the components are available from VW dealers in various combinations.

14 Renew all rubber seals, dust covers and caps disturbed on dismantling as a matter of course; these should never be re-used.

15 On reassembly, ensure that all components are clean and dry.

16 Smear a thin coat of brake fitting paste (VW part no G 052 150 A2) on the piston, seal and caliper bore. This should be included in the overhaul/repair kit. Fit the new piston (fluid) seal, using only the fingers (no tools) to manipulate into the cylinder bore groove.

17 Fit the new dust seal to the piston groove, then refit the piston assembly. Turn the piston in a clockwise direction, using the method employed on dismantling, until it is fully retracted into the caliper bore.

18 Press the dust seal into position in the caliper housing.

19 Apply the grease supplied in the repair kit, or a copper-based brake grease or anti-seize compound, to the guide pins. Fit the new gaiters to the guide pins and fit the pins to the caliper ensuring that the gaiters are correctly located in the grooves on both the pins and caliper.

20 Prior to refitting, fill the caliper with fresh hydraulic fluid by slackening the bleed screw and pumping the fluid through the caliper until bubble-free fluid is expelled from the union hole.

Refitting

21 Screw the caliper fully onto the flexible hose union.

22 Refit the brake pads as described in paragraphs 10 to 12 of Section 8.

23 Securely tighten the brake pipe union nut.

24 Remove the brake hose clamp or remove the polythene from the fluid reservoir, as applicable, and bleed the hydraulic system as described in Section 2. Note that, providing the precautions described were taken to minimise brake fluid loss, it should only be necessary to bleed the relevant rear brake.

25 Connect the handbrake cable to the caliper, and adjust the handbrake as described in Section 14.

26 Refit the roadwheel, then lower the vehicle to the ground and tighten the roadwheel bolts to the specified torque. On completion, check the hydraulic fluid level as described in *Weekly checks*.

10 Brake pedal –
removal and refitting

Removal

1 Disconnect the battery negative lead. **Note:** *Before disconnecting the battery, refer to 'Disconnecting the battery' in the reference section at the rear of this manual.*

2 With reference to Chapter 11, Section 28, remove the driver's side lower facia trim panels, and the trim panel below the dash.

3 Where fitted, unscrew the two retaining screws and remove the connecting plate between the clutch and brake pedals.

4 Remove the brake light switch as described in Section 18.

5 It is now necessary to release the brake pedal from the ball on the vacuum servo pushrod. To do this, a VW special tool is available, but a suitable alternative can be improvised **(see illustration)**. Note that the plastic lugs in the pedal are very stiff, and it will not be possible to release them by hand. Using the tool, release the securing lugs, and pull the pedal from the servo pushrod **(see illustrations)**.

6 Undo and remove the pedal bracket support retaining nut **(see illustration)**.

7 Unscrew the five nuts securing the pedal support bracket to the bulkhead/servo, sufficiently to allow the bracket some movement. Do not remove the nuts completely **(see illustration)**.

8 Undo the pivot shaft nut and slide the pivot shaft to the right, until the pedal is free.

10.6 Undo the support bracket nut

10.7 Slacken the five securing nuts

10.8 Recover the pivot bush

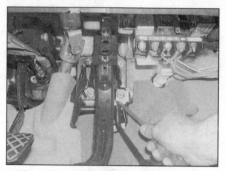

10.11 Lever the bracket away from the bulkhead

Remove the pedal and recover the pivot bush **(see illustration)**.
9 Carefully clean all components, and renew any that are worn or damaged.

Refitting

10 Prior to refitting, apply a smear of multi-purpose grease to the pivot shaft and pedal bearing surfaces.
11 Using a screwdriver, lever the pedal bracket away from the bulkhead **(see illustration)**.
12 Pull the servo unit pushrod down, and at the same time manoeuvre the pedal into position, ensuring that the pivot bush is correctly located.
13 Tighten the five pedal bracket retaining nuts securely, and refit the bracket support retaining nut.
14 Hold the servo unit pushrod, and push the pedal back onto the pushrod ball. Make sure the pedal is securely fastened to the pushrod.
15 Insert the pedal pivot bolt and tighten the retaining nut to the to the specified torque.
16 Refit the brake light switch, as described in Section 18.
17 Where fitted, refit the connecting plate between the clutch and brake pedals, and tighten the two retaining bolts securely.
18 Refit the facia trim panels as described in Chapter 11.

11 Servo unit –
testing, removal and refitting

Testing

1 To test the operation of the servo unit, depress the footbrake several times to exhaust the vacuum, then start the engine whilst keeping the pedal firmly depressed. As the engine starts, there should be a noticeable 'give' in the brake pedal as the vacuum builds-up. Allow the engine to run for at least two minutes, then switch it off. If the brake pedal is now depressed, it should feel normal, but further applications should result in the pedal feeling firmer, with the pedal stroke decreasing with each application.
2 If the servo does not operate as described, first inspect the servo unit non-return valve as

described in Section 12. On diesel models, also check the operation of the vacuum pump as described in Section 21 or 22.
3 If the servo unit still fails to operate satisfactorily, the fault lies within the unit itself. Repairs to the unit are not possible – if faulty, the servo unit must be renewed.

Removal

Note: *On left-hand drive models, it is not possible to remove the vacuum servo unit without first removing the hydraulic unit (see Section 20). Therefore, servo unit removal and refitting should be entrusted to a VW dealer. A new servo unit gasket will be required on refitting.*

4 Remove the master cylinder as described in Section 13.
5 Where applicable remove the heat shield from the servo, then carefully ease the vacuum hose out from the sealing grommet in the front of the servo.
6 Disconnect the servo vacuum sensor (where applicable).
7 With reference to Chapter 11, Section 28, remove the driver's side lower facia trim panels, and the trim panel below the dash.
8 Remove the brake light switch as described in Section 18.
9 Where fitted, unscrew the two retaining screws and remove the connecting plate between the clutch and brake pedals (manual transmission models only).
10 It is now necessary to release the brake pedal from the ball on the vacuum servo pushrod. To do this, a VW special tool is available, but a suitable alternative can be improvised. Note that the plastic lugs in the pedal are very stiff, and it will not be possible to release them by hand. Using the tool, release the securing lugs, and pull the pedal from the servo pushrod **(see illustration 10.5a)**.
11 Again working in the footwell, undo the five nuts securing the servo unit to the bulkhead, then return to the engine compartment and manoeuvre the servo unit out of position, noting the gasket which is fitted to the rear of the unit **(see illustration 10.7)**. Note that, on some models, it may be necessary to remove the inlet manifold (see Chapter 4A or 4B) to give sufficient clearance to withdraw the servo.

Refitting

12 Check the servo unit vacuum hose sealing grommet for signs of damage or deterioration, and renew if necessary.
13 Fit a new gasket to the rear of the servo unit, and reposition the unit in the engine compartment.
14 From inside the vehicle, ensure that the servo unit pushrod is correctly engaged with the brake pedal, and push the pedal onto the pushrod ball. Check the pushrod ball is securely engaged, then refit the servo unit mounting nuts and tighten them to the specified torque.
15 Where removed, refit the connecting plate between the clutch pedal and brake pedal, tighten the screws securely (manual transmission models only).
16 With reference to Section 18, refit the brake light switch.
17 Refit the facia trim panels.
18 Carefully ease the vacuum hose back into position in the servo, taking great care not to displace the sealing grommet. Refit the heat shield to the servo, and reconnect the vacuum sensor wiring plug (where applicable).
19 Refit the master cylinder as described in Section 13 of this Chapter.
20 Where applicable, refit the inlet manifold as described in Chapter 4A or 4B.
21 On completion, start the engine and check for air leaks at the vacuum hose-to-servo unit connection; check the operation of the braking system.

12 Servo non-return valve –
testing, removal and refitting

1 The non-return valve is located in the vacuum hose from the inlet manifold to the brake servo. If the valve is to be renewed, the complete hose/valve assembly should be replaced.

Removal

2 Ease the vacuum hose out of the servo unit, taking care not to displace the grommet.
3 Note the routing of the hose, then slacken the retaining clip(s) and disconnect the opposite end of the hose assembly from the manifold/pump hose, and remove it from the car.

Testing

4 Examine the check valve and vacuum hose for signs of damage, and renew if necessary.
5 The valve may be tested by blowing through it in both directions, air should flow through the valve in one direction only; when blown through from the servo unit end of the valve. Renew the valve if this is not the case.
6 Examine the servo unit rubber sealing grommet for signs of damage or deterioration, and renew as necessary.

Refitting

7 Ensure that the sealing grommet is correctly fitted to the servo unit.

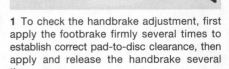

8 Ease the hose union into position in the servo, taking great care not to displace or damage the grommet.

9 Ensure that the hose is correctly routed, and connect it to the inlet manifold/pump hose, ensure that the hose is secured in the retaining clips.

10 On completion, start the engine and check the valve-to-servo unit connection for signs of air leaks.

13 Master cylinder – removal, overhaul and refitting

Note: *Before starting work, refer to the warning at the beginning of Section 2 concerning the dangers of hydraulic fluid. A new master cylinder O-ring will be required on refitting.*

Removal

1 On left-hand drive models, the ABS hydraulic unit must be removed before the master cylinder can be removed.

> ⚠ *Warning: Removal and refitting of the hydraulic unit should be entrusted to a VW dealer. Great care has to be taken not to allow any fluid to escape from the unit as the pipes are disconnected. If the fluid is allowed to escape, air can enter the unit, causing air locks which cause the hydraulic unit to malfunction.*

2 Disconnect the battery negative lead. **Note:** *Before disconnecting the battery, refer to 'Disconnecting the battery' in the Reference section at the rear of this manual.* Where necessary, to improve access to the master cylinder, remove the air inlet trunking.

3 Remove the master cylinder reservoir cap (disconnect the wiring plug from the brake fluid level sender unit), and syphon the hydraulic fluid from the reservoir. **Note:** *Do not syphon the fluid by mouth, as it is poisonous; use a syringe or an old poultry baster.*

4 Wipe clean the area around the brake pipe unions on the side of the master cylinder, and place absorbent rags beneath the pipe unions to catch any leaking fluid. Make a note of the correct fitted positions of the unions, then unscrew the union nuts and carefully withdraw the pipes. Plug or tape over the pipe ends and master cylinder orifices, to minimise the loss of brake fluid, and to prevent the entry of dirt into the system. Wash off any spilt fluid immediately with cold water.

5 Disconnect and plug the clutch master cylinder supply hose from the brake reservoir **(see illustration 13.7).**

6 On vehicles equipped with ESP (Electronic Stability Program – see Chapter 10), disconnect the two pressure sensors from the underside of the master cylinder.

7 Slacken and remove the two nuts and washers securing the master cylinder to the vacuum servo unit, remove the heat shield

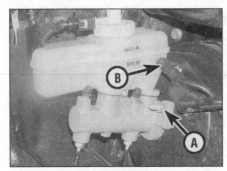

13.7 Brake cylinder nuts (A), and clutch cylinder supply hose (B)

(where fitted), then withdraw the unit from the engine compartment **(see illustration)**. Remove the O-ring from the rear of the master cylinder, and discard it.

Overhaul

8 If the master cylinder is faulty, it must be renewed. Repair kits are not available from VW dealer, so the cylinder must be treated as a sealed unit.

9 The only items which can be renewed are the mounting seals for the fluid reservoir; if these show signs of deterioration, withdraw the retaining pin, pull off the reservoir and remove the old seals. Lubricate the new seals with clean brake fluid, and press them into the master cylinder ports. Ease the fluid reservoir into position, push it fully home, and insert the retaining pin.

Refitting

10 Remove all traces of dirt from the master cylinder and servo unit mating surfaces, and fit a new O-ring to the groove on the master cylinder body.

11 Fit the master cylinder to the servo unit, ensuring that the servo unit pushrod enters the master cylinder bore centrally. Refit the heat shield (where applicable), master cylinder mounting nuts and washers, and tighten them to the specified torque.

12 Wipe clean the brake pipe unions, then refit them to the master cylinder ports and tighten them securely.

13 On vehicles equipped with ESP, reconnect the pressure sensors on the underside of the master cylinder.

14.5 Slacken the adjuster nut

14 Reconnect the clutch m⬛⬛⬛ supply hose to the reservoir.

15 Refill the master cylinder reser⬛⬛ new fluid, and bleed the complete hy⬛⬛ system as described in Section 2.

14 Handbrake – adjustment

1 To check the handbrake adjustment, first apply the footbrake firmly several times to establish correct pad-to-disc clearance, then apply and release the handbrake several times.

2 Applying normal moderate pressure, pull the handbrake lever to the fully-applied position, counting the number of clicks from the handbrake ratchet mechanism. If adjustment is correct, there should be approximately 4 to 7 clicks before the handbrake is fully applied. If this is not the case, adjust as follows.

3 Remove the handbrake cover or the centre console (see Chapter 11), as applicable, to gain access to the handbrake lever.

4 Chock the front wheels, then jack up the rear of the vehicle and support it on axle stands.

5 With the handbrake fully released, slacken the handbrake adjuster nut until both the rear caliper handbrake levers are back against their stops **(see illustration)**.

6 From this point, tighten the adjusting nuts until both handbrake levers just move off the caliper stops. Ensure that the gap between each caliper handbrake lever and its stop is between 1.0 and 1.5 mm, and ensure both the right- and left-hand gaps are equal **(see illustration)**. Check that both wheels/discs rotate freely, then check the adjustment by applying the handbrake fully and counting the clicks from the handbrake ratchet (see paragraph 2). If necessary, re-adjust.

7 Once adjustment is correct, refit the handbrake cover or centre console (as applicable).

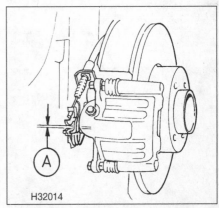

H32014

14.6 Turn the adjustment nuts until a gap (A) of between 1.0 and 1.5 mm can be seen between the caliper handbrake lever and the end stop

15.4 Disengage the cable

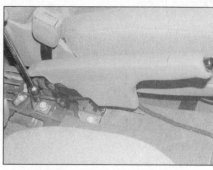

15.5 Unscrew the retaining nuts

2 If desired, ... handbrake lever cover sleeve by depressing the locating tag with a screwdriver, then sliding the sleeve from the lever.

3 Disconnect the wiring plug from the handbrake 'on' warning light switch.

4 Slacken the handbrake cable adjuster nut sufficiently to allow the ends of the cables to be disengaged from the equaliser plate **(see illustration)**.

5 Unscrew the three retaining nuts, and withdraw the lever **(see illustration)**.

Refitting

6 Refitting is a reversal of removal, bearing in mind the following points.

a) *Prior to refitting the handbrake cover, adjust the handbrake as described in Section 14.*

b) *Check the operation of the handbrake 'on' warning switch prior to refitting the centre console.*

16 Handbrake cables –
removal and refitting

Removal

1 Remove the centre console as described in Chapter 11, to gain access to the handbrake lever. The handbrake cable consists of two sections, a right- and a left-hand section, which are linked to the lever by an equaliser plate. Each section can be removed individually.

2 Slacken the handbrake cable adjuster nut sufficiently to allow the ends of the cables to be disengaged from the equaliser plate.

3 Chock the front wheels, then jack up the rear of the car and support it on axle stands.

4 Working back along the length of the cable,

noting its correct routing, and free it from all the relevant guides and retaining clips.

5 Disengage the inner cable from the caliper handbrake lever, then remove the outer cable retaining clip and detach the cable from the caliper **(see illustration)**. Withdraw the cable from underneath the vehicle.

Refitting

6 Refitting is a reversal of removal, bearing in mind the following points.

a) *When locating the handbrake cable sheath in the guide on the rear trailing arm, the cable clamping ring must lie in the middle of the clip.*

b) *Before refitting the centre console, adjust the handbrake as described in Section 14.*

17 Handbrake 'on'
warning light switch –
removal and refitting

Removal

1 Disconnect the battery negative lead. **Note:** *Before disconnecting the battery, refer to 'Disconnecting the battery' in the reference section at the rear of this manual.*

2 Remove the centre console, with reference to Chapter 11 if necessary.

3 Disconnect the wiring plug from the switch.

4 Squeeze the securing lugs, and withdraw the switch from the handbrake lever assembly **(see illustration)**.

Refitting

5 Refitting is a reversal of removal.

18 Brake light switch –
removal and refitting

Removal

1 The brake light switch is located on the pedal bracket beneath the facia. Disconnect the battery negative lead. **Note:** *Before disconnecting the battery, refer to 'Disconnecting the battery' in the Reference section at the rear of this manual.*

2 Working in the driver's footwell, remove the lower facia panel, see Chapter 11, Section 28.

3 Reach up behind the facia and disconnect the wiring connector from the switch **(see illustration)**.

4 Twist the switch through 90° and release it from the mounting bracket.

Refitting

5 Prior to installation, fully extend the brake light switch plunger.

6 Fully depress and hold the brake pedal, then manoeuvre the switch into position. Align the shaped lug of the switch with the corresponding cut-out in the bracket **(see illustration)**. Secure the switch in position it by pushing it into the bracket and twisting it through 90°, then release the brake pedal.

7 Reconnect the wiring connector, and check the operation of the brake lights. The brake

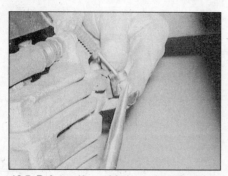

16.5 Release the cable inner from its lever and withdraw the cable from the caliper

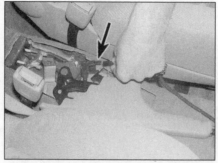

17.4 Handbrake warning switch (arrowed)

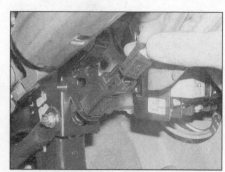

18.3 Disconnect the brake switch

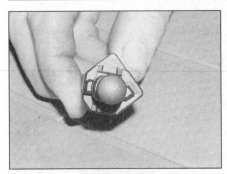

18.6 Align the shaped lug with the corresponding cut-out in the bracket

lights should illuminate after the brake pedal has travelled approximately 5 mm. If the switch is not functioning correctly, it is faulty and must be renewed; no adjustment is possible.

8 On completion, refit the lower facia panel.

19 Anti-lock braking system (ABS) – general information and precautions

Note: *On models equipped with traction control, the ABS unit is a dual function unit, controlling both the anti-lock braking system (ABS) and the electronic differential locking (EDL) system functions.*

ABS is standard on models covered in this manual; the system may also be referred to as including EBD (Electronic Brake Distribution) which means it adjusts the front and rear

braking forces according to the weight being carried. Two types of ABS are fitted: the Mark 20 IE and the Mark 60 **(see illustrations)**. The system comprises a hydraulic unit (which contains the hydraulic solenoid valves and accumulators), the electrically-driven fluid return pump, four roadwheel sensors (one fitted for each wheel), and the electronic control module (ECM). The purpose of the system is to prevent wheel(s) locking during heavy braking. This is achieved by automatic release of the brake on the relevant wheel, followed by re-application of the brake.

The solenoids are controlled by the ECM, which itself receives signals from the four wheel sensors, which monitor the speed of rotation of each wheel. By comparing these speed signals, the ECM can determine the speed at which the car is travelling. It can then use this speed to determine when a wheel is decelerating at an abnormal rate, compared to the speed of the car, and therefore predicts when a wheel is about to lock. During normal operation, the system functions in the same way as a non-ABS braking system.

If the ECM senses that a wheel is about to lock, it operates the relevant solenoid valve in the hydraulic unit, which then isolates the brake caliper on the wheel which is about to lock from the master cylinder, effectively sealing-in the hydraulic pressure.

If the speed of rotation of the wheel continues to decrease at an abnormal rate, the ECM switches on the electrically-driven return pump, which pumps the hydraulic fluid back into the master cylinder, releasing pressure on the brake caliper so that the brake is released.

Once the speed of rotation of the wheel returns to an acceptable rate, the pump stops; the solenoid valve opens, allowing the hydraulic master cylinder pressure to return to the caliper, which then re-applies the brake. This cycle can be carried out at up to 10 times a second.

The action of the solenoid valves and return pump creates pulses in the hydraulic circuit. When the ABS system is functioning, these pulses can be felt through the brake pedal.

The operation of the ABS system is entirely dependent on electrical signals. To prevent the system responding to any inaccurate signals, a built-in safety circuit monitors all signals received by the ECM. If an inaccurate signal or low battery voltage is detected, the ABS system is automatically shut down, and the warning light on the instrument panel is illuminated, to inform the driver that the ABS system is not operational. Normal braking should still be available, however.

If a fault does develop in the ABS system, the car must be taken to a VW dealer for fault diagnosis and repair.

20 Anti-lock braking system (ABS) components – removal and refitting

Hydraulic unit

1 Removal and refitting of the hydraulic unit is best entrusted to a VW dealer, as a fault diagnosis check must be performed on completion using specialist equipment.

Electronic control module (ECM)

2 The ECM is mounted underneath the hydraulic unit. Although it can be separated from the hydraulic unit, due to the delicacy of the components and the need for absolute cleanliness, it is recommended that the work be entrusted to a VW dealer.

Front wheel sensor

Removal

3 Chock the rear wheels, then firmly apply the handbrake, jack up the front of the car and support on axle stands (see *Jacking and vehicle support*). Remove the appropriate front roadwheel.

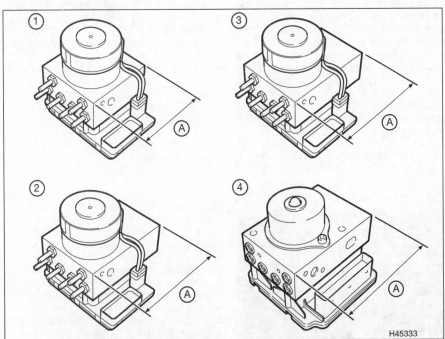

19.1a Distinguishing features of the Mark 20 IE ABS hydraulic unit

1 ABS version (A = 100 mm)
2 ABS/EDL version (A = 130 mm)
3 ABS/EDL/TCS version (A = 130 mm)
4 ABS/EDL/TCS/ESP version (A = 135 mm)

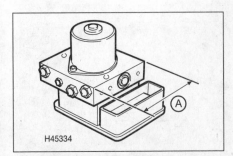

19.1b Distinguishing features of the Mark 60 ABS hydraulic unit

1 ABS/EDL/TCS/ESP version (A = 100 mm)

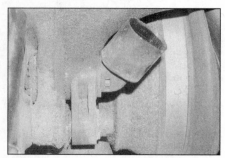

20.4 Disconnect the wheel speed sensor

4 Disconnect the electrical connector from the sensor by carefully lifting up the retaining tag, and pulling the connector from the sensor **(see illustration)**.

5 Slacken and remove the hexagon socket-head bolt securing the sensor to the hub carrier, and remove the sensor from the car.

Refitting

6 Ensure that the sensor and hub carrier sealing faces are clean.

7 Apply a thin coat of multi-purpose grease (VW recommend the use of lubricating paste G 000 650 – available from your dealer) to the mounting hole inner surface, then fit the sensor to the hub carrier. Refit the retaining bolt and tighten it to the specified torque.

8 Ensure that the sensor wiring is correctly routed and retained by all the necessary clips, and reconnect the wiring connector.

9 Refit the roadwheel, then lower the car to the ground and tighten the roadwheel bolts to the specified torque.

Rear wheel sensor

Removal

10 Chock the front wheels, then jack up the rear of the car and support it on axle stands (see *Jacking and vehicle support*). Remove the appropriate roadwheel.

11 Remove the sensor (paragraphs 4 and 5).

Refitting

12 Refit the sensor as described above in paragraphs 6 to 9.

Front reluctor rings

13 The front reluctor rings are integral with the wheel hubs. Examine the rings for damage

21.6 Undo the pump retaining nuts and bolt

21.5 Inlet and outlet hoses fitted to the vacuum pump on the diesel engine

such as chipped or missing teeth. If renewal is necessary, the complete hub assembly must be renewed with the bearings as described in Chapter 10.

Rear reluctor rings

14 The rear reluctor rings are integral with the rear wheel hub. Examine the rings for signs of damage such as chipped or missing teeth. If renewal is necessary, remove the disc as described in Section 6, renew the hub and bearings as described in Chapter 10.

---

21 Servo unit mechanical vacuum pump (diesel models) – testing, removal and refitting

Testing

1 The operation of the braking system vacuum pump can be checked using a vacuum gauge.

2 Disconnect the vacuum hose from the pump, and connect the gauge to the pump union using a suitable length of hose.

3 Start the engine and allow it to idle, then measure the vacuum created by the pump. As a guide, after one minute, a minimum of approximately 500 mm Hg should be recorded. If the vacuum registered is significantly less than this, it is likely that the pump is faulty. However, seek the advice of a VW dealer before condemning the pump.

4 Reconnect the vacuum hose. Overhaul of the vacuum pump is not possible, since no major components are available separately for it. If faulty, the complete pump assembly must be renewed.

21.9 Align the drive gear with the slot in the end of the camshaft

Removal

Note: *A new pump O-ring will be required on refitting.*

5 Release the retaining clip, and disconnect the vacuum hose from the top of pump. Also, where applicable, disconnect the outlet hose from the pump **(see illustration)**.

6 Slacken and remove the pump retaining bolt, and the two pump retaining nuts **(see illustration)**.

7 Withdraw the vacuum pump from the cylinder head, and recover the O-ring seal. Discard the O-ring – a new one should be used on refitting.

Refitting

8 Fit the new O-ring to the vacuum pump, and apply a smear of oil to the O-ring to aid installation.

9 Manoeuvre the vacuum pump into position, making sure that the slot in the pump drive gear aligns with the slot on the pump driveshaft **(see illustration)**.

10 Refit the pump retaining nuts and bolt, and tighten to the specified torque.

11 Reconnect the vacuum hose(s) to the pump, and secure in position with the retaining clip(s).

---

22 Servo unit electric vacuum pump (diesel models) – testing, removal and refitting

Note: *The electric vacuum pump is only fitted to models with ABS, EDL, TCS and ESP.*

Testing

1 With the engine stopped, depress the brake pedal several times to exhaust the vacuum in the servo unit. The pedal will become firm.

2 Start the engine, then slowly depress the brake pedal. An audible 'click' must be heard as the electric vacuum pump is activated, and the pedal will be easier to depress. Confirmation that the pump is running can be made by an assistant touching the pump as the pedal is depressed.

3 Overhaul of the electric vacuum pump is not possible, therefore, if faulty, the pump must be renewed.

Removal

4 The electric brake vacuum pump is located on the left-hand side of the front suspension subframe. Apply the handbrake, then jack up the front of the vehicle and support it on axle stands (see *Jacking and Vehicle Support*). Remove the left-hand front roadwheel.

5 Disconnect the wiring from the vacuum pump.

6 Unscrew the mounting bolts from the hydraulic unit bracket, then disconnect the vacuum hose from the pump.

7 Unbolt the bracket from the suspension subframe, and withdraw the vacuum pump.

Refitting

8 Refitting is a reversal of removal, but tighten the mounting bolts/nut to the specified torque.

Chapter 10
Suspension and steering systems

Contents

Front anti-roll bar – removal and refitting 7
Front anti-roll bar connecting link – removal and refitting 8
Front hub bearings – renewal 3
Front suspension and steering check . . . . See Chapter 1A or 1B
Front suspension lower arm – removal, overhaul and refitting 5
Front suspension lower arm balljoint – removal, inspection and
  refitting 6
Front suspension strut – removal, overhaul and refitting 4
Front wheel bearing housing – removal and refitting 2
General information 1
Ignition switch and steering column lock – removal and refitting . . . 18
Power steering fluid level check . . . . See Weekly checks
Power steering pump – removal and refitting 22
Power steering system – bleeding 21
Rear anti-roll bar – removal and refitting 12

Rear axle assembly – removal and refitting 13
Rear axle rubber mountings – renewal 14
Rear hub assembly – removal and refitting 9
Rear stub axle – removal and refitting 10
Rear suspension shock absorber and coil spring – removal and
  refitting 11
Steering column – removal, inspection and refitting 17
Steering gear assembly – removal, overhaul and refitting 19
Steering gear rubber gaiters and track rods – renewal 20
Steering wheel – removal and refitting 16
Track rod end – removal and refitting 23
Vehicle level sender – removal and refitting 15
Wheel alignment and steering angles – general information 24
Wheel and tyre maintenance and tyre pressure
  checks . . . . See Weekly checks

Degrees of difficulty

Easy, suitable for novice with little experience	**Fairly easy,** suitable for beginner with some experience	**Fairly difficult,** suitable for competent DIY mechanic	**Difficult,** suitable for experienced DIY mechanic 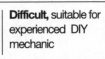	**Very difficult,** suitable for expert DIY or professional

Specifications

Front suspension

Type . . . .   Independent, with MacPherson struts incorporating coil springs and telescopic shock absorbers. Anti-roll bar fitted to all models

Rear suspension

Type . . . .   Transverse torsion beam axle with trailing arms. Separate gas-filled telescopic shock absorbers and coil springs. Anti-roll bar fitted to all models

Steering

Type . . . .   Rack-and-pinion. Power assistance standard

Wheel alignment and steering angles*

Front wheel:
  Camber angle:
    Standard suspension . . . .   -30' ± 30'
    Sports suspension . . . .   -33' ± 30'
    Heavy duty suspension . . . .   -16' ± 30'
    Maximum difference between sides (all models) . . . .   30'
  Castor angle:
    Standard suspension . . . .   7° 40' ± 30'
    Sports suspension . . . .   7° 50' ± 30'
    Heavy duty suspension . . . .   7° 15' ± 30'
    Maximum difference between sides (all models) . . . .   30'
  Toe setting . . . .   0° ± 10'
  Toe-out on turns (20° left or right):
    Standard suspension . . . .   1° 30' ± 20'
    Sports suspension . . . .   1° 31' ± 20'
    Heavy duty suspension . . . .   1° 27' ± 20'

Refer to a VW dealer for the latest recommendations.

Wheel alignment and steering angles (continued)

Rear wheel:

Camber angle	-1°27' ± 20'
Maximum difference between sides	30'

Toe setting:

Except Estate:

Standard suspension	20' ± 10'
Sports suspension	25' ± 10'
Heavy duty suspension	10' +10'/-7'

Estate:

Standard suspension	16' ± 10'
Sports suspension	22' ± 10'
Heavy duty suspension	10' +10'/-7'

Roadwheels

Type	Aluminium alloy

Tyres

Size	175/80R14, 195/65R15, 205/60R15, 205/55R16, 225/45R17 and 225/40ZR18
Pressures	see *Weekly checks* on page 0•17

Torque wrench settings

	Nm	lbf ft
Front suspension		
Anti-roll bar:		
Mounting clamp-to-subframe bolts	25	18
Connecting link-to-anti-roll bar bolt nut*	30	22
Connecting link-to-lower arm bolt	45	33
Hub nut/bolt*	See Chapter 8	
Lower arm:		
Pivot/mounting bolts*:		
Stage 1	70	52
Stage 2	Angle-tighten a further 90°	
Balljoint-to-lower arm bolts*:		
Stage 1	20	15
Stage 2	Angle-tighten a further 90°	
Balljoint nut*	45	33
Suspension strut:		
Bottom clamp bolt nut*:		
Stage 1	60	44
Stage 2	Angle-tighten a further 90°	
Upper mounting nut*	60	44
Spring seat retaining nut	60	44
Splash plate to wheel housing	10	7
Subframe-to-underbody bolts*:		
Stage 1	100	74
Stage 2	Angle-tighten a further 90°	
Vehicle level sender:		
Sender to underbody (pop-rivet screw)	8	6
Sender link to lower arm	6	4
Steering		
Power steering pump mounting bolts	25	18
Power steering pump pressure hose union bolt	30	22
Steering column universal joint clamp bolt*	30	22
Steering column:		
Upper mounting bolts	25	18
Lower mounting bolt nut	10	7
Fluid pipe union bolts:		
M14 union bolt	40	30
M16 union bolt	45	33
Steering gear mounting bolts*:		
Stage 1	20	15
Stage 2	Angle-tighten a further 90°	
Steering wheel bolt	50	37
Track rod balljoint locknut	50	37
Track rod balljoint nut*	45	33
Track rod inner balljoint to steering rack	75	55

Torque wrench settings (continued)

	Nm	lbf ft
Rear suspension		
Axle mounting bolts and nuts*	80	59
Hub nut*	175	129
Shock absorber:		
Lower mounting bolt and nut*	60	44
Upper mounting bolts*	75	55
Shock absorber-to-upper mounting nut*	25	18
Stub axle bolts*	60	44
Vehicle level sender to trailing arm	20	15
Vibration damper-to-axle bolts*:		
Stage 1	20	15
Stage 2	Angle-tighten a further 45°	
Roadwheels		
Roadwheel bolts	120	89

* Renew the nut/bolt every time it is removed

1 General information

The independent front suspension is of the MacPherson strut type, incorporating coil springs and integral telescopic shock absorbers. The struts are located by transverse lower suspension arms, which use rubber inner mounting bushes, and incorporate a balljoint at the outer ends. The front wheel bearing housings, which carry the wheel bearings, brake calipers and the hub/disc assemblies, are attached to the MacPherson struts by clamp bolts, and connected to the lower arms through the balljoints. A front anti-roll bar is fitted to all models. The anti-roll bar is rubber-mounted, and is connected to both lower suspension arms by short links.

The rear suspension consists of a torsion beam axle with telescopic shock absorbers and coil springs. An anti-roll bar is incorporated into the rear axle beam.

The safety steering column incorporates an intermediate shaft at its lower end. The intermediate shaft is connected to both the steering column and steering gear by universal joints, although the shaft is supplied as part of the column assembly and cannot be separated. Both the inner steering column and intermediate shaft have splined sections which collapse during a major frontal impact. The outer column is also telescopic with two sections, to facilitate reach adjustment.

The steering gear is mounted onto the front subframe, and is connected by two track rods, with balljoints at their inner and outer ends, to the steering arms projecting rearwards from the wheel bearing housings. The track rod ends are threaded to the track rods in order to allow adjustment of the front wheel toe setting.

Power-assisted steering is fitted as standard on all models. The hydraulic steering system is powered by a belt-driven pump, which is driven off the crankshaft pulley.

All models are fitted with an Anti-lock Brake System (ABS), and can also be fitted with a Traction Control System (TCS), an Electronic Differential Lock (EDL) system and an Electronic Stability Program (ESP). The ABS may also be referred to as including EBD (Electronic Brake Distribution) which means it adjusts the front and rear braking forces according to the weight being carried, and the TCS may also be referred to as ASR (Anti Slip Regulation).

The TCS system prevents the front wheels from losing traction during acceleration by reducing the engine output. The system is switched on automatically when the engine is started, and it utilises the ABS system sensors to monitor the rotational speeds of the front wheels.

The ESP system extends the ABS, TCS and EDL functions to reduce wheel spin in difficult driving conditions. It does this by using highly-sensitive sensors which monitor the speed of the vehicle, lateral movement of the vehicle, the brake pressure, and the steering angle of the front wheels. If, for example, the vehicle is tending to oversteer, the brake will be applied to the front outer wheel to correct the situation. If the vehicle is tending to understeer, the brake will be applied to the rear inside wheel. The steering angle of the front wheels is monitored by an angle sensor on the top of the steering column.

The TCS/ESP systems should always be switched on, except when driving with snow chains, driving in snow or driving on loose surfaces, when some wheel spin may be advantageous. The ESP switch is located in the centre of the facia.

Some models are also fitted with an Electronic Differential Lock (EDL) which reduces unequal traction from the front wheels. If one front wheel spins 100 rpm or more faster than the other, the faster wheel is slowed down by applying the brake to that wheel. The system is not the same as the traditional differential lock, where the actual differential gears are locked. Because the

system applies a front brake, in the event of a brake disc overheating the system will shut down until the disc has cooled. No warning light is displayed if the system shuts down. As is the case with the TCS system, the EDL system uses the ABS sensors to monitor front wheel speeds.

2 Front wheel bearing housing – removal and refitting

Note: *All self-locking nuts and bolts disturbed on removal must be renewed as a matter of course.*

Removal

1 Remove the wheel trim/hub cap (as applicable) and loosen the driveshaft retaining nut/bolt (hub nut/bolt) with the vehicle resting on its wheels. Also loosen the wheel bolts.

2 Apply the handbrake, then jack up the front of the vehicle and support it on axle stands (see *Jacking and vehicle support*). Remove the front roadwheel and also remove the splash guard from under the engine compartment.

3 Unscrew and remove the driveshaft retaining nut/bolt **(see illustration)**.

2.3 Removing the driveshaft retaining nut

2.4 The ABS wheel sensor on the inside of the wheel bearing housing

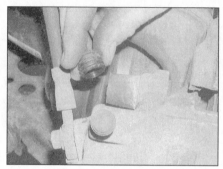

2.5a Remove the caps . . .

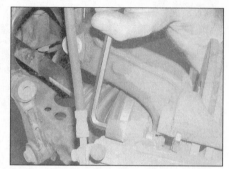

2.5b . . . then loosen the guide pins with an Allen key . . .

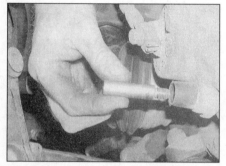

2.5c . . . remove the guide pins . . .

2.5d . . . withdraw the brake caliper . . .

2.5e . . . then undo the screws . . .

4 Remove the ABS wheel sensor as described in Chapter 9 **(see illustration)**.

5 Remove the brake disc as described in Chapter 9 **(see illustrations)**. This procedure includes removing the brake caliper, however do not disconnect the hydraulic brake hose from the caliper. Using a piece of wire or string, tie the caliper to the front suspension coil spring, to avoid placing any strain on the hydraulic brake hose.

6 Unbolt the splash plate from the wheel bearing housing.

7 Loosen the nut securing the steering track rod balljoint to the wheel bearing housing. To do this, fit a ring spanner to the nut, then hold the balljoint pin stationary using an Allen key. With the nut removed, it may be possible to release the balljoint from the wheel bearing housing by turning the balljoint pin with an Allen key. If not, leave the nut on by a few turns to protect the threads, then use a universal balljoint separator to release the balljoint. Remove the nut completely once the taper has been released.

8 Unscrew the front suspension lower balljoint-to-lower arm retaining bolts, and remove the retaining plate from the top of the lower arm. Now use a soft-faced mallet to tap the driveshaft from the hub splines while pulling out the bottom end of the wheel bearing housing. If the driveshaft is tight on the splines, it may be necessary to use a puller bolted to the hub to remove it **(see illustrations)**.

9 Note which way round it is fitted, then unscrew the nut and remove the clamp bolt securing the wheel bearing housing to the bottom of the strut.

10 The wheel bearing housing must now be released from the strut. To do this, VW technicians insert a special tool into the split wheel bearing housing, and turn it through 90° to open up the clamp. A similar tool can be made out of an old screwdriver, or alternatively a suitable cold chisel can be driven into the split as a wedge. Slightly press

2.5f . . . and remove the brake disc

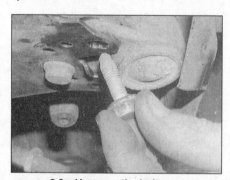

2.8a Unscrew the bolts . . .

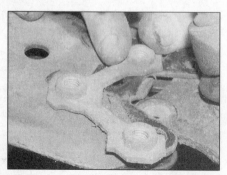

2.8b . . . and remove the retaining plate from the top of the lower arm

2.8c Pull out the wheel bearing housing and release the driveshaft from the hub

inwards the top of the wheel bearing housing, then push it downwards from the bottom of the strut (see illustrations).

Refitting

11 Note that all self-locking nuts and bolts disturbed on removal must be renewed as a matter of course.

12 Ensure that the driveshaft outer joint and hub splines are clean and dry, then lubricate the splines with fresh engine oil. Also lubricate the threads and contact surface of the hub nut/bolt with oil.

13 Lift the wheel bearing assembly into position, and engage the hub with the splines on the outer end of the driveshaft. Fit the new hub nut/bolt, tightening it by hand only at this stage.

14 Engage the wheel bearing housing with the bottom of the suspension strut, making sure that the hole in the side plate aligns with the holes in the split housing. Remove the tool used to open the split.

15 Insert the strut-to-wheel bearing housing clamp bolt from the front, and fit the new retaining nut. Tighten the nut to the specified torque.

16 Refit the lower arm balljoint and retaining plate, and tighten the bolts to the specified torque.

17 Refit the track rod balljoint to the wheel bearing housing, then fit a new retaining nut and tighten it to the specified torque. If necessary, hold the balljoint pin with an Allen key while tightening the nut.

18 Refit the splash plate and tighten the bolts.

19 Refit the brake disc and caliper with reference to Chapter 9.

20 Refit the ABS wheel sensor as described in Chapter 9, Section 20.

21 Ensure that the outer joint is drawn fully into the hub, then refit the roadwheel and splash guard. Lower the vehicle to the ground, and tighten the roadwheel bolts.

22 Tighten the driveshaft retaining nut/bolt in the stages given in the Specifications. It is recommended that an angle gauge is used to ensure the correct tightening angle.

3 Front hub bearings – renewal

Note: *The bearing is a sealed, pre-adjusted and prelubricated, double-row roller type, and requires no maintenance. A press will be required to remove the bearing, however, and if such a tool is not available, a large bench vice and spacers (such as large sockets) will serve as an adequate substitute. The bearing's inner races are an interference fit on the hub, and if the inner race remains on the hub when the latter is pressed out, a knife-edged bearing puller will be required to remove it. Note that the bearing is rendered unserviceable when it is removed.*

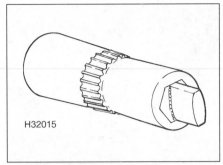

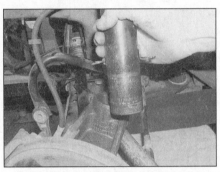

2.10a Tool used by VW technicians to open up the split wheel bearing housing

2.10b Using a cold chisel to open up the wheel bearing housing and release the suspension strut

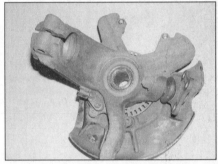

2.10c Withdrawing the wheel bearing housing from the bottom of the suspension strut

2.10d Wheel bearing housing

1 Remove the wheel bearing housing as described in Section 2.

2 Support the wheel bearing housing securely on blocks or in a vice. Using a metal tube which bears only on the inner end of the hub, press the hub out of the bearing. If the bearing's outboard inner race remains on the hub, remove it using a bearing puller. Take care not to damage the ABS rotor which is welded to the hub.

3 Extract the bearing retaining circlip from the outside of the wheel bearing housing.

4 Securely support the outer face of the wheel bearing housing. Using a suitable metal tube, press the complete bearing assembly out of the wheel bearing housing.

5 Thoroughly clean the hub and wheel bearing housing, removing all traces of dirt and grease, and polish away any burrs or raised edges which might hinder reassembly. Check both for cracks or any other signs of wear or damage, and renew them if necessary. It is recommended that the circlip is renewed, regardless of its apparent condition.

6 On reassembly, apply a light coating of molybdenum disulphide grease (VW recommend Molykote – available from your dealer) to the bearing outer race and bearing surface of the wheel bearing housing.

7 Securely support the wheel bearing housing, and locate the bearing in the hub. Press the bearing fully into position, ensuring that it enters the hub squarely, using a metal tube or suitable socket which bears only on the bearing outer race.

8 Once the bearing is correctly seated, secure the bearing in position with the new circlip, ensuring that it is correctly located in the groove in the wheel bearing housing.

9 Support the outer face of the hub, and locate the wheel bearing housing bearing inner race over the end of the hub. Press the bearing onto the hub, using a metal tube or socket which bears only on the inner race of the hub bearing, until it seats against the hub shoulder. Check that the hub rotates freely, and wipe off any excess oil or grease.

10 Refit the wheel bearing housing as described in Section 2.

4 Front suspension strut – removal, overhaul and refitting

Note: *All self-locking nuts and bolts disturbed on removal must be renewed as a matter of course.*

Removal

1 Apply the handbrake, then jack up the front of the vehicle and support it on axle stands (see *Jacking and vehicle support*). Remove the appropriate roadwheel.

2 Refer to Chapter 9 and unbolt the front brake caliper from the wheel bearing housing. **Do not** disconnect the hydraulic brake line. Support or tie the caliper to one side, taking care to avoid placing any strain on the brake line.

3 Unscrew the front suspension balljoint-to-

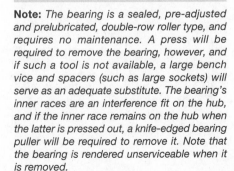

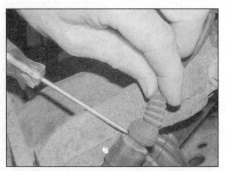

4.4a Disconnect the wiring from the ABS wheel sensor . . .

4.4b . . . and release the wiring from the strut support

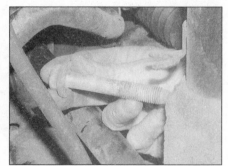

4.5 Removing the clamp bolt securing the wheel bearing housing to the strut

4.7a Use an Allen key to hold the piston rod while unscrewing the upper mounting nut

4.7b Remove the nut . . .

4.7c . . . and recover the mounting plate

lower arm retaining bolts, and remove the retaining plate from the top of the lower arm. This is necessary to provide additional room in order to lower the wheel bearing housing from the strut. If removing the left-hand suspension strut, it may be necessary to detach the automatic headlight range control sensor arm from the lower arm.

4 Disconnect the wiring from the ABS wheel sensor, and remove the wiring from the strut support **(see illustrations)**.

5 Note which way round it is fitted, then unscrew the nut and remove the clamp bolt securing the wheel bearing housing to the bottom of the strut **(see illustration)**.

6 Release the wheel bearing housing from the strut by slightly opening the split housing with reference to Section 2, then slightly pressing inwards the top of the wheel bearing housing,

and pushing it downwards from the bottom of the strut. There is no need to remove the driveshaft from the hub.

7 Unclip the plastic cover from the strut upper mounting, then unscrew and remove the upper mounting nut and recover the mounting plate. Note that it may be necessary to retain the strut piston rod with a suitable Allen key, to prevent it from rotating as the nut is loosened **(see illustrations)**.

8 Release the strut from the wheel bearing housing and manoeuvre it out from underneath the wheel arch **(see illustration)**.

Overhaul

⚠️ *Warning: Before attempting to dismantle the suspension strut, a suitable tool to hold the coil spring in compression must be obtained.*

Adjustable coil spring compressors are readily available, and are recommended for this operation. Any attempt to dismantle the strut without such a tool is likely to result in damage or personal injury.

9 With the strut removed from the car, clean away all external dirt. If necessary, mount it upright in a vice during the dismantling procedure.

10 Fit the spring compressor, and compress the coil spring until all tension is relieved from the upper spring seat **(see illustration)**.

11 Unscrew and remove the spring seat retaining nut, whilst retaining the strut piston with a suitable Allen key, then remove the bearing and mounting rubber, followed by the upper spring seat **(see illustrations)**. On models with heavy duty suspension, also remove the spacer/bush.

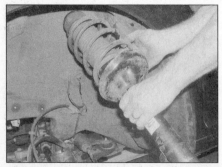

4.8 Removing the front suspension strut from underneath the wheel arch

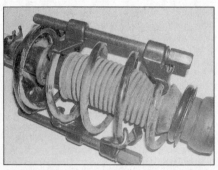

4.10 Compressor tool (double clamp type) fitted to the front suspension coil spring

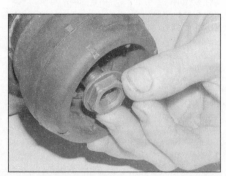

4.11a Unscrew the spring seat retaining nut . . .

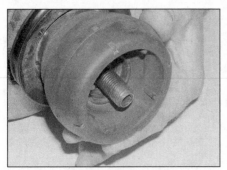

4.11b ... then remove the bearing and mounting rubber ...

4.11c ... followed by the upper spring seat ...

4.12a ... coil spring with compressor tool ...

4.12b ... protective gaiter ...

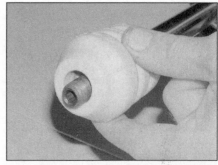

4.12c ... and rubber damper stop

12 Remove the coil spring (together with the compressor tool), then slide off the protective gaiter and rubber damper stop **(see illustrations)**.

13 With the strut assembly now completely dismantled **(see illustration)**, examine all the components for wear, damage or defor-mation, and check the bearing for smooth-ness of operation. Renew any of the components as necessary.

14 Examine the strut for signs of fluid leakage. Check the strut piston for signs of pitting along its entire length, and check the strut body for signs of damage. While holding it in an upright position, test the operation of the strut by moving the piston through a full stroke, and then through short strokes of 50 to 100 mm. In both cases, the resistance felt should be smooth and continuous. If the resistance is jerky, or uneven, or if there is any visible sign of wear or damage to the strut, renewal is necessary.

15 If any doubt exists about the condition of the coil spring, carefully remove the spring compressors, and check the spring for distortion and signs of cracking. Renew the spring if it is damaged or distorted, or if there is any doubt as to its condition.

16 Inspect all other components for signs of damage or deterioration, and renew as necessary.

17 Slide the rubber damper and protective gaiter onto the strut piston.

18 Fit the coil spring (together with the compressor tool) onto the strut, making sure its lower end is correctly located against the spring seat stop **(see illustration)**.

19 Refit the upper spring seat (and spacer/bush where fitted), followed by the bearing and mounting rubber. Screw on the new retaining nut, and tighten to the specified torque setting whilst retaining the strut piston with the Allen key.

Refitting

20 Manoeuvre the strut into position under the wheel arch, then locate the mounting plate on the suspension strut turret and screw on the new upper mounting nut. Tighten the nut to the specified torque, and refit the plastic cover.

21 Engage the wheel bearing housing with the bottom of the suspension strut, making sure that the hole in the side plate aligns with the holes in the split housing. Remove the tool used to open the split.

22 Insert the new strut-to-wheel bearing housing bolt from the front, and fit the new retaining nut. Tighten the nut to the specified torque.

23 Refit the lower arm balljoint and retaining plate, and tighten the bolts to the specified torque and angle. Where applicable, refit the headlight range control sensor arm to the lower arm and tighten the nut.

24 Reconnect the wiring to the ABS wheel sensor, and attach the wiring to the strut support.

25 Refer to Chapter 9 and refit the front brake caliper to the wheel bearing housing.

26 Refit the roadwheel and lower the vehicle to the ground. Tighten the roadwheel bolts.

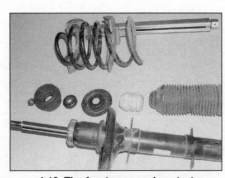

4.13 The front suspension strut completely dismantled

5 Front suspension lower arm – removal, overhaul and refitting

Note: *All self-locking nuts and bolts disturbed on removal must be renewed as a matter of course.*

Removal

1 Apply the handbrake, then jack up the front of the vehicle and support it on axle stands (see *Jacking and vehicle support*). Remove the appropriate front roadwheel and the engine compartment undershield.

2 If the left-hand lower arm is being removed on automatic transmission models, unscrew the bolts securing the engine/transmission rear mounting to the subframe. Discard the bolts, new ones should be used on refitting.

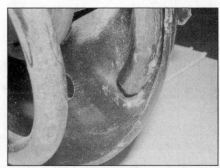

4.18 Make sure the lower end of the coil spring locates in the seat stop

5.6a Lower arm front mounting bolt . . .

5.6b . . . and rear mounting bolt

This is necessary to allow the engine/transmission unit to be moved slightly forwards when removing the lower arm front bolt.

3 If removing the left-hand lower arm on models with an automatic headlight range control system, mark the position of the level sender link on the plate on the front of the lower arm, then unscrew the nut and detach the sender link arm.

4 Unscrew and remove the bolt securing the anti-roll bar link to the front of the lower arm. Where applicable, remove the headlight range control adjustment plate.

5 Unscrew the front suspension lower balljoint-to-lower arm retaining bolts, and remove the retaining plate from the top of the lower arm.

6 Unscrew and remove the lower arm pivot bolt and rear mounting bolt **(see illustrations)**. On automatic transmission models it will be necessary to lever the engine/transmission slightly forwards in order to remove the front pivot bolt.

7 Remove the arm from the subframe and withdraw from under the vehicle. If necessary,

for additional working room, unbolt the driveshaft inner joint from the transmission drive flange with reference to Chapter 8, Section 2, and pull out the wheel bearing housing.

Overhaul

8 Thoroughly clean the lower arm, then check carefully for cracks or any other signs of wear or damage, paying particular attention to the pivot and rear mounting bushes. If either bush requires renewal, the lower arm should be taken to a VW dealer or suitably-equipped garage. A hydraulic press and suitable spacers are required to press the bushes out of the arm and install the new ones. When fitting a new rear mounting bush, make sure that it is located in the lower arm correctly **(see illustration)**. The cam must always point outwards.

Refitting

9 Locate the lower arm in the subframe, and insert the new pivot and rear mounting bolts. Tighten the rear mounting bolt to the specified torque and angle, however only hand-tighten the front pivot bolt at this stage.

10 Where removed, refit the driveshaft inner joint to the transmission flange with reference to Chapter 8.

11 Refit the balljoint and retaining plate to the lower arm using new bolts, and tighten the bolts to the specified torque and angle.

12 Refit the anti-roll bar link to the front of the lower arm and tighten to the specified torque. Where applicable, refit the headlight range control adjustment plate at the same time.

13 On models equipped with automatic headlight range control, refit the sender link arm to its previously noted position on the left-hand lower arm plate, and tighten the nut.

14 If the left-hand lower arm is being refitted on automatic transmission models, align the engine/transmission rear mounting with the subframe and fit the new mounting bolts. Tighten the bolts to the specified Stage 1 torque and through the specified Stage 2 angle (see Chapter 2A, 2B or 2C – as applicable).

15 Refit the roadwheel and undershield then lower the vehicle to the ground. With the weight of the vehicle on the suspension, tighten the lower arm front pivot bolt to the specified torque and angle.

---

6 Front suspension lower arm balljoint – removal, inspection and refitting

Note: *All self-locking nuts and bolts disturbed on removal must be renewed as a matter of course.*

Removal

Method 1

1 Remove the wheel bearing housing as described in Section 2.

2 Unscrew and remove the balljoint retaining nut, then release the balljoint from the wheel bearing housing using a universal balljoint separator **(see illustrations)**. Withdraw the balljoint.

Method 2

3 Apply the handbrake, then jack up the front of the vehicle and support it on axle stands (see *Jacking and vehicle support*). Remove the appropriate front roadwheel and the engine compartment undershield.

4 Unscrew and remove the bolts securing the inner driveshaft joint to the transmission flange (see Chapter 8, Section 2). Support the driveshaft by suspending it with wire or string.

5 Unscrew the balljoint-to-lower arm bolts and remove the retaining plate from the top of the lower arm.

6 Pull the wheel bearing housing outwards, and remove the balljoint from the lower arm.

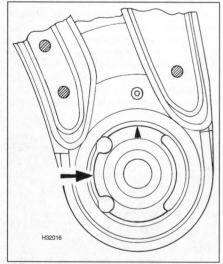

5.8 Fitting position of the lower arm rear mounting bush

Arrow indicates cam which must point outwards

6.2a The front suspension lower balljoint on the wheel bearing housing

6.2b Using a universal balljoint separator tool to remove the lower balljoint

Retain the wheel bearing housing away from the lower arm by inserting a block of wood between the strut and the inner body panel.

7 Unscrew and remove the balljoint retaining nut, then release the balljoint from the wheel bearing housing using a universal balljoint separator. Withdraw the balljoint.

Inspection

8 With the balljoint removed, check that it moves freely, without any sign of roughness. Check also that the balljoint rubber gaiter shows no sign of deterioration, and is free from cracks and splits. Renew as necessary.

Refitting

Method 1

9 Fit the balljoint to the wheel bearing housing and fit the new retaining nut. Tighten the nut to the specified torque setting, noting that the balljoint shank can be retained with an Allen key if necessary to prevent it from rotating.

10 Refit the wheel bearing housing with reference to Section 2.

Method 2

11 Fit the balljoint to the wheel bearing housing and fit the new retaining nut. Tighten the nut to the specified torque setting, noting that the balljoint shank can be retained with an Allen key if necessary to prevent it from rotating.

12 Remove the wooden block and move the strut inwards, then refit the balljoint and retaining plate to the lower arm using new bolts, and tighten the bolts to the specified torque and angle.

13 Refit the driveshaft inner joint to the transmission flange, and tighten its retaining bolts to the specified torque (see Chapter 8).

14 Refit the roadwheel and undershield, then lower the vehicle to the ground and tighten the wheel bolts to the specified torque.

---

7 Front anti-roll bar – removal and refitting

Note: All self-locking nuts and bolts disturbed on removal must be renewed as a matter of course.

Removal

1 Apply the handbrake, then jack up the front of the vehicle and support it on axle stands (see Jacking and vehicle support). Remove both front roadwheels.

2 Remove both anti-roll bar connecting links as described in Section 8.

3 Mark the anti-roll bar to indicate which way round it is fitted, and the position of the rubber mounting bushes. This will aid refitting. Unscrew and remove the anti-roll bar mounting clamp bolts from the subframe, and release the clamps from the lower slots. Note that it may be necessary to loosen the

8.2 Front anti-roll bar connecting link attachment to the lower arm

mounting bolts and lower the subframe for access to the clamp bolts.

4 Manoeuvre the anti-roll bar out from underneath the vehicle. Remove the rubber mounting bushes from the bar.

5 Carefully examine the anti-roll bar components for signs of wear, damage or deterioration, paying particular attention to the rubber mounting bushes. Renew worn components as necessary.

Refitting

6 Fit the rubber mounting bushes to the anti-roll bar, aligning them with the marks made prior to removal.

7 Offer up the anti-roll bar, and manoeuvre it into position. Refit the mounting clamps, ensuring that their ends are correctly located in the slots on the subframe, and refit the retaining bolts. Ensure that the bush markings are still aligned with the marks on the bars, then securely tighten the mounting clamp retaining bolts.

8 Where necessary, tighten the subframe mounting bolts to the specified torque.

9 Refit the connecting links with reference to Section 8.

10 Refit the roadwheels, then lower the vehicle to the ground and tighten the wheel bolts to the specified torque.

---

8 Front anti-roll bar connecting link – removal and refitting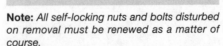

Note: All self-locking nuts and bolts disturbed on removal must be renewed as a matter of course.

Removal

1 Apply the handbrake, then jack up the front of the vehicle and support it on axle stands (see Jacking and vehicle support). Remove the relevant front roadwheel.

2 Unscrew and remove the bolt securing the link to the front of the lower arm (see illustration). If removing the link on the left-hand side on models equipped with an automatic headlight range control system, note that the sender link arm is located between the link and the lower arm.

8.3 Nut securing the connecting link to the front anti-roll bar

3 Using an Allen key to hold the link upper bolt, unscrew the nut and detach the link from the anti-roll bar (see illustration).

4 Inspect the link rubbers for signs of damage or deterioration. If evident, renew the link complete.

Refitting

5 Refitting is a reversal of removal, but delay fully tightening the link bolts until the weight of the car is on the front suspension.

---

9 Rear hub assembly – removal and refitting

Note: The rear wheel bearings cannot be renewed independently of the rear hub, because the outer races are formed in the hub itself. If excessive wear is evident, the rear hub must be renewed complete. The rear hub nut must always be renewed after removal.

Removal

1 Chock the front roadwheels, then jack up the rear of the vehicle and support on axle stands (see Jacking and vehicle support). Release the handbrake and remove the relevant rear roadwheel.

2 Remove the rear brake caliper and mounting bracket with reference to Chapter 9 (see illustrations). **Do not** disconnect the hydraulic brake pipe. Move the caliper just clear of the brake disc, without bending the hydraulic pipe excessively, and support it with welding rod or on an axle stand.

9.2a Unscrew the guide pin bolts . . .

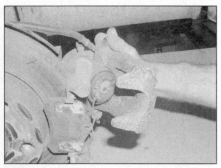

9.2b . . . remove the rear brake caliper . . .

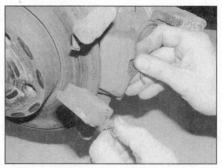

9.2c . . . then remove the brake pads . . .

9.2d . . . and caliper mounting bracket

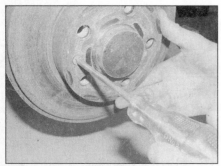

9.3a Undo the crosshead screw . . .

9.3b . . . and remove the rear brake disc

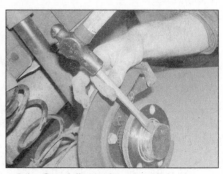

9.4a Carefully tap free the dust cap . . .

3 Undo the crosshead screw then withdraw the brake disc from the hub **(see illustrations)**.
4 Remove the dust cap from the centre of the hub using a screwdriver or cold chisel **(see illustrations)**.

5 Unscrew and remove the hub nut **(see illustrations)**. Note that it is tightened to a high torque and a socket extension bar may be required to loosen it. It is recommended that the nut is renewed whenever removed.

6 Using a suitable puller, pull the hub and bearings from the stub axle. The bearing inner race will remain on the stub axle, and a puller will be required to remove it; use a sharp cold chisel to move the race away from the stub

9.4b . . . and remove it from the hub

9.5a Use a socket extension bar to loosen the hub nut which is tightened to a high torque

9.5b Removing the hub nut

9.6a Using a puller to remove the rear hub

9.6b The ABS rotor may remain on the inner race – remove it before fitting the puller

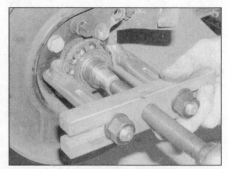

9.6c Using a puller to remove the inner race from the stub axle

axle base so that the puller legs can fully engage the race. The ABS rotor may come off of the hub and remain on the inner race as the hub is being removed, and it should be removed over the race before pulling off the race **(see illustrations)**.

7 Examine the hub and bearings for wear, pitting and damage. It is highly likely that the bearing surfaces will be damaged as a result of the inner race remaining on the stub axle, however if all the bearing surfaces and balls appear to be in good order upon inspection, the hub may be refitted.

Refitting

8 Wipe clean the stub axle, then check that the bearing races are adequately lubricated with suitable grease. Check that the inner bearing race is located correctly in the hub. Also make sure that the ABS rotor is pressed firmly onto the inner end of the hub.

9 Locate the hub as far as possible on the stub axle. VW technicians use a special elongated hub nut to pull the hub onto the stub axle, since the normal retaining nut is not long enough to reach the threads. If the special nut is unavailable, carefully drive on the hub using a metal tube or socket located only on the inner bearing race **(see illustrations)**.

10 Screw on the new nut and tighten it to the specified torque **(see illustration)**.

11 Check the dust cap for damage and renew it if necessary. Use a hammer to carefully tap the cap into the hub **(see illustration)**. **Note:** *A badly fitting dust cap will allow moisture to enter the bearing, reducing its service life.*

12 Refit the brake disc and tighten the crosshead screw.

13 Refit the rear brake mounting bracket and caliper with reference to Chapter 9.

14 Refit the roadwheel and lower the vehicle to the ground.

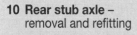

10 Rear stub axle –
removal and refitting

Note: *All self-locking nuts and bolts disturbed on removal must be renewed as a matter of course.*

Removal

1 Chock the front roadwheels, then jack up the rear of the vehicle and support on axle stands (see *Jacking and vehicle support*). Release the handbrake and remove the relevant roadwheel.

2 Remove the rear hub as described in Section 9.

3 Disconnect the wiring, then unscrew the bolt and remove the speed sensor from the rear axle trailing arm.

4 Unscrew the mounting bolts securing the

9.9a Locate the hub on the stub axle . . .

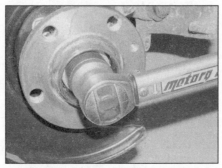

9.10 Torque-tightening the rear hub nut

stub axle and backplate to the rear axle trailing arm **(see illustration)**. Withdraw the backplate and stub axle.

5 Inspect the stub axle for signs of damage and renew if necessary. **Do not** attempt to straighten the stub axle.

Refitting

6 Ensure the mating surfaces of the axle, stub axle and backplate are clean and dry. Check the backplate for signs of damage.

7 Refit the stub axle together with the backplate, then insert the new bolts and progressively tighten to the specified torque.

8 Refit the speed sensor, tighten the bolt, and reconnect the wiring.

9 Refit the rear hub with reference to Section 9.

10 Refit the roadwheel and lower the vehicle to the ground.

10.4 Rear stub axle and mounting bolts

9.9b . . . then drive it on using a socket which locates only on the inner bearing race

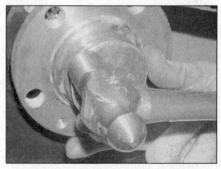

9.11 Tapping the cap into the hub

11 Rear suspension shock absorber and coil spring –
removal and refitting

Note: *All self-locking nuts and bolts disturbed on removal must be renewed as a matter of course.*

Shock absorber

Removal

1 Before removing the shock absorber, an idea of how effective it is can be gained by depressing the rear corner of the car. If the shock absorber is in good condition, the body should rise then settle in its normal position. If the body oscillates more than this, the shock absorber is defective. **Note:** *To ensure even rear suspension, both rear shock absorbers should be renewed at the same time.*

2 Chock the front roadwheels, then jack up the rear of the vehicle and support on axle stands (see *Jacking and vehicle support*). Remove the relevant rear roadwheel.

3 Position a trolley jack and block of wood beneath the coil spring position on the trailing arm, and raise the arm so that the shock absorber is slightly compressed **(see illustration)**. Note on some models, it may be necessary to remove the stone protection guard first.

4 Unscrew and remove the shock absorber lower mounting nut and bolt, and lever the bottom of the shock absorber from the trailing arm **(see illustrations)**.

5 Support the shock absorber, then unscrew

11.3 Position the trolley jack and block of wood beneath the trailing arm

11.4a Remove the lower mounting bolt . . .

11.4b . . . and withdraw the shock absorber from the trailing arm

the upper mounting bolts located in the rear wheel arch. Lower the shock absorber and withdraw from under the wheel arch **(see illustrations)**.

6 With the shock absorber on the bench, unscrew the nut from the top of the piston rod and remove the upper mounting bracket. The piston rod can be held stationary with a pair of grips on the raised peg on the top of the rod. Remove the rubber stop and protectors from the top of the rod.

7 If necessary, the action of the shock absorber can be checked by mounting it upright in a vice. Fully depress the rod, then pull it up fully. The piston rod must move smoothly over its complete length.

Refitting

8 Locate the rubber stop and protectors on the piston rod followed by the upper mounting bracket. Fit the new nut and tighten to the

specified torque while holding the piston rod as for removal.

9 Locate the shock absorber in the rear wheel arch, then insert the upper mounting bolts and tighten to the specified torque.

10 Locate the bottom of the shock absorber in the trailing arm, insert the bolt from the outside, then screw on the nut. Raise the trailing arm with the jack to take the weight of the rear suspension, then tighten the lower mounting bolt to the specified torque.

11 Lower the jack, and where necessary refit the stone protection guard.

12 Refit the roadwheel and lower the vehicle to the ground.

Coil spring

Note: *It is possible to remove the rear coil spring without the use of a coil spring compressor; both methods are described in the following paragraphs.*

⚠ *Warning: Adjustable coil spring compressors are readily available, and are recommended for this operation. Any attempt to remove the coil spring without such a tool is likely to result in damage or personal injury.*

13 Chock the front roadwheels, then jack up the rear of the vehicle and support on axle stands (see *Jacking and vehicle support*). Remove the relevant rear roadwheel.

Removal with a spring compressor

14 Fit the tool to the coil spring and compress it until it can be removed from the trailing arm and underbody. With the coil spring on the bench, carefully release the tension of the tool and remove it.

Removal without a spring compressor

15 Position a trolley jack and block of wood beneath the coil spring position on the trailing arm, and raise the arm so that the shock absorber is slightly compressed. Note on some models, it may be necessary to remove the stone protection guard first.

16 Unscrew and remove the shock absorber lower mounting nut and bolt, and lever the bottom of the shock absorber from the trailing arm.

17 Release the handbrake cable from the bracket on the trailing arm **(see illustration)**.

18 Lower the trolley jack and remove it from under the trailing arm, then carefully lever the arm down until the coil spring can be removed. Lever against a block of wood to prevent damage to the underbody. Make sure that the vehicle is adequately supported on the axle stands **(see illustrations)**.

Removal – all methods

19 With the coil spring removed, recover the upper and lower zinc spring seats and check them for damage **(see illustration)**. Obtain new ones if necessary. Also clean the spring locations on the underbody and trailing arm.

Refitting

20 Refitting is a reversal of removal, but make sure that the upper spring seat is located correctly on the top of the coil spring, with the spring end abutting the shoulder on the seat. The lower seat is circular and locates only in the centre of the spring. Before tightening the shock absorber lower mounting

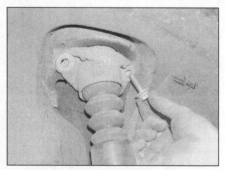

11.5a Unscrew the upper mounting bolts . . .

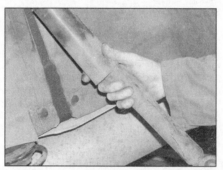

11.5b . . . and withdraw the rear shock absorber from under the wheel arch

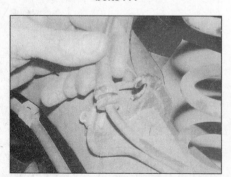

11.17 Release the handbrake cable from the bracket on the trailing arm

11.18a Lever down the trailing arm . . .

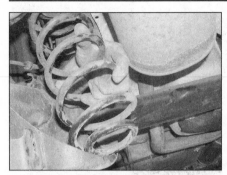

11.18b ... then release the coil spring from its lower seat ...

11.18c ... and underbody seat

11.19 Recover the upper and lower zinc spring seats

bolt to the specified torque, raise the trailing arm with the jack to take the weight of the rear suspension.

12 Rear anti-roll bar –
removal and refitting

The rear anti-roll bar runs along the length of the rear axle beam. It is an integral part of the axle assembly, and cannot be removed. If the anti-roll bar is damaged, which is unlikely, the complete axle assembly must be renewed.

13 Rear axle assembly –
removal and refitting

Note: *All self-locking nuts and bolts disturbed on removal must be renewed as a matter of course.*

Removal

1 Chock the front roadwheels, then jack up the rear of the vehicle and support on axle stands positioned beneath the underbody (see *Jacking and vehicle support*). Remove both rear roadwheels.
2 Working on each side at a time, slightly raise the trailing arm so that the shock absorber is not fully extended, then unscrew and remove the shock absorber upper mounting bolts from inside the rear wheel arch. Carefully lower the trailing arm to relieve the tension in the coil spring.
3 On models fitted with a vehicle level/ headlight range sender system, unbolt the link and arm from the left-hand trailing arm.
4 With both shock absorber upper mountings detached, lower the trailing arms until the coil springs and seats can be removed.
5 Remove the stone protection plates from the trailing arms, then unscrew the lower mounting bolts and remove the shock absorbers from the rear axle.
6 Release the handbrake cable from the supports/clips on the rear axle and underbody.
7 Pull out the clips and disconnect the flexible brake hoses from the supports on the rear axle and underbody bracket on both

sides **(see illustration)**. **Do not** disconnect the rigid brake lines from the hoses.
8 Refer to Chapter 9 and unbolt both brake calipers from the rear axle trailing arms. Release the rigid pipes from their clips and place the calipers to one side of the vehicle, together with the handbrake cables.
9 Disconnect the speed sensor wiring from the ABS speed sensors on each trailing arm and release the wiring from the supports.
10 Undo the screws and remove the brake discs, then remove the hubs and unbolt the stub axles and backplates. Refer to Sections 9 and 10 if necessary.
11 Support the rear axle with a trolley jack, then unscrew and remove the rear axle front mounting bolts from the underbody brackets.
12 Manoeuvre the rear axle down from the underbody brackets and withdraw from under the vehicle. The help of an assistant is recommended.
13 Inspect the rear axle mountings for signs or damage or deterioration, and refer to Section 14 if renewal is necessary. Where fitted, unbolt the vibration damper block from the top of the rear axle.

Refitting

14 Where fitted, refit the vibration damper to the top of the rear axle and tighten the bolts to the specified torque and angle.
15 Apply a little brake grease or soapy water to the kidney-shaped cavity in the front mounting rubbers, then manoeuvre the rear axle into the underbody brackets and insert the mounting bolts from the outside. Screw on the nuts finger-tight at this stage.

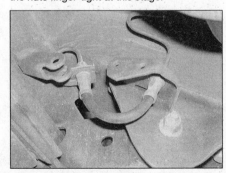

13.7 Flexible brake hose on the rear axle and underbody

16 Refer to Sections 9 and 10 and refit the backplates, stub axles and hubs, then refit the brake discs and secure with the screws tightened firmly.
17 Reconnect the wiring to the ABS speed sensors and clip the wiring in the supports.
18 Refit the brake calipers and secure the rigid hydraulic pipes in their clips with reference to Chapter 9.
19 Refit the hydraulic brake hoses to the supports and secure with the clips.
20 Refit the handbrake cables and locate them in the supports/clips.
21 Locate the shock absorbers on the trailing arms and insert the lower mounting bolts loosely.
22 Carefully locate the coil springs and zinc seats on the rear axle with reference to Section 11.
23 Working on each side at a time, raise the trailing arm until the upper mounting bolts can be inserted. Tighten the bolts to the specified torque.
24 Working on each side at a time, raise the trailing arm with a trolley jack until the weight of the car is taken on the coil spring. Fully tighten the relevant front mounting bolt to the specified torque, then tighten the relevant shock absorber lower mounting bolt to the specified torque.
25 Refit the stone protection plates under the trailing arms.
26 Check and if necessary adjust the handbrake as described in Chapter 9.
27 On models fitted with a vehicle level/headlight range sender system, refit the link and arm to the left-hand trailing arm and tighten the bolts to the specified torque.
28 Refit the roadwheels and lower the vehicle to the ground.

14 Rear axle rubber mountings
– renewal

Note: *It is recommended that the rubber mountings are renewed on both sides at the same time to ensure the correct rear wheel alignment.*
1 Most models covered by this manual are fitted with hydraulic type rubber mountings to

the rear axle when new, although, early 1.4 litre models may have the solid rubber type. In the event of leakage or excessive wear of the hydraulic type, both sides MUST be renewed with the solid rubber type. The following paragraphs describe renewal of the solid rubber type mountings, however the procedure for *removing* the hydraulic type is the same.

2 Chock the front roadwheels, then jack up the rear of the vehicle and support on axle stands positioned beneath the underbody (see *Jacking and vehicle support*). Remove both rear roadwheels.

3 Release the handbrake cables from the supports/clips on the rear axle and underbody.

4 Pull out the clips and disconnect the flexible brake hoses from the supports on the rear axle and underbody brackets.

5 Unscrew and remove both rear axle front mounting bolts from the underbody brackets.

6 Working on one side at a time, pull the front end of the trailing arm down from the underbody bracket and retain it in this position by placing a block of wood between the arm and underbody.

7 Note the fitted position of the rubber mounting to aid refitting.

8 VW technicians use a slide hammer tool to remove the rubber mounting from the rear axle. If a similar tool is not available, use a long bolt with suitable-sized metal tubing and washers to force out the mounting.

9 The new mounting must be located correctly in the rear axle **(see illustration)**. Using a suitable tool, pull the mounting into the rear axle until it is positioned as noted on removal.

10 Renew the mounting on the other side using the same procedure described in paragraphs 6 to 9 inclusive.

11 Apply a little brake grease or soapy water to the kidney-shaped cavity in the front mounting rubbers, then locate the rear axle in

the underbody brackets. Insert the mounting bolts from the outside, hand-tight at this stage.

12 Refit the flexible brake hoses and handbrake cables, and secure with the clips.

13 Working on one side at a time, raise the trailing arm with a trolley jack until the weight of the car is taken on the coil spring, then fully tighten the front mounting bolt to the specified torque.

14 Refit the roadwheels and lower the vehicle to the ground.

15 Vehicle level sender – removal and refitting

Removal

1 The front sender for the vehicle level/head-light range control system is located on the left-hand side of the underbody, and incorporates an arm and link attached to the left-hand front lower suspension arm. The rear sender is bolted to the underbody, and an arm and link is attached to a bracket on the left-hand trailing arm.

2 To remove the front sender, apply the handbrake then jack up the front of the vehicle and support it on axle stands (see *Jacking and vehicle support*). Remove the front roadwheel, then mark the position of the sender link on the lower arm plate – this will aid refitting. Unscrew the nut and disconnect the link from the plate. Disconnect the wiring then unscrew the nuts and remove the sender from the underbody. Note that pop-rivet screws are fitted to the underbody, and if they require renewal, a pop riveter will be necessary to fit them. The old rivets can be cut off with a hacksaw, or drilled out.

3 To remove the rear sender, chock the front roadwheels then jack up the rear of the vehicle and support on axle stands (see

Jacking and vehicle support). Unscrew the bolt and separate the link from the bracket on the rear axle. Disconnect the wiring then unbolt the sender.

Refitting

4 Refitting is a reversal of removal, but tighten the mounting nuts/bolts to the specified torque. If necessary, have the front sender adjustment checked by a VW dealer. This work requires the use a special equipment not available to the home mechanic.

16 Steering wheel – removal and refitting

> ⚠ **Warning: During the airbag removal and refitting procedures, avoid sitting in the front seats.**

Note: *The steering column, steering wheel and airbag are supplied by two independent manufacturers, and it is important that components from each manufacturer are not 'mixed'.*

Removal

1 Set the front wheels in the straight-ahead position, and release the steering lock by inserting the ignition key.

2 Disconnect the battery negative (earth) lead and position it away from the terminal.

3 Adjust the steering column to its lowest position by releasing the adjustment handle, then pull out the column and lower it as far as possible. Lock the column in this position by returning the adjustment handle.

4 With the spokes in the vertical position, insert a screwdriver approximately 45 mm into the hole in the upper rear of the steering wheel hub, then move it up to release the clip and free the airbag locking lug **(see illustrations)**. Now turn the steering wheel through 180° and release the remaining airbag locking lug.

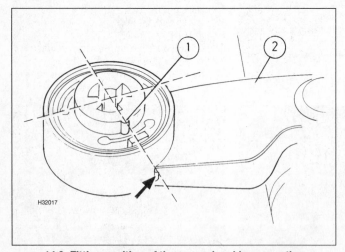

14.9 Fitting position of the rear axle rubber mounting

The cut-out (1) must align with the point indicated by the arrow on the trailing arm (2)

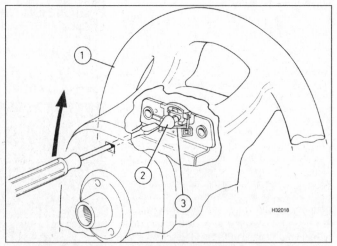

16.4a Airbag module removal on models with a four-spoke steering wheel

1 Steering wheel   2 Locking lug   3 Clip

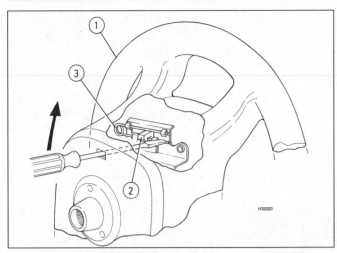

16.4b Airbag module removal on models with a three-spoke steering wheel

1 Steering wheel 2 Locking lug 3 Clip

16.4c Releasing the airbag module from the steering wheel

5 Turn the steering wheel to its central, straight-ahead position.

6 Carefully withdraw the airbag module and disconnect the wiring **(see illustration)**.

 Warning: Position the airbag in a safe and secure place, away from the work area (refer to Chapter 12).

7 Using a multi-spline socket, unscrew and remove the retaining bolt, while holding the steering wheel stationary **(see illustration)**. **Note:** *The steering wheel retaining bolt can be re-used up to 5 times, after which it must be renewed. It is recommended that the nut is marked with a centre punch to indicate the number of times it has been unscrewed.*

8 Use a dab of paint to mark the steering wheel in relation to the column in order to aid refitting, then ease the steering wheel from the column splines by firmly rocking it side-to-side.

Refitting

9 Note that if the combination switch has been removed from the column, it will be necessary to adjust the clearance between the steering wheel and switch before finally tightening the switch retaining clamp. The clearance must be approximately 2.5 mm. Refer to Chapter 12 for more information.

10 Locate the steering wheel on the column splines making sure that the previously-made marks are correctly aligned.

11 Apply suitable locking compound to the threads of the bolt, then screw it on and tighten to the specified torque while holding the steering wheel stationary.

12 With the steering wheel in the straight-ahead position, locate the airbag module in position and reconnect the wiring. Carefully press in the module until both locking lugs are heard to engage.

13 Reconnect the battery negative (earth) lead.

17 Steering column –
removal, inspection and refitting

Removal

1 Disconnect the battery negative (earth) lead and position it away from the terminal.

2 Remove the steering wheel as described in Section 16, and return the steering to the straight-ahead position.

3 Undo the screws and remove the column

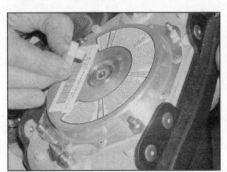

16.6 Disconnecting the wiring from the airbag module

17.3 Removing the steering column height and reach adjustment handle

height and reach adjustment handle **(see illustration)**

4 Undo the screws and remove the upper shroud from the steering column, then release the plastic clips and remove the lower shroud **(see illustrations)**. As the shroud is being removed, release it from the height and reach adjustment handle.

5 Remove the fusebox cover, then remove the facia lower trim panels and strengthening plate from under the steering column. Also remove the trim panel located under the facia in the driver's footwell **(see illustrations)**.

16.7 Hold the steering wheel stationary and unscrew the retaining bolt with a multi-spline socket

17.4a Undo the screws . . .

17.4b . . . then lift the upper shroud from the combination switch . . .

17.4c . . . and withdraw it from the facia

17.4d Undo the lower screws . . .

17.4e . . . and outer screws . . .

17.4f . . . and withdraw the lower shroud

Models without ESP/TCS

6 Disconnect the wiring from the bottom rear of the column combination switch.
7 Use a small screwdriver to release the locking lugs, then pull the airbag slip ring and

wiring connector from the combination switch.

Models with ESP/TCS

8 Note that on models equipped with ESP (electronic stability program) and TCS (traction control system), the slip-ring is different and incorporates a steering wheel angle sensor. To remove this type, make sure that the front wheels are still pointing straight-ahead, then check that a yellow spot is visible through the hole in the top, right-hand corner of the slip-ring housing. If necessary, temporarily refit the steering wheel and move the column until the spot is visible.
9 At the rear of the slip-ring housing, release the two retaining hooks and withdraw the slip ring and steering wheel angle sensor.

All models

10 Remove the plastic cover from the steering lock shear bolts on top of the steering column and release the cable tie securing the wiring loom **(see illustration)**.
11 Mark the position of the combination switch on the column, then unscrew the clamp bolt and withdraw the switch.

17.5a Remove the left-hand . . .

17.5b . . . and right-hand facia lower trim panels . . .

17.5c . . . then undo the screws . . .

17.5d . . . and remove the strengthening plate

17.5e Removing the trim panel from under the facia

17.10 Removing the plastic cover from the steering lock shear bolts

17.12a **Disconnecting the wiring from the ignition switch . . .**

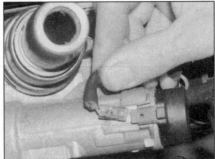

17.12b **. . . and from the ignition key sensor coil**

17.12c **Also remove the earth wire from the steering lock housing**

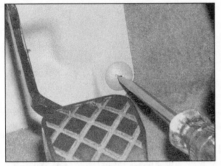

17.14a **Undo the plastic nuts . . .**

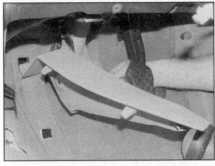

17.14b **. . . and remove the cover for access to the steering gear pinion shaft**

17.15a **Universal joint linking the bottom of the intermediate shaft to the steering gear pinion shaft**

12 Disconnect the wiring from the rear of the ignition switch and from the ignition key sensor coil. Also undo the bolt and remove the earth wire from the steering lock housing **(see illustrations)**.

13 On automatic transmission models, move the selector lever to position P, then turn the ignition key to the 'On' position. Release the wire clip by pressing it either up or down (according to type), then pull out the steering lock locking cable.

14 Beneath the pedal bracket, undo the plastic nuts and remove the cover for access to the steering column lower universal joint **(see illustrations)**.

15 Slacken and remove the clamp bolt and free the steering column universal joint from the steering gear pinion (the shaft is telescopic to enable it to be easily disconnected). Discard the clamp bolt; a new one should be used on refitting. Note that the pinion shaft has a cut-out to enable fitting of the clamp bolt, and the splined pinion shaft incorporates a flat making it impossible to assemble the joint to the shaft in the wrong position **(see illustrations)**.

16 Note that the inner and outer columns, and the intermediate shaft, are telescopic, to facilitate the reach adjustment. It is important to keep the splined sections of the inner steering column engaged with each other while the steering column is removed. If they become detached due to the outer column sections being separated, especially on a vehicle which has completed a high mileage, it is possible that rattling noises may occur. VW

technicians use a special plastic clip to hold the outer column sections together, although a retainer can be made out of a tapered wooden dowel, or the plastic end of a ballpoint pen can be put to good use. First, release the reach

17.15b **Removing the clamp bolt**

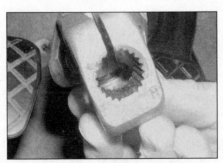

17.15d **The splined universal joint, showing the flat to ensure fitting in one position only**

adjustment handle and position the outer column tubes so that the transportation holes are in alignment. Insert the dowel or plug to hold the sections of the column together during removal **(see illustration)**.

17.15c **Splined pinion shaft on the steering gear**

17.16 **Insert a dowel or plug (arrowed) to hold the steering column outer sections together during removal**

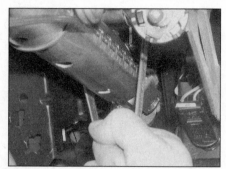

17.17a Loosen the nut . . .

17.17b . . . and remove the steering column lower mounting bolt

17.17c Unscrew the upper mounting bolts . . .

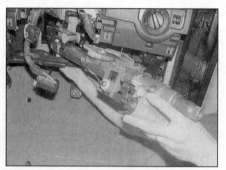

17.17d . . . and withdraw the steering column from inside the vehicle

17.17e The steering column removed from the car

17 Unscrew and remove the lower mounting bolt, then support the steering column and unscrew the upper mounting bolts. Withdraw the steering column from inside the vehicle **(see illustrations)**.

18 If necessary, remove the ignition switch/steering column lock with reference to Section 18.

Inspection

19 The steering column is designed to collapse in the event of a front-end crash, to prevent the steering wheel injuring the driver. Before refitting the steering column, examine the column and mountings for signs of

damage and deformation. Using vernier calipers, measure the distance between the bolt hole and the stop peg on the upper mounting plate **(see illustration)**. Insert the mounting bolt to make this check. If the distance is not 23.0 mm, the steering column is damaged and should be renewed.

20 Check the inner column sections for signs of free play in the column bushes. If any damage or wear is found on the steering column bushes, the column must be renewed as an assembly.

21 The intermediate shaft is permanently attached to the inner column and cannot be renewed separately **(see illustration)**. Inspect the universal joints for excessive wear. If evident, the complete steering column must be renewed.

Refitting

22 If a new steering column is being fitted,

the roller bracket must be removed from the old outer column and secured to the new one with a new shear-head bolt **(see illustration)**. Drill out the old shear-head bolt to remove the bracket, and unscrew the remains of the bolt. Locate the bracket on the new column and secure it with a new shear-head bolt. Tighten the bolt until its head breaks off.

23 Refit the ignition switch/steering column lock with reference to Section 18.

24 Apply a little locking fluid to the threads of the mounting bolts. Offer the steering column onto its mounting bracket and insert all of the mounting bolts loosely. Tighten the lower mounting bolt to the specified torque, then tighten the upper bolts to the specified torque.

25 Remove the clip securing the telescopic tube sections, and remove the retainer/wire from the inner column.

26 Locate the universal joint onto the steering gear pinion shaft so that the cut-out is aligned with the bolt holes. Insert the new clamp bolt and tighten to the specified torque.

27 Refit the plastic cover beneath the pedal bracket and secure with the plastic nuts.

28 On automatic transmission models, with the selector lever in position P and the ignition key in the 'On' position, slide the locking cable into the lock housing until the wire clip engages. Check that it is possible to move the selector lever out of the P position. If not, refer to Chapter 7B and adjust the cable. Check also that it is only possible to remove the ignition key with the selector in the P position. With the ignition key in the 'Off' position, it

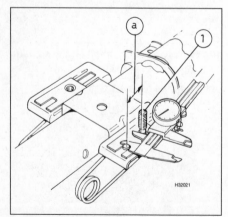

17.19 Using vernier calipers to measure the distance between the column mounting bolt hole and stop peg

1 Mounting bolt   a = 23.0 mm

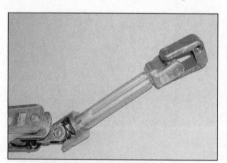

17.21 The intermediate shaft is permanently attached to the inner steering column

17.22 The roller bracket is secured to the steering column with a single shear-head bolt

must not be possible to move the selector lever out of the P position.

29 Locate the combination switch on the column, align it with the previously made mark, and tighten the clamp bolt.

30 Refit the plastic cover over the steering lock shear bolts, and refit the cable tie.

Models without ESP/TCS

31 Refit the airbag slip-ring and wiring connector to the combination switch.

32 Reconnect the wiring to the combination switch.

Models with ESP/TCS

33 Refit the steering wheel angle sensor and slip-ring, making sure that the retaining lugs are correctly engaged.

34 Make sure that the yellow spot is visible (see paragraph 8), then refit the steering wheel angle sensor in its central position **(see illustration)**. **Note:** *The basic setting of the sensor must be checked by a VW dealer whenever it is removed or whenever the steering wheel is repositioned.*

All models

35 Temporarily locate the steering wheel on the column splines and check that the clearance between the steering wheel and the clock spring housing is approximately 2.5 mm. If not, loosen the combination switch clamp bolt and reposition it, then retighten the bolt. Remove the steering wheel.

36 Refit the upper and lower steering column shrouds and secure with the screws.

37 Refit the height and reach adjustment handle and tighten the screws.

38 Refit the facia lower trim panels and strengthening plate. Also refit the trim panel under the facia in the driver's footwell.

39 Refit the steering wheel with reference to Section 16.

40 Reconnect the battery negative (earth) lead.

---

18 Ignition switch and steering column lock – removal and refitting

Ignition switch

Removal

1 Disconnect the battery negative (earth) lead and position it away from the terminal.

2 Remove the steering wheel as described in Section 16.

3 Undo the screws and remove the column height and reach adjustment handle.

4 Undo the screws and remove the lower shroud from the steering column, then release the plastic clips and remove the upper shroud.

5 Remove the plastic cover from the steering lock shear bolts on top of the steering column and release the cable tie securing the wiring loom.

6 Mark the position of the combination switch on the column, then unscrew the clamp bolt and withdraw the switch.

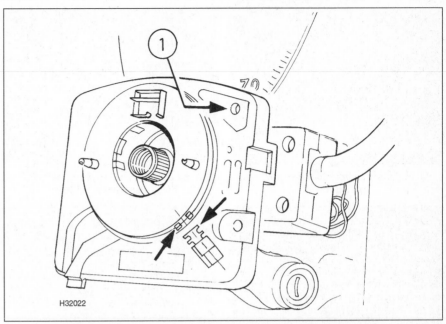

17.34 Steering wheel angle sensor on models with ESP and TCS

The yellow spot must be visible through the hole (1) with the steering angle sensor in its central position (arrowed)

7 Carefully pull the wiring plug from the ignition switch.

8 Remove the locking paint from the switch retaining screw heads, then loosen them slightly and pull out the switch from the steering lock housing.

Refitting

9 Insert the ignition key and turn it to the 'On' position. Also turn the switch in the same position.

10 Carefully insert the switch into the housing, then insert the screws and tighten securely. Lock the screws by applying some paint over their heads and onto the housing.

11 Reconnect the wiring plug to the ignition switch.

12 Locate the combination switch on the column, align it with the previously made mark, and tighten the clamp bolt.

13 Refit the plastic cover on the steering lock shear bolts, and secure the wiring loom with the cable tie.

14 Refit the upper and lower shrouds, and tighten the screws.

15 Refit the height and reach adjustment handle and tighten the screws.

16 Refit the steering wheel as described in Section 16.

17 Reconnect the battery negative (earth) lead.

Steering column lock

Removal

18 Disconnect the battery negative (earth) lead and position it away from the terminal.

19 Remove the steering wheel as described in Section 16.

20 Undo the screws and remove the column height and reach adjustment handle.

21 Undo the screws and remove the lower shroud from the steering column, then pull out and remove the upper shroud.

22 Remove the plastic cover from the steering lock shear bolts on top of the steering column and release the cable tie securing the wiring loom.

23 Mark the position of the combination switch on the column, then unscrew the clamp bolt and withdraw the switch.

24 On automatic transmission models, move the selector lever to position P, then turn the ignition key to the 'On' position. Release the wire clip by pressing it either up or down (according to type), then pull out the steering lock locking cable.

25 Carefully pull the wiring plug from the ignition switch. Also disconnect the wiring from the ignition key immobiliser coil.

26 The lock is secured to the outer column by shear-head bolts **(see illustration)**, and the

18.26 The steering column lock is secured to the outer column by shear-head bolts

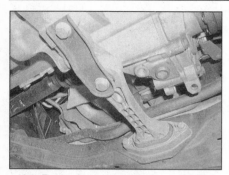

19.5 Engine/transmission rear mounting assembly

19.8 Hydraulic fluid lines connected to the power steering gear

19.10 Power steering gear mounting on the passenger side

heads are broken off in the tightening procedure. To remove the old bolts, either drill them out, or use a sharp cold chisel to cut off their heads or turn them anti-clockwise. Withdraw the lock from the steering column.

27 If necessary, the lock cylinder can be removed from the steering lock housing as follows. **Note:** *The lock cylinder can be removed with the lock in situ by removing the steering wheel, shrouds and combination switch.* Insert the ignition key and turn to the 'On' position. Insert a piece of wire 1.2 mm in diameter in the drilling next to the ignition key, depress it, then withdraw the lock cylinder from the housing.

Refitting

28 If removed, refit the lock cylinder with the ignition key in the 'On' position, then remove the wire. Make sure that the immobiliser coil connection is located correctly in the guide when inserting the lock cylinder.

29 Locate the lock on the outer column and insert the new shear-head bolts. Tighten the bolts until their heads break off.

30 Reconnect the wiring plug to the ignition switch and ignition key immobiliser coil.

31 On automatic transmission models, with the selector lever in position P and the ignition key in the 'On' position, slide the locking cable into the lock housing until the wire clip engages. Check that it is possible to move the selector lever out of the P position. If not, refer to Chapter 7B and adjust the cable. Check also that it is only possible to remove the ignition key with the selector in the P position. With the ignition key in the 'Off' position, it must not be possible to move the selector lever out of the P position.

32 Locate the combination switch on the column, align it with the previously made mark, and tighten the clamp bolt.

33 Refit the plastic cover on the steering lock shear bolts, and secure the wiring loom with the cable tie.

34 Refit the upper and lower shrouds, and tighten the screws.

35 Refit the height and reach adjustment handle and tighten the screws.

36 Refit the steering wheel as described in Section 16.

37 Reconnect the battery negative (earth) lead.

19 Steering gear assembly – removal, overhaul and refitting

Note: *New subframe mounting bolts, track rod balljoint nuts, steering gear retaining bolts, and an intermediate shaft universal joint clamp bolt will be required on refitting.*

Removal

1 Apply the handbrake, then jack up the front of the vehicle and support it on axle stands positioned on the underbody, leaving the subframe free (see *Jacking and vehicle support*). Position the steering straight-ahead, then remove both front roadwheels. Also remove the engine compartment undershield.

2 Inside the vehicle, undo the screws and remove the plastic cover for access to the universal joint connecting the steering inner column to the steering gear pinion. Unscrew and remove the clamp bolt, and pull the universal joint from the pinion splines. **Note:** *The steering gear pinion incorporates a cut-out for the clamp bolt, and therefore the joint can only be fitted in one position.* Discard the clamp bolt, a new one should be used on refitting.

3 Fit a hose clamp to the fluid return hose leading from the steering gear to the power steering fluid reservoir. Also fit a hose clamp to the power steering pump fluid inlet hose.

4 Working on each side at a time, unscrew the nuts from the track rod ends, then use a balljoint separator tool to release the ends from the steering arms on the front wheel bearing housings.

5 Unscrew the two bolts securing the rear engine/transmission mounting to the underside of the transmission unit **(see illustration)**. Discard both bolts, new ones must be used on refitting, and leave the mounting attached to the subframe.

6 Support the weight of the subframe with a trolley jack, then unscrew the bolts securing the subframe to the underbody. There are four bolts on each side of the subframe.

7 Position a suitable container beneath the steering gear to catch spilt fluid.

8 Lower the subframe a little to give sufficient access to the fluid supply and return unions on

the steering gear, at the same time guiding the pinion shaft from the rubber grommet in the floor. Unscrew the union bolts and disconnect the lines, then recover the copper sealing washers **(see illustration)**. Tape over or plug the ends of the lines and the apertures in the steering gear to prevent entry of dust and dirt into the hydraulic system. The line ends can be wrapped in a plastic bag if preferred.

9 Unscrew the bolt and nut, and release the return line from the subframe/steering gear. Move the return line to one side.

10 Unscrew the mounting bolts and withdraw the steering gear from the subframe to the rear. Note that the mounting on the passenger side of the gear incorporates a clamp and rubber mounting **(see illustration)**. Examine the mounting for wear and damage, and renew it if necessary. Discard the steering gear mounting bolts, new ones should be used on refitting.

Overhaul

11 Examine the steering gear assembly for signs of wear or damage, and check that the rack moves freely throughout the full length of its travel, with no signs of roughness or excessive free play between the steering gear pinion and rack. It is not possible to overhaul the steering gear assembly housing components, and if it is faulty, the assembly must be renewed. The only components which can be renewed individually are the steering gear gaiters, the track rod end balljoints and the track rods, as described later in this Chapter.

Refitting

12 Locate the steering gear on the subframe, and insert the new mounting bolts. Make sure that the location dowel is correctly fitted. Tighten the bolts to the specified torque and Stage 2 angle.

13 Attach the return line to the subframe /steering gear and tighten the bolt and nut. The clearance between the steering gear and return line must be approximately 10 mm.

14 Reconnect the fluid supply and return lines to the steering gear, together with new copper washers on each side of the unions. Tighten the union bolts to the specified torque.

15 Raise the subframe and at the same time guide the steering gear pinion shaft through the rubber grommet in the floor. Insert the new subframe bolts and tighten them to the specified torque and angle.

16 Align the engine/transmission rear mounting with the transmission unit and fit the new mounting bolts. Tighten the bolts to the specified Stage 1 torque and through the specified Stage 2 angle (see Chapter 2A, 2B or 2C – as applicable).

17 Refit the track rod ends to the steering arms, screw on the new nuts, and tighten them to the specified torque.

18 Remove the hose clamps from the fluid supply and return hoses.

19 Working inside the car, locate the steering column universal joint on the pinion shaft, making sure that the cut-out is aligned with the bolt holes. Insert the new bolt and tighten to the specified torque.

20 Check that the rubber grommet is located correctly in the floor, then refit the plastic cover and secure with the screws.

21 Refit the engine compartment undershield and roadwheels, then lower the vehicle to the ground. On completion check and, if necessary, adjust the front wheel alignment as described in Section 24.

20 Steering gear rubber gaiters and track rods – renewal

Steering gear rubber gaiters

1 Remove the track rod end balljoint as described in Section 23.

2 Note the fitted position of the gaiter on the track rod, then release the retaining clips and slide the gaiter off the steering gear housing and track rod.

3 Wipe clean the track rod and the steering gear housing, then apply a film of suitable grease to the surface of the rack. To do this, turn the steering wheel as necessary to fully extend the rack from the housing, then reposition it in its central position.

4 Carefully slide the new gaiter onto the track rod, and locate it on the steering gear housing. Position the gaiter as previously noted on removal, making sure that it is not twisted, then lift the outer sealing lip of the gaiter to equalise air pressure within the gaiter.

5 Secure the gaiter in position with new retaining clips. Where crimped-type clips are used, pull the clip as tight as possible, and locate the hooks in their slots. Remove any slack in the clip by carefully compressing the raised section. In the absence of the special crimping tool, a pair of side-cutters may be used, taking care not to actually cut the clip.

6 Refit the track rod end balljoint as described in Section 23.

Track rods

7 Remove the relevant steering gear rubber gaiter as described earlier. If there is insufficient working room with the steering gear mounted in the car, remove it as described in Section 19 and hold it in a vice while renewing the track rod.

8 Hold the steering rack stationary with one spanner on the flats provided, then loosen the balljoint nut with another spanner. Fully unscrew the nut and remove the track rod from the rack.

9 Locate the new track rod on the end of the steering rack and screw on the nut. Hold the rack stationary with one spanner and tighten the balljoint nut to the specified torque. A crow's foot adapter may be required since the track rod prevents access with a socket, and care must be taken to apply the exact torque in this situation.

10 Refit the steering gear or rubber gaiter with reference to the earlier paragraphs or Section 19. On completion check and, if necessary, adjust the front wheel alignment as described in Section 24.

21 Power steering system – bleeding

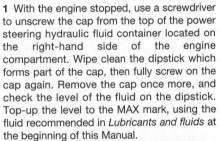

1 With the engine stopped, use a screwdriver to unscrew the cap from the top of the power steering hydraulic fluid container located on the right-hand side of the engine compartment. Wipe clean the dipstick which forms part of the cap, then fully screw on the cap again. Remove the cap once more, and check the level of the fluid on the dipstick. Top-up the level to the MAX mark, using the fluid recommended in *Lubricants and fluids* at the beginning of this Manual.

2 Slowly move the steering from lock-to-lock several times to purge out the trapped air, then top-up the level in the fluid reservoir. Repeat this procedure until the fluid level in the reservoir does not drop any further.

3 Have an assistant start the engine, whilst you keep watch on the fluid level. Be prepared to add more fluid as the engine starts, as the fluid level may drop quickly. The fluid level must be kept above the MIN mark at all times.

4 With the engine running at idle speed, turn the steering wheel slowly from lock-to-lock 10 times. Do not hold the wheel on either lock, as this imposes excessive strain upon the hydraulic system. Repeat this procedure until bubbles cease to appear in the fluid reservoir.

5 If, when turning the steering, an odd noise is heard from the fluid lines, it indicates there is still air in the system. Check this by turning the wheels to the straight-ahead position and switching off the engine. If the fluid level in the reservoir rises, then air is present in the system, and further bleeding is necessary.

6 Once all traces of air have been removed from the power steering hydraulic system, switch off the engine and allow the system to cool. Once cool, check that the fluid level is up to the maximum mark on the power

steering fluid reservoir, and top-up if necessary. Finally, tighten the cap onto the reservoir.

22 Power steering pump – removal and refitting

Note: *New feed pipe union copper sealing washers will be required on refitting*

Removal

1 Apply the handbrake, then jack up the front of the vehicle and support it on axle stands (see *Jacking and vehicle support*). Remove the engine compartment undershield.

2 Using an Allen key to hold the centre of the pump drive flange stationary, loosen **only** the bolts securing the pulley to the power steering pump. Do not remove them at this stage. Note that according to engine type, the power steering pump may be fitted either above or below the alternator.

3 Mark the auxiliary drivebelt for direction of rotation, then remove it as described in Chapter 1A or 1B.

4 Unscrew and remove the bolts and remove the pulley from the power steering pump.

5 Fit a hose clamp to the hose leading from the fluid reservoir to the power steering pump.

6 Position a suitable container beneath the pump to catch spilt fluid, then release the clip and disconnect the supply hose **(see illustration)**. Note that the hose and pump stub have alignment marks to ensure correct refitting. VW technicians use a special tool to remove the clip, but it should be possible to remove it using a pair of pliers.

7 Unscrew the union bolt and disconnect the pressure hose union from the pump. Recover the copper sealing washers. Tape over or plug the ends of the hoses and the apertures in the pump to prevent entry of dust and dirt into the hydraulic system. The end of the pressure line can be wrapped in a plastic bag if preferred. Note that on some models the power steering system pressure switch is located on the union bolt, and in this case it will be necessary to disconnect the wiring before unscrewing the bolt.

8 Unscrew and remove the three mounting

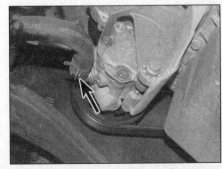

22.6 Clip securing the fluid supply hose to the power steering pump

23.4a Using an Allen key to hold the balljoint shank while loosening the nut

23.4b Using a balljoint separator to release the track rod balljoint from the steering arm on the wheel bearing housing

bolts from the pulley end of the pump, and the single mounting bolt from the engine side of the pump. Withdraw the power steering pump from the engine.

Refitting

9 Before refitting the pump (and especially if fitting a new pump), prime it with fresh fluid as follows. Place the pump in a container with the supply hose stub uppermost. Pour hydraulic fluid into the supply stub and turn the pulley drive flange clockwise by hand until fluid emerges from the pressure hose aperture.

10 Tilt the pump to retain the fluid, then locate it in the engine compartment and fit the supply hose and clip. Make sure that the alignment mark on the hose is in line with the seam on the pump supply stub.

11 Locate the pump in its mounting bracket and secure with the mounting bolts, tightened to the specified torque.

12 Reconnect the pressure hose union, together with new copper sealing washers, and tighten to the specified torque. Where necessary, reconnect the wiring to the pressure switch.

13 Remove the hose clamp from the supply hose.

14 Locate the pulley on the pump, insert the bolts, and tighten them securely while holding the drive flange with an Allen key.

15 Refit the auxiliary drivebelt with reference to Chapter 1A or 1B.

16 Refit the engine compartment under-shield, then lower the vehicle to the ground.

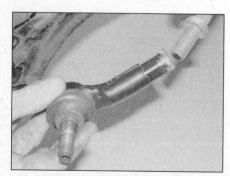

23.5 Unscrewing the track rod end from the track rod

17 Bleed the power steering hydraulic system as described in Section 21.

23 Track rod end – removal and refitting

Note: A new balljoint retaining nut will be required on refitting.

Removal

1 Apply the handbrake, then jack up the front of the vehicle and support it on axle stands (see *Jacking and vehicle support*). Remove the relevant roadwheel.

2 If the track rod end is to be re-used, mark its position in relation to the track rod to facilitate refitting.

3 Unscrew the track rod end locknut by a quarter of a turn. Do not move the locknut from this position, as it will serve as a handy reference mark on refitting.

4 Loosen and remove the nut securing the track rod end balljoint to the wheel bearing housing, and release the balljoint tapered shank using a universal balljoint separator. Note that the balljoint shank has a hexagon hole – hold the shank with an Allen key while loosening the nut **(see illustrations)**.

5 Counting the exact number of turns necessary to do so, unscrew the track rod end from the track rod **(see illustration)**.

6 Carefully clean the balljoint and the threads. Renew the balljoint if its movement is sloppy or too stiff, if excessively worn, or if damaged in any way; carefully check the stud taper and threads. If the balljoint gaiter is damaged, the complete balljoint assembly must be renewed; it is not possible to obtain the gaiter separately.

Refitting

7 Screw the track rod end onto the track rod by the number of turns noted on removal. This should bring the track rod end to within a quarter of a turn of the locknut, with the alignment marks that were made on removal (if applicable) lined up. Tighten the locknut.

8 Refit the balljoint shank to the steering arm on the wheel bearing housing, then fit a new retaining nut and tighten it to the specified

torque. Hold the shank with an Allen key if necessary.

9 Refit the roadwheel, then lower the car to the ground and tighten the roadwheel bolts to the specified torque.

10 Check and, if necessary, adjust the front wheel toe setting as described in Section 24.

24 Wheel alignment and steering angles – general information

Definitions

1 A car's steering and suspension geometry is defined in three basic settings – all angles are expressed in degrees; the steering axis is defined as an imaginary line drawn through the axis of the suspension strut, extended where necessary to contact the ground.

2 Camber is the angle between each roadwheel and a vertical line drawn through its centre and tyre contact patch, when viewed from the front or rear of the car. Positive camber is when the roadwheels are tilted outwards from the vertical at the top; negative camber is when they are tilted inwards.

3 Camber angle is only adjustable by loosening the front suspension subframe mounting bolts and moving it slightly to one side. This also alters the Castor angle. The camber angle can be checked using a camber checking gauge.

4 Castor is the angle between the steering axis and a vertical line drawn through each roadwheel's centre and tyre contact patch, when viewed from the side of the car. Positive castor is when the steering axis is tilted so that it contacts the ground ahead of the vertical; negative castor is when it contacts the ground behind the vertical. Slight castor angle adjustment is possible by loosening the front suspension subframe bolts and moving it slightly to one side. This also alters the Camber angle.

5 Castor is not easily adjustable, and is given for reference only; while it can be checked using a castor checking gauge, if the figure obtained is significantly different from that specified, the car must be taken for careful checking by a professional, as the fault can only be caused by wear or damage to the body or suspension components.

6 Toe is the difference, viewed from above, between lines drawn through the roadwheel centres and the car's centre-line. Toe-in is when the roadwheels point inwards, towards each other at the front, while toe-out is when they splay outwards from each other at the front.

7 The front wheel toe setting is adjusted by screwing the track rod(s) in/out of the outer balljoint(s) to alter the effective length of the track rod assembly.

8 Rear wheel toe setting is not adjustable, and is given for reference only. While it can be checked, if the figure obtained is significantly different from that specified, the car must be taken for careful checking by a professional, as the fault can only be caused by wear or damage to the body or suspension components.

Checking and adjustment

Front wheel toe setting

9 Due to the special measuring equipment necessary to check the wheel alignment, and the skill required to use it properly, the checking and adjustment of these settings is best left to a VW dealer or similar expert. Note that most tyre-fitting centres now possess sophisticated checking equipment.

10 To check the toe setting, a tracking gauge must first be obtained. Two types of gauge are available, and can be obtained from motor accessory shops. The first type measures the distance between the front and rear inside edges of the roadwheels, as previously described, with the car stationary. The second type, known as a 'scuff plate', measures the actual position of the contact surface of the tyre, in relation to the road surface, with the car in motion. This is achieved by pushing or driving the front tyre over a plate, which then moves slightly according to the scuff of the tyre, and shows this movement on a scale. Both types have their advantages and disadvantages, but either can give satisfactory results if used correctly and carefully.

11 Make sure that the steering is in the straight-ahead position when making measurements.

12 If adjustment is necessary, apply the handbrake, then jack up the front of the vehicle and support it securely on axle stands (see *Jacking and vehicle support*). Turn the steering wheel onto full-left lock, and record the amount of exposed thread on the right-hand track rod. Now turn the steering onto full-right lock, and record the number of threads on the left-hand track rod. If there is the same amount of thread visible on both sides, then subsequent adjustment should be made equally on both sides. If there are more thread is visible on one side than the other, it will be necessary to compensate for this during adjustment.

13 First clean the track rod threads; if they are corroded, apply penetrating fluid before starting adjustment. Release the rubber gaiter outer clips, peel back the gaiters and apply a smear of grease. This will ensure that both gaiters are free and will not be twisted or strained as their respective track rods are rotated.

14 Retain the track rod with a suitable spanner, and loosen the balljoint locknut fully. Alter the length of the track rod, by screwing it into or out of the balljoint. Rotate the track rod using an open-ended spanner fitted to the track rod flats provided; shortening the track rod (screwing it onto its balljoint) will reduce toe-in/increase toe-out.

15 When the setting is correct, hold the track rod and tighten the balljoint locknut to the specified torque setting. If after adjustment, the steering wheel spokes are no longer horizontal when the wheels are in the straight-ahead position, remove the steering wheel and reposition it (see Section 16).

16 Check that the toe setting has been correctly adjusted by lowering the car to the ground and rechecking the toe setting; re-adjust if necessary. Ensure that the rubber gaiters are seated correctly and are not twisted or strained, and secure them in position with the retaining clips; where necessary, fit a new retaining clip (refer to Section 20).

Rear wheel toe setting

17 The procedure for checking the rear toe setting is the same as described for the front setting in paragraph 10. The setting is not adjustable – see paragraph 8.

Front wheel camber and castor angles

18 Checking and adjusting the front wheel camber angle should be entrusted to a VW dealer or other suitably-equipped specialist. Note that most tyre-fitting centres now possess sophisticated checking equipment. For reference, adjustments are made by loosening the front suspension subframe mounting bolts, and repositioning the subframe.

Chapter 11
Bodywork and fittings

Contents

Body exterior fittings – removal and refitting 24
Bonnet – removal, refitting and adjustment 8
Bonnet lock – removal and refitting 10
Bonnet release cable – removal and refitting 9
Boot lid and support struts – removal and refitting 17
Boot lid lock components – removal and refitting 18
Central locking components – removal and refitting 19
Centre console – removal and refitting 29
Door – removal, refitting and adjustment 11
Door handle and lock components – removal and refitting 13
Door inner trim panel – removal and refitting 12
Door window glass and regulator – removal and refitting 14
Electric window components – removal and refitting 20
Exterior mirrors and associated components – removal and
  refitting 21
Facia panel assembly – removal and refitting 30

Front bumper – removal and refitting 6
Front seat belt tensioning mechanism – general information 26
General information 1
Interior trim – removal and refitting 28
Maintenance – bodywork and underframe 2
Maintenance – upholstery and carpets 3
Major body damage – repair 5
Minor body damage – repair 4
Rear bumper – removal and refitting 7
Seat belt components – removal and refitting 27
Seats – removal and refitting 25
Sunroof – general information 23
Tailgate and support struts – removal and refitting 15
Tailgate lock components – removal and refitting 16
Windscreen, tailgate and fixed rear quarter window glass – general
  information 22

Degrees of difficulty

Easy, suitable for novice with little experience	Fairly easy, suitable for beginner with some experience	Fairly difficult, suitable for competent DIY mechanic	Difficult, suitable for experienced DIY mechanic	Very difficult, suitable for expert DIY or professional

Specifications

Torque wrench settings	Nm	lbf ft
Bonnet hinge retaining bolts	23	17
Door hinges:		
Hinge retaining bolts*:		
Stage 1	20	15
Stage 2	Angle-tighten a further 90°	
Upper hinge pin bolt	13	9
Door lock/catch retaining bolts	20	15
Door lock/handle retaining bolt	18	13
Door regulator/assembly carrier retaining bolts	8	6
Door top hinge pin	13	10
Door window glass clamp bolts	10	7
Front seat mounting retaining bolts	23	17
Seat belt anchorage bolts	40	30
Tailgate hinge retaining bolts	22	16

Renew the bolt every time it is removed

1 General information

The body shell is made of pressed-steel sections, and is available in both three- and five-door Hatchback, four-door Saloon and Estate versions. Most components are welded together, and some use is made of structural adhesives; the front wings are bolted on.

The bonnet, door, and some other vulnerable panels are made of zinc-coated metal, and are further protected by being coated with an anti-chip primer before being sprayed.

Extensive use is made of plastic materials, mainly in the interior, but also in exterior components. The front and rear bumpers, and front grille, are injection-moulded from a synthetic material that is very strong and yet light. Plastic components such as wheel arch liners are fitted to the underside of the vehicle, to improve the body's resistance to corrosion.

2 Maintenance – bodywork and underframe

The general condition of a vehicle's bodywork is the one thing that significantly affects its value. Maintenance is easy, but needs to be regular. Neglect, particularly after minor damage, can lead quickly to further deterioration and costly repair bills. It is important also to keep watch on those parts of the vehicle not immediately visible, for instance the underside, inside all the wheel arches, and the lower part of the engine compartment.

The basic maintenance routine for the bodywork is washing – preferably with a lot of water, from a hose. This will remove all the loose solids which may have stuck to the vehicle. It is important to flush these off in such a way as to prevent grit from scratching the finish. The wheel arches and underframe need washing in the same way, to remove any accumulated mud, which will retain moisture and tend to encourage rust. Paradoxically enough, the best time to clean the underframe and wheel arches is in wet weather, when the mud is thoroughly wet and soft. In very wet weather, the underframe is usually cleaned of large accumulations automatically, and this is a good time for inspection.

Periodically, except on vehicles with a wax-based underbody protective coating, it is a good idea to have the whole of the underframe of the vehicle steam-cleaned, engine compartment included, so that a thorough inspection can be carried out to see what minor repairs and renovations are necessary. Steam-cleaning is available at many garages, and is necessary for the removal of the accumulation of oily grime, which sometimes is allowed to become thick in certain areas. If steam-cleaning facilities are not available,

there are some excellent grease solvents available which can be brush-applied; the dirt can then be simply hosed off. Note that these methods should not be used on vehicles with wax-based underbody protective coating, or the coating will be removed. Such vehicles should be inspected annually, preferably just prior to Winter, when the underbody should be washed down, and any damage to the wax coating repaired. Ideally, a completely fresh coat should be applied. It would also be worth considering the use of such wax-based protection for injection into door panels, sills, box sections, etc, as an additional safeguard against rust damage, where such protection is not provided by the vehicle manufacturer.

After washing paintwork, wipe off with a chamois leather to give an unspotted clear finish. A coat of clear protective wax polish will give added protection against chemical pollutants in the air. If the paintwork sheen has dulled or oxidised, use a cleaner/polisher combination to restore the brilliance of the shine. This requires a little effort, but such dulling is usually caused because regular washing has been neglected. Care needs to be taken with metallic paintwork, as special non-abrasive cleaner/polisher is required to avoid damage to the finish. Always check that the door and ventilator opening drain holes and pipes are completely clear, so that water can be drained out. Brightwork should be treated in the same way as paintwork. Windscreens and windows can be kept clear of the smeary film which often appears, by the use of proprietary glass cleaner. Never use any form of wax or other body or chromium polish on glass.

3 Maintenance – upholstery and carpets

Mats and carpets should be brushed or vacuum-cleaned regularly, to keep them free of grit. If they are badly stained, remove them from the vehicle for scrubbing or sponging, and make quite sure they are dry before refitting. Seats and interior trim panels can be kept clean by wiping with a damp cloth. If they do become stained (which can be more apparent on light-coloured upholstery), use a little liquid detergent and a soft nail brush to scour the grime out of the grain of the material. Do not forget to keep the headlining clean in the same way as the upholstery. When using liquid cleaners inside the vehicle, do not over-wet the surfaces being cleaned. Excessive damp could get into the seams and padded interior, causing stains, offensive odours or even rot.

If the inside of the vehicle gets wet accidentally, it is worthwhile taking some trouble to dry it out properly, particularly where carpets are involved. Do not leave oil or electric heaters inside the vehicle for this purpose.

4 Minor body damage – repair

Scratches

If the scratch is very superficial, and does not penetrate to the metal of the bodywork, repair is very simple. Lightly rub the area of the scratch with a paintwork renovator, or a very fine cutting paste, to remove loose paint from the scratch, and to clear the surrounding bodywork of wax polish. Rinse the area with clean water.

Apply touch-up paint to the scratch using a fine paint brush; continue to apply fine layers of paint until the surface of the paint in the scratch is level with the surrounding paintwork. Allow the new paint at least two weeks to harden, then blend it into the surrounding paintwork by rubbing the scratch area with a paintwork renovator or a very fine cutting paste. Finally, apply wax polish.

Where the scratch has penetrated right through to the metal of the bodywork, causing the metal to rust, a different repair technique is required. Remove any loose rust from the bottom of the scratch with a penknife, then apply rust-inhibiting paint to prevent the formation of rust in the future. Using a rubber or nylon applicator, fill the scratch with bodystopper paste. If required, this paste can be mixed with cellulose thinners to provide a very thin paste which is ideal for filling narrow scratches. Before the stopper-paste in the scratch hardens, wrap a piece of smooth cotton rag around the top of a finger. Dip the finger in cellulose thinners, and quickly sweep it across the surface of the stopper-paste in the scratch; this will ensure that the surface of the stopper-paste is slightly hollowed. The scratch can now be painted over as described earlier in this Section.

Dents

When deep denting of the vehicle's bodywork has taken place, the first task is to pull the dent out, until the affected bodywork almost attains its original shape. There is little point in trying to restore the original shape completely, as the metal in the damaged area will have stretched on impact, and cannot be reshaped fully to its original contour. It is better to bring the level of the dent up to a point which is about 3 mm below the level of the surrounding bodywork. In cases where the dent is very shallow anyway, it is not worth trying to pull it out at all. If the underside of the dent is accessible, it can be hammered out gently from behind, using a mallet with a wooden or plastic head. Whilst doing this, hold a suitable block of wood firmly against the outside of the panel, to absorb the impact from the hammer blows and thus prevent a large area of the bodywork from being 'belled-out'.

Should the dent be in a section of the

bodywork which has a double skin, or some other factor making it inaccessible from behind, a different technique is called for. Drill several small holes through the metal inside the area – particularly in the deeper section. Then screw long self-tapping screws into the holes, just sufficiently for them to gain a good purchase in the metal. Now the dent can be pulled out by pulling on the protruding heads of the screws with a pair of pliers.

The next stage of the repair is the removal of the paint from the damaged area, and from an inch or so of the surrounding 'sound' bodywork. This is accomplished most easily by using a wire brush or abrasive pad on a power drill, although it can be done just as effectively by hand, using sheets of abrasive paper. To complete the preparation for filling, score the surface of the bare metal with a screwdriver or the tang of a file, or alternatively, drill small holes in the affected area. This will provide a really good 'key' for the filler paste.

To complete the repair, see the Section on filling and respraying.

Rust holes or gashes

Remove all paint from the affected area, and from an inch or so of the surrounding 'sound' bodywork, using an abrasive pad or a wire brush on a power drill. If these are not available, a few sheets of abrasive paper will do the job most effectively. With the paint removed, you will be able to judge the severity of the corrosion, and therefore decide whether to renew the whole panel (if this is possible) or to repair the affected area. New body panels are not as expensive as most people think, and it is often quicker and more satisfactory to fit a new panel than to attempt to repair large areas of corrosion.

Remove all fittings from the affected area, except those which will act as a guide to the original shape of the damaged bodywork (eg headlight shells etc). Then, using tin snips or a hacksaw blade, remove all loose metal and any other metal badly affected by corrosion. Hammer the edges of the hole inwards, in order to create a slight depression for the filler paste.

Wire-brush the affected area to remove the powdery rust from the surface of the remaining metal. Paint the affected area with rust-inhibiting paint, if the back of the rusted area is accessible, treat this also.

Before filling can take place, it will be necessary to block the hole in some way. This can be achieved by the use of aluminium or plastic mesh, or aluminium tape.

Aluminium or plastic mesh, or glass-fibre matting, is probably the best material to use for a large hole. Cut a piece to the approximate size and shape of the hole to be filled, then position it in the hole so that its edges are below the level of the surrounding bodywork. It can be retained in position by several blobs of filler paste around its periphery.

Aluminium tape should be used for small or very narrow holes. Pull a piece off the roll, trim it to the approximate size and shape required, then pull off the backing paper (if used) and stick the tape over the hole; it can be overlapped if the thickness of one piece is insufficient. Burnish down the edges of the tape with the handle of a screwdriver or similar, to ensure that the tape is securely attached to the metal underneath.

Filling and respraying

Before using this Section, see the Sections on dent, deep scratch, rust holes and gash repairs.

Many types of bodyfiller are available, but generally speaking, those proprietary kits which contain a tin of filler paste and a tube of resin hardener are best for this type of repair. A wide, flexible plastic or nylon applicator will be found invaluable for imparting a smooth and well-contoured finish to the surface of the filler.

Mix up a little filler on a clean piece of card or board – measure the hardener carefully (follow the maker's instructions on the pack), otherwise the filler will set too rapidly or too slowly. Using the applicator, apply the filler paste to the prepared area; draw the applicator across the surface of the filler to achieve the correct contour and to level the surface. As soon as a contour that approximates to the correct one is achieved, stop working the paste – if you carry on too long, the paste will become sticky and begin to 'pick-up' on the applicator. Continue to add thin layers of filler paste at 20-minute intervals, until the level of the filler is just proud of the surrounding bodywork.

Once the filler has hardened, the excess can be removed using a metal plane or file. From then on, progressively-finer grades of abrasive paper should be used, starting with a 40-grade production paper, and finishing with a 400-grade wet-and-dry paper. Always wrap the abrasive paper around a flat rubber, cork, or wooden block – otherwise the surface of the filler will not be completely flat. During the smoothing of the filler surface, the wet-and-dry paper should be periodically rinsed in water. This will ensure that a very smooth finish is imparted to the filler at the final stage.

At this stage, the dent should be surrounded by a ring of bare metal, which in turn should be encircled by the finely 'feathered' edge of the good paintwork. Rinse the repair area with clean water, until all of the dust produced by the rubbing-down operation has gone.

Spray the whole area with a light coat of primer – this will show up any imperfections in the surface of the filler. Repair these imperfections with fresh filler paste or bodystopper, and once more smooth the surface with abrasive paper. Repeat this spray-and-repair procedure until you are satisfied that the surface of the filler, and the feathered edge of the paintwork, are perfect.

Clean the repair area with clean water, and allow to dry fully.

HAYNES HiNT *If bodystopper is used, it can be mixed with cellulose thinners to form a really thin paste which is ideal for filling small holes.*

The repair area is now ready for final spraying. Paint spraying must be carried out in a warm, dry, windless and dust-free atmosphere. This condition can be created artificially if you have access to a large indoor working area, but if you are forced to work in the open, you will have to pick your day very carefully. If you are working indoors, dousing the floor in the work area with water will help to settle the dust which would otherwise be in the atmosphere. If the repair area is confined to one body panel, mask off the surrounding panels; this will help to minimise the effects of a slight mis-match in paint colours. Bodywork fittings (eg chrome strips, door handles etc) will also need to be masked off. Use genuine masking tape, and several thicknesses of newspaper, for the masking operations.

Before commencing to spray, agitate the aerosol can thoroughly, then spray a test area (an old tin, or similar) until the technique is mastered. Cover the repair area with a thick coat of primer; the thickness should be built up using several thin layers of paint, rather than one thick one. Using 400-grade wet-and-dry paper, rub down the surface of the primer until it is really smooth. While doing this, the work area should be thoroughly doused with water, and the wet-and-dry paper periodically rinsed in water. Allow to dry before spraying on more paint.

Spray on the top coat, again building up the thickness by using several thin layers of paint. Start spraying at one edge of the repair area, and then, using a side-to-side motion, work until the whole repair area and about 2 inches of the surrounding original paintwork is covered. Remove all masking material 10 to 15 minutes after spraying on the final coat of paint.

Allow the new paint at least two weeks to harden, then, using a paintwork renovator, or a very fine cutting paste, blend the edges of the paint into the existing paintwork. Finally, apply wax polish.

Plastic components

With the use of more and more plastic body components by the vehicle manufacturers (eg bumpers, spoilers, and in some cases major body panels), rectification of more serious damage to such items has become a matter of either entrusting repair work to a specialist in this field, or renewing complete components. Repair of such damage by the DIY owner is not really feasible, owing to the cost of the equipment and materials required for effecting such repairs. The basic technique involves making a groove along the line of the

6.2 Unclip the release lever from the lock

6.3a Release the retaining lugs . . .

6.3b . . . and lift the radiator grille upwards

crack in the plastic, using a rotary burr in a power drill. The damaged part is then welded back together, using a hot-air gun to heat up and fuse a plastic filler rod into the groove. Any excess plastic is then removed, and the area rubbed down to a smooth finish. It is important that a filler rod of the correct plastic is used, as body components can be made of a variety of different types (eg polycarbonate, ABS, polypropylene).

Damage of a less serious nature (abrasions, minor cracks etc) can be repaired by the DIY owner using a two-part epoxy filler repair material. Once mixed in equal proportions, this is used in similar fashion to the bodywork filler used on metal panels. The filler is usually cured in twenty to thirty minutes, ready for sanding and painting.

If the owner is renewing a complete component himself, or if he has repaired it with epoxy filler, he will be left with the

problem of finding a suitable paint for finishing which is compatible with the type of plastic used. At one time, the use of a universal paint was not possible, owing to the complex range of plastics encountered in body component applications. Standard paints, generally speaking, will not bond to plastic or rubber satisfactorily. However, it is now possible to obtain a plastic body parts finishing kit which consists of a pre-primer treatment, a primer and coloured top coat. Full instructions are normally supplied with a kit, but basically, the method of use is to first apply the pre-primer to the component concerned, and allow it to dry for up to 30 minutes. Then the primer is applied, and left to dry for about an hour before finally applying the special-coloured top coat. The result is a correctly-coloured component, where the paint will flex with the plastic or rubber, a property that standard paint does not normally possess.

5 Major body damage – repair

Where serious damage has occurred, or large areas need renewal due to neglect, it means that complete new panels will need welding-in, and this is best left to professionals. If the damage is due to impact, it will also be necessary to check completely the alignment of the body shell, and this can only be carried out accurately by a VW dealer using special jigs. If the body is left misaligned, it is primarily dangerous, as the car will not handle properly, and secondly, uneven stresses will be imposed on the steering, suspension and possibly transmission, causing abnormal wear, or complete failure, particularly to such items as the tyres.

6 Front bumper – removal and refitting

Note : *Depending on the model, it is possible that slight changes to the removal and refitting procedures may be necessary.*

Removal

1 Apply the handbrake, then jack up the front of the vehicle and support it on axle stands (see *Jacking and vehicle support*).
2 Open the bonnet, and remove the bonnet release lever from the lock by lifting the securing clip, then using a flat-bladed screwdriver open out the end attached to the bonnet lock to disconnect **(see illustration)**.
3 Using a screwdriver, carefully release the radiator grille upper retaining lugs, then lift the grille upwards off the retaining pins **(see illustrations)**.
4 Remove the eight bolts (four each side) securing the wheel arch liners to the bumper ends **(see illustration)**.
5 Carefully unclip the air grilles in the lower part of the bumper cover to gain access to the two securing screws **(see illustrations)**.
6 Slacken and remove the five upper retaining screws **(see illustration)**.
7 On models with headlamp washers, remove the washer jets as described in Chapter 12.

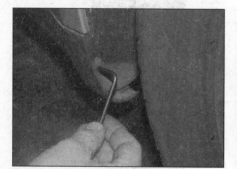

6.4 Removing the bolts securing the wheel arch liners to the bumper ends

6.5a Pull out the air grilles from the bumper cover . . .

6.5b . . . for access to the bumper securing screws

6.6 Undo the upper securing screws

8 Disconnect the wire connector below the headlamp for the temperature sensor as the bumper is being removed.

9 Carefully release the bumper left- and right-hand ends, and pull the bumper away from the vehicle in a forwards direction **(see illustration)**.

Refitting

10 Refitting is a reverse of the removal procedure, ensuring that the bumper ends engage correctly with the locating guides as the bumper is refitted.

7 Rear bumper – removal and refitting

Note : *Depending on the model, it is possible that slight changes to the removal and refitting procedures may be necessary.*

Removal

1 To improve access, chock the front wheels, then jack up the rear of the vehicle and support it on axle stands (see *Jacking and vehicle support*).

2 Remove the rear light clusters as described in Chapter 12, Section 7.

3 On Golf models, disconnect the wire connector for the number plate light below the left tail light.

4 Remove the six screws (three each side) securing the wheel arch liners to the bumper ends **(see illustration)**.

5 Slacken and remove the screws securing the bottom of the bumper in position **(see illustration)**.

6 Slacken and remove the upper retaining screws. On Golf models, push the centre pins out from the plastic rivets on the ends of the bumper and remove the rivets **(see illustrations)**.

7 Release the bumper cover off the guides at the left- and right-hand ends, then lift off the securing clip in the centre in a rearwards direction. Guide the wiring connector out of the grommet below the left tail light **(see illustration)**.

Refitting

8 Refitting is a reverse of the removal

6.9 Lift bumper off the locating guides

procedure, ensuring that the bumper ends engage correctly with the slides as the bumper is refitted. Retrieve the centre pins for the plastic rivets from the plastic slides before refitting the bumper – renew if necessary.

8 Bonnet – removal, refitting and adjustment

Removal

1 Open the bonnet and using a pencil or felt tip pen, mark the outline of each bonnet hinge relative to the bonnet, to use as a guide on refitting.

2 Disconnect the washer hose from the windscreen washer jets and, where necessary, disconnect the wiring from the jet heating elements.

7.5 Lower bumper retaining screws

7.6b Use a drift to push out the centre pin from the rivet

7.7 Unclip the wiring connector from below the left-hand tail light

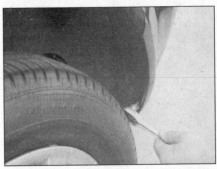

7.4 Remove wheel arch-to-rear bumper screws

3 With the help of an assistant to support the bonnet, disconnect the gas support strut as described in Section 15.

4 Undo the bonnet retaining bolts **(see illustration)** and carefully lift the bonnet clear. Store the bonnet out of the way in a safe place.

5 Unclip the hinge covers and then remove them from the hinge. Inspect the bonnet hinges for signs of wear and free play at the pivots, and if necessary renew. Each hinge is secured to the body by two bolts, mark the position of the hinge on the body then undo the retaining bolts and remove it from the vehicle. On refitting, align the new hinge with the marks and tighten the retaining bolts.

Refitting and adjustment

6 With the aid of an assistant, offer up the bonnet and loosely fit the retaining bolts. Align

7.6a Remove the upper retaining screws

8.4 Remove the bonnet securing bolts

9.1 The clip can be retrieved when the trim has been removed

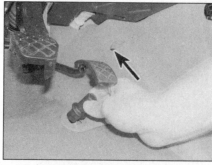

9.2 Remove the accelerator stop and plastic screw (arrowed)

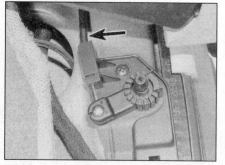

9.3 Push the outer cable in the direction of the arrow to disconnect

9.6 Disconnect the bonnet release cable

the hinges with the marks made on removal, then tighten the retaining bolts securely.

7 Refit the washer hose, wiring and gas strut in the reverse order of removal.

8 Close the bonnet, and check for alignment with the adjacent panels. If necessary, slacken the hinge bolts and re-align the bonnet. Once the bonnet is correctly aligned, tighten the hinge bolts. Check that the bonnet fastens and releases satisfactorily.

9 Bonnet release cable – removal and refitting

Removal

1 Working inside the vehicle, locate the release lever. Pull the lever approximately 2 cm, then

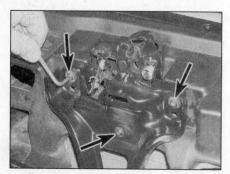
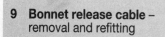

10.3 Remove the three securing bolts (arrowed)

insert a small screwdriver into the gap between release lever and its securing clip. Let the lever return to its original position, then release the clip with a screwdriver (note that the clip falls behind the trim) **(see illustration)**.

2 Unscrew the accelerator stop nut and plastic screw **(see illustration)**, then unclip the trim at the centre and at the lower edge from sill trim to remove.

3 Release the outer cable by unclipping forwards from the lever bracket and detach the inner cable from the lever **(see illustration)**.

4 Release the cable sealing grommet from the bulkhead.

5 Work along the length of the cable, noting its correct routing, and free it from the retaining clips and ties.

6 Disconnect the outer cable from under the crossmember on the lock housing and detach the inner cable **(see illustration)**.

7 Tie a length of string to the end of the cable

10.4 Pulling the support forward to release the lock

inside the vehicle, then withdraw the cable through into the engine compartment.

8 Once the cable is free, untie the string and leave it in position in the vehicle; the string can then be used to draw the new cable back into position.

Refitting

9 Tie the inner end of the string to the end of the cable, then use the string to draw the bonnet release cable back from the engine compartment. Once the cable is through, untie the string.

10 Refitting is a reversal of the removal. **Note:** *Before refitting the release lever, fit the securing clip into the lever first, then push the lever back into place.*

11 Ensure the rubber grommet in the bulkhead is fitted correctly, and the cable is correctly routed and secured to all the relevant retaining clips.

12 Before closing the bonnet, check the operation of the release lever and cable.

10 Bonnet lock – removal and refitting

Removal

1 Open the bonnet then remove the radiator grille, as described in Section 6.

2 Release the outer cable from the lock assembly as described in Section 9.

3 Remove the three bolts from the top of the lock support cover **(see illustration)**.

4 Pull the lock support cover forward and lift out the lock assembly **(see illustration)**; disconnecting the microswitch connector from the lock assembly where fitted.

Refitting

5 Before refitting, remove all traces of old locking compound from the lock retaining bolts and their threads in the body.

6 Refitting is then a reverse of removal procedure, ensuring bolts are securely tightened using thread-locking compound when required (VW recommend the use of D 185 400 A2 – available from your VW dealer).

7 Check that the bonnet fastens and releases satisfactorily. If adjustment is necessary, slacken the bonnet lock retaining bolts, and adjust the position of the lock to suit. Once the lock is operating correctly, tighten its retaining bolts.

11 Door – removal, refitting and adjustment

Note: *The hinge bolts must always be renewed if loosened.*

Removal

Front door

1 Disconnect the battery negative terminal.

Bodywork and fittings 11•7

Note: *Before disconnecting the battery, refer to 'Disconnecting the battery' at the rear of this manual.*

2 Open the door and unclip the lower trim from the front door pillar, carefully pull off at the centre and at the lower edge from the sill trim to remove (on the driver's door, remove the bonnet release lever as described in Section 9).

3 Disconnect the wiring connector from behind the trim **(see illustration)**.

4 Remove the gaiter from the door pillar, then guide wiring out through the hole in the pillar.

5 Lever off the cap from the top hinge pin and, with the aid of an assistant to support the door, remove the hinge pin from the top hinge. Also remove the two bolts from the lower hinge that secure the hinge to the door **(see illustrations)**. Lift the door upwards and out to remove.

6 Examine the hinges for signs of wear or damage. If renewal is necessary, mark the position of the hinge(s) then undo the retaining bolts and remove them from the vehicle. If there is a requirement to remove the top hinge from the front pillar, then the facia panel must be removed as described in Section 30. Fit the new hinge(s), aligning with the marks made before removal then tighten the retaining bolts and top hinge pin to the specified torque.

Rear door

7 Disconnect the battery negative terminal.
Note: *Before disconnecting the battery, refer to 'Disconnecting the battery' at the rear of this manual.*

8 Open the door and remove the gaiter from the door pillar, disconnect the wiring connector **(see illustration)**.

9 Carry out the operations described in paragraphs 5 and 6.

Refitting

10 With the aid of an assistant, offer up the door to the vehicle and fit the new hinge bolts. Align the hinges with the marks made before removal and tighten the retaining bolts to Stage 1 of their specified torque. Refit the cap to the top hinge pin.

11 Guide the wiring back through the hole in the pillar and refit the gaiter.

12 From inside the vehicle reconnect the wiring block connector.

13 Refit the lower trim securely back into the retaining clips (on the driver's door, refit the bonnet release lever as described in Section 9).

14 Check the door alignment and if necessary adjust. If the paintwork around the hinges has been damaged, paint the area with a suitable touch-in brush to prevent corrosion. Reconnect the battery negative terminal.

Adjustment

Note: *Always renew the hinge bolts after loosening.*
15 Close the door and check the door

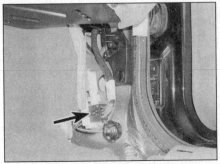

11.3 Disconnect the wiring connector (arrowed)

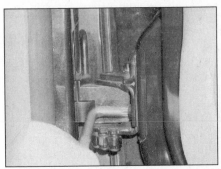

11.5b . . . then remove the bottom hinge bolts

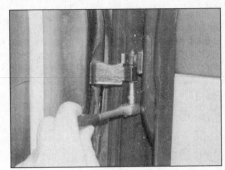

11.5a Remove the top hinge pin . . .

11.8 Pull back the gaiter and disconnect the wiring

alignment with the surrounding body panels. If necessary, slight adjustment of the door position can be made by slackening the hinge retaining bolts and repositioning the hinge/door as necessary. If there is a requirement to loosen the top hinge on the door pillar (front doors only), then the facia panel must be removed as described in Section 30. Once the door is correctly positioned, tighten the hinge bolts to Stage 2 of their specified torque. If the paintwork around the hinges has been damaged, paint the affected area with a suitable touch-in brush to prevent corrosion.

---

12 Door inner trim panel – removal and refitting

Note: *Before disconnecting the battery lower*

the window to ease the removal of the interior door handle assembly, also refer to 'Disconnecting the battery' at the rear of this manual.

Removal

Front passenger door

1 Disconnect the battery negative terminal then open the door.

2 Using a flat-bladed screwdriver, carefully unclip the upper trim cover from the door grab handle and remove it from the vehicle **(see illustration)**.

3 Slacken and remove the screws securing the inner trim and armrest to the door **(see illustrations)**.

4 Release the door trim panel studs, carefully levering between the panel and door with a flat-bladed lever. Work around the outside of the panel, and when all the studs are

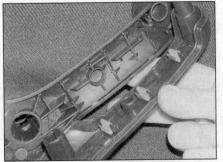

12.2 Carefully prise the trim off the three securing clips

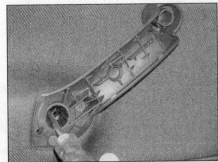

12.3a Slacken and remove the screws from inside the handle . . .

12.3b . . . also the screw from the top front edge of the panel . . .

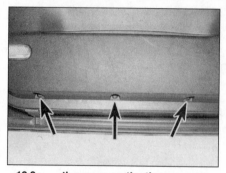

12.3c . . . then remove the three screws (arrowed)

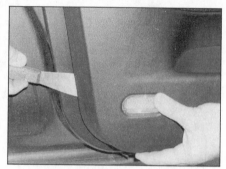

12.4 Release the trim panel carefully

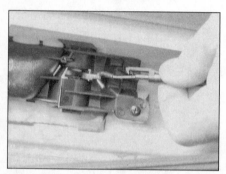

12.5 Unclip the outer cable, then unhook the inner cable

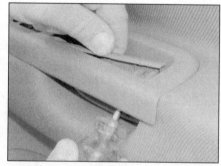

12.8a Push the trim out of its retaining clips . . .

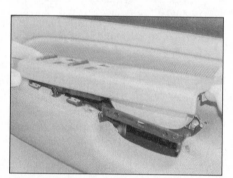

12.8b . . . then carefully lever out from the door trim panel

released, lift the door trim panel upwards and off the window slot **(see illustration)**.

5 As the panel is being removed disconnect the outer cable from the release handle

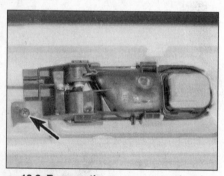

13.2 Remove the screw arrowed and unclip from door trim panel

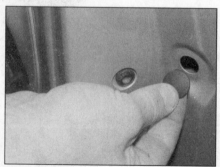

13.3 Remove the plastic cap . . .

assembly using a flat-bladed screwdriver, then unhook inner cable **(see illustration)**.

6 Disconnect wiring connectors as they become accessible.

Driver's door

7 Disconnect the battery negative terminal then open the door.

8 Insert flat-bladed screwdriver under the trim on the grip handle, and carefully lever trim off towards the door trim. The grip recess with switches can then be unclipped upwards to remove **(see illustrations)**. Press the lug on the connector to disconnect the wiring connector from the switch panel.

9 Remove the door trim panel as described in paragraphs 3 to 6.

Rear doors

10 Remove the trim panel as described in paragraphs 1 to 6.

13.4 . . . then hold the door handle in the open position while loosening the screw to the stop

Refitting

11 Before refitting, check whether any of the trim panel retaining studs were broken on removal, renew them as necessary. Refitting of the trim panel is then a reverse of removal. After connecting the battery, check the operation of the door electrical equipment.

---

13 Door handle and lock components – removal and refitting

Removal

Interior door handle

1 Remove the door inner trim panel as described in Section 12.

2 Undo the screw on the inside of the door trim panel, then unclip the door handle to remove it **(see illustration)**.

Front door lock cylinder

Note: *This task can be performed with the door inner trim panel in position.*

3 Open the door, then remove the plastic cap in the rear edge of the door to locate the retaining screw **(see illustration)**.

4 Pull the door handle out, hold it in this position whilst undoing the Torx retaining screw until it comes to its stop. Do not remove the screw too far or the locking ring may fall into the door **(see illustration)**.

5 Pull the lock cylinder housing out of the door handle, and release the handle to the

13.5a Withdraw the lock cylinder from the handle

13.5b The lock cylinder removed

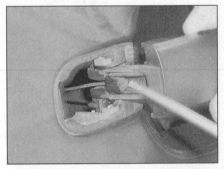

13.6a Detach the release cable from the door handle . . .

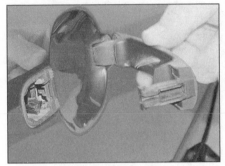

13.6b . . . then pivot the handle from the door

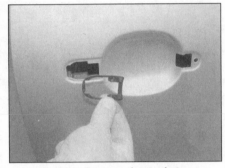

13.6c Recover the gasket

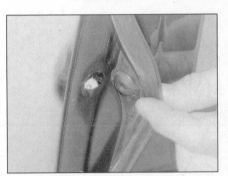

13.7 On the rear door, pull back the door seal to locate the handle housing screw

original position (see illustrations). On older vehicles, the housing may be corroded into the door aperture making it difficult to remove. **Note:** *Do not drop the locking ring into the door, as it will be necessary to remove the inner trim panel to recover it.*

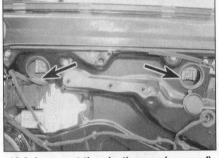

13.9 Lever out the plastic caps (arrowed)

Exterior door handle

6 On the front door, remove the door lock cylinder housing as described in paragraphs 3 to 5. Working via the lock cylinder aperture, disconnect the lock release cable from the handle then manoeuvre the handle out from the door. Recover the gasket (see illustrations).

7 On the rear door, pull the door seal to one side to gain access to the housing retaining screw, then undo the screw and remove the housing and end cap from the handle as described in paragraphs 4 and 5 (see illustration). Working via the housing aperture, disconnect the lock release cable from the handle then manoeuvre the handle out from the door.

Front door lock

Note: *The window regulator, the door lock and the speaker are secured to an assembly carrier.*

8 Remove the door inner trim panel as described in Section 12. Carry out the operations described in paragraphs 3 to 7.

9 Lever out the plastic cap(s) in the cut-outs on the inside of the door to gain access to the window securing bolts (see illustration).

10 Lower the window until the window securing bolts are in line with the cut-outs. If this cannot be carried out because there is a fault with the electric windows, then remove the motor so as to slide the window down.

11 Loosen the securing bolts approximately two turns (do not remove) to release the clamps securing the window, then push the window upwards and secure it in position (see illustrations).

12 Disconnect all the wiring connectors on the assembly carrier. Unscrew the two bolts on the rear edge of the door from the door lock (see illustration).

13 Undo the bolts securing the assembly

13.11a Slacken off the securing bolts. Do not remove

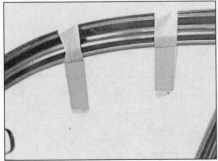

13.11b Push the glass up and secure (eg, with adhesive tape)

13.12 Slacken and remove the two retaining bolts

13.13a Guide the lock out when removing the assembly carrier

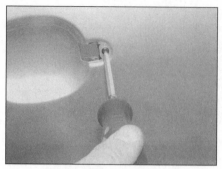

13.13b Undo the screw . . .

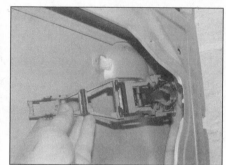

13.13c . . . and withdraw the security plate from inside the door

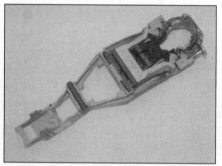

13.13d Security plate removed from the door

13.14 Disconnect the lock wiring

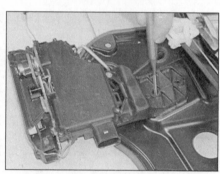

13.15a Push out the plastic pin with a suitable drift

carrier to the door. Pull the top of the assembly carrier from the door, then remove towards the front of the door by lifting and turning the carrier. At this stage, the security plate may be removed from inside the door

after removing the exterior door handle, by undoing the single screw **(see illustrations)**.
14 The wiring cable retaining clips can then be unclipped from the carrier. Disconnect the wiring connector from the door lock **(see illustration)**.

15 The lock can now be removed from the carrier. By using a drift, remove the pins from the retaining bracket **(see illustrations)** then lever off using a flat-bladed screwdriver. Disconnect the cable and the linkage rod by unclipping from the lock. **Note:** *The retaining bracket is not part of the items supplied with the door lock. It is secured to the door lock by a bolt and pop rivet.*

Rear door lock

Note: *The window regulator, the door lock and the speaker are secured to an assembly carrier.*
16 Carry out the operations described above in paragraphs 1 to 10.
17 Screw a 5 mm bolt, approximately 70 mm long into the inner window securing plug and pull out. Using a piece of rod with a hook on one end, pull the outer securing plug from the window guide **(see illustrations)**, holding window cable to one side. **Note:** *Do not exert too much pressure on the plug otherwise the plug will fall into the door.*
18 Remove the plastic cap from the bottom of the window guide rail at the middle of the door, and remove the bolt **(see illustration)**.
19 Pull the seal out from the window guide rail, and with a small flat-bladed screwdriver, lift the locking tab at the bottom of the guide rail to remove the filler piece upwards from the guide **(see illustrations)**.
20 Carefully remove the inner sealing strip from the top of the door, by gripping with pliers at the centre and rotating inwards **(see illustration)**.

13.15b Front door lock removed

13.17a Screw a bolt into the plug then pull out with a pair of pliers

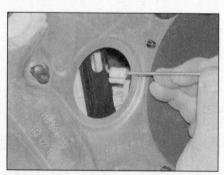

13.17b Hook the outer plug out, by using a suitable piece of rod

13.18 Remove the plastic cap to locate the guide rail bolt

13.19a Lever out the plastic clip under the seal . . .

13.19b . . . then slide upwards out of the guide rail

13.20 A wedge can be used to assist the removal of the trim

13.21 Carefully remove the glass inwards from the door

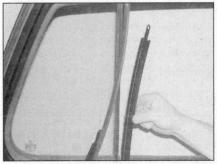

13.23a Remove the plastic cap to locate the bottom guide rail bolt

13.23b Pull the guide rail down first, to unclip from frame at the top

21 Slide the door window upwards and inwards to remove from the door **(see illustration)**.

22 Pull the window guide seal off at the top of the guide rail and unclip, or remove the securing screw if fitted.

23 Remove the bolt from the rear edge of the door, at the bottom of the window guide rail. Pull the guide from the small fixed window and remove upwards and out from the door **(see illustrations)**.

24 With the door open, remove the wiring gaiter from the door pillar and disconnect the wiring connectors.

25 Undo the bolts securing the assembly carrier to the door, and the two bolts on the rear edge of the door for the lock. Pull the top of the assembly carrier from the door, then lift and remove towards the front of the door. Release the wiring clip from the door and pull the wiring out from the gaiter **(see illustration)**.

26 The lock can now be removed from the carrier, as described in paragraph 15.

Refitting

Interior door handle

27 Clip the handle back into position and secure with the screw on the inside of the door trim. Refit the door trim panel as described in Section 12.

Exterior door handle

28 Locate the door handle into the door at the front end, then pivot the handle into position. Refit the cable into the door handle and clip into recess. Refit the lock cylinder housing (front door) or housing and end cap (rear door) to the handle and secure it in position with the retaining screw.

Front door lock cylinder

29 Refit the lock cylinder into the door handle

housing, then tighten the screw in the rear edge of the door to secure door lock cylinder. Refit the plastic cap to cover the screw.

Front door lock

30 Before refitting, pull the operating lever on the door lock, and locate the tension spring into slot **(see illustration)**. **Note:** *Locating the spring into the operating lever locks the lock, preventing incorrect fitting of the cable later.*

31 Refitting is a reversal of removal as described in paragraphs 8 to 15. **Note:** *When tightening bolts on assembly carrier, tighten the two locating bolts first to allow the location pegs to align in door **(see illustration)**. Tighten all the bolts to the specified torque, where given.*

Rear door lock

Note: *Do not refit the bolts to the bottom of the guide rail before refitting the filler piece back into the guide rail or this will prevent it locating into the guide rail correctly.*

13.25 Guide the lock out when removing the assembly carrier

13.30 Locate the spring clip into the slot on the lever (arrowed)

13.31 Refit the two screws arrowed first, to locate the carrier

32 See refitting of front door lock procedure.
33 Relocate the securing inner and outer plugs in the window ensuring they project either side of the glass. Guide the window into the door so that the securing plug locates in the window lifting rail slot **(see illustrations)**. Lightly tap the top of the window to locate into the lifting rail.
34 Refitting is then a reversal of removal, as described in paragraphs 16 to 26.

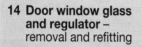

14 Door window glass and regulator – removal and refitting

Note: *The window regulator mechanism is part of the assembly carrier and cannot be obtained individually.*

Removal

Front door window glass

1 Remove the door inner trim panel as described in Section 12.
2 Carry out the procedure as described in Section 13, paragraphs 3 to 11.
3 Lift the rear of glass up and forwards to remove from the door **(see illustration)**.

Rear door window glass

4 Remove the door inner trim panel as described in Section 12.
5 Remove the door glass as described in Section 13, paragraphs 16 to 21.
6 If necessary, the fixed window can then be

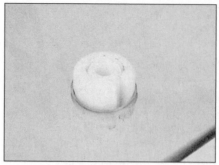

13.33a Fit the plastic plugs into the glass before assembly . . .

removed from the door while removing the window seal **(see illustration)**.

Front window regulator

7 Carry out the operations described in Section 13 for the removal of the front door lock.
8 If there is a fault with the motor, then it can be removed from the assembly carrier by removing the securing screws and wiring connector **(see illustration)**.
9 If the window mechanism is to be renewed, the lock will need to be removed from the carrier as described in Section 13.

Rear window regulator

10 Carry out the operations described in Section 13 for the removal of the rear door lock.
11 If there is a fault with the motor, then it can be removed from the assembly carrier by removing the securing screws and wiring connector **(see illustration)**.

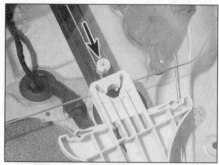

13.33b . . . arrow shows the direction to locate the glass into the lifting rail

12 If the window mechanism is to be renewed, the lock will need to be removed from the carrier as described in Section 13.

Refitting

Front door window glass

13 Manoeuvre the window glass into position and engage it with the regulator clamps. Make sure the glass is correctly seated then lightly tighten the regulator clamp bolts.
14 Refitting is a reversal of removal as described above.
15 Check that the window glass moves smoothly and easily and closes fully. If necessary, slacken the regulator clamp bolts then reposition the glass as necessary. Once the window operation is correct, tighten the clamp nuts to the specified torque.

Rear door window glass

16 Relocate the securing inner and outer plugs in the window ensuring they project either side of the glass. Guide the window into the door so that the securing plug locates into the window lifting rail slot. Lightly tap the top of the window to locate into the lifting rail (see illustrations for the refitting of the rear door lock in Section 13).
17 Refitting is a reversal of removal as described above.
18 Check that the window glass moves smoothly and easily and closes fully. If necessary, slacken the regulator clamp bolts then reposition the glass as necessary. Once the window operation is correct, tighten the clamp nuts to the specified torque.

Front window regulator

19 Refitting is a reversal of removal as described in the refitting of the front door lock in Section 13.

Rear window regulator

20 Refitting is then a reversal of removal as described in the refitting of the rear door lock in Section 13. **Note:** *When installing a new regulator/carrier, before removing the cable tie from the gearing, slide a hammer shaft between the window guide and the assembly carrier to prevent any movement* **(see illustration)**. *The gearing will then stay centralised while the motor is being fitted, enabling the motor to locate correctly.*

14.3 Lift the rear of the glass upwards and out of the door frame

14.6 Push the fixed glass forwards with the seal

14.8 Undo the three window motor securing screws

14.11 Unclip the wiring block connector

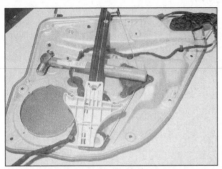

14.20 Hammer positioned to hold the regulator while motor is fitted

15 Tailgate and support struts – removal and refitting

Removal

Tailgate

1 Open up the tailgate then disconnect the battery negative terminal.

2 Slacken and remove the tailgate lower trim panel retaining screws inside the grab handles (see illustration). Release the trim panel clips, carefully levering between the panel and tailgate with a flat-bladed screwdriver. Work around the outside of the panel, and when all the clips are released, unclip from the upper trim and remove the panel.

3 Remove the parcel shelf retainers (Hatchback models only) from the upper trim

by pulling out the centre pins, then remove both the retainers. Unclip the upper trim from the tailgate starting from the outer ends and working towards the middle (see illustrations).

4 Disconnect the wiring connectors situated behind the trim panel and free the washer hose from the tailgate wiper motor. Disconnect the wiring connectors from the heated rear screen terminals and free the wiring grommets from the tailgate (see illustrations).

5 Tie a piece of string to each end of the wiring then, noting the correct routing of the wiring harness, release the harness rubber grommets from the tailgate and withdraw the wiring. When the end of the wiring appears, untie the string and leave it in position in the tailgate; it can then be used on refitting to draw the wiring into position.

6 Using a suitable marker pen, draw around the outline of each hinge marking its correct position on the tailgate.

7 With the help of an assistant to support the tailgate, remove the support struts as described below.

8 Slacken and remove the bolts securing the hinges to the tailgate (see illustration). Where necessary, recover the gaskets which are fitted between the hinge and vehicle body.

9 Inspect the hinges for signs of wear or damage and renew if necessary. The hinges are secured to the vehicle by nuts or bolts (depending on model) which can be accessed once the headlining rear cover strip has been removed.

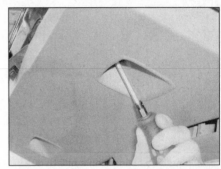

15.2 Remove the handle retaining screw inside tailgate

Support struts

⚠ Warning : The support struts are filled with a gas and must be disposed of safely.

10 With the help of an assistant, support the tailgate in the open position.

11 Using a small flat-bladed screwdriver lift the locking clip, and pull the gas support strut off its balljoint mounting on the tailgate (see illustrations). Repeat the procedure on the lower strut mounting and remove the strut from the vehicle body. Note: If the gas strut is to be re-used, the locking clip must not be taken all the way out, or the clip will be damaged.

Refitting

Tailgate

12 Refitting is the reverse of removal,

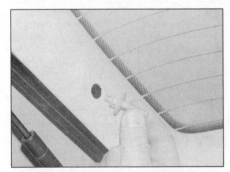

15.3a Pull out centre from parcel shelf clip

15.3b Pull trim away from the outer ends first

15.4a Disconnect washer hose from the wiper motor . . .

15.4b . . . then pull grommet from tailgate to release the wiring

15.8 Remove tailgate hinge securing bolts

15.11a Lift locking clip upwards; do not remove clip completely . . .

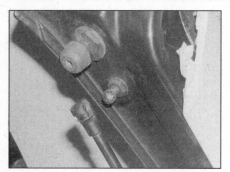

15.11b . . . then pull strut off balljoint

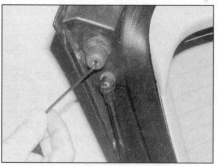

15.14a Slacken the centre screw to adjust the tailgate buffer . . .

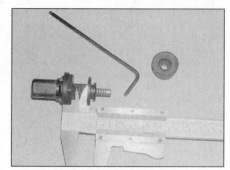

15.14b . . . check the setting on each buffer to line up tailgate

aligning the hinges with the marks made before removal. Tighten retaining bolts to the specified torque.

13 On completion, close the tailgate and check its alignment with the surrounding panels. If necessary slight adjustment can be made by slackening the retaining bolts and repositioning the tailgate on its hinges. If the tailgate buffers are in need of adjustment, continue as follows.

14 Locate the adjustment buffers on the tailgate. Through the hole in the rubber cap, insert an Allen key and slacken the screw until the centre notched slide will move freely in or out, in the housing. When the adjustment buffer has been set to the correct position tighten the centre screw. When renewing buffers the notched slide is preset at 12.5 mm from the housing **(see illustrations)**. To remove the adjustment buffer, turn anti-clockwise 90° with a spanner.

Support struts

15 Refitting is a reverse of the removal procedure, ensuring that the strut is securely retained by its retaining clips.

16 Tailgate lock components – removal and refitting

Removal

Tailgate lock

1 Open up the tailgate, remove the trim panel as described in Section 15.

2 Detach the linkage rod from the lock assembly **(see illustration)**.

3 Undo the retaining bolts and remove the lock from the tailgate, disconnect the wiring connector where applicable **(see illustration)**.

Tailgate handle – Hatchback

4 Remove the tailgate trim panel as described in Section 15.

5 Unclip the securing clip and the linkage rods to remove the lock cylinder out of the handle **(see illustrations)**.

6 Where necessary, disconnect the wiring connector from the lock switch.

7 Slacken and remove the retaining bolts then remove the handle from the tailgate **(see illustration)**. Recover the handle seal (where fitted) and check it for signs of damage, renewing it if necessary.

Tailgate handle – Estate

8 Remove the tailgate trim panel as described in Section 15.

9 Disconnect the wiring connector from the lock release switch. Slacken and remove the retaining screws, then remove the handle from the tailgate **(see illustration)**.

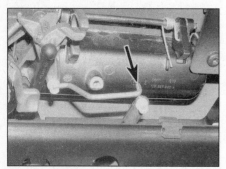

16.2 Unclip the linkage rod (arrowed)

16.3 Disconnect wiring connector

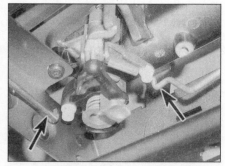

16.5a Disconnect two linkage rods (arrowed) . . .

16.5b . . . prise out securing clip to remove lock (shown out of tailgate)

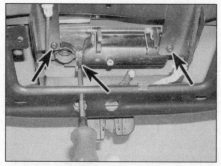

16.7 Remove three screws to release the handle (arrowed)

16.9 Unclip the handle from the tailgate

Tailgate lock cylinder – Hatchback

10 Remove the lock cylinder as described in paragraphs 4 to 6.

Tailgate lock cylinder – Estate

11 Open up the tailgate and remove the trim panel as described in Section 15, then remove the lock cylinder as described in Section 18 paragraphs 5 to 7.

Refitting

12 On the Hatchback the securing clip for the lock cylinder should be refitted back into the handle before assembly **(see illustration)**; the lock can then be pressed back into the handle. Refitting is then a reversal of the relevant removal procedure. Before refitting the trim panel, check the operation of the lock components and (where necessary) the central locking system.

17 Boot lid and support struts – removal and refitting

Removal

Boot lid

1 Open up the boot lid then disconnect the battery negative terminal.

2 Remove the warning triangle from the retaining bracket, then undo the two screws in the retaining bracket and lift out to remove **(see illustration)**. Undo all the remaining screws from around the boot trim and release trim from boot lid.

3 Disconnect all the wiring connectors from the number plate lights and the boot lock assembly **(see illustration)**, tie a piece of string to each end of the wiring. Noting the correct routing of the wiring harness, release the harness rubber grommets from the boot lid and withdraw the wiring. When the end of the wiring appears, untie the string and leave it in position in the boot lid; it can then be used on refitting to draw the wiring into position

4 Unclip the plastic wiring cover from the left-hand hinge to release the wiring **(see illustration)**. Remove the support struts as described below.

5 Draw around the outline of each hinge with a suitable marker pen then slacken and remove the hinge retaining nuts and remove the boot lid from the vehicle.

6 Inspect the hinges for signs of wear or damage and renew if necessary; the hinges are secured to the vehicle body by bolts.

Support struts

⚠ **Warning! The support struts are filled with a gas and must be disposed of safely.**

7 With the help of an assistant, support the boot lid in the open position.

8 Using a small flat-bladed screwdriver lift the locking clip, and pull the gas support strut off

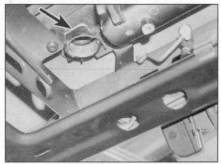
16.12 Arrow shows securing clip in place before fitting the lock cylinder

17.3 Unclip the block connectors and disconnect wiring plugs

its balljoint mounting on the boot lid. Repeat the procedure on the lower strut mounting and remove the strut from the vehicle body. **Note:** *If the gas strut is to be reused, the locking clip must not be taken all the way out, or the clip will be damaged.*

Refitting

Boot lid

9 Refitting is the reverse of removal, aligning the hinges with the marks made before removal.

10 On completion, close the boot lid and check its alignment with the surrounding panels. If necessary slight adjustment can be made by slackening the retaining nuts and repositioning the boot lid on its hinges. If further adjustment is required see the tailgate refitting procedure in Section 15.

18.2 Unclipping the linkage rod from the lock unit

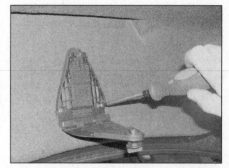
17.2 Remove the screws in the warning triangle retaining bracket

17.4 Unclip plastic cover from hinge to free wiring

Support struts

11 Refitting is a reverse of removal, ensuring the strut is securely retained by its clips.

18 Boot lid lock components – removal and refitting

Removal

Boot lid lock

1 Open up the boot lid, remove the trim panel as described in Section 17.

2 Detach the link rod from the lock assembly and disconnect the wiring connector **(see illustration)**.

3 Undo the retaining nuts and remove the lock from the boot lid.

Boot lid lock cylinder

4 Open up the boot lid, remove the trim panel as described in Section 17.

5 Unclip the linkage rod from the lock cylinder and disconnect the wiring connector **(see illustration)**.

6 Undo the three retaining screws and remove the lock cylinder assembly from the boot lid **(see illustration)**.

7 Remove the two screws in the back of the VW badge to remove the lock cylinder.

Boot lid handle

8 Open up the boot lid, remove the trim panel as described in Section 17.

9 Disconnect the wiring connector and

18.5 Unclipping the linkage rod from the lock cylinder

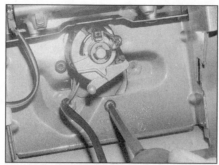

18.6 Removing the three securing screws

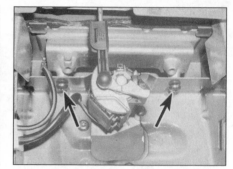

18.9 Remove the two retaining screws (arrowed)

remove the two retaining screws **(see illustration)**.

Refitting

Boot lid lock

10 Reconnect the wiring connector and securely attach the link rod. Seat the lock in the boot lid and securely tighten the nuts.

Boot lid lock cylinder

11 Refitting is a reversal of removal. Check the operation of the lock cylinder assembly on completion.

Boot lid handle

12 Refitting is a reversal of removal. Securely tighten the retaining screws.

19 Central locking components – removal and refitting

Note: *Before disconnecting the battery, refer to 'Disconnecting the battery' at the rear of this manual.*

Removal

Internal central locking switch

1 Remove the door switch assembly as described in Section 12, paragraphs 7 and 8.
2 Undo the screws on the rear of the switch trim panel **(see illustration)**, the switch assembly can now be removed by unclipping from the switch panel.

Central locking control unit

Note: *On models fitted with the 'convenience system', this is the central control unit which also operates the alarm, sunroof and the electric windows and exterior mirrors (via the separate control unit in each door).*
3 Remove the securing screws from the facia panel lower trims, then carefully unclip the top of the trims from the facia **(see illustration)**. Unscrew the plastic reinforcement panel from under the lower trim panels and remove.
4 Unscrew the control unit from the steering column bracket and disconnect the wiring connector **(see illustration)**.

Door locking motors

5 Remove the door lock as described in Section 13.
6 The locking motors are part of the door lock assembly and cannot be obtained separately.

Tailgate lock motor

7 Remove the tailgate trim panel as described in Section 15, paragraphs 1 and 2.
8 Disconnect the linkage rod from the lock motor **(see illustration)**.
9 Using a suitable spanner/pliers slacken the retaining screws in a clockwise direction, and remove by sliding the lock motor out of the elongated holes in tailgate **(see illustration)**. Disconnect the wiring block connector.

Boot lid lock motor

10 Remove the boot lid trim panel as described in Section 17, paragraphs 1 and 2.
11 Unclip the linkage rods from the boot lock

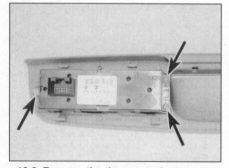

19.2 Remove the three securing screws (arrowed)

19.3 Unclip lower trims from facia

19.4 Remove the two screws securing the control unit (arrowed)

19.8 Disconnect the linkage rod

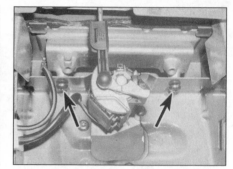

19.9 Turn the securing screws clockwise to remove the lock motor

assembly, then disconnect the wiring block connector **(see illustration)**.

12 Remove the three securing nuts from the lock motor bracket, then remove the lock motor from the bracket by removing the retaining screws **(see illustration)**.

Fuel filler flap lock motor – Hatchback

13 Carry out the operations as described in Section 27, for removing the inner trim panels on the rear seat side belt.

14 Disconnect the wiring connector and operating rod from the motor. Using a suitable spanner/pliers slacken the retaining screws in a clockwise direction, and remove by sliding the lock motor out of the elongated holes in the body **(see illustration)**.

Fuel filler flap lock motor – Saloon

15 Carry out the operations as described in Section 27 for the appropriate side.

16 Disconnect the wiring connector and operating rod from the motor. Slacken the retaining screws and remove by sliding the lock motor out of the elongated holes in the mounting bracket **(see illustration)**.

Refitting

17 Refitting is a reverse of the relevant removal procedure making sure all connections are securely remade. On completion check the operation of all central locking system components.

---

20 Electric window components – removal and refitting

Window switches

1 Refer to Chapter 12, Section 4.

Window winder motors

Removal

2 Remove the relevant window regulator assemblies as described in Section 14.

3 To remove the motor from the window regulator undo the three retaining screws **(see illustration)**.

4 Disconnect the wiring block connector from the window motor assembly **(see illustration)**.

19.11 Disconnect the two linkage rods and unplug the wiring connector (arrowed)

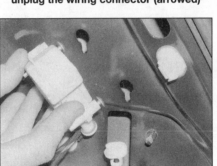

19.14 Slacken and remove the locking motor

Refitting

5 If a new motor is being fitted, remove the protective cover from the gearing.

6 Make sure that the motor drive gear components are sufficiently lubricated (VW recommend grease G 000 450 02 – available from your VW dealer) and free from dust and dirt.

7 Carefully align the motor and engage it with the regulator **(see illustration)**. If the motor does not engage correctly, refit the motor as described in Section 14.

8 Refit the window motor retaining screws and screw them in loosely; when the motor drive gears engage correctly, tighten the screws. Refit the wiring connector to the window motor.

9 Refitting of the trim panel is then a reversal of removal.

19.12 Remove the lock motor assembly

19.16 Slacken the two screws (arrowed)

---

21 Exterior mirrors and associated components – removal and refitting

Removal

Electrically-operated mirror

1 Remove the door inner trim panel as described in Section 12. Disconnect the mirror wiring connector and speaker connector if fitted **(see illustration)**.

2 Remove the screw from the mirror inner trim/speaker panel and unclip from the door **(see illustration)**.

3 Remove the insulation from the door frame and undo the mirror retaining bolt. Free the wiring and remove the mirror assembly from the door **(see illustrations)**.

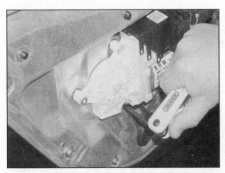

20.3 Remove the three retaining screws

20.4 Disconnect the wiring block connector

20.7 Check the gear on the motor locates correctly

21.1 Disconnecting the mirror wiring plug

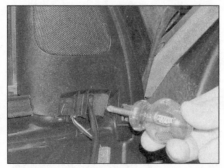

21.2 Remove securing screw from trim

21.3a Undo the retaining bolt . . .

Manually-operated mirror

4 Carry out the procedures as described in paragraphs 1 to 3. Remove the retaining screws from the inner trim panel to disconnect the mirror adjustment cable.

Mirror glass

Note: *The mirror glass is clipped into place. Removal of the glass without the VW special tool (number 80-200) is likely to result in breakage of the glass.*

5 Insert special tool between the mirror glass and mirror housing. First press the mirror downwards and carefully prise the glass from the motor. Disconnect the wiring connectors from the mirror heating element **(see illustration)**.

6 Take great care when removing the glass; do not use excessive force as the glass is easily broken. If the VW special tool is not available, use a flat-bladed lever with tape around to prevent any damage to the mirror housing **(see illustration)**.

Mirror housing

7 Fold the mirror assembly forwards and position the glass vertical to ease the removal of the housing.

8 Remove the small plastic plug in the bottom of the mirror assembly, then insert a screwdriver. Carefully push the screwdriver forwards to release the securing clip, pulling the cover upwards over the mirror glass to remove **(see illustrations)**.

Mirror switch

9 Refer to Chapter 12.

Electrically-operated mirror motor

10 Remove the mirror glass as described above.

11 Undo the retaining screws and remove the motor, disconnecting its wiring connector as it becomes accessible.

Refitting

12 Refitting is the reverse of the relevant removal procedure.

13 When refitting the mirror glass, press firmly at the centre taking care not to use excessive force, as the glass is easily broken.

22 Windscreen, tailgate and fixed rear quarter window glass – general information

These areas of glass are secured by the tight fit of the weather-strip in the body aperture, and are bonded in position with a special adhesive. Renewal of such fixed glass is a difficult, messy and time-consuming task, which is beyond the scope of the home mechanic. It is difficult, unless one has plenty of practice, to obtain a secure, waterproof fit. Furthermore, the task carries a high risk of breakage; this applies especially to the laminated glass windscreen. In view of this, owners are strongly advised to have this sort of work carried out by one of the many specialist windscreen fitters.

If the fixed rear door window glass requires renewal then follow the procedures as described in Section 14.

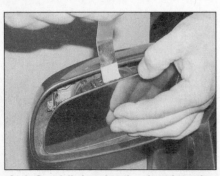

21.3b . . . and remove the mirror from the door

21.5 Disconnect the wiring from the mirror glass

21.6 Carefully levering the glass from the motor

21.8a Push the screwdriver forward . . .

21.8b . . . then lift the cover upwards over mirror glass

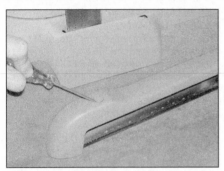

25.2 Unclip the caps to remove the screws

25.3 Remove the two securing bolts

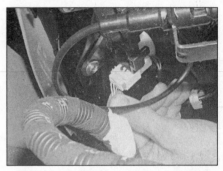

25.4 Disconnect the wiring connectors from under the seat

23 Sunroof –
general information

Due to the complexity of the sunroof mechanism, considerable expertise is needed to repair, renew or adjust the sunroof components successfully. Removal of the roof first requires the headlining to be removed, which is a complex and tedious operation, and not a task to be undertaken lightly. Therefore, any problems with the sunroof should be referred to a VW dealer. On models with an electric sunroof, if the sunroof motor fails to operate, first check the relevant fuse. If the fault cannot be traced and rectified, the sunroof can be opened and closed manually using an Allen key to turn the motor spindle (a suitable key is supplied with the vehicle, and should be clipped onto the inside of the sunroof motor trim). To gain access to the motor, unclip the rear of the trim cover to open. Unclip the Allen key, then insert it fully into the motor opening (against spring pressure). Rotate the key to move the sunroof to the required position.

24 Body exterior fittings –
removal and refitting

Wheel arch liners and body under-panels

1 The various plastic covers fitted to the underside of the vehicle are secured in position by a mixture of screws, nuts and retaining clips and removal will be fairly obvious on inspection. Work methodically around the panel removing its retaining screws and releasing its retaining clips until the panel is free and can be removed from the underside of the vehicle. Most clips used on the vehicle are simply prised out of position. Remove the wheels to ease the removal of the wheel arch liners.

2 On refitting, renew any retaining clips that may have been broken on removal, and ensure that the panel is securely retained by all the relevant clips and screws.

Body trim strips and badges

3 The various body trim strips and badges are held in position with a special adhesive tape and locating lugs. Removal requires the trim/badge to be heated, to soften the adhesive, and then carefully lifted away from the surface. Due to the high risk of damage to the vehicle's paintwork during this operation, it is recommended that this task should be entrusted to a VW dealer.

25 Seats –
removal and refitting
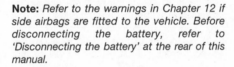

Note: *Refer to the warnings in Chapter 12 if side airbags are fitted to the vehicle. Before disconnecting the battery, refer to 'Disconnecting the battery' at the rear of this manual.*

Removal

Front seats

Note: *The amount of wiring connectors under the seat may vary depending on the vehicle specification.*

1 Disconnect the battery negative terminal.
2 Slide the seat forwards and unclip the caps, on the trim covering the seat runner guide rails **(see illustration)**. Remove the securing screws and pull out the trim covers.
3 Slide the seat backwards, remove the two bolts under the front of the seat **(see illustration)**.
4 Slide the seat fully backwards, disengaging

25.5 Pull the outer cable out; unclipping the inner cable

it from the outer guide rails. Tilt the seat backwards and disconnect the wiring connectors from under the front of the seat **(see illustration)**. Remove the seat from the vehicle.
5 To remove the seat slide locking cable, remove the screw holding the handle on the lever. Unclip the outer cable from the bracket and disengage the inner cable from the lever **(see illustration)**.
6 Using a suitable screwdriver lever the clip off the other end of the cable and remove from the seat sliding rail **(see illustration)**. To remove the seat belt stalk from the seat assembly see Section 27.

Rear seat assembly

7 Lift up the rear seat cushion(s) then unhook the hinge rods from their retaining brackets and remove from the vehicle.
8 On Estate models, unclip the caps on the hinges and remove the retaining screws. Pull out the hinge pins and remove the seat cushion(s).
9 Fold down the rear seat backs.
10 Using a small flat-bladed screwdriver, release the outer hinge pivot retaining catch and lift the seat back upwards to disengage. Pull the seat back out from the centre hinge pivot and remove it from the vehicle **(see illustrations)**. Remove the opposite seat back in the same way.

Refitting

Front seats

11 Before refitting examine the seat guide rails for signs of wear or damage and renew if

25.6 Pulling the cable free from the rail

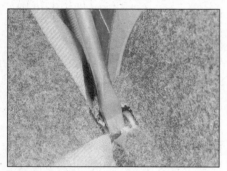

25.10a Lever the catch back to release the seat from the wheel arch . . .

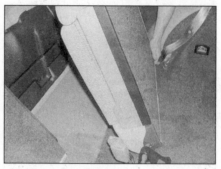

25.10b . . . then pull the seat out from the centre pivot

necessary. Refitting is a reverse of the removal procedure. Ensure that the seat adjustment lever engages correctly with the centre guide rail when the seat has been refitted and the seat bolts are tightened to their specified torque.

Rear seat assembly

12 Refitting is the reverse of removal, making sure the seat backs are clipped securely in position and the seat bolts are tightened securely.

26 Front seat belt tensioning mechanism – general information

Most models covered in this manual are fitted with a front seat belt tensioner system. The system is designed to instantaneously take up any slack in the seat belt in the case of a sudden frontal impact, therefore reducing

the possibility of injury to the front seat occupants. Each front seat is fitted with its system, the tensioner being situated behind the sill trim panel.

The seat belt tensioner is triggered by a frontal impact above a predetermined force. Lesser impacts, including impacts from behind, will not trigger the system.

When the system is triggered, the explosive gas in the tensioner mechanism retracts and locks the seat belt through a cable which acts on the inertia reel. This prevents the seat belt moving and keeps the occupant firmly in position in the seat. Once the tensioner has been triggered, the seat belt will be permanently locked and the assembly must be renewed.

There is a risk of injury if the system is triggered inadvertently when working on the vehicle, and it is therefore strongly recommended that any work involving the seat belt tensioner system is entrusted to a VW dealer.

Note the following warnings before contemplating any work on the front seat belts.

 Warning: Do not expose the tensioner mechanism to temperatures in excess of 100°C (212°F).
• *If the tensioner mechanism is dropped, it must be renewed, even it has suffered no apparent damage.*
• *Do not allow any solvents to come into contact with the tensioner mechanism.*
• *Do not attempt to open the tensioner mechanism as it contains explosive gas.*
• *Tensioners must be discharged before they are disposed of, but this task should be entrusted to a VW dealer.*
• *If the battery is to be disconnected, refer to 'Disconnecting the battery' at the rear of this manual.*

27 Seat belt components – removal and refitting

 Warning: On models equipped with seat belt tensioners refer to Section 26 before proceeding; under no circumstances should you attempt to separate the tensioner assembly from the inertia reel.

Front seat belt removal

Four- and five-door models

Note: *Before disconnecting the battery, refer to 'Disconnecting the battery' at the rear of this manual.*

1 Disconnect the battery negative lead. Unclip the front lower trim panel from the sill trim and pull out from under the facia panel off retaining clip (see illustration). On the driver's side remove the trim as described in Section 9.
2 Unclip the cover on the upper seat belt mounting and remove the securing bolt. Unclip the seat belt pillar lower trim panel, carefully release from the door seal and prise off trim lifting up off the securing pegs (see illustrations).
3 Fold the rear seat cushion up and unscrew the fastener at the bottom of the rear wheel arch trim (see illustration).
4 Remove the two screws securing the sill trim at the bottom of the seat belt pillar (see illustration). Clips may be fitted instead of screws.

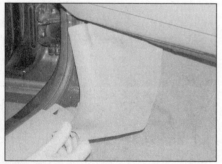

27.1 Carefully prise out lower trim panel

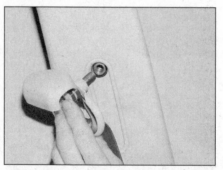

27.2a Remove the top seat belt securing bolt . . .

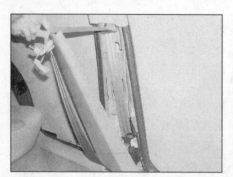

27.2b . . . then unclip the lower pillar trim panel

27.3 Unscrew the plastic retaining plug

27.4 Sill trim securing screws (arrowed)

27.5 Removing the sill trim from around the seat belt

27.6 Unclip the centre locking clip before removing the wiring connector

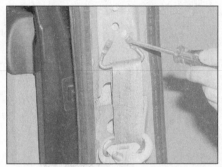

27.7 Remove the belt guide securing screws to free the belt

5 Unclip the sill trim upwards and remove from the sill. Carefully slide the seat belt out from the sill trim (see illustration).

6 On vehicles with side airbags, disconnect the wiring connector from the seat belt tensioner reel (see illustration).

7 Carefully unclip the upper pillar trim, then undo the screws in the belt guide (see illustration).

8 Slacken and remove the seat belt lower mounting bolt and free the seat belt from its lower anchorage (see illustration).

9 Slacken and remove the inertia reel mounting bolt and remove the seat belt assembly from the vehicle (see illustration).

10 To remove the belt height adjustment, remove the securing bolt and lift upwards from pillar (see illustration).

Three-door models

11 Remove the relevant rear seat as described in Section 25.

12 Unclip the rear inner side trim panel from the door pillar and carefully prise out from the speaker bracket. Lift upwards to remove, disconnecting the speaker wiring where fitted.

13 Unclip the front lower trim panel from the sill trim and pull out from under the facia panel off retaining clip. On the driver's side remove the trim as described in Section 9.

14 Slacken and remove the retaining screws from the rear of the sill trim, unscrew the fastener at the bottom of the rear wheel arch trim. Unclip the sill panel and lift upwards to remove it from the vehicle.

15 Unclip the cover on the upper seat belt mounting and remove the securing bolt, then remove the seat belt as described in paragraphs 6 to 10. On some earlier models remove the retaining bolt(s) and free the seat belt lower fixing rail from the floor, disengage the rail from the belt and remove it from the vehicle.

Front seat belt stalk removal

16 Remove the front seat assembly as described in Section 25.

17 Slacken and remove the bolt securing the stalk to the seat, and remove the stalk (see illustration).

Rear seat side belt removal

Hatchback

18 Open the tailgate and remove the rear parcel shelf.

19 Remove the retaining screw from the rear of the parcel shelf support trim, pull upwards to unclip from the upper pillar trim (see illustrations).

20 Unclip the cover from the top seat belt mounting bolt, slacken and remove the bolt. Where necessary, recover the spacer from behind the belt anchorage (see illustration).

21 Remove the plastic retaining plugs and

27.8 Seat belt lower mounting bolt (arrowed)

27.9 Inertia reel mounting bolt (arrowed)

27.10 Securing bolt to remove the seat belt height adjuster (arrowed)

27.17 Remove the securing bolt from the seat frame

27.19a Remove the screw securing the support trim . . .

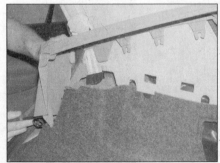

27.19b . . . then unclip the support trim upwards to remove

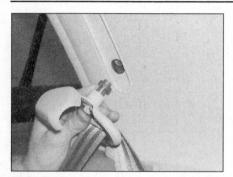

27.20 Taking care not to drop spacer when removing the seat belt top mounting bolt

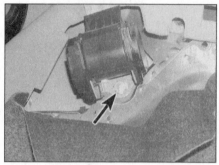

27.21 Inertia reel mounting bolt (arrowed)

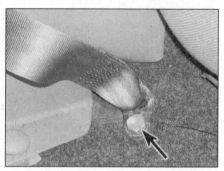

27.22 Seat belt lower mounting bolt (arrowed)

pull back the lower wheel arch cover. Remove the insulation, then undo the bolt to free the inertia reel from the pillar **(see illustration)**.

22 Lift up the rear seat base to remove the seat belt lower mounting bolt from in front of the wheel arch **(see illustration)**.

23 To remove the belt height adjustment, undo the two retaining nuts on the bottom of the upper pillar trim. Unclip the trim from the top and remove from the vehicle **(see illustrations)**, remove the securing bolt and lift the height adjustment rail upwards from the pillar.

Saloon

24 Unclip the cover from the top seat belt mounting bolt, slacken and remove the bolt. Where necessary, recover the spacer from behind the belt anchorage.

25 Lift up the rear seat base to remove the seat belt lower mounting bolt at the wheel arch.

26 Fold the rear seat backrests forward, disconnect the additional brake light connector under the rear shelf and unclip the rear shelf.

27 Lift out the boot carpet and unclip the rear lock cover trim by unclipping from the outer ends, then working towards the middle, lift off from the rear panel **(see illustration)**.

28 Remove the plastic plugs from around the inner wheel housing trim and unclip from the wheel arch **(see illustration)**.

29 Remove the trim from the side of the boot compartment, disconnect any wiring connectors and unscrew the lashing hooks if required **(see illustration)**.

30 Remove the insulation then undo the bolt to free the inertia reel from the pillar **(see illustration)**. Remove the seat belt assembly from the vehicle out through the boot compartment.

Estate

31 Remove the rear seat assembly as described in Section 25.

32 Open the tailgate and remove the luggage compartment cover.

33 Remove the inner wheel housing trim and seat belt as described in paragraphs 20 to 22.

34 Make a careful check that all the fasteners have been removed, before unclipping the panel.

Rear seat centre belt and buckle removal

35 Fold the rear seat cushion forwards then slacken and remove the bolt and washers securing the centre belt and/or buckle assembly to the floor, and remove it from the vehicle **(see illustration)**.

36 On Estate models, the centre inertia seat

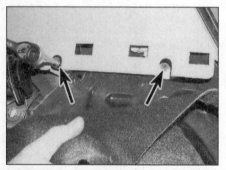

27.23a Remove the two retaining nuts (arrowed) . . .

27.23b . . . then unclip at the top to remove

27.27 Removing the rear trim panel

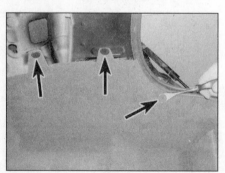

27.28 Remove the retaining clips (arrowed)

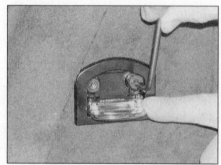

27.29 Removing the lashing hooks

27.30 Inertia reel mounting bolt (arrowed)

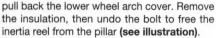

belt can only be removed from the seat back if the seat cover and padding is removed first. The seat belt reel can then be unbolted from the seat frame.

Refitting

37 Refitting is a reversal of the removal procedure, ensuring that all the seat belt units are located correctly and mounting bolts are securely tightened to their specified torque. Check all the trim panels are securely retained by all the relevant retaining clips. When refitting the upper trim panels, ensure that the height adjustment levers engage correctly with the seat belt upper mounting bolt head.

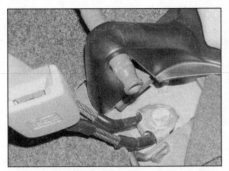

27.35 Rear seat belt stalk securing bolts

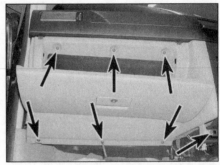

28.7 Remove the seven retaining screws (arrowed)

28 Interior trim – removal and refitting

Interior trim panels

Note: *Specific details for most interior panels are contained within Section 27.*

1 The interior trim panels are secured using either screws or various types of trim fasteners, usually studs or clips.
2 Check that there are no other panels overlapping the one to be removed; usually there is a sequence that has to be followed, and this will only become obvious on close inspection.
3 Remove all obvious fasteners, such as screws. If the panel will not come free, it is held by hidden clips or fasteners. These are usually situated around the edge of the panel and can be prised up to release them; note, however that they can break quite easily so new ones should be available. The best way of releasing such clips, without the correct type of tool, is to use a large flat-bladed screwdriver. Note in many cases that the adjacent sealing strip must be prised back to release a panel.
4 When removing a panel, **never** use excessive force or the panel may be damaged; always check carefully that all fasteners or other relevant components have been removed or released before attempting to withdraw a panel.
5 Refitting is the reverse of the removal procedure; secure the fasteners by pressing them firmly into place and ensure that all disturbed components are correctly secured to prevent rattles.

Glovebox

6 Before the glovebox can be removed, the centre console front section has to be removed to gain access to one of the screws, see Section 29.
7 Open up the glovebox lid then slacken and remove the seven retaining screws **(see illustration)**. Slide the glovebox out of position, disconnecting the wiring connector from the glovebox illumination light (where fitted) as it becomes accessible.

8 Refitting is the reverse of removal.

Carpets

9 The passenger compartment floor carpet is in one piece and is secured at its edges by screws or clips, usually the same fasteners used to secure the various adjoining trim panels.
10 Carpet removal and refitting is reasonably straightforward but very time-consuming because all adjoining trim panels must be removed first, as must components such as the seats, the centre console and seat belt lower anchorages.

Headlining

11 The headlining is clipped to the roof and can be withdrawn only once all fittings such as the grab handles, sun visors, sunroof (if fitted), and related upper trim panels have been removed and the door, tailgate and sunroof aperture sealing strips have been prised clear. To remove the sun visors and grab handles the plastic covers have to be unclipped first, to gain access to the securing screws.
12 Note that headlining removal requires considerable skill and experience if it is to be carried out without damage and is therefore best entrusted to an expert.

Interior mirror

13 Pull the mirror downwards off its retaining clip to remove. When refitting, place the mirror at 90° to the mounted position; then turn until

the locking clip locks into place to secure the mirror. On models fitted with rain sensor, unclip the trim around the stem of the mirror and disconnect the wiring connector.

Facia lower trim panels

14 See Section 30.

29 Centre console – removal and refitting

Rear section

1 Unclip the end cover caps from the ashtray; release the clips each side of the ashtray and remove from the console **(see illustrations)**.
2 On high specification models, unclip the end cover cap on the passenger side of the armrest, remove the retaining bolt and pull out the arm rest from the centre console. To remove the rear drinks holder, press the retaining hooks down and slide the holder out of the console **(see illustrations)**.
3 Slacken and remove the two retaining screws located under the ashtray, then lever out the caps located at the front sides of the rear console and remove the screws. Lift the centre console upwards and off the handbrake lever disconnecting the wiring connector from the switch as it becomes accessible **(see illustrations)**.

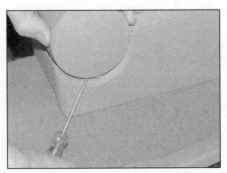

29.1a Unclip the end covers . . .

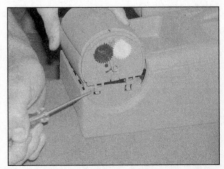

29.1b . . . then release the clips to remove the ashtray

29.2a Unclip the cover on the left-hand side . . .

29.2b . . . then remove the securing bolt and lift out from console

29.2c Push the retaining hooks down and slide the holder out

29.3a Remove the two rear console screws . . .

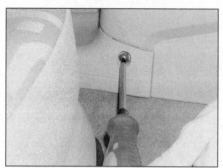

29.3b . . . then the two front console screws . . .

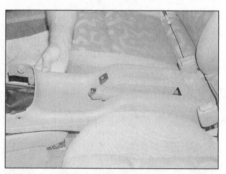

29.3c . . . lift the console upwards off the handbrake lever

Front section

4 On manual transmission models, free the gear lever gaiter from the console then carefully unclip the gaiter trim panel and lift it off over the gear lever **(see illustration)**. On automatic transmission models, the selector lever does not need to be removed.

5 On all models, slacken and remove the retaining screws from the left- and right-hand front edges of the console **(see illustration)**.

6 If the rear section has not already been removed, lever out the caps located at the rear sides of the front console and remove the screws.

7 Open the ashtray and pull out the insert

29.4 Remove the gaiter retaining trim

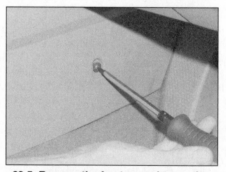

29.5 Remove the front console securing screws

29.7a Remove the ashtray securing screw . . .

29.7b . . . then slide the ashtray assembly out

29.8a Lift the console up over the gear lever . . .

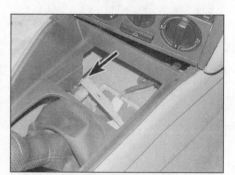

29.8b . . . unclip the metal brace to ease the removal (arrowed)

30.4a Remove the two screws up through the lower cover . . .

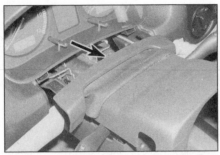

30.4b . . . then unclip the top trim away from the instrument panel in the direction of the arrow

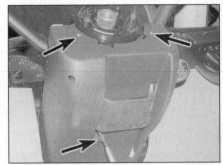

30.5 Remove the three screws (arrowed)

30.6 Remove the switch assembly securing bolt

30.8 Unclip the facia end panels

30.9 Remove the two fusebox securing screws

then remove the retaining screw inside. Slide the ashtray assembly out slightly, close the lid and pull out from the console **(see illustrations)**. Disconnect the cigarette lighter wiring when it comes into view.

8 Pull the centre console off upwards over the gear lever. Unclip the metal brace under the ashtray to ease the removal if required **(see illustrations)**.

Refitting

9 Refitting is the reverse of removal making sure all fasteners are securely tightened.

---

30 Facia panel assembly –
 removal and refitting

Note : *Refer to the warnings in Chapter 12 for airbags.*
Note: *Before disconnecting the battery, refer to 'Disconnecting the battery' at the rear of this manual.*

Label each wiring connector as it is disconnected from its component. The labels will prove useful on refitting, when routing the wiring and feeding the wiring through the facia apertures.

Removal

1 Disconnect the battery negative terminal.
2 Remove the centre console (Section 29).

3 Remove the steering wheel (Chapter 10).
4 Remove the two screws up through the lower steering column cover to release the top cover. Unclip from the bottom cover and pull away from the instrument panel, carefully unclipping from the retaining clips **(see illustrations)**.
5 Release the height adjustment lever and remove the two screws securing the handle to the lever. Undo the remaining three screws in the lower steering cover and remove from the steering column **(see illustration)**.
6 Remove the securing bolt from the top of the switch assembly **(see illustration)**, disconnect the wiring to the switches and remove from the steering column.
7 Remove the instrument panel as described in Chapter 12.
8 Using a flat-bladed screwdriver, unclip the right- and left-hand end panels on the facia panel **(see illustration)**.

30.10 Unscrew the reinforcement panel

9 On the driver's side, remove the two screws securing the fusebox assembly **(see illustration)**. To remove the lower trims on the facia panel, undo the two screws on the bottom then unclip from the top (the outer trim first).
10 Remove the seven screws from the plastic reinforcement panel under the steering column **(see illustration)**.
11 Unclip the cover above the pedals and remove from the vehicle **(see illustration)** (on some models this could be secured with screws).
12 To remove the glovebox see Section 28.
13 To remove the radio/cassette see Chapter 12.
14 To remove the heater control panel see Chapter 3.
15 Unclip the cover from the bottom of the centre panel below heater controls. Remove the five screws securing the centre panel to

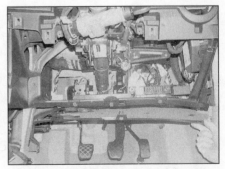

30.11 Unclip the cover from above the pedals

30.15 Undo the five screws to remove centre panel

30.17a Push the switch in and turn clockwise to remove . . .

30.17b . . . undo the screw in the air vent . . .

30.17c . . . then disconnect the wiring connectors as the air vent assembly is removed

30.18 Disconnect the airbag connector from under the facia

the facia – unclip the diagnostic connector as it is removed **(see illustration)**.

16 Remove the switches from below the centre air vents on the facia panel. Unclip the outer switches first, to ease the removal of the inner ones as they have stronger retaining clips (on Bora models disconnect the wiring connectors for the lighting on the air vents).

17 On the driver's side air vent, push the centre dial of the light switch in and turn clockwise, pull assembly out and disconnect the wiring connector (on the Golf models unclip the air vent and remove the retaining screw). Remove the screw from the air vent assembly, then unclip the vent from the facia panel, disconnecting the wiring connectors where applicable **(see illustrations)**.

18 Disconnect the wiring connector under the facia panel for the passenger side airbag **(see illustration)**, if fitted.

19 On models with air conditioning, unclip the temperature sensor from the centre of the air vent, in the top of the facia panel.

20 Remove the seven retaining bolts from the facia assembly, then pull out from the crossmember to remove from the vehicle.

Refitting

21 Refitting is a reversal of the removal procedure, noting the following points:

a) Clip the facia back into position, making sure all the wiring connectors are fed through their respective apertures, then refit all the facia fasteners, and tighten them securely.

b) On completion, reconnect the battery and check that all the electrical components and switches function correctly.

Chapter 12
Body electrical system

Contents

Airbag system – general information and precautions 25
Airbag system components – removal and refitting 26
Anti-theft alarm system and engine immobiliser – general
   information 24
Battery – removal and refitting . . . . .See Chapter 5A
Battery check and maintenance . . . . .See Weekly checks
Bulbs (exterior lights) – renewal 5
Bulbs (interior lights) – renewal 6
Cigarette lighter – removal and refitting 14
Clock – removal and refitting 13
Electrical fault finding – general information 2
Exterior light units – removal and refitting 7
Fuses and relays – general information 3
General information and precautions 1
Headlight beam adjustment components – removal and refitting . . . 8
Headlight beam alignment – general information 9
Horn – removal and refitting 15
Instrument panel – removal and refitting 10
Instrument panel components – removal and refitting 11
Loudspeakers – removal and refitting 22
Parking aid components – general information, removal and
   refitting 27
Radio aerial – removal and refitting 23
Radio/cassette/CD player/changer – removal and refitting 21
Rear wiper motor – removal and refitting 19
Service interval indicator – general information and resetting 12
Speedometer sensor – general information 16
Switches – removal and refitting 4
Washer fluid level check . . . . .See Weekly checks
Washer system components – removal and refitting 20
Windscreen wiper motor and linkage – removal and refitting 18
Wiper arm – removal and refitting 17
Wiper blade check and renewal . . . . .See Weekly checks

Degrees of difficulty

Easy, suitable for novice with little experience	**Fairly easy,** suitable for beginner with some experience	**Fairly difficult,** suitable for competent DIY mechanic	**Difficult,** suitable for experienced DIY mechanic	**Very difficult,** suitable for expert DIY or professional

Specifications

System type	12 volt negative earth
Fuses	See Wiring diagrams on page 12•20

Bulbs	Wattage	Type
Direction indicators	21	Bayonet
Front foglight	55	H3 Halogen
Glovebox light	3	Wedge
Headlight:		
Halogen:		
Golf:		
Main beam	55	H1 Halogen
Dipped beam	55	H7 Halogen
Bora	60/55	H4 Halogen
Gas discharge:		
Main beam	55	H1 Halogen
Dipped beam	35	DS2 (80-117 volt)
Interior light	3	Festoon
Sidelight:		
With halogen headlight	5	Wedge
With gas discharge headlight	6	Wedge

1 General information and precautions

⚠️ **Warning: Before carrying out any work on the electrical system, read through the precautions given in 'Safety first!' at the beginning of this manual, and in Chapter 5A.**

The electrical system is of 12 volt negative earth type. Power for the lights and all electrical accessories is supplied by a lead-acid type battery, which is charged by the alternator.

This Chapter covers repair and service procedures for the various electrical components not associated with the engine. Information on the battery, alternator and starter motor can be found in Chapter 5A.

It should be noted that prior to working on any component in the electrical system, the ignition and all electrical consumers must be switched off. Additionally, where stated, the battery negative lead must be disconnected, however, note the information given in 'Disconnecting the battery' in the Reference section at the end of this manual, as special procedures have to be carried out when reconnecting the battery.

Early Golf and Bora models were only fitted with halogen headlights, however, later models may be fitted with gas discharge headlight systems. These vehicles are also equipped with automatic range control, to reduce the possibility of dazzling oncoming drivers. Note the special precautions which apply to these systems as given in Section 5.

2 Electrical fault finding – general information

Note: *Refer to the precautions given in 'Safety first!' and in Chapter 5A before starting work. The following tests relate to testing of the main electrical circuits, and should not be used to test delicate electronic circuits (such as anti-lock braking systems), particularly where an electronic control module is used.*

General

1 A typical electrical circuit consists of an electrical component, any switches, relays, motors, fuses, fusible links or circuit breakers related to that component, and the wiring and connectors which link the component to both the battery and the chassis. To help to pinpoint a problem in an electrical circuit, wiring diagrams are included at the end of this Chapter.

2 Before attempting to diagnose an electrical fault, first study the appropriate wiring diagram to obtain a complete understanding of the components included in the particular circuit concerned. The possible sources of a fault can be narrowed down by noting if other components related to the circuit are operating properly. If several components or circuits fail at one time, the problem is likely to be related to a shared fuse or earth connection.

3 Electrical problems usually stem from simple causes, such as loose or corroded connections, a faulty earth connection, a blown fuse, a melted fusible link, or a faulty relay (refer to Section 3 for details of testing relays). Visually inspect the condition of all fuses, wires and connections in a problem circuit before testing the components. Use the wiring diagrams to determine which terminal connections will need to be checked in order to pinpoint the trouble spot.

4 The basic tools required for electrical fault finding include a circuit tester or voltmeter (a 12 volt bulb with a set of test leads can also be used for certain tests); a self-powered test light (sometimes known as a continuity tester); an ohmmeter (to measure resistance); a battery and set of test leads; and a jumper wire, preferably with a circuit breaker or fuse incorporated, which can be used to bypass suspect wires or electrical components. Before attempting to locate a problem with test instruments, use the wiring diagram to determine where to make the connections.

5 To find the source of an intermittent wiring fault (usually due to a poor or dirty connection, or damaged wiring insulation), a wiggle test can be performed on the wiring. This involves wiggling the wiring by hand to see if the fault occurs as the wiring is moved. It should be possible to narrow down the source of the fault to a particular section of wiring. This method of testing can be used in conjunction with any of the tests described in the following sub-Sections.

6 Apart from problems due to poor connections, two basic types of fault can occur in an electrical circuit – open-circuit, or short-circuit.

7 Open-circuit faults are caused by a break somewhere in the circuit, which prevents current from flowing. An open-circuit fault will prevent a component from working, but will not cause the relevant circuit fuse to blow.

8 Short-circuit faults are caused by a short somewhere in the circuit, which allows the current flowing in the circuit to escape along an alternative route, usually to earth. Short-circuit faults are normally caused by a breakdown in wiring insulation, which allows a feed wire to touch either another wire, or an earthed component such as the bodyshell. A short-circuit fault will normally cause the relevant circuit fuse to blow.

Finding an open-circuit

9 To check for an open-circuit, connect one lead of a circuit tester or voltmeter to either the negative battery terminal or a known good earth.

10 Connect the other lead to a connector in the circuit being tested, preferably nearest to the battery or fuse.

11 Switch on the circuit, bearing in mind that some circuits are live only when the ignition switch is moved to a particular position.

12 If voltage is present (indicated either by the tester bulb lighting or a voltmeter reading, as applicable), this means that the section of the circuit between the relevant connector and the battery is problem-free.

13 Continue to check the remainder of the circuit in the same fashion.

14 When a point is reached at which no voltage is present, the problem must lie between that point and the previous test point with voltage. Most problems can be traced to a broken, corroded or loose connection.

Finding a short-circuit

15 To check for a short-circuit, first disconnect the load(s) from the circuit (loads are the components which draw current from a circuit, such as bulbs, motors, heating elements, etc).

16 Remove the relevant fuse from the circuit, and connect a circuit tester or voltmeter to the fuse connections.

17 Switch on the circuit, bearing in mind that some circuits are live only when the ignition switch is moved to a particular position.

18 If voltage is present (indicated either by the tester bulb lighting or a voltmeter reading, as applicable), this means that there is a short circuit.

19 If no voltage is present, but the fuse still blows with the load(s) connected, this indicates an internal fault in the load(s).

Finding an earth fault

20 The battery negative terminal is connected to earth – the metal of the engine/transmission and the car body – and most systems are wired so that they only receive a positive feed, the current returning through the metal of the car body. This means that the component mounting and the body form part of that circuit. Loose or corroded mountings can therefore cause a range of electrical faults, ranging from total failure of a circuit, to a puzzling partial fault. In particular, lights may shine dimly (especially when another circuit sharing the same earth point is in operation), motors (eg, wiper motors or the radiator cooling fan motor) may run slowly, and the operation of one circuit may have an apparently unrelated effect on another. Note that on many vehicles, earth straps are used between certain components, such as the engine/transmission and the body, usually where there is no metal-to-metal contact between components due to flexible rubber mountings, etc.

21 To check whether a component is properly earthed, disconnect the battery (refer to the warnings given in the Reference section at the rear of the manual) and connect one lead of an ohmmeter to a known good earth point. Connect the other lead to the wire or earth connection being tested. The resistance reading should be zero; if not, check the connection as follows.

22 If an earth connection is thought to be faulty, dismantle the connection and clean back to bare metal both the bodyshell and the wire terminal or the component earth connection mating surface. Be careful to remove all traces of dirt and corrosion, then use a knife to trim away any paint, so that a clean metal-to-metal joint is made. On reassembly, tighten the joint fasteners securely; if a wire terminal is being refitted, use serrated washers between the terminal and the bodyshell to ensure a clean and secure connection. When the connection is remade, prevent the onset of corrosion in the future by applying a coat of petroleum jelly or silicone-based grease or by spraying on (at regular intervals) a proprietary ignition sealer or a water dispersant lubricant.

3 Fuses and relays – general information

Fuses and fusible links

1 Fuses are designed to break a circuit when a predetermined current is reached, in order to protect the components and wiring which could be damaged by excessive current flow. Any excessive current flow will be due to a fault in the circuit, usually a short-circuit (see Section 2).
2 The main fuses are located in the fusebox on the driver's side of the facia. Open the driver's door and unclip the fusebox cover from the end of the facia to gain access to the fuses. The fuse locations are marked onto the rear of the fusebox cover.
3 To remove a fuse, first switch off the circuit concerned (or the ignition), then pull the fuse out of its terminals (see illustration).
4 The wire within the fuse should be visible; if the fuse has blown it will be broken or melted.
5 Always renew a fuse with one of the correct rating, never use a fuse with a different rating from that specified.
6 Refer to the wiring diagrams for details of the fuse ratings and the circuits protected. The fuse rating is stamped on the top of the fuse, the fuses are also colour-coded as follows.

Colour	Rating
Light brown	5A
Red	10A
Blue	15A
Yellow	20A
Green	30A

7 Never renew a fuse more than once without tracing the source of the trouble. If the new fuse blows immediately, find the cause before renewing it again; a short to earth as a result of faulty insulation is most likely. Where a fuse protects more than one circuit, try to isolate the fault by switching on each circuit in turn (where possible) until the fuse blows again. Always carry a supply of spare fuses of each relevant rating on the vehicle.

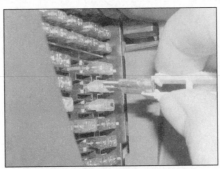

3.3 Removing a fuse from the facia fusebox

8 Additional heavy-duty fusible links are located in the fuse holder which is fitted to the top of the battery. Unclip and open the fuse holder cover to gain access to these links.
9 To renew a fusible link, first disconnect the battery negative terminal. Unscrew the retaining nuts then remove the blown link from the holder. Fit the new link to its terminals and reconnect the lead. Ensure the link and lead are correctly seated then refit the retaining nuts and tighten securely. Clip the cover back into position then reconnect the battery.

Relays

10 A relay is an electrically-operated switch, which is used for the following reasons:
  a) A relay can switch a heavy current remotely from the circuit in which the current is flowing, allowing the use of lighter-gauge wiring and switch contacts.
  b) A relay can receive more than one control input, unlike a mechanical switch.
  c) A relay can have a timer function – for example, the intermittent wiper relay.
11 Most of the relays are located on the relay plate behind the driver's side facia.
12 Access to the relays can be obtained after removing the driver's side lower facia panel as described in Chapter 11, Section 28, then removing the two relay plate retaining screws (one at either end), and lowering the plate complete with relays (see illustration). Identification details of the relays are given at the start of the wiring diagrams.
13 If a circuit or system controlled by a relay develops a fault, and the relay is suspect, operate the system. If the relay is functioning,

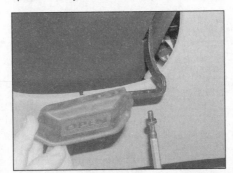

4.3a Remove the column adjustment handle screws

3.12 Relays located behind the facia

it should be possible to hear it click as it is energised. If this is the case, the fault lies with the components or wiring of the system. If the relay is not being energised, then either the relay is not receiving a main supply or a switching voltage, or the relay itself is faulty. Testing is by the substitution of a known good unit, but be careful – while some relays are identical in appearance and in operation, others look similar but perform different functions.
14 To remove a relay, first ensure that the relevant circuit is switched off. The relay can then simply be pulled out from the socket, and pushed back into position.
15 The direction indicator/hazard flasher relay is integral with the hazard warning switch. Refer to Section 4 for the switch removal procedure.

4 Switches – removal and refitting

Ignition switch/ steering column lock

Note: Disconnect the battery negative lead (refer to 'Disconnecting the battery' in the Reference section at the end of this manual) before removing this switch, and reconnect the lead after refitting.
1 Refer to Chapter 10.

Steering column switch

Note: Disconnect the battery negative lead (refer to 'Disconnecting the battery' in the Reference section at the end of this manual) before removing this switch, and reconnect the lead after refitting.
2 Remove the steering wheel as described in Chapter 10.
3 Slacken and remove the two retaining screws, and remove the steering column adjustment handle from the lever. Then unscrew the two retaining screws and unclip the upper steering column shroud. Remove the three retaining screws and remove the lower shroud (see illustrations).
4 Separate the wiring plug to the coil connector, release the locking lugs and pull

4.3b Undo two screws . . .

4.3c . . . and unclip the upper shroud

4.3d Remove the screw underneath . . .

the coil connector with the slip ring from the column.

5 Slacken the switch clamp screw and pull the switch assembly from the column **(see illustration)**.

6 Refitting is a reversal of removal, but the switch must be accurately positioned as follows:
  a) *Refit the switch to the column, but only lightly tighten the clamp screw.*
  b) *Refit the coil connector and slip ring to the switch. Ensure that the locking lugs are correctly engaged.*
  c) *Temporarily refit the steering wheel, and measure the clearance between the wheel and coil connector with slip-ring. The correct clearance is approximately 2.5 mm.*
  d) *Once the correct clearance is achieved, tighten the switch clamp screw securely.*

Lighting switch

Note: *Disconnect the battery negative lead (refer to 'Disconnecting the battery' in the Reference section at the end of this manual) before removing this switch, and reconnect the lead after refitting.*

7 With the light switch in position O, press the switch centre inwards and turn it slightly to the right. Hold this position and pull the switch from the dash.

8 As the switch is withdrawn from the dash, disconnect the wiring plug **(see illustration)**.

9 Reconnect the wiring plug.

10 Hold the switch and press the rotary part inwards and slightly to the right.

11 Insert the switch into the dash, turn the rotary part to position O and release. Check the switch for correct operation.

Headlamp range control and instrument illumination switches

Note: *Switch off the ignition and all electrical consumers before commencing work.*

12 Remove the light switch with reference to paragraphs 7 and 8. Prise out the air vent, with reference to Chapter 3, and undo the two Torx screws **(see illustration)**.

13 Prise of the switch surround. Withdraw the switch from the housing and unplug the wiring connector.

14 Refitting is a reversal of removal.

Heated front seat switches

Note: *Switch off the ignition and all electrical consumers before commencing work.*

15 Carefully prise the switch from its location in the facia panel, using a small flat-bladed screwdriver. Take care not to damage the surrounding trim.

16 Disconnect the wiring plug(s) and withdraw the switch.

17 Reconnect the switch wiring plug, and push the switch firmly into position.

Hazard warning, heated rear window and ESP switches

Note: *Disconnect the battery negative lead (refer to 'Disconnecting the battery' in the Reference section at the end of this manual) before removing this switch, and reconnect the lead after refitting.*

18 Due to the strong retaining clips, these switches have to be pushed out of the dash instead of prised.

19 Remove the heated front seat switch next to the switch to be removed.

20 Reaching through the aperture vacated by the heated seat switch, push the ESP or heated rear window switch from the dash.

21 In order to remove the hazard warning switch, it is necessary to remove the ESP or heated rear window switch, and then push the switch from the dash as previously described.

22 Disconnect the switch wiring plug.

23 Reconnect the switch wiring plug, and push the switch firmly into position.

4.3e . . . and the upper screws

4.5 Slacken the clamp screw

4.8 In the correct position, pull the switch from the facia

4.12 Undo the Torx screws

Electric window switches

Driver's door

Note: *Disconnect the battery negative lead (refer to 'Disconnecting the battery' in the Reference section at the end of this manual) before removing this switch, and reconnect the lead after refitting.*

24 Unclip the interior door handle grip trim **(see illustration)**.

25 Carefully prise the control panel up from the door trim, and disconnect the wiring plug **(see illustration)**.

26 Remove the three retaining screws and withdraw the control unit from the trim.

27 If a window switch is faulty, the complete control unit must be renewed.

28 Refitting is a reversal of removal.

Passenger's door

Note: *Disconnect the battery negative lead (refer to 'Disconnecting the battery' in the Reference section at the end of this manual) before removing this switch, and reconnect the lead after refitting.*

29 Remove the relevant door trim as described in Chapter 11.

30 Disconnect the wiring plug from the switch.

31 Release the switch from the mounting frame.

32 Refitting is a reversal of removal.

Electric mirror switch

Note: *Switch off the ignition and all electrical consumers before commencing work.*

33 The procedure is the same as that described in paragraphs 29 to 31 above.

34 Refitting is a reversal of removal.

Air conditioning switches

Note: *Switch off the ignition and all electrical consumers before commencing work.*

35 The switches are integral with the heater control panel, and cannot be removed separately. Refer to Chapter 3 for details of heater control panel removal and refitting.

Heater blower motor switch

Note: *Switch off the ignition and all electrical consumers before commencing work.*

36 The switch is integral with the heater control panel, and cannot be removed separately. Refer to Chapter 3 for details of heater control panel removal and refitting.

Handbrake 'on' warning switch

Note: *Switch off the ignition and all electrical consumers before commencing work.*

37 Refer to Chapter 9.

Brake light switch

Note: *Switch off the ignition and all electrical consumers before commencing work.*

38 Refer to Chapter 9.

Reversing light switch

Note: *Switch off the ignition and all electrical consumers before commencing work.*

39 Refer to Chapter 7A.

Courtesy light switches

Note: *Switch off the ignition and all electrical consumers before commencing work.*

40 The courtesy light switch is integrated into the door lock mechanism, and cannot be renewed independently. If the courtesy light switch is faulty, renew the door lock mechanism as described in Chapter 11.

Luggage area light switch

Note: *Switch off the ignition and all electrical consumers before commencing work.*

41 The luggage compartment light switch is integrated into the tailgate/boot lid lock mechanism, and cannot be renewed independently. If the luggage compartment light switch is faulty, renew the tailgate/boot lid lock mechanism as described in Chapter 11.

Glovebox light switch

Note: *Switch off the ignition and all electrical consumers before commencing work.*

42 The switch is integral with the light assembly. Carefully prise the light assembly from the glovebox and disconnect the wiring plug, refer to Section 6.

43 Refitting is a reversal of removal.

Fuel filler flap release switch

Note: *Switch off the ignition and all electrical consumers before commencing work.*

44 Carefully prise the switch from the housing, and disconnect the wiring plug.

45 Refitting is a reversal of removal.

Interior monitoring deactivation switch

Note: *Switch off the ignition and all electrical consumers before commencing work.*

46 Carefully prise the switch from the inner sill trim, and disconnect the wiring plug.

47 Refitting is a reversal of removal.

Central locking switch

Note: *Disconnect the battery negative lead (refer to 'Disconnecting the battery' in the Reference section at the end of this manual) before removing this switch, and reconnect the lead after refitting.*

48 The central locking switch is integral with the electric window switch located in the driver's door internal handle. Proceed as described in paragraphs 24 to 27.

49 Refitting is a reversal of removal.

Rain sensor

Note: *Switch off the ignition and all electrical consumers before commencing work.*

50 The windscreen wipers are automatically activated when droplets of water are detected by the rain sensor, located in the front of the interior mirror base. Separate the left and right mirror base covers, and disconnect the sensor wiring plug.

51 Pull the mirror downwards from the mirror base.

52 The mirror base is bonded to the windscreen. Whilst it is possible to remove the

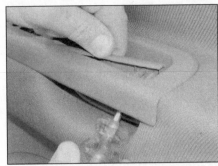

4.24 Unclip the handle grip trim

base by means of a scraper, great care must be exercised to avoid scratching the windscreen.

53 Due to the hazardous chemicals involved, it is recommended that the bonding of the mirror base to the windscreen be entrusted to a VW dealer or suitably-equipped specialist.

54 With the base in place, refit the mirror to the base.

55 Reconnect the sensor wiring plugs.

56 Refit the two halves of the mirror base covers.

5 Bulbs (exterior lights) – renewal

General

1 Whenever a bulb is renewed, note the following points:

a) Switch off the ignition and all electrical consumers before commencing work.

b) Remember that if the light has just been in use the bulb may be extremely hot.

c) Always check the bulb contacts and holder, ensuring that there is clean metal-to-metal contact between the bulb and its live(s) and earth. Clean off any corrosion or dirt before fitting a new bulb.

d) Wherever bayonet-type bulbs are fitted ensure that the live contact(s) bear firmly against the bulb contact.

e) Always ensure that the new bulb is of the correct rating and that it is completely clean before fitting it.

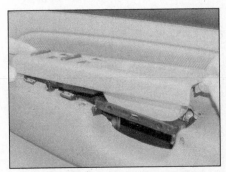

4.25 Prise up the switch panel

5.2a Release the securing clip . . .

5.2b . . . and remove the small plastic cover

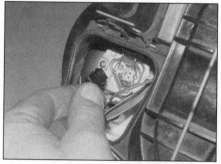

5.3 Disconnect the wiring plug

Headlight main beam

Golf models with halogen headlights

2 Working in the engine compartment, release the securing clip, and remove the small plastic cover from the rear of the headlight **(see illustrations)**. Since access to the left-hand headlight is difficult, either remove the headlight completely or remove the battery (see Chapter 5A).

3 Disconnect the wiring plug from the rear of the bulb **(see illustration)**.

4 Unhook and release the ends of the bulb retaining clip from the light unit, then withdraw the bulb **(see illustrations)**.

5 When handling the new bulb, use a tissue or clean cloth to avoid touching the glass with the fingers; moisture and grease from the skin can cause blackening and rapid failure of this type of bulb. If the glass is accidentally touched, wipe it clean using methylated spirit.

6 Install the new bulb, ensuring that its locating tabs are correctly located in the light cut-outs, and secure it in position with the retaining clip.

7 Reconnect the wiring plug and refit the headlight cover, making sure that it is secure.

Gas discharge headlights

8 Right-hand headlight – remove the head-lamp assembly as described in Section 7. Left-hand headlight – either remove the headlamp assembly as described in Section 7 or remove the battery as described in Chapter 5A.

9 Release the retaining clip and remove the cap cover **(see illustration)**.

10 Disconnect the wiring plug from the rear of the bulb **(see illustration)**.

11 Unhook and release the ends of the bulb retaining clip and release it from the light unit, then withdraw the bulb.

12 When handling the new bulb, use a tissue

or clean cloth to avoid touching the glass with the fingers; moisture and grease from the skin can cause blackening and rapid failure of this type of bulb. If the glass is accidentally touched, wipe it clean using methylated spirit.

13 Install the new bulb, ensuring that its locating tabs are correctly located in the light cut-outs, and secure it in position with the retaining clip.

14 Reconnect the wiring plug and refit the headlight cover, making sure that it is secure.

15 Refit the headlamp or battery as applicable.

Caution: After refitting a gas discharge headlamp, the basic setting of the Automatic Range Control system should be checked. Because of the requirement for specialised equipment, this can only be carried out by a VW dealer or suitably-equipped specialist.

Headlight dip beam

Golf models with halogen headlights

16 Working in the engine compartment, release the securing clip, and remove the large plastic cover from the rear of the headlight **(see illustrations)**. Since access to the left-hand headlight is difficult, either remove the headlight completely or remove the battery (see Chapter 5A).

17 Disconnect the wiring plug from the rear of the bulb **(see illustration)**.

18 Unhook and release the ends of the bulb retaining clip and release it from the light unit, then withdraw the bulb **(see illustrations)**.

19 When handling the new bulb, use a tissue

5.4a Unhook the retaining clip . . .

5.4b . . . and remove the bulb

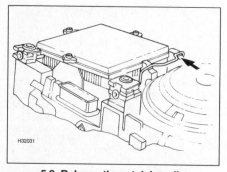

5.9 Release the retaining clip

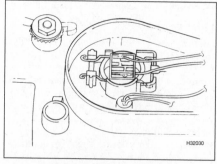

5.10 Remove the connector

5.16a Release the retaining clip . . .

5.16b . . . and remove the cover

5.17 Disconnect the wiring plug

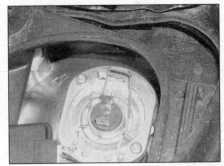

5.18a Unhook the retaining clip . . .

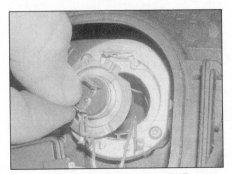

5.18b . . . and remove the bulb

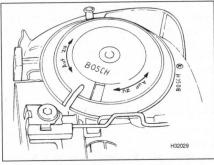

5.23 Twist the cover anti-clockwise –
Golf

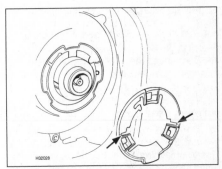

5.27 Align the bulb retaining lugs with the
corresponding grooves in the ring (arrowed)

or clean cloth to avoid touching the glass with the fingers; moisture and grease from the skin can cause blackening and rapid failure of this type of bulb. If the glass is accidentally touched, wipe it clean using methylated spirit.
20 Install the new bulb, ensuring that its locating tabs are correctly located in the light cut-outs, and secure it in position with the retaining clip.
21 Reconnect the wiring plug and refit the headlight cover, making sure that it is secure.

Gas discharge headlights

Caution: Before attempting to remove the dipped beam bulb, it is absolutely necessary to disconnect the battery negative lead (refer to 'Disconnecting the battery' in the Reference section at the rear of this manual), and then turn the relevant beam on and off to dissipate any residual voltage. It is also strongly recommended that safety goggles/glasses are worn prior to handling gas discharge bulbs, as the interior of the bulb is pressurised to in excess of 10 bar.
22 Right-hand headlight – remove the headlamp assembly as described in Section 7. Left-hand headlight – either remove the headlamp assembly as described in Section 7 or remove the battery as described in Chapter 5A.
23 Golf models: Remove the cover by turning it anti-clockwise. On Bora models, the cover is secured by three screws **(see illustration)**.
24 Release the bulb connector by turning it 90° anti-clockwise.
25 Turn the bulb retaining ring anti-clockwise and remove it.

26 Carefully pull the bulb from the reflector.
27 Install the new bulb, ensuring that its locating tabs are correctly located in the light cut-outs, and secure it in position with the retaining clip **(see illustration)**. When handling the new bulb, use a tissue or clean cloth to avoid touching the glass with the fingers; moisture and grease from the skin can cause blackening and rapid failure of this type of bulb. If the glass is accidentally touched, wipe it clean using methylated spirit.
28 The remainder of the procedure is a reversal of removal procedure.

Caution: After refitting a gas discharge headlamp, the basic setting of the Automatic Range Control system should be checked. Because of the requirement for specialised equipment, this can only be carried out by a VW dealer or suitably-equipped specialist.

Headlight main/dipped beam

Bora models with halogen headlights

29 Working in the engine compartment, release the securing clip, and remove the plastic cover from the rear of the headlight. Since access to the left-hand headlight is difficult, either remove the headlight completely or remove the battery (see Chapter 5A).
30 Disconnect the wiring plug from the rear of the bulb **(see illustration)**.
31 Unhook and release the ends of the bulb retaining clip from the light unit, then withdraw the bulb **(see illustration)**.
32 When handling the new bulb, use a tissue or clean cloth to avoid touching the glass with the fingers; moisture and grease from the skin can cause blackening and rapid failure of this type of bulb. If the glass is accidentally touched, wipe it clean using methylated spirit.

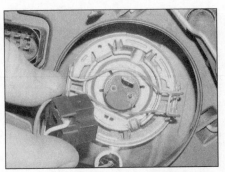

5.30 Remove the connector

5.31 Release the retaining clip

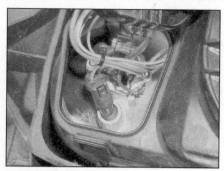

**5.36a Sidelight bulb –
Golf**

**5.36b Sidelight bulb –
Bora**

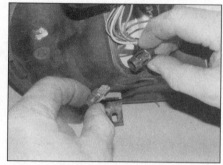

**5.36c Removing the wedge-type bulb from
the front sidelight bulbholder**

33 Install the new bulb, ensuring that its locating tabs are correctly located in the light cut-outs, and secure it in position with the retaining clip.

34 Reconnect the wiring plug and refit the headlight cover, making sure that it is secure.

Front sidelight

Halogen headlights

35 Working in the engine compartment, release the securing clip, and remove the plastic cover from the rear of the headlight. Since access to the left-hand headlight is difficult, either remove the headlight completely or remove the battery (see Chapter 5A).

36 Carefully pull the sidelight bulbholder from the headlight unit. The bulb is a push-fit in the holder and can be removed by grasping the end of the bulb and pulling it out (see illustrations).

37 Refitting is a reversal of removal, making sure that the headlight cover is securely refitted.

Gas discharge headlights

38 Right-hand headlight – remove the headlamp assembly as described in Section 7. Left-hand headlight – either remove the headlamp assembly as described in Section 7 or remove the battery as described in Chapter 5A.

39 Open the bulb cover by releasing the retaining clip (see illustration 5.9).

40 Carefully pull the sidelight bulbholder from the headlight unit. The bulb is a push-fit in the holder and can be removed by grasping the

end of the bulb and pulling it out. When handling the new bulb, use a tissue or clean cloth to avoid touching the glass with the fingers; moisture and grease from the skin can cause blackening and rapid failure of this type of bulb. If the glass is accidentally touched, wipe it clean using methylated spirit.

41 Refitting is a reversal of removal, making sure that the headlight cover is securely refitted.

Caution: After refitting a gas discharge headlamp, the basic setting of the Automatic Range Control system should be checked. Because of the requirement for specialised equipment, this can only be carried out by a VW dealer or suitably-equipped specialist.

Front direction indicator

Halogen headlights

42 Working in the engine compartment, release the securing clip, and remove the plastic cover from the rear of the headlight. Since access to the left-hand headlight is difficult, either remove the headlight completely or remove the battery (see Chapter 5A). Turn the bulbholder anti-clockwise to release it. The bulb is a bayonet-fit in the bulbholder – push the bulb into the holder and twist anti-clockwise (see illustrations).

43 Fit the new bulb using a reversal of the removal procedure.

Gas discharge headlights

44 Right-hand headlight – remove the headlamp assembly as described in Section 7. Left-

hand headlight – either remove the headlamp assembly as described in Section 7 or remove the battery as described in Chapter 5A.

45 Open the bulb cover by releasing the retaining clip (see illustration 5.9).

46 Turn the bulbholder anti-clockwise, and pull the bulb from the holder. When handling the new bulb, use a tissue or clean cloth to avoid touching the glass with the fingers; moisture and grease from the skin can cause blackening and rapid failure of this type of bulb. If the glass is accidentally touched, wipe it clean using methylated spirit.

47 Refitting is a reversal of removal.

Caution: After refitting a gas discharge headlamp, the basic setting of the Automatic Range Control system should be checked. Because of the requirement for specialised equipment, this can only be carried out by a VW dealer or suitably-equipped specialist.

Front foglight

48 Working in the engine compartment, release the securing clip, and remove the plastic cover from the rear of the headlight. Since access to the left-hand headlight is difficult, either remove the headlight completely or remove the battery (see Chapter 5A).

49 Disconnect the wire leading to the foglight from the connector (see illustration).

50 Unhook and release the ends of the bulb retaining clip and release it from the light unit, then withdraw the bulb (see illustrations).

51 When handling the new bulb, use a tissue

**5.42a Direction indicator bulb –
Golf**

**5.42b Direction indicator bulb –
Bora**

5.49 Disconnect the foglight wiring

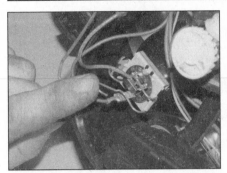

5.50a Unhook the retaining clip . . .

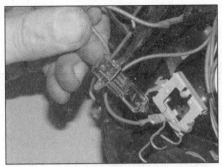

5.50b . . . and withdraw the foglight bulb from the light unit

5.55a Push the repeater in the direction of the spring clip . . .

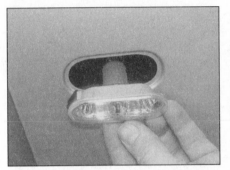

5.55b . . . and ease the side repeater from the aperture

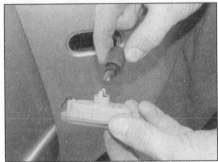

5.56a Pull the bulb from the holder . . .

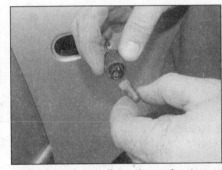

5.56b . . . then pull out the wedge-type bulb

or clean cloth to avoid touching the glass with the fingers; moisture and grease from the skin can cause blackening and rapid failure of this type of bulb. If the glass is accidentally touched, wipe it clean using methylated spirit.
52 Install the new bulb, ensuring that its locating tabs are correctly located in the light cut-outs, and secure it in position with the retaining clip.
53 Reconnect the wiring and refit the headlight cover, making sure that it is secure.

Direction indicator side repeater

54 Great care must be taken when removing the direction indicator side repeater, as it is only possible to be removed in one direction, and it is not possible to determine which end of the repeater the spring clip or mounting sits. Consequently, there is a high risk of damaging the vehicle paintwork.
55 Carefully push the repeater sideways in the direction of the spring clip. Once the spring clip is compressed, it should be possible to ease the mounting end of the repeater out of the aperture, and manoeuvre the assembly from the wing **(see illustrations)**.
56 Pull the rubber bulbholder from the repeater. The bulb is a push-fit in the holder **(see illustrations)**.
57 Refitting is a reversal of removal.

Rear light cluster

58 Working in the luggage compartment, remove the relevant side panel trim.
59 Depress the two retaining tabs and remove the bulbholder from the light unit. The bulbs are a bayonet-fit in the bulbholder – push the bulb into the holder and twist anti-clockwise **(see illustrations)**.
60 Fit the new bulb using a reversal of the removal procedure.

High level brake light

Golf models

61 With reference to Chapter 11, Section 15, remove the upper and lower tailgate trim.
62 Undo the two retaining screws, unplug the wiring connector, and remove the light unit **(see illustration)**.
63 Depress the retaining clips and separate the bulb holder from the cover.
64 As the 32 LEDs are soldered in position and covered with a plastic strip, it is not possible to renew individual LEDs. The complete bulbholder must be renewed.
65 Refitting is a reversal of removal.

Bora models

66 Disconnect the wiring plug from the light unit.
67 Remove the parcel shelf.
68 Unclip the light unit from the parcel shelf.

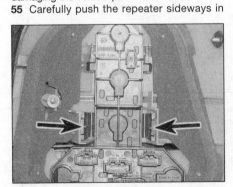

5.59a Depress the retaining tabs (arrowed)

5.59b The bulbs are a bayonet fit

5.62 Remove the retaining screws (arrowed)

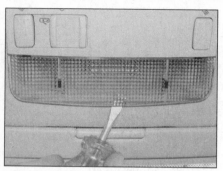

6.2 Carefully prise the lens from the unit

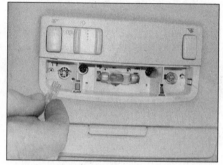

6.3 The reading light bulb is a bayonet fit

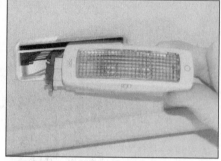

6.5 Prise the lamp from the mounting

69 Depress the retaining clips and separate the bulb holder from the cover.
70 As the 32 LEDs are soldered in position and covered with a plastic strip, it is not possible to renew individual LEDs. The complete bulbholder must be renewed.
71 Refitting is a reversal of removal.

Rear number plate light

72 Unscrew the two securing screws, and withdraw the light unit from the tailgate/boot lid.
73 Unclip the lens from the light unit. The bulb is a push-fit in the bulbholder.
74 Fit the new bulb using a reversal of the removal procedure.

6 Bulbs (interior lights) – renewal

General

1 Whenever a bulb is renewed, note the following points:
 a) Switch off the ignition and all electrical consumers before commencing work.
 b) Remember that if the light has just been in use the bulb may be extremely hot.
 c) Always check the bulb contacts and holder, ensuring that there is clean metal-to-metal contact between the bulb and its live(s) and earth. Clean off any corrosion or dirt before fitting a new bulb.

 d) Wherever bayonet-type bulbs are fitted ensure that the live contact(s) bear firmly against the bulb contact.
 e) Always ensure that the new bulb is of the correct rating and that it is completely clean before fitting it.

Front courtesy/reading light

2 Carefully prise the lens from the light unit, using a small flat-bladed screwdriver (see illustration).
3 Pull the courtesy light bulb from the spring contacts. The reading lamp bulbs are a bayonet fitting (see illustration).
4 Fit the new bulb using a reversal of the removal procedure.

Rear courtesy/reading lights

Without interior monitoring sensors

5 Carefully prise the assembly from the headlining (see illustration).
6 Pull the bulb from the spring contacts.
7 Fit the new bulb using a reversal of the removal procedure.

With interior monitoring sensors

8 Carefully prise the assembly from the mounting frame.
9 Pull the bulb from the spring contacts.
10 Fit the new bulb using a reversal of the removal procedure.

Luggage compartment light

11 Carefully prise the light unit from its

location in the luggage compartment or boot lid, as applicable. The bulb is a push-fit in the spring contacts (see illustration).
12 Fit the new bulb using a reversal of the removal procedure.

Make-up lights

13 Proceed as described previously for the luggage compartment light (see illustration). The make-up light is activated by lifting the cover of the mirror built into the sunvisor. No renewal procedure is recommended for the microswitch in the sunvisor. If the switch is faulty, the visor must be renewed.

Glovebox illumination light

14 Proceed as described previously for the luggage compartment light (see illustration).

Instrument panel illumination/ warning lights

15 The instrument panel illumination/warning lights are non-renewable LEDs.

Cigarette lighter/ ashtray illumination

16 Remove the centre console, as described in Chapter 11.
17 Lift the retaining clip, and pull the bulbholder from the rear of the assembly and disconnect the wiring plug. The bulb is integral with the bulbholder (see illustration).
18 Fit the new bulb using a reversal of the removal procedure.

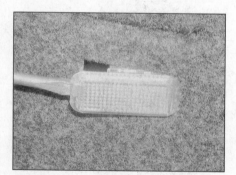

6.11 Lever the light from the trim

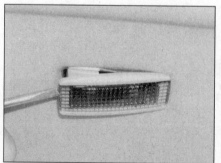

6.13 Prise the make-up light from the headlining

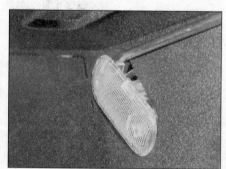

6.14 Carefully prise out the glovebox light

Heater/ventilation control panel illumination

19 The control panel is illuminated by LEDs built into the panel. Consequently, if a fault develops, renewal of the panel is necessary. However, the centre rotary control of the panel is illuminated by a bulb. Carefully pull the control from the panel, and with a length of washer tube (or similar), pull the capless bulb from the holder **(see illustration)**.
20 Fit the new bulb using a reversal of the removal procedure.

Switch illumination

21 The switch illumination bulbs are integral with the switches. If a bulb fails, the complete switch must be renewed.

Air vent illumination

Bora models

22 Remove the relevant air vent, as described in Chapter 3.
23 Twist the bulb holder anti-clockwise and remove it from the vent.
24 The bulb is integral with the holder, and if faulty must be renewed as a unit.
25 Refitting is a reversal of removal.

Door warning lights

26 Open the relevant door, and carefully prise out the light unit **(see illustration)**.
27 Unplug the wiring connector.
28 Unclip the lens from the unit, and release the bulb from the spring contacts **(see illustration)**.
29 Refitting is a reversal of removal.

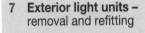

7 Exterior light units – removal and refitting

Headlight

Golf with halogen headlights

1 Remove the front bumper cover, as described in Chapter 11.
2 Undo the four retaining bolts, and pull the headlight unit slightly forward **(see illustrations)**.
3 Unplug the wiring multi-pin connector **(see illustration)**.
4 Remove the headlamp forwards.
5 Refitting is a reversal of removal, but on completion, have the headlight alignment checked at the earliest opportunity.

Bora and gas discharge headlights

6 Remove the front bumper, as described in Chapter 11.
7 Unscrew the two screws, and pull the headlight cover up and out.
8 Unplug the wiring multi-pin connector(s) **(see illustration)**.
9 Remove the two upper and two lower retaining bolts **(see illustration)**.
10 Remove the headlight forwards.

6.17 The bulb is integral with the holder

6.26 Prise the light unit from the trim

11 Refitting is a reversal of removal, but on completion, have the headlight alignment checked at the earliest opportunity.
Caution: After refitting a gas discharge headlamp, the basic setting of the

7.2a Unscrewing the headlight lower retaining bolts . . .

7.3 Disconnecting the headlight wiring

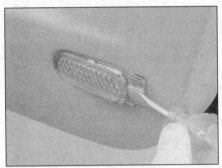

6.19 Use a length of washer tube to extract the bulb

6.28 Unclip the lens from the unit

Automatic Range Control system should be checked. Because of the requirement for specialised equipment, this can only be carried out by a VW dealer or suitably-equipped specialist.

7.2b . . . and upper retaining bolts

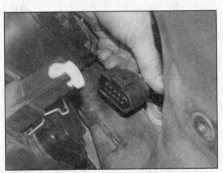

7.8 Disconnect the headlamp wiring plug

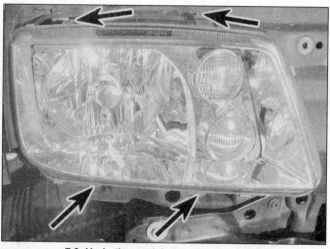

7.9 Undo the retaining screws (arrowed)

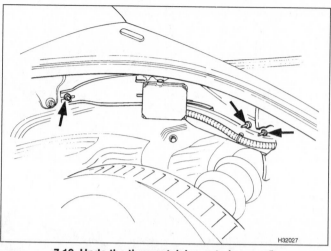

7.13 Undo the three retaining nuts (arrowed)

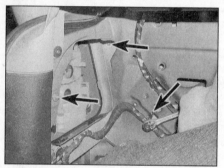

**7.19a Undo the securing nuts (arrowed) –
Golf**

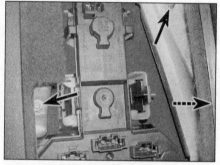

**7.19b Rear light securing nuts (arrowed) –
Bora**

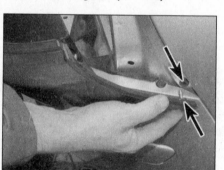

**7.19c Rear light cluster locating pin and
hole**

Gas discharge light starter unit

12 The gas discharge headlight starter unit is located under the left wheel arch, for the left headlight, and the right wheel arch for the right headlight. With reference to Chapter 11, remove the wheel arch liner from the relevant side.

13 Undo the three nuts securing the starter unit retaining plate to the wheel arch **(see illustration)**.

14 Unplug the wiring connector, and remove the starter unit with the retaining plate.

15 Remove the three retaining screws and separate the starter unit from the retaining plate.

16 Refitting is a reversal of removal.

8.5 Disconnect the wiring plug

Direction indicator side repeater

17 The procedure is described as part of the bulb renewal procedure in Section 5.

Rear light cluster

18 Remove the rear light bulbholder, as described in Section 5.

19 Working inside the wing panel, unscrew the three securing nuts, and withdraw the light unit from the location holes in the wing panel **(see illustrations)**.

20 Refitting is a reversal of removal.

High level brake light

21 The procedure is described as part of the bulb renewal procedure in Section 5.

Rear number plate light

22 The procedure is described as part of the rear number plate light bulb renewal procedure in Section 5.

**8 Headlight beam
adjustment components –
removal and refitting**

Headlight adjustment switch

1 The switch is integral with the instrument illumination switch.

2 Removal and refitting of the switch assembly is covered in Section 4.

Headlight adjustment motor

Halogen headlights

3 Remove the headlight (see Section 7).

4 Release the retaining clip and remove the sealing cover.

5 Disconnect the wiring plug connector **(see illustration)**.

6 Release the left-hand motor by twisting it clockwise and sliding it out of the mounting on the reflector, and the right-hand motor by twisting it anti-clockwise and sliding it out of the mounting on the reflector **(see illustration)**.

**8.6 Slide the adjustment shaft from the
mounting**

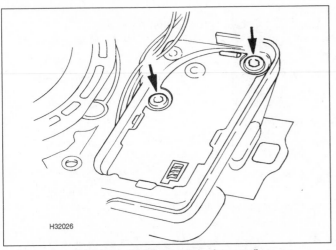

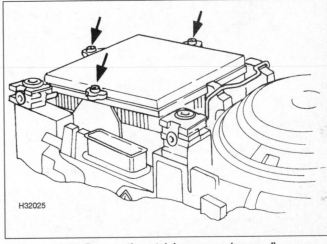

8.11 Undo the Torx screws (arrowed)

8.15 Remove the retaining screws (arrowed)

7 Refitting is a reversal of removal. On completion, check the operation of the headlight beam adjustment mechanism, and have the headlight alignment checked at the earliest opportunity.

Gas discharge headlights – Golf

8 The headlight adjustment motor is integral with the headlight unit and cannot be renewed separately.

Gas discharge headlights – Bora

9 Remove the headlight as described in Section 7.

10 Undo the three securing screws and remove the gas discharge bulb sealing cover.

11 Unscrew the two Torx screws and pull the positioning motor shaft ball head from the mounting on the reflector **(see illustration)**.

12 Unplug the wiring connector.

13 Refitting is a reversal of removal, but on completion, have the headlight alignment checked at the earliest opportunity.

Automatic range control ECU

Note: *Although it is possible to remove and refit the ECU, the new unit will need to be 'coded' before it will function correctly. This task can only be carried out by a VW dealer or suitably-equipped specialist.*

14 The ECU is located on the left-hand head-

light. On Golf models, remove the battery as described in Chapter 5A. On Bora models, remove the headlight as described in Section 7.

15 Undo the three screws securing the control unit **(see illustration)**.

16 Pull the ECU from the headlight, and unplug the wiring connector.

17 Refitting is a reversal of removal.

Vehicle level sender

18 Refer to Chapter 10.

<hr>

9	Headlight beam alignment – general information

1 Accurate adjustment of the headlight beam is only possible using optical beam setting equipment and this work should therefore be carried out by a VW dealer or suitably-equipped workshop.

2 For reference, the headlights can be adjusted using the adjuster assemblies fitted to the top of each light unit. The inner adjuster alters the vertical position of the beam whilst the outer adjuster alters the horizontal aim of the beam **(see illustration)**.

3 On models quipped with gas discharge headlights, the 'dipping' characteristics of the unit can be set for countries who drive on the

left or right. Remove the headlight with reference to Section 7, remove the gas discharge bulb end cap. The adjustment lever, next to the bulb, should be set downwards for driving on the right, and upwards for driving on the left **(see illustration)**.

10	Instrument panel – removal and refitting

Removal

1 Disconnect the battery negative lead. **Note:** *Before disconnecting the battery, refer to 'Disconnecting the battery' in the Reference section at the rear of this manual.* Release the steering wheel adjustment lock, pull the wheel out as far as possible, and set it in the lowest position.

2 Unclip the instrument panel lower centre trim and lay it on the upper steering column cover.

3 Remove the two instrument panel retaining screws, and lift the panel out of the facia sufficiently to allow the wiring plugs on the rear of the unit to be disconnected **(see illustrations)**.

4 Withdraw the instrument panel from the facia.

9.2 Headlamp horizontal adjustment screw (arrowed)

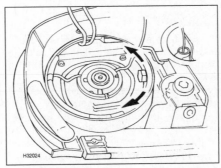

9.3 Move the lever up for driving on the left, and down for driving on the right

10.3a Undo the screws ...

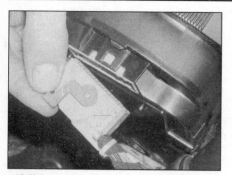

10.3b . . . and disconnect the wiring plug

Refitting

5 Refitting is a reversal of removal, making sure that the wiring plugs are securely reconnected.

11 Instrument panel components – removal and refitting

It is not possible to dismantle the instrument panel. If any of the gauges are faulty, the complete instrument panel must be renewed.

12 Service interval indicator – general information and resetting

1 All Golf and Bora models are equipped with a service interval indicator. After all necessary maintenance work has been completed (see the relevant part of Chapter 1), the service interval display code must be reset. If more than one service schedule is carried out, note that the relevant display intervals must be reset individually.
2 The display is reset using the button on the left-hand side of the instrument panel (below the speedometer) and the clock setting button on the right-hand side of the panel (below the clock/tachometer). Resetting is described in the relevant part of Chapter 1.

15.3 Undo the mounting nut (arrowed)

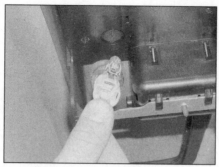

14.4 Push out the centre element

13 Clock – removal and refitting

The clock is integral with the instrument panel, and cannot be removed separately. The instrument panel is a sealed unit, and if the clock, or any other components, are faulty, the complete instrument panel must be renewed. Refer to Section 10 to remove it.

14 Cigarette lighter – removal and refitting

Removal

1 Disconnect the battery negative lead. **Note:** *Before disconnecting the battery, refer to 'Disconnecting the battery' in the Reference section at the rear of this manual.*
2 Remove the centre console as described in Chapter 11.
3 Remove the bulbholder as described in Section 6.
4 Push the centre element of the lighter out of the mounting **(see illustration)**.

Refitting

5 Refitting is a reversal of removal.

15 Horn – removal and refitting

Removal

1 Disconnect the battery negative lead. **Note:** *Before disconnecting the battery, refer to 'Disconnecting the battery' in the Reference section at the rear of this manual.*
2 Remove the right-hand vent from the bumper, as described in Chapter 11.
3 Working through the vent aperture, disconnect the horn wiring plug, then unscrew the securing nut, and withdraw the horn from its mounting bracket **(see illustration)**.

Refitting

4 Refitting is a reversal of removal.

16 Speedometer sensor – general information

All models are fitted with an electronic speedometer sensor. This device measures the rotational speed of the transmission final drive and converts the information into an electronic signal, which is then sent to the speedometer module in the instrument panel. On certain models, the signal is also used as an input by the engine management system ECU, and the trip computer.

Refer to Chapter 7A or 7B for details of the removal procedure.

17 Wiper arm – removal and refitting

Removal

1 Operate the wiper motor, then switch off so that the wiper arms return to the at-rest position.
2 Stick a piece of masking tape to the glass along the edge of the wiper blade to use as an alignment aid on refitting.
3 Prise off the wiper arm spindle nut cover, then slacken but do not completely remove the spindle nut. Lift the blade off the glass and pull the wiper arm until it releases from the spindle **(see illustration)**. Remove the spindle nut. If necessary the arm can be levered off the spindle using a suitable flat-bladed screwdriver. **Note:** *If both windscreen wiper arms are to be removed at the same time mark them for identification; the arms are not interchangeable.*

Refitting

4 Ensure that the wiper arm and spindle splines are clean and dry, then refit the arm to the spindle, aligning the wiper blade with the tape fitted on removal. Refit the spindle nut, tightening it securely, and clip the nut cover back in position.

17.3 Remove the cap and slacken the nut

18 Windscreen wiper motor and linkage – removal and refitting

Removal

1 Remove the wiper arms as described in Section 17.

2 Remove the rubber sealing strip from the top of the bulkhead then undo the retaining screws and remove the pollen filter cover from the passenger side of the windscreen cowling.

3 The windscreen cowling can then be unclipped from the base of the windscreen and removed from the vehicle. To unclip the cowling first free the ends of the panel from behind the windscreen pillar panels then carefully unclip the panel from the windscreen and remove it from the vehicle.

Caution: Do not use a screwdriver lever between the cowling and windscreen as this is likely to result in the windscreen cracking.

4 Unscrew the three securing bolts, then carefully manipulate the windscreen wiper motor and linkage out from the scuttle and disconnect the wiring plug **(see illustrations)**.

5 Recover the washers and spacers from the motor mounting rubbers, noting their locations, then inspect the rubbers for signs of damage or deterioration, and renew if necessary.

6 To separate the motor from the linkage, proceed as follows.

 a) *Make alignment marks between the motor spindle and the linkage to ensure correct alignment on refitting, and note the orientation of the linkage.*

 b) *Unscrew the nut securing the linkage to the motor spindle.*

 c) *Unscrew the three bolts securing the motor to the mounting plate, then withdraw the motor.*

Refitting

7 Refitting is a reversal of removal, bearing in mind the following points.

 a) *If the motor has been separated from the linkage, ensure that the marks made on the motor spindle and linkage before removal are aligned, and ensure that the*

18.4a Remove the three mounting bolts . . .

linkage is orientated as noted before removal.

 b) *Ensure that the washers and spacers are fitted to the motor mounting rubbers as noted before removal.*

 c) *Lubricate the windscreen cowling mounting slots with a silicone-based spray lubricant to ease installation. Do not strike the cowling to seat it in position as this could result in the windscreen cracking.*

 d) *Refit the wiper arms as described in Section 17.*

19 Rear wiper motor – removal and refitting

Removal

1 Remove the wiper arm as described in Section 17.

2 Recover the wiper motor shaft sealing ring.

3 Open the tailgate, then with reference to Chapter 11, Section 15, remove the tailgate trim panel.

4 Unplug the wiring connector from the motor.

5 Disconnect the washer fluid hose from the washer nozzle connector on the motor assembly.

6 Unscrew the three nuts securing the motor, then withdraw the assembly **(see illustration)**.

Refitting

7 Refitting is a reversal of removal, but ensure that the motor shaft rubber sealing ring is

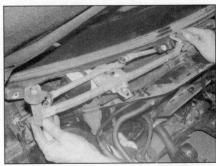

18.4b . . . and manoeuvre the motor from the scuttle

correctly refitted to prevent water leaks, and refit the wiper arm with reference to Section 17.

20 Washer system components – removal and refitting

Washer fluid reservoir

Removal

1 Switch off the ignition and all electrical consumers.

2 Undo the coolant expansion bottle securing bolts and move the bottle to one side. Do not disconnect the hoses.

3 Remove the activated charcoal canister retaining bolts, and move the unit to one side.

4 Unscrew the two plastic nuts, disconnect the hose(s), and remove the washer reservoir **(see illustration)**. Be prepared for fluid spillage.

Refitting

5 Refitting is a reversal of removal.

Washer fluid pumps

Removal

6 Switch off the ignition and all electrical consumers.

7 Remove the washer fluid reservoir as described previously in this Section.

8 Carefully pull the pump from its grommet in the reservoir **(see illustration)**. If not already done, disconnect the washer fluid hose(s) and the wiring plug from the pump.

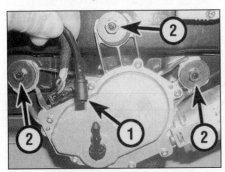

19.6 Tailgate wiper motor

1 *Washer pipe*
2 *Wiper motor mounting nuts*

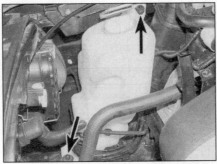

20.4 Undo the two plastic nuts (arrowed)

20.8 Pull the pump from the grommet

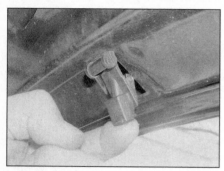

20.10a Pull the jet from the bonnet . . .

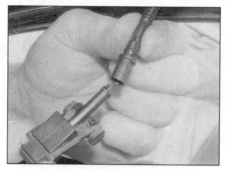

20.10b . . . and disconnect the pipe

20.11 Turn the eccentric to adjust the jet

20.12 Pull the jet from the centre of the spindle

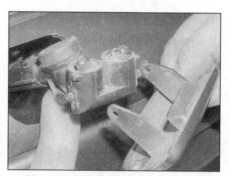

20.14 Prise the end cap from the jet

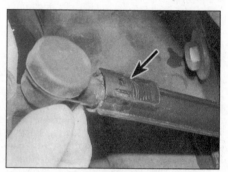

20.15 Lift the clip and pull out the jet (arrowed)

Refitting

9 Refitting is a reversal of removal, but take care not to push the pump grommet into the reservoir. Use a little soapy water to ease the pump into the grommet.

Windscreen washer jets

Removal

10 Open the bonnet, and pull the washer jet towards the front of the bonnet, and down. Disconnect the washer tube as the jet is withdrawn from the bonnet **(see illustrations)**.

Refitting

11 Refitting is a reversal of removal. Note that the aim of the jet can be adjusted using a screwdriver and turning the eccentric shaft at the base of the washer jet **(see illustration)**.

Tailgate washer jet

Removal

12 Unclip the cover from the wiper arm spindle for access to the washer jet, and pull the jet from the centre of the spindle **(see illustration)**.

Refitting

13 On refitting, ensure that the jet is securely pushed into position. Check the operation of the jet. If necessary, adjust the nozzle, aiming the spray at a point slightly above the area of glass swept by the wiper blade.

Headlight washer jets

Removal

14 Carefully pull the washer jet out from the front bumper to its full extent, and hold it. Carefully prise the end cap from the washer jet **(see illustration)**.

15 Still holding the washer jet, lift the securing clip slightly, and pull the jet from the lift cylinder **(see illustration)**.

Refitting

16 Refitting is a reversal of removal.

Headlight washer jet lift cylinder

Removal

17 Remove the washer jet end cap as described in paragraph 14. Remove the front bumper as described in Chapter 11.

18 Undo the two retaining screws, and withdraw the cylinder **(see illustration)**.

19 Clamp the hose, squeeze the retaining clip, and disconnect the hose.

Refitting

20 Refitting is a reversal of removal.

21 Radio/cassette/CD player/changer – removal and refitting

Note: *This Section only applies to standard-fit audio equipment.*

Radio/cassette player

Removal

1 The radio is fitted with special mounting clips, requiring the use of special removal tools, which should be supplied with the vehicle, or may be obtained from an in-car entertainment specialist. Alternatively, two feeler blades can be used **(see illustration)**.

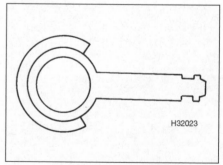

21.1 Radio removal tool

20.18 Undo the lift cylinder mounting screws (arrowed)

2 Switch off the ignition and all electrical consumers.

3 Insert the tools into the slots on each side of the unit and push them until they snap into place. The radio/cassette player can then be pulled out of the facia using the tools, and the wiring connectors and aerial disconnected (see illustrations).

Refitting

4 Reconnect the wiring connectors and aerial lead then push the unit into the facia until the retaining lugs snap into place.

CD player

Removal

5 The CD player is fitted with special mounting clips, requiring the use of special removal tools, which should be supplied with the vehicle, or may be obtained from an in-car entertainment specialist. Alternatively, two feeler blades can be used.

6 Switch off the ignition and all electrical consumers, then remove the radio/cassette player as described earlier in this Section.

7 Insert the tools or feeler blades into the slots on each side of the unit and push them until they snap into place. The CD player can then be pulled out of the facia using the tools, and the wiring disconnected (see illustrations).

Refitting

8 Reconnect the wiring then push the unit into the facia until the retaining lugs snap into place.

CD changer

Removal

9 The CD changer is located in the luggage compartment, behind the left-hand side trim. It is installed horizontally in Golf models and vertically in Bora models.

10 Switch off the ignition and all electrical consumers.

11 Turn the retaining fasteners anticlockwise and remove the trim panel from the luggage compartment.

12 Disconnect the wiring from the rear of the CD player and unclip them from the bracket.

13 Undo the mounting screws and withdraw the CD player from the bracket.

21.3a Using feeler blades to remove the radio/cassette player

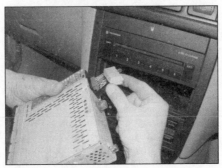

21.3c Disconnecting the wiring . . .

Refitting

14 Refitting is a reversal of removal.

22	Loudspeakers – removal and refitting

Front door-mounted treble

Removal

1 Switch off the ignition and all electrical consumers.

2 Remove the door trim as described in Chapter 11.

3 Disconnect the speaker wiring plug.

4 Remove the single retaining screw, and push the mirror triangular cover upwards.

5 The loudspeaker is integral with the triangular mirror cover.

21.3b The feeler blades bend the retaining clips inwards from the surrounding panel

21.3d . . . and aerial

Refitting

6 Refitting is a reversal of removal.

Rear door-mounted treble

Removal

7 Switch off the ignition and all electrical consumers.

8 Remove the door trim as described in Chapter 11.

9 With reference to Chapter 11, remove the door internal handle. The speaker is integral with the handle cover.

Refitting

10 Refitting is a reversal of removal.

Door-mounted bass

Removal

11 Switch off the ignition and all electrical consumers.

21.7a Using feeler blades to remove the CD player

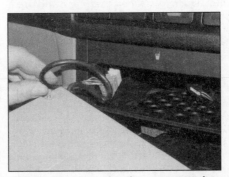

21.7b Disconnecting the power supply wiring . . .

21.7c . . . and speaker wiring

12 Remove the door trim with reference to Chapter 11.

13 Disconnect the wiring plug from the loudspeaker.

14 Drill out the retaining rivets, and withdraw the speaker from the door. Recover the rubber sealing ring between the speaker and door trim.

Refitting

15 Refitting is a reversal of removal. The special-sized rivets should be available from VW dealers and in-car entertainment specialists.

23 Radio aerial – removal and refitting

Removal

1 The aerial mast can be unscrewed from the base by twisting anti-clockwise.

2 If the aerial base is to be removed, the rear of the headlining must be lowered for access.

3 Once the headlining has been lowered, disconnect the aerial lead at the connector, then unscrew the securing nut, and withdraw the aerial base from the roof. Hold the aerial base as the nut is being unscrewed to prevent the base from rotating and scratching the roof panel. Recover the rubber spacer.

Refitting

4 Refitting is a reversal of removal.

24 Anti-theft alarm system and engine immobiliser – general information

Note: *This information is applicable only to the anti-theft alarm system fitted by VW as standard equipment.*

Models in the range are fitted with an anti-theft alarm system as standard equipment. The alarm has switches on all the doors (including the tailgate/boot lid), the bonnet and the ignition switch. If the tailgate/boot lid, bonnet or any of the doors are opened, or the ignition switch is switched on whilst the alarm is set, the alarm horn will sound and the

26.4 Free the airbag locking lug

hazard warning lights will flash. Some models are equipped with an internal monitoring system, which will activate the alarm system if any movement in the cabin is detected.

The alarm is set using the key in the driver's or passenger's front door lock, and tailgate/boot lid lock, or via the central locking remote control transmitter. The alarm system will then start to monitor its various switches approximately 30 seconds later.

With the alarm set, if the tailgate/boot lid is unlocked, the lock switch sensing will automatically be switched off but the door and bonnet switches will still be active. Once the tailgate/boot lid is shut and locked again, the switch sensing will be switched back on.

Certain models are fitted with an immobiliser system, which is activated via the ignition switch. A module incorporated in the ignition switch reads a code contained within the ignition key. The module sends a signal to the engine management electronic control unit (ECU) which allows the engine to start if the code is correct. If an incorrect ignition key is used, the engine will not start.

If a fault is suspected with the alarm or immobiliser systems, the vehicle should be taken to a VW dealer for examination. They will have access to a special diagnostic tester which will quickly trace any fault present in the system.

25 Airbag system – general information and precautions

⚠ **Warning: Before carrying out any operations on the airbag system, disconnect the battery negative terminal (refer to 'Disconnecting the battery' in the Reference section at the rear of this manual). When operations are complete, make sure no one is inside the vehicle when the battery is reconnected.**

• **Note that the airbag(s) must not be subjected to temperatures in excess of 90°C (194°F). When the airbag is removed, ensure that it is stored the with the pad upwards to prevent possible inflation.**

• **Do not allow any solvents or cleaning agents to contact the airbag assemblies. They must be cleaned using only a damp cloth.**

• **The airbags and control unit are both sensitive to impact. If either is dropped or damaged they should be renewed.**

• **Remove the airbag units prior to using arc-welding equipment on the vehicle.**

A driver's airbag, passenger's airbag and side airbags were fitted as standard to the Golf/Bora range. The airbag system comprises of the airbag unit (complete with gas generator) which is fitted to the steering wheel (driver's side), facia (passenger's side) and front seats, an impact sensor, the control unit and a warning light in the instrument panel.

The airbag system is triggered in the event of a heavy frontal or side impact above a predetermined force; depending on the point of impact. The airbag is inflated within milliseconds and forms a safety cushion between the driver and the steering wheel, the passenger and the facia, and in the case of side impact, between front seat occupants and the sides of the cabin. This prevents contact between the upper body and cabin interior, and therefore greatly reduces the risk of injury. The airbag then deflates almost immediately.

Every time the ignition is switched on, the airbag control unit performs a self-test. The self-test takes approximately 3 seconds and during this time the airbag warning light on the facia is illuminated. After the self-test has been completed the warning light should go out. If the warning light fails to come on, remains illuminated after the initial 3 second period or comes on at any time when the vehicle is being driven, there is a fault in the airbag system. The vehicle should then be taken to a VW dealer for examination at the earliest possible opportunity.

26 Airbag system components – removal and refitting

Note: *Refer to the warnings in Section 25 before carrying out the following operations.*

1 Disconnect the battery negative terminal, then continue as described under the relevant heading. **Note:** *Before disconnecting the battery, refer to 'Disconnecting the battery' in the Reference section at the rear of this manual.*

Driver's side airbag

Removal

2 Set the front wheels in the straight-ahead position, and release the steering lock by inserting the ignition key.

3 Adjust the steering column to its lowest position by releasing the adjustment handle, then pull out the column and lower it as far as possible. Lock the column in this position by returning the adjustment handle.

4 With the spokes in the vertical position, insert a screwdriver approximately 45 mm into the hole in the upper rear of the steering wheel hub, then move it up to release the clip and free the airbag locking lug **(see illustration)**. Now turn the steering wheel through 180° and release the remaining airbag locking lug.

5 Turn the steering wheel to its central, straight-ahead position.

6 Carefully withdraw the airbag module and disconnect the wiring **(see illustration)**.

Refitting

7 On refitting, reconnect the wiring connector and seat the airbag unit in the steering wheel, making sure that the wire does not become trapped. Reconnect the battery negative lead,

26.6 Disconnect the wiring plug

26.9 Undo the Torx screws

26.15 Airbag ECU location

ensuring that no-one is inside the vehicle as the lead is connected.

Passenger's side airbag

Removal

8 With reference to Chapter 11, Section 28, remove the passenger side glovebox.
9 Unscrew the four Torx screws securing the airbag support bracket to the facia crossmember **(see illustration)**.
10 Carefully withdraw the airbag unit from the facia, and disconnect the wiring connector.

Refitting

11 On refitting, manoeuvre the airbag into position and reconnect the wiring connector.
12 Refit the airbag securing screws, and tighten it securely.
13 Refit the glovebox, then reconnect the battery negative lead, ensuring that no-one is inside the vehicle as the lead is connected.

Front seat side impact airbags

14 The side impact air bags are integral with the seats. As seat upholstery removal requires considerable skill and experience, if it is to be carried out without damage, it is best entrusted to an expert.

Airbag control unit

Removal

15 The control unit is located under the facia, beneath the heater matrix housing **(see illustration)**.
16 Disconnect the battery negative lead.
Note: *Before disconnecting the battery, refer to 'Disconnecting the battery' in the Reference section at the rear of this manual.*
17 Remove the passenger's side footwell trim, as described in Chapter 11, Section 28.
18 Working on the passenger's side of the facia centre section, reach under the heater housing, move the retaining clip to the open position, and disconnect the control unit wiring plug.
19 Unscrew the four nuts securing the control unit to the floor, then manipulate the control unit out from behind the facia.

Refitting

20 Refitting is the reverse of removal making sure the wiring connector is securely reconnected. Reconnect the battery negative lead, ensuring that no-one is inside the vehicle as the lead is connected.

Airbag wiring contact unit

Removal

Note: *When removing or installing the contact unit, use tape to ensure that the coil connector remains in the centre position.*
21 Remove the steering wheel as described in Chapter 10.
22 Undo the two screws through the holes in the lower steering column shroud, and remove the upper shroud. Undo the three retaining screws for the lower shroud, release the height adjustment lever, and withdraw the lower shroud.
23 Disconnect the wiring plug on the underside on the unit. Release the three locking lugs, and pull the unit with the slip ring from the column.

Refitting

24 Refitting is a reversal of removal. Ensure that no-one is inside the vehicle as the wiring plug is reconnected.

24 Parking aid components – general information, removal and refitting

General information

1 The parking aid system is available as a standard fitment on highline models, and optional on other models. Four ultrasound sensors located in the rear bumper measure the distance to the closest object behind the car, and inform the driver using acoustic signals from a buzzer located under the rear luggage compartment trim. The nearer the object, the more frequent the acoustic signals.
2 The system includes a control unit and self-diagnosis program, and therefore, in the event of a fault, the vehicle should be taken to a VW dealer.

Control unit

Hatchback and Saloon models

3 Switch off the ignition and all electrical consumers, then open (Golf) or remove (Bora) the right-hand trim in the luggage compartment.
4 Undo the two mounting screws, disconnect the wiring, and remove the control unit.
5 Refitting is a reversal of removal.

Estate models

6 Switch off the ignition and all electrical consumers, then open the flap in the right-hand luggage compartment trim.
7 Remove the plastic insert for the first aid box.
8 Undo the screw, disconnect the wiring, and remove the control unit together with the holder.
9 Unbolt the control unit from the holder.
10 Refitting is a reversal of removal.

Range/distance sensor

11 It is not necessary to remove the rear bumper. Reach under the bumper and squeeze the retaining clips on the top and bottom of the sensor. Now press out the sensor from the outside of the bumper.
12 Disconnect the wiring and remove the sensor.
13 Refitting is a reversal of removal. Press the sensor firmly into position until the retaining clips engage.

Warning buzzer

14 Switch off the ignition and all electrical consumers, then remove the right-hand luggage compartment cover on hatchback and estate models, and remove the rear shelf on Bora saloon models.
15 Release the clips or undo the nuts, then disconnect the wiring and remove the buzzer.
16 Refitting is a reversal of removal.

Volkswagen Golf and Bora 2001 to 2004

Diagram 1

Key to symbols

Bulb

Switch

Fuse/fusible
link and current
rating

F5
10A

Multiple contact
switch (ganged)

Resistor

Variable
resistor

Connecting
wires

Item no.

2

Pump/motor

Earth point
and location

E12

Wire joint

Solenoid
actuator

Diode

Light emitting
diode (LED)

Wire colour
(brown with black tracer)

Br/Bk

Screened cable

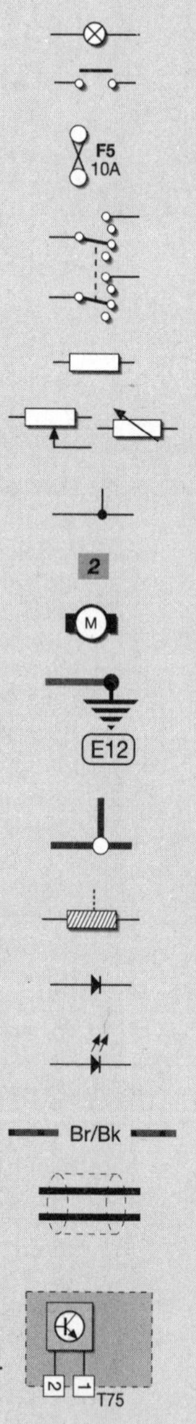

Dashed outline denotes part of a
larger item, containing in this case
an electronic or solid state device.
Pin types:
2 - Unspecified connector, pin 2.
T75 1 - Connector T75, pin 1.

Main fuse box layout

	8	12	16	20
	5	9	13	17	21
1	3	6	10	14	18	22
2	4	7	11	15	19	23

24	31	38
25	32	39
26	33	40
27	34	41
28	35	42
29	36	43
30	37	44

Earth points

E1	Battery earth	E8	Driver's door earth 3	E15	Passenger's door earth 2
E2	Gearbox earth	E9	Lower left A pillar	E16	Passenger's door earth 3
E3	Airbag earth	E10	Lower right A pillar	E17	LH engine compartment
E4	Centre of the dashboard	E11	Lower left B pillar	E18	Front cross member
E5	Radio earth 2	E12	Lower right B pillar	E19	Instrument panel earth
E6	Radio earth 1	E13	Steering column		
E7	Driver's door earth 2	E14	LH luggage compartment		

Key to circuits

Diagram 1	Information for wiring diagrams
Diagram 2	Starting and charging, airbag and radio with CD player
Diagram 3	Central locking, electric windows and mirrors
Diagram 4	Central locking control unit and interior lights, horn, fuel tank filler flap release, typical radiator fan, diagnostic connector supply, cigarette lighter and 12V socket
Diagram 5	ABS, heater blower, heated rear window, wash/wipe, brake lights and reversing lights
Diagram 6	Headlights, licence plate lights, taillights and side lights, rear fog light, hazard warning lights and direction indicators
Diagram 7	Headlight leveling, lighting rheostat, front fog lights, gas discharge headlights, gas discharge headlight range control
Diagram 8	Instrument panel, glove box light, interior lights not convenience system

Fuse table

Battery fuse holder

Fuses	Rating	
F162	50A	Glow pin heating
F163	50A	Engine management
F164	40A	Radiator fan
F176	110A	Interior
F177	110A	Alternator (90A)
	150A	Alternator (120A)
F178	30A	ABS (pump)
F179	30A	ABS
F180	30A	Radiator fan

Relay plate fuses

Fuses	Rating	
F37	30A	Central locking, electric windows
F111	15A	Convenience system
F144	15A	Convenience system

Main fuse box

Fuses	Rating	Circuit protected	Fuses	Rating	Circuit protected
F1	10A	Glove box light, electric mirrors	F20	15A	Headlight range control,
F2	10A	Indicators, hazard lights, headlight adjusters			RH headlight (dipped beam), RH gas discharge headlight
F3	5A	Fog light relay, lighting rheostat	F21	15A	LH headlight (dipped beam), LH gas discharge headlight
F4	5A	Licence plate lights	F22	5A	RH sidelights, instrument panel
F5	7.5A	Air conditioning, heater blower convenience system, sunroof CCS, electric mirrors, radiator fan, heated seats diagnostic connector	F23	5A	LH sidelights, instrument panel
			F24	20A	Wash/wipe
			F25	20A	Air conditioning, heater blower engine management
F6	–	Not used	F26	25A	Heated rear window
F7	10A	Reversing lights	F27	15A	Rear window wiper
F8	5A	Mobile phone	F28	15A	Fuel pump
F9	5A	ABS	F29	15A	Engine management (petrol)
F10	15A	Engine management (petrol)		10A	Engine management (diesel)
	5A	Engine management (diesel)	F30	20A	Sunroof
	10A	Radio	F31	20A	Brake servo, automatic transmission
F11	5A	Automatic transmission, instrument panel		5A	4 wheel drive unit (4 motion)
F12	7.5A	Alarm, mobile phone, diagnostic connector	F32	15A	Injectors (petrol)
			F33	30A	Engine management
F13	10A	Brake lights, ABS, engine management		20A	Wash/wipe
			F34	10A	Engine management
F14	10A	Central locking, interior lights	F35	30A	12V socket
F15	5A	Automatic transmission, instrument panel, ABS	F36	15A	Fog lights, instrument panel
			F37	10A	Engine management
F16	10A	Air conditioning, radiator fan	F38	15A	Central locking, filler flap
F17	–	Not used	F39	15A	Indicators, gas discharge headlights
F18	10A	RH headlight (main beam), instrument panel	F40	20A	Horn
			F41	15A	Cigarette lighter
F19	20A	LH headlight (main beam)	F42	25A	Radio
			F43	10A	Engine management
			F44	15A	Heated seats

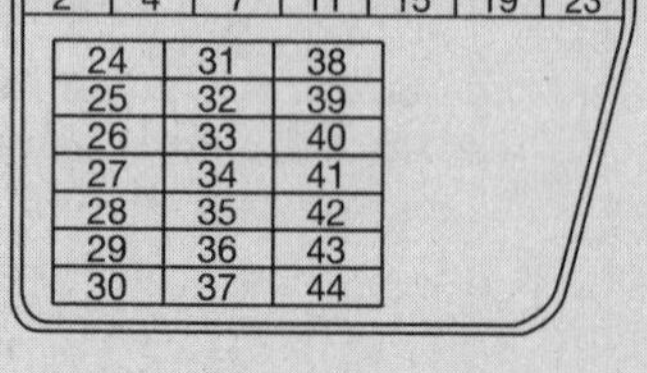

H33004

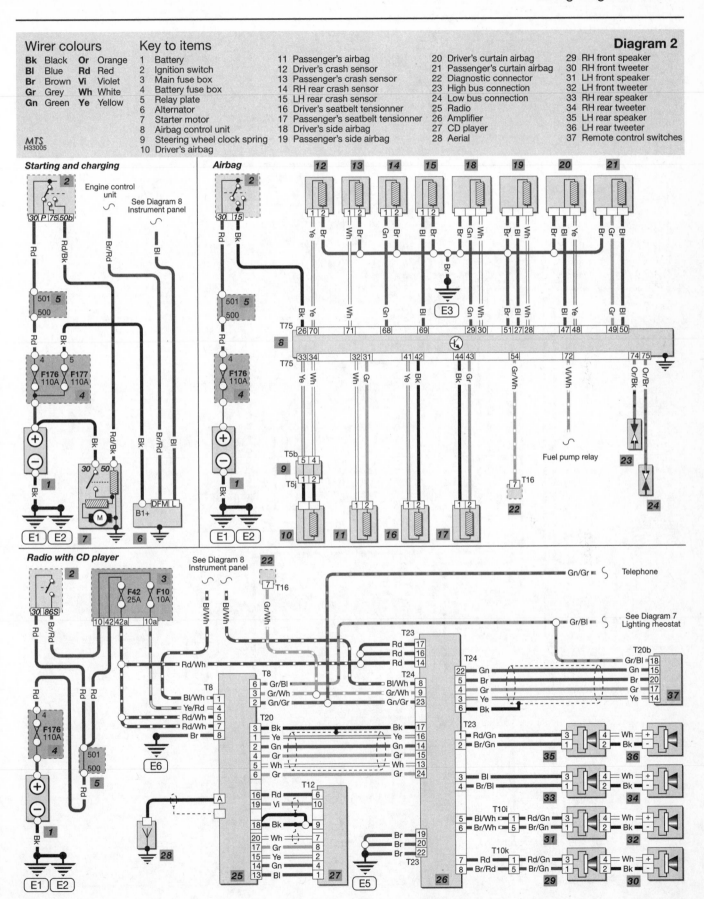

Wirer colours

Bk	Black	**Or**	Orange
Bl	Blue	**Rd**	Red
Br	Brown	**Vi**	Violet
Gr	Grey	**Wh**	White
Gn	Green	**Ye**	Yellow

MTS
H33005

Key to items

1 Battery
2 Ignition switch
3 Main fuse box
4 Battery fuse box
5 Relay plate
6 Alternator
7 Starter motor
8 Airbag control unit
9 Steering wheel clock spring
10 Driver's airbag
11 Passenger's airbag
12 Driver's crash sensor
13 Passenger's crash sensor
14 RH rear crash sensor
15 LH rear crash sensor
16 Driver's seatbelt tensioner
17 Passenger's seatbelt tensioner
18 Driver's side airbag
19 Passenger's side airbag
20 Driver's curtain airbag
21 Passenger's curtain airbag
22 Diagnostic connector
23 High bus connection
24 Low bus connection
25 Radio
26 Amplifier
27 CD player
28 Aerial
29 RH front speaker
30 RH front tweeter
31 LH front speaker
32 LH front tweeter
33 RH rear speaker
34 RH rear tweeter
35 LH rear speaker
36 LH rear tweeter
37 Remote control switches

Diagram 2

Starting and charging

Airbag

Radio with CD player

Wirer colours

Bk Black **Or** Orange
Bl Blue **Rd** Red
Br Brown **Vi** Violet
Gr Grey **Wh** White
Gn Green **Ye** Yellow

Key to items

1 Battery
2 Ignition switch
3 Main fuse box
4 Battery fuse box
5 Relay plate
23 High bus connection
24 Low bus connection
38 Driver's door unit
    with window motor

39 Driver's electric
    window switch unit
40 Central locking warning light
41 Driver's door locking unit
42 Driver's mirror heater and motors
43 Mirror adjustment switches
44 Passengers's door unit
    with window motor
45 Passenger's door locking unit

46 Passenger's mirror heater
    and motors
47 Passenger's electric
    window switch
48 LH rear door unit
    with window motor
49 LH rear door locking unit
50 LH rear electric
    window switch

51 LH rear door unit
    with window motor
52 LH rear door locking unit
53 LH rear electric
    window switch

Diagram 3

MTS
H33006

* Separate heater only

Central locking, electric windows and mirrors

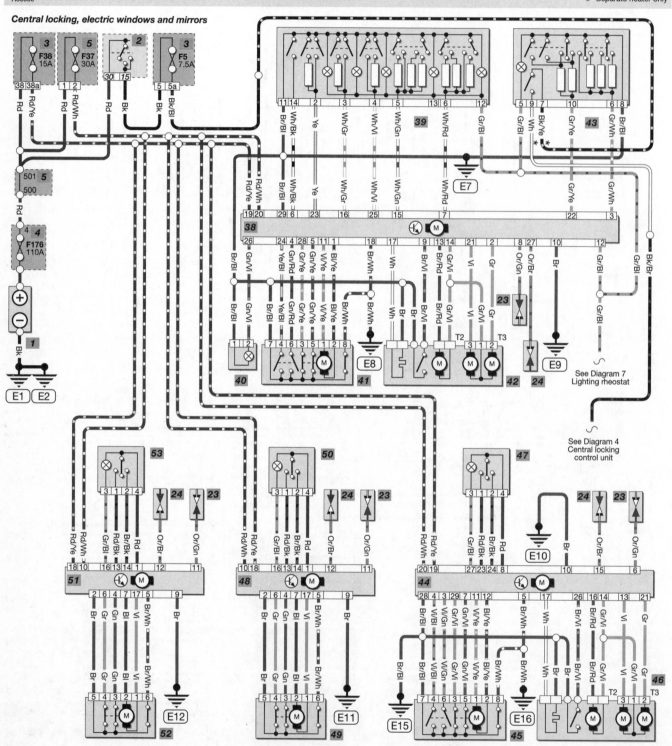

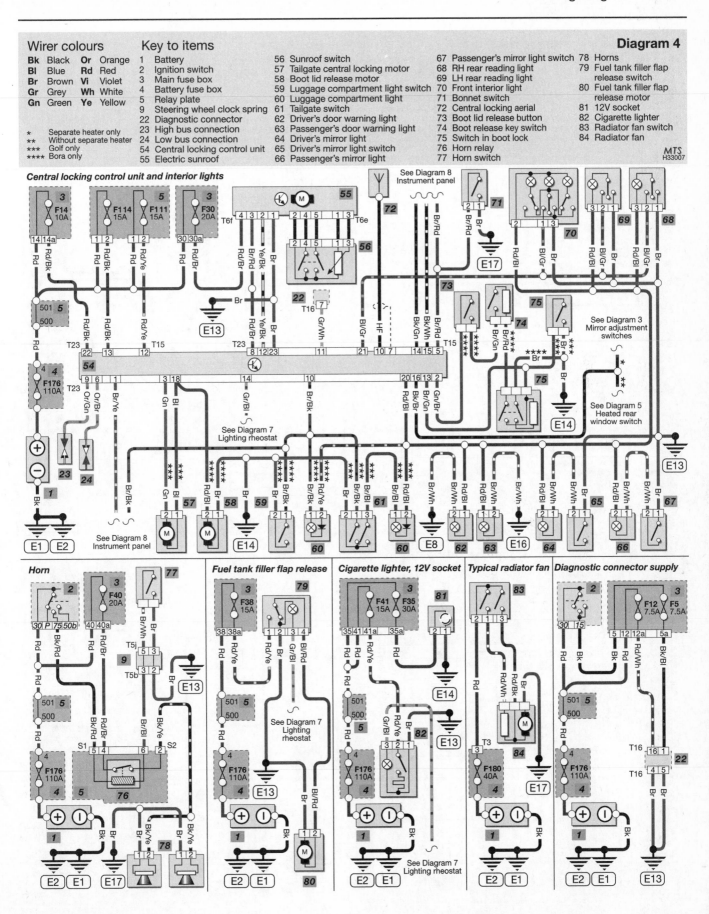

Wirer colours

Bk	Black
Bl	Blue
Br	Brown
Gr	Grey
Gn	Green
Or	Orange
Rd	Red
Vi	Violet
Wh	White
Ye	Yellow

* Separate heater only
** Without separate heater
*** Golf only
**** Bora only

Key to items

1 Battery
2 Ignition switch
3 Main fuse box
4 Battery fuse box
5 Relay plate
9 Steering wheel clock spring
22 Diagnostic connector
23 High bus connection
24 Low bus connection
54 Central locking control unit
55 Electric sunroof
56 Sunroof switch
57 Tailgate central locking motor
58 Boot lid release motor
59 Luggage compartment light switch
60 Luggage compartment light
61 Tailgate switch
62 Driver's door warning light
63 Passenger's door warning light
64 Driver's mirror light
65 Driver's mirror light switch
66 Passenger's mirror light
67 Passenger's mirror light switch
68 RH rear reading light
69 LH rear reading light
70 Front interior light
71 Bonnet switch
72 Central locking aerial
73 Boot lid release button
74 Boot release key switch
75 Switch in boot lock
76 Horn relay
77 Horn switch
78 Horns
79 Fuel tank filler flap release switch
80 Fuel tank filler flap release motor
81 12V socket
82 Cigarette lighter
83 Radiator fan switch
84 Radiator fan

Diagram 4

MTS
H33007

Central locking control unit and interior lights

Horn

Fuel tank filler flap release

Cigarette lighter, 12V socket

Typical radiator fan

Diagnostic connector supply

Wirer colours

Bk	Black	Or	Orange
Bl	Blue	Rd	Red
Br	Brown	Vi	Violet
Gr	Grey	Wh	White
Gn	Green	Ye	Yellow

Key to items

1 Battery
2 Ignition switch
3 Main fuse box
4 Battery fuse box
5 Relay plate
23 High bus connection
24 Low bus connection
85 ABS control unit
86 Traction control switch
87 Steering angle sensor

88 LH front wheel speed sensor
89 LH rear wheel speed sensor
90 RH front wheel speed sensor
91 RH rear wheel speed sensor
92 ESP sensor
93 Brake pressure sensor
94 X contact relay
95 Blower controls
96 Blower motor
97 Resistor pack

98 Air recirculation flap motor
99 Heated rear window switch
100 Heated rear window
101 Rear wiper motor
102 Washer pump
103 Wash wipe relay
104 Windscreen wiper motor
105 Intermittent wiper control
106 Wash/wipe switch

107 Brake light switch
108 LH rear light cluster
  a) brake light
  b) reversing light
109 RH rear light cluster
  (as 108)
110 High level brake light
111 Reversing light switch

★ Golf only

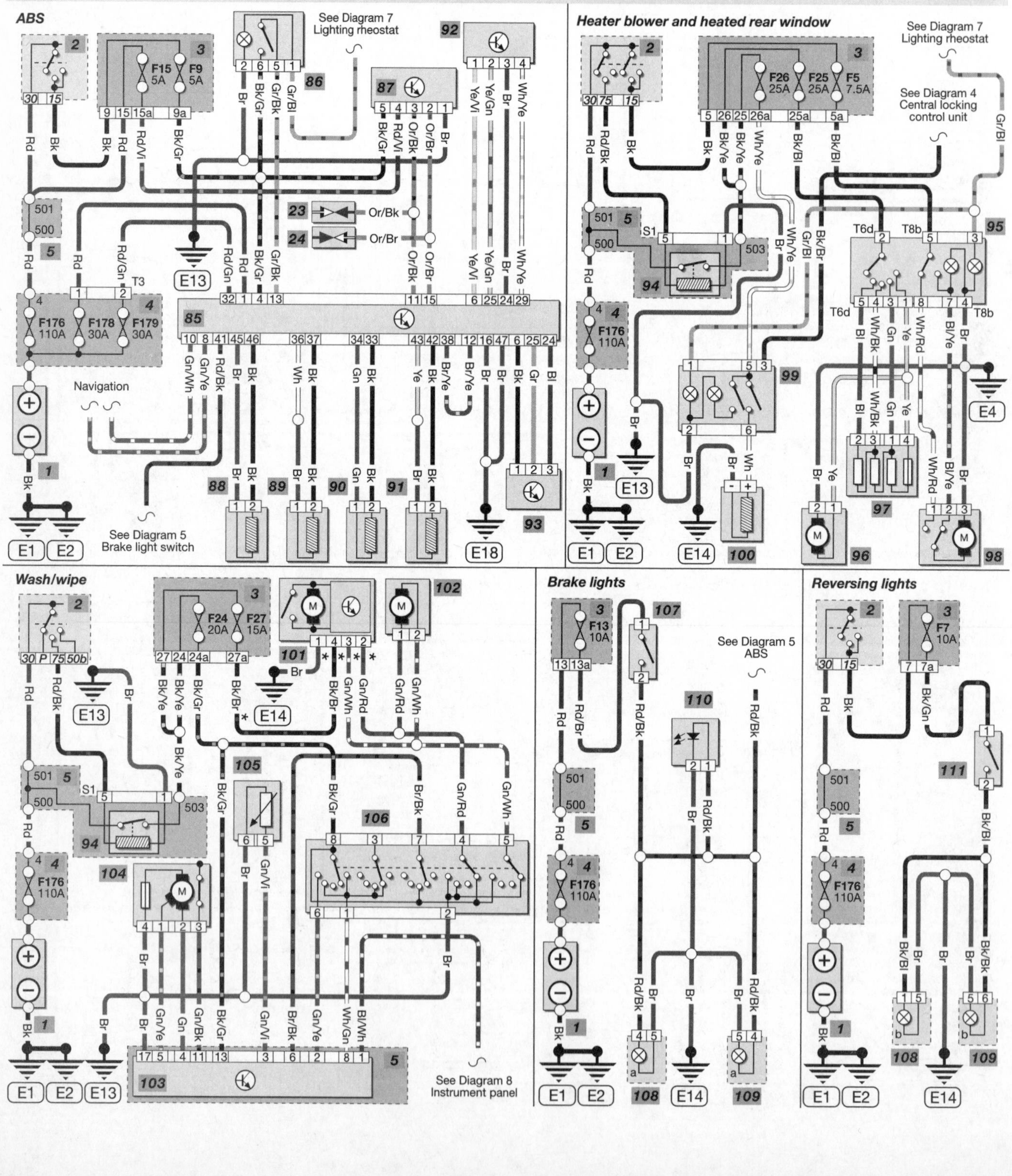

Diagram 5

MTS
H33008

ABS

Heater blower and heated rear window

Wash/wipe

Brake lights

Reversing lights

See Diagram 7
Lighting rheostat

See Diagram 4
Central locking
control unit

See Diagram 5
Brake light switch

See Diagram 5
ABS

See Diagram 8
Instrument panel

Navigation

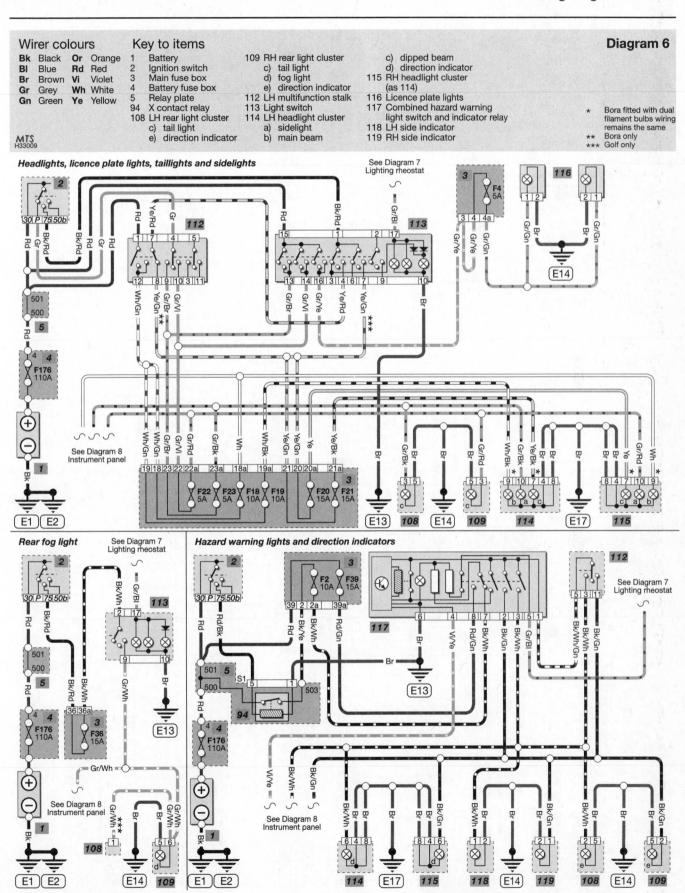

Diagram 6

Wirer colours

Bk	Black	**Or**	Orange
Bl	Blue	**Rd**	Red
Br	Brown	**Vi**	Violet
Gr	Grey	**Wh**	White
Gn	Green	**Ye**	Yellow

MTS
H33009

Key to items

1 Battery
2 Ignition switch
3 Main fuse box
4 Battery fuse box
5 Relay plate
94 X contact relay
108 LH rear light cluster
   c) tail light
   e) direction indicator

109 RH rear light cluster
   c) tail light
   d) fog light
   e) direction indicator
112 LH multifunction stalk
113 Light switch
114 LH headlight cluster
   a) sidelight
   b) main beam

   c) dipped beam
   d) direction indicator
115 RH headlight cluster
   (as 114)
116 Licence plate lights
117 Combined hazard warning
   light switch and indicator relay
118 LH side indicator
119 RH side indicator

* Bora fitted with dual
   filament bulbs wiring
   remains the same
** Bora only
*** Golf only

Headlights, licence plate lights, taillights and sidelights

Rear fog light

Hazard warning lights and direction indicators

Wirer colours

Bk	Black	**Or**	Orange
Bl	Blue	**Rd**	Red
Br	Brown	**Vi**	Violet
Gr	Grey	**Wh**	White
Gn	Green	**Ye**	Yellow

Key to items

1 Battery
2 Ignition switch
3 Main fuse box
4 Battery fuse box
5 Relay plate
94 X contact relay
112 LH multifunction stalk
113 Light switch
114 LH headlight cluster
   e) fog light
115 RH headlight cluster
   (as 114)
120 Headlight range switch
   and lighting rheostat
121 LH headlight motor
122 RH headlight motor

123 Front fog light relay
124 LH gas discharge starter
125 LH gas discharge control unit
126 LH gas discharge bulb
127 RH gas discharge starter
128 RH gas discharge control unit
129 RH gas discharge bulb
130 Range control unit

131 LH range control motor
132 RH range control motor
133 LH front vehicle level sensor
134 LH rear vehicle level sensor

     ★   Bora only
     ★★ Golf only

Diagram 7

MTS
H33010

Headlight leveling, lighting rheostat

Front fog lights

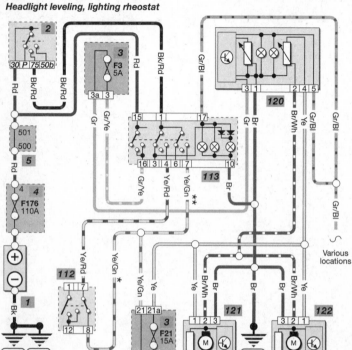

Gas discharge headlights

Gas discharge headlight range control

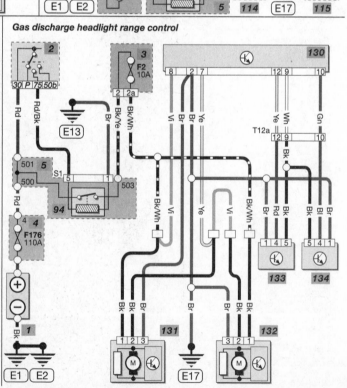

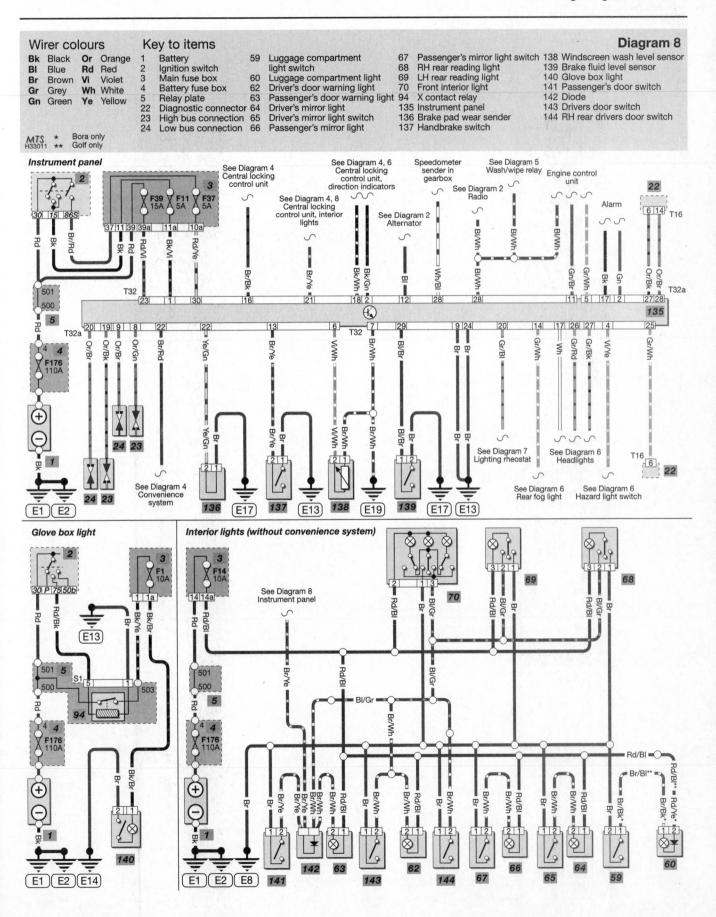

Wirer colours

Bk	Black	Or	Orange
Bl	Blue	Rd	Red
Br	Brown	Vi	Violet
Gr	Grey	Wh	White
Gn	Green	Ye	Yellow

MTS * Bora only
H33011 ** Golf only

Key to items

1	Battery	59	Luggage compartment light switch
2	Ignition switch	60	Luggage compartment light
3	Main fuse box	62	Driver's door warning light
4	Battery fuse box	63	Passenger's door warning light
5	Relay plate	64	Driver's mirror light
22	Diagnostic connector	65	Driver's mirror light switch
23	High bus connection	66	Passenger's mirror light
24	Low bus connection	67	Passenger's mirror light switch
		68	RH rear reading light
		69	LH rear reading light
		70	Front interior light
		94	X contact relay
		135	Instrument panel
		136	Brake pad wear sender
		137	Handbrake switch
		138	Windscreen wash level sensor
		139	Brake fluid level sensor
		140	Glove box light
		141	Passenger's door switch
		142	Diode
		143	Drivers door switch
		144	RH rear drivers door switch

Diagram 8

Instrument panel

Glove box light

Interior lights (without convenience system)

Notes

Dimensions and weights ....**REF•1**
Conversion factors ....**REF•2**
Buying spare parts ....**REF•3**
Vehicle identification numbers ....**REF•3**
General repair procedures ....**REF•4**
Jacking and vehicle support ....**REF•5**

Disconnecting the battery ....**REF•5**
Tools and working facilities ....**REF•6**
MOT test checks ....**REF•8**
Fault finding ....**REF•12**
Glossary of technical terms ....**REF•19**
Index ....**REF•24**

Dimensions and weights

Note: *All figures and dimensions are approximate and may vary according to model. Refer to manufacturer's data for exact figures.*

Overall length

Golf Hatchback models .... 4149 mm
Golf Estate models .... 4397 mm
Bora Saloon models .... 4376 mm

Overall width

All models .... 1735 mm

Overall height (unladen)

Golf Hatchback models .... 1444 mm
Golf Estate models .... 1473 mm
Bora Saloon models .... 1446 mm

Wheelbase

Golf Hatchback models .... 2511 mm
Golf Estate models .... 2515 mm
Bora Saloon models .... 2513 mm

Turning circle

All models .... 10.9 m

Weights

Kerb weight *

Golf Hatchback models .... 1090 to 1234 kg
Golf Estate models .... 1189 to 1340 kg
Bora Saloon models .... 1165 to 1303 kg

Maximum gross vehicle weight **

Golf Hatchback models .... 1640 to 1770 kg
Golf Estate models .... 1735 to 1880 kg
Bora Saloon models .... 1710 to 1840 kg

* *Exact kerb weights depend upon model and specification – details are given the owner's handbook, and on a sticker affixed to the left-hand front suspension turret.*
** *Exact maximum gross vehicle weights depend upon model and specifications – details are given in the owner's handbook, and on a sticker affixed to the left-hand front suspension turret.*

Maximum roof rack load

All models .... 75 kg

Maximum towing weights*	Unbraked trailer	Braked trailer
Petrol engines	550 to 600 kg	1000 to 1400 kg
Diesel engines	500 to 650 kg	850 to 1500 kg

* *Exact towing weights depend upon model and specification – details are given the owner's handbook.*

Conversion factors

Length (distance)
Inches (in)	x 25.4	= Millimetres (mm)	x 0.0394	= Inches (in)
Feet (ft)	x 0.305	= Metres (m)	x 3.281	= Feet (ft)
Miles	x 1.609	= Kilometres (km)	x 0.621	= Miles

Volume (capacity)
Cubic inches (cu in; in³)	x 16.387	= Cubic centimetres (cc; cm³)	x 0.061	= Cubic inches (cu in; in³)
Imperial pints (Imp pt)	x 0.568	= Litres (l)	x 1.76	= Imperial pints (Imp pt)
Imperial quarts (Imp qt)	x 1.137	= Litres (l)	x 0.88	= Imperial quarts (Imp qt)
Imperial quarts (Imp qt)	x 1.201	= US quarts (US qt)	x 0.833	= Imperial quarts (Imp qt)
US quarts (US qt)	x 0.946	= Litres (l)	x 1.057	= US quarts (US qt)
Imperial gallons (Imp gal)	x 4.546	= Litres (l)	x 0.22	= Imperial gallons (Imp gal)
Imperial gallons (Imp gal)	x 1.201	= US gallons (US gal)	x 0.833	= Imperial gallons (Imp gal)
US gallons (US gal)	x 3.785	= Litres (l)	x 0.264	= US gallons (US gal)

Mass (weight)
Ounces (oz)	x 28.35	= Grams (g)	x 0.035	= Ounces (oz)
Pounds (lb)	x 0.454	= Kilograms (kg)	x 2.205	= Pounds (lb)

Force
Ounces-force (ozf; oz)	x 0.278	= Newtons (N)	x 3.6	= Ounces-force (ozf; oz)
Pounds-force (lbf; lb)	x 4.448	= Newtons (N)	x 0.225	= Pounds-force (lbf; lb)
Newtons (N)	x 0.1	= Kilograms-force (kgf; kg)	x 9.81	= Newtons (N)

Pressure
Pounds-force per square inch (psi; lbf/in²; lb/in²)	x 0.070	= Kilograms-force per square centimetre (kgf/cm²; kg/cm²)	x 14.223	= Pounds-force per square inch (psi; lbf/in²; lb/in²)
Pounds-force per square inch (psi; lbf/in²; lb/in²)	x 0.068	= Atmospheres (atm)	x 14.696	= Pounds-force per square inch (psi; lbf/in²; lb/in²)
Pounds-force per square inch (psi; lbf/in²; lb/in²)	x 0.069	= Bars	x 14.5	= Pounds-force per square inch (psi; lbf/in²; lb/in²)
Pounds-force per square inch (psi; lbf/in²; lb/in²)	x 6.895	= Kilopascals (kPa)	x 0.145	= Pounds-force per square inch (psi; lbf/in²; lb/in²)
Kilopascals (kPa)	x 0.01	= Kilograms-force per square centimetre (kgf/cm²; kg/cm²)	x 98.1	= Kilopascals (kPa)
Millibar (mbar)	x 100	= Pascals (Pa)	x 0.01	= Millibar (mbar)
Millibar (mbar)	x 0.0145	= Pounds-force per square inch (psi; lbf/in²; lb/in²)	x 68.947	= Millibar (mbar)
Millibar (mbar)	x 0.75	= Millimetres of mercury (mmHg)	x 1.333	= Millibar (mbar)
Millibar (mbar)	x 0.401	= Inches of water (inH₂O)	x 2.491	= Millibar (mbar)
Millimetres of mercury (mmHg)	x 0.535	= Inches of water (inH₂O)	x 1.868	= Millimetres of mercury (mmHg)
Inches of water (inH₂O)	x 0.036	= Pounds-force per square inch (psi; lbf/in²; lb/in²)	x 27.68	= Inches of water (inH₂O)

Torque (moment of force)
Pounds-force inches (lbf in; lb in)	x 1.152	= Kilograms-force centimetre (kgf cm; kg cm)	x 0.868	= Pounds-force inches (lbf in; lb in)
Pounds-force inches (lbf in; lb in)	x 0.113	= Newton metres (Nm)	x 8.85	= Pounds-force inches (lbf in; lb in)
Pounds-force inches (lbf in; lb in)	x 0.083	= Pounds-force feet (lbf ft; lb ft)	x 12	= Pounds-force inches (lbf in; lb in)
Pounds-force feet (lbf ft; lb ft)	x 0.138	= Kilograms-force metres (kgf m; kg m)	x 7.233	= Pounds-force feet (lbf ft; lb ft)
Pounds-force feet (lbf ft; lb ft)	x 1.356	= Newton metres (Nm)	x 0.738	= Pounds-force feet (lbf ft; lb ft)
Newton metres (Nm)	x 0.102	= Kilograms-force metres (kgf m; kg m)	x 9.804	= Newton metres (Nm)

Power
Horsepower (hp)	x 745.7	= Watts (W)	x 0.0013	= Horsepower (hp)

Velocity (speed)
Miles per hour (miles/hr; mph)	x 1.609	= Kilometres per hour (km/hr; kph)	x 0.621	= Miles per hour (miles/hr; mph)

Fuel consumption*
Miles per gallon, Imperial (mpg)	x 0.354	= Kilometres per litre (km/l)	x 2.825	= Miles per gallon, Imperial (mpg)
Miles per gallon, US (mpg)	x 0.425	= Kilometres per litre (km/l)	x 2.352	= Miles per gallon, US (mpg)

Temperature
Degrees Fahrenheit = (°C x 1.8) + 32   Degrees Celsius (Degrees Centigrade; °C) = (°F - 32) x 0.56

It is common practice to convert from miles per gallon (mpg) to litres/100 kilometres (l/100km), where mpg x l/100 km = 282

Spare parts are available from many sources, including maker's appointed garages, accessory shops, and motor factors. To be sure of obtaining the correct parts, it will sometimes be necessary to quote the vehicle identification number. If possible, it can also be useful to take the old parts along for positive identification. Items such as starter motors and alternators may be available under a service exchange scheme – any parts returned should be clean.

Our advice regarding spare parts is as follows.

Officially appointed garages

This is the best source of parts which are peculiar to your car, and which are not otherwise generally available (eg, badges, interior trim, certain body panels, etc). It is also the only place at which you should buy parts if the vehicle is still under warranty.

Accessory shops

These are very good places to buy materials and components needed for the maintenance of your car (oil, air and fuel filters, light bulbs, drivebelts, greases, brake pads, touch-up paint, etc). Components of this nature sold by a reputable shop are usually of the same standard as those used by the car manufacturer.

Besides components, these shops also sell tools and general accessories, usually have convenient opening hours, charge lower prices, and can often be found close to home. Some accessory shops have parts counters where components needed for almost any repair job can be purchased or ordered.

Motor factors

Good factors will stock all the more important components which wear out comparatively quickly, and can sometimes supply individual components needed for the overhaul of a larger assembly (eg, brake seals and hydraulic parts, bearing shells, pistons, valves). They may also handle work such as cylinder block reboring, crankshaft regrinding, etc.

Tyre and exhaust specialists

These outlets may be independent, or members of a local or national chain. They frequently offer competitive prices when compared with a main dealer or local garage, but it will pay to obtain several quotes before making a decision. When researching prices, also ask what extras may be added – for instance fitting a new valve and balancing the wheel are both commonly charged on top of the price of a new tyre.

Other sources

Beware of parts or materials obtained from market stalls, car boot sales or similar outlets. Such items are not invariably sub-standard, but there is little chance of compensation if they do prove unsatisfactory. in the case of safety-critical components such as brake pads, there is the risk not only of financial loss, but also of an accident causing injury or death.

Second-hand components or assemblies obtained from a car breaker can be a good buy in some circumstances, but this sort of purchase is best made by the experienced DIY mechanic.

Vehicle identification numbers

Modifications are a continuing and unpublicised process in vehicle manufacture, quite apart from major model changes. Spare parts manuals and lists are compiled upon a numerical basis, the individual vehicle identification numbers being essential to correct identification of the component concerned.

When ordering spare parts, always give as much information as possible. Quote the car model, year of manufacture and registration, chassis and engine numbers as appropriate.

The *Vehicle Identification Number plate* is stamped on the bulkhead panel at the front left-hand corner of the windscreen, visible through a cut-out in the windscreen cowl panel, and on the left-hand side front suspension turret **(see illustrations)**.

The engine number is stamped into the left-hand end of the cylinder block and on the right-hand end of the cylinder head on petrol engines. On diesel engines it is stamped into the front of the cylinder block, next to the engine-to-transmission joint. A barcode identification sticker is located on the top of the timing cover or cylinder head **(see illustrations)**.

Vehicle Identification Number (VIN) located on the scuttle panel in front of the windscreen

Vehicle Identification Number (VIN) located on the left-hand front suspension turret

Vehicle Identification Number (VIN) located on the left-hand front edge of the windscreen

Engine number located on the block

Engine code located on the cylinder head

Engine code sticker on the cylinder head

Whenever servicing, repair or overhaul work is carried out on the car or its components, observe the following procedures and instructions. This will assist in carrying out the operation efficiently and to a professional standard of workmanship.

Joint mating faces and gaskets

When separating components at their mating faces, never insert screwdrivers or similar implements into the joint between the faces in order to prise them apart. This can cause severe damage which results in oil leaks, coolant leaks, etc upon reassembly. Separation is usually achieved by tapping along the joint with a soft-faced hammer in order to break the seal. However, note that this method may not be suitable where dowels are used for component location.

Where a gasket is used between the mating faces of two components, a new one must be fitted on reassembly; fit it dry unless otherwise stated in the repair procedure. Make sure that the mating faces are clean and dry, with all traces of old gasket removed. When cleaning a joint face, use a tool which is unlikely to score or damage the face, and remove any burrs or nicks with an oilstone or fine file.

Make sure that tapped holes are cleaned with a pipe cleaner, and keep them free of jointing compound, if this is being used, unless specifically instructed otherwise.

Ensure that all orifices, channels or pipes are clear, and blow through them, preferably using compressed air.

Oil seals

Oil seals can be removed by levering them out with a wide flat-bladed screwdriver or similar implement. Alternatively, a number of self-tapping screws may be screwed into the seal, and these used as a purchase for pliers or some similar device in order to pull the seal free.

Whenever an oil seal is removed from its working location, either individually or as part of an assembly, it should be renewed.

The very fine sealing lip of the seal is easily damaged, and will not seal if the surface it contacts is not completely clean and free from scratches, nicks or grooves. If the original sealing surface of the component cannot be restored, and the manufacturer has not made provision for slight relocation of the seal relative to the sealing surface, the component should be renewed.

Protect the lips of the seal from any surface which may damage them in the course of fitting. Use tape or a conical sleeve where possible. Lubricate the seal lips with oil before fitting and, on dual-lipped seals, fill the space between the lips with grease.

Unless otherwise stated, oil seals must be fitted with their sealing lips toward the lubricant to be sealed.

Use a tubular drift or block of wood of the appropriate size to install the seal and, if the seal housing is shouldered, drive the seal down to the shoulder. If the seal housing is unshouldered, the seal should be fitted with its face flush with the housing top face (unless otherwise instructed).

Screw threads and fastenings

Seized nuts, bolts and screws are quite a common occurrence where corrosion has set in, and the use of penetrating oil or releasing fluid will often overcome this problem if the offending item is soaked for a while before attempting to release it. The use of an impact driver may also provide a means of releasing such stubborn fastening devices, when used in conjunction with the appropriate screwdriver bit or socket. If none of these methods works, it may be necessary to resort to the careful application of heat, or the use of a hacksaw or nut splitter device.

Studs are usually removed by locking two nuts together on the threaded part, and then using a spanner on the lower nut to unscrew the stud. Studs or bolts which have broken off below the surface of the component in which they are mounted can sometimes be removed using a stud extractor. Always ensure that a blind tapped hole is completely free from oil, grease, water or other fluid before installing the bolt or stud. Failure to do this could cause the housing to crack due to the hydraulic action of the bolt or stud as it is screwed in.

When tightening a castellated nut to accept a split pin, tighten the nut to the specified torque, where applicable, and then tighten further to the next split pin hole. Never slacken the nut to align the split pin hole, unless stated in the repair procedure.

When checking or retightening a nut or bolt to a specified torque setting, slacken the nut or bolt by a quarter of a turn, and then retighten to the specified setting. However, this should not be attempted where angular tightening has been used.

For some screw fastenings, notably cylinder head bolts or nuts, torque wrench settings are no longer specified for the latter stages of tightening, "angle-tightening" being called up instead. Typically, a fairly low torque wrench setting will be applied to the bolts/nuts in the correct sequence, followed by one or more stages of tightening through specified angles.

Locknuts, locktabs and washers

Any fastening which will rotate against a component or housing during tightening should always have a washer between it and the relevant component or housing.

Spring or split washers should always be renewed when they are used to lock a critical component such as a big-end bearing retaining bolt or nut. Locktabs which are folded over to retain a nut or bolt should always be renewed.

Self-locking nuts can be re-used in non-critical areas, providing resistance can be felt when the locking portion passes over the bolt or stud thread. However, it should be noted that self-locking stiffnuts tend to lose their effectiveness after long periods of use, and should then be renewed as a matter of course.

Split pins must always be replaced with new ones of the correct size for the hole.

When thread-locking compound is found on the threads of a fastener which is to be re-used, it should be cleaned off with a wire brush and solvent, and fresh compound applied on reassembly.

Special tools

Some repair procedures in this manual entail the use of special tools such as a press, two or three-legged pullers, spring compressors, etc. Wherever possible, suitable readily-available alternatives to the manufacturer's special tools are described, and are shown in use. In some instances, where no alternative is possible, it has been necessary to resort to the use of a manufacturer's tool, and this has been done for reasons of safety as well as the efficient completion of the repair operation. Unless you are highly-skilled and have a thorough understanding of the procedures described, never attempt to bypass the use of any special tool when the procedure described specifies its use. Not only is there a very great risk of personal injury, but expensive damage could be caused to the components involved.

Environmental considerations

When disposing of used engine oil, brake fluid, antifreeze, etc, give due consideration to any detrimental environmental effects. Do not, for instance, pour any of the above liquids down drains into the general sewage system, or onto the ground to soak away. Many local council refuse tips provide a facility for waste oil disposal, as do some garages. If none of these facilities are available, consult your local Environmental Health Department, or the National Rivers Authority, for further advice.

With the universal tightening-up of legislation regarding the emission of environmentally-harmful substances from motor vehicles, most vehicles have tamperproof devices fitted to the main adjustment points of the fuel system. These devices are primarily designed to prevent unqualified persons from adjusting the fuel/air mixture, with the chance of a consequent increase in toxic emissions. If such devices are found during servicing or overhaul, they should, wherever possible, be renewed or refitted in accordance with the manufacturer's requirements or current legislation.

OIL CARE
FOLLOW THE CODE
OIL BANK LINE
0800 66 33 66
www.oilbankline.org.uk

Note: It is antisocial and illegal to dump oil down the drain. To find the location of your local oil recycling bank, call this number free.

Jacking and vehicle s

The jack supplied with the vehicle tool kit should only be used for changing the roadwheels – see *Wheel changing* at the front of this book. When carrying out any other kind of work, raise the vehicle using a hydraulic (or 'trolley') jack, and always supplement the jack with axle stands positioned under the vehicle jacking points.

When using a hydraulic jack or axle stands, always position the jack head or axle stand head under one of the relevant jacking points.

To raise the front and/or rear of the vehicle, use the jacking/support points at the front and rear ends of the door sills, indicated by the triangular depressions in the sill panel **(see illustration)**. Position a block of wood with a groove cut in it on the jack head to prevent the vehicle weight resting on the sill edge; align the sill edge with the groove in the wood so that the vehicle weight is spread evenly over the surface of the block. Supplement the jack with axle stands (also with slotted blocks

of wood) positione
the jacking points (

Do not jack the ve
the sill, sump, floor p
suspension compone
an axle stand should
vehicle jack location p

⚠️ **Warning: Never work under, around, or near a raised car, unless it is adequately supported in at least two places.**

Front and rear jacking points (arrowed)

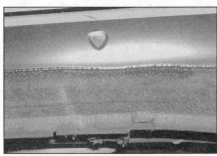

The jacking points are indicated by an arrow on the sill

Use an axle stand with a suitable block of wood

Disconnecting the battery

Caution: After reconnecting the battery, the safety function of the electric windows will not be re-instated until the windows have been reprogrammed. This could potentially cause severe pinching injuries.
Several of the systems require battery power to be available at all times (permanent live). This is either to ensure their continued operation (such as the clock), or to maintain electronic memory settings which would otherwise be erased. Whenever the battery is to be disconnected, first note the following points, to ensure there are no unforeseen consequences:

a) Firstly, on any vehicle with central door locking, it is a wise precaution to remove the key from the ignition, and to keep it with you. This avoids the possibility of the key being locked inside the car, should the central locking engage when the battery is reconnected.

b) If a security-coded audio unit is fitted, and the unit and/or the battery is disconnected, the unit will not function until the correct security code has been entered. Therefore, if you do not know the correct security code for the radio/cassette unit, **do not** disconnect either of the battery terminals, or remove the radio/cassette unit from the vehicle. The code appears on a code card suplied with the car when new. Details for entering the code appear in the vehicle handbook. Should the code have been misplaced or forgotten, on production of proof of ownership, a VW dealer or in-car entertainment specialist may be able to help.

c) The engine management system ECU is of the 'self-learning' type, meaning that, as it operates, it adapts to changes in operating conditions, and stores the optimum settings found (this is especially true for idle speed settings). When the battery is disconnected, these 'learned' settings are lost, and the ECU reverts to the base factory settings. When the engine is restarted, it may idle and run roughly until the ECU has 'relearned' the best settings. To further this 'learning' process, take the car for a road test of at least 15 minutes' duration, covering as many engine speeds and loads as possible, and concentrating on the 2000 to 4000 rpm range. On completion, let the engine idle for at least 10 minutes, turning the steering wheel occasionally and switching on high-current-draw equipment such as the heater fan or heated rear window. If the engine does not regain its normal performance, have the system checked for faults by a VW dealer.

d) On vehicles equipped with an original equipment anti-theft alarm system, before disconnecting the battery, de-activate the alarm system, otherwise the alarm will be triggered.

e) After the battery has been reconnected, the electric window 'closed' positions must be reprogrammed as follows. With the windows and sunroof closed, close all the doors and lock the vehicle manually at the driver's or passenger's door. Unlock the vehicle, then lock it again while

holding the key in the locked position for at least one second. The windows are now reprogrammed. Similarly, reprogram the electrically-adjustable driver's seat as follows. Open the driver's door and switch on the ignition, then move the seat cushion forwards and upwards onto the stop limit. Now move the seat backrest forwards onto its stop limit, and switch off the ignition.

f) When starting a petrol engine for the first time after having disconnected the battery, turn on the ignition for 30 seconds, then switch off the ignition – the engine may now be started.

Devices known as 'memory-savers' or 'code-savers' can be used to avoid some of the above problems. Precise details of use vary according to the device used. Typically, it is plugged into the cigarette lighter socket, and is connected by its own wiring to a spare battery; the vehicle battery is then disconnected from the electrical system, leaving the memory-saver to pass sufficient current to maintain audio unit security codes, and other memory values, and also to run permanently-live circuits such as the clock.

⚠️ **Warning: Some of these devices allow a considerable amount of currect to pass, which can mean that many of the vehicle's systems are still operational when the main battery is disconnected. If a memory-saver is used, ensure that the circuit concerned is actually 'dead' before carrying out any work on it.**

Tools and working facilities

Introduction

A selection of good tools is a fundamental requirement for anyone contemplating the maintenance and repair of a motor vehicle. For the owner who does not possess any, their purchase will prove a considerable expense, offsetting some of the savings made by doing-it-yourself. However, provided that the tools purchased meet the relevant national safety standards and are of good quality, they will last for many years and prove an extremely worthwhile investment.

To help the average owner to decide which tools are needed to carry out the various tasks detailed in this manual, we have compiled three lists of tools under the following headings: *Maintenance and minor repair*, *Repair and overhaul*, and *Special*. Newcomers to practical mechanics should start off with the *Maintenance and minor repair* tool kit, and confine themselves to the simpler jobs around the vehicle. Then, as confidence and experience grow, more difficult tasks can be undertaken, with extra tools being purchased as, and when, they are needed. In this way, a *Maintenance and minor repair* tool kit can be built up into a *Repair and overhaul* tool kit over a considerable period of time, without any major cash outlays. The experienced do-it-yourselfer will have a tool kit good enough for most repair and overhaul procedures, and will add tools from the *Special* category when it is felt that the expense is justified by the amount of use to which these tools will be put.

Maintenance and minor repair tool kit

The tools given in this list should be considered as a minimum requirement if routine maintenance, servicing and minor repair operations are to be undertaken. We recommend the purchase of combination spanners (ring one end, open-ended the other); although more expensive than open-ended ones, they do give the advantages of both types of spanner.

☐ *Combination spanners:*
  Metric - 8 to 19 mm inclusive
☐ *Adjustable spanner - 35 mm jaw (approx.)*
☐ *Spark plug spanner (with rubber insert) - petrol models*
☐ *Spark plug gap adjustment tool - petrol models*
☐ *Set of feeler gauges*
☐ *Brake bleed nipple spanner*
☐ *Screwdrivers:*
  Flat blade - 100 mm long x 6 mm dia
  Cross blade - 100 mm long x 6 mm dia
  Torx - various sizes (not all vehicles)
☐ *Combination pliers*
☐ *Hacksaw (junior)*
☐ *Tyre pump*
☐ *Tyre pressure gauge*
☐ *Oil can*
☐ *Oil filter removal tool*
☐ *Fine emery cloth*
☐ *Wire brush (small)*
☐ *Funnel (medium size)*
☐ *Sump drain plug key (not all vehicles)*

Repair and overhaul tool kit

These tools are virtually essential for anyone undertaking any major repairs to a motor vehicle, and are additional to those given in the *Maintenance and minor repair* list. Included in this list is a comprehensive set of sockets. Although these are expensive, they will be found invaluable as they are so versatile - particularly if various drives are included in the set. We recommend the half-inch square-drive type, as this can be used with most proprietary torque wrenches.

The tools in this list will sometimes need to be supplemented by tools from the *Special* list:

☐ *Sockets (or box spanners) to cover range in previous list (including Torx sockets)*
☐ *Reversible ratchet drive (for use with sockets)*
☐ *Extension piece, 250 mm (for use with sockets)*
☐ *Universal joint (for use with sockets)*
☐ *Flexible handle or sliding T "breaker bar" (for use with sockets)*
☐ *Torque wrench (for use with sockets)*
☐ *Self-locking grips*
☐ *Ball pein hammer*
☐ *Soft-faced mallet (plastic or rubber)*
☐ *Screwdrivers:*
  Flat blade - long & sturdy, short (chubby), and narrow (electrician's) types
  Cross blade - long & sturdy, and short (chubby) types
☐ *Pliers:*
  Long-nosed
  Side cutters (electrician's)
  Circlip (internal and external)
☐ *Cold chisel - 25 mm*
☐ *Scriber*
☐ *Scraper*
☐ *Centre-punch*
☐ *Pin punch*
☐ *Hacksaw*
☐ *Brake hose clamp*
☐ *Brake/clutch bleeding kit*
☐ *Selection of twist drills*
☐ *Steel rule/straight-edge*
☐ *Allen keys (inc. splined/Torx type)*
☐ *Selection of files*
☐ *Wire brush*
☐ *Axle stands*
☐ *Jack (strong trolley or hydraulic type)*
☐ *Light with extension lead*
☐ *Universal electrical multi-meter*

Sockets and reversible ratchet drive

Brake bleeding kit

Angular-tightening gauge

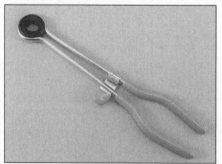

Hose clamp

Torx key, socket and bit

Special tools

The tools in this list are those which are not used regularly, are expensive to buy, or which need to be used in accordance with their manufacturers' instructions. Unless relatively difficult mechanical jobs are undertaken frequently, it will not be economic to buy many of these tools. Where this is the case, you could consider clubbing together with friends (or joining a motorists' club) to make a joint purchase, or borrowing the tools against a deposit from a local garage or tool hire specialist. It is worth noting that many of the larger DIY superstores now carry a large range of special tools for hire at modest rates.

The following list contains only those tools and instruments freely available to the public, and not those special tools produced by the vehicle manufacturer specifically for its dealer network. You will find occasional references to these manufacturers' special tools in the text of this manual. Generally, an alternative method of doing the job without the vehicle manufacturers' special tool is given. However, sometimes there is no alternative to using them. Where this is the case and the relevant tool cannot be bought or borrowed, you will have to entrust the work to a dealer.

☐ Angular-tightening gauge
☐ Valve spring compressor
☐ Valve grinding tool
☐ Piston ring compressor
☐ Piston ring removal/installation tool
☐ Cylinder bore hone
☐ Balljoint separator
☐ Coil spring compressors (where applicable)
☐ Two/three-legged hub and bearing puller
☐ Impact screwdriver
☐ Micrometer and/or vernier calipers
☐ Dial gauge
☐ Stroboscopic timing light
☐ Dwell angle meter/tachometer
☐ Fault code reader
☐ Cylinder compression gauge
☐ Hand-operated vacuum pump and gauge
☐ Clutch plate alignment set
☐ Brake shoe steady spring cup removal tool
☐ Bush and bearing removal/installation set
☐ Stud extractors
☐ Tap and die set
☐ Lifting tackle
☐ Trolley jack

Buying tools

Reputable motor accessory shops and superstores often offer excellent quality tools at discount prices, so it pays to shop around.

Remember, you don't have to buy the most expensive items on the shelf, but it is always advisable to steer clear of the very cheap tools. Beware of 'bargains' offered on market stalls or at car boot sales. There are plenty of good tools around at reasonable prices, but always aim to purchase items which meet the relevant national safety standards. If in doubt, ask the proprietor or manager of the shop for advice before making a purchase.

Care and maintenance of tools

Having purchased a reasonable tool kit, it is necessary to keep the tools in a clean and serviceable condition. After use, always wipe off any dirt, grease and metal particles using a clean, dry cloth, before putting the tools away. Never leave them lying around after they have been used. A simple tool rack on the garage or workshop wall for items such as screwdrivers and pliers is a good idea. Store all normal spanners and sockets in a metal box. Any measuring instruments, gauges, meters, etc, must be carefully stored where they cannot be damaged or become rusty.

Take a little care when tools are used. Hammer heads inevitably become marked, and screwdrivers lose the keen edge on their blades from time to time. A little timely attention with emery cloth or a file will soon restore items like this to a good finish.

Working facilities

Not to be forgotten when discussing tools is the workshop itself. If anything more than routine maintenance is to be carried out, a suitable working area becomes essential.

It is appreciated that many an owner-mechanic is forced by circumstances to remove an engine or similar item without the benefit of a garage or workshop. Having done this, any repairs should always be done under the cover of a roof.

Wherever possible, any dismantling should be done on a clean, flat workbench or table at a suitable working height.

Any workbench needs a vice; one with a jaw opening of 100 mm is suitable for most jobs. As mentioned previously, some clean dry storage space is also required for tools, as well as for any lubricants, cleaning fluids, touch-up paints etc, which become necessary.

Another item which may be required, and which has a much more general usage, is an electric drill with a chuck capacity of at least 8 mm. This, together with a good range of twist drills, is virtually essential for fitting accessories.

Last, but not least, always keep a supply of old newspapers and clean, lint-free rags available, and try to keep any working area as clean as possible.

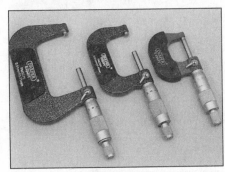

Micrometers

Dial test indicator ("dial gauge")

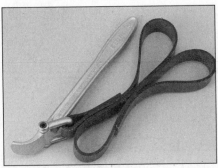

Strap wrench

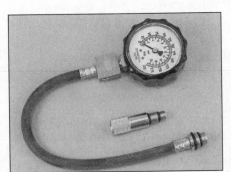

Compression tester

Fault code reader

This is a guide to getting your vehicle through the MOT test. Obviously it will not be possible to examine the vehicle to the same standard as the professional MOT tester. However, working through the following checks will enable you to identify any problem areas before submitting the vehicle for the test.

Where a testable component is in borderline condition, the tester has discretion in deciding whether to pass or fail it. The basis of such discretion is whether the tester would be happy for a close relative or friend to use the vehicle with the component in that condition. If the vehicle presented is clean and evidently well cared for, the tester may be more inclined to pass a borderline component than if the vehicle is scruffy and apparently neglected.

It has only been possible to summarise the test requirements here, based on the regulations in force at the time of printing. Test standards are becoming increasingly stringent, although there are some exemptions for older vehicles.

An assistant will be needed to help carry out some of these checks.

The checks have been sub-divided into four categories, as follows:

1 Checks carried out **FROM THE DRIVER'S SEAT**

2 Checks carried out **WITH THE VEHICLE ON THE GROUND**

3 Checks carried out **WITH THE VEHICLE RAISED AND THE WHEELS FREE TO TURN**

4 Checks carried out on **YOUR VEHICLE'S EXHAUST EMISSION SYSTEM**

---

1 Checks carried out **FROM THE DRIVER'S SEAT**

Handbrake

□ Test the operation of the handbrake. Excessive travel (too many clicks) indicates incorrect brake or cable adjustment.
□ Check that the handbrake cannot be released by tapping the lever sideways. Check the security of the lever mountings.

Footbrake

□ Depress the brake pedal and check that it does not creep down to the floor, indicating a master cylinder fault. Release the pedal, wait a few seconds, then depress it again. If the pedal travels nearly to the floor before firm resistance is felt, brake adjustment or repair is necessary. If the pedal feels spongy, there is air in the hydraulic system which must be removed by bleeding.

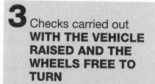

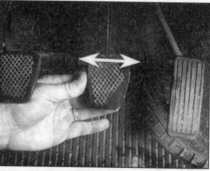

□ Check that the brake pedal is secure and in good condition. Check also for signs of fluid leaks on the pedal, floor or carpets, which would indicate failed seals in the brake master cylinder.
□ Check the servo unit (when applicable) by operating the brake pedal several times, then keeping the pedal depressed and starting the engine. As the engine starts, the pedal will move down slightly. If not, the vacuum hose or the servo itself may be faulty.

Steering wheel and column

□ Examine the steering wheel for fractures or looseness of the hub, spokes or rim.
□ Move the steering wheel from side to side and then up and down. Check that the steering wheel is not loose on the column, indicating wear or a loose retaining nut. Continue moving the steering wheel as before, but also turn it slightly from left to right.
□ Check that the steering wheel is not loose on the column, and that there is no abnormal

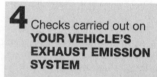

movement of the steering wheel, indicating wear in the column support bearings or couplings.

Windscreen, mirrors and sunvisor

□ The windscreen must be free of cracks or other significant damage within the driver's field of view. (Small stone chips are acceptable.) Rear view mirrors must be secure, intact, and capable of being adjusted.

290mm

□ The driver's sunvisor must be capable of being stored in the "up" position.

Seat belts and seats

Note: *The following checks are applicable to all seat belts, front and rear.*

☐ Examine the webbing of all the belts (including rear belts if fitted) for cuts, serious fraying or deterioration. Fasten and unfasten each belt to check the buckles. If applicable, check the retracting mechanism. Check the security of all seat belt mountings accessible from inside the vehicle.

☐ Seat belts with pre-tensioners, once activated, have a "flag" or similar showing on the seat belt stalk. This, in itself, is not a reason for test failure.

☐ The front seats themselves must be securely attached and the backrests must lock in the upright position.

Doors

☐ Both front doors must be able to be opened and closed from outside and inside, and must latch securely when closed.

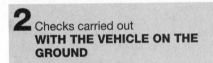

2 Checks carried out WITH THE VEHICLE ON THE GROUND

Vehicle identification

☐ Number plates must be in good condition, secure and legible, with letters and numbers correctly spaced – spacing at (A) should be at least twice that at (B).

☐ The VIN plate and/or homologation plate must be legible.

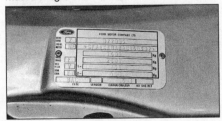

Electrical equipment

☐ Switch on the ignition and check the operation of the horn.

☐ Check the windscreen washers and wipers, examining the wiper blades; renew damaged or perished blades. Also check the operation of the stop-lights.

☐ Check the operation of the sidelights and number plate lights. The lenses and reflectors must be secure, clean and undamaged.

☐ Check the operation and alignment of the headlights. The headlight reflectors must not be tarnished and the lenses must be undamaged.

☐ Switch on the ignition and check the operation of the direction indicators (including the instrument panel tell-tale) and the hazard warning lights. Operation of the sidelights and stop-lights must not affect the indicators - if it does, the cause is usually a bad earth at the rear light cluster.

☐ Check the operation of the rear foglight(s), including the warning light on the instrument panel or in the switch.

☐ The ABS warning light must illuminate in accordance with the manufacturers' design. For most vehicles, the ABS warning light should illuminate when the ignition is switched on, and (if the system is operating properly) extinguish after a few seconds. Refer to the owner's handbook.

Footbrake

☐ Examine the master cylinder, brake pipes and servo unit for leaks, loose mountings, corrosion or other damage.

☐ The fluid reservoir must be secure and the fluid level must be between the upper (**A**) and lower (**B**) markings.

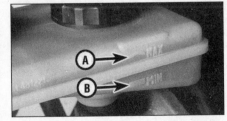

☐ Inspect both front brake flexible hoses for cracks or deterioration of the rubber. Turn the steering from lock to lock, and ensure that the hoses do not contact the wheel, tyre, or any part of the steering or suspension mechanism. With the brake pedal firmly depressed, check the hoses for bulges or leaks under pressure.

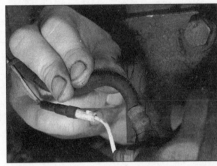

Steering and suspension

☐ Have your assistant turn the steering wheel from side to side slightly, up to the point where the steering gear just begins to transmit this movement to the roadwheels. Check for excessive free play between the steering wheel and the steering gear, indicating wear or insecurity of the steering column joints, the column-to-steering gear coupling, or the steering gear itself.

☐ Have your assistant turn the steering wheel more vigorously in each direction, so that the roadwheels just begin to turn. As this is done, examine all the steering joints, linkages, fittings and attachments. Renew any component that shows signs of wear or damage. On vehicles with power steering, check the security and condition of the steering pump, drivebelt and hoses.

☐ Check that the vehicle is standing level, and at approximately the correct ride height.

Shock absorbers

☐ Depress each corner of the vehicle in turn, then release it. The vehicle should rise and then settle in its normal position. If the vehicle continues to rise and fall, the shock absorber is defective. A shock absorber which has seized will also cause the vehicle to fail.

Exhaust system

☐ Start the engine. With your assistant holding a rag over the tailpipe, check the entire system for leaks. Repair or renew leaking sections.

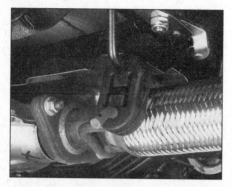

3 Checks carried out **WITH THE VEHICLE RAISED AND THE WHEELS FREE TO TURN**

Jack up the front and rear of the vehicle, and securely support it on axle stands. Position the stands clear of the suspension assemblies. Ensure that the wheels are clear of the ground and that the steering can be turned from lock to lock.

Steering mechanism

☐ Have your assistant turn the steering from lock to lock. Check that the steering turns smoothly, and that no part of the steering mechanism, including a wheel or tyre, fouls any brake hose or pipe or any part of the body structure.
☐ Examine the steering rack rubber gaiters for damage or insecurity of the retaining clips. If power steering is fitted, check for signs of damage or leakage of the fluid hoses, pipes or connections. Also check for excessive stiffness or binding of the steering, a missing split pin or locking device, or severe corrosion of the body structure within 30 cm of any steering component attachment point.

Front and rear suspension and wheel bearings

☐ Starting at the front right-hand side, grasp the roadwheel at the 3 o'clock and 9 o'clock positions and rock gently but firmly. Check for free play or insecurity at the wheel bearings, suspension balljoints, or suspension mountings, pivots and attachments.
☐ Now grasp the wheel at the 12 o'clock and 6 o'clock positions and repeat the previous inspection. Spin the wheel, and check for roughness or tightness of the front wheel bearing.

☐ If excess free play is suspected at a component pivot point, this can be confirmed by using a large screwdriver or similar tool and levering between the mounting and the component attachment. This will confirm whether the wear is in the pivot bush, its retaining bolt, or in the mounting itself (the bolt holes can often become elongated).

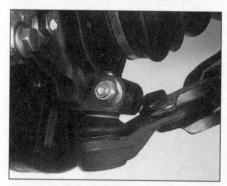

☐ Carry out all the above checks at the other front wheel, and then at both rear wheels.

Springs and shock absorbers

☐ Examine the suspension struts (when applicable) for serious fluid leakage, corrosion, or damage to the casing. Also check the security of the mounting points.
☐ If coil springs are fitted, check that the spring ends locate in their seats, and that the spring is not corroded, cracked or broken.
☐ If leaf springs are fitted, check that all leaves are intact, that the axle is securely attached to each spring, and that there is no deterioration of the spring eye mountings, bushes, and shackles.

☐ The same general checks apply to vehicles fitted with other suspension types, such as torsion bars, hydraulic displacer units, etc. Ensure that all mountings and attachments are secure, that there are no signs of excessive wear, corrosion or damage, and (on hydraulic types) that there are no fluid leaks or damaged pipes.
☐ Inspect the shock absorbers for signs of serious fluid leakage. Check for wear of the mounting bushes or attachments, or damage to the body of the unit.

Driveshafts (fwd vehicles only)

☐ Rotate each front wheel in turn and inspect the constant velocity joint gaiters for splits or damage. Also check that each driveshaft is straight and undamaged.

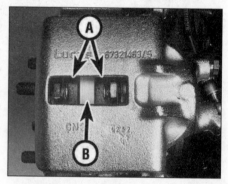

Braking system

☐ If possible without dismantling, check brake pad wear and disc condition. Ensure that the friction lining material has not worn excessively, (A) and that the discs are not fractured, pitted, scored or badly worn (B).

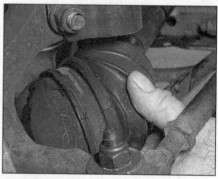

☐ Examine all the rigid brake pipes underneath the vehicle, and the flexible hose(s) at the rear. Look for corrosion, chafing or insecurity of the pipes, and for signs of bulging under pressure, chafing, splits or deterioration of the flexible hoses.
☐ Look for signs of fluid leaks at the brake calipers or on the brake backplates. Repair or renew leaking components.
☐ Slowly spin each wheel, while your assistant depresses and releases the footbrake. Ensure that each brake is operating and does not bind when the pedal is released.

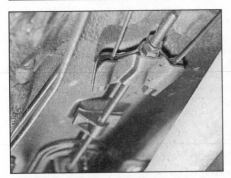

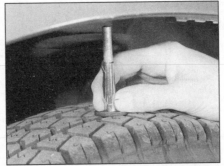

□ Examine the handbrake mechanism, checking for frayed or broken cables, excessive corrosion, or wear or insecurity of the linkage. Check that the mechanism works on each relevant wheel, and releases fully, without binding.

□ It is not possible to test brake efficiency without special equipment, but a road test can be carried out later to check that the vehicle pulls up in a straight line.

Fuel and exhaust systems

□ Inspect the fuel tank (including the filler cap), fuel pipes, hoses and unions. All components must be secure and free from leaks.

□ Examine the exhaust system over its entire length, checking for any damaged, broken or missing mountings, security of the retaining clamps and rust or corrosion.

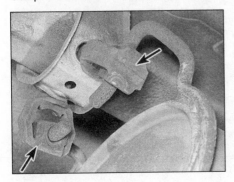

Wheels and tyres

□ Examine the sidewalls and tread area of each tyre in turn. Check for cuts, tears, lumps, bulges, separation of the tread, and exposure of the ply or cord due to wear or damage. Check that the tyre bead is correctly seated on the wheel rim, that the valve is sound and properly seated, and that the wheel is not distorted or damaged.

□ Check that the tyres are of the correct size for the vehicle, that they are of the same size

and type on each axle, and that the pressures are correct.

□ Check the tyre tread depth. The legal minimum at the time of writing is 1.6 mm over at least three-quarters of the tread width. Abnormal tread wear may indicate incorrect front wheel alignment.

Body corrosion

□ Check the condition of the entire vehicle structure for signs of corrosion in load-bearing areas. (These include chassis box sections, side sills, cross-members, pillars, and all suspension, steering, braking system and seat belt mountings and anchorages.) Any corrosion which has seriously reduced the thickness of a load-bearing area is likely to cause the vehicle to fail. In this case professional repairs are likely to be needed.

□ Damage or corrosion which causes sharp or otherwise dangerous edges to be exposed will also cause the vehicle to fail.

4 Checks carried out on YOUR VEHICLE'S EXHAUST EMISSION SYSTEM

Petrol models

□ The engine should be warmed up, and running well (ignition system in good order, air filter element clean, etc).

□ Before testing, run the engine at around 2500 rpm for 20 seconds. Let the engine drop to idle, and watch for smoke from the exhaust. If the idle speed is too high, or if dense blue or black smoke emerges for more than 5 seconds, the vehicle will fail. Typically, blue smoke signifies oil burning (engine wear); black smoke means unburnt fuel (dirty air cleaner element, or other fuel system fault).

□ An exhaust gas analyser for measuring carbon monoxide (CO) and hydrocarbons (HC) is now needed. If one cannot be hired or borrowed, have a local garage perform the check.

CO emissions (mixture)

□ The MOT tester has access to the CO limits for all vehicles. The CO level is measured at idle speed, and at 'fast idle' (2500 to 3000 rpm). The following limits are given as a general guide:

At idle speed – Less than 0.5% CO
At 'fast idle' – Less than 0.3% CO
Lambda reading – 0.97 to 1.03

□ If the CO level is too high, this may point to poor maintenance, a fuel injection system problem, faulty lambda (oxygen) sensor or catalytic converter. Try an injector cleaning treatment, and check the vehicle's ECU for fault codes.

HC emissions

□ The MOT tester has access to HC limits for all vehicles. The HC level is measured at 'fast idle' (2500 to 3000 rpm). The following limits are given as a general guide:

At 'fast idle' – Less then 200 ppm

□ Excessive HC emissions are typically caused by oil being burnt (worn engine), or by a blocked crankcase ventilation system ('breather'). If the engine oil is old and thin, an oil change may help. If the engine is running badly, check the vehicle's ECU for fault codes.

Diesel models

□ The only emission test for diesel engines is measuring exhaust smoke density, using a calibrated smoke meter. The test involves accelerating the engine at least 3 times to its maximum unloaded speed.

Note: *On engines with a timing belt, it is VITAL that the belt is in good condition before the test is carried out.*

□ With the engine warmed up, it is first purged by running at around 2500 rpm for 20 seconds. A governor check is then carried out, by slowly accelerating the engine to its maximum speed. After this, the smoke meter is connected, and the engine is accelerated quickly to maximum speed three times. If the smoke density is less than the limits given below, the vehicle will pass:

Non-turbo vehicles: 2.5m-1
Turbocharged vehicles: 3.0m-1

□ If excess smoke is produced, try fitting a new air cleaner element, or using an injector cleaning treatment. If the engine is running badly, where applicable, check the vehicle's ECU for fault codes. Also check the vehicle's EGR system, where applicable. At high mileages, the injectors may require professional attention.

Engine

- [ ] Engine fails to rotate when attempting to start
- [ ] Engine rotates, but will not start
- [ ] Engine difficult to start when cold
- [ ] Engine difficult to start when hot
- [ ] Starter motor noisy or excessively-rough in engagement
- [ ] Engine starts, but stops immediately
- [ ] Engine idles erratically
- [ ] Engine misfires at idle speed
- [ ] Engine misfires throughout the driving speed range
- [ ] Engine hesitates on acceleration
- [ ] Engine stalls
- [ ] Engine lacks power
- [ ] Engine backfires
- [ ] Oil pressure warning light illuminated with engine running
- [ ] Engine runs-on after switching off
- [ ] Engine noises

Cooling system

- [ ] Overheating
- [ ] Overcooling
- [ ] External coolant leakage
- [ ] Internal coolant leakage
- [ ] Corrosion

Fuel and exhaust systems

- [ ] Excessive fuel consumption
- [ ] Fuel leakage and/or fuel odour

Clutch

- [ ] Pedal travels to floor – no pressure or very little resistance
- [ ] Clutch fails to disengage (unable to select gears).
- [ ] Clutch slips (engine speed increases, with no increase in vehicle speed).
- [ ] Judder as clutch is engaged
- [ ] Noise when depressing or releasing clutch pedal

Manual transmission

- [ ] Noisy in neutral with engine running
- [ ] Noisy in one particular gear
- [ ] Difficulty engaging gears
- [ ] Vibration
- [ ] Jumps out of gear
- [ ] Lubricant leaks

Automatic transmission

- [ ] Fluid leakage
- [ ] General gear selection problems
- [ ] Transmission fluid brown, or has burned smell
- [ ] Transmission will not downshift (kickdown) with accelerator fully depressed
- [ ] Engine will not start in any gear, or starts in gears other than Park or Neutral
- [ ] Transmission slips, shifts roughly, is noisy, or has no drive in forward or reverse gears

Braking system

- [ ] Vehicle pulls to one side under braking
- [ ] Noise (grinding or high-pitched squeal) when brakes applied
- [ ] Brakes binding
- [ ] Excessive brake pedal travel
- [ ] Brake pedal feels spongy when depressed
- [ ] Excessive brake pedal effort required to stop vehicle
- [ ] Judder felt through brake pedal or steering wheel when braking
- [ ] Rear wheels locking under normal braking

Driveshafts

- [ ] Clicking or knocking noise on turns (at slow speed on full-lock)

Suspension and steering

- [ ] Vehicle pulls to one side
- [ ] Excessive pitching and/or rolling around corners, or during braking
- [ ] Lack of power assistance
- [ ] Wandering or general instability
- [ ] Excessively-stiff steering
- [ ] Excessive play in steering
- [ ] Wheel wobble and vibration
- [ ] Tyre wear excessive

Electrical system

- [ ] Battery will not hold a charge for more than a few days
- [ ] Ignition/no-charge warning light remains illuminated with engine running
- [ ] Ignition/no-charge warning light fails to come on
- [ ] Lights inoperative
- [ ] Instrument readings inaccurate or erratic
- [ ] Horn inoperative, or unsatisfactory in operation
- [ ] Windscreen wipers inoperative, or unsatisfactory in operation
- [ ] Windscreen washers inoperative, or unsatisfactory in operation
- [ ] Electric windows inoperative, or unsatisfactory in operation
- [ ] Central locking system inoperative, or unsatisfactory in operation

Introduction

The vehicle owner who does his or her own maintenance according to the recommended service schedules should not have to use this section of the manual very often. Modern component reliability is such that, provided those items subject to wear or deterioration are inspected or renewed at the specified intervals, sudden failure is comparatively rare. Faults do not usually just happen as a result of sudden failure, but develop over a period of time. Major mechanical failures in particular are usually preceded by characteristic symptoms over hundreds or even thousands of miles. Those components that do

occasionally fail without warning are often small and easily carried in the vehicle.

With any fault-finding, the first step is to decide where to begin investigations. Sometimes this is obvious, but on other occasions, a little detective work will be necessary. The owner who makes half a dozen haphazard adjustments or component renewals may be successful in curing a fault (or its symptoms). However, will be none the wiser if the fault recurs, and ultimately may have spent more time and money than was necessary. A calm and logical approach will be found to be more satisfactory in the long

run. Always take into account any warning signs or abnormalities that may have been noticed in the period preceding the fault – power loss, high or low gauge readings, unusual smells, etc – and remember that failure of components such as fuses or spark plugs may only be pointers to some underlying fault.

The pages which follow provide an easy-reference guide to the more common problems which may occur during the operation of the vehicle. These problems and their possible causes are grouped under headings denoting various components or systems, such as

Engine, Cooling system, etc. The general Chapter which deals with the problem is also shown in brackets; refer to the relevant part of that Chapter for system-specific information. Whatever the fault, certain basic principles apply. These are as follows:

Verify the fault. This is simply a matter of being sure that you know what the symptoms are before starting work. This is particularly important if you are investigating a fault for someone else, who may not have described it very accurately.

Do not overlook the obvious. For example, if the vehicle will not start, is there petrol in the tank? (Do not take anyone else's word on this particular point, and do not trust the fuel gauge either!) If an electrical fault is indicated, look for loose or broken wires before digging out the test gear.

Cure the disease, not the symptom. Substituting a flat battery with a fully-charged one will get you off the hard shoulder, but if the underlying cause is not attended to, the new battery will go the same way. Similarly, changing oil-fouled spark plugs for a new set will get you moving again, but remember that the reason for the fouling (if it was not simply an incorrect grade of plug) will have to be established and corrected.

Do not take anything for granted. Particularly, do not forget that a new component may itself be defective (especially if it's been rattling around in the boot for months). Also do not leave components out of a fault diagnosis sequence just because they are new or recently fitted. When you do finally diagnose a difficult fault, you will probably realise that all the evidence was there from the start.

Engine

Engine fails to rotate when attempting to start

- [ ] Battery terminal connections loose or corroded (Weekly checks).
- [ ] Battery discharged or faulty (Chapter 5A).
- [ ] Broken, loose or disconnected wiring in the starting circuit (Chapter 5A).
- [ ] Defective starter solenoid or switch (Chapter 5A).
- [ ] Defective starter motor (Chapter 5A).
- [ ] Starter pinion or flywheel ring gear teeth loose or broken (Chapters 2A, 2B, 2C and 5A).
- [ ] Engine earth strap broken or disconnected (Chapter 5A).

Engine rotates, but will not start

- [ ] Fuel tank empty.
- [ ] Battery discharged (engine rotates slowly) (Chapter 5A).
- [ ] Battery terminal connections loose or corroded (Weekly checks).
- [ ] Ignition components damp or damaged – petrol models (Chapters 1A and 5B).
- [ ] Broken, loose or disconnected wiring in the ignition circuit – petrol models (Chapters 1A and 5B).
- [ ] Worn, faulty or incorrectly gapped spark plugs – petrol models (Chapter 1A).
- [ ] Fuel injection system fault (Chapter 4A and 4B).
- [ ] Stop solenoid faulty – diesel models (Chapter 4B).
- [ ] Air in fuel system – diesel models (Chapter 4B).
- [ ] Major mechanical failure (eg, timing belt) (Chapter 2A, 2B or 2C).

Engine difficult to start when cold

- [ ] Battery discharged (Chapter 5A).
- [ ] Battery terminal connections loose or corroded (Weekly checks).
- [ ] Worn, faulty or incorrectly gapped spark plugs – petrol models (Chapter 1A).
- [ ] Fuel injection system fault (Chapter 4A and 4B).
- [ ] Other ignition system fault – petrol models (Chapters 1A and 5B).
- [ ] Preheating system fault – diesel models (Chapter 5C).
- [ ] Low cylinder compressions (Chapter 2A, 2B or 2C).

Engine difficult to start when hot

- [ ] Air filter element dirty or clogged (Chapter 1A or 1B).
- [ ] Fuel injection system fault (Chapter 4A and 4B).
- [ ] Low cylinder compressions (Chapter 2A, 2B or 2C).

Starter motor noisy or excessively rough in engagement

- [ ] Starter pinion or flywheel ring gear teeth loose or broken (Chapters 2A, 2B, 2C and 5A).
- [ ] Starter motor mounting bolts loose or missing (Chapter 5A).
- [ ] Starter motor internal components worn or damaged (Chapter 5A).

Engine starts, but stops immediately

- [ ] Loose or faulty electrical connections in the ignition circuit – petrol models (Chapters 1A and 5B).
- [ ] Vacuum leak at the throttle body or inlet manifold – petrol models (Chapter 4A).
- [ ] Blocked injector/fuel injection system fault (Chapter 4A or 4B).
- [ ] Faulty injector(s) – diesel models (Chapter 4B).
- [ ] Air in fuel system – diesel models (Chapter 4B).

Engine idles erratically

- [ ] Air filter element clogged (Chapter 1A or 1B).
- [ ] Vacuum leak at the throttle body, inlet manifold or associated hoses – petrol models (Chapter 4A).
- [ ] Worn, faulty or incorrectly gapped spark plugs – petrol models (Chapter 1A).
- [ ] Uneven or low cylinder compressions (Chapter 2A, 2B or 2C).
- [ ] Camshaft lobes worn (Chapter 2A, 2B or 2C).
- [ ] Timing belt incorrectly tensioned (Chapter 2A, 2B or 2C).
- [ ] Blocked injector/fuel injection system fault (Chapter 4A or 4B).
- [ ] Faulty injector(s) – diesel models (Chapter 4B).

Engine misfires at idle speed

- [ ] Worn, faulty or incorrectly gapped spark plugs – petrol models (Chapter 1A).
- [ ] Faulty spark plug HT leads – petrol models (Chapter 5B).
- [ ] Vacuum leak at the throttle body, inlet manifold or associated hoses (Chapter 4A or 4B).
- [ ] Blocked injector/fuel injection system fault (Chapter 4A and 4B).
- [ ] Faulty injector(s) – diesel models (Chapter 4B).
- [ ] Uneven or low cylinder compressions (Chapter 2A, 2B or 2C).
- [ ] Disconnected, leaking, or perished crankcase ventilation hoses (Chapter 4C and 4D).

Engine misfires throughout the driving speed range

- [ ] Fuel filter choked (Chapter 1A or 1B).
- [ ] Fuel pump faulty, or delivery pressure low (Chapter 4A or 4B).
- [ ] Fuel tank vent blocked, or fuel pipes restricted (Chapter 4A or 4B).
- [ ] Vacuum leak at the throttle body, inlet manifold or associated hoses – petrol models (Chapter 4A).
- [ ] Worn, faulty or incorrectly gapped spark plugs – petrol models (Chapter 1A).
- [ ] Faulty spark plug HT leads (Chapter 5B).
- [ ] Faulty injector(s) – diesel models (Chapter 4B).
- [ ] Faulty ignition coil – petrol models (Chapter 5B).
- [ ] Uneven or low cylinder compressions (Chapter 2A, 2B or 2C).
- [ ] Blocked injector/fuel injection system fault (Chapter 4A or 4B).

Engine (continued)

Engine hesitates on acceleration

- ☐ Worn, faulty or incorrectly gapped spark plugs – petrol models (Chapter 1A).
- ☐ Vacuum leak at the throttle body, inlet manifold or associated hoses – petrol models (Chapter 4A).
- ☐ Blocked injector/fuel injection system fault (Chapter 4A or 4B).
- ☐ Faulty injector(s) – diesel models (Chapter 4B).
- ☐ Incorrect injection pump timing – diesel models (Chapter 4B).

Engine stalls

- ☐ Vacuum leak at the throttle body, inlet manifold or associated hoses – petrol models (Chapter 4A).
- ☐ Fuel filter choked (Chapter 1A or 1B).
- ☐ Fuel pump faulty, or delivery pressure low – petrol models (Chapter 4A).
- ☐ Fuel tank vent blocked, or fuel pipes restricted (Chapter 4A or 4B).
- ☐ Blocked injector/fuel injection system fault (Chapter 4A or 4B).
- ☐ Faulty injector(s) – diesel models (Chapter 4B).
- ☐ Air in fuel system – diesel models (Chapter 4B).

Engine lacks power

- ☐ Timing belt incorrectly fitted or tensioned (Chapter 2A, 2B or 2C).
- ☐ Fuel filter choked (Chapter 1A or 1B).
- ☐ Fuel pump faulty, or delivery pressure low – petrol models (Chapter 4A).
- ☐ Uneven or low cylinder compressions (Chapter 2A, 2B or 2C).
- ☐ Worn, faulty or incorrectly gapped spark plugs – petrol models (Chapter 1A).
- ☐ Vacuum leak at the throttle body, inlet manifold or associated hoses – petrol models (Chapter 4A).
- ☐ Blocked injector/fuel injection system fault (Chapter 4A or 4B).
- ☐ Injection pump timing incorrect – diesel models (Chapter 4B).
- ☐ Brakes binding (Chapters 1A or 1B and 9).
- ☐ Clutch slipping (Chapter 6).

Engine backfires

- ☐ Timing belt incorrectly fitted or tensioned (Chapter 2A, 2B or 2C).
- ☐ Vacuum leak at the throttle body, inlet manifold or associated hoses – petrol models (Chapter 4A).
- ☐ Blocked injector/fuel injection system fault (Chapter 4A or 4B).

Oil pressure warning light illuminated with engine running

- ☐ Low oil level, or incorrect oil grade (Weekly checks).
- ☐ Faulty oil pressure warning light switch (Chapter 2A, 2B or 2C).

- ☐ Worn engine bearings and/or oil pump (Chapter 2A, 2B or 2C).
- ☐ High engine operating temperature (Chapter 3).
- ☐ Oil pressure relief valve defective (Chapter 2A, 2B or 2C).
- ☐ Oil pick-up strainer clogged (Chapter 2A, 2B or 2C).

Engine runs-on after switching off

- ☐ Excessive carbon build-up in engine (Chapter 2A, 2B or 2C).
- ☐ High engine operating temperature (Chapter 3).
- ☐ Fuel injection system fault – petrol models (Chapter 4A).
- ☐ Faulty stop solenoid – diesel models (Chapter 4B).

Engine noises

Pre-ignition (pinking) or knocking during acceleration or under load

- ☐ Ignition timing incorrect/ignition system fault – petrol models (Chapters 1A and 5B).
- ☐ Incorrect grade of spark plug – petrol models (Chapter 1A).
- ☐ Incorrect grade of fuel (Chapter 4A).
- ☐ Vacuum leak at the throttle body, inlet manifold or associated hoses – petrol models (Chapter 4A).
- ☐ Excessive carbon build-up in engine (Chapter 2A, 2B or 2C).
- ☐ Blocked injector/fuel injection system fault – petrol models (Chapter 4A).

Whistling or wheezing noises

- ☐ Leaking inlet manifold or throttle body gasket – petrol models (Chapter 4A).
- ☐ Leaking exhaust manifold gasket or pipe-to-manifold joint (Chapter 4C or 4D).
- ☐ Leaking vacuum hose (Chapters 4A, 4B, 4C, 4D and 9).
- ☐ Blowing cylinder head gasket (Chapter 2A, 2B or 2C).

Tapping or rattling noises

- ☐ Worn valve gear or camshaft (Chapter 2A, 2B or 2C).
- ☐ Ancillary component fault (coolant pump, alternator, etc) (Chapters 3, 5A, etc).

Knocking or thumping noises

- ☐ Worn big-end bearings (regular heavy knocking, perhaps worsening under load) (Chapter 2D).
- ☐ Worn main bearings (rumbling and knocking, perhaps less under load) (Chapter 2D).
- ☐ Piston slap (most noticeable when cold) (Chapter 2D).
- ☐ Ancillary component fault (coolant pump, alternator, etc) (Chapters 3, 5A, etc).

Cooling system

Overheating

- ☐ Insufficient coolant in system (Weekly checks).
- ☐ Thermostat faulty (Chapter 3).
- ☐ Radiator core blocked, or grille restricted (Chapter 3).
- ☐ Electric cooling fan or thermoswitch faulty (Chapter 3).
- ☐ Pressure cap faulty (Chapter 3).
- ☐ Ignition timing incorrect/ignition system fault – petrol engines (Chapters 1A and 5B).
- ☐ Inaccurate temperature gauge sender unit (Chapter 3).
- ☐ Airlock in cooling system.

Overcooling

- ☐ Thermostat faulty (Chapter 3).
- ☐ Inaccurate temperature gauge sender unit (Chapter 3).

External coolant leakage

- ☐ Deteriorated or damaged hoses or hose clips (Chapter 1A or 1B).
- ☐ Radiator core or heater matrix leaking (Chapter 3).
- ☐ Pressure cap faulty (Chapter 3).
- ☐ Water pump seal leaking (Chapter 3).
- ☐ Boiling due to overheating (Chapter 3).
- ☐ Core plug leaking (Chapter 2D).

Internal coolant leakage

- ☐ Leaking cylinder head gasket (Chapter 2A, 2B or 2C).
- ☐ Cracked cylinder head or cylinder bore (Chapter 2D).

Corrosion

- ☐ Infrequent draining and flushing (Chapter 1A or 1B).
- ☐ Incorrect coolant mixture or inappropriate coolant type (Chapter 1A or 1B).

Fuel and exhaust systems

Excessive fuel consumption

☐ Air filter element dirty or clogged (Chapter 1A or 1B).
☐ Fuel injection system fault (Chapter 4A or 4B).
☐ Ignition timing incorrect/ignition system fault – petrol models (Chapters 1A and 5B).
☐ Faulty injector(s) – diesel models (Chapter 4B).
☐ Tyres under-inflated (Weekly checks).

Fuel leakage and/or fuel odour

☐ Damaged or corroded fuel tank, pipes or connections (Chapter 4A or 4B).
☐ Excessive noise or fumes from exhaust system
☐ Leaking exhaust system or manifold joints (Chapters 1A, 1B, 4C or 4D).
☐ Leaking, corroded or damaged silencers or pipe (Chapters 1A, 1B, 4C or 4D).
☐ Broken mountings causing body or suspension contact (Chapter 1A or 1B).

Clutch

Pedal travels to floor – no pressure or very little resistance

☐ Hydraulic fluid level low/air in hydraulic system (Chapter 6).
☐ Broken clutch release bearing or fork (Chapter 6).
☐ Broken diaphragm spring in clutch pressure plate (Chapter 6).

Clutch fails to disengage (unable to select gears)

☐ Clutch disc sticking on transmission input shaft splines (Chapter 6).
☐ Clutch disc sticking to flywheel or pressure plate (Chapter 6).
☐ Faulty pressure plate assembly (Chapter 6).
☐ Clutch release mechanism worn or incorrectly assembled (Chapter 6).

Clutch slips (engine speed increases, with no increase in vehicle speed)

☐ Clutch disc linings excessively worn (Chapter 6).

☐ Clutch disc linings contaminated with oil or grease (Chapter 6).
☐ Faulty pressure plate or weak diaphragm spring (Chapter 6).

Judder as clutch is engaged

☐ Clutch disc linings contaminated with oil or grease (Chapter 6).
☐ Clutch disc linings excessively worn (Chapter 6).
☐ Faulty or distorted pressure plate or diaphragm spring (Chapter 6).
☐ Worn or loose engine or transmission mountings (Chapter 2A, 2B or 2C).
☐ Clutch disc hub or transmission input shaft splines worn (Chapter 6).

Noise when depressing or releasing clutch pedal

☐ Worn clutch release bearing (Chapter 6).
☐ Worn or dry clutch pedal bushes (Chapter 6).
☐ Faulty pressure plate assembly (Chapter 6).
☐ Pressure plate diaphragm spring broken (Chapter 6).
☐ Broken clutch disc cushioning springs (Chapter 6).

Manual transmission

Noisy in neutral with engine running

☐ Input shaft bearings worn (noise apparent with clutch pedal released, but not when depressed) (Chapter 7A).*
☐ Clutch release bearing worn (noise apparent with clutch pedal depressed, possibly less when released) (Chapter 6).

Noisy in one particular gear

☐ Worn, damaged or chipped gear teeth (Chapter 7A).*

Difficulty engaging gears

☐ Clutch fault (Chapter 6).
☐ Worn or damaged gear linkage (Chapter 7A).
☐ Incorrectly adjusted gear linkage (Chapter 7A).
☐ Worn synchroniser units (Chapter 7A).*

Vibration

☐ Lack of oil (Chapter 1A or 1B).
☐ Worn bearings (Chapter 7A).*

Jumps out of gear

☐ Worn or damaged gear linkage (Chapter 7A).
☐ Incorrectly adjusted gear linkage (Chapter 7A).
☐ Worn synchroniser units (Chapter 7A).*
☐ Worn selector forks (Chapter 7A).*

Lubricant leaks

☐ Leaking differential output oil seal (Chapter 7A).
☐ Leaking housing joint (Chapter 7A).*
☐ Leaking input shaft oil seal (Chapter 7A).*

* Although the corrective action necessary to remedy the symptoms described is beyond the scope of the home mechanic, the above information should be helpful in isolating the cause of the condition. This should enable the owner can communicate clearly with a professional mechanic.

Automatic transmission

Note: *Due to the complexity of the automatic transmission, it is difficult for the home mechanic to properly diagnose and service this unit. For problems other than the following, the vehicle should be taken to a dealer service department or automatic transmission specialist. Do not be too hasty in removing the transmission if a fault is suspected, as most of the testing is carried out with the unit still fitted.*

Fluid leakage

☐ Automatic transmission fluid is usually dark in colour. Fluid leaks should not be confused with engine oil, which can easily be blown onto the transmission by airflow.

☐ To determine the source of a leak, first remove all built-up dirt and grime from the transmission housing and surrounding areas using a degreasing agent, or by steam-cleaning. Drive the vehicle at low speed, so airflow will not blow the leak far from its source. Raise and support the vehicle, and determine where the leak is coming from.

General gear selection problems

☐ Chapter 7B deals with checking and adjusting the selector cable on automatic transmissions. The following are common problems which may be caused by a poorly-adjusted cable:
a) Engine starting in gears other than Park or Neutral.
b) Indicator panel indicating a gear other than the one actually being used.
c) Vehicle moves when in Park or Neutral.
d) Poor gear shift quality or erratic gearchanges.

Transmission fluid brown, or has burned smell

☐ Transmission fluid level low (Chapter 1A or 1B). If the fluid appears to have deteriorated badly it is recommended that it is renewed.

Transmission will not downshift (kickdown) with accelerator pedal fully depressed

☐ Low transmission fluid level (Chapter 1A or 1B).
☐ Incorrect selector cable adjustment (Chapter 7B).

Engine will not start in any gear, or starts in gears other than Park or Neutral

☐ Incorrect selector cable adjustment (Chapter 7B).

Transmission slips, shifts roughly, is noisy, or has no drive in forward or reverse gears

☐ There are many probable causes for the above problems, but unless there is a very obvious reason (such as a loose or corroded wiring plug connection on or near the transmission), the car should be taken to a franchise dealer for the fault to be diagnosed. The transmission control unit incorporates a self-diagnosis facility, and any fault codes can quickly be read and interpreted by a dealer with the proper diagnostic equipment.

Braking system

Note: *Before assuming that a brake problem exists, make sure that the tyres are in good condition and correctly inflated, that the front wheel alignment is correct, and that the vehicle is not loaded with weight in an unequal manner. Apart from checking the condition of all pipe and hose connections, any faults occurring on the anti-lock braking system should be referred to a VW dealer for diagnosis.*

Vehicle pulls to one side under braking

☐ Worn, defective, damaged or contaminated brake pads on one side (Chapters 1A or 1B and 9).
☐ Seized or partially seized brake caliper piston (Chapters 1A or 1B and 9).
☐ A mixture of brake pad lining materials fitted between sides (Chapters 1A or 1B and 9).
☐ Brake caliper mounting bolts loose (Chapter 9).
☐ Worn or damaged steering or suspension components (Chapters 1A or 1B and 10).

Noise (grinding or high-pitched squeal) when brakes applied)

☐ Brake pad friction lining material worn down to metal backing (Chapters 1A or 1B and 9).
☐ Excessive corrosion of brake disc. This may be apparent after the vehicle has been standing for some time (Chapters 1A or 1B and 9).
☐ Foreign object (stone chipping, etc.) trapped between brake disc and shield (Chapters 1A or 1B and 9).

Brakes binding

☐ Seized brake caliper piston(s) (Chapter 9).
☐ Incorrectly adjusted handbrake mechanism (Chapter 9).
☐ Faulty master cylinder (Chapter 9).

Excessive brake pedal travel

☐ Faulty master cylinder (Chapter 9).

☐ Air in hydraulic system (Chapters 1A or 1B and 9).
☐ Faulty vacuum servo unit (Chapter 9).

Brake pedal feels spongy when depressed

☐ Air in hydraulic system (Chapters 1A or 1B and 9).
☐ Deteriorated flexible rubber brake hoses (Chapters 1A or 1B and 9).
☐ Master cylinder mounting nuts loose (Chapter 9).
☐ Faulty master cylinder (Chapter 9).

Excessive brake pedal effort required to stop vehicle

☐ Faulty vacuum servo unit (Chapter 9).
☐ Faulty brake vacuum pump – diesel models (Chapter 9).
☐ Disconnected, damaged or insecure brake servo vacuum hose (Chapter 9).
☐ Primary or secondary hydraulic circuit failure (Chapter 9).
☐ Seized brake caliper piston(s) (Chapter 9).
☐ Brake pads incorrectly fitted (Chapters 1A or 1B and 9).
☐ Incorrect grade of brake pads fitted (Chapters 1A or 1B and 9).
☐ Brake pads contaminated (Chapters 1A or 1B and 9).

Judder felt through brake pedal or steering wheel when braking

Note: *Judder felt through the brake pedal is a normal feature of models fitted with ABS.*
☐ Excessive run-out or distortion of discs (Chapters 1A or 1B and 9).
☐ Brake pad worn (Chapters 1A or 1B and 9).
☐ Brake caliper mounting bolts loose (Chapter 9).
☐ Wear in suspension or steering components or mountings (Chapters 1A or 1B and 10).

Rear wheels locking under normal braking

☐ Rear brake pads contaminated (Chapters 1A or 1B and 9).
☐ ABS system fault (Chapter 9).

Driveshafts

Clicking or knocking noise on turns (at slow speed on full-lock)

☐ Lack of constant velocity joint lubricant, possibly due to damaged gaiter (Chapter 8).

☐ Worn outer constant velocity joint (Chapter 8).
☐ Vibration when accelerating or decelerating
☐ Worn inner constant velocity joint (Chapter 8).
☐ Bent or distorted driveshaft (Chapter 8).

Suspension and steering

Note: *Before diagnosing suspension or steering faults, be sure that the trouble is not due to incorrect tyre pressures, mixtures of tyre types, or binding brakes.*

Vehicle pulls to one side

☐ Defective tyre (Weekly checks).
☐ Excessive wear in suspension or steering components (Chapters 1A or 1B and 10).
☐ Incorrect front wheel alignment (Chapter 10).
☐ Accident damage to steering or suspension components (Chapter 1A or 1B and 10).

Excessive pitching and/or rolling around corners, or during braking

☐ Defective shock absorbers (Chapters 1A or 1B and 10).
☐ Broken or weak spring and/or suspension component (Chapters 1A or 1B and 10).
☐ Worn or damaged anti-roll bar or mountings – where applicable (Chapter 10).

Lack of power assistance

☐ Broken or incorrectly adjusted auxiliary drivebelt (Chapter 1A or 1B).
☐ Incorrect power steering fluid level (Weekly checks).
☐ Restriction in power steering fluid hoses (Chapter 1A or 1B).
☐ Faulty power steering pump (Chapter 10).
☐ Faulty rack-and-pinion steering gear (Chapter 10).

Wandering or general instability

☐ Incorrect front wheel alignment (Chapter 10).
☐ Worn steering or suspension joints, bushes or components (Chapters 1A or 1B and 10).
☐ Roadwheels out of balance (Chapters 1A or 1B and 10).
☐ Faulty or damaged tyre (Weekly checks).
☐ Wheel bolts loose (refer to Chapters 1A or 1B and 10 for correct torque).
☐ Defective shock absorbers (Chapters 1A or 1B and 10).

Excessively stiff steering

☐ Lack of steering gear lubricant (Chapter 10).
☐ Seized track rod end balljoint or suspension balljoint Chapters 1A or 1B and 10).
☐ Broken or incorrectly adjusted auxiliary drivebelt – power steering (Chapter 1A or 1B).
☐ Incorrect front wheel alignment (Chapter 10).
☐ Steering rack or column bent or damaged (Chapter 10).

Excessive play in steering

☐ Worn steering column intermediate shaft universal joint (Chapter 10).
☐ Worn steering track rod end balljoints (Chapters 1A or 1B and 10).
☐ Worn rack-and-pinion steering gear (Chapter 10).
☐ Worn steering or suspension joints, bushes or components (Chapters 1A or 1B and 10).

Wheel wobble and vibration

☐ Front roadwheels out of balance (vibration felt mainly through the steering wheel) (Chapters 1A or 1B and 10).
☐ Rear roadwheels out of balance (vibration felt throughout the vehicle) (Chapters 1A or 1B and 10).
☐ Roadwheels damaged or distorted (Chapters 1A or 1B and 10).
☐ Faulty or damaged tyre (Weekly checks).
☐ Worn steering or suspension joints, bushes or components (Chapters 1A or 1B and 10).
☐ Wheel bolts loose (Chapter 10).

Tyre wear excessive

Tyres worn on inside or outside edges

☐ Tyres under-inflated (wear on both edges) (Weekly checks).
☐ Incorrect camber or castor angles (wear on one edge only) (Chapter 10).
☐ Worn steering or suspension joints, bushes or components (Chapters 1A or 1B and 10).
☐ Excessively hard cornering.
☐ Accident damage.

Tyre treads exhibit feathered edges

☐ Incorrect toe setting (Chapter 10).

Tyres worn in centre of tread

☐ Tyres over-inflated (Weekly checks).

Tyres worn on inside and outside edges

☐ Tyres under-inflated (Weekly checks).

Tyres worn unevenly

☐ Tyres/wheels out of balance (Chapter 1A, 1B or 10).
☐ Excessive wheel or tyre run-out (Chapter 1A, 1B or 10).
☐ Worn shock absorbers (Chapters 1A or 1B and 10).
☐ Faulty tyre (Weekly checks).

Electrical system

Note: *For problems associated with the starting system, refer to the faults listed under 'Engine' earlier in this Section.*

Battery will not hold a charge for more than a few days

- ☐ Battery defective internally (Chapter 5A).
- ☐ Battery terminal connections loose or corroded (Weekly checks).
- ☐ Auxiliary drivebelt worn or incorrectly adjusted (Chapter 1A or 1B).
- ☐ Alternator not charging at correct output (Chapter 5A).
- ☐ Alternator or voltage regulator faulty (Chapter 5A).
- ☐ Short-circuit causing continual battery drain (Chapters 5A and 12).

Ignition/no-charge warning light remains illuminated with engine running

- ☐ Auxiliary drivebelt broken, worn, or incorrectly adjusted (Chapter 1A or 1B).
- ☐ Alternator brushes worn, sticking, or dirty (Chapter 5A).
- ☐ Alternator brush springs weak or broken (Chapter 5A).
- ☐ Internal fault in alternator or voltage regulator (Chapter 5A).
- ☐ Broken, disconnected, or loose wiring in charging circuit (Chapter 5A).

Ignition/no-charge warning light fails to come on

- ☐ Warning light LED defective (Chapter 12).
- ☐ Broken, disconnected, or loose wiring in warning light circuit (Chapter 12).
- ☐ Alternator faulty (Chapter 5A).

Lights inoperative

- ☐ Bulb blown (Chapter 12).
- ☐ Corrosion of bulb or bulbholder contacts (Chapter 12).
- ☐ Blown fuse (Chapter 12).
- ☐ Faulty relay (Chapter 12).
- ☐ Broken, loose, or disconnected wiring (Chapter 12).
- ☐ Faulty switch (Chapter 12).

Instrument readings inaccurate or erratic

Fuel or temperature gauges give no reading

- ☐ Faulty gauge sender unit (Chapters 3, 4A or 4B).
- ☐ Wiring open-circuit (Chapter 12).
- ☐ Faulty gauge (Chapter 12).

Fuel or temperature gauges give continuous maximum reading

- ☐ Faulty gauge sender unit (Chapters 3, 4A or 4B).
- ☐ Wiring short-circuit (Chapter 12).
- ☐ Faulty gauge (Chapter 12).

Horn inoperative, or unsatisfactory in operation

Horn operates all the time

- ☐ Horn push either earthed or stuck down (Chapter 12).
- ☐ Horn cable-to-horn push earthed (Chapter 12).

Horn fails to operate

- ☐ Blown fuse (Chapter 12).
- ☐ Cable or cable connections loose, broken or disconnected (Chapter 12).
- ☐ Faulty horn (Chapter 12).

Horn emits intermittent or unsatisfactory sound

- ☐ Cable connections loose (Chapter 12).
- ☐ Horn mountings loose (Chapter 12).
- ☐ Faulty horn (Chapter 12).

Windscreen/tailgate wipers inoperative, or unsatisfactory in operation

Wipers fail to operate, or operate very slowly

- ☐ Wiper blades stuck to screen, or linkage seized or binding (Weekly checks and Chapter 12).
- ☐ Blown fuse (Chapter 12).
- ☐ Cable or cable connections loose, broken or disconnected (Chapter 12).
- ☐ Faulty relay (Chapter 12).
- ☐ Faulty wiper motor (Chapter 12).

Wiper blades sweep over too large or too small an area of the glass

- ☐ Wiper arms incorrectly positioned on spindles (Chapter 12).
- ☐ Excessive wear of wiper linkage (Chapter 12).
- ☐ Wiper motor or linkage mountings loose or insecure (Chapter 12).

Wiper blades fail to clean the glass effectively

- ☐ Wiper blade rubbers worn or perished (Weekly checks).
- ☐ Wiper arm tension springs broken, or arm pivots seized (Chapter 12).
- ☐ Insufficient windscreen washer additive to adequately remove road film (Weekly checks).

Windscreen/tailgate washers inoperative, or unsatisfactory in operation

One or more washer jets inoperative

- ☐ Blocked washer jet (Chapter 1A or 1B).
- ☐ Disconnected, kinked or restricted fluid hose (Chapter 12).
- ☐ Insufficient fluid in washer reservoir (Chapter 1A or 1B).

Washer pump fails to operate

- ☐ Broken or disconnected wiring or connections (Chapter 12).
- ☐ Blown fuse (Chapter 12).
- ☐ Faulty washer switch (Chapter 12).
- ☐ Faulty washer pump (Chapter 12).

Electric windows inoperative, or unsatisfactory in operation

Window glass will only move in one direction

- ☐ Faulty switch (Chapter 12).

Window glass slow to move

- ☐ Regulator seized or damaged, or in need of lubrication (Chapter 11).
- ☐ Door internal components or trim fouling regulator (Chapter 11).
- ☐ Faulty motor (Chapter 11).

Window glass fails to move

- ☐ Blown fuse (Chapter 12).
- ☐ Faulty relay (Chapter 12).
- ☐ Broken or disconnected wiring or connections (Chapter 12).
- ☐ Faulty motor (Chapter 11).

Central locking system inoperative, or unsatisfactory in operation

Complete system failure

- ☐ Blown fuse (Chapter 12).
- ☐ Faulty relay (Chapter 12).
- ☐ Broken or disconnected wiring or connections (Chapter 12).
- ☐ Faulty control module (Chapter 11).

Latch locks but will not unlock, or unlocks but will not lock

- ☐ Faulty master switch (Chapter 11).
- ☐ Broken or disconnected latch operating rods or levers (Chapter 11).
- ☐ Faulty relay (Chapter 12).
- ☐ Faulty control module (Chapter 11).

One actuator fails to operate

- ☐ Broken or disconnected wiring or connections (Chapter 12).
- ☐ Faulty actuator (Chapter 11).
- ☐ Broken, binding or disconnected latch operating rods or levers (Chapter 11).
- ☐ Fault in door lock (Chapter 11).

A

ABS (Anti-lock brake system) A system, usually electronically controlled, that senses incipient wheel lockup during braking and relieves hydraulic pressure at wheels that are about to skid.

Air bag An inflatable bag hidden in the steering wheel (driver's side) or the dash or glovebox (passenger side). In a head-on collision, the bags inflate, preventing the driver and front passenger from being thrown forward into the steering wheel or windscreen.

Air cleaner A metal or plastic housing, containing a filter element, which removes dust and dirt from the air being drawn into the engine.

Air filter element The actual filter in an air cleaner system, usually manufactured from pleated paper and requiring renewal at regular intervals.

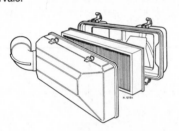

Air filter

Allen key A hexagonal wrench which fits into a recessed hexagonal hole.

Alligator clip A long-nosed spring-loaded metal clip with meshing teeth. Used to make temporary electrical connections.

Alternator A component in the electrical system which converts mechanical energy from a drivebelt into electrical energy to charge the battery and to operate the starting system, ignition system and electrical accessories.

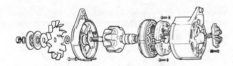

Alternator (exploded view)

Ampere (amp) A unit of measurement for the flow of electric current. One amp is the amount of current produced by one volt acting through a resistance of one ohm.

Anaerobic sealer A substance used to prevent bolts and screws from loosening. Anaerobic means that it does not require oxygen for activation. The Loctite brand is widely used.

Antifreeze A substance (usually ethylene glycol) mixed with water, and added to a vehicle's cooling system, to prevent freezing of the coolant in winter. Antifreeze also contains chemicals to inhibit corrosion and the formation of rust and other deposits that would tend to clog the radiator and coolant passages and reduce cooling efficiency.

Anti-seize compound A coating that reduces the risk of seizing on fasteners that are subjected to high temperatures, such as exhaust manifold bolts and nuts.

Anti-seize compound

Asbestos A natural fibrous mineral with great heat resistance, commonly used in the composition of brake friction materials. Asbestos is a health hazard and the dust created by brake systems should never be inhaled or ingested.

Axle A shaft on which a wheel revolves, or which revolves with a wheel. Also, a solid beam that connects the two wheels at one end of the vehicle. An axle which also transmits power to the wheels is known as a live axle.

Axle assembly

Axleshaft A single rotating shaft, on either side of the differential, which delivers power from the final drive assembly to the drive wheels. Also called a driveshaft or a halfshaft.

B

Ball bearing An anti-friction bearing consisting of a hardened inner and outer race with hardened steel balls between two races.

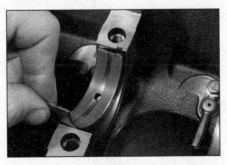

Bearing

Bearing The curved surface on a shaft or in a bore, or the part assembled into either, that permits relative motion between them with minimum wear and friction.

Big-end bearing The bearing in the end of the connecting rod that's attached to the crankshaft.

Bleed nipple A valve on a brake wheel cylinder, caliper or other hydraulic component that is opened to purge the hydraulic system of air. Also called a bleed screw.

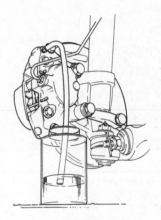

Brake bleeding

Brake bleeding Procedure for removing air from lines of a hydraulic brake system.

Brake disc The component of a disc brake that rotates with the wheels.

Brake drum The component of a drum brake that rotates with the wheels.

Brake linings The friction material which contacts the brake disc or drum to retard the vehicle's speed. The linings are bonded or riveted to the brake pads or shoes.

Brake pads The replaceable friction pads that pinch the brake disc when the brakes are applied. Brake pads consist of a friction material bonded or riveted to a rigid backing plate.

Brake shoe The crescent-shaped carrier to which the brake linings are mounted and which forces the lining against the rotating drum during braking.

Braking systems For more information on braking systems, consult the *Haynes Automotive Brake Manual*.

Breaker bar A long socket wrench handle providing greater leverage.

Bulkhead The insulated partition between the engine and the passenger compartment.

C

Caliper The non-rotating part of a disc-brake assembly that straddles the disc and carries the brake pads. The caliper also contains the hydraulic components that cause the pads to pinch the disc when the brakes are applied. A caliper is also a measuring tool that can be set to measure inside or outside dimensions of an object.

Camshaft A rotating shaft on which a series of cam lobes operate the valve mechanisms. The camshaft may be driven by gears, by sprockets and chain or by sprockets and a belt.

Canister A container in an evaporative emission control system; contains activated charcoal granules to trap vapours from the fuel system.

Canister

Carburettor A device which mixes fuel with air in the proper proportions to provide a desired power output from a spark ignition internal combustion engine.

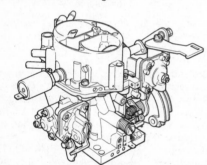

Carburettor

Castellated Resembling the parapets along the top of a castle wall. For example, a castellated balljoint stud nut.

Castellated nut

Castor In wheel alignment, the backward or forward tilt of the steering axis. Castor is positive when the steering axis is inclined rearward at the top.

Catalytic converter A silencer-like device in the exhaust system which converts certain pollutants in the exhaust gases into less harmful substances.

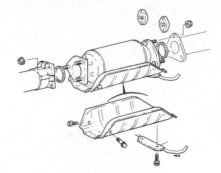

Catalytic converter

Circlip A ring-shaped clip used to prevent endwise movement of cylindrical parts and shafts. An internal circlip is installed in a groove in a housing; an external circlip fits into a groove on the outside of a cylindrical piece such as a shaft.

Clearance The amount of space between two parts. For example, between a piston and a cylinder, between a bearing and a journal, etc.

Coil spring A spiral of elastic steel found in various sizes throughout a vehicle, for example as a springing medium in the suspension and in the valve train.

Compression Reduction in volume, and increase in pressure and temperature, of a gas, caused by squeezing it into a smaller space.

Compression ratio The relationship between cylinder volume when the piston is at top dead centre and cylinder volume when the piston is at bottom dead centre.

Constant velocity (CV) joint A type of universal joint that cancels out vibrations caused by driving power being transmitted through an angle.

Core plug A disc or cup-shaped metal device inserted in a hole in a casting through which core was removed when the casting was formed. Also known as a freeze plug or expansion plug.

Crankcase The lower part of the engine block in which the crankshaft rotates.

Crankshaft The main rotating member, or shaft, running the length of the crankcase, with offset "throws" to which the connecting rods are attached.

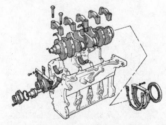

Crankshaft assembly

Crocodile clip See Alligator clip

D

Diagnostic code Code numbers obtained by accessing the diagnostic mode of an engine management computer. This code can be used to determine the area in the system where a malfunction may be located.

Disc brake A brake design incorporating a rotating disc onto which brake pads are squeezed. The resulting friction converts the energy of a moving vehicle into heat.

Double-overhead cam (DOHC) An engine that uses two overhead camshafts, usually one for the intake valves and one for the exhaust valves.

Drivebelt(s) The belt(s) used to drive accessories such as the alternator, water pump, power steering pump, air conditioning compressor, etc. off the crankshaft pulley.

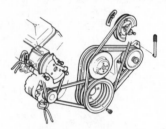

Accessory drivebelts

Driveshaft Any shaft used to transmit motion. Commonly used when referring to the axleshafts on a front wheel drive vehicle.

Driveshaft

Drum brake A type of brake using a drum-shaped metal cylinder attached to the inner surface of the wheel. When the brake pedal is pressed, curved brake shoes with friction linings press against the inside of the drum to slow or stop the vehicle.

Drum brake assembly

E

EGR valve A valve used to introduce exhaust gases into the intake air stream.

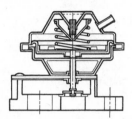

EGR valve

Electronic control unit (ECU) A computer which controls (for instance) ignition and fuel injection systems, or an anti-lock braking system. For more information refer to the *Haynes Automotive Electrical and Electronic Systems Manual.*

Electronic Fuel Injection (EFI) A computer controlled fuel system that distributes fuel through an injector located in each intake port of the engine.

Emergency brake A braking system, independent of the main hydraulic system, that can be used to slow or stop the vehicle if the primary brakes fail, or to hold the vehicle stationary even though the brake pedal isn't depressed. It usually consists of a hand lever that actuates either front or rear brakes mechanically through a series of cables and linkages. Also known as a handbrake or parking brake.

Endfloat The amount of lengthwise movement between two parts. As applied to a crankshaft, the distance that the crankshaft can move forward and back in the cylinder block.

Engine management system (EMS) A computer controlled system which manages the fuel injection and the ignition systems in an integrated fashion.

Exhaust manifold A part with several passages through which exhaust gases leave the engine combustion chambers and enter the exhaust pipe.

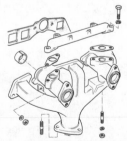

Exhaust manifold

F

Fan clutch A viscous (fluid) drive coupling device which permits variable engine fan speeds in relation to engine speeds.

Feeler blade A thin strip or blade of hardened steel, ground to an exact thickness, used to check or measure clearances between parts.

Feeler blade

Firing order The order in which the engine cylinders fire, or deliver their power strokes, beginning with the number one cylinder.

Flywheel A heavy spinning wheel in which energy is absorbed and stored by means of momentum. On cars, the flywheel is attached to the crankshaft to smooth out firing impulses.

Free play The amount of travel before any action takes place. The "looseness" in a linkage, or an assembly of parts, between the initial application of force and actual movement. For example, the distance the brake pedal moves before the pistons in the master cylinder are actuated.

Fuse An electrical device which protects a circuit against accidental overload. The typical fuse contains a soft piece of metal which is calibrated to melt at a predetermined current flow (expressed as amps) and break the circuit.

Fusible link A circuit protection device consisting of a conductor surrounded by heat-resistant insulation. The conductor is smaller than the wire it protects, so it acts as the weakest link in the circuit. Unlike a blown fuse, a failed fusible link must frequently be cut from the wire for replacement.

G

Gap The distance the spark must travel in jumping from the centre electrode to the side

Adjusting spark plug gap

electrode in a spark plug. Also refers to the spacing between the points in a contact breaker assembly in a conventional points-type ignition, or to the distance between the reluctor or rotor and the pickup coil in an electronic ignition.

Gasket Any thin, soft material - usually cork, cardboard, asbestos or soft metal - installed between two metal surfaces to ensure a good seal. For instance, the cylinder head gasket seals the joint between the block and the cylinder head.

Gasket

Gauge An instrument panel display used to monitor engine conditions. A gauge with a movable pointer on a dial or a fixed scale is an analogue gauge. A gauge with a numerical readout is called a digital gauge.

H

Halfshaft A rotating shaft that transmits power from the final drive unit to a drive wheel, usually when referring to a live rear axle.

Harmonic balancer A device designed to reduce torsion or twisting vibration in the crankshaft. May be incorporated in the crankshaft pulley. Also known as a vibration damper.

Hone An abrasive tool for correcting small irregularities or differences in diameter in an engine cylinder, brake cylinder, etc.

Hydraulic tappet A tappet that utilises hydraulic pressure from the engine's lubrication system to maintain zero clearance (constant contact with both camshaft and valve stem). Automatically adjusts to variation in valve stem length. Hydraulic tappets also reduce valve noise.

I

Ignition timing The moment at which the spark plug fires, usually expressed in the number of crankshaft degrees before the piston reaches the top of its stroke.

Inlet manifold A tube or housing with passages through which flows the air-fuel mixture (carburettor vehicles and vehicles with throttle body injection) or air only (port fuel-injected vehicles) to the port openings in the cylinder head.

J

Jump start Starting the engine of a vehicle with a discharged or weak battery by attaching jump leads from the weak battery to a charged or helper battery.

L

Load Sensing Proportioning Valve (LSPV) A brake hydraulic system control valve that works like a proportioning valve, but also takes into consideration the amount of weight carried by the rear axle.

Locknut A nut used to lock an adjustment nut, or other threaded component, in place. For example, a locknut is employed to keep the adjusting nut on the rocker arm in position.

Lockwasher A form of washer designed to prevent an attaching nut from working loose.

M

MacPherson strut A type of front suspension system devised by Earle MacPherson at Ford of England. In its original form, a simple lateral link with the anti-roll bar creates the lower control arm. A long strut - an integral coil spring and shock absorber - is mounted between the body and the steering knuckle. Many modern so-called MacPherson strut systems use a conventional lower A-arm and don't rely on the anti-roll bar for location.

Multimeter An electrical test instrument with the capability to measure voltage, current and resistance.

N

NOx Oxides of Nitrogen. A common toxic pollutant emitted by petrol and diesel engines at higher temperatures.

O

Ohm The unit of electrical resistance. One volt applied to a resistance of one ohm will produce a current of one amp.

Ohmmeter An instrument for measuring electrical resistance.

O-ring A type of sealing ring made of a special rubber-like material; in use, the O-ring is compressed into a groove to provide the sealing action.

O-ring

Overhead cam (ohc) engine An engine with the camshaft(s) located on top of the cylinder head(s).

Overhead valve (ohv) engine An engine with the valves located in the cylinder head, but with the camshaft located in the engine block.

Oxygen sensor A device installed in the engine exhaust manifold, which senses the oxygen content in the exhaust and converts this information into an electric current. Also called a Lambda sensor.

P

Phillips screw A type of screw head having a cross instead of a slot for a corresponding type of screwdriver.

Plastigage A thin strip of plastic thread, available in different sizes, used for measuring clearances. For example, a strip of Plastigage is laid across a bearing journal. The parts are assembled and dismantled; the width of the crushed strip indicates the clearance between journal and bearing.

Plastigage

Propeller shaft The long hollow tube with universal joints at both ends that carries power from the transmission to the differential on front-engined rear wheel drive vehicles.

Proportioning valve A hydraulic control valve which limits the amount of pressure to the rear brakes during panic stops to prevent wheel lock-up.

R

Rack-and-pinion steering A steering system with a pinion gear on the end of the steering shaft that mates with a rack (think of a geared wheel opened up and laid flat). When the steering wheel is turned, the pinion turns, moving the rack to the left or right. This movement is transmitted through the track rods to the steering arms at the wheels.

Radiator A liquid-to-air heat transfer device designed to reduce the temperature of the coolant in an internal combustion engine cooling system.

Refrigerant Any substance used as a heat transfer agent in an air-conditioning system. R-12 has been the principle refrigerant for many years; recently, however, manufacturers have begun using R-134a, a non-CFC substance that is considered less harmful to the ozone in the upper atmosphere.

Rocker arm A lever arm that rocks on a shaft or pivots on a stud. In an overhead valve engine, the rocker arm converts the upward movement of the pushrod into a downward movement to open a valve.

Rotor In a distributor, the rotating device inside the cap that connects the centre electrode and the outer terminals as it turns, distributing the high voltage from the coil secondary winding to the proper spark plug. Also, that part of an alternator which rotates inside the stator. Also, the rotating assembly of a turbocharger, including the compressor wheel, shaft and turbine wheel.

Runout The amount of wobble (in-and-out movement) of a gear or wheel as it's rotated. The amount a shaft rotates "out-of-true." The out-of-round condition of a rotating part.

S

Sealant A liquid or paste used to prevent leakage at a joint. Sometimes used in conjunction with a gasket.

Sealed beam lamp An older headlight design which integrates the reflector, lens and filaments into a hermetically-sealed one-piece unit. When a filament burns out or the lens cracks, the entire unit is simply replaced.

Serpentine drivebelt A single, long, wide accessory drivebelt that's used on some newer vehicles to drive all the accessories, instead of a series of smaller, shorter belts. Serpentine drivebelts are usually tensioned by an automatic tensioner.

Serpentine drivebelt

Shim Thin spacer, commonly used to adjust the clearance or relative positions between two parts. For example, shims inserted into or under bucket tappets control valve clearances. Clearance is adjusted by changing the thickness of the shim.

Slide hammer A special puller that screws into or hooks onto a component such as a shaft or bearing; a heavy sliding handle on the shaft bottoms against the end of the shaft to knock the component free.

Sprocket A tooth or projection on the periphery of a wheel, shaped to engage with a chain or drivebelt. Commonly used to refer to the sprocket wheel itself.

Starter inhibitor switch On vehicles with an automatic transmission, a switch that prevents starting if the vehicle is not in Neutral or Park.

Strut See MacPherson strut.

T

Tappet A cylindrical component which transmits motion from the cam to the valve stem, either directly or via a pushrod and rocker arm. Also called a cam follower.

Thermostat A heat-controlled valve that regulates the flow of coolant between the cylinder block and the radiator, so maintaining optimum engine operating temperature. A thermostat is also used in some air cleaners in which the temperature is regulated.

Thrust bearing The bearing in the clutch assembly that is moved in to the release levers by clutch pedal action to disengage the clutch. Also referred to as a release bearing.

Timing belt A toothed belt which drives the camshaft. Serious engine damage may result if it breaks in service.

Timing chain A chain which drives the camshaft.

Toe-in The amount the front wheels are closer together at the front than at the rear. On rear wheel drive vehicles, a slight amount of toe-in is usually specified to keep the front wheels running parallel on the road by offsetting other forces that tend to spread the wheels apart.

Toe-out The amount the front wheels are closer together at the rear than at the front. On front wheel drive vehicles, a slight amount of toe-out is usually specified.

Tools For full information on choosing and using tools, refer to the *Haynes Automotive Tools Manual.*

Tracer A stripe of a second colour applied to a wire insulator to distinguish that wire from another one with the same colour insulator.

Tune-up A process of accurate and careful adjustments and parts replacement to obtain the best possible engine performance.

Turbocharger A centrifugal device, driven by exhaust gases, that pressurises the intake air. Normally used to increase the power output from a given engine displacement, but can also be used primarily to reduce exhaust emissions (as on VW's "Umwelt" Diesel engine).

U

Universal joint or U-joint A double-pivoted connection for transmitting power from a driving to a driven shaft through an angle. A U-joint consists of two Y-shaped yokes and a cross-shaped member called the spider.

V

Valve A device through which the flow of liquid, gas, vacuum, or loose material in bulk may be started, stopped, or regulated by a movable part that opens, shuts, or partially obstructs one or more ports or passageways. A valve is also the movable part of such a device.

Valve clearance The clearance between the valve tip (the end of the valve stem) and the rocker arm or tappet. The valve clearance is measured when the valve is closed.

Vernier caliper A precision measuring instrument that measures inside and outside dimensions. Not quite as accurate as a micrometer, but more convenient.

Viscosity The thickness of a liquid or its resistance to flow.

Volt A unit for expressing electrical "pressure" in a circuit. One volt that will produce a current of one ampere through a resistance of one ohm.

W

Welding Various processes used to join metal items by heating the areas to be joined to a molten state and fusing them together. For more information refer to the *Haynes Automotive Welding Manual.*

Wiring diagram A drawing portraying the components and wires in a vehicle's electrical system, using standardised symbols. For more information refer to the *Haynes Automotive Electrical and Electronic Systems Manual.*

Note: *References throughout this index are in the form* "**Chapter number**" • "**Page number**"

A

Absolute pressure (altitude) sensor – 4B•5
Accelerator cable – 4A•5, 4B•4
Accessory shops – REF•3
Acknowledgements – 0•6
Air bags – 0•5
Air cleaner assembly – 4A•3, 4B•3
Air conditioning
    components – 3•11
    switches – 12•5
    system – 3•10
Air filter element – 1A•13, 1B•14
Air mass meter – 4B•5
Air pump – 4C•5
Air supply combi-valve – 4C•5
Air vent illumination – 12•11
Airbag
    system – 12•18
    unit check – 1A•12, 1B•13
Alternator – 5A•3, 5A•4
Anti roll bar – 10•9, 10•13
Antifreeze – 0•13, 0•17
    check – 1A•10, 1B•11
    mixture – 1A•19, 1B•18
Anti-lock braking system (ABS) – 9•13
Anti-roll bar connecting link – 10•9
Anti-theft alarm system and engine immobiliser – 12•18
Asbestos – 0•5
Automatic range control ECU – 12•13
Automatic transmission – 7B•1 *et seq*
    fault finding – REF•16
    final drive oil level check – 1A•17, 1B•16
    fluid level check – 0•17, 1A•16, 1B•16
Auxiliary drivebelt – 1A•10, 1A•15, 1B•11, 1B•15

B

Balancer shaft unit – 2A•19
Battery – 0•5, 0•15, 5A•2, REF•5
    check – 1A•12, 1B•13
Bearings
    hub – 10•5
    main and big-end – 2D•23, 2D•26
Bleeding
    power steering system – 10•21
    brakes – 9•2
    clutch – 6•2
Body electrical system – 12•1 *et seq*
    corrosion – REF•11
    exterior fittings – 11•19
    trim strips and badges – 11•19
    under-panels – 11•19
Bodywork and fittings – 11•1 *et seq*
Bonnet – 11•5
    lock – 11•6
    release cable – 11•6

Boost pressure
    solenoid valve – 4D•5
    wastegate valve – 4D•6
Boot lid
    lock components – 11•15
    lock motor – 11•16
    support struts – 11•15
Brakes – REF•8, REF•9
Braking system – 1A•13, 1B•14, 9•1 *et seq*, REF•10
    caliper – 9•6, 9•8
    disc – 9•6, 9•7
    fault finding – REF•16
    fluid – 0•13, 0•17, 1B•17, 1A•18
    hydraulic circuit check – 1A•10, 1B•11
    light switch – 9•12, 12•5
    pads – 1A•9, 1B•9, 9•4, 9•7
    pedal – 9•9
Bulbs – 12•5, 12•10
Bumper – 11•4
Burning – 0•5
Buying spare parts – REF•3

C

Cable
    accelerator – 4A•5, 4B•4
    automatic transmission selector – 7B•3
    handbrake – 9•12
    Park Lock system – 7B•4
Camber angles – 10•23
Camshaft – 2A•8, 2B•19, 2D•16
    carrier – 2B•18
    chain adjuster solenoid valve – 4A•10
    cover – 2A•5, 2B•8, 2C•6
    hub – 2C•13
    oil seal – 2A•10, 2B•24, 2C•15
    position sensor – 4A•9
    sprocket – 2A•7, 2B•16, 2C•13
Camshaft and hydraulic tappets – 2B•20, 2C•14
Carpets – 11•23
Castor angles – 10•23
Catalytic converter – 4C•14, 4D•8
CD player/changer – 12•17
Central facia vents – 3•10
Central locking
    components – 11•16
    switch – 12•5
Centre console – 11•23
Centre silencer – 4C•13, 4D•8
Changeover flap housing and vacuum control – 4B•13
Changeover valve and diaphragm unit – 4A•16, 4B•14
Changing the wheel – 0•9
Charging – 5A•2, 5A•3
Cigarette lighter/ashtray illumination – 12•10, 12•14

Climatronic system components – 3•11
Clock – 12•14
Clutch – 6•1 *et seq*
    fault finding – REF•15
    Clutch fluid – 0•13, 0•17, 1A•18, 1B•17
    friction disc and pressure plate – 6•4, 2C•19
    pedal – 6•2
    switch petrol engines – 4A•10, 4B•6
Coil spring – 10•12
Coil(s) – 5B•3
Compression test – 2A•4, 2B•5, 2C•4
Connecting rod assemblies – 2D•18, 2D•21, 2D•25, 2D•26
Control and display unit – 3•11
Conversion factors – REF•2
Coolant – 0•13, 0•17
    pump – 3•6
    pump sprocket – 2A•8, 2B•17, 2C•14
    renewal – 1A•18, 1B•17
    temperature sensor – 3•5, 4A•9, 4B•4
Cooling fan thermostatic switch – 3•5
Cooling system
    draining – 1A•18, 1B•17
    electrical switches and sensors – 3•5
    fault finding – REF•14
    filling – 1A•18, 1B•18
    flushing – 1A•18, 1B•17
    hoses – 3•2
Cooling, heating and air conditioning systems – 3•1 *et seq*
Courtesy light – 12•5, 12•10
Crankcase emission control – 4C•2, 4C•3, 4D•1, 4D•2
Crankshaft – 2D•19, 2D•22, 2D•24
    oil seals – 2A•15, 2B•29, 2C•19
    pulley – 2A•5, 2B•9, 2C•8
    sprocket – 2A•8, 2B•16, 2B•17, 2C•12
Cruise control system – 4A•18
Crushing – 0•5
Cylinder
    block/crankcase – 2D•20
    head – 2A•11, 2B•24, 2C•16, 2D•15, 2D•16, 2D•17
Cylinder head gasket selection – 2C•17

D

Dents – 11•2
Depressurisation fuel injection system
    petrol engines – 4A•13
Diesel engine fuel system – 4B•1 *et seq*
Diesel engine in-car repair procedures – 2C•1 *et seq*
Diesel engine management system components – 4B•4
Diesel injection equipment – 0•5
Dimensions – REF•1
Direction indicator – 12•8, 12•12

Disconnecting the battery – REF•5
DOHC petrol engine in-car repair procedures – 2B•1 *et seq*
Doors – 11•6, REF•9
  handle and lock components – 11•8
  inner trim panel – 11•7
  locking motors – 11•16
  warning lights – 12•11
  window glass and regulator – 11•12
Drivebelt – 1A•10, 1A•15, 1B•11, 1B•15
Driveplate – 2A•14, 2B•29, 2C•19
Driveshafts – 8•1 *et seq*, REF•10
  gaiters – 1A•11, 1B•12, 8•2
  fault finding – REF•17
Drivetrain – 1A•13, 1B•14

E

Earth fault – 12•2
EGR
  damper – 4D•3
  solenoid – 4C•3, 4D•2
  valve – 4C•3, 4D•2
Electric shock – 0•5
Electric
  cooling fan – 3•5
  window components – 11•17
Electrical equipment – 0•16, 1A•13, 1B•14, REF•9
  fault finding – 12•2, REF•18
Electronic control module (ECM) – 9•13
Electronic control unit (ECU) – 4A•10, 4B•6
Emission control and exhaust systems – 4C•1 *et seq*, 4D•1 *et seq*, REF•11
Engine
  fault finding – REF•13
  flushing – 1A•18, 1B•18
  management self-diagnosis – 1A•13, 1B•13
  mountings – 2A•15, 2B•30, 2C•20
  oil and filter renewal – 0•12, 0•17, 1A•8, 1B•7
  oil cooler – 2C•20
  speed sensor – 4A•9, 4B•5
Engine removal and overhaul procedures – 2D•1 *et seq*
Environmental considerations – REF•4
ESP switches – 12•4
Evaporative emission control – 4C•2
Exhaust
  emission control – 4C•2, 4D•1
  emissions check – 1A•13, 1B•14
  gas recirculation (EGR) system – 4C•3, 4D•2
  manifold – 4C•10, 4D•6
  specialists – REF•3
Exhaust system – 1A•9, 1B•9, 4C•2, 4C•12, 4D•2, 4D•7, REF•10, REF•11
Exterior light units – 12•11

Exterior mirrors and associated components – 11•17

F

Facia assembly – 11•23, 11•25
Fan cooling – 3•5
Fault finding – REF•12
  automatic transmission – REF•16
  braking system – REF•16
  clutch – REF•15
  cooling system – REF•14
  driveshafts – REF•17
  electrical system – 12•2
  electrical system – REF•18
  engine – REF•13
  fuel and exhaust systems – REF•15
  manual transmission – REF•15
  suspension and steering – REF•17
Filling and respraying – 11•3
Filter
  air – 1A•13, 1B•14
  fuel – 1B•8, 1B•10, 1B•14, 4A•11, 4B•12
  oil – 1A•8, 1B•7
  pollen – 1A•10, 1B•11
Final crankshaft refitting – 2D•25
Fire – 0•5
Fluids – 0•17
  leak check – 1A•9, 1B•9
Flywheel – 2A•14, 2B•29, 2C•19
Foglight – 12•8
Footwell vent temperature sender – 3•11
Fresh/recirculating air flap positioning motor – 3•10
Front pipe and catalytic converter – 4C•12, 4D•7
Front wheel toe setting – 10•23
Fuel and exhaust systems fault finding – REF•15
Fuel cut-off solenoid valve – 4B•11
Fuel filler flap
  lock motor – 11•17
  release switch – 12•5
Fuel filter – 1B•8, 1B•10, 1B•14, 4A•11, 4B•12
Fuel gauge sender unit – 4A•11, 4B•12
Fuel injection pump
  sprocket – 2C•13
  timing – 4B•11
Fuel injection system – 4A•17
Fuel injectors and fuel rail – 4A•6
Fuel pressure regulator – 4A•7
Fuel pump and gauge sender unit – 4A•11
Fuel system – 4A•6, REF•11
Fuel tank – 4A•13, 4B•12
Fuel temperature sensor – 4B•4
Fume or gas intoxication – 0•5
Fuses – 12•3

G

Gaiters
  driveshaft – 1A•11, 1B•12, 8•2
  inner CV joint – 8•5
  outer CV joint – 8•3
  steering gear – 10•21
Gaskets – REF•4
Gearchange linkage – 7A•2
General information petrol engines – 4A•11, 11•2
General repair procedures – REF•4
Glossary of technical terms – REF•19
Glovebox – 11•23
  illumination light – 12•10
  light switch – 12•5
Glow plugs – 5C•1

H

Handbrake – REF•8
  adjustment – 9•11
  cable – 9•12
  lever – 9•12
  warning light switch – 9•12, 12•5
Hazard warning light – 12•4
Headlamp range control – 12•4
Headlight – 12•11
  beam adjustment – 1A•10, 1B•11, 12•13
  components – 12•12
  dip/main beam – 12•6, 12•7
  gas discharge light starter unit – 12•12
Headlight washer jets – 12•16
  lift cylinder – 12•16
  system check – 1A•12, 1B•13
Headlining – 11•23
Heated front seat switches – 12•4
Heated rear window – 12•4
Heater blower motor – 3•10
  resistor – 3•10
  switch – 12•5
Heater control unit – 3•10
Heater matrix – 3•8, 3•10
Heater/ventilation control cables – 3•7
  panel illumination – 12•11
Heating and ventilation system – 3•7, 3•10
High level brake light – 12•9, 12•12
Hinge lubrication – 1A•12, 1B•13
Horn – 12•14
Hose and fluid leak check – 1A•9, 1B•9
Hoses
  braking system – 9•3
  cooling system – 3•2
HT coil(s) – 5B•3
Hub assembly – 10•9
Hub bearings – 10•5
Hydraulic pipes and hoses – 9•3
Hydraulic tappets – 2A•10, 2C•15
Hydrofluoric acid – 0•5

I

Identification numbers – REF•3
Identifying leaks – 0•10
Idler pulley – 2B•17, 2C•12
Ignition switch – 10•19, 12•3
Ignition system – 5B•1 *et seq*
Indicator – 12•8
Injection pump – 4B•9
Injectors – 4B•6
Inlet air temperature control system – 4A•5
    sensor – 4A•8, 4B•5
Inlet camshaft timing
components/camshaft adjuster – 2B•17
Inlet manifold and associated
    components – 4A•14, 4B•11
    changeover flap and valve – 4B•13
Inner CV joint gaiter – 8•5
Instrument illumination switches – 12•4
Instrument panel – 12•13
    illumination/warning lights – 12•10
Instruments – 1A•13, 1B•14
Intercooler – 4C•8, 4D•6
Interior mirror – 11•23
Interior monitoring deactivation switch –
    12•5
Interior trim – 11•23
Internal central locking switch – 11•16

J

Jacking and vehicle support – REF•5
Joint mating faces – REF•4
Jump starting – 0•8

K

Knock sensor(s) – 5B•4

L

Leak check – 0•10, 1A•9, 1B•9
Leakdown test – 2C•5
Lighting switch – 12•4
Lock
    bonnet – 11•6
    boot – 11•15, 11•16
    door – 11•8
    fuel filer – 11•17
    lubrication – 1A•12, 1B•13
    steering column – 10•19, 12•3
    tailgate – 11•14, 11•16
Locknuts, locktabs and washers – REF•4
Loudspeakers – 12•17
Lubricants and fluids – 0•17
Luggage area light switch – 12•5, 12•10

M

Main and big-end bearings – 2D•23
    clearance check – 2D•24
Maintenance – bodywork and underframe
    – 11•2
Maintenance – upholstery and carpets –
    11•2
Make-up lights – 12•10
Manual transmission – 7A•1 *et seq*
    fault finding – REF•15
    oil level check – 1A•11, 1B•12
Master cylinder
    brake – 9•11
    clutch – 6•3
Mirrors – REF•8
    switch – 11•18, 12•5
MOT test checks – REF•8 *et seq*
Motor factors – REF•3

N

Needle lift sender – 4B•6
Number plate light – 12•10

O

Officially appointed garages – REF•3
Oil
    engine – 0•12, 0•17, 1A•8, 1B•7
    manual transmission – 1A•11, 1B•12
    oil cooler – 2A•17, 2B•31, 2C•20
    filter – 1A•8, 1B•7
Oil level temperature sender – 2A•18,
    2B•31
Oil pressure relief valve – 2A•18, 2B•31,
    2C•20
Oil pressure warning light switch – 2A•18,
    2B•31, 2C•20
Oil pump and drive chain – 2A•13, 2B•28,
    2B•29, 2C•19
Oil seals – REF•4
    camshaft – 2B•24, 2C•15
    crankshaft – 2A•15, 2B•29, 2C•19
Open-circuit – 12•2
Outer CV joint gaiter – 8•3
Oxygen (lambda) sensor(s) – 4A•9

P

Park Lock system – 7B•4
Parking aid components – 12•19
Pedal brake – 9•9
Petrol engine fuel systems – 4A•1 *et seq*
Pipes – 9•3
Pistons – 2D•18, 2D•21, 2D•24, 2D•25,
    2D•26

Plastic components – 11•3
Poisonous or irritant substances – 0•5
Pollen filter – 1A•10, 1B•11
Power steering
    hydraulic fluid – 0•17, 1A•16, 1B•15
    pressure switch – 4A•10
    pump – 10•21
Preheating system – diesel engines –
    5C•1 *et seq*
Pump
    air – 4C•5
    coolant – 2B•17, 2C•14, 3•6
    fuel injection – 2C•13, 4B•9
    oil – 2A•13, 2B•28, 2B•29, 2C•19
    power steering – 10•21
    tandem fuel – 4B•13
    washer fluid – 12•15

R

Radiator – 3•3
    flushing – 1A•18, 1B•18
Radio
    aerial – 12•18
    cassette player – 12•16
Rain sensor – 12•5
Range/distance sensor – 12•19
Rear axle assembly – 10•13
Rear bumper – 11•5
Rear courtesy/reading lights – 12•10
Rear light cluster – 12•9, 12•12
Rear number plate light – 12•10, 12•12
Rear pipe and silencers – 4C•12, 4C•13,
    4D•8
Rear wheel toe setting – 10•23
Rear wiper motor – 12•15
Relays – 12•3
    air pump – 4C•5
Release bearing and lever – 6•7
Reluctor rings – 9•14
Repair procedures – REF•4
Reversing light switch – 7A•5, 12•5
Road test – 1A•13, 1B•14
Roadside repairs – 0•7 *et seq*
Roadspeed sensor/speedometer drive –
    4A•9, 7A•5
Rockers and tappets – 2B•20
Roller rocker fingers – 2A•10
*Routine maintenance and servicing –
    diesel models* – 1B•1 *et seq*
*Routine maintenance and servicing –
    petrol models* – 1A•1 *et seq*
Rust holes or gashes – 11•3

S

Safety first! – 0•5, 0•13
Scalding – 0•5

Scratches – 11•2
Screw threads and fastenings – REF•4
Seat belt components – 11•20
Seats – 11•19
Secondary air injection system – 4C•5
Selector cable – 7B•3
Sender oil level temperature – 2A•18
Sensor
  absolute pressure (altitude) – 4B•5
  camshaft position – 4A•9
  coolant temperature – 3•5, 4A•9, 4B•4
  engine speed – 4A•9, 4B•5
  fuel temperature – 4B•4
  inlet air temperature – 4A•8, 4B•5
  knock – 5B•4
  rain – 12•5
  oxygen (lambda) – 4A•9
  range/distance – 12•19
  roadspeed/speedometer drive – 4A•9, 7A•5
  speedometer – 12•14
  sunlight penetration – 3•11
  throttle position – 4A•8, 4B•4
  wheel – 9•13, 9•14
Service interval display – 1A•9, 1B•9, 12•14
Servo non-return valve – 9•10
Servo unit – 9•10
  electric vacuum pump – 9•14
  mechanical vacuum pump – 9•14
Setting No 1 cylinder to TDC – 2A•5, 2B•7, 2C•5
Shock absorber – 10•11, REF•9, REF•10
Short-circuit – 12•2
Side repeater – 12•9
Side vents – 3•10
Sidelight – 12•8
Slave cylinder – 6•4
SOHC petrol engine in-car repair procedures – 2A•1 *et seq*
Spare parts – REF•3
Spark plug renewal – 1A•13
Speedometer drive – 7A•5
Speedometer sensor – 12•14
Springs – 10•12, REF•10
Starter motor – 5A•5
Starting and charging systems – 5A•1 *et seq*
Start-up after overhaul and reassembly – 2D•27
Steering – REF•9, REF•10
Steering and suspension – 1A•13, 1A•12, 1B•14
Steering angles – 10•22
Steering check – 1B•12
Steering column – 10•15, REF•8
  lock – 10•19, 12•3
  switch – 12•3
Steering gear assembly – 10•20
Steering gear rubber gaiters and track rods – 10•21
Steering wheel – 10•14, REF•8
Stub axle – 10•11
Sump – 2A•12, 2B•27, 2C•19
Sunlight penetration sensor – 3•11

Sunroof – 11•19
  check and lubrication – 1A•13, 1B•13
Suspension – 1A•13, REF•9, REF•10
Suspension and steering systems – 10•1 *et seq*
  fault finding – REF•17
Suspension
  check – 1B•12
  lower arm – 10•7, 10•8
  strut – 10•5
Switches – 12•3
  air conditioning – 12•5
  brake light – 9•12, 12•5
  central locking – 12•5
  clutch and brake pedal – 4A•10, 4B•6
  cooling system – 3•5
  courtesy light – 12•5
  electric mirror – 12•5
  electric window – 12•5
  ESP – 12•4
  fuel filler release flap – 12•5
  glovebox light – 12•5
  handbrake 'on' – 9•12, 12•5
  hazard warning light – 12•4
  heated front seats – 12•4
  heater blower – 12•5
  ignition – 10•19, 12•3
  instrument illumination – 12•4, 12•11
  interior monitoring deactivation – 12•5
  internal central locking – 11•16
  lighting – 12•4
  luggage area light – 12•5
  mirror – 11•18
  oil pressure warning light – 2A•18, 2B•31, 2C•20
  power steering – 4A•10
  reversing light – 7A•5, 12•5
  steering column – 12•3
  window – 11•17

Tailgate
  support struts – 11•13
  lock components – 11•14
  lock motor – 11•16
  washer jet – 12•16
  washer system check – 1A•12, 1B•13
Tandem fuel pump – 4B•13
Tappets – 2A•10, 2B•20, 2C•15
Tensioner assembly – 2A•8
Thermostat – 3•3
Throttle housing – 4A•6
Throttle position sensor – 4A•8, 4B•4
Throttle valve potentiometer/positioner – 4A•8
Timing belt – 1A•17, 1B•17, 2A•6, 2B•12, 2C•9
Timing belt covers – 2A•6, 2B•10, 2C•9
Timing belt tensioner and sprockets – 2A•7, 2B•16, 2B•17, 2C•12
Timing ignition – 5B•4

Toe setting
  front – 10•23
  rear – 10•23
Tools and working facilities – REF•6 *et seq*
Towing – 0•10
Track rods – 10•21, 10•22
Transmission mountings – 2A•15, 2B•30, 2C•20
Turbocharger boost control system components – 4D•5
Turbocharger – 4C•7, 4D•3
Tyres – REF•11
  condition and pressure – 0•14, 0•17
  specialists – REF•3

U

Underbody protection check – 1A•11, 1B•12
Underbonnet check points – 0•11
Unleaded petrol – 4A•18

V

Vacuum solenoid valve – 4C•6
Valve timing marks – 2A•4, 2B•6
Valves – 2D•16
Vehicle Identification – REF•3, REF•9
Vehicle level sender – 10•14, 12•13
Vehicle support – REF•5
VW Golf and Bora Manual – 0•6

W

Warning buzzer – 12•19
Washer fluid
  pump – 0•15, 12•15
  reservoir – 12•15
Washer system check – 1A•12, 1B•13
Wastegate – 4D•6
Weekly checks – 0•11 *et seq*
Weights – REF•1
Wheel
  alignment – 10•22
  bearings – REF•10
  camber – 10•23
  changing – 0•9
  sensor – 9•13, 9•14
Wheel arch liners – 11•19
Wheels – REF•11
Window switches – 11•17, 12•5
Window winder motors – 11•17
Windscreen – REF•8
Windscreen washer jets – 1A•12, 1B•13, 12•15, 12•16
Windscreen wiper motor and linkage – 12•15
Windscreen, tailgate and fixed rear quarter window glass – 11•18
Wiper arm/blades – 0•16, 12•14
Working facilities – REF•7

Haynes Manuals – The Complete UK Car List

Title	Book No.
ALFA ROMEO Alfasud/Sprint (74 - 88) up to F *	0292
Alfa Romeo Alfetta (73 - 87) up to E *	0531
AUDI 80, 90 & Coupe Petrol (79 - Nov 88) up to F	0605
Audi 80, 90 & Coupe Petrol (Oct 86 - 90) D to H	1491
Audi 100 & 200 Petrol (Oct 82 - 90) up to H	0907
Audi 100 & A6 Petrol & Diesel (May 91 - May 97) H to P	3504
Audi A3 Petrol & Diesel (96 - May 03) P to 03	4253
Audi A4 Petrol & Diesel (95 - Feb 00) M to V	3575
AUSTIN A35 & A40 (56 - 67) up to F *	0118
Austin/MG/Rover Maestro 1.3 & 1.6 Petrol (83 - 95) up to M	0922
Austin/MG Metro (80 - May 90) up to G	0718
Austin/Rover Montego 1.3 & 1.6 Petrol (84 - 94) A to L	1066
Austin/MG/Rover Montego 2.0 Petrol (84 - 95) A to M	1067
Mini (59 - 69) up to H *	0527
Mini (69 - 01) up to X	0646
Austin/Rover 2.0 litre Diesel Engine (86 - 93) C to L	1857
Austin Healey 100/6 & 3000 (56 - 68) up to G *	0049
BEDFORD CF Petrol (69 - 87) up to E	0163
Bedford/Vauxhall Rascal & Suzuki Supercarry (86 - Oct 94) C to M	3015
BMW 316, 320 & 320i (4-cyl) (75 - Feb 83) up to Y *	0276
BMW 320, 320i, 323i & 325i (6-cyl) (Oct 77 - Sept 87) up to E	0815
BMW 3- & 5-Series Petrol (81 - 91) up to J	1948
BMW 3-Series Petrol (Apr 91 - 99) H to V	3210
BMW 3-Series Petrol (Sept 98 - 03) S to 53	4067
BMW 520i & 525e (Oct 81 - June 88) up to E	1560
BMW 525, 528 & 528i (73 - Sept 81) up to X *	0632
BMW 5-Series 6-cyl Petrol (April 96 - Aug 03) N to 03	4151
BMW 1500, 1502, 1600, 1602, 2000 & 2002 (59 - 77) up to S *	0240
CHRYSLER PT Cruiser Petrol (00 - 03) W to 53	4058
CITROËN 2CV, Ami & Dyane (67 - 90) up to H	0196
Citroën AX Petrol & Diesel (87 - 97) D to P	3014
Citroën Berlingo & Peugeot Partner Petrol & Diesel (96 - 05) P to 55	4281
Citroën BX Petrol (83 - 94) A to L	0908
Citroën C15 Van Petrol & Diesel (89 - Oct 98) F to S	3509
Citroën C3 Petrol & Diesel (02 - 05) 51 to 05	4197
Citroën CX Petrol (75 - 88) up to F	0528
Citroën Saxo Petrol & Diesel (96 - 04) N to 54	3506
Citroën Visa Petrol (79 - 88) up to F	0620
Citroën Xantia Petrol & Diesel (93 - 01) K to Y	3082
Citroën XM Petrol & Diesel (89 - 00) G to X	3451
Citroën Xsara Petrol & Diesel (97 - Sept 00) R to W	3751
Citroën Xsara Picasso Petrol & Diesel (00 - 02) W to 52	3944
Citroën ZX Diesel (91 - 98) J to S	1922
Citroën ZX Petrol (91 - 98) H to S	1881
Citroën 1.7 & 1.9 litre Diesel Engine (84 - 96) A to N	1379
FIAT 126 (73 - 87) up to E *	0305
Fiat 500 (57 - 73) up to M *	0090
Fiat Bravo & Brava Petrol (95 - 00) N to W	3572
Fiat Cinquecento (93 - 98) K to R	3501
Fiat Panda (81 - 95) up to M	0793
Fiat Punto Petrol & Diesel (94 - Oct 99) L to V	3251
Fiat Punto Petrol (Oct 99 - July 03) V to 03	4066
Fiat Regata Petrol (84 - 88) A to F	1167
Fiat Tipo Petrol (88 - 91) E to J	1625
Fiat Uno Petrol (83 - 95) up to M	0923

Title	Book No.
Fiat X1/9 (74 - 89) up to G *	0273
FORD Anglia (59 - 68) up to G *	0001
Ford Capri II (& III) 1.6 & 2.0 (74 - 87) up to E *	0283
Ford Capri II (& III) 2.8 & 3.0 V6 (74 - 87) up to E	1309
Ford Cortina Mk III 1300 & 1600 (70 - 76) up to P *	0070
Ford Escort Mk I 1100 & 1300 (68 - 74) up to N *	0171
Ford Escort Mk I Mexico, RS 1600 & RS 2000 (70 - 74) up to N *	0139
Ford Escort Mk II Mexico, RS 1800 & RS 2000 (75 - 80) up to W *	0735
Ford Escort (75 - Aug 80) up to V *	0280
Ford Escort Petrol (Sept 80 - Sept 90) up to H	0686
Ford Escort & Orion Petrol (Sept 90 - 00) H to X	1737
Ford Escort & Orion Diesel (Sept 90 - 00) H to X	4081
Ford Fiesta (76 - Aug 83) up to Y	0334
Ford Fiesta Petrol (Aug 83 - Feb 89) A to F	1030
Ford Fiesta Petrol (Feb 89 - Oct 95) F to N	1595
Ford Fiesta Petrol & Diesel (Oct 95 - Mar 02) N to 02	3397
Ford Fiesta Petrol & Diesel (Apr 02 - 05) 02 to 54	4170
Ford Focus Petrol & Diesel (98 - 01) S to Y	3759
Ford Focus Petrol & Diesel (Oct 01 - 04) 51 to 54	4167
Ford Galaxy Petrol & Diesel (95 - Aug 00) M to W	3984
Ford Granada Petrol (Sept 77 - Feb 85) up to B *	0481
Ford Granada & Scorpio Petrol (Mar 85 - 94) B to M	1245
Ford Ka (96 - 02) P to 52	3570
Ford Mondeo Petrol (93 - Sept 00) K to X	1923
Ford Mondeo Petrol & Diesel (Oct 00 - Jul 03) X to 03	3990
Ford Mondeo Diesel (93 - 96) L to N	3465
Ford Orion Petrol (83 - Sept 90) up to H	1009
Ford Sierra 4-cyl Petrol (82 - 93) up to K	0903
Ford Sierra V6 Petrol (82 - 91) up to J	0904
Ford Transit Petrol (Mk 2) (78 - Jan 86) up to C	0719
Ford Transit Petrol (Mk 3) (Feb 86 - 89) C to G	1468
Ford Transit Diesel (Feb 86 - 99) C to T	3019
Ford 1.6 & 1.8 litre Diesel Engine (84 - 96) A to N	1172
Ford 2.1, 2.3 & 2.5 litre Diesel Engine (77 - 90) up to H	1606
FREIGHT ROVER Sherpa Petrol (74 - 87) up to E	0463
HILLMAN Avenger (70 - 82) up to Y	0037
Hillman Imp (63 - 76) up to R *	0022
HONDA Civic (Feb 84 - Oct 87) A to E	1226
Honda Civic (Nov 91 - 96) J to N	3199
Honda Civic Petrol (Mar 95 - 00) M to X	4050
HYUNDAI Pony (85 - 94) C to M	3398
JAGUAR E Type (61 - 72) up to L *	0140
Jaguar MkI & II, 240 & 340 (55 - 69) up to H *	0098
Jaguar XJ6, XJ & Sovereign; Daimler Sovereign (68 - Oct 86) up to D	0242
Jaguar XJ6 & Sovereign (Oct 86 - Sept 94) D to M	3261
Jaguar XJ12, XJS & Sovereign; Daimler Double Six (72 - 88) up to F	0478
JEEP Cherokee Petrol (93 - 96) K to N	1943
LADA 1200, 1300, 1500 & 1600 (74 - 91) up to J	0413
Lada Samara (87 - 91) D to J	1610
LAND ROVER 90, 110 & Defender Diesel (83 - 95) up to N	3017
Land Rover Discovery Petrol & Diesel (89 - 98) G to S	3016
Land Rover Discovery Diesel (99 - 04) S to 54	4606
Land Rover Freelander Petrol & Diesel (97 - 02) R to 52	3929
Land Rover Series IIA & III Diesel (58 - 85) up to C	0529
Land Rover Series II, IIA & III 4-cyl Petrol (58 - 85) up to C	0314
MAZDA 323 (Mar 81 - Oct 89) up to G	1608
Mazda 323 (Oct 89 - 98) G to R	3455
Mazda 626 (May 83 - Sept 87) up to E	0929

Title	Book No.
Mazda B1600, B1800 & B2000 Pick-up Petrol (72 - 88) up to F	0267
Mazda RX-7 (79 - 85) up to C *	0460
MERCEDES-BENZ 190, 190E & 190D Petrol & Diesel (83 - 93) A to L	3450
Mercedes-Benz 200D, 240D, 240TD, 300D & 300TD 123 Series Diesel (Oct 76 - 85) up to C	1114
Mercedes-Benz 250 & 280 (68 - 72) up to L *	0346
Mercedes-Benz 250 & 280 123 Series Petrol (Oct 76 - 84) up to B *	0677
Mercedes-Benz 124 Series Petrol & Diesel (85 - Aug 93) C to K	3253
Mercedes-Benz C-Class Petrol & Diesel (93 - Aug 00) L to W	3511
MGA (55 - 62) *	0475
MGB (62 - 80) up to W	0111
MG Midget & Austin-Healey Sprite (58 - 80) up to W *	0265
MINI Petrol (July 01 - 05) Y to 05	4273
MITSUBISHI Shogun & L200 Pick-Ups Petrol (83 - 94) up to M	1944
MORRIS Ital 1.3 (80 - 84) up to B	0705
Morris Minor 1000 (56 - 71) up to K	0024
NISSAN Almera Petrol (95 - Feb 00) N to V	4053
Nissan Bluebird (May 84 - Mar 86) A to C	1223
Nissan Bluebird Petrol (Mar 86 - 90) C to H	1473
Nissan Cherry (Sept 82 - 86) up to D	1031
Nissan Micra (83 - Jan 93) up to K	0931
Nissan Micra (93 - 02) K to 52	3254
Nissan Primera Petrol (90 - Aug 99) H to T	1851
Nissan Stanza (82 - 86) up to D	0824
Nissan Sunny Petrol (May 82 - Oct 86) up to D	0895
Nissan Sunny Petrol (Oct 86 - Mar 91) D to H	1378
Nissan Sunny Petrol (Apr 91 - 95) H to N	3219
OPEL Ascona & Manta (B Series) (Sept 75 - 88) up to F *	0316
Opel Ascona Petrol (81 - 88)	3215
Opel Astra Petrol (Oct 91 - Feb 98)	3156
Opel Corsa Petrol (83 - Mar 93)	3160
Opel Corsa Petrol (Mar 93 - 97)	3159
Opel Kadett Petrol (Nov 79 - Oct 84) up to B	0634
Opel Kadett Petrol (Oct 84 - Oct 91)	3196
Opel Omega & Senator Petrol (Nov 86 - 94)	3157
Opel Rekord Petrol (Feb 78 - Oct 86) up to D	0543
Opel Vectra Petrol (Oct 88 - Oct 95)	3158
PEUGEOT 106 Petrol & Diesel (91 - 04) J to 53	1882
Peugeot 205 Petrol (83 - 97) A to P	0932
Peugeot 206 Petrol & Diesel (98 - 01) S to X	3757
Peugeot 206 Petrol & Diesel (01 - 06) Y to 56	4613
Peugeot 306 Petrol & Diesel (93 - 02) K to 02	3073
Peugeot 307 Petrol & Diesel (01 - 04) Y to 54	4147
Peugeot 309 Petrol (86 - 93) C to K	1266
Peugeot 405 Petrol (88 - 97) E to P	1559
Peugeot 405 Diesel (88 - 97) E to P	3198
Peugeot 406 Petrol & Diesel (96 - Mar 99) N to T	3394
Peugeot 406 Petrol & Diesel (Mar 99 - 02) T to 52	3982
Peugeot 505 Petrol (79 - 89) up to G	0762
Peugeot 1.7/1.8 & 1.9 litre Diesel Engine (82 - 96) up to N	0950
Peugeot 2.0, 2.1, 2.3 & 2.5 litre Diesel Engines (74 - 90) up to H	1607
PORSCHE 911 (65 - 85) up to C	0264
Porsche 924 & 924 Turbo (76 - 85) up to C	0397
PROTON (89 - 97) F to P	3255
RANGE ROVER V8 Petrol (70 - Oct 92) up to K	0606

* Classic reprint

Title	Book No.
RELIANT Robin & Kitten (73 - 83) up to A *	0436
RENAULT 4 (61 - 86) up to D *	0072
Renault 5 Petrol (Feb 85 - 96) B to N	1219
Renault 9 & 11 Petrol (82 - 89) up to F	0822
Renault 18 Petrol (79 - 86) up to D	0598
Renault 19 Petrol (89 - 96) F to N	1646
Renault 19 Diesel (89 - 96) F to N	1946
Renault 21 Petrol (86 - 94) C to M	1397
Renault 25 Petrol & Diesel (84 - 92) B to K	1228
Renault Clio Petrol (91 - May 98) H to R	1853
Renault Clio Diesel (91 - June 96) H to N	3031
Renault Clio Petrol & Diesel (May 98 - May 01) R to Y	3906
Renault Clio Petrol & Diesel (June 01 - 04) Y to 54	4168
Renault Espace Petrol & Diesel (85 - 96) C to N	3197
Renault Laguna Petrol & Diesel (94 - 00) L to W	3252
Renault Laguna Petrol & Diesel (Feb 01 - Feb 05) X to 54	4283
Renault Mégane & Scénic Petrol & Diesel (96 - 98) N to R	3395
Renault Mégane & Scénic Petrol & Diesel (Apr 99 - 02) T to 52	3916
Renault Megane Petrol & Diesel (Oct 02 - 05) 52 to 55	4284
Renault Scenic Petrol & Diesel (Sept 03 - 06) 53 to 06	4297
ROVER 213 & 216 (84 - 89) A to G	1116
Rover 214 & 414 Petrol (89 - 96) G to N	1689
Rover 216 & 416 Petrol (89 - 96) G to N	1830
Rover 211, 214, 216, 218 & 220 Petrol & Diesel (Dec 95 - 99) N to V	3399
Rover 25 & MG ZR Petrol & Diesel (Oct 99 - 04) V to 54	4145
Rover 414, 416 & 420 Petrol & Diesel (May 95 - 98) M to R	3453
Rover 45 / MG ZS Petrol & Diesel (99 - 05) V to 55	4384
Rover 618, 620 & 623 Petrol (93 - 97) K to P	3257
Rover 75 / MG ZT Petrol & Diesel (99 - 06) S to 06	4292
Rover 820, 825 & 827 Petrol (86 - 95) D to N	1380
Rover 3500 (76 - 87) up to E *	0365
Rover Metro, 111 & 114 Petrol (May 90 - 98) G to S	1711
SAAB 95 & 96 (66 - 76) up to R *	0198
Saab 90, 99 & 900 (79 - Oct 93) up to L	0765
Saab 900 (Oct 93 - 98) L to R	3512
Saab 9000 (4-cyl) (85 - 98) C to S	1686
Saab 9-3 Petrol & Diesel (98 - May 02) R to 02	4614
Saab 9-5 4-cyl Petrol (97 - 04) R to 54	4156
SEAT Ibiza & Cordoba Petrol & Diesel (Oct 93 - Oct 99) L to V	3571
Seat Ibiza & Malaga Petrol (85 - 92) B to K	1609
SKODA Estelle (77 - 89) up to G	0604
Skoda Fabia Petrol & Diesel (00 - 06) W to 06	4376
Skoda Favorit (89 - 96) F to N	1801
Skoda Felicia Petrol & Diesel (95 - 01) M to X	3505
Skoda Octavia Petrol & Diesel (98 - Apr 04) R to 04	4285
SUBARU 1600 & 1800 (Nov 79 - 90) up to H *	0995
SUNBEAM Alpine, Rapier & H120 (67 - 74) up to N *	0051
SUZUKI Supercarry & Bedford/Vauxhall Rascal (86 - Oct 94) C to M	3015
Suzuki SJ Series, Samurai & Vitara (4-cyl) Petrol (82 - 97) up to P	1942
TALBOT Alpine, Solara, Minx & Rapier (75 - 86) up to D	0337
Talbot Horizon Petrol (78 - 86) up to D	0473
Talbot Samba (82 - 86) up to D	0823
TOYOTA Avensis Petrol (98 - Jan 03) R to 52	4264
Toyota Carina E Petrol (May 92 - 97) J to P	3256

Title	Book No.
Toyota Corolla (80 - 85) up to C	0683
Toyota Corolla (Sept 83 - Sept 87) A to E	1024
Toyota Corolla (Sept 87 - Aug 92) E to K	1683
Toyota Corolla Petrol (Aug 92 - 97) K to P	3259
Toyota Corolla Petrol (July 97 - Feb 02) P to 51	4286
Toyota Hi-Ace & Hi-Lux Petrol (69 - Oct 83) up to A	0304
Toyota Yaris Petrol (99 - 05) T to 05	4265
TRIUMPH GT6 & Vitesse (62 - 74) up to N *	0112
Triumph Herald (59 - 71) up to K *	0010
Triumph Spitfire (62 - 81) up to X	0113
Triumph Stag (70 - 78) up to T *	0441
Triumph TR2, TR3, TR3A, TR4 & TR4A (52 - 67) up to F *	0028
Triumph TR5 & 6 (67 - 75) up to P *	0031
Triumph TR7 (75 - 82) up to Y *	0322
VAUXHALL Astra Petrol (80 - Oct 84) up to B	0635
Vauxhall Astra & Belmont Petrol (Oct 84 - Oct 91) B to J	1136
Vauxhall Astra Petrol (Oct 91 - Feb 98) J to R	1832
Vauxhall/Opel Astra & Zafira Petrol (Feb 98 - Apr 04) R to 04	3758
Vauxhall/Opel Astra & Zafira Diesel (Feb 98 - Apr 04) R to 04	3797
Vauxhall/Opel Calibra (90 - 98) G to S	3502
Vauxhall Carlton Petrol (Oct 78 - Oct 86) up to D	0480
Vauxhall Carlton & Senator Petrol (Nov 86 - 94) D to L	1469
Vauxhall Cavalier Petrol (81 - Oct 88) up to F	0812
Vauxhall Cavalier Petrol (Oct 88 - 95) F to N	1570
Vauxhall Chevette (75 - 84) up to B	0285
Vauxhall/Opel Corsa Diesel (Mar 93 - Oct 00) K to X	4087
Vauxhall Corsa Petrol (Mar 93 - 97) K to R	1985
Vauxhall/Opel Corsa Petrol (Apr 97 - Oct 00) P to X	3921
Vauxhall/Opel Corsa Petrol & Diesel (Oct 00 - Sept 03) X to 53	4079
Vauxhall/Opel Frontera Petrol & Diesel (91 - Sept 98) J to S	3454
Vauxhall Nova Petrol (83 - 93) up to K	0909
Vauxhall/Opel Omega Petrol (94 - 99) L to T	3510
Vauxhall/Opel Vectra Petrol & Diesel (95 - Feb 99) N to S	3396
Vauxhall/Opel Vectra Petrol & Diesel (Mar 99 - May 02) T to 02	3930
Vauxhall/Opel 1.5, 1.6 & 1.7 litre Diesel Engine (82 - 96) up to N	1222
VOLKSWAGEN 411 & 412 (68 - 75) up to P *	0091
Volkswagen Beetle 1200 (54 - 77) up to S	0036
Volkswagen Beetle 1300 & 1500 (65 - 75) up to P	0039
Volkswagen Beetle 1302 & 1302S (70 - 72) up to L *	0110
Volkswagen Beetle 1303, 1303S & GT (72 - 75) up to P	0159
Volkswagen Beetle Petrol & Diesel (Apr 99 - 01) T to 51	3798
Volkswagen Golf & Jetta Mk 1 Petrol 1.1 & 1.3 (74 - 84) up to A	0716
Volkswagen Golf, Jetta & Scirocco Mk 1 Petrol 1.5, 1.6 & 1.8 (74 - 84) up to A	0726
Volkswagen Golf & Jetta Mk 1 Diesel (78 - 84) up to A	0451
Volkswagen Golf & Jetta Mk 2 Petrol (Mar 84 - Feb 92) A to J	1081
Volkswagen Golf & Vento Petrol & Diesel (Feb 92 - Mar 98) J to R	3097
Volkswagen Golf & Bora Petrol & Diesel (April 98 - 00) R to X	3727

Title	Book No.
Volkswagen Golf & Bora 4-cyl Petrol & Diesel (01 - 03) X to 53	4169
Volkswagen LT Petrol Vans & Light Trucks (76 - 87) up to E	0637
Volkswagen Passat & Santana Petrol (Sept 81 - May 88) up to E	0814
Volkswagen Passat 4-cyl Petrol & Diesel (May 88 - 96) E to P	3498
Volkswagen Passat 4-cyl Petrol & Diesel (Dec 96 - Nov 00) P to X	3917
Volkswagen Passat Petrol & Diesel (Dec 00 - May 05) X to 05	4279
Volkswagen Polo & Derby (76 - Jan 82) up to X	0335
Volkswagen Polo (82 - Oct 90) up to H	0813
Volkswagen Polo Petrol (Nov 90 - Aug 94) H to L	3245
Volkswagen Polo Hatchback Petrol & Diesel (94 - 99) M to S	3500
Volkswagen Polo Hatchback Petrol (00 - Jan 02) V to 51	4150
Volkswagen Polo Petrol & Diesel (Feb 02 - June 05) 51 to 05	4608
Volkswagen Scirocco (82 - 90) up to H *	1224
Volkswagen Transporter 1600 (68 - 79) up to V	0082
Volkswagen Transporter 1700, 1800 & 2000 (72 - 79) up to V *	0226
Volkswagen Transporter (air-cooled) Petrol (79 - 82) up to Y *	0638
Volkswagen Transporter (water-cooled) Petrol (82 - 90) up to H	3452
Volkswagen Type 3 (63 - 73) up to M *	0084
VOLVO 120 & 130 Series (& P1800) (61 - 73) up to M *	0203
Volvo 142, 144 & 145 (66 - 74) up to N *	0129
Volvo 240 Series Petrol (74 - 93) up to K	0270
Volvo 262, 264 & 260/265 (75 - 85) up to C *	0400
Volvo 340, 343, 345 & 360 (76 - 91) up to J	0715
Volvo 440, 460 & 480 Petrol (87 - 97) D to P	1691
Volvo 740 & 760 Petrol (82 - 91) up to J	1258
Volvo 850 Petrol (92 - 96) J to P	3260
Volvo 940 Petrol (90 - 96) H to N	3249
Volvo S40 & V40 Petrol (96 - Mar 04) N to 04	3569
Volvo S70, V70 & C70 Petrol (96 - 99) P to V	3573
Volvo V70 / S80 Petrol & Diesel (98 - 05) S to 55	4263
AUTOMOTIVE TECHBOOKS	
Automotive Air Conditioning Systems	3740
Automotive Electrical and Electronic Systems Manual	3049
Automotive Gearbox Overhaul Manual	3473
Automotive Service Summaries Manual	3475
Automotive Timing Belts Manual – Austin/Rover	3549
Automotive Timing Belts Manual – Ford	3474
Automotive Timing Belts Manual – Peugeot/Citroën	3568
Automotive Timing Belts Manual – Vauxhall/Opel	3577
DIY MANUAL SERIES	
The Haynes Air Conditioning Manual	4192
The Haynes Manual on Bodywork	4198
The Haynes Manual on Brakes	4178
The Haynes Manual on Carburettors	4177
The Haynes Car Electrical Systems Manual	4251
The Haynes Manual on Diesel Engines	4174
The Haynes Manual on Engine Management	4199
The Haynes Manual on Fault Codes	4175
The Haynes Manual on Practical Electrical Systems	4267
The Haynes Manual on Small Engines	4250
The Haynes Manual on Welding	4176

* Classic reprint

Preserving Our Motoring Heritage

<
The Model J Duesenberg
Derham Tourster.
Only eight of these
magnificent cars were
ever built – this is the
only example to be found
outside the United States
of America

Almost every car you've ever loved, loathed or desired is gathered under one roof at the Haynes Motor Museum. Over 300 immaculately presented cars and motorbikes represent every aspect of our motoring heritage, from elegant reminders of bygone days, such as the superb Model J Duesenberg to curiosities like the bug-eyed BMW Isetta. There are also many old friends and flames. Perhaps you remember the 1959 Ford Popular that you did your courting in? The magnificent 'Red Collection' is a spectacle of classic sports cars including AC, Alfa Romeo, Austin Healey, Ferrari, Lamborghini, Maserati, MG, Riley, Porsche and Triumph.

A Perfect Day Out

Each and every vehicle at the Haynes Motor Museum has played its part in the history and culture of Motoring. Today, they make a wonderful spectacle and a great day out for all the family. Bring the kids, bring Mum and Dad, but above all bring your camera to capture those golden memories for ever. You will also find an impressive array of motoring memorabilia, a comfortable 70 seat video cinema and one of the most extensive transport book shops in Britain. The Pit Stop Cafe serves everything from a cup of tea to wholesome, home-made meals or, if you prefer, you can enjoy the large picnic area nestled in the beautiful rural surroundings of Somerset.

>
John Haynes O.B.E.,
Founder and
Chairman of the
museum at the wheel
of a Haynes Light 12.

<
Graham Hill's Lola
Cosworth Formula 1
car next to a 1934
Riley Sports.

The Museum is situated on the A359 Yeovil to Frome road at Sparkford, just off the A303 in Somerset. It is about 40 miles south of Bristol, and 25 minutes drive from the M5 intersection at Taunton.
Open 9.30am - 5.30pm (10.00am - 4.00pm Winter) 7 days a week, *except Christmas Day, Boxing Day and New Years Day*
Special rates available for schools, coach parties and outings Charitable Trust No. 292048